THE REPUBLIC

 OF

PLATO

SECOND EDITION

TRANSLATED WITH NOTES AND
AN INTERPRETIVE ESSAY BY
ALLAN BLOOM

BASIC
BOOKS

A Member of The Perseus Books Group

To my mother and father

PREFACE TO THE
SECOND EDITION

When I teach the *Republic* now, the reactions to it are more urgent and more intense than they were a quarter-century ago when I was working on this translation and this interpretation. The *Republic* is, of course, a permanent book, one of the small number of books that engage the interest and sympathy of thoughtful persons wherever books are esteemed and read in freedom. No other philosophic book so powerfully expresses the human longing for justice while satisfying the intellect's demands for clarity. The problems of justice as presented by Plato arouse more interest, excitement, and disagreement at some points than at others. When non-philosophers begin their acquaintance with philosophers, they frequently say, "This is nonsense." But sometimes they say, "This is outrageous nonsense," and at such moments their passions really become involved with the philosophers, frequently culminating in hatred or in love. Right now Plato is both attractive and repulsive to the young.

This is most obvious when they reach the section of the *Republic* where Socrates legislates about music. Between the late 1940s and the mid-1960s there was a lull in music's power over the soul, between the declining magnetism of high romanticism and the surge of rock, and music was not much of a practical or theoretical problem for students. They took note of the fact that Socrates is for censorship—a no-no, of course—and went on, not taking much account of what in particular is being censored. If forced to think about it, they tended to be surprised that music above all should be the theme of censorship when what seemed to them to be the likely candidates were science, politics, and sex. But now that musical frenzy has resumed its natural place, Socrates is seen to be both pertinent and dangerous. Discussion is real and intense, for Socrates understands the charms—erotic, military, political, and religious—of music, which he takes to be the most authentic primitive expressions of the soul's hopes and terrors. But, precisely because music is central to the soul and the musicians are such virtuosos at plucking its chords, Socrates argues that it is imperative to think about how the development of the passions affects the whole of life and how musical pleasures may conflict with duties or other, less immediate pleasures. This is intolerable, and many students feel that the whole Socratic understanding is subversive of their establishment. As I said, the *Republic* is perennial; it always returns with the change of human seasons.

Another theme, not unrelated to music, also suddenly became current in the late 1960s and remains central to general and professional discussion about politics: community, or roots. And again the *republic* becomes peculiarly attractive and repulsive because no book describes community so precisely and so completely or undertakes so rigorously to turn cold politics into family warmth. In the period just after World War II, no criticism of what Karl Popper called "the open society" was brooked. The open society was understood to be simply unproblematic, having solved the difficulties presented by older thinkers. The progress of science was understood to be strictly paralleled by that of society; individualism seemed no threat to human ties, and *mass* society no threat to meaningful participation. The softening in this narrow liberal position can be seen in the substitution in common discourse of the less positively charged term *technology* for *science,* the pervasive doubt about whether the mastery of nature is a very good idea, and a commonly expressed sentiment of lostness and powerlessness on the part of individual citizens.

In the days of thoughtless optimism, Plato was considered irrelevant and his criticism was not available to warn us of possible dangers. Now it is recognized that he had all the doubts we have today and that the founding myth of his city treats men and women as literally rooted in its soil. Everybody is sure that Plato knew something about community, but he makes today's comfortable communitarians uncomfortable by insisting that so much individuality must be sacrificed to community. Moreover, they rightly sense that Plato partly parodies the claims and the pretensions of community. The uninvolved Socrates, distrustful of neat solutions, does not appear to be a very reliable ally of movements. Plato, criticized in the recent past for not being a good liberal, is now shunned for not being a wholehearted communitarian. He is, however, back in the game.

But, above all, the Platonic text is now gripping because of its very radical, more than up-to-date treatment of the "gender question." In a stunning demonstration of the power of the philosophic imagination, Plato treats the question as it was never again treated up to our own day— proving thereby that reason can penetrate to the essentials at any time or place. Perfect justice, Socrates argues in the dialogue, can be achieved only by suppression of the distinction between the sexes in all important matters and the admission of women on an equal footing to all activities of the city, particularly the most important, fighting and thinking. Corollary to this is the virtual suppression of the bodily differences between the sexes and all the psychic affects habitually accompanying those differences, especially shame, which effectively separates women from men.

In consequence, Socrates further recognizes that there must be a revolution in the family in which its functions are transferred to the community, so that women will not have to bear the double burden of career mothers. Day-care centers, abortion, and the desacralization of marriage are only a few of the easily recognizable elements of this revolution in favor of synthesizing the opposites man/woman into the unity, human being. Some activists even find Socrates' analysis too radical, sacrificing all the charms of family ties to rational considerations of justice. Reason, it seems, is corrosive of the mysteries of human connectedness. Others rightly suspect that Socrates is not sufficiently convinced of the factual equality of women. Socrates is again the questionable ally, but he marks the starting point of something that would be unimaginable if he had not thought it through. One can search in other historical epochs and cultures, but the foundations of this perspective will not be found elsewhere. They are inextricably linked to the founder of political philosophy.

For students the story of man bound in the cave and breaking the bonds, moving out and up into the light of the sun, is the most memorable from their encounter with the *Republic*. This is the image of every serious student's profoundest longing, the longing for liberation from convention in order to live according to nature, and one of the book's evidently permanent aspects. The story still exercises some of its old magic, but it now encounters a fresh obstacle, for the meaning of the story is that truth is substituted for myth. Today students are taught that no such substitution is possible and that there is nothing beyond myth or "narrative." The myths of the most primitive cultures are not, it is said, qualitatively different from the narratives of the most rigorous science. Men and women must bend to the power of myth rather than try to shuck it off as philosophy wrongly used to believe. Socrates, who gaily abandons the founding myth or noble lie he himself made up for the sake of the city, looks quixotic in this light. This can be disheartening to the young person who cares, but it can be a beginning of philosophy, for he is perplexed by a real difficulty in his own breast. This is another case where Platonic radicalism is particularly timely for us.

Finally, in terms of my own experience of these last twenty-five years, after the *Republic* I translated Rousseau's *Emile*, the greatest modern book on education. Rousseau was one of the great readers of Plato, and from my time on that work I gained an even greater respect for the *Republic*. *Emile* is its natural companion, and Rousseau proved his greatness by entering the lists in worthy combat with it. He shows that Plato articulated first and best all the problems, and he himself differs only with respect to some of the solutions. If one takes the two books together, one has the basic training necessary for the educational wars. And wars they are, now that doctrine tells us that these two books are cornerstones of an outlived canon. So, I conclude, the *Republic* is always useful to students who read it, but now more than ever.

I have corrected many minor mistranslations or misleading formulations for this second edition. I must also add that there are certainly many more I did not catch. This is regrettable but inherent in the nature of the task and the nature of this translator.

Paris, 1991

PREFACE

This is intended to be a literal translation. My goal—unattained—was the accuracy of William of Moerbeke's Latin translations of Aristotle. These versions are so faithful to Aristotle's text that they are authorities for the correction of the Greek manuscripts, and they enabled Thomas Aquinas to become a supreme interpreter of Aristotle without knowing Greek.

Such a translation is intended to be useful to the serious student, the one who wishes and is able to arrive at his own understanding of the work. He must be emancipated from the tyranny of the translator, given the means of transcending the limitations of the translator's interpretation, enabled to discover the subtleties of the elusive original. The only way to provide the reader with this independence is by a slavish, even if sometimes cumbersome, literalness—insofar as possible always using the same English equivalent for the same Greek word. Thus the little difficulties which add up to major discoveries become evident to, or at least are not hidden from, the careful student. The translator should conceive of himself as a medium between a master whose depths he has not plumbed and an audience of potential students of that master who may be much better endowed than is the translator. His greatest vice is to believe he has adequately grasped the teaching of his author. It is least of all his function to render the work palatable to those who do not wish, or are unable, to expend the effort requisite to the study of difficult texts. Nor should he try to make an ancient mode of thought sound "contemporary." Such translations become less useful as more attention is paid to the text. At the very least, one can say that a literal translation is a necessary supplement to more felicitous renditions which deviate widely from their original.

The difference from age to age in the notions of the translator's responsibility is in itself a chapter of intellectual history. Certainly the popularization of the classics is one part of that chapter. But there seem to be two major causes for the current distaste for literal translations—one rooted in the historical science of our time, the other rooted in a specific, and I believe erroneous, view of the character of Platonic books.

The modern historical consciousness has engendered a general scepticism about the truth of all "world views," except for that one of which it is itself a product. There seems to be an opinion that the thought of the past is immediately accessible to us, that, although we may not accept it, we at least understand it. We apply the tools of our science to the past without reflecting that those tools are also historically limited. We do not sufficiently realize that the only true historical objectivity is to understand the ancient authors as they understood themselves; and we are loath to assume that perhaps *they* may be able to criticize *our* framework and our methods. We should, rather, try to see our historical science in the perspective of their teachings rather than the other way around. Most of all, we must accept, at least tentatively, the claim of the older thinkers that the truth is potentially attainable by the efforts of unaided human reason at all times and in all places. If we begin by denying the fundamental contention of men like Plato and Aristotle, they are refuted for us from the outset, not by any immanent criticism but by our unreflecting acceptance of the self-contradictory principle that all thought is related to a specific age and has no grasp of reality beyond that age. On this basis, it is impossible to take them seriously. One often suspects that this is what is lacking in many translations: they are not animated by the passion for the truth; they are really the results of elegant trifling. William of Moerbeke was motivated by the concern that he might miss the most important counsels about the most important things, counsels emanating from a man wiser than he. His knowledge of the world and his way of life, nay, his very happiness, depended on the success of his quest to get at Aristotle's real meaning.

Today men do not generally believe so much is at stake in their studies of classic thinkers, and there is an inclination to smile at naive scholastic reverence for antiquity. But that smile should fade when it is realized that this sense of superiority is merely the perseveration of the confidence, so widespread in the nineteenth century, that science had reached a plateau overlooking broader and more comprehensible horizons than those previously known, a confidence that our intellectual progress could suffer no reverse. This confidence has almost vanished; few scholars believe that our perspective is *the* authoritative one any longer; but much scholarship still clings to the habits which grew up in the shadow of that conviction. However, if that is not a justified conviction, if we are really at sea so far as the truth of things goes, then our most evident categories are questionable, and we do not even know whether we understand the simplest questions Plato poses. It then behooves us to rediscover the perspective of the ancient authors, for the sake both of accurate scholarship and of trying to find alternatives to the current mode of understanding things.

It is not usually understood how difficult it is to see the phenomena as they were seen by the older writers. It is one of the most awesome undertakings of the mind, for we have divided the world up differently, and willy-nilly we apply our terms, and hence the thoughts behind them, to the things discussed. It is always the most popular and questionable terms of our own age that seem most natural; it is virtually impossible to speak without using them. For example, H. D. P. Lee, in describing his view of a translator's responsibility, says, "The translator must go behind what Plato said and discover what he means, and if, for example, he says 'examining the beautiful and the good' must not hesitate to render this as 'discussing moral values' if that is in fact the way in which the same thought would be expressed today." (*The Republic* [London: Penguin, 1956], p. 48.) But if one hurries too quickly "behind" Plato's speech, one loses the sense of the surface. Lee shares with Cornford and many other translators the assurance that they have a sufficient understanding of Plato's meaning, and that that meaning is pretty much the kind of thing Englishmen or Americans already think. However, it might be more prudent to let the reader decide whether "the beautiful and the good" are simply equivalent to "moral values." If they are the same, he will soon enough find out. And if they are not, as may be the case, he will not be prevented from finding that out and thereby putting his own opinions to the test.

In fact "values," in this sense, is a usage of German origin popularized by sociologists in the last seventy-five years. Implicit in this usage is the distinction between "facts and values" and the consequence that ends or goals are not based on facts but are mere individual subjective preferences or, at most, ideal creations of the human spirit.

Whether the translator intends it or not, the word "values" conjures up a series of thoughts which are alien to Plato. Every school child knows that values are relative, and thus that the Plato who seems to derive them from facts, or treat them as facts themselves, is unsophisticated. When the case is prejudged for him in this way, how could the student ever find out that there was once another way of looking at these things that had some plausibility? The text becomes a mirror in which he sees only himself. Or, as Nietzsche put it, the scholars dig up what they themselves buried.

Even if Plato is wrong, the pre-history of our current wisdom is still of some importance so that the inadequacies of the traditional teaching, which necessitated its replacement, may become clear.

Similarly, the word "moral" is inappropriate. It is questionable whether Plato had a "moral philosophy." There is a teaching about the virtues, some of which find their roots in the city, some in philosophy. But in Plato there are no moral virtues, as we find them first described in Aristotle's *Ethics*. This is a subtle question, one that requires long study, but one that leads to the heart of the difference between Plato and Aristotle, and beyond to the whole dispute about the status of morality. Thus the translator hides another issue. And even if "the beautiful and the good" do add up to what we mean by morality, it is well that the student should know that for Plato morality is composed of two elements, one of which lends a certain splendor to it which is lacking in, say, Kantian morality. And it may also be the case that these two elements are not always wholly in harmony. The good or the just need not always be beautiful or noble, for example, punishment; and the beautiful or noble need not always be good or just, for example, Achilles' wrath. There is further matter for reflection here: one might learn a great deal if one could follow such problems throughout Plato's works. It is only in this way that a student might reconstruct a plausible and profound Platonic view of the world rather than find the dialogues a compendium of unconvincing platitudes.

F. M. Cornford, whose translation is now the one most widely used, ridicules literal translation and insists that it is often ". . . misleading, or tedious, or grotesque and silly, or pompous and verbose" (*The Republic* [New York: Oxford University Press, 1956], p. v.). I doubt that it is often misleading, although I admit that it may often lack the beauty of the original. The issue is whether a certain spurious charm—for it is not Plato's charm—is worth the loss of awareness of Plato's problems necessitated by Cornford's notions about translation. It is only because he did not see the extent of the loss that he could be so cavalier with the original. He made a rather heavy joke at the expense of an earlier translator:

One who opened Jowett's version at random and lighted on the statement (at 549B) that the best guardian for a man's "virtue" is "philosophy tempered with music," might run away with the idea that in order to avoid irregular relations with women, he had better play the violin in the intervals of studying metaphysics. There may be some truth in this; but only after reading widely in other parts of the book would he discover that it was not quite what Plato meant by describing *logos*, combined with *musikē*, as the only sure safeguard of *aretē* (*ibid.*, p. vi.).

But no matter how widely one reads in Cornford's translation, one cannot clarify this sentence or connect it with the general problems developed throughout the *Republic*; for the only possible sources of clarification or connection, the original terms, have disappeared and have been replaced by a sentence meaningless in itself and unillumined by the carefully prepared antecedents which were intended to give the thought special significance. Cornford's version reads as follows, ". . . his character is not thoroughly sound, for lack of the only safeguard that can preserve it throughout life, a thoughtful and cultivated mind." A literal rendering would be "'. . . [he is] not pure in his attachment to virtue, having been abandoned by the best guardian . . .' 'What's that?' Adeimantus said. 'Argument [or speech or reason] mixed with music. . . .'" There is no doubt that one can read the sentence as it appears in Cornford without being drawn up short, without being puzzled. But this is only because it says nothing. It uses commonplace terms which have no precise significance; it is the kind of sentence one finds in newspaper editorials. From having been shocking or incomprehensible, Plato becomes boring. There is no food for reflection here. Virtue has become character. But virtue has been a theme from the beginning of the *Republic*, and it has received a most subtle treatment. As a matter of fact, the whole issue of the book is whether one of the virtues, justice, is choiceworthy in itself or only for its accessory advantages. Socrates in this passage teaches that a man of the Spartan type—the kind of man most reputed for virtue—really does not love virtue for its own sake, but for other advantages following upon it. Secretly he believes money is truly good. This is the same critique Aristotle makes of Sparta. The question raised here is whether all vulgar virtue, all nonphilosophic practice of the virtues, is based upon expectation of some kind of further reward or not. None of this would appear from Cornford's version, no matter how hard the student of the text might think about it. He even suppresses Adeimantus' question so that the entire atmosphere of perplexity disappears. Now, Adeimantus is an admirer of Sparta, and Socrates has been trying to correct and purify that admiration. Adeimantus' question indicates his difficulty in understanding Socrates' criticism of what he admires; it shows how little he has learned. The dramatic aspect of the dialogue is not without significance.

Cornford is undoubtedly right that virtue no longer means what it used to mean and that it has lost its currency. (However, if one were to assert that courage, for example, is a virtue, most contemporaries would have some divination of what one is talking about.) But is this senility of the word only an accident? It has been said that it is one of the great mysteries of Western thought "how a word which used to mean the manliness of man has come to mean the chastity of woman." This change in significance is the product of a new understanding of the nature of man which began with Machiavelli. (If there were a translation of the *Prince* which always translated *virtù* by *virtue*, the student who compared it with the *Republic* would be in a position to make the most exciting of discoveries.) "Freedom" took the place of "virtue" as the most important term of political discourse, and virtue came to mean social virtue—that is, the disposition which would lead men to be obedient to civil authority and live in peace together rather than the natural perfection of the soul. The man who begins his studies should not be expected to know these things, but the only tolerable result of learning is that he become aware of them and be able to reflect on which of the alternatives most adequately describes the human condition. As it now stands, he may well be robbed of the greatest opportunity for enlightenment afforded by the classic literature. A study of the use of the word "virtue" in the *Republic* is by itself most revealing; and when, in addition, its sense is compared in Cicero, Thomas Aquinas, Hobbes, and Rousseau, the true history of political thought comes to light, and a series of alternatives is presented to the mind. These authors all self-consciously used the same term and in their disagreement were referring to the same issues. The reader must be sensitized by the use of the term to a whole ethos in which "virtue" was still a political issue.

Cornford uses *safeguard* instead of *guardian*. This is unobjectionable in itself, but *guardian* is a word that has been laden with significance by what has preceded in the book. The rulers, in particular those who fight and thus hold the power in the city, have been called guardians since their introduction in Book II. In a sense the problem of the *Republic* was to educate a ruling class which is such as to possess the characteristics of both the citizen, who cares for his country and has the spirit to fight for it, and the philosopher, who is gentle and cosmopolitan. This is a quasi-impossibility, and it is the leading theme of the onerous and complex training prescribed in the succeeding five books. If the education does not succeed, justice must be fundamentally compromised with the nature of those who hold power. In the context under discussion here Socrates is discussing the regimes which have to be founded on the fundamental compromise because of the flawed character of the guardians' virtues. Regimes depend on men's virtues, not on institutions; if the highest virtues are not present in the rulers, an inferior regime must be instituted. There are no guardians above the guardians; the only guardian of the guardians is a proper education. It is this theme to which the reader's attention must be brought.

And Socrates tells us something important about that education: it consists of reason but not reason alone. It must be mixed with a non-rational element which tempers the wildness and harshness of both the pre-philosophic and philosophic natures. Reason does not suffice in the formation of the good ruler. This is not the place to enter into a discussion of the full bearing of this lesson, but it is of utmost significance. The term *music* is indeed a difficult one for the modern reader, but there has been a full discussion of it in several passages of the *Republic,* and any other word would surely be most misleading. And, in fact, the sense we give to music is not totally alien to the understanding Glaucon and Adeimantus had at the start. It is Socrates who transformed their view by concentrating on the speech and its truth while subordinating rhythm and harmony. It is Socrates who rationalized *music*.

Is it not conceivable that the *Republic* is a book meant for people who are going to read widely in it, and that it would be unfair to cheat them for the sake of the subjective satisfaction of those who pick out sentences aimlessly? Is the man who comes away from the text with the interpretation feared by Cornford a reader about whom Plato would care? And does the gain in immediate intelligibility or beauty offset the loss in substance? Only unawareness of the problems can account for such a perverse skewing of the emphases. And this was a sentence chosen by Cornford to demonstrate the evident superiority of his procedure!

There are a whole series of fundamental terms like *virtue. Nature* and *city* are but two of the most important which are most often mistranslated. I have tried to indicate a number of them in the notes when they first occur. They are translated as they have been by the great authors in the philosophic tradition. Above all, I have avoided using terms of recent origin for which it is difficult to find an exact Greek equivalent, inasmuch as they are likely to be the ones which most reflect specifically modern thought. It is, of course, impossible always to translate every Greek word in the same way. But the only standard for change was the absolute unintelligibility of the rendition and not any desire to make Plato sound better or to add variety where he might seem monotonous. And the most crucial words, like those just mentioned and *form* and *regime*, etc., are always the same in spite of the difficulties this procedure sometimes causes. Ordinarily in contemporary translations the occurrence of, for example, *nature* in the English is no indication that there is anything related to *physis* in the Greek, and the occurrence of *physis* in the Greek does not regularly call forth any word related to *nature* from the translator. But, since *nature* is *the* standard for Plato, this confusion causes the reader either to be ignorant of the fact that nature is indeed Plato's standard or to mistake which phenomena he considers natural. Literal translation makes the *Republic* a difficult book to read; but it is in itself a difficult book, and our historical situation makes it doubly difficult for us. This must not be hidden. Plato intended his works essentially for the intelligent and industrious few, a natural aristocracy determined neither by birth nor wealth, and this translation attempts to do nothing which would contradict that intention.

In addition to unawareness of the need for precision, unwillingness to accept certain unpalatable or shocking statements or teachings is another cause of deviation from literalness. This unwillingness is due either to a refusal to believe Plato says what he means or to a desire to make him respectable. Cornford provides again a spectacular example of a not too uncommon tendency. At Book III 414 Socrates tells of the need for a "noble lie" to be believed in the city he and his companions are founding (in speech). Cornford calls it a"bold flight of invention" and adds the following note: "This phrase is commonly rendered 'noble lie,' a self-contradictory expression no more applicable to Plato's harmless allegory than to a New Testament parable or the Pilgrim's Progress, and liable to suggest that he would countenance the lies, for the most part ignoble, now called propaganda . . ." (*ibid.*, p. 106). But Socrates calls it a lie. The difference between a parable and this tale is that the man who hears a parable is conscious that it is an invention the truth of which is not in its literal expression, whereas the inhabitants of Socrates' city are to believe the untrue story to be true. His interlocutors are shocked by the notion, but—according to Cornford—we are to believe it is harmless because it might conjure up unpleasant associations.

This whole question of lying has been carefully prepared by Plato from the very outset, starting with the discussion with old Cephalus (331 b–c). It recurs again with respect to the lies of the poets (377 d), and in the assertions that gods cannot lie (381 e–382 e) and that rulers may lie (380 b–c). Now, finally, it is baldly stated that the only truly just civil society must be founded on a lie. Socrates prefers to face up to the issue with clarity. A good regime cannot be based on enlightenment; if there is no lie, a number of compromises—among them private property—must be made and hence merely conventional inequalities must be accepted. This is a radical statement about the relationship between truth and justice, one which leads to the paradox that wisdom can rule only in an element dominated by falsehood. It is hardly worth obscuring this issue for the sake of avoiding the crudest of misunderstandings. And perhaps the peculiarly modern phenomenon of propaganda might become clearer to the man who sees that it is somehow related to a certain myth of enlightenment which is itself brought into question by the Platonic analysis.

Beyond the general problems affecting the translation of all Greek and Latin texts, the Platonic dialogues present a particular difficulty. It is not too hard to find acceptable versions of Aristotle's treatises. This is because they are not entirely unlike modern books. There is, on the other hand, frequently a lack of clarity about the purposes of the dialogue form. Plato is commonly understood to have had a teaching like that of Aristotle and to have enclosed it in a sweet coating designed to perform certain didactic or artistic functions but which must be stripped away to get to the philosophic core. We then have Plato the poet and Plato the philosopher, two beings rolled into one and coexisting in an uneasy harmony. This is the fatal error which leads to the distinction between form and substance. The student of philosophy then takes one part of the dialogue as his special domain and the student of literature another as his; the translator follows suit, using great license in the bulk of the book and reverting to a care appropriate to Aristotle when philosophy appears to enter.

Cornford, as in all other things, expresses the current tendency in a radical form. He cuts out many of the exchanges of the interlocutors and suppresses entire arguments which do not seem to him to contribute to the movement of the dialogue. Although he claims his wish is to fulfill Plato's intentions in a modern context, he finally confesses that "the convention of question and answer becomes formal and frequently tedious. Plato himself came near to abandoning it in his latest work, the *Laws* . . ." (*ibid.*, p. vii). Cornford thus improves on Plato, correcting him in what he believes to be the proper direction. He thinks the dialogue form is only a convention, and, when it fatigues him, *he* abandons it. It is at precisely this point that one should begin to ask whether we understand what a dialogue really is. It is neither poetry nor philosophy; it is something of both, but it is itself and not a mere combination of the two. The fact that sometimes it does not meet the standards of the dramatic art reveals the same thing as the fact that sometimes the arguments are not up to the standards of philosophical rigor: Plato's intention is different from that of the poet or the philosopher as we understand them. To call the dialogue a convention is to hide the problem. Perhaps this very tedium of which Cornford complains is the test which Plato gives to the potential philosopher to see whether he is capable of overcoming the charm of external form; for a harsh concentration on often ugly detail is requisite to the philosophic enterprise. It is the concentration on beauty to the detriment of truth which constitutes the core of his critique of poetry, just as the indifference to forms, and hence to man, constitutes the core of his criticism of pre-Socratic philosophy. The dialogue is the synthesis of these two poles and is an organic unity. Every argument must be interpreted dramatically, for every argument is incomplete in itself and only the context can supply the missing links. And every dramatic detail must be interpreted philosophically, because these details contain the images of the problems which complete the arguments. Separately these two aspects are meaningless; together they are an invitation to the philosophic quest.

Cornford cites the *Laws* as proof that Plato gradually mended his ways; thus he has a certain Platonic justification for his changes in the text. But the difference in form between the *Republic* and the *Laws* is not a result of Plato's old age having taught him the defects of his mannered drama, as Cornford would have it, or its having caused him to lose his dramatic flair, as others assert. Rather the difference reflects the differences in the participants in the dialogues and thereby the difference of intention of the two works. This is just one example of what is typical of every part of the Platonic works. By way of the drama one comes to the profoundest issues. In the *Republic* Socrates discusses the best regime, a regime which can never be actualized, with two young men of some theoretical gifts whom he tries to convert from the life of political ambition to one in which philosophy plays a role. He must persuade them; every step of the argument is directed to their particular opinions and characters. Their reasoned assent is crucial to the whole process. The points at which they object to Socrates' reasoning are always most important, and so are the points when they assent when they should not. Each of the exchanges reveals something, even when the responses seem most uninteresting. In the *Laws* the Athenian Stranger engages in the narrower task of prescribing a code of laws for a possible but inferior regime. His interlocutors are old men who have no theoretical gifts or openness. The Stranger talks to them not for the end of any conversion but only because one of them has the political power the Stranger lacks. The purpose of his rhetoric is to make his two companions receptive to this unusual code. The Stranger must have the consent of the other two to operate his reforms of existing orders. Their particular prejudices must be overcome, but not by true persuasion of the truth; the new teaching must be made to appear to be in accord with their ancestrally hallowed opinions. Important concessions must be made to those opinions, since they are inalterable. The discussions indicate such difficulties and are preliminary to the essential act of lawgiving. Laws by their nature have the character of monologue rather than dialogue, and they are not supposed to discuss or be discussed; thus the presentation of the laws tends to be interrupted less. The strength and weakness of law lies in the fact that it is the polar opposite of philosophic discussion. The intention of a dialogue is the cause of its form, and that intention comes to light only to those who reflect on its form.

The Platonic dialogues do not present a doctrine; they prepare the way for philosophizing. They are intended to perform the function of a living teacher who makes his students think, who knows which ones should be led further and which ones should be kept away from the mysteries, and who makes them exercise the same faculties and virtues in studying his words as they would have to use in studying nature independently. One must philosophize to understand them. There is a Platonic teaching, but it is no more to be found in any of the speeches than is the thought of Shakespeare to be found in the utterances of any particular character. That thought is in none of the parts but is somehow in the whole, and the process of arriving at it is more subtle than that involved in reading a treatise. One must look at the microcosm of the drama just as one would look at the macrocosm of the world which it represents. Every detail of that world is an effect of the underlying causes which can be grasped only by the mind but which can be unearthed only by using all the senses as well. Those causes are truly known only when they are come to by way of the fullest consciousness of the world which they cause. Otherwise one does not know what to look for nor can one know the full power of the causes. A teaching which gives only the principles remains abstract and is mere dogma, for the student himself does not know what the principles explain nor does he know enough of the world to be sure that their explanations are anything more than partial. It is this rich consciousness of the phenomena on which the dialogues insist, and they themselves provide a training in it.

The human world is characterized by the distinction between speech and deed, and we all recognize that in order to understand a man or what he says both aspects must be taken into account. Just as no action of a man can be interpreted without hearing what he says about it himself, no speech can be accepted on its face value without comparing it to the actions of its author. The understanding of the man and his speeches is a result of a combination of the two perspectives. Thrasymachus' blush is as important as any of his theoretical arguments. A student who has on his own pieced together the nature of the rhetorician on the basis of his representation in the *Republic* has grasped his nature with a sureness grounded on a perception of the universal seen through the particular. This is his own insight, and he knows it more authentically and surely than someone who has been given a definition. This joins the concreteness of *l'esprit de finesse* to the science of *l'esprit de géometrie;* it avoids the pitfalls of particularistic sensitivity, on the one hand, and abstractness on the other. Poet and scientist become one, for the talents of both are necessary to the attainment of the only end—the truth.

The Platonic dialogues are a representation of the world; they are a cosmos in themselves. To interpret them, they must be approached as one would approach the world, bringing with one all one's powers. The only difference between the dialogues and the world is that the dialogues are so constructed that each part is integrally connected with every other part; there are no meaningless accidents. Plato reproduced the essential world as he saw it. Every word has its place and its meaning, and when one cannot with assurance explain any detail, he can know that his understanding is incomplete. When something seems boring or has to be explained away as a convention, it means that the interpreter has given up and has taken his place among the ranks of those Plato intended to exclude from the center of his thought. It is always that which strikes us as commonplace or absurd which indicates that we are not open to one of the mysteries, for such sentiments are the protective mechanisms which prevent our framework from being shaken.

The dialogues are constructed with an almost unbelievable care and subtlety. The drama is everywhere, even in what seem to be the most stock responses or the most purely theoretical disquisitions. In the discussion of the divided line, for example, the particular illustrations chosen fit the nature of Socrates' interlocutor; in order to see the whole problem, the reader must ponder not only the distinction of the kinds of knowing and being but its particular effect on Glaucon and what Socrates might have said to another man. One is never allowed to sit and passively receive the words of wisdom from the mouth of the master. And this means that the translation must, insofar as humanly possible, present all the nuances of the original—the oaths, the repetitions of words, the slight changes in the form of responses, etc.—so that the reader can look at the progress of the drama with all the perceptiveness and sharpness of which his nature permits him, which he would bring to bear on any real situation which concerned him. The translator cannot hope to have understood it all, but he must not begrudge his possible moral and intellectual superiors their possibility of insight. It is in the name of this duty that one risks the ridiculousness of pedantry in preserving the uncomfortable details which force a sacrifice of the easygoing charms of a more contemporary style.

I have used the Oxford text of the *Republic*, edited by John Burnet. I have deviated from it only rarely and in the important instances have made mention of it in the notes. Always at my hand was, of course, James Adam's valuable commentary (New York: Cambridge University Press, 1963). Schleiermacher's old German version was the most useful translation I found. Although his text was inferior to ours, he seems to have had the best grasp of the character and meaning of the dialogues. Robin's French is also quite careful. The best English translations are Paul Shorey's (Loeb) and A. D. Lindsay's (Everyman's). The latter is probably the more useful of the two because it is so unpretentious and straightforward.

The notes are not intended to be interpretive but merely to present necessary information the reader could not be expected to know, explain difficulties in translation, present the meaning of certain key terms, and, above all, give the known sources for the citations from other authors and the changes Plato makes in them. The dialogue is so rich in connections with other Platonic works and the rest of classical literature that it would be impossible to begin to supply even the most important. Moreover, it is the reader's job to discover these things himself, not only because it is good for him but also because the editor might very well be wrong in his emphases. The text is as much as possible Plato's, to be confronted directly by the reader. I have saved my own opinions for the interpretive essay. The index is also intended to serve as a glossary; its categories are drawn only from Plato's usage and not from contemporary interests or problems.

Whatever merit this translation may have is due in large measure to the help of Seth Benardete and Werner J. Dannhauser. The former gave me unsparingly of his immense classical learning and insight; the latter was almost unbelievably generous with his time and brought his sensitivity and sound judgment to the entire manuscript. I am also grateful to Ralph Lerner for his suggestions after a thorough reading of the text. Walter F. Berns, Jr., Richard H. Kennington, and Myron Rush were very helpful with the introduction. I wish to thank my students, who were the first to use the translation in their studies; particularly Carnes Lord, James Nichols, and Marc Plattner for their suggestions and detection of omissions and errors. Mr. Plattner also did the bulk of the work on the index and deserves the credit for this useful addition to my translation. The interpretive essay relies heavily on Leo Strauss' authoritative discussion of the *Republic* in *The City and Man* (Chicago: Rand McNally, 1964).

I must thank the Relm Foundation and Cornell University for their support. And I must also thank the Centre Universitaire International and its staff for the lovely office and the thoughtful assistance they gave me during my stay in Paris where I did the bulk of this work.

Allan Bloom

Ithaca, New York
July 1968

CONTENTS

THE REPUBLIC OF PLATO

THE REPUBLIC [1] (ON THE JUST) [2]

Dramatis Personae:

SOCRATES

GLAUCON

POLEMARCHUS

ADEIMANTUS

CEPHALUS

THRASYMACHUS

CLEITOPHON

CHARMANTIDES

EUTHYDEMUS

LYSIAS

NICERATUS

BOOK I

Socrates: I went down to the Piraeus[3] yesterday with Glaucon, son of
Ariston,[4] to pray to the goddess; and, at the same time, I wanted to observe how they would put on the festival,[5] since they were now holding it for the first time. Now, in my opinion, the procession of the native
inhabitants was fine; but the one the Thracians conducted was no less
fitting a show. After we had prayed and looked on, we went off toward
town.

327 *a*

b

Catching sight of us from afar as we were pressing homewards,
Polemarchus, son of Cephalus, ordered his slave boy to run after us and
order us to wait for him. The boy took hold of my cloak from behind
and said, "Polemarchus orders you to wait."

And I turned around and asked him where his master was. "He is
coming up behind," he said, "just wait."

"Of course we'll wait," said Glaucon.

A moment later Polemarchus came along with Adeimantus, Glaucon's brother, Niceratus, son of Nicias, and some others—apparently
from the procession. Polemarchus said, "Socrates, I guess you two are
hurrying to get away to town."

c

"That's not a bad guess," I said.

"Well," he said, "do you see how many of us there are?"

"Of course."

"Well, then," he said, "either prove stronger than these men
or stay here."

327 c   "Isn't there still one other possibility . . . ," I said, "our persuading you that you must let us go?"

"Could you really persuade," he said, "if we don't listen?"

"There's no way," said Glaucon.

"Well, then, think it over, bearing in mind we won't listen."

328 a   Then Adeimantus said, "Is it possible you don't know that at sunset there will be a torch race on horseback for the goddess?"

"On horseback?" I said. "That is novel. Will they hold torches
and pass them to one another while racing the horses, or what do you
mean?"

"That's it," said Polemarchus, "and, besides, they'll put on an all-
night festival that will be worth seeing. We'll get up after dinner and go
to see it; there we'll be together with many of the young men and we'll
b   talk. So stay and do as I tell you."

And Glaucon said, "It seems we must stay."

"Well, if it is so resolved,"[6] I said, "that's how we must act."

Then we went to Polemarchus' home; there we found Lysias[7] and
Euthydemus, Polemarchus' brothers, and, in addition, Thrasymachus,[8]
the Chalcedonian and Charmantides, the Paeanian,[9] and Cleitophon,[10] the son of Aristonymus.

Cephalus,[11] Polemarchus' father, was also at home; and he
c   seemed very old to me, for I had not seen him for some time. He was
seated on a sort of cushioned stool and was crowned with a wreath, for
he had just performed a sacrifice in the courtyard. We sat down beside
him, for some stools were arranged in a circle there. As soon as Cephalus saw me, he greeted me warmly and said:

"Socrates, you don't come down to us in the Piraeus very often,
yet you ought to. Now if I still had the strength to make the trip to
town easily, there would be no need for you to come here; rather we
d   would come to you. As it is, however, you must come here more frequently. I want you to know that as the other pleasures, those connected with the body, wither away in me, the desires and pleasures that
have to do with speeches grow the more. Now do as I say: be with these
young men, but come here regularly to us as to friends and your very
own kin."

"For my part, Cephalus, I am really delighted to discuss with the
e   very old," I said. "Since they are like men who have proceeded on a
certain road that perhaps we too will have to take, one ought, in my
opinion, to learn from them what sort of road it is—whether it is rough
and hard or easy and smooth. From you in particular I should like to
learn how it looks to you, for you are now at just the time of life the

poets call 'the threshold of old age.'¹² Is it a hard time of life, or what   328 c
have you to report of it?"

"By Zeus, I shall tell you just how it looks to me, Socrates," he
said. "Some of us who are about the same age often meet together and   329 a
keep up the old proverb.¹³ Now then, when they meet, most of the
members of our group lament, longing for the pleasures of youth and
reminiscing about sex, about drinking bouts and feasts and all that goes
with things of that sort; they take it hard as though they were deprived
of something very important and had then lived well but are now not
even alive. Some also bewail the abuse that old age receives from   b
relatives, and in this key they sing a refrain about all the evils old age
has caused them. But, Socrates, in my opinion these men do not put
their fingers on the cause. For, if this were the cause, I too would have
suffered these same things insofar as they depend on old age and so
would everyone else who has come to this point in life. But as it is, I
have encountered others for whom it was not so, especially Sophocles. I
was once present when the poet was asked by someone, 'Sophocles,
how are you in sex? Can you still have intercourse with a woman?'   c
'Silence, man,' he said. 'Most joyfully did I escape it, as though I had
run away from a sort of frenzied and savage master.' I thought at the
time that he had spoken well and I still do. For, in every way, old age
brings great peace and freedom from such things. When the desires
cease to strain and finally relax, then what Sophocles says comes to pass
in every way; it is possible to be rid of very many mad masters. But of   d
these things and of those that concern relatives, there is one just
cause: not old age, Socrates, but the character of the human beings.¹⁴
If they are orderly and content with themselves,¹⁵ even old age is only
moderately troublesome; if they are not, then both age, Socrates, and
youth alike turn out to be hard for that sort."

Then I was full of wonder at what he said and, wanting him to say
still more, I stirred him up, saying: "Cephalus, when you say these   e
things, I suppose that the many¹⁶ do not accept them from you, but
believe rather that it is not due to character that you bear old age so
easily but due to possessing great substance. They say that for the rich
there are many consolations."

"What you say is true," he said. "They do not accept them. And
they do have something there, but not, however, quite as much as they
think; rather, the saying of Themistocles holds good. When a Seriphian
abused him—saying that he was illustrious not thanks to himself but   330 a
thanks to the city—he answered that if he himself had been a Seriphian
he would not have made a name, nor would that man have made one

330 a   had he been an Athenian. And the same argument also holds good for those who are not wealthy and bear old age with difficulty: the decent man would not bear old age with poverty very easily, nor would the one who is not a decent sort ever be content with himself even if he were wealthy."

"Cephalus," I said, "did you inherit or did you earn most of what you possess?"

b   "What do you mean, earned, Socrates!" he said. "As a money-maker, I was a sort of mean between my grandfather and my father. For my grandfather, whose namesake I am, inherited pretty nearly as much substance as I now possess, and he increased it many times over. Lysanias, my father, used it to a point where it was still less than it is now. I am satisfied if I leave not less, but rather a bit more than I inherited, to my sons here."

"The reason I asked, you see," I said, "is that to me you didn't

c   seem overly fond of money. For the most part, those who do not make money themselves are that way. Those who do make it are twice as attached to it as the others. For just as poets are fond of their poems and fathers of their children, so money-makers too are serious about money—as their own product; and they also are serious about it for the same reason other men are—for its use. They are, therefore, hard even to be with because they are willing to praise nothing but wealth."

"What you say is true," he said.

d   "Indeed it is," I said. "But tell me something more. What do you suppose is the greatest good that you have enjoyed from possessing great wealth?"

"What I say wouldn't persuade many perhaps. For know well, Socrates," he said, "that when a man comes near to the realization that he will be making an end, fear and care enter him for things to which he gave no thought before. The tales[17] told about what is in Hades—that the one who has done unjust deeds[18] here must pay the penalty there—at which he laughed up to then, now make his soul twist

e   and turn because he fears they might be true. Whether it is due to the debility of old age, or whether he discerns something more of the things in that place because he is already nearer to them, as it were—he is, at any rate, now full of suspicion and terror; and he reckons up his accounts and considers whether he has done anything unjust to anyone. Now, the man who finds many unjust deeds in his life often even wakes from his sleep in a fright as children do, and lives in anticipation of evil. To the man who is conscious in himself of no unjust deed, sweet

331 a   and good hope is ever beside him—a nurse of his old age, as Pindar puts it. For, you know, Socrates, he put it charmingly when he said that whoever lives out a just and holy life

Sweet hope accompanies,   *If you live a just*
Fostering his heart, a nurse of his old age,   *life.*   331 a
Hope which most of all pilots
The ever-turning opinion of mortals.

How very wonderfully well he says that. For this I count the possession
of money most wroth-while, not for any man, but for the decent and orderly one. The possession of money contributes a great deal to not   b
cheating or lying to any man against one's will, and, moreover, to
not departing for that other place frightened because one owes some
sacrifices to a god or money to a human being. It also has many other
uses. But, still, one thing reckoned against another, I wouldn't count
this as the least thing, Socrates, for which wealth is very useful to an intelligent man."

"What you say is very fine[19] indeed, Cephalus," I said. "But as   c
to this very thing, justice, shall we so simply assert that it is the truth
and giving back what a man has taken from another, or is to do these
very things sometimes just and sometimes unjust? Take this case as an
example of what I mean: everyone would surely say that if a man takes
weapons from a friend when the latter is of sound mind, and the friend
demands them back when he is mad, one shouldn't give back such
things, and the man who gave them back would not be just, and
moreover, one should not be willing to tell someone in this state the
whole truth."

"What you say is right," he said.   d

"Then this isn't the definition of justice, speaking the truth and
giving back what one takes."

"It most certainly is, Socrates," interrupted Polemarchus, "at least
if Simonides should be believed at all."

"Well, then," said Cephalus, "I hand down the argument to you,
for it's already time for me to look after the sacrifices."

"Am I not the heir of what belongs to you?" said Polemarchus.[20]

"Certainly," he said and laughed. And with that he went away to
the sacrifices.[21]

"Tell me, you, the heir of the argument," I said, "what was it Si-   e
monides said about justice that you assert he said correctly?"

"That it is just to give to each what is owed," he said. "In saying
this he said a fine thing, at least in my opinion."

"Well, it certainly isn't easy to disbelieve a Simonides," I said.
"He is a wise and divine man. However, you, Polemarchus, perhaps
know what on earth he means, but I don't understand. For plainly he
doesn't mean what we were just saying—giving back to any man whatsoever something he has deposited when, of unsound mind, he demands
it. And yet, what he deposited is surely owed to him, isn't it?"   332 a

332 a   "Yes."

"But, when of unsound mind he demands it, it should under no condition be given back to him?"

"True," he said.

"Then Simonides, it seems, means something different from this sort of thing when he says that it is just to give back what is owed."

"Of course it's different, by Zeus," he said. "For he supposes that friends owe it to friends to do some good and nothing bad."

"I understand," I said. "A man does not give what is owed in giving back gold to someone who has deposited it, when the giving and the
b   taking turn out to be bad, assuming the taker and the giver are friends. Isn't this what you assert Simonides means?"

"Most certainly."

"Now, what about this? Must we give back to enemies whatever is owed to them?"

"That's exactly it," he said, "just what's owed to them. And I suppose that an enemy owes his enemy the very thing which is also fitting: some harm."

"Then," I said, "it seems that Simonides made a riddle, after the
c   fashion of poets, when he said what the just is. For it looks as if he thought that it is just to give to everyone what is fitting, and to this he gave the name 'what is owed.'"

"What else do you think?" he said.

"In the name of Zeus," I said, "if someone were to ask him, 'Simonides, the art[22] called medicine gives what that is owed and fitting to which things?' what do you suppose he would answer us?"

"It's plain," he said, "drugs, foods and drinks to bodies."

"The art called cooking gives what that is owed and fitting to which things?"
d   "Seasonings to meats."

"All right. Now then, the art that gives what to which things would be called justice?"

"If the answer has to be consistent with what preceded, Socrates," he said, "the one that gives benefits and harms to friends and enemies."

"Does he mean that justice is doing good to friends and harm to enemies?"

"In my opinion."

"With respect to disease and health, who is most able to do good to sick friends and bad to enemies?"

"A doctor."

"And with respect to the danger of the sea, who has this power   332 *e*
over those who are sailing?"

"A pilot."

"And what about the just man, in what action and with respect to
what work is he most able to help friends and harm enemies?"

"In my opinion it is in making war and being an ally in battle."

"All right. However, to men who are not sick, my friend Polemarchus, a doctor is useless."

"True."

"And to men who are not sailing, a pilot."

"Yes."

"Then to men who are not at war, is the just man useless?"

"Hardly so, in my opinion."

"Then is justice also useful in peacetime?"

"It is useful."   333 *a*

"And so is farming, isn't it?"

"Yes."

"For the acquisition of the fruits of the earth?"

"Yes."

"And, further, is shoemaking also useful?"

"Yes."

"You would say, I suppose, for the acquisition of shoes?"

"Certainly."

"What about justice then? For the use or acquisition of what
would you say it is useful in peacetime?"

"Contracts, Socrates."

"Do you mean by contracts, partnerships,²³ or something else?"

"Partnerships, of course."

"Then is the just man a good and useful partner in setting down   *b*
draughts, or is it the skilled player of draughts?"²⁴

"The skilled player of draughts."

"In setting down bricks and stones, is the just man a more useful
and better partner than the housebuilder?"

"Not at all."

"But in what partnership then is the just man a better partner than
the harp player, just as the harp player is better than the just man when
one has to do with notes?"

"In money matters, in my opinion."

"Except perhaps in using money, Polemarchus, when a horse
must be bought or sold with money in partnership; then, I suppose, the
expert on horses is a better partner. Isn't that so?"   *c*

333 c

"It looks like it."

"And, further, when it's a ship, the shipbuilder or pilot is better?"

"It seems so."

"Then, when gold or silver must be used in partnership, in what case is the just man more useful than the others?"

"When they must be deposited and kept safe, Socrates."

"Do you mean when there is no need to use them, and they are left lying?"

"Certainly."

d

"Is it when money is useless that justice is useful for it?"

"I'm afraid so."

"And when a pruning hook must be guarded, justice is useful both in partnership and in private; but when it must be used, vine-culture."

"It looks like it."

"Will you also assert that when a shield and a lyre must be guarded and not used, justice is useful; but when they must be used, the soldier's art and the musician's art are useful?"

"Necessarily."

"And with respect to everything else as well, is justice useless in the use of each and useful in its uselessness?"

"I'm afraid so."

e

"Then justice, my friend, wouldn't be anything very serious, if it is useful for useless things. Let's look at it this way. Isn't the man who is cleverest at landing a blow in boxing, or any other kind of fight, also the one cleverest at guarding against it?"

"Certainly."

"And whoever is clever at guarding against disease is also cleverest at getting away with producing it?"

"In my opinion, at any rate."

"And, of course, a good guardian of an army is the very same man

334 a

who can also steal the enemy's plans and his other dispositions?"

"Certainly."

"So of whatever a man is a clever guardian, he is also a clever thief?"

"It seems so."

"So that if a man is clever at guarding money, he is also clever at stealing it?"

"So the argument[25] indicates at least," he said.

"The just man, then, as it seems, has come to light as a kind of robber, and I'm afraid you learned this from Homer. For he admires

b

Autolycus, Odysseus' grandfather[26] on his mother's side, and says he

surpassed all men 'in stealing and in swearing oaths.' Justice, then,   *334 b*
seems, according to you and Homer and Simonides, to be a certain art
of stealing, for the benefit, to be sure, of friends and the harm of enemies. Isn't that what you meant?"

"No, by Zeus," he said. "But I no longer know what I did mean.
However, it is still my opinion that justice is helping friends and harming
enemies."

"Do you mean by friends those who seem to be good to an in-   *c*
dividual, or those who are, even if they don't seem to be, and similarly
with enemies?"

"It's likely," he said, "that the men one believes to be good, one
loves, while those he considers bad one hates."

"But don't human beings make mistakes about this, so that many
seem to them to be good although they are not, and vice versa?"

"They do make mistakes."

"So for them the good are enemies and the bad are friends?"

"Certainly."

"But nevertheless it's still just for them to help the bad and harm
the good?"   *d*

"It looks like it."

"Yet the good are just and such as not to do injustice?"

"True."

"Then, according to your argument, it's just to treat badly men who
have done nothing unjust?"

"Not at all, Socrates," he said. "For the argument seems to be
bad."

"Then, after all," I said, "it's just to harm the unjust and help the
just?"

"This looks finer than what we just said."

"Then for many, Polemarchus—all human beings who make
mistakes—it will turn out to be just to harm friends, for their friends   *e*
are bad; and just to help enemies, for they are good. So we shall say the
very opposite of what we asserted Simonides means."

"It does really turn out that way," he said. "But let's change what
we set down at the beginning. For I'm afraid we didn't set down the
definition of friend and enemy correctly."

"How did we do it, Polemarchus?"

"We set down that the man who seems good is a friend."

"Now," I said, "how shall we change it?"

"The man who seems to be, and is, good, is a friend," he said,
"while the man who seems good and is not, seems to be but is not a   *335 a*
friend. And we'll take the same position about the enemy."

335 *a*   "Then the good man, as it seems, will by this argument be a friend, and the good-for-nothing man an enemy?"

"Yes."

"You order us to add something to what we said at first about the just. Then we said that it is just to do good to the friend and bad to the enemy, while now we are to say in addition that it is just to do good to the friend, if he is good, and harm to the enemy, if he is bad."

b   "Most certainly," he said. "Said in that way it would be fine in my opinion."

"Is it, then," I said, "the part of a just man to harm any human being whatsoever?"

"Certainly," he said, "bad men and enemies ought to be harmed."

"Do horses that have been harmed become better or worse?"

"Worse."

"With respect to the virtue[27] of dogs or to that of horses?"

"With respect to that of horses."

"And when dogs are harmed, do they become worse with respect to the virtue of dogs and not to that of horses?"

"Necessarily."

c   "Should we not assert the same of human beings, my comrade— that when they are harmed, they become worse with respect to human virtue?"

"Most certainly."

"But isn't justice human virtue?"

"That's also necessary."

"Then, my friend, human beings who have been harmed necessarily become more unjust."

"It seems so."

"Well, are musicians able to make men unmusical by music?"

"Impossible."

"Are men skilled in horsemanship able to make men incompetent riders by horsemanship?"

"That can't be."

"But are just men able to make others unjust by justice, of all
d   things? Or, in sum, are good men able to make other men bad by virtue?"

"Impossible."

"For I suppose that cooling is not the work of heat, but of its opposite."

"Yes."

"Nor wetting the work of dryness but of its opposite."

"Certainly."

"Nor is harming, in fact, the work of the good but of its opposite." 335 *d*

"It looks like it."

"And it's the just man who is good?"

"Certainly."

"Then it is not the work of the just man to harm either a friend or anyone else, Polemarchus, but of his opposite, the unjust man."

"In my opinion, Socrates," he said, "what you say is entirely true."

"Then if someone asserts that it's just to give what is owed to each *e* man—and he understands by this that harm is owed to enemies by the just man and help to friends—the man who said it was not wise. For he wasn't telling the truth. For it has become apparent to us that it is never just to harm anyone."

"I agree," he said.

"We shall do battle then as partners, you and I," I said, "if someone asserts that Simonides, or Bias, or Pittacus[28] or any other wise and blessed man said it."

"I, for one," he said, "am ready to be your partner in the battle."

"Do you know," I said, "to whom, in my opinion, that saying 336 *a* belongs which asserts that it is just to help friends and harm enemies?"

"To whom?" he said.

"I suppose it belongs to Periander, or Perdiccas, or Xerxes, or Ismenias the Theban,[29] or some other rich man who has a high opinion of what he can do."

"What you say is very true," he said.

"All right," I said, "since it has become apparent that neither justice nor the just is this, what else would one say they are?"

Now Thrasymachus had many times started out to take over the *b* argument in the midst of our discussion, but he had been restrained by the men sitting near him, who wanted to hear the argument out. But when we paused and I said this, he could no longer keep quiet; hunched up like a wild beast, he flung himself at us as if to tear us to pieces. Then both Polemarchus and I got all in a flutter from fright. And he shouted out into our midst and said, "What is this nonsense that has possessed you for so long, Socrates? And why do you act like *c* fools making way for one another? If you truly want to know what the just is, don't only ask and gratify your love of honor by refuting whatever someone answers—you know that it is easier to ask than to answer—but answer yourself and say what you assert the just to be. And see to it you don't tell me that it is the needful, or the helpful, *d* or the profitable, or the gainful, or the advantageous; but tell me

336 d   clearly and precisely what you mean, for I won't accept it if you say such inanities."

I was astounded when I heard him, and, looking at him, I was frightened. I think that if I had not seen him before he saw me, I would have been speechless.[30] As it was, just when he began to be exasperated by the argument, I had looked at him first, so that I was able

e   to answer him; and with just a trace of a tremor, I said: "Thrasymachus, don't be hard on us. If we are making any mistake in the consideration of the arguments, Polemarchus and I, know well that we're making an unwilling mistake. If we were searching for gold we would never willingly make way for one another in the search and ruin our chances of finding it; so don't suppose that when we are seeking for justice, a thing more precious than a great deal of gold, we would ever foolishly give in to one another and not be as serious as we can be about bringing it to light. Don't you suppose that, my friend! Rather, as I suppose, we are not competent. So it's surely far more fitting for us to

337 a   be pitied by you clever men than to be treated harshly."

He listened, burst out laughing very scornfully, and said, "Heracles! Here is that habitual irony of Socrates. I knew it, and I predicted to these fellows that you wouldn't be willing to answer, that you would be ironic and do anything rather than answer if someone asked you something."

"That's because you are wise, Thrasymachus," I said. "Hence you knew quite well that if you asked someone how much twelve is and in

b   asking told him beforehand, 'See to it you don't tell me, you human being, that it is two times six, or three times four, or six times two, or four times three; I won't accept such nonsense from you'—it was plain to you, I suppose, that no one would answer a man who asks in this way. And if he asked, 'Thrasymachus, what do you mean? Shall I answer none of those you mentioned before? Even if it happens to be one of these, shall I say something other than the truth, you surprising

c   man? Or what do you mean?'—what would you say to him in response?"

"Very well," he said, "as if this case were similar to the other."

"Nothing prevents it from being," I said. "And even granting that it's not similar, but looks like it is to the man who is asked, do you think he'll any the less answer what appears to him, whether we forbid him to or not?"

"Well, is that what you are going to do?" he said. "Are you going to give as an answer one of those I forbid?"

"I shouldn't be surprised," I said, "if that were my opinion upon consideration."

"What if I could show you another answer about justice besides   337 d
all these and better than they are?" he said. "What punishment do you
think you would deserve to suffer?"

"What else than the one it is fitting for a man who does not know
to suffer?" I said. "And surely it is fitting for him to learn from the man
who knows. So this is what I think I deserve to suffer."

"That's because you are an agreeable chap!" he said. "But in addition to learning, pay a fine in money too."

"When I get some," I said.

"He has some," said Glaucon. "Now, for money's sake, speak,
Thrasymachus. We shall all contribute for Socrates."[31]

"I certainly believe it," he said, "so that Socrates can get away   e
with his usual trick; he'll not answer himself, and when someone else
has answered he gets hold of the argument and refutes it."

"You best of men," I said, "how could a man answer who, in the
first place, does not know and does not profess to know; and who, in
the second place, even if he does have some supposition about these
things, is forbidden to say what he believes by no ordinary man? It's
more fitting for you to speak; for you are the one who says he knows   338 a
and can tell. Now do as I say; gratify me by answering and don't begrudge your teaching to Glaucon here and the others."

After I said this, Glaucon and the others begged him to do as I
said. And Thrasymachus evidently desired to speak so that he could
win a good reputation, since he believed he had a very fine answer. But
he kept up the pretense of wanting to prevail on me to do the answering. Finally, however, he conceded and then said:

"Here is the wisdom of Socrates; unwilling himself to teach, he   b
goes around learning from others, and does not even give thanks to
them."

"When you say I learn from others," I said, "you speak the truth,
Thrasymachus; but when you say I do not make full payment in thanks,
you lie. For I pay as much as I can. I am only able to praise. I have no
money. How eagerly I do so when I think someone speaks well, you
will well know as soon as you have answered; for I suppose you will
speak well."

"Now listen," he said. "I say that the just is nothing other than the   c
advantage of the stronger.[32] Well, why don't you praise me? But you
won't be willing."

"First I must learn what you mean," I said. "For, as it is, I don't
yet understand. You say the just is the advantage of the stronger. What
ever do you mean by that, Thrasymachus? You surely don't assert such
a thing as this: if Polydamas, the pancratiast,[33] is stronger than we are

338 *d* and beef is advantageous for his body, then this food is also advantageous and just for us who are weaker than he is."

"You are disgusting, Socrates," he said. "You take hold of the argument in the way you can work it the most harm."

"Not at all, best of men," I said. "Just tell me more clearly what you mean."

"Don't you know," he said, "that some cities are ruled tyrannically, some democratically, and some aristocratically?"

"Of course."

"In each city, isn't the ruling group master?"

"Certainly."

e "And each ruling group sets down laws for its own advantage; a democracy sets down democratic laws; a tyranny, tyrannic laws; and the others do the same. And they declare that what they have set down—their own advantage—is just for the ruled, and the man who departs from it they punish as a breaker of the law and a doer of unjust

339 *a* deeds. This, best of men, is what I mean: in every city the same thing is just, the advantage of the established ruling body. It surely is master; so the man who reasons rightly concludes that everywhere justice is the same thing, the advantage of the stronger."

"Now," I said, "I understand what you mean. Whether it is true or not, I'll try to find out. Now, you too answer that the just is the advantageous, Thrasymachus—although you forbade me to give that answer. Of course, 'for the stronger' is added on to it."

b "A small addition, perhaps," he said.

"It isn't plain yet whether it's a big one. But it is plain that we must consider whether what you say is true. That must be considered, because, while I too agree that the just is something of advantage, you add to it and assert that it's the advantage of the stronger, and I don't know whether it's so."

"Go ahead and consider," he said.

"That's what I'm going to do," I said. "Now, tell me: don't you say though that it's also just to obey the rulers?"

"I do."

c "Are the rulers in their several cities infallible, or are they such as to make mistakes too?"

"By all means," he said, "they certainly are such as to make mistakes too."

"When they put their hands to setting down laws, do they set some down correctly and some incorrectly?"

"I suppose so."

"Is that law correct which sets down what is advantageous for themselves, and that one incorrect which sets down what is disadvantageous?—Or, how do you mean it?"   339 c

"As you say."

"But whatever the rulers set down must be done by those who are ruled, and this is the just?"

"Of course."

"Then, according to your argument, it's just to do not only what is advantageous for the stronger but also the opposite, what is disadvantageous."   d

"What do you mean?" he said.

"What you mean, it seems to me. Let's consider it better. Wasn't it agreed that the rulers, when they command the ruled to do something, sometimes completely mistake what is best for themselves, while it is just for the ruled to do whatever the rulers command? Weren't these things agreed upon?"

"I suppose so," he said.

"Well, then," I said, "also suppose that you're agreed that it is just to do what is disadvantageous for those who are the rulers and the stronger, when the rulers unwillingly command what is bad for themselves, and you assert it is just to do what they have commanded. In this case, most wise Thrasymachus, doesn't it necessarily follow that it is just for the others to do the opposite of what you say? For the weaker are commanded to do what is doubtless disadvantageous for the stronger."   e

"Yes, by Zeus, Socrates," said Polemarchus, "most clearly."   340 a

"If it's you who are to witness for him, Polemarchus," said Cleitophon interrupting.

"What need is there of a witness?" he said. "Thrasymachus himself agrees that the rulers sometimes command what is bad for themselves and that it is just for the others to do these things."

"That's because Thrasymachus set down that to do what the rulers bid is just, Polemarchus."

"And because, Cleitophon, he also set down that the advantage of the stronger is just. Once he had set both of these principles down, he further agreed that sometimes the stronger order those who are weaker and are ruled to do what is to the disadvantage of the stronger. On the basis of these agreements, the advantage of the stronger would be no more just than the disadvantage."   b

"But," said Cleitophon, "he said that the advantage of the stronger is what the stronger believes to be his advantage. This is what

[17]

340 b   must be done by the weaker, and this is what he set down as the just."

"That's not what was said," said Polemarchus.

c   "It doesn't make any difference, Polemarchus," I said, "if Thrasymachus says it that way now, let's accept it from him. Now tell me, Thrasymachus, was this what you wanted to say the just is, what *seems* to the stronger to be the advantage of the stronger, whether it is advantageous or not? Shall we assert that this is the way you mean it?"

"Not in the least," he said. "Do you suppose that I call a man who makes mistakes 'stronger' at the moment when he is making mistakes?"

"I did suppose you to mean this," I said, "when you agreed that the rulers are not infallible but also make mistakes in some things."

d   "That's because you're a sycophant[34] in arguments, Socrates," he said. "To take an obvious example, do you call a man who makes mistakes about the sick a doctor because of the very mistake he is making? Or a man who makes mistakes in calculation a skilled calculator, at the moment he is making a mistake, in the very sense of his mistake? I suppose rather that this is just our manner of speaking—the doctor made a mistake, the calculator made a mistake, and the grammarian. But I suppose that each of these men, insofar as he is what we address

e   him as, never makes mistakes. Hence, in precise speech, since you too speak precisely, none of the craftsmen makes mistakes. The man who makes mistakes makes them on account of a failure in knowledge and is in that respect no craftsman. So no craftsman, wise man, or ruler makes mistakes at the moment when he is ruling, although everyone would say that the doctor made a mistake and the ruler made a mistake. What I answered you earlier, then, you must also take in this way. But what follows is the most precise way: the ruler, insofar as he

341 a   is a ruler, does not make mistakes; and not making mistakes, he sets down what is best for himself. And this must be done by the man who is ruled. So I say the just is exactly what I have been saying from the beginning, to do the advantage of the stronger."

"All right, Thrasymachus," I said, "so in your opinion I play the sycophant?"

"You most certainly do," he said.

"Do you suppose I ask as I asked because I am plotting to do harm[35] to you in the argument?"

"I don't suppose," he said, "I know it well. But it won't profit you. You

b   won't get away with doing harm unnoticed and, failing to get away unnoticed, you won't be able to overpower me in the argument."

"Nor would I even try, you blessed man," I said. "But, so that the same sort of thing doesn't happen to us again, make it clear whether

you meant by the ruler and stronger the man who is such only in com-   341 *b*
mon parlance or the man who is such in precise speech, whose advantage you said a moment ago it will be just for the weaker to serve
because he is stronger?"

"The one who is the ruler in the most precise sense," he said. "Do
harm to that and play the sycophant, if you can—I ask for no
favors—but you won't be able to."

"Do you suppose me to be so mad," I said, "as to try to shave a   *c*
lion and play the sycophant with Thrasymachus?"

"At least you tried just now," he said, "although you were a
nonentity at that too."

"Enough of this," I said. "Now tell me, is the doctor in the precise
sense, of whom you recently spoke, a money-maker or one who cares
for the sick? Speak about the man who is really a doctor."

"One who cares for the sick," he said.

"And what about the pilot? Is the man who is a pilot in the correct sense a ruler of sailors or a sailor?"

"A ruler of sailors."

"I suppose it needn't be taken into account that he sails in the   *d*
ship, and he shouldn't be called a sailor for that. For it isn't because of
sailing that he is called a pilot but because of his art and his rule over
sailors."

"True," he said.

"Is there something advantageous for each of them?"

"Certainly."

"And isn't the art," I said, "naturally directed toward seeking and
providing for the advantage of each?"

"Yes, that is what it is directed toward."

"And is there then any advantage for each of the arts other than to
be as perfect as possible?"

"How do you mean this question?"   *e*

"Just as," I said, "if you should ask me whether it's enough for a
body to be a body or whether it needs something else, I would say: 'By
all means, it needs something else. And the art of medicine has now
been discovered because a body is defective,[36] and it won't do for it to
be like that. The art was devised for the purpose of providing what is
advantageous for a body.' Would I seem to you to speak correctly in
saying that or not?"

"You would," he said.

"And what about medicine itself, is it or any other art defective,   342 *a*
and does it need some supplementary virtue? Just as eyes need sight
and ears hearing and for this reason an art is needed that will consider
and provide what is advantageous for them, is it also the case that there

342 a   is some defect in the art itself and does each art have need of another
        art that considers its advantage, and does the art that considers it need
        in its turn another of the same kind, and so on endlessly? Or does each
b   consider its own advantage by itself? Or does it need neither itself nor
        another to consider what is advantageous for its defect? Is it that there
        is no defect or error present in any art, and that it isn't fitting for an art
        to seek the advantage of anything else than that of which it is the art,
        and that it is itself without blemish or taint because it is correct so long
        as it is precisely and wholly what it is? And consider this in that precise
        sense. Is it so or otherwise?"

        "That's the way it looks," he said.
c   "Then," I said, "medicine doesn't consider the advantage of
        medicine, but of the body."

        "Yes," he said.

        "Nor does horsemanship consider the advantage of horsemanship,
        but of horses. Nor does any other art consider its own advantage—for
        it doesn't have any further need to—but the advantage of that of which
        it is the art."

        "It looks that way," he said.

        "But, Thrasymachus, the arts rule and are masters of that of
        which they are arts."

        He conceded this too, but with a great deal of resistance.

        "Then, there is no kind of knowledge that considers or commands
        the advantage of the stronger, but rather of what is weaker and ruled by
d   it."

        He finally agreed to this, too, although he tried to put up a fight
        about it. When he had agreed, I said:

        "Then, isn't it the case that the doctor, insofar as he is a doctor,
        considers or commands not the doctor's advantage, but that of the sick
        man? For the doctor in the precise sense was agreed to be a ruler of
        bodies and not a money-maker. Wasn't it so agreed?"

        He assented.

        "And was the pilot in the precise sense agreed to be a ruler of
        sailors and not a sailor?"

e   "It was agreed."

        "Then such a pilot and ruler will consider or command the benefit
        not of the pilot, but of the man who is a sailor and is ruled."

        He assented with resistance.

        "Therefore, Thrasymachus," I said, "there isn't ever anyone who
        holds any position of rule, insofar as he is ruler, who considers or
        commands his own advantage rather than that of what is ruled and of
        which he himself is the craftsman; and it is looking to this and what is

advantageous and fitting for it that he says everything he says and does   *342 e*
everything he does."

When we came to this point in the argument and it was evident to   *343 a*
everyone that the argument about the just had turned around in the opposite direction, Thrasymachus, instead of answering, said, "Tell me,
Socrates, do you have a wet nurse?"

"Why this?" I said. "Shouldn't you answer instead of asking such
things?"

"Because," he said, "you know she neglects your sniveling nose
and doesn't give it the wiping you need, since it's her fault you do not
even recognize sheep or shepherd."

"Because of what, in particular?" I said.

"Because you suppose shepherds or cowherds consider the good   *b*
of the sheep or the cows and fatten them and take care of them looking
to something other than their masters' good and their own; and so you
also believe that the rulers in the cities, those who truly rule, think
about the ruled differently from the way a man would regard sheep,
and that night and day they consider anything else than how they will
benefit themselves. And you are so far off about the just and justice,   *c*
and the unjust and injustice, that you are unaware that justice and the
just are really someone else's good, the advantage of the man who is
stronger and rules, and a personal harm to the man who obeys and
serves. Injustice is the opposite, and it rules the truly simple and just;   *d*
and those who are ruled do what is advantageous for him who is
stronger, and they make him whom they serve happy but themselves
not at all. And this must be considered, most simple Socrates: the just
man everywhere has less than the unjust man. First, in contracts, when
the just man is a partner of the unjust man, you will always find that
at the dissolution of the partnership the just man does not have more
than the unjust man, but less. Second, in matters pertaining to the city,
when there are taxes, the just man pays more on the basis of equal property, the unjust man less; and when there are distributions, the one makes
no profit, the other much. And, further, when each holds some ruling   *e*
office, even if the just man suffers no other penalty, it is his lot to see
his domestic affairs deteriorate from neglect, while he gets no advantage from the public store, thanks to his being just; in addition to
this, he incurs the ill will of his relatives and his acquaintances when he
is unwilling to serve them against what is just. The unjust man's situation is the opposite in all of these respects. I am speaking of the man
I just now spoke of, the one who is able to get the better[37] in a big   *344 a*
way. Consider him, if you want to judge how much more to his private
advantage the unjust is than the just. You will learn most easily of all if

344 a   you turn to the most perfect injustice, which makes the one who does injustice most happy, and those who suffer it and who would not be willing to do injustice, most wretched. And that is tyranny, which by stealth and force takes away what belongs to others, both what is sacred and profane, private and public, not bit by bit, but all at once. When

b   someone does some part of this injustice and doesn't get away with it, he is punished and endures the greatest reproaches—temple robbers, kidnappers, housebreakers,[38] defrauders, and thieves are what they call those partially unjust men who do such evil deeds. But when someone, in addition to the money of the citizens, kidnaps and enslaves them too, instead of these shameful names, he gets called happy and

c   blessed, not only by the citizens but also by whomever else hears that he has done injustice entire. For it is not because they fear doing unjust deeds, but because they fear suffering them, that those who blame injustice do so. So, Socrates, injustice, when it comes into being on a sufficient scale, is mightier, freer, and more masterful than justice; and, as I have said from the beginning, the just is the advantage of the stronger, and the unjust is what is profitable and advantageous for oneself."

d   When Thrasymachus had said this, he had it in mind to go away, just like a bathman,[39] after having poured a great shower of speech into our ears all at once. But those present didn't let him and forced him to stay put and present an argument for what had been said. And I, too, on my own begged him and said:

"Thrasymachus, you demonic man, do you toss in such an argument, and have it in mind to go away before teaching us adequately or finding out whether it is so or not? Or do you suppose you are

e   trying to determine a small matter and not a course of life on the basis of which each of us would have the most profitable existence?"

"What? Do I suppose it is otherwise?" said Thrasymachus.

"You seemed to," I said, "or else you have no care for us and aren't a bit concerned whether we shall live worse or better as a result of our ignorance of what you say you know. But, my good man, make

345 a   an effort to show it to us—it wouldn't be a bad investment for you to do a good deed for so many as we are. I must tell you that for my part I am not persuaded; nor do I think injustice is more profitable than justice, not even if one gives it free rein and doesn't hinder it from doing what it wants. But, my good man, let there be an unjust man, and let him be able to do injustice, either by stealth or by fighting out in the open; nevertheless, he does not persuade me that this is more profitable

b   than justice. And perhaps, someone else among us—and not only

I—also has this sentiment. So persuade us adequately, you blessed   345 *b*
man, that we don't deliberate correctly in having a higher regard for
justice than injustice."

"And how," he said, "shall I persuade you? If you're not persuaded by what I've just now said, what more shall I do for you? Shall I
take the argument and give your soul a forced feeding?"[40]

"By Zeus, don't you do it," I said. "But, first, stick to what you
said, or if you change what you set down, make it clear that you're
doing so, and don't deceive us. As it is, Thrasymachus, you see
that—still considering what went before—after you had first defined   *c*
the true doctor, you later thought it no longer necessary to keep a precise guard over the true shepherd. Rather you think that he, insofar as
he is a shepherd, fattens the sheep, not looking to what is best for the
sheep, but, like a guest who is going to be feasted, to good cheer, or in   *d*
turn, to the sale, like a money-maker and not a shepherd. The
shepherd's art surely cares for nothing but providing the best for what
it has been set over. For that the art's own affairs be in the best possible
way is surely adequately provided for so long as it lacks nothing of
being the shepherd's art. And, similarly, I for my part thought just now
that it is necessary for us to agree that every kind of rule, insofar as it is
rule, considers what is best for nothing other than for what is ruled
and cared for, both in political and private rule. Do you think that   *e*
the rulers in the cities, those who truly rule, rule willingly?"

"By Zeus, I don't think it," he said. "I know it well."

"But, Thrasymachus," I said, "what about the other kinds of rule?   *Salary*
Don't you notice that no one wishes to rule voluntarily, but they demand wages as though the benefit from ruling were not for them but for
those who are ruled? Now tell me this much: don't we, at all events, al-   346 *a*
ways say that each of the arts is different on the basis of having a different capacity? And don't answer contrary to your opinion, you
blessed man, so that we can reach a conclusion."

"Yes," he said, "this is the way they differ."

"And does each of them provide us with some peculiar[41] benefit
and not a common one, as the medical art furnishes us with health, the
pilot's art with safety in sailing, and so forth with the others?"

"Certainly."

"And does the wage-earner's art furnish wages? For this is its   *b*
power. Or do you call the medical art the same as the pilot's art? Or, if
you wish to make precise distinctions according to the principle you set
down, even if a man who is a pilot becomes healthy because sailing on
the sea is advantageous to him, nonetheless you don't for that reason
call what he does the medical art?"

"Surely not," he said.

346 b   "Nor do you, I suppose, call the wage-earner's art the medical art, even if a man who is earning wages should be healthy?"

"Surely not," he said.

"And, what about this? Do you call the medical art the wage-earner's art, even if a man practicing medicine should earn wages?"

c   He said that he did not.

"And we did agree that the benefit of each art is peculiar?"

"Let it be," he said.

"Then whatever benefit all the craftsmen derive in common is plainly derived from their additional use of some one common thing that is the same for all."

"It seems so," he said.

"And we say that the benefit the craftsmen derive from receiving wages comes to them from their use of the wage-earner's art in addition."

He assented with resistance.

d   "Then this benefit, getting wages, is for each not a result of his own art; but, if it must be considered precisely, the medical art produces health, and the wage-earner's art wages; the housebuilder's art produces a house and the wage-earner's art, following upon it, wages; and so it is with all the others: each accomplishes its own work and benefits that which it has been set over. And if pay were not attached to it, would the craftsman derive benefit from the art?"

e   "It doesn't look like it," he said.

"Does he then produce no benefit when he works for nothing?"

"I suppose he does."

"Therefore, Thrasymachus, it is plain by now that no art or kind of rule provides for its own benefit, but, as we have been saying all along, it provides for and commands the one who is ruled, considering his advantage—that of the weaker—and not that of the stronger. It is for just this reason, my dear Thrasymachus, that I said a moment ago that no one willingly chooses to rule and get mixed up in straightening out other people's troubles; but he asks for wages, because the man

347 a   who is to do anything fine by art never does what is best for himself nor does he command it, insofar as he is commanding by art, but rather what is best for the man who is ruled. It is for just this reason, as it seems, that there must be wages for those who are going to be willing to rule—either money, or honor, or a penalty if he should not rule."

"What do you mean by that, Socrates?" said Glaucon. "The first two kinds of wages I know, but I don't understand what penalty you mean and how you can say it is a kind of wage."

"Then you don't understand the wages of the best men," I said,   347 *a*
"on account of which the most decent men rule, when they are willing   *b*
to rule. Or don't you know that love of honor and love of money are
said to be, and are, reproaches?"

"I do indeed," he said.

"For this reason, therefore," I said, "the good aren't willing to
rule for the sake of money or honor. For they don't wish openly to exact wages for ruling and get called hirelings, nor on their own secretly
to take a profit from their ruling and get called thieves. Nor, again, will
they rule for the sake of honor. For they are not lovers of honor.
Hence, necessity and a penalty must be there in addition for them, if   *c*
they are going to be willing to rule—it is likely that this is the source of
its being held to be shameful to seek to rule and not to await
necessity—and the greatest of penalties is being ruled by a worse man
if one is not willing to rule oneself. It is because they fear this, in my
view, that decent men rule, when they do rule; and at that time they
proceed to enter on rule, not as though they were going to something
good, or as though they were going to be well off in it; but they enter on
it as a necessity and because they have no one better than or like them-   *d*
selves to whom to turn it over. For it is likely that if a city of good men
came to be, there would be a fight over not ruling, just as there is now
over ruling; and there it would become manifest that a true ruler really
does not naturally consider his own advantage but rather that of the one
who is ruled. Thus everyone who knows would choose to be benefited
by another rather than to take the trouble of benefiting another. So I
can in no way agree with Thrasymachus that the just is the advantage
of the stronger. But this we shall consider again at another time. What   *e*
Thrasymachus now says is in my own opinion a far bigger thing—he
asserts that the life of the unjust man is stronger[42] than that of the just
man. Which do you choose, Glaucon," I said, "and which speech is
truer in your opinion?"

"I for my part choose the life of the just man as more profitable."

"Did you hear," I said, "how many good things Thrasymachus
listed a moment ago as belonging to the life of the unjust man?"   348 *a*

"I heard," he said, "but I'm not persuaded."

"Then do you want us to persuade him, if we're able to find a way,
that what he says isn't true?"

"How could I not want it?" he said.

"Now," I said, "if we should speak at length against him, setting
speech against speech, telling how many good things belong to being
just, and then he should speak in return, and we again, there'll be need

348 b   of counting the good things and measuring how many each of us has in each speech, and then we'll be in need of some sort of judges[43] who will decide. But if we consider just as we did a moment ago, coming to agreement with one another, we'll ourselves be both judges and pleaders at once."

"Most certainly," he said.

"Which way do you like?" I said.

"The latter," he said.

"Come now, Thrasymachus," I said, "answer us from the beginning. Do you assert that perfect injustice is more profitable than justice when it is perfect?"

c   "I most certainly do assert it," he said, "and I've said why."

"Well, then, how do you speak about them in this respect? Surely you call one of them virtue and the other vice?"

"Of course."

"Then do you call justice virtue and injustice vice?"

"That's likely, you agreeable man," he said, "when I also say that injustice is profitable and justice isn't."

"What then?"

"The opposite," he said.

"Is justice then vice?"

"No, but very high-minded innocence."

d   "Do you call injustice corruption?"[44]

"No, rather good counsel."

"Are the unjust in your opinion good as well as prudent, Thrasymachus?"

"Yes, those who can do injustice perfectly," he said, "and are able to subjugate cities and tribes of men to themselves. You, perhaps, suppose I am speaking of cutpurses. Now, such things, too, are profitable," he said, "when one gets away with them; but they aren't worth mentioning compared to those I was just talking about."

e   "As to that," I said, "I'm not unaware of what you want to say. But I wondered about what went before, that you put injustice in the camp of virtue and wisdom, and justice among their opposites?"

"But I do indeed set them down as such."

"That's already something more solid, my comrade," I said, "and it's no longer easy to know what one should say. For if you had set injustice down as profitable but had nevertheless agreed that it is viciousness or shameful, as do some others, we would have something to say, speaking according to customary usage. But as it is, plainly you'll say that injustice is fair and mighty, and, since you also dared to set it down in the camp of virtue and wisdom, you'll set down to its ac-

count all the other things which we used to set down as belonging to the   349 *a*
just."

"Your divination is very true," he said.

"But nonetheless," I said, "one oughtn't to hesitate to pursue the consideration of the argument as long as I understand you to say what you think. For, Thrasymachus, you seem really not to be joking now, but to be speaking the truth as it seems to you."

"And what difference does it make to you," he said, "whether it seems so to me or not, and why don't you refute the argument?"

"No difference," I said. "But try to answer this in addition to the   *b*
other things: in your opinion would the just man be willing to get the better of the just man in anything?"

"Not at all," he said. "Otherwise he wouldn't be the urbane innocent he actually is."

"And what about this: would he be willing to get the better of the just action?"

"Not even of the just action," he said.

"And does he claim he deserves to get the better of the unjust man, and believe it to be just, or would he not believe it to be so?"

"He'd believe it to be just," he said, "and he'd claim he deserves to get the better, but he wouldn't be able to."

"That," I said, "is not what I am asking, but whether the just man wants, and claims he deserves, to get the better of the unjust and not of   *c*
the just man?"

"He does," he said.

"And what about the unjust man? Does he claim he deserves to get the better of the just man and the just action?"

"How could it be otherwise," he said, "since he claims he deserves to get the better of everyone?"

"Then will the unjust man also get the better of the unjust human being and action, and will he struggle to take most of all for himself?"

"That's it."

"Let us say it, then, as follows," I said, "the just man does not get the better of what is like but of what is unlike, while the unjust man gets the better of like and unlike?"   *d*

"What you said is very good," he said.

"And," I said, "is the unjust man both prudent and good, while the just man is neither?"

"That's good too," he said.

"Then," I said, "is the unjust man also like the prudent and the good, while the just man is not like them?"

349 d   "How," he said, "could he not be like such men, since he is such as they, while the other is not like them."

"Fine. Then is each of them such as those to whom he is like?"

"What else could they be?" he said.

e   "All right, Thrasymachus. Do you say that one man is musical and that another is unmusical?"

"I do."

"Which is prudent and which thoughtless?"

"Surely the musical man is prudent and the unmusical man thoughtless."

"Then, in the things in which he is prudent, is he also good, and in those in which he is thoughtless, bad?"

"Yes."

350 a   "And what about a medical man? Is it not the same with him?"

"It is the same."

"Then, you best of men, is any musical man who is tuning a lyre in your opinion willing to get the better of another musical man in tightening and relaxing the strings, or does he claim he deserves more?"

"Not in my opinion."

"But the better of the unmusical man?"

"Necessarily," he said.

"And what about a medical man? On questions of food and drink, would he want to get the better of a medical man or a medical action?"

"Surely not."

"But the better of what is not medical?"

"Yes."

"Now, for every kind of knowledge and lack of knowledge, see if in your opinion any man at all who knows chooses voluntarily to say or do more than another man who knows, and not the same as the man who is like himself in the same action."

b   "Perhaps," he said, "it is necessarily so."

"And what about the ignorant man? Would he not get the better of both the man who knows and the man who does not?"

"Perhaps."

"The man who knows is wise?"

"I say so."

"And the wise man is good?"

"I say so."

"Then the man who is both good and wise will not want to get the better of the like, but of the unlike and opposite?"

"It seems so," he said.

"But the bad and unlearned will want to get the better of both the like and the opposite?"

"It looks like it."

"Then, Thrasymachus," I said, "does our unjust man get the better of both like and unlike? Weren't you saying that?"

"I was," he said.

"And the just man will not get the better of like but of unlike?"   *c*

"Yes."

"Then," I said, "the just man is like the wise and good, but the unjust man like the bad and unlearned."

"I'm afraid so."

"But we were also agreed that each is such as the one he is like."

"We were."

"Then the just man has revealed himself to us as good and wise, and the unjust man unlearned and bad."

Now, Thrasymachus did not agree to all of this so easily as I tell it now, but he dragged his feet and resisted, and he produced a wonderful   *d* quantity of sweat, for it was summer. And then I saw what I had not yet seen before—Thrasymachus blushing. At all events, when we had come to complete agreement about justice being virtue and wisdom, and injustice both vice and lack of learning, I said, "All right, let that be settled for us; but we did say that injustice is mighty as well. Or don't you remember, Thrasymachus?"

"I remember," he said. "But even what you're saying now doesn't satisfy me, and I have something to say about it. But if I should speak, I know well that you would say that I am making a public harangue. So   *e* then, either let me say as much as I want; or, if you want to keep on questioning, go ahead and question, and, just as with old wives who tell tales, I shall say to you, 'All right,' and I shall nod and shake my head."

"Not, in any case, contrary to your own opinion," I said.

"To satisfy you," he said, "since you won't let me speak. What else do you want?"

"Nothing, by Zeus," I said, "but if that's what you are going to do, go ahead and do it. And I'll ask questions."

"Then ask."

"I ask what I asked a moment ago so that we can in an orderly fashion make a thorough consideration of the argument about the   *351 a* character of justice as compared to injustice. Surely it was said that injustice is more powerful and mightier than justice. But now," I said,

351 a   "if justice is indeed both wisdom and virtue, I believe it will easily
come to light that it is also mightier than injustice, since injustice is
lack of learning—no one could still be ignorant of that. But, Thrasymachus, I do not desire it to be so simply considered, but in this

b   way: would you say that a city is unjust that tries to enslave other
cities unjustly, and has reduced them to slavery, and keeps many
enslaved to itself?"

"Of course," he said. "And it's this the best city will most do, the
one that is most perfectly unjust."

"I understand," I said, "that this argument was yours, but I am
considering this aspect of it: will the city that becomes stronger than
another have this power without justice, or is it necessary for it to have
this power with justice?"

c   "If," he said, "it's as you said a moment ago, that justice is
wisdom—with justice. But if it's as I said—with injustice."

"I am full of wonder, Thrasymachus," I said, "because you not
only nod and shake your head, but also give very fine answers."

"It's because I am gratifying you," he said.

"It's good of you to do so. But gratify me this much more and tell
me: do you believe that either a city, or an army, or pirates, or robbers,
or any other tribe which has some common unjust enterprise would be
able to accomplish anything, if its members acted unjustly to one
another?"

d   "Surely not," he said.

"And what if they didn't act unjustly? Wouldn't they be more able
to accomplish something?"

"Certainly," he said.

"For surely, Thrasymachus, it's injustice that produces factions,
hatreds, and quarrels among themselves, and justice that produces
unanimity and friendship. Isn't it so?"

"Let it be so, so as not to differ with you."

"And it's good of you to do so, you best of men. Now tell me this:
if it's the work of injustice, wherever it is, to implant hatred, then,
when injustice comes into being, both among free men and slaves, will
it not also cause them to hate one another and to form factions, and to

e   be unable to accomplish anything in common with one another?"

"Certainly."

"And what about when injustice comes into being between two?
Will they not differ and hate and be enemies to each other and to just
men?"

"They will," he said.

"And if, then, injustice should come into being within one man, you surprising fellow, will it lose its power or will it remain undiminished?"

"Let it remain undiminished," he said.

"Then does it come to light as possessing a power such that, wherever it comes into being, be it in a city, a clan, an army, or whatever else, it first of all makes that thing unable to accomplish anything together with itself due to faction and difference, and then it makes that thing an enemy both to itself and to everything opposite and to the just? Isn't it so?"

352 *a*

"Certainly."

"And then when it is in one man, I suppose it will do the same thing which it naturally accomplishes. First it will make him unable to act, because he is at faction and is not of one mind with himself, and, second, an enemy both to himself and to just men, won't it?"

"Yes."

"And the gods, too, my friend, are just?"

"Let it be," he said.

b

"Then the unjust man will also be an enemy to the gods, Thrasymachus, and the just man a friend."

"Feast yourself boldly on the argument," he said, "for I won't oppose you, so as not to irritate these men here."

"Come, then," I said, "fill out the rest of the banquet for me by answering just as you have been doing. I understand that the just come to light as wiser and better and more able to accomplish something, while the unjust can't accomplish anything with one another—for we don't speak the complete truth about those men who we say vigorously accomplished some common object with one another although they were unjust; they could never have restrained themselves with one another if they were completely unjust, but it is plain that there was a certain justice in them which caused them at least not to do injustice to one another at the same time that they were seeking to do it to others; and as a result of this they accomplished what they accomplished, and they pursued unjust deeds when they were only half bad from injustice, since the wholly bad and perfectly unjust are also perfectly unable to accomplish anything—I say that I understand that these things are so and not as you set them down at first. But whether the just also live better than the unjust and are happier, which is what we afterwards proposed for consideration, must be considered. And now, in my opinion, they do also look as though they are, on the basis of what we have said. Nevertheless, this must still be considered better: for the argument is not about just any question, but about the way one should live."

c

d

"Well, go ahead and consider," he said.

352 d   "I shall," I said. "Tell me, in your opinion is there some work that belongs to a horse?"

e   "Yes."

"Would you take the work of a horse or of anything else whatsoever to be that which one can do only with it, or best with it?"

"I don't understand," he said.

"Look at it this way: is there anything with which you could see other than eyes?"

"Surely not."

"And what about this? Could you hear with anything other than ears?"

"By no means."

"Then wouldn't we justly assert that this is the work of each?"

"Certainly."

353 a   "And what about this: you could cut a slip from a vine with a dagger or a leather-cutter or many other things?"

"Of course."

"But I suppose you could not do as fine a job with anything other than a pruning knife made for this purpose."

"True."

"Then shall we take this to be its work?"

"We shall indeed."

"Now I suppose you can understand better what I was asking a moment ago when I wanted to know whether the work of each thing is what it alone can do, or can do more finely than other things."

"Yes, I do understand," he said, "and this is, in my opinion, the

b   work of each thing."

"All right," I said, "does there seem to you also to be a virtue for each thing to which some work is assigned? Let's return again to the same examples. We say that eyes have some work?"

"They do."

"Is there then a virtue of eyes, too?"

"A virtue, too."

"And what about ears? Wasn't it agreed that they have some work?"

"Yes."

"And do they have a virtue, too?"

"Yes, they do."

"And what about all other things? Aren't they the same?"

"They are."

"Stop for a moment. Could eyes ever do a fine job of their work if

they did not have their proper virtue but, instead of the virtue,   353 c
vice?"

"How could they?" he said. "For you probably mean blindness
instead of sight."

"Whatever their virtue may be," I said. "For I'm not yet asking
that, but whether their work, the things to be done by them, will be
done well with their proper virtue, and badly with vice."

"What you say is true," he said.

"Will ears, too, do their work badly when deprived of their vir-
tue?"

"Certainly."   d

"Then, shall we include everything else in the same argument?"

"In my opinion, at least."

"Come, let's consider this now: is there some work of a soul that
you couldn't ever accomplish with any other thing that is? For example, managing, ruling, and deliberating, and all such things—could we
justly attribute them to anything other than a soul and assert that they
are peculiar to it?"

"To nothing else."

"And, further, what about living? Shall we not say that it is the
work of a soul?"

"Most of all," he said.

"Then, do we say that there is also some virtue of a soul?"

"We do."

"Then, Thrasymachus, will a soul ever accomplish its work well if   e
deprived of its virtue, or is that impossible?"

"Impossible."

"Then a bad soul necessarily rules and manages badly while a
good one does all these things well."

"Necessarily."

"Didn't we agree that justice is virtue of soul, and injustice,
vice?"

"We did so agree."

"Then the just soul and the just man will have a good life, and the
unjust man a bad one."

"It looks like it," he said, "according to your argument."

"And the man who lives well is blessed and happy, and the man   354 a
who does not is the opposite."

"Of course."

"Then the just man is happy and the unjust man wretched."

"Let it be so," he said.

354 a   "But it is not profitable to be wretched; rather it is profitable to be happy."

"Of course."

"Then, my blessed Thrasymachus, injustice is never more profitable than justice."

"Let that," he said, "be the fill of your banquet at the festival of Bendis,[45] Socrates."

"I owe it to you, Thrasymachus," I said, "since you have grown gentle and have left off being hard on me. However, I have not had a

b   fine banquet, but it's my own fault, not yours. For in my opinion, I am just like the gluttons who grab at whatever is set before them to get a taste of it, before they have in proper measure enjoyed what went before. Before finding out what we were considering at first—what the just is—I let go of that and pursued the consideration of whether it is vice and lack of learning, or wisdom and virtue. And later, when in its turn an argument that injustice is more profitable than justice fell in my way, I could not restrain myself from leaving the other one and going after this one, so that now as a result of the discussion I know nothing.

c   So long as I do not know what the just is, I shall hardly know whether it is a virtue or not and whether the one who has it is unhappy or happy."

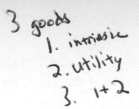

3 goods
1. intrinsic
2. utility
3. 1+2

1. Compact

2. Ring of Gyges

3 "perfect injustice" > justice

A   B

BOOK II

Now, when I had said this, I thought I was freed from argument. But after all, as it seems, it was only a prelude. For Glaucon is always most courageous in everything, and so now he didn't accept Thrasymachus' giving up but said, "Socrates, do you want to seem to have persuaded us, or truly to persuade us, that it is in every way better to be just than unjust?"

"I would choose to persuade you truly," I said, "if it were up to me."

"Well, then," he said, "you're not doing what you want. Tell me, is there in your opinion a kind of good that we would choose to have not because we desire its consequences, but because we delight in it for its own sake—such as enjoyment and all the pleasures which are harmless and leave no after effects other than the enjoyment in having them?"

"In my opinion, at least," I said, "there is a good of this kind."

"And what about this? Is there a kind we like both for its own sake and for what comes out of it, such as thinking and seeing and being healthy? Surely we delight in such things on both accounts."

"Yes," I said.

"And do you see a third form[1] of good, which includes gymnastic exercise, medical treatment when sick as well as the practice of medicine, and the rest of the activities from which money is made? We

357 c
d

would say that they are drudgery but beneficial to us; and we would not choose to have them for themselves but for the sake of the wages and whatever else comes out of them."

"Yes, there is also this third," I said, "but what of it?"

"In which of them," he said, "would you include justice?"

358 a

"I, for my part, suppose," I said, "that it belongs in the finest kind, which the man who is going to be blessed should like both for itself and for what comes out of it."

"Well, that's not the opinion of the many," he said, "rather it seems to belong to the form of drudgery, which should be practiced for the sake of wages and the reputation that comes from opinion;[2] but all by itself it should be fled from as something hard."

"I know this is the popular opinion," I said, "and a while ago justice, taken as being such, was blamed by Thrasymachus while injustice was praised. But I, as it seems, am a poor learner."

b

"Come, now," he said, "hear me too, and see if you still have the same opinion. For it looks to me as though Thrasymachus, like a snake, has been charmed more quickly than he should have been; yet to my way of thinking there was still no proof about either. For I desire to hear what each is and what power it has all alone by itself when it is in the soul—dismissing its wages and its consequences. So I shall do it

c

this way, if you too consent: I'll restore Thrasymachus' argument, and first I'll tell what kind of thing they say justice is and where it came from; second, that all those who practice it do so unwillingly, as necessary but not good; third, that it is fitting that they do so, for the life of the unjust man is, after all, far better than that of the just man, as they say. For, Socrates, though that's not at all my own opinion, I am at a loss: I've been talked deaf by Thrasymachus and countless others, while the argument on behalf of justice—that it is better than in-

d

justice—I've yet to hear from anyone as I want it. I want to hear it extolled all by itself, and I suppose I would be most likely to learn that from you. That's the reason why I'll speak in vehement praise of the unjust life, and in speaking I'll point out to you how I want to hear you, in your turn, blame injustice and praise justice. See if what I'm saying is what you want."

"Most of all," I said. "What would an intelligent man enjoy talking and hearing about more again and again?"

e

"What you say is quite fine," he said. "Now listen to what I said I was going to tell first—what justice is and where it came from.

"They say that doing injustice is naturally good, and suffering injustice bad, but that the bad in suffering injustice far exceeds the good in doing it; so that, when they do injustice to one another and suffer it

and taste of both, it seems profitable—to those who are not able to   *358 e*
escape the one and choose the other—to set down a compact among   *359 a*
themselves neither to do injustice nor to suffer it. And from there they
began to set down their own laws and compacts and to name what the
law commands lawful and just. And this, then, is the genesis and being
of justice; it is a mean between what is best—doing injustice without
paying the penalty—and what is worst—suffering injustice without
being able to avenge oneself. The just is in the middle between these
two, cared for not because it is good but because it is honored due to a
want of vigor in doing injustice. The man who is able to do it and is   *b*
truly a man would never set down a compact with anyone not to do injustice and not to suffer it. He'd be mad. Now the nature of justice is
this and of this sort, and it naturally grows out of these sorts of things.
So the argument goes.

"That even those who practice it do so unwillingly, from an incapacity to do injustice, we would best perceive if we should in thought
do something like this: give each, the just man and the unjust, license to   *c*
do whatever he wants, while we follow and watch where his desire will
lead each. We would catch the just man red-handed going the same way
as the unjust man out of a desire to get the better; this is what any
nature naturally pursues as good, while it is law[3] which by force per-
verts it to honor equality. The license of which I speak would best be
realized if they should come into possession of the sort of power that it
is said the ancestor of Gyges,[4] the Lydian, once got. They say he was a   *d*
shepherd toiling in the service of the man who was then ruling Lydia.
There came to pass a great thunderstorm and an earthquake; the earth
cracked and a chasm opened at the place where he was pasturing.
He saw it, wondered at it, and went down. He saw, along with other
quite wonderful things about which they tell tales, a hollow bronze
horse. It had windows; peeping in, he saw there was a corpse inside
that looked larger than human size. It had nothing on except a gold ring
on its hand; he slipped it off and went out. When there was the usual   *e*
gathering of the shepherds to make the monthly report to the king
about the flocks, he too came, wearing the ring. Now, while he was sitting with the others, he chanced to turn the collet of the ring to himself,
toward the inside of his hand; when he did this, he became invisible to
those sitting by him, and they discussed him as though he were away.   *360 a*
He wondered at this, and, fingering the ring again, he twisted the collet
toward the outside; when he had twisted it, he became visible. Thinking this over, he tested whether the ring had this power, and that was
exactly his result: when he turned the collet inward, he became invisible, when outward, visible. Aware of this, he immediately contrived to

360 a

b be one of the messengers to the king. When he arrived, he committed adultery with the king's wife and, along with her, set upon the king and killed him. And so he took over the rule.

"Now if there were two such rings, and the just man would put one on, and the unjust man the other, no one, as it would seem, would be so adamant as to stick by justice and bring himself to keep away from what belongs to others and not lay hold of it, although he had license to take what he wanted from the market without fear, and to go into houses and have intercourse with whomever he wanted, and to

c slay or release from bonds whomever he wanted, and to do other things as an equal to a god among humans. And in so doing, one would act no differently from the other, but both would go the same way. And yet, someone could say that this is a great proof that no one is willingly just but only when compelled to be so. Men do not take it to be a good for them in private, since wherever each supposes he can do injustice, he does it. Indeed, all men suppose injustice is far more to their private

d profit than justice. And what they suppose is true, as the man who makes this kind of an argument will say, since if a man were to get hold of such license and were never willing to do any injustice and didn't lay his hands on what belongs to others, he would seem most wretched to those who were aware of it, and most foolish too, although they would praise him to each others' faces, deceiving each other for fear of suffering injustice. So much for that.

e "As to the judgment itself about the life of these two of whom we are speaking, we'll be able to make it correctly if we set the most just man and the most unjust in opposition; if we do not, we won't be able to do so. What, then, is this opposition? It is as follows: we shall take away nothing from the injustice of the unjust man nor from the justice of the just man, but we shall take each as perfect in his own pursuit. So, first, let the unjust man act like the clever craftsmen. An outstanding pilot or doctor is aware of the difference between what is impossible in

361 a his art and what is possible, and he attempts the one, and lets the other go; and if, after all, he should still trip up in any way, he is competent to set himself aright. Similarly, let the unjust man also attempt unjust deeds correctly, and get away with them, if he is going to be extremely unjust. The man who is caught must be considered a poor chap. For the extreme of injustice is to seem to be just when one is not. So the perfectly unjust man must be given the most perfect injustice, and nothing must be taken away; he must be allowed to do the greatest injustices while having provided himself with the greatest reputation for justice.

b And if, after all, he should trip up in anything, he has the power to set himself aright; if any of his unjust deeds should come to light, he is

capable both of speaking persuasively and of using force, to the extent   *361 b*
that force is needed, since he is courageous and strong and since he has
provided for friends and money. Now, let us set him down as such, and
put beside him in the argument the just man in his turn, a man simple
and noble, who, according to Aeschylus,⁵ does not wish to seem, but
rather to be, good. The seeming must be taken away. For if he should
seem just, there would be honors and gifts for him for seeming to be   *c*
such. Then it wouldn't be plain whether he is such for the sake of the
just or for the sake of the gifts and honors. So he must be stripped of
everything except justice, and his situation must be made the opposite
of the first man's. Doing no injustice, let him have the greatest reputation for injustice, so that his justice may be put to the test to see if it is
softened by bad reputation and its consequences. Let him go un-
changed till death, seeming throughout life to be unjust although he is   *d*
just, so that when each has come to the extreme—the one of justice, the
other of injustice—they can be judged as to which of the two is happier."

"My, my," I said, "my dear Glaucon, how vigorously you polish
up each of the two men—just like a statue—for their judgment."

"As much as I can," he said. "With two such men it's no longer
hard, I suppose, to complete the speech by a description of the kind of
life that awaits each. It must be told, then. And if it's somewhat   *e*
rustically told, don't suppose that it is I who speak, Socrates, but rather
those who praise injustice ahead of justice. They'll say that the just man
who has such a disposition will be whipped; he'll be racked; he'll be
bound; he'll have both his eyes burned out; and, at the end, when he   *362 a*
has undergone every sort of evil, he'll be crucified and know that one
shouldn't wish to be, but to seem to be, just. After all, Aeschylus' saying applies far more correctly to the unjust man. For really, they will
say, it is the unjust man, because he pursues a thing dependent on truth
and does not live in the light of opinion, who does not wish to seem unjust but to be unjust,

> Reaping a deep furrow in his mind
> From which trusty plans bear fruit.⁶   *b*

First, he rules in the city because he seems to be just. Then he takes in
marriage from whatever station he wants and gives in marriage to
whomever he wants; he contracts and has partnerships with whomever
he wants, and, besides benefiting himself in all this, he gains because he
has no qualms about doing injustice. So then, when he enters contests,
both private and public, he wins and gets the better of his enemies. In
getting the better, he is wealthy and does good to friends and harm to   *c*

362 c   enemies. To the gods he makes sacrifices and sets up votive offerings, adequate and magnificent, and cares for the gods and those human beings he wants to care for far better than the just man. So, in all likelihood, it is also more appropriate for him to be dearer to the gods than is the just man. Thus, they say, Socrates, with gods and with humans, a better life is provided for the unjust man than for the just man."

d   When Glaucon had said this, I had it in mind to say something to it, but his brother Adeimantus said in his turn, "You surely don't believe, Socrates, that the argument has been adequately stated?"

"Why not?" I said.

"What most needed to be said has not been said," he said.

"Then," I said, "as the saying goes, 'let a man stand by his brother.'[7] So, you too, if he leaves out anything, come to his defense. And yet, what he said was already enough to bring me to my knees and make it impossible to help out justice."

e   And he said, "Nonsense. But still hear this too. We must also go through the arguments opposed to those of which he spoke, those that praise justice and blame injustice, so that what Glaucon in my opinion wants will be clearer. No doubt, fathers say to their sons and exhort

363 a   them, as do all those who have care of anyone, that one must be just. However, they don't praise justice by itself but the good reputations that come from it; they exhort their charges to be just so that, as a result of the opinion, ruling offices and marriages will come to the one who seems to be just, and all the other things that Glaucon a moment ago attributed to the just man as a result of his having a good reputation. And these men tell even more of the things resulting from the opinions. For by throwing in good reputation with the gods, they can tell of an inexhaustible store of goods that they say gods give to the holy. And in this way they join both the noble Hesiod and Homer. The former says that for the just the gods make the oaks

b   Bear acorns on high, and bees in the middle,
            And the fleecy sheep heavily laden with wool[8]

and many other very good things connected with these. And the other has pretty much the same to tell, as when he says,

c   As for some blameless king who in fear of the gods
            Upholds justice, the black earth bears
            Barley and wheat, the trees are laden with fruit,
            The sheep bring forth without fail, and the
               sea provides fish.[9]

And Musaeus and his son give the just even headier goods than these from the gods. In their speech they lead them into Hades and lay them

down on couches; crowning them, they prepare a symposium of the   *363 c*
holy, and they then make them go through the rest of time drunk, in the
belief that the finest wage of virtue is an eternal drunk.¹⁰ Others ex-   *d*
tend the wages from the gods yet further than these. For they say that a
holy and oath-keeping man leaves his children's children and a whole
tribe behind him. So in these and like ways they extol justice. And, in
turn, they bury the unholy and unjust in mud in Hades and compel
them to carry water in a sieve; and they bring them into bad reputation
while they are still alive. Thus, those penalties that Glaucon described   *e*
as the lot of the just men who are reputed to be unjust, these people
say are the lot of the unjust. But they have nothing else to say. This
then is the praise and blame attached to each.

"Furthermore, Socrates, consider still another form of speeches
about justice and injustice, spoken in prose¹¹ and by poets. With one
tongue they all chant that moderation and justice are fair, but hard and   *364 a*
full of drudgery, while intemperance and injustice are sweet and easy to
acquire, and shameful only by opinion and law. They say that the unjust is for the most part more profitable than the just; and both in
public and in private, they are ready and willing to call happy and to
honor bad men who have wealth or some other power and to dishonor
and overlook those who happen in some way to be weak or poor, although they agree they are better than the others. But the most won-   *b*
derful of all these speeches are those they give about gods and virtue.
They say that the gods, after all, allot misfortune and a bad life to many
good men too, and an opposite fate to opposite men. Beggar priests and
diviners go to the doors of the rich man and persuade him that the gods
have provided them with a power based on sacrifices and incantations.
If he himself, or his ancestors, has committed some injustice, they can   *c*
heal it with pleasures and feasts; and if he wishes to ruin some enemies
at small expense, he will injure just and unjust alike with certain evoca-
tions and spells. They, as they say, persuade the gods to serve them.
And they bring the poets forward as witnesses to all these arguments
about vice, and they present it as easy, saying that,

> Vice in abundance is easy to choose,   *d*
> The road is smooth and it lies very near,
> While the gods have set sweat before virtue,
> And it is a long road, rough and steep.¹²

And they use Homer as a witness to the perversion of the gods by human beings because he too said:

> The very gods can be moved by prayer too.   *e*
> With sacrifices and gentle vows and

364 e
>The odor of burnt and drink offerings, human beings
>turn them aside with their prayers,
>When someone has transgressed and made a mistake.[13]

And they present a babble of books by Musaeus and Orpheus, off-spring of the Moon and the Muses, as they say, according to whose prescriptions they busy themselves about their sacrifices. They persuade not only private persons, but cities as well, that through sacrifices and pleasurable games there are, after all, deliverances and purifica-

365 a tions from unjust deeds for those still living. And there are also rites for those who are dead. These, which they call initiations,[14] deliver us from the evils in the other place; while, for those who did not sacrifice, terrible things are waiting.

"My dear Socrates," he said, "with all these things being said—of this sort and in this quantity—about virtue and vice and how human beings and gods honor them, what do we suppose they do to the souls of the young men who hear them? I mean those who have good natures and have the capacity, as it were, to fly to all the things that are said and gather from them what sort of man one should be and what way

b one must follow to go through life best. In all likelihood he would say to himself, after Pindar, will I 'with justice or with crooked deceits scale the higher wall' where I can fortify myself all around and live out my life? For the things said indicate that there is no advantage in my being just, if I don't also seem to be, while the labors and penalties involved are evident. But if I'm unjust, but have provided myself with a reputation for justice, a divine life is promised. Therefore, since as the

c wise make plain to me, 'the seeming overpowers even the truth'[15] and is the master of happiness, one must surely turn wholly to it. As facade and exterior I must draw a shadow painting[16] of virtue all around me, while behind it I must trail the wily and subtle fox of the most wise Archilochus.[17] 'But,' says someone, 'it's not always easy to do bad and get

d away with it unnoticed.' 'Nothing great is easy,' we'll say. 'But at all events, if we are going to be happy we must go where the tracks of the arguments lead. For, as to getting away with it, we'll organize secret societies and clubs; and there are teachers of persuasion who offer the wisdom of the public assembly and the court. On this basis, in some things we'll persuade and in others use force; thus we'll get the better and not pay the penalty.' 'But it surely isn't possible to get away from the gods or overpower them.' 'But, if there are no gods, or if they have no care for human things, why should we care at all about getting

e away? And if there are gods and they care, we know of them or have heard of them from nowhere else than the laws[18] and the poets who have given genealogies; and these are the very sources of our being told that they are such as to be persuaded and perverted by sacrifices, sooth-

ing vows, and votive offerings. Either both things must be believed or   *365 e*
neither. If they are to be believed, injustice must be done and sacrifice
offered from the unjust acquisitions. For if we are just, we won't be   *366 a*
punished by the gods. That is all. And we'll refuse the gains of injustice. But if we are unjust, we shall gain and get off unpunished as
well, by persuading the gods with prayers when we transgress and make
mistakes.' 'But in Hades we'll pay the penalty for our injustices here,
either we ourselves or our children's children.' 'But, my dear,' will say
the man who calculates, 'the initiations and the delivering gods have   *b*
great power, as say the greatest cities and those children of gods who
have become poets and spokesmen of the gods and reveal that this is
the case.'

"Then, by what further argument could we choose justice before
the greatest injustice? For, if we possess it with a counterfeited seemly
exterior, we'll fare as we are minded with gods and human beings both
while we are living and when we are dead, so goes the speech of both
the many and the eminent. After all that has been said, by what device,
Socrates, will a man who has some power—of soul, money, body or   *c*
family—be made willing to honor justice and not laugh when he hears
it praised? So, consequently, if someone can show that what we have
said is false and if he has adequate knowledge that justice is best, he
undoubtedly has great sympathy for the unjust and is not angry with
them; he knows that except for someone who from a divine nature cannot stand doing injustice or who has gained knowledge and keeps away
from injustice, no one else is willingly just; but because of a lack of   *d*
courage, or old age, or some other weakness, men blame injustice because they are unable to do it. And that this is so is plain. For the first
man of this kind to come to power is the first to do injustice to the best
of his ability. And there is no other cause of all this than that which
gave rise to this whole argument of his and mine with you, Socrates.
We said, 'You surprising man, of all you who claim to be praisers of   *e*
justice—beginning with the heroes[19] at the beginning (those who have
left speeches) up to the human beings of the present—there is not one
who has ever blamed injustice or praised justice other than for the
reputations, honors, and gifts that come from them. But as to what each
itself does with its own power when it is in the soul of a man who
possesses it and is not noticed by gods and men, no one has ever, in
poetry or prose, adequately developed the argument that the one is the
greatest of evils a soul can have in it, and justice the greatest good. For
if all of you had spoken in this way from the beginning and persuaded   *367 a*
us, from youth onwards, we would not keep guard over each other for
fear injustice be done, but each would be his own best guard, afraid
that in doing injustice he would dwell with the greatest evil.'

367 a   "This, Socrates, and perhaps yet more than this, would Thrasymachus and possibly someone else say about justice and injustice, vulgarly
turning their powers upside down, in my opinion at least. But I—for I

b   need hide nothing from you—out of my desire to hear the opposite
from you, speak as vehemently as I can. Now, don't only show us by
the argument that justice is stronger[20] than injustice, but show what
each in itself does to the man who has it that makes the one bad and the
other good. And take away the reputations, as Glaucon told you to. For
if you don't take the true reputation from each and attach the false one
to it, we'll say that you aren't praising the just but the seeming, nor

c   blaming being unjust but the seeming; and that you're exhorting one to
be unjust and to get away with it; and that you agree with Thrasymachus that the just is someone else's good, the advantage of the stronger,
while the unjust is one's own advantage and profitable, but disadvantageous to the weaker. Now, since you agreed that justice is among the
greatest goods—those that are worth having for what comes from them
but much more for themselves, such as seeing, hearing, thinking, and,

d   of course, being healthy and all the other goods that are fruitful by their
own nature and not by opinion—praise this aspect of justice. Of what
profit is justice in itself to the man who possesses it, and what harm does
injustice do? Leave wages and reputations to others to praise. I could
endure other men's praising justice and blaming injustice in this way,
extolling and abusing them in terms of reputations and wages; but from
you I couldn't, unless you were to order me to, because you have spent

e   your whole life considering nothing other than this. So, don't only show
us by the argument that justice is stronger than injustice, but show what
each in itself does to the man who has it—whether it is noticed by gods
and human beings or not—that makes the one good and the other
bad."

I listened, and although I had always been full of wonder at the
nature of Glaucon and Adeimantus, at this time I was particularly

368 a   delighted and said, "That wasn't a bad beginning, you children of that
man,[21] that Glaucon's lover made to his poem about your distinguishing yourselves in the battle at Megara:

Sons of Ariston,[22] divine offspring of a famous man.

That, my friends, in my opinion is good. For something quite divine
must certainly have happened to you, if you are remaining unper-
suaded that injustice is better than justice when you are able to speak

b   that way on its behalf. Now you truly don't seem to me to be being persuaded. I infer it from the rest of your character, since, on the basis of
the arguments themselves, I would distrust you. And the more I trust
you, the more I'm at a loss as to what I should do. On the one hand, I

can't help out. For in my opinion I'm not capable of it; my proof is that   368 *b*
when I thought I showed in what I said to Thrasymachus that justice is
better than injustice, you didn't accept it from me. On the other hand, I
can't not help out. For I'm afraid it might be impious to be here when
justice is being spoken badly of and give up and not bring help while I   *c*
am still breathing and able to make a sound. So the best thing is to suc-
cour her as I am able."

Glaucon and the others begged me in every way to help out and
not to give up the argument, but rather to seek out what each is and the
truth about the benefit of both. So I spoke my opinion.

"It looks to me as though the investigation we are undertaking is
no ordinary thing, but one for a man who sees sharply. Since we're not
clever men," I said, "in my opinion we should make this kind of   *d*
investigation of it: if someone had, for example, ordered men who
don't see very sharply to read little letters from afar and then someone
had the thought that the same letters are somewhere else also, but bigger and in a bigger place, I suppose it would look like a godsend to be
able to consider the littler ones after having read these first, if, of
course, they do happen to be the same."

"Most certainly," said Adeimantus. "But, Socrates, what do you
notice in the investigation of the just that's like this?"   *e*

"I'll tell you," I said. "There is, we say, justice of one man; and
there is, surely, justice of a whole city too?"

"Certainly," he said.

"Is a city bigger[23] than one man?"

"Yes, it is bigger," he said.

"So then, perhaps there would be more justice in the bigger and it
would be easier to observe closely. If you want, first we'll investigate
what justice is like in the cities. Then, we'll also go on to consider it in   369 *a*
individuals, considering the likeness of the bigger in the *idea*[24] of the
littler?"

"What you say seems fine to me," he said.

"If we should watch a city coming into being in speech," I said,
"would we also see its justice coming into being, and its injustice?"

"Probably," he said.

"When this has been done, can we hope to see what we're looking
for more easily?"   *b*

"Far more easily."

"Is it resolved[25] that we must try to carry this out? I suppose it's
no small job, so consider it."

"It's been considered," said Adeimantus. "Don't do anything
else."

"Well, then," I said, "a city, as I believe, comes into being be-

369 b   cause each of us isn't self-sufficient but is in need of much. Do you believe there's another beginning to the founding of a city?"

"None at all," he said.

c   "So, then, when one man takes on another for one need and another for another need, and, since many things are needed, many men gather in one settlement as partners and helpers, to this common settlement we give the name city, don't we?"

"Most certainly."

"Now, does one man give a share to another, if he does give a share, or take a share, in the belief that it's better for himself?"

"Certainly."

"Come, now," I said, "let's make a city in speech from the beginning. Our need, as it seems, will make it."

"Of course."

d   "Well, now, the first and greatest of needs is the provision of food for existing and living."

"Certainly."

"Second, of course, is housing, and third, clothing, and such."

"That's so."

"Now wait," I said. "How will the city be sufficient to provide for this much? Won't one man be a farmer, another the housebuilder, and still another, a weaver? Or shall we add to it a shoemaker or some other man who cares for what has to do with the body?"

"Certainly."

"The city of utmost necessity[26] would be made of four or five men."

e   "It looks like it."

"Now, what about this? Must each one of them put his work at the disposition of all in common—for example, must the farmer, one man, provide food for four and spend four times as much time and labor in the provision of food and then give it in common to the others; or must he neglect them and produce a fourth part of the food in a

370 a   fourth part of the time and use the other three parts for the provision of a house, clothing,[27] and shoes, not taking the trouble to share in common with others, but minding his own business for himself?"

And Adeimantus said, "Perhaps, Socrates, the latter is easier than the former."

"It wouldn't be strange, by Zeus," I said. "I myself also had the thought when you spoke that, in the first place, each of us is naturally not quite like anyone else, but rather differs in his nature; different

b   men are apt for the accomplishment of different jobs. Isn't that your opinion?"

"It is."

"And, what about this? Who would do a finer job, one man prac-   370 b
ticing many arts, or one man one art?"

"One man, one art," he said.

"And, further, it's also plain, I suppose, that if a man lets the crucial moment in any work pass, it is completely ruined."

"Yes, it is plain."

"I don't suppose the thing done is willing to await the leisure of
the man who does it; but it's necessary for the man who does it to
follow close upon the thing done, and not as a spare-time occupation."   c

"It is necessary."

"So, on this basis each thing becomes more plentiful, finer, and
easier, when one man, exempt from other tasks, does one thing according to nature and at the crucial moment."

"That's entirely certain."

"Now, then, Adeimantus, there's need of more citizens than four
for the provisions of which we were speaking. For the farmer, as it
seems, won't make his own plow himself, if it's going to be a fine one,
or his hoe, or the rest of the tools for farming; and the housebuilder   d
won't either—and he needs many too. And it will be the same with the
weaver and the shoemaker, won't it?"

"True."

"So, carpenters, smiths, and many other craftsmen of this sort become partners in our little city, making it into a throng."

"Most certainly."

"But it wouldn't be very big yet, if we added cowherds, shepherds,
and the other kinds of herdsmen, so that the farmers would have oxen
for plowing, the housebuilders teams to use with the farmers for   e
hauling, and the weavers and cobblers hides and wool."

"Nor would it be a little city," he said, "when it has all this."

"And, further," I said, "just to found the city itself in the sort of
place where there will be no need of imports is pretty nearly impossible."

"Yes, it is impossible."

"Then, there will also be a need for still other men who will bring
to it what's needed from another city."

"Yes, they will be needed."

"Now, if the agent comes empty-handed, bringing nothing needed
by those from whom they take what they themselves need, he'll go   371 a
away empty-handed, won't he?"

"It seems so to me."

"Then they must produce at home not only enough for themselves
but also the sort of thing and in the quantity needed by these others of
whom they have need."

371 a   "Yes, they must."

"So our city needs more farmers and other craftsmen."

"It does need more."

"And similarly, surely, other agents as well, who will import and export the various products. They are merchants, aren't they?"

"Yes."

"Then, we'll need merchants too."

"Certainly."

"And if the commerce is carried on by sea, there will also be need

b   of throngs of other men who know the business of the sea."

"Throngs, indeed."

"Now what about this? In the city itself, how will they exchange what they have produced with one another? It was for just this that we made a partnership and founded the city."

"Plainly," he said, "by buying and selling."

"Out of this we'll get a market[28] and an established currency[29] as a token for exchange."

"Most certainly."

c   "If the farmer or any other craftsman brings what he has produced to the market, and he doesn't arrive at the same time as those who need what he has to exchange, will he sit in the market idle, his craft unattended?"

"Not at all," he said. "There are men who see this situation and set themselves to this service; in rightly governed cities they are usually those whose bodies are weakest and are useless for doing any other job.

d   They must stay there in the market and exchange things for money with those who need to sell something and exchange, for money again, with all those who need to buy something."

"This need, then, produces tradesmen in our city," I said. "Don't we call tradesmen those men who are set up in the market to serve in buying and selling, and merchants those who wander among the cities?"

"Most certainly."

e   "There are, I suppose, still some other servants who, in terms of their minds, wouldn't be quite up to the level of partnership, but whose bodies are strong enough for labor. They sell the use of their strength and, because they call their price a wage, they are, I suppose, called wage earners, aren't they?"

"Most certainly."

"So the wage earners too, as it seems, go to fill out the city."

"It seems so to me."

"Then has our city already grown to completeness, Adeimantus?"

"Perhaps."   *371 e*

"Where in it, then, would justice and injustice be? Along with which of the things we considered did they come into being?"

"I can't think, Socrates," he said, "unless it's somewhere in   *372 a* some need these men have of one another."

"Perhaps what you say is fine," I said. "It really must be considered and we mustn't back away. First, let's consider what manner of life men so provided for will lead. Won't they make bread, wine, clothing, and shoes? And, when they have built houses, they will work in the summer, for the most part naked and without shoes, and in the winter adequately clothed and shod. For food they will prepare barley meal   *b* and wheat flour; they will cook it and knead it. Setting out noble loaves of barley and wheat on some reeds or clean leaves, they will stretch out on rushes strewn with yew and myrtle and feast themselves and their children. Afterwards they will drink wine and, crowned with wreathes, sing of the gods. So they will have sweet intercourse with one another, and not produce children beyond their means, keeping an eye out against poverty or war."   *c*

And Glaucon interrupted, saying: "You seem to make these men have their feast without relishes."

"What you say is true," I said. "I forgot that they'll have relishes, too—it's plain they'll have salt, olives, cheese; and they will boil onions and greens, just as one gets them in the country. And to be sure, we'll set desserts before them—figs, pulse and beans; and they'll roast myrtle-berries and acorns before the fire and drink in measure along with it.   *d* And so they will live out their lives in peace with health, as is likely, and at last, dying as old men, they will hand down other similar lives to their offspring."

And he said, "If you were providing for a city of sows, Socrates, on what else would you fatten them than this?"

"Well, how should it be, Glaucon?" I said.

"As is conventional," he said. "I suppose men who aren't going to be wretched recline on couches[30] and eat from tables and have relishes and desserts just like men have nowadays."   *e*

"All right," I said. "I understand. We are, as it seems, considering not only how a city, but also a luxurious city, comes into being. Perhaps that's not bad either. For in considering such a city too, we could probably see in what way justice and injustice naturally grow in cities. Now, the true[31] city is in my opinion the one we just described—a healthy city, as it were. But, if you want to, let's look at a feverish city, too. Nothing stands in the way. For these things, as it seems, won't satisfy some, or this way of life, but couches, tables, and other furniture   *373 a*

373 a   will be added, and, of course, relishes, perfume, incense, courtesans and cakes—all sorts of all of them. And, in particular, we can't still postulate the mere necessities we were talking about at first—houses, clothes, and shoes; but painting and embroidery must also be set in motion; and gold, ivory, and everything of the sort must be obtained. Isn't that so?"

b   "Yes," he said.

"Then the city must be made bigger again. This healthy one isn't adequate any more, but must already be gorged with a bulky mass of things, which are not in cities because of necessity—all the hunters and imitators, many concerned with figures and colors, many with music; and poets and their helpers, rhapsodes, actors, choral dancers, contractors, and craftsmen of all sorts of equipment, for feminine adorn-

c   ment as well as other things. And so we'll need more servants too. Or doesn't it seem there will be need of teachers, wet nurses, governesses, beauticians, barbers, and, further, relish-makers and cooks? And, what's more, we're in addition going to need swineherds. This animal wasn't in our earlier city—there was no need—but in this one there will be need of it in addition. And there'll also be need of very many other fatted beasts if someone will eat them, won't there?"

"Of course."

d   "Won't we be in much greater need of doctors if we follow this way of life rather than the earlier one?"

"Much greater."

"And the land, of course, which was then sufficient for feeding the men who were then, will now be small although it was sufficient. Or how should we say it?"

"Like that," he said.

"Then must we cut off a piece of our neighbors' land, if we are going to have sufficient for pasture and tillage, and they in turn from ours, if they let themselves go to the unlimited acquisition of money, overstepping the boundary of the necessary?"

e   "Quite necessarily, Socrates," he said.

"After that won't we go to war as a consequence, Glaucon? Or how will it be?"

"Like that," he said.

"And let's not yet say whether war works evil or good," I said, "but only this much, that we have in its turn found the origin of war—in those things whose presence in cities most of all produces evils both private and public."

"Most certainly."

"Now, my friend, the city must be still bigger, and not by a small

374 a   number but by a whole army, which will go out and do battle with in-

vaders for all the wealth and all the things we were just now talking   374 *a*
about."

"What," he said, "aren't they adequate by themselves?"

"Not if that was a fine agreement you and all we others made
when we were fashioning the city," I said. "Surely we were in agreement, if you remember, that it's impossible for one man to do a fine job
in many arts."

"What you say is true," he said.

"Well then," I said, "doesn't the struggle for victory in war seem   *b*
to be a matter for art?"

"Very much so," he said.

"Should one really care for the art of shoemaking more than for
the art of war?"

"Not at all."

"But, after all, we prevented the shoemaker from trying at the
same time to be a farmer or a weaver or a housebuilder; he had to stay
a shoemaker just so the shoemaker's art would produce fine work for
us. And in the same way, to each one of the others we assigned one
thing, the one for which his nature fitted him, at which he was to work
throughout his life, exempt from the other tasks, not letting the crucial   *c*
moments pass, and thus doing a fine job. Isn't it of the greatest importance that what has to do with war be well done? Or is it so easy that a
farmer or a shoemaker or a man practicing any other art whatsoever
can be at the same time skilled in the art of war, while no one could become an adequate draughts or dice player who didn't practice it from
childhood on, but only gave it his spare time? Will a man, if he picks
up a shield or any other weapon or tool of war, on that very day be an   *d*
adequate combatant in a battle of heavy-armed soldiers,[32] or any other
kind of battle in war, even though no other tool if picked up will make
anyone a craftsman or contestant, nor will it even be of use to the man
who has not gained knowledge of it or undergone adequate training?"

"In that case," he said, "the tools would be worth a lot."

"Then," I said, "to the extent that the work of the guardians is
more important, it would require more leisure time than the other tasks   *e*
as well as greater art and diligence."

"I certainly think so," he said.

"And also a nature fit for the pursuit?"

"Of course."

"Then it's our job, as it seems, to choose, if we're able, which are
the natures, and what kind they are, fit for guarding the city."

"Indeed it is our job."

"By Zeus," I said, "it's no mean thing we've taken upon our-

374 e   selves. But nevertheless, we mustn't be cowardly, at least as far as it's in
our power."

375 a   "No," he said, "we mustn't."

"Do you suppose," I said, "that for guarding there is any difference between the nature of a noble puppy and that of a well-born
young man?"

"What do you mean?"

"Well, surely both of them need sharp senses, speed to catch what
they perceive, and, finally, strength if they have to fight it out with what
they have caught."

"Yes, indeed," he said, "both need all these things."

"To say nothing of courage, if they are to fight well."

"Of course."

"Then, will horse or dog—or any other animal whatsoever—be
willing to be courageous if it's not spirited? Haven't you noticed how
b   irresistible and unbeatable spirit[33] is, so that its presence makes every
soul fearless and invincible in the face of everything?"

"Yes, I have noticed it."

"As for the body's characteristics, it's plain how the guardian
must be."

"Yes."

"And as for the soul's—that he must be spirited."

"That too."

"Glaucon," I said, "with such natures, how will they not be
savage to one another and the rest of the citizens?"

"By Zeus," he said, "it won't be easy."

c   "Yet, they must be gentle to their own and cruel to enemies. If
not, they'll not wait for others to destroy them, but they'll do it themselves beforehand."

"True," he said.

"What will we do?" I said. "Where will we find a disposition at
the same time gentle and great-spirited? Surely a gentle nature is opposed to a spirited one."

"It looks like it."

"Yet, if a man lacks either of them, he can't become a good
guardian. But these conditions resemble impossibilities, and so it fol-
d   lows that a good guardian is impossible."

"I'm afraid so," he said.

I too was at a loss, and, looking back over what had gone before, I
said, "It is just, my friend, that we're at a loss. For we've abandoned
the image we proposed."

"How do you mean?"

"We didn't notice that there are, after all, natures such as we thought impossible, possessing these opposites."   *375 d*

"Where, then?"

"One could see it in other animals too, especially, however, in the
one we compared to the guardian. You know, of course, that by nature   *e*
the disposition of noble dogs is to be as gentle as can be with their
familiars and people they know and the opposite with those they don't
know."

"I do know that."

"Then," I said, "it is possible, after all; and what we're seeking for
in the guardian isn't against nature."

"It doesn't seem so."

"In your opinion, then, does the man who will be a fit guardian
need, in addition to spiritedness, also to be a philosopher in his
nature?"[34]

"How's that?" he said. "I don't understand."   *376 a*

"This, too, you'll observe in dogs," I said, "and it's a thing in the
beast worthy of our wonder."

"What?"

"When it sees someone it doesn't know, it's angry, although it
never had any bad experience with him. And when it sees someone it
knows, it greets him warmly, even if it never had a good experience
with him. Didn't you ever wonder about this before?"

"No, I haven't paid very much attention to it up to now. But it's
plain that it really does this."

"Well, this does look like an attractive affection of its nature and
truly philosophic."   *b*

"In what way?"

"In that it distinguishes friendly from hostile looks by nothing
other than by having learned the one and being ignorant of the other," I
said. "And so, how can it be anything other than a lover of learning
since it defines what's its own and what's alien by knowledge and
ignorance?"

"It surely couldn't be anything but," he said.

"Well," I said, "but aren't love of learning and love of wisdom the
same?"

"Yes, the same," he said.

"So shall we be bold and assert that a human being too, if he is
going to be gentle to his own and those known to him, must by nature   *c*
be a philosopher and a lover of learning?"

"Yes," he said, "let's assert it."

"Then the man who's going to be a fine and good[35] guardian of
the city for us will in his nature be philosophic, spirited, swift, and
strong."

376 c   "That's entirely certain," he said.

"Then he would be of this sort to begin with. But how, exactly, will they be reared and educated by us? And does our considering this contribute anything to our goal of discerning that for the sake of which

d   we are considering all these things—in what way justice and injustice come into being in a city? We don't want to scant the argument, but we don't want an overlong one either."

And Glaucon's brother said, "I most certainly expect that this present consideration will contribute to that goal."

"By Zeus," I said, "then, my dear Adeimantus, it mustn't be given up even if it turns out to be quite long."

"No, it mustn't."

"Come, then, like men telling tales in a tale and at their leisure, let's educate the men in speech."

e   "We must."

"What is the education? Isn't it difficult to find a better one than that discovered over a great expanse of time? It is, of course, gymnastic for bodies and music[36] for the soul."

"Yes, it is."

"Won't we begin educating in music before gymnastic?"

"Of course."

"You include speeches in music, don't you?" I said.

"I do."

"Do speeches have a double form, the one true, the other false?"

"Yes."

377 a   "Must they be educated in both, but first in the false?"

"I don't understand how you mean that," he said.

"Don't you understand," I said, "that first we tell tales to children? And surely they are, as a whole, false, though there are true things in them too. We make use of tales with children before exercises."

"That's so."

"That's what I meant by saying music must be taken up before gymnastic."

"That's right," he said.

"Don't you know that the beginning is the most important part of

b   every work and that this is especially so with anything young and tender? For at that stage it's most plastic, and each thing assimilates itself to the model whose stamp anyone wishes to give to it."

"Quite so."

"Then shall we so easily let the children hear just any tales fashioned by just anyone and take into their souls opinions for the most part opposite to those we'll suppose they must have when they are grown up?"   377 *b*

"In no event will we permit it."

"First, as it seems, we must supervise the makers of tales; and if they make[37] a fine tale, it must be approved, but if it's not, it must be rejected. We'll persuade nurses and mothers to tell the approved tales to their children and to shape their souls with tales more than their bodies with hands. Most of those they now tell must be thrown out."   *c*

"Which sort?" he said.

"In the greater tales we'll also see the smaller ones," I said. "For both the greater and the smaller must be taken from the same model and have the same power. Don't you suppose so?"   *d*

"I do," he said. "But I don't grasp what you mean by the greater ones."

"The ones Hesiod and Homer told us, and the other poets too. They surely composed false tales for human beings and used to tell them and still do tell them."

"But what sort," he said, "and what do you mean to blame in them?"

"What ought to be blamed first and foremost," I said, "especially if the lie a man tells isn't a fine one."

"What's that?"

"When a man in speech makes a bad representation of what gods and heroes are like, just as a painter who paints something that doesn't resemble the things whose likeness he wished to paint."   *e*

"Yes, it's right to blame such things," he said. "But how do we mean this and what sort of thing is it?"

"First," I said, "the man who told the biggest lie about the biggest things didn't tell a fine lie—how Uranus did what Hesiod says he did, and how Cronos in his turn took revenge on him.[38] And Cronos' deeds   378 *a*
and his sufferings at the hands of his son,[39] not even if they were true would I suppose they should so easily be told to thoughtless young things; best would be to keep quiet, but if there were some necessity to tell, as few as possible ought to hear them as unspeakable secrets, after making a sacrifice, not of a pig but of some great offering that's hard to come by, so that it will come to the ears of the smallest possible number."

"These speeches are indeed harsh," he said.

"And they mustn't be spoken in our city, Adeimantus," I said.   *b*
"Nor must it be said within the hearing of a young person that in doing the extremes of injustice, or that in punishing the unjust deeds of his father in every way, he would do nothing to be wondered at, but would

378 b   be doing only what the first and the greatest of the gods did."

"No, by Zeus," he said. "To say this doesn't seem fitting to me either."

c   "Above all," I said, "it mustn't be said that gods make war on gods, and plot against them and have battles with them—for it isn't even true—provided that those who are going to guard the city for us must consider it most shameful[40] to be easily angry with one another. They are far from needing to have tales told and embroideries woven[41] about battles of giants and the many diverse disputes of gods and heroes with their families and kin. But if we are somehow going to persuade them that no citizen ever was angry with another and that to be so is not holy, it's just such things that must be told the children right

d   away by old men and women; and as they get older, the poets must be compelled to make up speeches for them which are close to these. But Hera's bindings by her son,[42] and Hephaestus' being cast out by his father when he was about to help out his mother who was being beaten,[43] and all the battles of the gods Homer[44] made, must not be accepted in the city, whether they are made with a hidden sense or without a hidden sense. A young thing can't judge what is hidden sense and what is not; but what he takes into his opinions at that age has a

e   tendency to become hard to eradicate and unchangeable. Perhaps it's for this reason that we must do everything to insure that what they hear first, with respect to virtue, be the finest told tales for them to hear."

"That's reasonable," he said. "But if someone should at this point ask us what they are and which tales we mean, what would we say?"

And I said, "Adeimantus, you and I aren't poets right now but

379 a   founders of a city. It's appropriate for founders to know the models according to which the poets must tell their tales. If what the poets produce goes counter to these models, founders must not give way; however, they must not themselves make up tales."

"That's correct," he said. "But, that is just it; what would the models for speech about the gods[45] be."

"Doubtless something like this," I said. "The god must surely always be described such as he is, whether one presents him in epics, lyrics, or tragedies."

"Yes, he must be."

b   "Then, is the god really good, and, hence, must he be said to be so?"

"Of course."

"Well, but none of the good things is harmful, is it?"

"Not in my opinion."

"Does that which isn't harmful do harm?"

"In no way."

"Does that which does not harm do any evil?"   *379 b*

"Not that, either."

"That which does no evil would not be the cause of any evil?"

"How could it be?"

"What about this? Is the good beneficial?"

"Yes."

"Then it's the cause of doing well?"

"Yes."

"Then the good is not the cause of everything; rather it is the cause of the things that are in a good way, while it is not responsible for the bad things."

"Yes," he said, "that's entirely so."   *c*

"Then," I said, "the god, since he's good, wouldn't be the cause of everything, as the many say, but the cause of a few things for human beings and not responsible for most. For the things that are good for us are far fewer than those that are bad; and of the good things, no one else must be said to be the cause; of the bad things, some other causes must be sought and not the god."

"What you say," he said, "is in my opinion very true."

"Then," I said, "we mustn't accept Homer's—or any other poet's—foolishly making this mistake about the gods and saying that   *d*

> Two jars stand on Zeus's threshold
> Full of dooms—the one of good,
>   the other of wretched;

and the man to whom Zeus gives a mixture of both,

> At one time he happens on evil,
>   at another good;

but the man to whom he doesn't give a mixture, but the second pure,

> Evil misery, drives him over the divine
>   earth;[46]

nor that Zeus is the dispenser to us   *e*

> Of good and evil alike.[47]

And, as to the violation of the oaths and truces that Pandarus committed, if someone says Athena and Zeus were responsible for its happening,[48] we'll not praise him; nor must the young be allowed to hear that Themis and Zeus were responsible for strife and contention among   *380 a* the gods,[49] nor again, as Aeschylus says, that

> God plants the cause in mortals
> When he wants to destroy a house utterly.

380 a   And if someone produces a 'Sorrows of Niobe,'[50] the work where these iambics are, or a 'Sorrows of the Pelopidae,' or the 'Trojan Sorrows,' or anything else of the sort, either he mustn't be allowed to say that they are the deeds of a god, or, if of a god, he must find a speech for them pretty much like the one we're now seeking; and he must say

b   the god's works were just and good, and that these people profited by being punished. But the poet mustn't be allowed to say that those who pay the penalty are wretched and that the one who did it was a god. If, however, he should say that the bad men were wretched because they needed punishment and that in paying the penalty they were benefited by the god, it must be allowed. As for the assertion that a god, who is good, is the cause of evil to anyone, great exertions must be made against anyone's saying these things in his own city, if its laws are going to be well observed, or anyone's hearing them, whether he is younger or

c   older, whether the tale is told in meter or without meter. For these are to be taken as sayings that, if said, are neither holy, nor advantageous for us, nor in harmony with one another."

"I give my vote to you in support of this law," he said, "and it pleases me."[51]

"Now, then," I said, "this would be one of the laws and models concerning the gods, according to which those who produce speeches will have to do their speaking and those who produce poems will have to do their making: the god is not the cause of all things, but of the good."

"And it's very satisfactory," he said.

d   "Now, what about this second one? Do you suppose the god is a wizard, able treacherously to reveal himself at different times in different *ideas*, at one time actually himself changing and passing from his own form into many shapes, at another time deceiving us and making us think such things about him? Or is he simple and does he least of all things depart from his own *idea*?"

"On the spur of the moment, I can't say," he said.

"What about this? Isn't it necessary that, if something steps out of

e   its own *idea*, it be changed either by itself or something else?"

"Yes, it is necessary."

"Are things that are in the best condition least altered and moved by something else—for example, a body by food, drink, and labor, and all plants by the sun's heat, winds, and other affections of the sort;

381 a   aren't the healthiest and strongest least altered?"

"Of course."

"And a soul that is most courageous and most prudent, wouldn't an external affection least trouble and alter it?"

"Yes."

"And, again, the same argument surely also holds for all com-   *381 a*
posites, implements, houses, and clothing; those that are well made and
in good condition are least altered by time and the other affections."

"That's so."

"Hence everything that's in fine condition, whether by nature or   *b*
art or both, admits least transformation by anything else."

"It seems so."

"Now, the god and what belongs to the god are in every way in the
best condition."

"Of course."

"So, in this way, the god would least of all have many shapes."

"Least of all, surely."

"But would he be the one to transform and alter himself?"

"It's plain," he said, "if he's altered at all."

"Does he transform himself into what's better and fairer, or what's
worse and uglier than himself?"

"Necessarily into what's worse," he said, "if he's altered at all.   *c*
For surely we won't say that the god is wanting in beauty or virtue."

"What you say is very right," I said. "And, if this is so, in your
opinion, Adeimantus, does anyone, either god or human being,
willingly make himself worse in any way at all?"

"It's impossible," he said.

"Then it's impossible," I said, "for a god to want to alter himself,
but since, as it seems, each of them is as fair and as good as possible, he
remains forever simply in his own shape."

"That's entirely necessary, in my opinion at least," he said.

"Then, you best of men," I said, "let none of the poets tell us   *d*
that

> The gods, like wandering strangers,
> Take on every sort of shape and visit
> the cities[52]

and let none tell lies about Proteus and Thetis[53] or bring on an altered
Hera, either in tragedies or the other kinds of poetry, as a priestess

> Making a collection for the life-giving children
> of Inachus, Argos' river[54]

and let them not lie to us in many other such ways. Nor should the   *e*
mothers, in their turn, be convinced by these things and frighten the
children with tales badly told—that certain gods go around nights looking like all sorts of strangers—lest they slander the gods while at the
same time making the children more cowardly."

"No, they shouldn't," he said.

"But," I said, "while the gods themselves can't be transformed, do

381 e   they make us think they appear in all sorts of ways, deceiving and
bewitching us?"

"Perhaps," he said.

382 a   "What?" I said. "Would a god want to lie, either in speech or
deed by presenting an illusion?"

"I don't know," he said.

"Don't you know," I said, "that all gods and human beings hate
the true lie, if that expression can be used?"

"What do you mean?" he said.

"That surely no one," I said, "voluntarily wishes to lie about the
most sovereign things to what is most sovereign in himself. Rather, he
fears holding a lie there more than anything."

"I still don't understand," he said.

b   "That's because you suppose I mean something exalted," I said.
"But I mean that to lie and to have lied to the soul about the things that
are, and to be unlearned, and to have and to hold a lie there is what
everyone would least accept; and that everyone hates a lie in that place
most of all."

"Quite so," he said.

"Now what I was just talking about would most correctly be
called truly a lie—the ignorance in the soul of the man who has been
lied to. For the lie in speeches is a kind of imitation of the affection in
the soul, a phantom of it that comes into being after it, and not quite an
c   unadulterated lie. Isn't that so?"

"Most certainly."

"So the real lie is hated not only by gods, but also by human
beings."

"Yes, in my opinion."

"Now, what about the one in speeches? When and for whom is it
also useful, so as not to deserve hatred? Isn't it useful against enemies,
and, as a preventive, like a drug, for so-called friends when from
madness or some folly they attempt to do something bad? And, in the
d   telling of the tales we were just now speaking about—those told because we don't know where the truth about ancient things lies—likening the lie to the truth as best we can, don't we also make it useful?"

"It is very useful in such cases," he said.

"Then in which of these cases is a lie useful to the god? Would he
lie in making likenesses because he doesn't know ancient things?"

"That," he said, "would be ridiculous."

"Then there is no lying poet in a god?"

"Not in my opinion."

"Would he lie because he's frightened of enemies?"

"Far from it."   *382 e*

"Because of the folly or madness of his intimates?"

"None of the foolish or the mad is a friend of the gods," he said.

"Then, there's nothing for the sake of which a god would lie?"

"There is nothing."

"Then the demonic[55] and the divine are wholly free from lie."

"That's completely certain," he said.

"Then the god is altogether simple and true in deed and speech, and he doesn't himself change or deceive others by illusions, speeches, or the sending of signs either in waking or dreaming."

"That's how it looks to me too when you say it," he said.

"Do you then agree," I said, "that this is the second model ac-   *383 a* cording to which speeches and poems about gods must be made: they are neither wizards who transform themselves, nor do they mislead us by lies in speech or in deed?"

"I do agree."

"So, although we praise much in Homer, we'll not praise Zeus' sending the dream to Agamemnon,[56] nor Thetis' saying in Aeschylus that Apollo sang at her wedding, foretelling good things for her off-spring,   *b*

> Free from sickness and living long lives,
> Telling all that the friendship of the gods
>   would do for my fortunes,
> He sang the paean, gladdening my spirit.
> And I expected Phoebus' divine mouth
> To be free of lie, full with the diviner's art.
> And he, he who sang, who was at this feast, who
>   said this, he is the one who slew my son.

When someone says such things about gods, we'll be harsh and not pro-   *c* vide a chorus;[57] and we'll not let the teachers use them for the education of the young, if our guardians are going to be god-revering and divine insofar as a human being can possibly be."

"I am in complete agreement with these models," he said, "and would use them as laws."

BOOK III

"About gods, then," I said, "such, it seems, are the things that should and should not be heard, from childhood on, by men who would honor gods and ancestors and not take lightly their friendship with each other."

"And I," he said, "suppose our impression is right."

"And what if they are to be courageous? Mustn't they also be told things that will make them fear death least? Or do you believe that anyone who has this terror in him would ever become courageous?"

"By Zeus, I don't," he said.

"What about this? Do you suppose anyone who believes Hades' domain exists and is full of terror will be fearless in the face of death and choose death in battles above defeat and slavery?"

"Not at all."

"Then, concerning these tales too, it seems we must supervise those who undertake to tell them and ask them not simply to disparage Hades' domain in this way but rather to praise it, because what they say is neither true nor beneficial for men who are to be fighters."

"Indeed, we must," he said.

"Then, we'll expunge all such things," I said, "beginning with this verse:

> I would rather be on the soil, a serf to another,
> To a man without lot whose means of life are not great,
> Than rule over all the dead who have perished[1]

386 c   and this,

d

> [Lest] his house appear to mortals and immortals,
> Dreadful, moldy, and even the gods hate it[2]

and,

> Oh woe, so there is in Hades' house, too,
> Both soul and phantom, but no mind in it at all[3]

and this,

> He alone possesses understanding; the others are
>   fluttering shadows[4]

and,

> The soul flew from his limbs and went to
>   Hades,
> Wailing his fate, leaving manliness and the bloom
>   of youth[5]

387 a   and this,

> Under the earth, like smoke,
> Went the gibbering soul[6]

and,

> Like bats who in a corner of an enchanted cave
> Fly gibbering when one falls off
> The cluster hanging from the rock, and
> Rise holding on to each other,
> So they went together gibbering.[7]

b   "We'll beg Homer and the other poets not to be harsh if we strike out these and all similar things. It's not that they are not poetic and sweet for the many to hear, but the more poetic they are, the less should they be heard by boys and men who must be free and accustomed to fearing slavery more than death."

"That's entirely certain."

"And we must, further, also throw out all those terrible and fearful names applied to this domain: Cocytus, Styx, 'those below,' 'the
c withered dead,' and all the other names that are part of this model and which make all those who hear them shiver, as is thought.[8] Perhaps they're good for something else, but we fear that our guardians, as a result of such shivers, will get hotter and softer than they ought."

"And," he said, "our fear is right."

"Then they must be deleted?"

"Yes."

"Must the model opposite to these be used in speaking and writ-   387 *c*
ing?"

"Plainly."

"Will we then take out the laments and wailings of famous men,   *d*
too?"

"If," he said, "what went before was necessary, so is this."

"Now, consider whether we'll be right in taking them out or not,"
I said. "We surely say that a decent[9] man will believe that for the decent man—who happens to be his comrade—being dead is not a terrible thing."

"Yes, we do say that."

"Then, he wouldn't lament him as though he had suffered something terrible."

"Surely not."

"Moreover, we also say that such a man is most of all sufficient
unto himself for living well and, in contrast to others, has least need of
another."   *e*

"True," he said.

"Then for him it is least terrible to be deprived of a son, or a
brother, or money, or of anything else of the sort."

"Yes, least of all."

"Then he laments the least and bears it most gently when some
such misfortune overtakes him."

"Quite so."

"So, we'd be right in taking out the wailings of renowned men and
we'd give them to women—and not to the serious ones, at that—and to
all the bad men. Thus the men we say we are rearing for the guard-   388 *a*
ianship of the country won't be able to stand doing things similar to
those such people do."

"Yes," he said, "we would be right."

"Then, again, we'll ask Homer and the other poets not to make
Achilles, son of a goddess,

> Now lying on his side, now again
> On his belly, and now on his side,
> Then standing upright, roaming distraught along the
>   shore of the unharvested sea[10]

nor taking black ashes in both hands and pouring them over his   *b*
head,[11] nor crying and lamenting as much as, or in the ways, Homer
made him do; nor Priam, a near offspring of the gods, entreating and

> Rolling around in dung,
> Calling out to each man by name.[12]

388 b   And yet far more than this, we'll ask them under no condition to make
gods who lament and say,

c   Ah me, wretched me, ah me, unhappy mother of the
best man.[13]

But, if they do make gods so, at least they shouldn't dare to make so
unlikely an imitation of the greatest of the gods as when he says,

Ah woe, dear is the man I see with my own eyes being
Chased around the town, and my heart is grieved[14]

and,

Oh, oh, Sarpedon, dearest of men to me, is fated
d   To be vanquished by Patroclus, Menoetius' son.[15]

For, my dear Adeimantus, if our young should seriously hear such
things and not laugh scornfully at them as unworthy speeches, it's not
very likely that any one of them would believe these things to be unworthy of himself, a human being, and would reproach himself for
them, if it should enter into his head to say or do any such thing.
Rather, with neither shame nor endurance, he would chant many dirges
and laments at the slightest sufferings."

e   "What you say is very true," he said.

"But that mustn't be, as the argument was just indicating to us.
We must be persuaded by it until someone persuades us with another
and finer one."

"No, it mustn't be."

"Further, they shouldn't be lovers of laughter either. For when a
man lets himself go and laughs mightily, he also seeks a mighty change
to accompany his condition."

"That's my opinion," he said.

"If, then, someone makes noteworthy human beings overpowered
389 a   by laughter, it mustn't be accepted, far less if they are gods."

"Indeed," he said, "that is far less acceptable."

"So, we won't accept from Homer such things about the gods as,

Unquenchable laughter rose among the immortal gods,
When they saw Hephaestus hastening breathlessly
through the halls.[16]

They mustn't be accepted according to your argument."

"If you want to consider it mine," he said. "At any rate, it mustn't
b   be accepted."

"Further, truth must be taken seriously too. For if what we were   389 *b*
just saying was correct, and a lie is really useless to gods and useful to
human beings as a form of remedy, it's plain that anything of the sort
must be assigned to doctors while private men[17] must not put their
hands to it."

"Yes," he said, "it is plain."

"Then, it's appropriate for the rulers, if for anyone at all, to lie for
the benefit of the city in cases involving enemies or citizens, while all
the rest must not put their hands to anything of the sort. We'll say that
for a private man to lie to such rulers is a fault the same as, and even   *c*
greater than, for a sick man or a man in training not to tell the truth
about the affections of his body to the doctor or the trainer, or for a
man not to say to the pilot the things that are[18] concerning the ship
and the sailors, lying about how he himself or his fellow sailors are faring."

"Very true," he said.

"Then, if he[19] catches anyone else in the city lying,   *d*

> Anyone of those who are craftsmen,
> Whether diviner or doctor of sickness
> or carpenter of wood,[20]

he'll punish him for introducing a practice as subversive and destructive of a city as of a ship."

"That is, at least," he said, "if deeds are to fulfill speech."

"And what about this? Won't our youngsters need moderation?"[21]

"Of course."

"Aren't these the most important elements of moderation for the
multitude: being obedient to the rulers, and being themselves rulers of   *e*
the pleasures of drink, sex, and eating?"

"They are, at least in my opinion."

"So I suppose we'll assert that it's fine to say the sort of thing
Diomede says in Homer,

> Friend, keep quiet, and obey my word[22]

and what's connected with this,

> Breathing might the Achaeans went,
> In silence, afraid of their leaders,[23]

and everything else of the sort."

"Yes, these things are fine."

"And what about this?

389 e   Heavy with wine, with eyes of a dog and heart of
                         a deer.[24]

390 a   And what comes right after, and all the rest of the youthful insolence of
          private men to rulers that anyone has ever said in speech or in poem,
          are they fine things to say?"
              "No, they are not fine."
              "I don't suppose they're fit for the young to hear, so far as
          moderation is concerned. But, if they provide some other pleasure, it's
          no surprise. How does it look to you?"
              "As you say," he said.
              "And what about making the wisest of men say that, in his
          opinion, the finest of all things is when

                    The tables are full of bread and meat
   b   And the wine bearer draws wine from the bowl
                    And brings it to pour in the goblets?[25]

          Do you think that's fit for a young man to hear for his self-mastery? Or
          this:

                    Hunger is the most pitiful way to die and find one's fate?[26]

          Or Zeus, alone and awake, making plans while the other gods and men
   c   sleep, easily forgetting all of them because of sexual desire, and so
          struck when he sees Hera that he isn't even willing to go into the house,
          but wants to have intercourse right there on the ground, saying that he
          wasn't so full of desire even when they first went unto one another,
          'unbeknownst to their dear parents?'[27] Nor is Hephaestus' binding of
          Ares and Aphrodite fit, for similar reasons."[28]
              "No, by Zeus," he said, "it doesn't look fit to me."
   d   "But," I said, "if there are any speeches and deeds of endurance
          by famous men in the face of everything, surely they must be seen and
          heard, such as,

                    Smiting his breast, he reproached his heart with word.
                    Endure, heart; you have endured worse before.[29]

              "That's entirely certain," he said.
              "Of course the men mustn't be allowed to be receivers of gifts or
          lovers of money."
   e   "Not at all."
              "Nor must it be sung to them that

                    Gifts persuade gods, gifts persuade venerable kings.[30]

          Nor must Achilles' teacher, Phoenix, be praised for making a sen-

sible[31] speech in advising him to come to the aid of the Achaeans pro-   *390 e*
vided he gets gifts, but failing gifts not to desist from wrath. Nor should
we think it worthy of Achilles himself. Nor shall we agree that he was
such a lover of money as to take gifts from Agamemnon, or, again, to
give up a corpse when getting paid for it, but otherwise not to be
willing."[32]   *391 a*

"It's not just, in any case," he said, "to praise such things."

"And, for Homer's sake," I said, "I hesitate to say that it's not
holy to say these things against Achilles and to believe them when said
by others; or, again, to believe that he said to Apollo,

> You've hindered me, Far-Darter, most destructive of
> all gods.
> And I would revenge myself on you, if I had the
> power;[33]

and that he was disobedient to the river, who was a god, and ready to   *b*
do battle with it;[34] and that he said about the locks consecrated to
another river, Spercheius,

> To the hero Patroclus I would give my hair
> To take with him,[35]

although he was a corpse. It must not be believed that he did. The drag-
ging of Hector around Patroclus' tomb, the slaughter in the fire of the
men captured alive: we'll deny that all this is truly told. And we'll not
let our men believe that Achilles—the son of a goddess and Peleus, a   *c*
most moderate man and third from Zeus, Achilles who was reared by
the most wise Chiron—was so full of confusion as to contain within
himself two diseases that are opposite to one another—illiberality accompanying love of money, on the one hand, and arrogant disdain for
gods and human beings, on the other."

"What you say is correct," he said.

"Then let's not believe it," I said, "and let us not believe, or let it
be said, that Theseus, Poseidon's son, and Perithous, Zeus' son, so
eagerly undertook terrible rapes, or that any other child of a god and   *d*
himself a hero would have dared to do terrible and impious deeds such as
the current lies accuse them of. Rather we should compel the poets to deny
either that such deeds are theirs, or that they are children of gods, but not
to say both, nor to attempt to persuade our youngsters that the gods
produce evil and that heroes are no better than human beings. For, as
we were saying before, these things are neither holy nor true. For,
surely, we showed that it's impossible for evil to be produced by   *e*
gods."

391 e   "Of course."

"And, further, they are harmful to those who hear them. Everyone will be sympathetic with himself when he is bad, persuaded that after all similar things are done and were done even by

> The close relations of gods,
> Near to Zeus, whose altar to patriarchal Zeus
> Is on Ida's peak in the ether

and

> In them the blood of demons has not yet faded.[36]

On that account such tales must cease, for fear that they sow a strong proclivity for badness in our young."

392 a

"Entirely so," he said.

"So," I said, "what form of speeches still remains for which we are to define the sort of thing that must and must not be said? It has been stated how gods must be spoken about, and demons and heroes, and Hades' domain."

"Most certainly."

"Wouldn't it be human beings who remain?"

"Plainly."

"Well, my friend, it's impossible for us to arrange that at present."

"Why?"

b

"Because I suppose we'll say that what both poets and prose writers[37] say concerning the most important things about human beings is bad—that many happy men are unjust, and many wretched ones just, and that doing injustice is profitable if one gets away with it, but justice is someone else's good and one's own loss. We'll forbid them to say such things and order them to sing and to tell tales about the opposites of these things. Or don't you suppose so?"

"I know it quite well," he said.

"Then, if you were to agree that what I say is correct, wouldn't I say you've agreed about what we've been looking for all along?"

"Your supposition is correct," he said.

c

"Won't we come to an agreement that such speeches must be made about human beings when we find out what sort of a thing justice is and how it by nature profits the man who possesses it, whether he seems to be just or not?"

"Very true," he said.

"So then let that be the end of what has to do with speeches. After this, I suppose, style[38] must be considered, and then we'll have made a

[70]

complete consideration of what must be said and how it must be   392 *c*
said."

And Adeimantus said, "I don't understand what you mean."   *d*

"But, you just have to," I said. "Perhaps you'll grasp it better in
this way. Isn't everything that's said by tellers of tales or poets a narrative of what has come to pass, what is, or what is going to be?"

"What else could it be?" he said.

"Now, don't they accomplish this with a narrative that is either
simple or produced by imitation, or by both together?"

"I need," he said, "a still clearer understanding of this as well."

"I seem to be a ridiculous teacher, and an unclear one," I said.
"So, just like men who are incompetent at speaking, instead of speaking about the whole in general, I'll cut off a part and with it attempt to   *e*
make plain to you what I want. Tell me, do you know the first things in
the *Iliad*[39] where the poet tells of Chryses' begging Agamemnon to
ransom his daughter, and Agamemnon's harshness, and Chryses'
calling down curses from the god on the Achaeans when he failed?"   393 *a*

"I do."

"Then you know that up to these lines,

> And he entreated all the Achaeans,
> But especially Atreus' two sons, the marshallers of
> the host,[40]

the poet himself speaks and doesn't attempt to turn our thought elsewhere, as though someone other than he were speaking. But, in what
follows, he speaks as though he himself were Chryses and tries as hard
as he can to make it seem to us that it's not Homer speaking, but the   *b*
priest, an old man. And in this way he made pretty nearly all the rest of
the narrative about the events in Ilium as well as about those in Ithaca
and the whole Odyssey."

"Most certainly," he said.

"Isn't it narrative when he gives all the speeches and also what
comes between the speeches?"

"Of course."

"But, when he gives a speech as though he were someone else,   *c*
won't we say that he then likens his own style as much as possible to
that of the man he has announced as the speaker?"

"We'll say that, surely."

"Isn't likening himself to someone else, either in voice or in looks,
the same as imitating the man he likens himself to?"

"Surely."

"Then, in this case, it seems, he and the other poets use imitation
in making their narrative."

"Most certainly."
                "If the poet nowhere hid himself, his poetic work and narrative as
d   a whole would have taken place without imitation. So that you won't
           say you don't understand again, I'll tell you how this would be. If
           Homer said that Chryses came bringing ransom for his daughter and as
           a suppliant to the Achaeans, especially to the kings, and after that
           didn't speak as though he had become Chryses but still as Homer, you
           know that it wouldn't be imitation but simple narrative. It would be
           something like this—I'll speak without meter; I'm not poetic: The
e   priest came and prayed that the gods grant them the capture of Troy
           and their own safety, and that they accept compensation and free his
           daughter out of reverence for the god. When he had said this, the others
           there showed pious respect and consented, but Agamemnon was angry
           and ordered him to leave immediately and not to come back again or
           else his scepter and the god's chaplets wouldn't protect him. Before his
           daughter would be freed, he said she'd grow old with him in Argos. He
           ordered him to go away and not provoke him if he wished to get home
394 a   safely. The old man heard and was frightened; he went away in silence.
           But when he had withdrawn from the camp, he made a great prayer to
           Apollo, calling upon the god with his special names,[41] reminding him
           and asking a return if anything he had ever given had been pleasing,
           whether it was in the building of temples or the sacrifice of victims. In
           return for them he called down the god's arrows on the Achaeans in
           payment for his tears. That, my comrade," I said, "is the way simple
b   narrative without imitation comes to pass."
                "I understand," he said.
                "Now," I said, "understand that the opposite of this comes to pass
           when someone takes out the poet's connections between the speeches
           and leaves the exchanges."
                "That I understand, too," he said. "That's the way it is with trage-
           dies."
                "Your supposition is most correct," I said. "And now I suppose I
           can make plain to you what I couldn't before. Of poetry and tale-
c   telling, one kind proceeds wholly by imitation—as you say, tragedy
           and comedy; another, by the poet's own report—this, of course, you
           would find especially in dithyrambs; and still another by both—this is
           found in epic poetry and many other places too, if you understand
           me."
                "Now," he said, "I grasp what you wanted to say then."
                "And remember, too, that before this we asserted that what must
           be said had already been stated, but that how it must be said had still to
           be considered."

"I do remember."

"Now this is exactly what I meant: we must come to an agreement as to whether we'll let the poets make their narratives for us by imitation; or whether they are to imitate some things and not others, and what sort belongs to each group; or whether they are not to imitate at all."

"I divine," he said, "that you're considering whether we'll admit tragedy and comedy into the city or not."

"Perhaps," I said, "and perhaps something still more than this. You see, I myself really don't know yet, but wherever the argument, like a wind, tends, thither must we go."

"What you say is fine," he said.

"Now, Adeimantus, reflect on whether our guardians ought to be imitators or not. Or does this follow from what went before—that each one would do a fine job in one activity, but not in many, and if he should try to put his hand to many, he would surely fail of attaining fame in all?"

"Of course that's what would happen."

"Doesn't the same argument also hold for imitation—the same man isn't able to imitate many things as well as one?"

"No, he isn't."

"Then, he'll hardly pursue any of the noteworthy activities while at the same time imitating many things and being a skilled imitator. For even in two kinds of imitation that seem close to one another, like writing comedy and tragedy, the same men aren't capable of producing good imitations in both at the same time. Weren't you just calling these two imitations?"

"I was, and what you say is true. The same men aren't capable of doing both."

"Nor are they able to be rhapsodes and actors at the same time."

"True."

"Nor are the same actors, you know, even able to do both comic and tragic poets. But all these are imitations, aren't they?"

"Yes, they are imitations."

"Human nature, Adeimantus, looks to me to be minted in even smaller coins than this, so that it is unable either to make a fine imitation of many things or to do the things themselves of which the imitations are in fact only likenesses."

"Very true," he said.

"If, then, we are to preserve the first argument—that our guardians must give up all other crafts and very precisely be craftsmen of the city's freedom and practice nothing other than what tends to

394 c
d

e

395 a

b

c

395 c   it—they also mustn't do or imitate anything else. And if they do imitate, they must imitate what's appropriate to them from childhood: men who are courageous, moderate, holy, free, and everything of the sort; and what is slavish, or anything else shameful, they must neither do nor be clever at imitating, so that they won't get a taste for the being

d   from its imitation. Or haven't you observed that imitations, if they are practiced continually from youth onwards, become established as habits and nature, in body and sounds and in thought?"

"Quite so," he said.

"So then," I said, "we won't allow those whom we claim we care for and who must themselves become good men to imitate women—since they are men—either a young woman or an older one, or one who's abusing her husband, or one who's striving with gods and boasting because she supposes herself to be happy, or one who's caught

e   in the grip of misfortune, mourning and wailing. And we'll be far from needing one who's sick or in love or in labor."

"That's entirely certain," he said.

"Nor must they in any event imitate slaves, women or men, who are doing the slavish things."

"No, they mustn't."

"Nor, as it seems, bad men who are cowards and doing the opposite of what we just now said, insulting and making fun of one another, and using shameful language, drunk or sober, or committing

396 a   the other faults that such men commit against themselves and others in speeches and deeds. Nor do I suppose they should be accustomed to likening themselves to madmen in speeches or in deeds. For, although they must know both mad and worthless men and women, they must neither do nor imitate anything of theirs."

"Very true," he said.

"And what about this," I said. "Should they imitate smiths at work, or men exercising any other craft, or men rowing triremes or

b   calling time to those who do, or anything that has to do with these things?"

"How could that be," he said, "since they won't even be permitted to pay attention to any of these things?"

"And what about this? Horses neighing, bulls lowing, the roaring of rivers, the crashing of the sea, thunder, and everything of the sort—will they imitate them?"

"But," he said, "they're forbidden to be mad or to liken themselves to the mad."

"Then, if I understand what you mean," I said, "there is a certain form of style and narrative in which the real gentleman[42] narrates

c   whenever he must say something, and, again, another form, unlike this

one, in the man who is by nature and rearing the opposite of this   *396 c*
other, always keeps and in which he narrates."

"Which are they?" he said.

"In my opinion," I said, "when the sensible man comes in his narrative to some speech or deed of a good man, he will be willing to
report it as though he himself were that man and won't be ashamed of
such an imitation. He will imitate the good man most when he is acting
steadily and prudently; less, and less willingly, when he's unsteadied by   *d*
diseases, loves,[43] drink, or some other misfortune. But when he meets
with someone unworthy of himself, he won't be willing seriously to represent himself as an inferior, unless, of course, it's brief, when the
man does something good; rather, he'll be ashamed, both because he's
unpracticed at imitating such men and because he can't stand forming
himself according to, and fitting himself into, the models of worse men.   *e*
In his mind he despises this, unless it's done in play."

"It's likely," he said.

"Then, won't he use a narration like the one we described a little
while ago concerning Homer's verses, and won't his style participate in
both imitation and the other kind of narrative, but there'll be a little bit
of imitation in a great deal of speech? Or am I talking nonsense?"

"That," he said, "is just the way the model of such a speaker must
be."

"Now, then," I said, "as for the man who's not of this sort, the
more common he is, the more he'll narrate everything and think noth-   *397 a*
ing unworthy of himself; hence he'll undertake seriously to imitate in
the presence of many everything we were just mentioning—thunder,
the noises of winds, hailstorms, axles and pulleys, the voices of
trumpets, flutes, and all the instruments, and even the sound of dogs,
sheep, and birds. And this man's whole style will be based on imitation   *b*
of voice and looks, or else include only a bit of narrative."

"That," he said, "is also the way it must be."

"Well, then," I said, "these are the two forms of style I meant."

"So they are," he said.

"Then, of the two, one involves only small changes, and, if
someone assigns the appropriate harmonic mode and rhythm[44] to the
style, it turns out that the man who speaks correctly speaks mostly in
the same style and in one mode, for the changes are small, and likewise
in a similar rhythm."   *c*

"That's exactly the way it is," he said.

"And what about the form of the other? Doesn't it need the opposites—all modes and all rhythms—if it's going to be spoken in its
own way, because it involves all species of changes?"

"Yes, indeed, that's very much the way it is."

397 c
"Do all the poets and the men who say anything fall into one of these patterns of style or the other, or make some mixture of them both?"

"Necessarily," he said.

d
"What will we do then?" I said. "Shall we admit all of them into the city, or one of the unmixed, or the one who is mixed?"

"If my side wins," he said, "it will be the unmixed imitator of the decent."

"However, Adeimantus, the man who is mixed is pleasing; and by far the most pleasing to boys and their teachers, and to the great mob too, is the man opposed to the one you choose."

"Yes," he said, "he is the most pleasing."

"But," I said, "perhaps you would say he doesn't harmonize with

e
our regime because there's no double man among us, nor a manifold one, since each man does one thing."

"No, he doesn't harmonize."

"Isn't it for this reason that it's only in such a city that we'll find the shoemaker a shoemaker, and not a pilot along with his shoemaking, and the farmer a farmer, and not a judge along with his farming, and the skilled warrior a skilled warrior, and not a moneymaker along with his warmaking, and so on with them all?"

"True," he said.

398 a
"Now, as it seems, if a man who is able by wisdom to become every sort of thing and to imitate all things should come to our city, wishing to make a display of himself and his poems, we would fall on our knees before him as a man sacred, wonderful, and pleasing; but we would say that there is no such man among us in the city, nor is it lawful[45] for such a man to be born there. We would send him to another city, with myrrh poured over his head and crowned with wool, while we ourselves would use a more austere and less pleasing poet and

b
teller of tales for the sake of benefit, one who would imitate the style of the decent man and would say what he says in those models that we set down as laws at the beginning, when we undertook to educate the soldiers."

"Indeed that is what we would do," he said, "if it were up to us."

"Now, my friend," I said, "it's likely we are completely finished with that part of music that concerns speeches and tales. What must be told and how it must be told have been stated."

"That's my opinion too," he said.

c
"After that," I said, "doesn't what concerns the manner of song and melody remain?"

"Plainly."

"Couldn't everyone by now discover what we have to say about   *398 c*
how they must be if we're going to remain in accord with what has
already been said?"

And Glaucon laughed out and said, "I run the risk of not being
included in everyone. At least I'm not at present capable of suggesting
what sort of things we must say. However, I've a suspicion."

"At all events," I said, "you are, in the first place, surely capable   *d*
of saying that melody is composed of three things—speech, harmonic
mode, and rhythm."

"Yes," he said, "that I can do."

"What's speech in it surely doesn't differ from the speech that
isn't sung insofar as it must be spoken according to the same models
we prescribed a while ago and in the same way."

"True," he said.

"And, further, the harmonic mode and the rhythm must follow
the speech."

"Of course."

"Moreover, we said there is no further need of wailing and lamentations in speeches."

"No, there isn't."

"What are the wailing modes? Tell me, for you're musical."   *e*

"The mixed Lydian," he said, "and the 'tight' Lydian and some
similar ones."

"Aren't they to be excluded?" I said. "They're useless even for
women who are to be decent, let alone for men."

"Certainly."

"Then again, drunkenness, softness, and idleness are most unseemly for guardians."

"Of course."

"What modes are soft and suitable for symposia?"⁴⁶

"There are some Ionian," he said, "and some Lydian, too, which
are called 'slack.'"

"Could you, my friend, use them for war-making men?"   *399 a*

"Not at all," he said. "So, you've probably got the Dorian and the
Phrygian left."

"I don't know the modes," I said. "Just leave that mode which
would appropriately imitate the sounds and accents of a man who is
courageous in warlike deeds and every violent work, and who in failure
or when going to face wounds or death or falling into some other   *b*
disaster, in the face of all these things stands up firmly and patiently
against chance. And, again, leave another mode for a man who performs a peaceful deed, one that is not violent but voluntary, either per-

399 *b*   suading someone of something and making a request—whether a god by prayer or a human being by instruction and exhortation—or, on the contrary, holding himself in check for someone else who makes a request or instructs him or persuades him to change, and as a result acting intelligently, not behaving arrogantly, but in all these things acting

c   moderately and in measure and being content with the consequences. These two modes—a violent one and a voluntary one, which will produce the finest imitation of the sounds of unfortunate and fortunate, moderate and courageous men—leave these."

"You're asking me to leave none other than those I was just speaking of."

"Then," I said, "there'll be no need of many-toned or panharmonic instruments for our songs and melodies."

"It doesn't look like it to me," he said.

"Then we'll not support the craftsmen who make lutes, harps, and

d   all the instruments that are many-stringed and play many modes."

"It doesn't look like we will," he said.

"And what about this? Will you admit flutemakers and flutists into the city? Or, isn't the flute the most many-stringed of all, and aren't the panharmonic instruments themselves imitations of it?"

"Plainly," he said.

"The lyre and the cither are left you as useful for the city," I said. "And, further, for the country, there'd be a sort of pipe for the herdsmen."

"At least so our argument indicates," he said.

e   "It's nothing new we're doing, my friend," I said, "in choosing Apollo and Apollo's instruments ahead of Marsyas and his instruments."[47]

"No, by Zeus," he said. "We don't look to me as though we were."

"And, by the dog," I said, "unawares we've again purged the city that a while ago we said was luxurious."

"That's a sign of our moderation," he said.

"Come, then," I said, "and let's purge the rest. Now, following on harmonic modes would be our rule about rhythms: we mustn't seek subtle ones nor all sorts of feet, but we'll see which are the rhythms of an orderly and courageous life; and when we have seen them, we'll compel the foot and the tune to follow the speech of such a man, rather

400 *a*   than the speech following the foot and the tune. Whatever these rhythms might be is your job to tell, just as with the harmonic modes."

"But, by Zeus, I can't say," he said. "There are three forms out of

which the feet are woven, just as there are four for sounds from which   *400 a*
all the modes are compounded—this I've observed and could tell. But
as to which sort are imitations of which sort of life, I can't say."[48]

"We'll consult with Damon[49] too," I said, "about which feet are   *b*
appropriate for illiberality and insolence or madness and the rest of
vice, and which rhythms must be left for their opposites. I think I
heard him, but not clearly, naming a certain enoplion foot, which is a
composite, and a dactyl and an heroic—I don't know how, but he arranged it and presented it so that it's equal up and down, passing into a
short and a long; and, I think, he named one iambic and another
trochaic and attached longs and shorts to them. With some of these I   *c*
think he blamed and praised the tempo of the foot no less than the
rhythms themselves, or it was the two together—I can't say. But, as I
said, let these things be turned over to Damon. To separate them out[50]
is no theme for a short argument. Or do you think so?"[51]

"Not I, by Zeus."

"But you are able to determine that grace and gracelessness[52] accompany rhythm and lack of it?"

"Of course."

"Further, rhythm and lack of it follow the style, the one likening   *d*
itself to a fine style, the other to its opposite; and it's the same with harmony and lack of it, provided, that is, rhythm and harmonic mode
follow speech, as we were just saying, and not speech them."

"But, of course," he said, "they must accompany speech."

"What about the manner of the style and the speech?" I said.
"Don't they follow the disposition of the soul?"

"Of course."

"And the rest follow the style?"

"Yes."

"Hence, good speech, good harmony, good grace, and good
rhythm accompany good disposition,[53] not the folly that we endear-   *e*
ingly call 'good disposition,' but that understanding truly trained to a
good and fair disposition."

"That's entirely certain," he said.

"Mustn't the young pursue them everywhere if they are to do their
own work?"

"Indeed they must be pursued."

"Surely painting is full of them, as are all crafts of this sort; weav-   *401 a*
ing is full of them, and so are embroidery, housebuilding, and also all
the crafts that produce the other furnishings; so, furthermore, is the
nature of bodies and the rest of what grows. In all of them there is
grace or gracelessness. And gracelessness, clumsiness, inhar-

401 a   moniousness, are akin to bad speech and bad disposition, while their
opposites are akin to, and imitations of, the opposite—moderate and
good disposition."

"Entirely so," he said.

b   "Must we, then, supervise only the poets and compel them to impress the image of the good disposition on their poems or not to make
them among us? Or must we also supervise the other craftsmen and
prevent them from impressing this bad disposition, a licentious,
illiberal, and graceless one, either on images of animals or on houses or
on anything else that their craft produces? And the incapable craftsman
we mustn't permit to practice his craft among us, so that our guardians

c   won't be reared on images of vice, as it were on bad grass, every day
cropping and grazing on a great deal little by little from many places,
and unawares put together some one big bad thing in their soul?
Mustn't we, rather, look for those craftsmen whose good natural en-
dowments make them able to track down the nature of what is fine and
graceful, so that the young, dwelling as it were in a healthy place, will
be benefited by everything; and from that place something of the fine
works will strike their vision or their hearing, like a breeze bringing

d   health from good places; and beginning in childhood, it will, without
their awareness, with the fair speech lead them to likeness and friendship
as well as accord?"

"In this way," he said, "they'd have by far the finest rearing."

"So, Glaucon," I said, "isn't this why the rearing in music is most
sovereign? Because rhythm and harmony most of all insinuate themselves into the inmost part of the soul and most vigorously lay hold of it
in bringing grace with them; and they make a man graceful if he is cor-

e   rectly reared, if not, the opposite. Furthermore, it is sovereign because
the man properly reared on rhythm and harmony would have the
sharpest sense for what's been left out and what isn't a fine product of
craft or what isn't a fine product of nature. And, due to his having the
right kind of dislikes, he would praise the fine things; and, taking
pleasure in them and receiving them into his soul, he would be reared

402 a   on them and become a gentleman. He would blame and hate the ugly in
the right way while he's still young, before he's able to grasp reasonable
speech. And when reasonable speech comes, the man who's reared in
this way would take most delight in it, recognizing it on account of its
being akin?"

"In my opinion, at least," he said, "it's for such reasons that
there's rearing in music."

"Then," I said, "just as we were competent at reading only when
the few letters there are didn't escape us in any of the combinations in

b   which they turn up, and we didn't despise them as not needing to be

noticed in either small writing or large, but were eager to make them   *402 b*
out everywhere, since we wouldn't be skilled readers before we could
do so—"

"True."

"Now isn't it also true that if images of writings should appear
somewhere, in water or in mirrors, we wouldn't recognize them before
we knew the things themselves, but both belong to the same art and
discipline?"

"That's entirely certain."

"So, in the name of the gods, is it as I say: we'll never be
musical—either ourselves or those whom we say we must educate to be   *c*
guardians—before we recognize the forms of moderation, courage,
liberality, magnificence, and all their kin, and, again, their opposites,
everywhere they turn up, and notice that they are in whatever they are
in, both themselves and their images, despising them neither in little nor
big things, but believing that they all belong to the same art and
discipline?"

"Quite necessarily," he said.

"Then," I said, "if the fine dispositions that are in the soul and   *d*
those that agree and accord with them in the form should ever coincide
in anyone, with both partaking of the same model, wouldn't that be the
fairest sight for him who is able to see?"

"By far."

"Now the fairest is the most lovable?"

"Of course."

"It's the musical man who would most of all love such human
beings, while if there were one who lacked harmony, he wouldn't love
him."

"No, he wouldn't," he said, "at least if there were some defect in the
soul. If, however, there were some bodily defect, he'd be patient and
would willingly take delight in him."   *e*

"I understand," I said. "You have, or had, such a boy and I concede your point. But tell me this: does excessive pleasure have anything
in common with moderation?"

"How could it," he said, "since it puts men out of their minds no
less than pain?"

"But, then, with the rest of virtue?"

"Nothing at all."   *403 a*

"But with insolence and licentiousness?"

"Most of all."

"Can you tell of a greater or keener pleasure than the one connected with sex?"

"I can't," he said, "nor a madder one either."

403 a

"Is the naturally right kind of love to love in a moderate and musical way what's orderly and fine?"

"Quite so," he said.

"Nothing that's mad or akin to licentiousness must approach the right kind of love?"

"No, it mustn't."

b

"Then this pleasure mustn't approach love, and lover and boy who love and are loved in the right way mustn't be partner to it?"

"By Zeus, no, Socrates," he said, "this pleasure certainly mustn't approach love."

"So then, as it seems, you'll set down a law in the city that's being founded: that a lover may kiss, be with, and touch his boy as though he were a son, for fair purposes, if he persuades him; but, as for the rest, his intercourse with the one for whom he cares will be such that their

c

relationship will never be reputed to go further than this. If not, he'll be subject to blame as unmusical and inexperienced in fair things."

"Just so," he said.

"Does it look to you too as though our argument concerning music has reached an end?" I said. "At least it's ended where it ought to end. Surely musical matters should end in love matters that concern the fair."

"I am in accord," he said.

"Now, after music, the youths must be trained in gymnastic."

"Of course."

"In this too they must then receive a precise training from child-

d

hood throughout life. And it would, I believe, be something like this; and you consider it too. It doesn't look to me as though it's a sound body that by its virtue makes the soul good, but the opposite: a good soul by its own virtue makes the body as good as it can be. How does it look to you?"

"It looks that way to me too," he said.

"If we gave adequate care to the intellect and turned over to it the concern for the precise details about the body, while we, so as not to

e

talk too much, showed the way only to the models, would we be doing the right thing?"

"Most certainly."

"Now we said that they must keep away from drunkenness. Surely it's more permissible for anyone, other than a guardian, to be drunk and not to know where on earth he is."

"It's ridiculous," he said, "if the guardian needs a guardian."

"Now, what about food? For the men are champions in the greatest contest, aren't they?"

"Yes."

"Then would the habit of the ordinary athletes be proper for them?"

"Perhaps."

"But," I said, "this is a sort of sleepy habit and not a very steady one so far as health is concerned. Or don't you see that they sleep their life away; and if they depart a bit from their fixed way of life, these athletes get very critically ill?"

"I do see that."

"There's need then," I said, "for a subtler exercise for these combatants in war, since they must be sleepless like hounds, see and hear as sharply as possible, and in their campaigns undergo many changes of water, food, the sun's heat, and winds without being too highly tuned for steadiness in health."

"It looks like it to me."

"Would the best gymnastic be a kin of the simple music we were describing a little while ago?"

"How do you mean?"

"A simple and decent gymnastic, of course, especially in matters of war."

"How would it be?"

"From Homer too," I said, "one could learn things very much of this sort. For you know that, during the campaign, at the feasts of the heroes, he doesn't feast them on fish—and that, although they are by the sea at the Hellespont—nor on boiled meats but only roasted, which would be especially easy for soldiers to come by; for, so to speak, everywhere it's easier to come by the use of fire alone than to carry pots around."

"Quite so."

"Nor does Homer, I believe, ever make mention of sweets. Don't even the other athletes know that if a body is going to be in good shape it must keep away from everything of the sort?"

"Yes," he said, "and they are right in knowing it and keeping away."

"My friend, you don't seem to recommend a Syracusan table and Sicilian refinement at cooking, if you think this is right."

"No, I think not."

"Then you also blame a Corinthian girl's being the mistress of men who are going to have good bodies."

"That's entirely certain."

"And the reputed joys of Attic cakes?"

"Necessarily."

404 d

"In likening such food and such a way of life as a whole to melodies and songs written in the panharmonic mode and with all rhythms,

e

we would make a correct likeness, I suppose."

"Of course."

"Just as refinement there gave birth to licentiousness, does it give birth to illness here? And just as simplicity in music produced moderation in souls, does it in gymnastic produce health in bodies?"

"That's very true," he said.

405 a

"When licentiousness and illness multiply in a city, aren't many courts and hospitals opened, and aren't the arts of the law court and medicine full of pride when even many free men take them very seriously?"

"How could it turn out differently?"

"Will you be able to produce a greater sign of a bad and base education in a city than its needing eminent doctors and judges not only for the common folk and the manual artisans but also for those who pretend to have been reared in a free fashion? Or doesn't it

b

seem base, and a great sign of lack of education, to be compelled— because of a shortage at home—to use a justice imported from others who are thus masters and umpires?"

"Certainly," he said, "basest of all."

"In your opinion, is this really baser," I said, "than when someone not only wastes most of his life in courtrooms defending and accusing, but, from inexperience in fair things, is also persuaded to pride himself on this very thing, because he is clever at doing injustice and

c

competent at practicing every dodge, escaping through every loophole by writhing and twisting and thereby not paying the penalty, and all this for the sake of little and worthless things; ignorant of how much finer and better it is to arrange his life so as to have no need of a dozing judge?"

"No," he said, "but this case is even baser than the other one."

"And," I said, "needing medicine, not because one has met with wounds or some of the seasonal maladies, but as a result of idleness and

d

a way of life such as we described, full of humors and winds like a marsh, compelling the subtle Asclepiads[54] to give names like 'flatulences' and 'catarrhs' to diseases, doesn't that seem base?"

"Quite so," he said. "How truly new and strange are these names for diseases."

"Such," I said, "as didn't exist in the time of Asclepius, as I sup-

e

pose. I infer this from the fact that at Troy his sons didn't blame the woman who gave the wounded Eurypylus Pramneian wine to drink

406 a

with a great deal of barley and grated cheese sprinkled on it; and it's

just these that are thought to be inflammatory; nor did they criticize   *406 a*
Patroclus who was healing."[55]

"But for all of that," he said, "the drink is certainly strange for
one in that condition."

"No, it isn't," I said, "if only you recognize that this current art of
medicine which is an education in disease was not used by the Asclepiads of former times, or so they say, until Herodicus came on the
scene. He was a gymnastic master and became sickly; so he mixed
gymnastic with medicine, and he first and foremost worried himself   *b*
to death, then many others afterwards."

"In what way?" he said.

"He drew out his death," I said. "Attending the mortal disease, he
wasn't able to cure it, I suppose, and spent his whole life treating it
with no leisure for anything else, mightily distressed if he departed a bit
from his accustomed regimen. So, finding it hard to die, thanks to his
wisdom, he came to an old age."

"Well," he said, "that was a fine prize[56] he won for his art."

"Such as is fitting," I said, "for one who didn't know that it wasn't   *c*
from ignorance or inexperience in this form of medicine that Asclepius
didn't reveal it to his offspring, but rather because he knew that for all
men obedient to good laws a certain job has been assigned to each in
the city at which he is compelled to work, and no one has the leisure to
be sick throughout life and treat himself. It's laughable that we
recognize this for the craftsmen, while for the rich and reputed happy
we don't."

"How's that?" he said.

"A carpenter," I said, "when he's sick, thinks fit to drink some   *d*
medicine from the doctor and vomit up his disease or have it purged
out from below, or submit to burning or cutting and be rid of it. If
someone prescribes a lengthy regimen for him, putting bandages
around his head and what goes with them, he soon says that he has
no leisure to be sick nor is a life thus spent—paying attention to a
disease while neglecting the work at hand—of any profit. And, with
that, he says goodbye to such a doctor and returns to his accus-   *e*
tomed regimen; regaining his health, he lives minding his own business; if his body is inadequate to bearing up under it, he dies and is
rid of his troubles."

"For this kind of man at least," he said, "it's thought proper to
use medicine in this way."

"Is it," I said, "because he had a definite job, and if he couldn't do   *407 a*
it, it would be of no profit to go on living?"

"Plainly," he said.

[85]

407 a   "While the rich man, as we claim, has no such job at hand that makes his life unlivable if he's compelled to keep away from it."

"At least there's not said to be."

"That," I said, "is because you don't listen to how Phocylides[57] says that when someone already has a livelihood he must practice virtue."

"I, for my part," he said, "suppose he must also do so before that."

"Let's not fight with him about that," I said. "But let's instruct ourselves as to whether the rich man must practice it and whether life is

b   unlivable for the one who doesn't practice it, or whether care of sickness is a hindrance in paying attention to carpentry and the other arts, but doesn't hinder Phocylides' exhortation."

"Yes, by Zeus," he said, "this excessive care of the body, if it's over and above gymnastic, hinders it just about more than anything. And it's troublesome in the management of a household, on a campaign, and in sedentary offices in the city."

"But most important of all, surely, is that it also makes any kind

c   of learning, thought, or meditation by oneself hard; it is always on the lookout for tensions and spinning in the head and holds philosophy to blame. So that wherever virtue is practiced and made to undergo scrutiny in this way, this care of the body is in every way a hindrance. It always makes one suppose he's sick and never cease to take pains about his body."

"Quite likely," he said.

"Then won't we say that Asclepius, too, knew this and revealed an art of medicine for those whose bodies are by nature and regimen in a

d   healthy condition but have some distinct and definite disease in them? His medicine is for these men and this condition; with drugs and cutting to drive out the diseases, he prescribed their customary regimen so as not to harm the city's affairs. But with bodies diseased through and through, he made no attempt by regimens—drawing off a bit at one time, pouring in a bit at another—to make a lengthy and bad life for a human being and have him produce offspring likely to be such as he; he didn't think he should care for the man who's not able to live in his established round, on the grounds that he's of no profit to himself or to

e   the city."

"You speak," he said, "of a statesmanlike Asclepius."[58]

"Plainly," I said. "And don't you see that his sons, because he was

408 a   like that, both showed themselves to be good men in the war at Troy and made use of the art of medicine in the way I say? Or don't you remember that as well from the wound Pandarus inflicted on Menelaus,

They sucked out the blood and sprinkled gentle drugs on it[59]

and that after this they didn't prescribe what he must drink or eat   *408 a*
any more than with Eurypylus, believing the drugs to be sufficient
to cure men who before their wounds were healthy and orderly in
their regimen, even if they should happen to take a drink mixed with   *b*
barley, cheese, and wine right away? And, as for those with a naturally
sickly and licentious body, they thought that living is of no profit
either to themselves or others, that the art shouldn't be applied to
them, and that they mustn't be treated—not even if they were richer
than Midas."

"You speak," he said, "of quite subtle sons of Asclepius."

"It's appropriate," I said. "And yet it's in just this that the tragic
poets as well as Pindar[60] don't obey us. Although they claim Asclepius was the son of Apollo, they also say he was persuaded by gold to
cure a rich man who was as good as dead and it's for this that he was
struck with a thunderbolt. But we, in accord with what was said before,   *c*
won't believe both things from them; rather if he was a god's son, we'll
say he wasn't basely greedy, and if he was basely greedy, he wasn't a
god's son."

"Quite right in that," he said. "But what do you say about this,
Socrates? Won't we need to get good doctors in the city? And, of
course, those who have handled the most healthy men and the most   *d*
sick ones would be the best, and the best judges, similarly, would be
those who have been familiar with all sorts of natures."

"Yes indeed, I mean good ones," I said. "But do you know whom I
consider to be such?"

"I would, if you'd tell me," he said.

"Well, I'll try," I said. "However you asked about dissimilar matters in the same speech."

"How's that?" he said.

"Doctors," I said, "would prove cleverest if, beginning in childhood, in addition to learning the art, they should be familiar with very
many and very bad bodies and should themselves suffer all diseases and   *e*
not be quite healthy by nature. For I don't suppose they care for a body
with a body—in that case it wouldn't be possible for the bodies themselves ever to be, or to have been, bad—but for a body with a soul; and
it's not possible for a soul to have been, and to be, bad and to care for
anything well."

"Correct," he said.

"A judge, on the other hand, my friend, rules a soul with a soul,   *409 a*
and it's not possible for it to have been reared and been familiar with
bad souls from youth on, and to have gone through the list of all unjust
deeds and to have committed them itself so as to be sharp at inferring
from itself the unjust deeds of others like diseases in the body. Rather,

409 a   it must have been inexperienced and untainted by bad dispositions
when it was young, if, as a fine and good soul, it's going to make
healthy judgments about what is just. This is exactly why decent men,
when they are young, look as though they were innocents[61] and easily

b   deceived by unjust men, because they have in themselves no patterns of
affections similar to those of bad men."

"Yes, indeed," he said, "this is the very thing that happens to
them."

"That, you see, is why," I said, "the good judge must not be young
but old, a late learner of what injustice is; he must not have become
aware of it as kindred, dwelling in his own soul. Rather, having studied
it as something alien in alien souls, over a long time, he has become
thoroughly aware of how it is naturally bad, having made use of
knowledge, not his own personal experience."

"Well," he said, "a judge who's like that seems to be most noble."

"And good, too," I said, "which is what you asked. The man who
has a good soul is good. That clever and suspicious man, the one who
has himself done many unjust things and supposes he's a master crim-
inal and wise, looks clever, because he is on his guard, when he keeps
company with his likes—taking his bearings by the patterns within
himself. But when he has contact with good men who are older, he now

d   looks stupid, distrustful out of season, and ignorant of a healthy
disposition, because he does not possess a pattern for such a man. But
since he meets bad men more often than good ones, he seems to be
rather more wise than unlearned, both to himself and to others."

"That is," he said, "quite certainly true."

"Then it's not in such a man that the good and wise judge must be
looked for but in the former," I said. "For badness would never know
virtue and itself, while virtue in an educated nature will in time gain a

e   knowledge of both itself and badness simultaneously. This man, in my
opinion, and not the bad one, becomes wise."

"And I," he said, "share your opinion."

"Will you set down a law in the city providing as well for an art of
medicine such as we described along with such an art of judging, which

410 a   will care for those of your citizens who have good natures in body and
soul; while as for those who haven't, they'll let die the ones whose bodies are such, and the ones whose souls have bad natures and are incurable, they themselves will kill?"

"Well," he said, "that's the way it looked best for those who undergo it and for the city."

"Then your young," I said, "will plainly beware of falling into
need of the judge's art, since they use that simple music which we claimed
engenders moderation."

"Of course," he said.   410 *a*

"Won't the musical man hunt for a gymnastic by following these   *b*
same tracks, and, if he wishes, catch it, so that he will require no art of
medicine except in case of necessity?"

"That's my opinion."

"Moreover, he'll undergo these very exercises and labors looking
less to strength than to the spirited part of his nature and for the purpose
of arousing it, unlike the other kinds of contestants who treat diets and
labors as means to force."

"Quite right," he said.

"Then, Glaucon," I said, "did those who established an education
in music and gymnastic do so for other reasons than the one supposed   *c*
by some, that the latter should care for the body and the former for the
soul?"

"For what else, then?" he said.

"It's likely," I said, "that they established both chiefly for the
soul."

"How's that?"

"Don't you notice," I said, "the turn of mind of those who maintain a lifelong familiarity with gymnastic but don't touch music; or,
again, that of those who do the opposite?"

"What are you talking about?" he said.

"Savageness and hardness on the one hand," I said, "softness and   *d*
tameness on the other."

"I do notice," he said, "that those who make use of unmixed gymnastic turn out more savage than they ought, while those who make use
of music become in their turn softer than is fine for them."

"And, surely," I said, "the savage stems from the spirited part of
their nature, which, if rightly trained, would be courageous; but, if
raised to a higher pitch than it ought to have, would be likely to become cruel and harsh."

"That is my opinion," he said.

"And what about this? Wouldn't the philosophic nature have the   *e*
tame; and if it is relaxed somewhat more, would it be softer than it
ought to be, while if it is finely reared, it would be tame and orderly?"

"That's so."

"And we do say that the guardians must have both of these two
natures."

"Yes, they must."

"Then mustn't they be harmonized with one another?"

"Of course."

"And the soul of the man thus harmonized is moderate and
courageous?"   411 *a*

411 a

"Certainly."

"And that of the inharmonious man is cowardly and crude?"

"Of course."

"Then, when a man gives himself to music and lets the flute play and pour into his soul through his ears, as it were into a funnel—using those sweet, soft, wailing harmonies we were just speaking of—and spends his whole life humming and exulting in song, at first, whatever spiritedness he had, he softened like iron and made useful from having

b   been useless and hard. But when he keeps at it without letting up and charms his spirit, he, as the next step, already begins to melt and liquefy his spirit, until he dissolves it completely and cuts out, as it were, the sinews from his soul and makes it 'a feeble warrior.' "[62]

"Most certainly," he said.

"And," I said, "if from the start he got a spiritless soul from nature, he accomplishes this quickly. But if it's spirited, the spirit is weakened and made temperamental, quickly inflamed by little things and quickly extinguished. Thus these men have become quick-

c   tempered and irritable from having been spirited, and they are filled with discontent."

"Quite so."

"Now what about the man who labors a great deal at gymnastic and feasts himself really well but never touches music and philosophy? At first, with his body in good condition, isn't he filled with high thought and spirit, and doesn't he become braver than himself?"

"Very much."

"But what about when he does nothing else and never communes

d   with a Muse? Even if there was some love of learning in his soul, because it never tastes of any kind of learning or investigation nor partakes in speech or the rest of music, doesn't it become weak, deaf, and blind because it isn't awakened or trained and its perceptions aren't purified?"

"That's so," he said.

"Then, I suppose, such a man becomes a misologist[63] and unmusical. He no longer makes any use of persuasion by means of speech

e   but goes about everything with force and savageness, like a wild beast; and he lives ignorantly and awkwardly without rhythm or grace."

"Exactly," he said, "that's the way it is."

"Now I, for one, would assert that some god gave two arts to human beings for these two things, as it seems—music and gymnastic for the spirited and the philosophic—not for soul and body, except incidentally, but rather for these two. He did so in order that they might be

412 a   harmonized with one another by being tuned to the proper degree of tension and relaxation."

"Yes, it does seem so," he said.

"Then the man who makes the finest mixture of gymnastic with music and brings them to his soul in the most proper measure is the one of whom we would most correctly say that he is the most perfectly musical and well harmonized, far more so than of the man who tunes the strings to one another."

"That's fitting, Socrates," he said.

"Won't we also always need some such man as overseer in the city, Glaucon, if the regime is going to be saved?"

"Indeed, we will need him more than anything."

"These, then, would be the models of education and rearing. Why should one go through the dances of such men and the hunts, chases, gymnastic contests, and horseraces? It's pretty plain, surely, that they must follow these models, and they are no longer difficult to discover."

"Perhaps," he said, "they aren't."

"All right," I said. "After that, what would it be that we must determine? Isn't it who among these men will rule and who be ruled?"

"Of course."

"That the rulers must be older and the ruled younger is plain, isn't it?"

"Yes, it is."

"And that they must be the best among them?"

"That's plain, too."

"And the best of the farmers, aren't they the most skillful at farming?"

"Yes."

"Now since they must be the best of the guardians, mustn't they be the most skillful at guarding the city?"

"Yes."

"Mustn't they, to begin with, be prudent in such matters as well as powerful, and, moreover, mustn't they care for the city?"

"That's so."

"A man would care most for that which he happened to love."

"Necessarily."

"And wouldn't he surely love something most when he believed that the same things are advantageous to it and to himself, and when he supposed that if it did well, he too himself would do well along with it, and if it didn't, neither would he?"

"That's so," he said.

"Then we must select from the other guardians the sort of men who, upon our consideration, from everything in their lives, look as if

412 e   they were entirely eager to do what they believe to be advantageous to
the city and would in no way be willing to do what is not."

"Yes," he said, "they would be suitable."

"Then, in my opinion, they must be watched at every age to see if
they are skillful guardians of this conviction[64] and never under the
influence of wizardry or force forget and thus banish the opinion that
one must do what is best for the city."

"What do you mean by 'banishment'?" he said.

"I'll tell you," I said. "It looks to me as though an opinion departs
from our minds either willingly or unwillingly; the departure of the
false opinion from the man who learns otherwise is willing, that of
413 a   every true opinion is unwilling."

"I understand the case of the willing departure," he said, "but I
need to learn about the unwilling."

"What?" I said. "Don't you too believe that human beings are unwillingly deprived of good things and willingly of bad ones? Or isn't
being deceived about the truth bad, and to have the truth good? Or isn't
it your opinion that to opine the things that are, is to have the truth?"

"What you say is correct," he said, "and in my opinion men are
unwillingly deprived of true opinion."

b   "Don't they suffer this by being robbed, bewitched by wizards, or
forced?"

"Now I don't understand again," he said.

"I'm afraid I am speaking in the tragic way," I said. "By the
robbed I mean those who are persuaded to change and those who
forget, because in the one case, time, in the other, speech, takes
away their opinions unawares. Now you surely understand?"

"Yes."

"And, then, by the forced I mean those whom some grief or pain
causes to change their opinions."

"I understand that too," he said, "and what you say is correct."

c   "And, further, the bewitched you too, I suppose, would say are
those who change their opinions either because they are charmed by
pleasure or terrified by some fear."

"Yes," he said, "that's because everything that deceives seems to
bewitch."

"Now then, as I said a while ago, we must look for some men who
are the best guardians of their conviction that they must do what on
each occasion seems best for the city. So we must watch them straight
from childhood by setting them at tasks in which a man would most
likely forget and be deceived out of such a conviction. And the man
who has a memory and is hard to deceive must be chosen, and the one
d   who's not must be rejected, mustn't he?"

"Yes."   413 d

"And again, they must be set to labors, pains, and contests in which these same things must be watched."

"Correct," he said.

"Then," I said, "we must also make them a competition for the third form, wizardry, and we must look on. Just as they lead colts to noises and confusions and observe if they're fearful, so these men when they are young must be brought to terrors and then cast in turn into pleasures, testing them far more than gold in fire. If a man appears   e
hard to bewitch and graceful in everything, a good guardian of himself and the music he was learning, proving himself to possess rhythm and harmony on all these occasions—such a man would certainly be most useful to himself and the city. And the one who on each occasion, among the children and youths and among the men, is tested and comes through untainted, must be appointed ruler of the city and guardian;   414 a
and he must be given honors, both while living and when dead, and must be allotted the greatest prizes in burial and the other memorials. And the man who's not of this sort must be rejected. The selection and appointment of the rulers and guardians is, in my opinion, Glaucon," I said, "something like this, not described precisely, but by way of a model."

"That," he said, "is the way it looks to me too."

"Isn't it then truly most correct to call these men complete guard-   b
ians? They can guard over enemies from without and friends from within—so that the ones will not wish to do harm and the others will be unable to. The young, whom we were calling guardians up to now, we shall call auxiliaries and helpers of the rulers' convictions."

"In my opinion," he said, "that is what they should be called."

"Could we," I said, "somehow contrive one of those lies that come into being in case of need, of which we were just now speaking, some one noble[65] lie to persuade, in the best case, even the rulers,   c
but if not them, the rest of the city?"

"What sort of a thing?" he said.

"Nothing new," I said, "but a Phoenician thing,[66] which has already happened in many places before, as the poets assert and have caused others to believe, but one that has not happened in our time—and I don't know if it could—one that requires a great deal of persuasion."

"How like a man who's hesitant to speak you are," he said.

"You'll think my hesitation quite appropriate, too," I said, "when I do speak."

"Speak," he said, "and don't be afraid."

"I shall speak—and yet, I don't know what I'll use for daring or   d

414 d   speeches in telling it—and I'll attempt to persuade first the rulers and
the soldiers, then the rest of the city, that the rearing and education we
gave them were like dreams; they only thought they were undergoing
all that was happening to them, while, in truth, at that time they
were under the earth within, being fashioned and reared themselves,

e   and their arms and other tools being crafted. When the job had been
completely finished, then the earth, which is their mother, sent them
up. And now, as though the land they are in were a mother and nurse,
they must plan for and defend it, if anyone attacks, and they must think
of the other citizens as brothers and born of the earth."

"It wasn't," he said, "for nothing that you were for so long
ashamed to tell the lie."

415 a   "It was indeed appropriate," I said. "All the same, hear out the
rest of the tale. 'All of you in the city are certainly brothers,' we shall
say to them in telling the tale, 'but the god, in fashioning those of you
who are competent to rule, mixed gold in at their birth; this is why they
are most honored; in auxiliaries, silver; and iron and bronze in the farmers and the other craftsmen. So, because you're all related, although for
the most part you'll produce offspring like yourselves, it sometimes hap-

b   pens that a silver child will be born from a golden parent, a golden
child from a silver parent, and similarly all the others from each other.
Hence the god commands the rulers first and foremost to be of nothing
such good guardians and to keep over nothing so careful a watch as the
children, seeing which of these metals is mixed in their souls. And, if a
child of theirs should be born with an admixture of bronze or iron, by

c   no manner of means are they to take pity on it, but shall assign the
proper value to its nature and thrust it out among the craftsmen or the
farmers; and, again, if from these men one should naturally grow who
has an admixture of gold or silver, they will honor such ones and lead
them up, some to the guardian group, others to the auxiliary, believing that there is an oracle that the city will be destroyed when an iron
or bronze man is its guardian.' So, have you some device for persuading them of this tale?"

d   "None at all," he said, "for these men themselves; however for
their sons and their successors and the rest of the human beings who
come afterwards."

"Well, even that would be good for making them care more for
the city and one another," I said. "For I understand pretty much what
you mean.

"Well, then, this will go where the report[67] of men shall lead it.
And when we have armed these earth-born men, let's bring them forth
led by the rulers. When they've come, let them look out for the fairest

place in the city for a military camp, from which they could most con-   *415 d*
trol those within, if anyone were not willing to obey the laws, and ward   *e*
off those from without, if an enemy, like a wolf, should attack the
flock. When they have made the camp and sacrificed to whom they
ought, let them make sleeping places. Or how should it be?"

"Like that," he said.

"Won't these places be such as to provide adequate shelter in both
winter and summer?"

"Yes, of course," he said. "For you seem to me to mean houses."

"Yes," I said, "those of soldiers, not moneymakers."

"How," he said, "do you mean to distinguish the one from the   *416 a*
other?"

"I shall try to tell you," I said. "Surely the most terrible and
shameful thing of all is for shepherds to rear dogs as auxiliaries for the
flocks in such a way that due to licentiousness, hunger or some other
bad habit, they themselves undertake to do harm to the sheep and instead of dogs become like wolves."

"Terrible," he said. "Of course."

"Mustn't we in every way guard against the auxiliaries doing any-   *b*
thing like that to the citizens, since they are stronger than they, becoming like savage masters instead of well-meaning allies?"

"Yes," he said, "we must."

"And wouldn't they have been provided with the greatest
safeguard if they have been really finely educated?"

"But they have been," he said.

And I said, "It's not fit to be too sure about that, my dear Glaucon. However, it is fit to be sure about what we were saying a while
ago, that they must get the right education, whatever it is, if they're   *c*
going to have what's most important for being tame with each other
and those who are guarded by them."

"That's right," he said.

"Now, some intelligent man would say that, in addition to this
education, they must be provided with houses and other property such
as not to prevent them from being the best possible guardians and not
to rouse them up to do harm to the other citizens."   *d*

"And he'll speak the truth."

"Well, then," I said, "see if this is the way they must live and be
housed if they're going to be such men. First, no one will possess any
private property except for what's entirely necessary. Second, no one
will have any house or storeroom into which everyone who wishes cannot come. The sustenance, as much as is needed by moderate and
courageous men who are champions of war, they'll receive in fixed   *e*

416 e   installments from the other citizens as a wage for their guarding, in
such quantity that there will be no surplus for them in a year and no
lack either. They'll go regularly to mess together[68] like soldiers in a
camp and live a life in common. We'll tell them that gold and silver of a
divine sort from the gods they have in their soul always and have no
further need of the human sort; nor is it holy to pollute the possession
of the former sort by mixing it with the possession of the mortal sort,
because many unholy things have been done for the sake of the currency
417 a   of the many, while theirs is untainted. But for them alone of those in the
city it is not lawful to handle and to touch gold and silver, nor to go
under the same roof with it, nor to hang it from their persons, nor to
drink from silver or gold. And thus they would save themselves as well
as save the city. Whenever they'll possess private land, houses, and currency, they'll be householders and farmers instead of guardians, and
b   they'll become masters and enemies instead of allies of the other
citizens; hating and being hated, plotting and being plotted against,
they'll lead their whole lives far more afraid of the enemies within than
those without. Then they themselves as well as the rest of the city are
already rushing toward a destruction that lies very near. So, for all
these reasons," I said, "let's say that the guardians must be provided
with houses and the rest in this way, and we shall set this down as a law,
shall we not?"

"Certainly," said Glaucon.

BOOK IV

And Adeimantus interrupted and said, "What would your apology[1] be, Socrates, if someone were to say that you're hardly making these men happy, and further, that it's their own fault—they to whom the city in truth belongs but who enjoy nothing good from the city as do others, who possess lands, and build fine big houses, and possess all the accessories that go along with these things, and make private sacrifices to gods, and entertain foreigners, and, of course, also acquire what you were just talking about, gold and silver and all that's conventionally held to belong to men who are going to be blessed? But, he would say, they look exactly like mercenary auxiliaries who sit in the city and do nothing but keep watch."

"Yes," I said, "and besides they do it for food alone; they get no wages beyond the food, as do the rest. So, if they should wish to make a private trip away from home, it won't even be possible for them, or give gifts to lady companions, or make expenditures wherever else they happen to wish, such as those made by the men reputed to be happy. You leave these things and a throng of others like them out of the accusation."

"Well," he said, "let them too be part of the accusation."

"You ask what our apology will then be?"

b

"Yes."

420 b   "Making our way by the same road," I said, "I suppose we'll find
what has to be said. We'll say that it wouldn't be surprising if these
men, as they are, are also happiest. However, in founding the city we
are not looking to the exceptional happiness of any one group among
us but, as far as possible, that of the city as a whole. We supposed we
would find justice most in such a city, and injustice, in its turn, in the
c   worst-governed one, and taking a careful look at them, we would judge
what we've been seeking for so long. Now then, we suppose we're
fashioning the happy city—a whole city, not setting apart a happy few
and putting them in it. We'll consider its opposite presently. Just as if we
were painting statues² and someone came up and began to blame
us, saying that we weren't putting the fairest colors on the fairest parts
of the animal—for the eyes, which are fairest, had not been painted
d   purple but black—we would seem to make a sensible apology to him
by saying: 'You surprising man, don't suppose we ought to paint eyes so
fair that they don't even look like eyes, and the same for the other parts;
but observe whether, assigning what's suitable to each of them, we
make the whole fair. So now too, don't compel us to attach to the
guardians a happiness that will turn them into everything except guard-
e   ians. We know how to clothe the farmers in fine robes and hang gold on
them and bid them work the earth at their pleasure, and how to make
the potters recline before the fire, drinking in competition from left to
right³ and feasting, and having their wheel set before them as often as
they get a desire to make pots, and how to make all the others blessed
in the same way just so the city as a whole may be happy. But
don't give us this kind of advice, since, if we were to be persuaded by
421 a   you, the farmer won't be a farmer, nor the potter a potter, nor will
anyone else assume any of those roles that go to make up a city. The
argument has less weight for these others. That men should become
poor menders of shoes, corrupted and pretending to be what they're
not, isn't so terrible for a city. But you surely see that men who are not
guardians of the laws and the city, but seem to be, utterly destroy an
entire city, just as they alone are masters of the occasion to govern it
well and to make it happy.' Now if we're making true guardians, men
b   least likely to do harm to the city, and the one who made that speech is
making some farmers and happy banqueters, like men at a public
festival and not like members of a city, then he must be speaking of
something other than a city. So we have to consider whether we are
establishing the guardians looking to their having the most happiness.
Or else, whether looking to this happiness for the city as a whole, we
must see if it comes to be in the city, and must compel and persuade
c   these auxiliaries and guardians to do the same, so that they'll be the
best possible craftsmen at their jobs, and similarly for all the others,
and, with the entire city growing thus and being fairly founded, we

must let nature assign to each of the groups its share of happiness."   *421 c*

"You seem to me," he said, "to speak finely."

"Then, will I," I said, "also seem to you to speak sensibly if I say what is akin to that?"

"What exactly?"

"Take the other craftsmen again and consider whether these things   *d*
corrupt them so as to make them bad."

"What are they?"

"Wealth and poverty," I said.

"How?"

"Like this: in your opinion, will a potter who's gotten rich still be willing to attend to his art?"

"Not at all," he said.

"And will he become idler and more careless than he was?"

"By far."

"Doesn't he become a worse potter then?"

"That, too, by far," he said.

"And further, if from poverty he's not even able to provide himself with tools or anything else for his art, he'll produce shoddier works, and he'll make worse craftsmen of his sons or any others he teaches."   *e*

"Of course."

"Then from both poverty and wealth the products of the arts are worse and the men themselves are worse."

"It looks like it."

"So, as it seems, we've found other things for the guardians to guard against in every way so that these things never slip into the city without their awareness."

"What are they?"

"Wealth and poverty," I said, "since the one produces luxury,   *422 a*
idleness, and innovation, while the other produces illiberality and wrongdoing as well as innovation."

"Most certainly," he said. "However, Socrates, consider this: how will our city be able to make war when it possesses no money, especially if it's compelled to make war against a wealthy one?"

"It's plain," I said, "that against one it would be harder, but against two of that sort it would be easier."   *b*

"How do you mean?" he said.

"Well," I said, "in the first place, if the guardians should have to fight, won't it be as champions in war fighting with rich men?"

"Yes," he said, "that's so."

"Now, then, Adeimantus," I said, in your opinion, wouldn't one boxer with the finest possible training in the art easily fight with two rich, fat nonboxers?"

"Perhaps not at the same time," he said.

422 b
c

"Not even if it were possible for him to withdraw a bit," I said, "and turning on whichever one came up first, to strike him, and if he did this repeatedly in sun and stifling heat? Couldn't such a man handle even more of that sort?"

"Undoubtedly," he said, "that wouldn't be at all surprising."

"But don't you suppose the rich have more knowledge and experience of boxing than of the art of war?"

"I do," he said.

"Then in all likelihood our champions will easily fight with two or three times their number."

"I'll grant you that," he said, "for what you say is right in my opinion."

d

"What if they sent an embassy to the other city and told the truth? 'We make use of neither gold nor silver, nor is it lawful for us, while it is for you. So join us in making war and keep the others' property.' Do you suppose any who hear that will choose to make war against solid, lean dogs[4] rather than with the dogs against fat and tender sheep?"

"Not in my opinion," he said. "But if the money of the others is

e

gathered into one city, look out that it doesn't endanger the city that isn't rich."

"You are a happy one," I said, "if you suppose it is fit to call 'city' another than such as we have been equipping."

"What else then?" he said.

"The others ought to get bigger names," I said. "For each of them is very many cities but not a city, as those who play say.[5] There are

423 a

two, in any case, warring with each other, one of the poor, the other of the rich. And within each of these there are very many. If you approach them as though they were one, you'll be a complete failure; but if you approach them as though they were many, offering to the ones the money and the powers or the very persons of the others, you'll always have the use of many allies and few enemies. And as long as your city is moderately governed in the way it was just arranged, it will be biggest; I do not mean in the sense of good reputation but truly biggest, even if it should be made up of only one thousand defenders. You'll not easily find one city so big as this, either among the Greeks or the bar-

b

barians, although many seem to be many times its size. Or do you suppose otherwise?"

"No, by Zeus," he said.

"Therefore," I said, "this would also be the fairest boundary for our rulers; so big must they make the city, and, bounding off enough land so that it will be of that size, they must let the rest go."

"What boundary?" he said.

"I suppose this one," I said, "up to that point in its growth at   *423 b*
which it's willing to be one, let it grow, and not beyond."

"That's fine," he said.   *c*

"Therefore, we'll also set this further command on the guardians,
to guard in every way against the city's being little or seemingly big;
rather it should be sufficient and one."

"This is," he said, "perhaps a slight task we will impose on them."

"And still slighter than that," I said, "is what we mentioned
earlier when we said that if a child of slight ability were born of the
guardians, he would have to be sent off to the others, and if a serious
one were born of the others, he would have to be sent off to the   *d*
guardians. This was intended to make plain that each of the other
citizens too must be brought to that which naturally suits him—one
man, one job—so that each man, practicing his own, which is one,
will not become many but one; and thus, you see, the whole city
will naturally grow to be one and not many."

"This is indeed," he said, "a lesser task than the other."

"Yet, my good Adeimantus," I said, "these are not, as one might
think, many great commands we are imposing on them, but they are all
slight if, as the saying goes, they guard the one great—or, rather than   *e*
great, sufficient—thing."

"What's that?" he said.

"Their education and rearing," I said. "If by being well educated
they become sensible men, they'll easily see to all this and everything
else we are now leaving out—that the possession of women, marriage,
and procreation of children must as far as possible be arranged according to the proverb that friends have all things in common."   *424 a*

"Yes," he said, "that would be the most correct way."

"And hence," I said, "the regime, once well started, will roll on
like a circle in its growth. For sound rearing and education, when they
are preserved, produce good natures; and sound natures, in their turn
receiving such an education, grow up still better than those before
them, for procreation as well as for the other things, as is also the case
with the other animals."   *b*

"It's likely," he said.

"Now, to state it briefly, the overseers of the city must cleave to
this, not letting it be corrupted unawares, but guarding it against all
comers: there must be no innovation in gymnastic and music contrary
to the established order; but they will guard against it as much as they
can, fearing that when someone says

> Human beings esteem most that song
> Which floats newest from the singer[6]

424 c   someone might perchance suppose the poet means not new songs, but a
new way of song, and praises that. Such a saying shouldn't be praised,
nor should this one be taken in that sense. For they must beware of change
to a strange form of music, taking it to be a danger to the whole.
For never are the ways[7] of music moved without the greatest political
laws being moved, as Damon says, and I am persuaded."

"Include me, too," said Adeimantus, "among those who are persuaded."

d   "So it's surely here in music, as it seems," I said, "that the guardians must build the guardhouse."

"At least," he said, "this kind of lawlessness[8] easily creeps in
unawares."

"Yes," I said, "since it's considered to be a kind of play and to do
no harm."

"It doesn't do any, either," he said, "except that, establishing itself bit by bit, it flows gently beneath the surface into the dispositions
and practices, and from there it emerges bigger in men's contracts with
one another; and it's from the contracts, Socrates, that it attacks laws
e   and regimes with much insolence until it finally subverts everything
private and public."

"Well, well," I said. "Is that so?"

"In my opinion," he said.

"Then, as we were saying at the beginning, mustn't our boys take
part in more lawful play straight away, since, if play becomes lawless
itself and the children along with it, it's not possible that they'll grow
425 a   up to be law-abiding, good men?"

"Of course, they must," he said.

"It's precisely when the boys make a fine beginning at play and
receive lawfulness from music that it—as opposed to what happened in
the former case—accompanies them in everything and grows, setting
right anything in the city that may have previously been neglected."

"Quite true," he said.

"Then, these men," I said, "will also find out the seemingly small
conventions that were all destroyed by their predecessors."

"What kind of things?"

b   "Such as the appropriate silence of younger men in the presence
of older ones, making way for them and rising, care of parents; and
hair-dos, clothing, shoes, and, as a whole, the bearing of the body, and
everything else of the sort. Or don't you think so?"

"I do."

"But to set them down as laws is, I believe, foolish.[9] Surely they

don't come into being, nor would they be maintained, by being set   425 *b*
down as laws in speech and in writing."

"How could they?"

"At least it's likely, Adeimantus," I said, "that the starting point
of a man's education sets the course of what follows too. Or doesn't like   *c*
always call forth like?"

"Of course."

"Then, I suppose we'd also say that the final result is some one
complete and hardy thing, whether good or the opposite."

"Of course," he said.

"That," I said, "is why I for one wouldn't go further and undertake to set down laws about such things."

"That's proper," he said.

"And, in the name of the gods," I said, "what about that market
business—the contracts individuals make with one another in the
market, and, if you wish, contracts with manual artisans, and libel, in-   *d*
sult, lodging of legal complaints, and the appointment of judges, and,
of course, whatever imposts might have to be collected or assessed in
the markets or harbors, or any market, town, or harbor regulations, or
anything else of the kind—shall we bring ourselves to set down laws for
any of these things?"

"It isn't worth-while," he said, "to dictate to gentlemen. Most of
these things that need legislation they will, no doubt, easily find for   *e*
themselves."

"Yes, my friend," I said, "provided, that is, a god grants them the
preservation of the laws we described before."

"And if not," he said, "they'll spend their lives continually setting
down many such rules and correcting them, thinking they'll get hold of
what's best."

"You mean," I said, "that such men will live like those who are
sick but, due to licentiousness, aren't willing to quit their worthless way
of life."

"Most certainly."

"And don't they go on charmingly? For all their treatment, they   426 *a*
get nowhere, except, of course, to make their illnesses more complicated and bigger, always hoping that if someone would just recommend a drug, they will be—thanks to it—healthy."

"Yes," he said, "the affections of men who are sick in this way are
exactly like that."

"What about this?" I said. "Isn't it charming in them that they
believe the greatest enemy of all is the man who tells the

426 a   truth—namely, that until one gives up drinking, stuffing oneself, sex
   b   and idleness, there will be no help for one in drugs, burning, or cutting,
nor in charms, pendants, or anything of the sort."

"Not quite charming," he said. "Being harsh with the man who
says something good isn't charming."

"You are not," I said, "as it seems, a praiser of such men."

"No, indeed, by Zeus."

"Therefore, if, as we were just saying, the city as a whole behaves
like that, you won't praise it either. Or isn't it your impression that the
very same thing these men do is done by all cities with bad regimes,
   c   which warn the citizens they must not disturb the city's constitution as
a whole, under pain of death for the man who does; while the man who
serves them most agreeably, with the regime as it is, and gratifies them
by flattering them and knowing their wishes beforehand and being
clever at fulfilling them, will on that account be the good man and the
one wise in important things and be honored by them?"

"They certainly do," he said, "seem to me to act in the same way,
and I don't praise them in any respect whatsoever."

   d   "And what about the men who are willing and eager to serve such
cities? Don't you admire their courage and facility?"

"I do," he said, "except for those who are deceived by them and
suppose they are truly statesmen because they are praised by the many."

"How do you mean?" I said. "Don't you sympathize with these
men? Or do you suppose it's possible for a man who doesn't know how
   e   to take measurements not to believe it when many other men like him
say he's a six-footer?"

"No," he said, "that I don't suppose."

"Then don't be harsh. For such men are surely the most charming
of all, setting down laws like the ones we described a moment ago and
correcting them, always thinking they'll find some limit to wrongdoing
in contracts and the other things I was just talking about, ignorant that
they are really cutting off the heads of a Hydra."

427 a   "Well," he said, "they do nothing but that."

"I, for one," I said, "therefore thought that the true lawgiver
wouldn't have to bother with that class of things[10] in the laws and the
regime, either in a city with a bad regime or in one with a good
regime—in the one case because it's useless and accomplishes nothing;
in the other, partly because anyone at all could find some of these
things, and partly because the rest follow of themselves from the practices already established."

   b   "Then what," he said, "might still remain for our legislation?"

And I said, "For us, nothing. However for the Apollo at Del-   427 *b*
phi[11] there remain the greatest, fairest, and first of the laws which are
given."

"What are they about?" he said.

"Foundings of temples, sacrifices, and whatever else belongs to
the care of gods, demons, and heroes; and further, burial of the dead
and all the services needed to keep those in that other place gracious.
For such things as these we neither know ourselves, nor in founding a
city shall we be persuaded by any other man, if we are intelligent, nor   *c*
shall we make use of any interpreter other than the ancestral one. Now
this god is doubtless the ancestral interpreter of such things for all humans, and he sits in the middle of the earth at its navel and delivers his
interpretations."

"What you say is fine," he said. "And that's what must be done."

"So then, son of Ariston," I said, "your city would now be
founded. In the next place, get yourself an adequate light somewhere;   *d*
and look yourself—and call in your brother and Polemarchus and the
others—whether we can somehow see where the justice might be and
where the injustice, in what they differ from one another, and which
the man who's going to be happy must possess, whether it escapes the
notice of all gods and humans or not."

"You're talking nonsense," said Glaucon. "You promised you
would look for it because it's not holy for you not to bring help to   *e*
justice in every way in your power."

"What you remind me of is true," I said, "and though I must do
so, you too have to join in."

"We'll do so," he said.

"Now, then," I said, "I hope I'll find it in this way. I suppose our
city—if, that is, it has been correctly founded—is perfectly good."

"Necessarily," he said.

"Plainly, then, it's wise, courageous, moderate and just."

"Plainly."

"Isn't it the case that whichever of them we happen to find will
leave as the remainder what hasn't been found?"

"Of course."   428 *a*

"Therefore, just as with any other four things, if we were seeking
any one of them in something or other and recognized it first, that
would be enough for us; but if we recognized the other three first, this
would also suffice for the recognition of the thing looked for. For
plainly it couldn't be anything but what's left over."

"What you say is correct," he said.

428 *a*   "With these things too, since they happen to be four, mustn't we look for them in the same way?"

"Plainly."

"Well, it's wisdom, in my opinion, which first comes plainly to

b   light in it. And something about it looks strange."

"What?" he said.

"The city we described is really wise, in my opinion. That's because it's of good counsel,[12] isn't it?"

"Yes."

"And further, this very thing, good counsel, is plainly a kind of knowledge. For it's surely not by lack of learning, but by knowledge, that men counsel well."

"Plainly."

"But, on the other hand, there's much knowledge of all sorts in the city."

"Of course."

"Then, is it thanks to the carpenters' knowledge that the city must be called wise and of good counsel?"

"Not at all," he said, "thanks to that it's called skilled in carpen-

c   try."

"Then, it's not thanks to the knowledge that counsels about how wooden implements would be best that a city must be called wise."

"Surely not."

"And what about this? Is it thanks to the knowledge of bronze implements or any other knowledge of such things?"

"Not to any knowledge of the sort," he said.

"And not to the knowledge about the production of the crop from the earth; for that, rather, it is called skilled in farming."

"That's my opinion."

"What about this?" I said. "Is there in the city we just founded a kind of knowledge belonging to some of the citizens that counsels not

d   about the affairs connected with some particular thing in the city, but about how the city as a whole would best deal with itself and the other cities?"

"There is indeed."

"What and in whom is it?" I said.

"It's the guardian's skill," he said, "and it's in those rulers whom we just now named perfect guardians."

"Thanks to this knowledge, what do you call the city?"

"Of good counsel," he said, "and really wise."

"Then, do you suppose," I said, "that there will be more smiths in

e   our city than these true guardians?"

"Far more smiths," he said.

"Among those," I said, "who receive a special name for possess-   *428 e*
ing some kind of knowledge, wouldn't the guardians be the fewest of all
in number?"

"By far."

"It is, therefore, from the smallest group and part of itself and the
knowledge in it, from the supervising[13] and ruling part, that a city
founded according to nature would be wise as a whole. And this class,
which properly has a share in that knowledge which alone among the   *429 a*
various kinds of knowledge ought to be called wisdom, has, as it seems,
the fewest members by nature."

"What you say," he said, "is very true."

"So we've found—I don't know how—this one of the four, both it
and where its seat in the city is."

"In my opinion, at least," he said, "it has been satisfactorily
discovered."

"And, next, courage, both itself as well as where it's situated in
the city—that courage thanks to which the city must be called
courageous—isn't very hard to see."

"How's that?"

"Who," I said, "would say a city is cowardly or courageous while   *b*
looking to any part other than the one that defends it and takes the field
on its behalf?"

"There's no one," he said, "who would look to anything else."

"I don't suppose," I said, "that whether the other men in it are
cowardly or courageous would be decisive for its being this or that."

"No, it wouldn't."

"So a city is also courageous by a part of itself, thanks to that
part's having in it a power that through everything will preserve the   *c*
opinion about which things are terrible—that they are the same ones
and of the same sort as those the lawgiver transmitted in the education.
Or don't you call that courage?"

"I didn't quite understand what you said," he said. "Say it again."

"I mean," I said, "that courage is a certain kind of preserving."

"Just what sort of preserving?"

"The preserving of the opinion produced by law through education about what—and what sort of thing—is terrible. And by preserving through everything I meant preserving that opinion and not casting
it out in pains and pleasures and desires and fears. If you wish I'm   *d*
willing to compare it to what I think it's like."

"But I do wish."

"Don't you know," I said, "that the dyers, when they want to dye
wool purple, first choose from all the colors the single nature belonging
to white things; then they prepare it beforehand and care for it with no

429 d
e

little preparation so that it will most receive the color; and it is only then that they dye? And if a thing is dyed in this way, it becomes color-fast, and washing either without lyes or with lyes can't take away its color. But those things that are not so dyed—whether one dyes other colors or this one without preparatory care—you know what they be-come like."

"I do know," he said, "that they're washed out and ridiculous."

"Hence," I said, "take it that we too were, to the extent of our power, doing something similar when we selected the soldiers and

430 a

educated them in music and gymnastic. Don't think we devised all that for any other purpose than that—persuaded by us—they should receive the laws from us in the finest possible way like a dye, so that their opinion about what's terrible and about everything else would be color-fast because they had gotten the proper nature and rearing, and their dye could not be washed out by those lyes so terribly effective at scour-ing, pleasure—more terribly effective for this than any Chalestrean

b

soda[14] and alkali; and pain, fear, and desire—worse than any other lye. This kind of power and preservation, through everything, of the right and lawful opinion about what is terrible and what not, I call courage; and so I set it down, unless you say something else."

"But I don't say anything else," he said. "For, in my opinion, you regard the right opinion about these same things that comes to be without education—that found in beasts and slaves—as not at all lawful[15] and call it something other than courage."

c

"What you say," I said, "is very true."

"Well, then, I accept this as courage."

"Yes, do accept it, but as political courage,"[16] I said, "and you'd be right in accepting it. Later, if you want, we'll give it a still finer treatment. At the moment we weren't looking for it, but for justice. For that search, I suppose, this is sufficient."

"What you say is fine," he said.

"Well, now," I said, "there are still two left that must be seen in

d

the city, moderation and that for the sake of which we are making the whole search, justice."

"Most certainly."

"How could we find justice so we won't have to bother about moderation any further?"

"I for my part don't know," he said, "nor would I want it to come to light before, if we aren't going to consider moderation any further. If you want to gratify me, consider this before the other."

e

"But I do want to," I said, "so as not to do an injustice."

"Then consider it," he said.

430 e

"It must be considered," I said. "Seen from here, it's more like a kind of accord and harmony than the previous ones."

"How?"

"Moderation," I said, "is surely a certain kind of order and mastery of certain kinds of pleasures and desires, as men say when they use—I don't know in what way—the phrase 'stronger than himself'; and some other phrases of the sort are used that are, as it were, its tracks.[17] Isn't that so?"

"Most surely," he said.

"Isn't the phrase 'stronger than himself' ridiculous though? For, of course, the one who's stronger than himself would also be weaker than himself, and the weaker stronger. The same 'himself' is referred to in all of them."

431 a

"Of course it is."

"But," I said, "this speech looks to me as if it wants to say that, concerning the soul, in the same human being there is something better and something worse. The phrase 'stronger than himself' is used when that which is better by nature is master over that which is worse. At least it's praise. And when, from bad training or some association, the smaller and better part is mastered by the inferior multitude, then this, as though it were a reproach, is blamed and the man in this condition is called weaker than himself and licentious."

b

"Yes," he said, "that's likely."

"Now, then," I said, "take a glance at our young city, and you'll find one of these conditions in it. For you'll say that it's justly designated stronger than itself, if that in which the better rules over the worse must be called moderate and 'stronger than itself.' "

"Well, I am glancing at it," he said, "and what you say is true."

"And, further, one would find many diverse desires, pleasures, and pains, especially in children, women, domestics, and in those who are called free among the common many."

c

"Most certainly."

"But the simple and moderate desires, pleasures and pains, those led by calculation accompanied by intelligence and right opinion, you will come upon in few, and those the ones born with the best natures and best educated."

"True," he said.

"Don't you see that all these are in your city too, and that there the desires in the common many are mastered by the desires and the prudence in the more decent few?"

d

431 d   "I do," he said.

"If, therefore, any city ought to be designated stronger than pleasures, desires, and itself, then this one must be so called."

"That's entirely certain," he said.

"And then moderate in all these respects too?"

"Very much so," he said.

"And, moreover, if there is any city in which the rulers and the

e   ruled have the same opinion about who should rule, then it's this one. Or doesn't it seem so?"

"Very much so indeed," he said.

"In which of the citizens will you say the moderation resides, when they are in this condition? In the rulers or the ruled?"

"In both, surely," he said.

"You see," I said, "we divined pretty accurately a while ago that moderation is like a kind of harmony."

"Why so?"

"Because it's unlike courage and wisdom, each of which resides in

432 a   a part, the one making the city wise and the other courageous. Moderation doesn't work that way, but actually stretches throughout the whole, from top to bottom of the entire scale,[18] making the weaker, the stronger and those in the middle—whether you wish to view them as such in terms of prudence, or, if you wish, in terms of strength, or multitude, money or anything else whatsoever of the sort—sing the same chant together. So we would quite rightly claim that this unanimity is moderation, an accord of worse and better, according to nature, as to which must rule in the city and in each one."

b   "I am," he said, "very much of the same opinion."

"All right," I said. "Three of them have been spied out in our city, at least sufficiently to form some opinion. Now what would be the remaining form thanks to which the city would further partake in virtue? For, plainly, this is justice."

"Plainly."

"So then, Glaucon, we must, like hunters, now station ourselves in a circle around the thicket and pay attention so that justice doesn't slip through somewhere and disappear into obscurity. Clearly it's

c   somewhere hereabouts. Look to it and make every effort to catch sight of it; you might somehow see it before me and could tell me."

"If only I could," he said. "However, if you use me as a follower and a man able to see what's shown him, you'll be making quite sensible use of me."

"Follow," I said, "and pray with me."

"I'll do that," he said, "just lead."

"The place really appears to be hard going and steeped in   432 c
shadows," I said. "At least it's dark and hard to search out. But, all the
same, we've got to go on."

"Yes," he said, "we've got to go on."

And I caught sight of it and said, "Here! Here![19] Glaucon.   d
Maybe we've come upon a track; and, in my opinion, it will hardly get
away from us."

"That's good news you report," he said.

"My, my," I said, "that was a stupid state we were in."

"How's that?"

"It appears, you blessed man, that it's been rolling around[20] at
our feet from the beginning and we couldn't see it after all, but were
quite ridiculous. As men holding something in their hand sometimes
seek what they're holding, we too didn't look at it but turned our gaze   e
somewhere far off, which is also perhaps just the reason it escaped our
notice."

"How do you mean?" he said.

"It's this way," I said. "In my opinion, we have been saying and
hearing it all along without learning from ourselves that we were in a
way saying it."

"A long prelude," he said, "for one who desires to hear."

"Listen whether after all I make any sense," I said. "That rule we   433 a
set down at the beginning as to what must be done in everything when
we were founding the city—this, or a certain form of it, is, in my opinion, justice. Surely we set down and often said, if you remember, that
each one must practice one of the functions in the city, that one for
which his nature made him naturally most fit."

"Yes, we were saying that."

"And further, that justice is the minding of one's own business
and not being a busybody, this we have both heard from many others
and have often said ourselves."   b

"Yes, we have."

"Well, then, my friend," I said, "this—the practice of minding
one's own business—when it comes into being in a certain way is
probably justice. Do you know how I infer this?"

"No," he said, "tell me."

"In my opinion," I said, "after having considered moderation,
courage, and prudence, this is what's left over in the city; it provided
the power by which all these others came into being; and, once having
come into being, it provides them with preservation as long as it's in
the city. And yet we were saying that justice would be what's left over   c
from the three if we found them."

433 c   "Yes, we did," he said, "and it's necessarily so."

"Moreover," I said, "if one had to judge which of them by coming to be will do our city the most good, it would be a difficult judgment. Is it the unity of opinion among rulers and ruled? Or is it the coming into being in the soldiers of that preserving of the lawful opinion as to which things are terrible and which are not? Or is it the prudence and

d   guardianship present in the rulers? Or is the city done the most good by the fact that—in the case of child, woman, slave, freeman, craftsman, ruler and ruled—each one minded his own business and wasn't a busybody?"

"It would, of course," he said, "be a difficult judgment."

"Then, as it seems, with respect to a city's virtue, this power that consists in each man's minding his own business in the city is a rival to wisdom, moderation and courage."

"Very much so," he said.

"Wouldn't you name justice that which is the rival of these others

e   in contributing to a city's virtue?"

"That's entirely certain."

"Now consider if it will seem the same from this viewpoint too. Will you assign the judging of lawsuits in the city to the rulers?"

"Of course."

"Will they have any other aim in their judging than that no one have what belongs to others, nor be deprived of what belongs to him?"

"None other than this."

"Because that's just?"

"Yes."

"And therefore, from this point of view too, the having and doing

434 a   of one's own and what belongs to oneself would be agreed to be justice."

"That's so."

"Now see if you have the same opinion as I do. A carpenter's trying to do the job of a shoemaker or a shoemaker that of a carpenter, or their exchanging tools or honors with one another, or even the same man's trying to do both, with everything else being changed along with it, in your opinion, would that do any great harm to the city?"

"Hardly," he said.

"But, I suppose, when one who is a craftsman or some other kind

b   of money-maker by nature, inflated by wealth, multitude, strength, or something else of the kind, tries to get into the class[21] of the warrior, or one of the warriors who's unworthy into that of the adviser and guardian, and these men exchange tools and honors with one another;

or when the same man tries to do all these things at once—then I sup-   434 b
pose it's also your opinion that this change in them and this meddling
are the destruction of the city."

"That's entirely certain."

"Meddling among the classes, of which there are three, and ex-   c
change with one another is the greatest harm for the city and would
most correctly be called extreme evil-doing."

"Quite certainly."

"Won't you say that the greatest evil-doing against one's own city
is injustice?"

"Of course."

"Then, that's injustice. Again, let's say it this way. The opposite
of this—the money-making, auxiliary, and guardian classes doing
what's appropriate, each of them minding its own business in a city—
would be justice and would make the city just."   *[handwritten: Everyone doing their part = Justice]*   d

"My opinion," he said, "is also that and no other."

"Let's not assert it so positively just yet," I said. "But, if this form
is applied to human beings singly and also agreed by us to be justice
there, then we'll concede it. What else will there be for us to say? And
if not, then we'll consider something else. Now let's complete the consideration by means of which we thought that, if we should attempt to
see justice first in some bigger thing that possessed it, we would more
easily catch sight of what it's like in one man. And it was our opinion
that this bigger thing is a city; so we founded one as best we could,   e
knowing full well that justice would be in a good one at least. Let's apply what came to light there to a single man, and if the two are in
agreement, everything is fine. But if something different should turn up
in the single man, we'll go back again to the city and test it; perhaps,
considering them side by side and rubbing them together like sticks,   435 a
we would make justice burst into flame, and once it's come to light,
confirm it for ourselves."

"The way to proceed is as you say," he said, "and it must be
done."

"Then," I said, "is that which one calls the same, whether it's bigger or smaller, unlike or like in that respect in which it's called the
same?"

"Like," he said.

"Then the just man will not be any different from the just city   b
with respect to the form itself of justice, but will be like it."

"Yes," he said, "he will be like it."

"But a city seemed to be just when each of the three classes of

435 b   natures present in it minded its own business and, again, moderate, courageous, and wise because of certain other affections and habits of these same classes."

"True," he said.

"Then it's in this way, my friend, that we'll claim that the single
c   man—with these same forms in his soul—thanks to the same affections as those in the city, rightly lays claim to the same names."

"Quite necessarily," he said.

"Now it's a slight question about the soul we've stumbled upon, you surprising man," I said. "Does it have these three forms in it or not?"

"In my opinion, it's hardly a slight question," he said. "Perhaps, Socrates, the saying that fine things are hard is true."

"It looks like it," I said. "But know well, Glaucon, that in my
d   opinion, we'll never get a precise grasp of it on the basis of procedures[22] such as we're now using in the argument. There is another longer and further road leading to it. But perhaps we can do it in a way worthy of what's been said and considered before."

"Mustn't we be content with that?" he said. "It would be enough for me to present."

"Well, then," I said, "it will quite satisfy me too."

"So don't grow weary," he said, "but go ahead with the consideration."

e   "Isn't it quite necessary for us to agree that the very same forms and dispositions as are in the city are in each of us?" I said. "Surely they haven't come there from any other place. It would be ridiculous if someone should think that the spiritedness didn't come into the cities from those private men who are just the ones imputed with having this character,[23] such as those in Thrace, Scythia, and pretty nearly the whole upper region; or the love of learning, which one could most im
436 a   pute to our region, or the love of money, which one could affirm is to be found not least among the Phoenicians and those in Egypt."[24]

"Quite so," he said.

"This is so, then," I said, "and not hard to know."

"Surely not."

"But this now is hard. Do we act in each of these ways as a result of the same part of ourselves, or are there three parts and with a different one we act in each of the different ways? Do we learn with one, become spirited with another of the parts within us, and desire the pleasures of nourishment and generation and all their kin with a third;
b   or do we act with the soul as a whole in each of them once we are started? This will be hard to determine in a way worthy of the argument."

"That's my opinion too," he said.

"Now let's try to determine whether these things are the same or different from each other in this way."

"How?"

"It's plain that the same thing won't be willing at the same time to do or suffer opposites with respect to the same part and in relation to the same thing.25 So if we should ever find that happening in these things, we'll know they weren't the same but many."   *c*

"All right."

"Now consider what I say."

"Say on," he said.

"Is it possible that the same thing at the same time and with respect to the same part should stand still and move?"

"Not at all."

"Now let's have a still more precise agreement so that we won't have any grounds for dispute as we proceed. If someone were to say of a human being standing still, but moving his hands and his head, that the same man at the same time stands still and moves, I don't suppose we'd claim that it should be said like that, but rather that one part of him stands still and another moves. Isn't that so?"   *d*

"Yes, it is."

"Then if the man who says this should become still more charming and make the subtle point that tops as wholes stand still and move at the same time when the peg is fixed in the same place and they spin, or that anything else going around in a circle on the same spot does this too, we wouldn't accept it because it's not with respect to the same part of themselves that such things are at that time both at rest and in motion. But we'd say that they have in them both a straight and a circumference; and with respect to the straight they stand still since they don't lean in any direction—while with respect to the circumference they move in a circle; and when the straight inclines to the right, the left, forward, or backward at the same time that it's spinning, then in no way does it stand still."   *e*

"And we'd be right," he said.

"Then the saying of such things won't scare us, or any the more persuade us that something that is the same, at the same time, with respect to the same part and in relation to the same thing, could ever suffer, be, or do opposites."   *437 a*

"Not me at least," he said.

"All the same," I said, "so we won't be compelled to go through all such objections and spend a long time assuring ourselves they're not true, let's assume that this is so and go ahead, agreed that if it should ever appear otherwise, all our conclusions based on it will be undone."

437 a   "That," he said, "is what must be done."

  b   "Then, would you set down all such things as opposites to one another," I said, "acceptance to refusal, longing to take something to rejecting it, embracing to thrusting away, whether they are actions or affections?" That won't make any difference."

          "Yes," he said, "they are opposites."

          "What about this?" I said. "Being thirsty and hungry and generally the desires, and further, willing and wanting—wouldn't you
  c   set all these somewhere in those classes²⁶ we just mentioned? For example, won't you say that the soul of a man who desires either longs for what it desires or embraces that which it wants to become its own; or again, that, insofar as the soul wills that something be supplied to it, it nods assent to itself as though someone had posed a question and reaches out toward the fulfillment of what it wills?"

          "I shall."

          "And what about this? Won't we class not-wanting, and not-willing and not-desiring with the soul's thrusting away from itself and driving out of itself and along with all the opposites of the previously mentioned acts?"

  d   "Of course."

          "Now since this is so, shall we assert that there is a form of desires and that what we call being thirsty and hungry are the most vivid of them?"

          "Yes," he said, "we shall assert it."

          "Isn't the one for drink and the other for food?"

          "Yes."

          "Insofar as it's thirst, would it be a desire in the soul for something more than that of which we say it is a desire? For example, is thirst thirst for hot drink or cold, or much or little, or, in a word, for any particular kind of drink? Or isn't it rather that in the case where heat is present in addition to the thirst, the heat would cause the desire
  e   to be also for something cold as well; and where coldness, something hot; and where the thirst is much on account of the presence of muchness, it will cause the desire to be for much, and where it's little, for little? But, thirsting itself will never be a desire for anything other than that of which it naturally is a desire—for drink alone—and, similarly, hungering will be a desire for food?"

          "That's the way it is," he said. "Each particular desire itself is only for that particular thing itself of which it naturally is, while the desire for this or that kind depends on additions."

438 a   "Now let no one catch us unprepared," I said, "and cause a disturbance, alleging that no one desires drink, but good drink, nor

[116]

food, but good food; for everyone, after all, desires good things; if,   438 a
then, thirst is a desire, it would be for good drink or for good whatever
it is, and similarly with the other desires."

"Perhaps," he said, "the man who says that would seem to make
some sense."

"However," I said, "of all things that are such as to be related to
something, those that are of a certain kind are related to a thing of a
certain kind, as it seems to me, while those that are severally them-   b
selves are related only to a thing that is itself."

"I don't understand," he said.

"Don't you understand," I said, "that the greater is such as to be
greater than something?"

"Certainly."

"Than the less?"

"Yes."

"And the much-greater than the much-less, isn't that so?"

"Yes."

"And, then, also the once-greater than the once-less, and the-
going-to-be-greater than the-going-to-be-less?"

"Of course," he said.

"And, further, the more in relation to the fewer, the double to the   c
half, and everything of the sort; and, again, heavier to lighter, faster to
slower; and further, the hot to the cold, and everything like them—
doesn't the same thing hold?"

"Most certainly."

"And what about the various sorts of knowledge? Isn't it the same
way? Knowledge itself is knowledge of learning itself, or of whatever it
is to which knowledge should be related; while a particular kind of
knowledge is of a particular kind of thing. I mean something like this.   d
When knowledge of constructing houses came to be, didn't it differ
from the other kinds of knowledge and was thus called housebuilding?"

"Of course."

"Wasn't this by its being a particular kind of thing that is different
from the others?"

"Yes."

"Since it was related to a particular kind of thing, didn't it too become a particular kind of thing itself? And isn't this the way with the
other arts and sorts of knowledge too?"

"It is."

"Well, then," I said, "say that what I wanted to say then, if you
now understand after all, is that of all things that are such as to be

438 d   related to something, those that are only themselves are related to
things that are only themselves, while those that are related to things of
a particular kind are of a particular kind. And I in no sense mean that
e   they are such as the things to which they happen to be related, so that it
would follow that the knowledge of things healthy and sick is healthy
and sick and that of bad and good is itself bad and good. But when
knowledge became knowledge not of that alone to which knowledge is
related but of a particular sort of thing, and this was health and
sickness, it as a consequence also became of a certain sort itself; and
this caused it not to be called knowledge simply any more but, with the
particular kind having been added to it, medicine."

"I understand," he said, "and, in my opinion, that's the way it is."

439 a   "And then, as for thirst," I said, "won't you include it among
those things that are related to something? Surely thirst is in relation to . . ."

"I will," he said, "and it's related to drink."

"So a particular sort of thirst is for a particular kind of drink, but
thirst itself is neither for much nor little, good nor bad, nor, in a word,
for any particular kind, but thirst itself is naturally only for drink."

"That's entirely certain."

"Therefore, the soul of the man who's thirsty, insofar as it thirsts,
b   wishes nothing other than to drink, and strives for this and is impelled
toward it."

"Plainly."

"If ever something draws it back when it's thirsting, wouldn't that
be something different in it from that which thirsts and leads it like a
beast to drink? For of course, we say, the same thing wouldn't perform
opposed actions concerning the same thing with the same part of itself
at the same time."

"No, it wouldn't."

"Just as, I suppose, it's not fair to say of the archer that his hands
at the same time thrust the bow away and draw it near, but that one
hand pushes it away and the other pulls it in."

c   "That's entirely certain," he said.

"Now, would we assert that sometimes there are some men who
are thirsty but not willing to drink?"

"Surely," he said, "many and often."

"What should one say about them?" I said. "Isn't there something
in their soul bidding them to drink and something forbidding them to
do so, something different that masters that which bids?"

"In my opinion there is," he said.

"Doesn't that which forbids such things come into being—when it

comes into being—from calculation,[27] while what leads and draws   439 *d*
is present due to affections and diseases?"

"It looks like it."

"So we won't be irrational," I said, "if we claim they are two and
different from each other, naming the part of the soul with which it calculates, the calculating, and the part with which it loves, hungers,
thirsts and is agitated by the other desires, the irrational[28] and desiring, companion of certain replenishments and pleasures."

"No, we won't," he said. "It would be fitting for us to believe   *e*
that."

"Therefore," I said, "let these two forms in the soul be distinguished. Now, is the part that contains spirit and with which we are
spirited a third, or would it have the same nature as one of these
others?"

"Perhaps," he said, "the same as one of them, the desiring."

"But," I said, "I once heard something that I trust. Leontius, the
son of Aglaion, was going up from the Piraeus under the outside of the
North Wall[29] when he noticed corpses lying by the public executioner.[30] He desired to look, but at the same time he was disgusted
and made himself turn away; and for a while he struggled and covered
his face. But finally, overpowered by the desire, he opened his eyes   440 *a*
wide, ran toward the corpses and said: 'Look, you damned wretches,
take your fill of the fair sight.'"

"I too have heard it," he said.

"This speech," I said, "certainly indicates that anger sometimes
makes war against the desires as one thing against something else."

"Yes," he said, "it does indicate that."

"And in many other places, don't we," I said, "notice that, when
desires force someone contrary to calculation, he reproaches him-   *b*
self and his spirit is roused against that in him which is doing the forcing; and, just as though there were two parties at faction, such a man's
spirit becomes the ally of speech? But as for its making common cause
with the desires to do what speech has declared must not be done,
I suppose you'd say you had never noticed anything of the kind happening in yourself, nor, I suppose, in anyone else."

"No, by Zeus," he said.

"And what about when a man supposes he's doing injustice?" I   *c*
said. "The nobler he is, won't he be less capable of anger at suffering
hunger, cold or anything else of the sort inflicted on him by one whom
he supposes does so justly; and, as I say, won't his spirit be unwilling to
rouse itself against that man?"

"True," he said.

440 c   "And what about when a man believes he's being done injustice?
Doesn't his spirit in this case boil and become harsh and form an
alliance for battle with what seems just; and, even if it suffers in
hunger, cold and everything of the sort, doesn't it stand firm and con-

d   quer, and not cease from its noble efforts before it has succeeded, or
death intervenes, or before it becomes gentle, having been called in by
the speech within him like a dog by a herdsman?"31

"Most certainly, it resembles the likeness you make. And, of
course, we put the auxiliaries in our city like dogs obedient to the
rulers, who are like shepherds of a city."

"You have," I said, "a fine understanding of what I want to say.
But beyond that, are you aware of this too?"

e   "What?"

"That what we are now bringing to light about the spirited is the
opposite of our recent assertion. Then we supposed it had something to
do with the desiring part; but now, far from it, we say that in the faction of the soul it sets its arms on the side of the calculating part."

"Quite so," he said.

"Is it then different from the calculating part as well, or is it a particular form of it so that there aren't three forms in the soul but two,
the calculating and the desiring? Or just as there were three classes in

441 a   the city that held it together, money-making, auxiliary, and delibera-
tive, is there in the soul too this third, the spirited, by nature an
auxiliary to the calculating part, if it's not corrupted by bad rearing?"

"Necessarily," he said, "there is the third."

"Yes," I said, "if it should come to light as something other than
the calculating part, just as it has come to light as different from the
desiring part."

"But it's not hard," he said, "for it to come to light as such. For,
even in little children, one could see that they are full of spirit straight
from birth, while, as for calculating, some seem to me never to get a

b   share of it, and the many do so quite late."

"Yes, by Zeus," I said, "what you have said is fine. Moreover, in
beasts one could see that what you say is so. And to them can be added
the testimony of Homer that we cited in that other place somewhere
earlier,

> He smote his breast and reproached
> his heart with word. . .32

c   Here, you see, Homer clearly presents that which has calculated about
better and worse and rebukes that which is irrationally spirited as
though it were a different part."

"What you say is entirely correct," he said.   *441 c*

"Well," I said, "we've had a hard swim through that and pretty much agreed that the same classes that are in the city are in the soul of each one severally and that their number is equal."

"Yes, that's so."

"Isn't it by now necessary that the private man be wise in the same way and because of the same thing as the city was wise?"

"Of course."

"And, further, that a city be courageous because of the same thing   *d* and in the same way as a private man is courageous, and that in everything else that has to do with virtue both are alike?"

"Yes, that is necessary."

"And, further, Glaucon, I suppose we'll say that a man is just in the same manner that a city too was just."

"This too is entirely necessary."

"Moreover, we surely haven't forgotten that this city was just because each of the three classes in it minds its own business."

"We haven't in my opinion forgotten," he said.

"Then we must remember that, for each of us too, the one within whom each of the parts minds its own business will be just and mind   *e* his own business."

"Indeed," he said, "that must be remembered."

"Isn't it proper for the calculating part to rule, since it is wise and has forethought about all of the soul, and for the spirited part to be obedient to it and its ally?"

"Certainly."

"So, as we were saying, won't a mixture of music and gymnastic make them accordant, tightening the one and training it in fair speeches and learning, while relaxing the other with soothing tales,   *442 a* taming it by harmony and rhythm?"

"Quite so," he said.

"And these two, thus trained and having truly learned their own business and been educated, will be set over the desiring—which is surely most of the soul in each and by nature most insatiable for money—and they'll watch it for fear of its being filled with the so-called pleasures of the body and thus becoming big and strong, and then not minding its own business, but attempting to enslave and rule   *b* what is not appropriately ruled by its class and subverting everyone's entire life."

"Most certainly," he said.

"So," I said, "wouldn't these two do the finest job of guarding against enemies from without on behalf of all of the soul and the body,

442 b the one deliberating, the other making war, following the ruler, and
with its courage fulfilling what has been decided?"

"Yes, that's so."

c "And then I suppose we call a single man courageous because of
that part—when his spirited part preserves, through pains and
pleasures, what has been proclaimed by the speeches about that which
is terrible and that which is not."

"Correct," he said.

"And wise because of that little part which ruled in him and proclaimed these things; it, in its turn, possesses within it the knowledge of
that which is beneficial for each part and for the whole composed of the
community of these three parts."

"Most certainly."

"And what about this? Isn't he moderate because of the friendship
and accord of these parts—when the ruling part and the two ruled parts
are of the single opinion that the calculating part ought to rule and

d don't raise faction against it?"

"Moderation, surely," he said, "is nothing other than this, in city
or in private man."

"Now, of course, a man will be just because of that which we are
so often saying, and in the same way."

"Quite necessarily."

"What about this?" I said. "Has our justice in any way been
blunted so as to seem to be something other than what it came to light
as in the city?"

"Not in my opinion," he said.

"If there are still any doubts in our soul," I said, "we could

e reassure ourselves completely by testing our justice in the light of the
vulgar standards."

"Which ones?"

"For example, if, concerning this city and the man who by nature
and training is like it, we were required to come to an agreement about
whether, upon accepting a deposit of gold or silver, such a man would
seem to be the one to filch it—do you suppose anyone would suppose
that he would be the man to do it and not rather those who are not such

443 a as he is?"

"No one would," he said.

"And as for temple robberies, thefts, and betrayals, either of comrades in private or cities in public, wouldn't this man be beyond
them?"

"Yes, he would be beyond them."

"And, further, he would in no way whatsoever be faithless in
oaths or other agreements."

"Of course not."   443 a

"Further, adultery, neglect of parents, and failure to care for the gods are more characteristic of every other kind of man than this one."

"Of every other kind, indeed," he said.

"Isn't the cause of all this that, so far as ruling and being ruled are   b
concerned, each of the parts in him minds its own business?"

"That and nothing else is the cause."

"Are you still looking for justice to be something different from this power which produces such men and cities?"

"No, by Zeus," he said. "I'm not."

"Then that dream of ours has reached its perfect fulfillment.[33] I mean our saying that we suspected that straight from the beginning of the city's founding, through some god, we probably hit upon an origin and model for justice."   c

"That's entirely certain."

"And this, Glaucon, turns out to be after all a kind of phantom of justice—that's also why it's helpful—the fact that the shoemaker by nature rightly practices shoemaking and does nothing else, and the carpenter practices carpentry, and so on for the rest."

"It looks like it."

"But in truth justice was, as it seems, something of this sort; however, not with respect to a man's minding his external business, but with respect to what is within, with respect to what truly concerns him   d
and his own. He doesn't let each part in him mind other people's business or the three classes in the soul meddle with each other, but really sets his own house in good order and rules himself; he arranges himself, becomes his own friend, and harmonizes the three parts, exactly like three notes in a harmonic scale, lowest, highest and middle. And if there are some other parts in between, he binds them together and becomes entirely one from many, moderate and harmonized. Then, and only then, he acts, if he does act in some   e
way—either concerning the acquisition of money, or the care of the body, or something political, or concerning private contracts. In all these actions he believes and names a just and fine action one that preserves and helps to produce this condition, and wisdom the knowledge that supervises[34] this action; while he believes and names an unjust action one that undoes this condition, and lack of learning, in its turn, the opinion that supervises this action."   444 a

"Socrates," he said, "what you say is entirely true."

"All right," I said. "If we should assert that we have found the just man and city and what justice really is in them, I don't suppose we'd seem to be telling an utter lie."

444 a

"By Zeus, no indeed," he said.

"Shall we assert it then?"

"Let's assert it."

"So be it," I said. "After that, I suppose injustice must be considered."

"Plainly."

b   "Mustn't it, in its turn, be a certain faction among those three—a meddling, interference, and rebellion of a part of the soul against the whole? The purpose of the rebellious part is to rule in the soul although this is not proper, since by nature it is fit to be a slave to that which belongs to the ruling class.[35] Something of this sort I suppose we'll say, and that the confusion and wandering of these parts are injustice, licentiousness, cowardice, lack of learning, and, in sum, vice entire."

"Certainly," he said, "that is what they are."

c   "Then," I said, "as for performing unjust actions and being unjust and, again, doing just things, isn't what all of them are by now clearly manifest, if injustice and justice are also manifest?"

"How so?"

"Because," I said, "they don't differ from the healthy and the sick; what these are in a body, they are in a soul."

"In what way?" he said.

"Surely healthy things produce health and sick ones sickness."

"Yes."

"Doesn't doing just things also produce justice and unjust ones in-
d justice?"

"Necessarily."

"To produce health is to establish the parts of the body in a relation of mastering, and being mastered by, one another that is according to nature, while to produce sickness is to establish a relation of ruling, and being ruled by, one another that is contrary to nature."

"It is."

"Then, in its turn," I said, "isn't to produce justice to establish the parts of the soul in a relation of mastering, and being mastered by, one another that is according to nature, while to produce injustice is to establish a relation of ruling, and being ruled by, one another that is contrary to nature?"

"Entirely so," he said.

"Virtue, then, as it seems, would be a certain health, beauty and
e good condition of a soul, and vice a sickness, ugliness and weakness."

"So it is."

"Don't fine practices also conduce to the acquisition of virtue and base ones to vice?"

"Necessarily."

"So, as it seems, it now remains for us to consider whether it is   *444 e*
profitable to do just things, practice fine ones, and be just—whether or   *445 a*
not one's being such remains unnoticed; or whether it is profitable to do
injustice and be unjust—provided one doesn't pay the penalty and become better as a result of punishment."

"But Socrates," he said, "that inquiry looks to me as though it has
become ridiculous by now. If life doesn't seem livable with the body's
nature corrupted, not even with every sort of food and drink and every
sort of wealth and every sort of rule, will it then be livable when the
nature of that very thing by which we live is confused and corrupted,   *b*
even if a man does whatever else he might want except that which will
rid him of vice and injustice and will enable him to acquire justice and
virtue? Isn't this clear now that all of these qualities have manifested
their characters in our description?"

"Yes, it is ridiculous," I said. "But all the same, since we've come
to the place from which we are able to see most clearly that these things
are so, we mustn't weary."

"Least of all, by Zeus," he said, "must we shrink back."

"Now come here," I said, "so you too can see just how many   *c*
forms vice, in my opinion, has; those, at least, that are worth looking
at."

"I am following," he said. "Just tell me."

"Well," I said, "now that we've come up to this point in the argument, from a lookout as it were, it looks to me as though there is one
form for virtue and an unlimited number for vice, but some four among
them are also worth mentioning."

"How do you mean?"

"There are," I said, "likely to be as many types of soul as there
are types of regimes possessing distinct forms."

"How many is that?"

"Five of regimes," I said, "and five of soul."   *d*

"Tell me what they are," he said.

"I say that one type of regime would be the one we've described,
but it could be named in two ways," I said. "If one exceptional man
arose among the rulers, it would be called a kingship, if more, an
aristocracy."

"True," he said.

"Therefore," I said, "I say that this is one form. For whether it's
many or one who arise, none of the city's laws that are worth mention-   *e*
ing would be changed, if he uses that rearing and education we described."

"It's not likely," he said.

BOOK V

"Good, then, and right, is what I call such a city and regime and such a man, while the rest I call bad and mistaken, if this one is really right; and this applies to both governments of cities and the organization of soul in private men. There are four forms of badness."

"What are they?" he said.

And I was going to speak of them in the order that each appeared to me to pass from one to the other. But Polemarchus[1]—he was sitting at a little distance from Adeimantus—stretched out his hand and took hold of his cloak from above by the shoulder, began to draw him toward himself, and, as he stooped over, said some things in his ear, of which we overheard nothing other than his saying: "Shall we let it go or what shall we do?"

"Not in the least," said Adeimantus, now speaking aloud.

And I said, "What in particular aren't you letting go?"

"You," he said.

"Because of what in particular?" I said.

"In our opinion you're taking it easy," he said, "and robbing us of a whole section[2] of the argument, and that not the least, so you won't have to go through it. And you supposed you'd get away with it by saying, as though it were something quite ordinary, that after all it's plain to everyone that, as for women and children, the things of friends will be in common."[3]

449 c   "Isn't that right, Adeimantus?" I said.

"Yes," he said, "but this 'right,' like the rest, is in need of argument as to what the manner of the community is. There could be many

d   ways. So don't pass over the particular one you mean, since we've been waiting all this time supposing you would surely mention begetting of children—how they'll be begotten and, once born, how they'll be reared—and that whole community of women and children of which you speak. We think it makes a big difference, or rather, the whole difference, in a regime's being right or not right. Now, since you're taking on another regime before having adequately treated these things, we've

450 a   resolved what you heard—not to release you before you've gone through all this just as you did the rest."

"Include me too as a partner in this vote," said Glaucon.

"In fact," said Thrasymachus, "you can take this as a resolution approved by all of us, Socrates."[4]

"What a thing you've done in arresting me," I said. "How much discussion you've set in motion, from the beginning again as it were, about the regime I was delighted to think I had already described, content if one were to leave it at accepting these things as they were stated then. You don't know how great a swarm of arguments you're

b   stirring up with what you are now summoning to the bar. I saw it then and passed by so as not to cause a lot of trouble."

"What," said Thrasymachus, "do you suppose these men have come here now to look for fool's gold[5] and not to listen to arguments?"

"Yes," I said, "but in due measure."

"For intelligent men, Socrates," said Glaucon, "the proper measure of listening to such arguments is a whole life. Never mind

c   about us. And as for you, don't weary in going through your opinion about the things we ask: what the community of children and women will be among our guardians, and their rearing when they are still young, in the time between birth and education, which seems to be the most trying. Attempt to say what the manner of it must be."

"It's not easy to go through, you happy man," I said. "Even more than what we went through before, it admits of many doubts. For, it could be doubted that the things said are possible; and, even if, in the best possible conditions, they could come into being, that they would be what is best will also be doubted. So that is why there's a certain

d   hestitation about getting involved in it, for fear that the argument might seem to be a prayer, my dear comrade."

"Don't hesitate," he said. "Your audience won't be hard-hearted, or distrustful, or ill-willed."

And I said, "Best of men, presumably you're saying that because   *450 d*
you wish to encourage me?"

"I am," he said.

"Well, you're doing exactly the opposite," I said. "If I believed I
knew whereof I speak, it would be a fine exhortation. To speak knowing the truth, among prudent and dear men, about what is greatest and
dear, is a thing that is safe and encouraging. But to present arguments   *e*
at a time when one is in doubt and seeking—which is just what I am   *451 a*
doing—is a thing both frightening and slippery. It's not because I'm
afraid of being laughed at—that's childish—but because I'm afraid that
in slipping from the truth where one least ought to slip, I'll not only fall
myself but also drag my friends down with me. I prostrate myself
before Adrasteia,[6] Glaucon, for what I'm going to say. I expect that
it's a lesser fault to prove to be an unwilling murderer of someone than
a deceiver about fine, good, and just things in laws. It's better to run
that risk with enemies than friends. So you've given me a good exhorta-   *b*
tion."

And Glaucon laughed and said, "But, Socrates, if we are affected
in some discordant way by the argument, we'll release you like a man
who is guiltless of murder and you won't be our deceiver. Be bold and
speak."

"The man who is released in the case of involuntary murder is indeed guiltless, as the law says. And it's probably so in this case too, if it
is in the other."[7]

"Well, then, as far as this goes, speak," he said.

"Then," I said, "I must now go back again and say what perhaps
should have been said then in its turn. However, maybe it would be   *c*
right this way—after having completely finished the male drama, to
complete the female,[8] especially since you are so insistent about issu-
ing this summons.

"For human beings born and educated as we described, there is,
in my opinion, no right acquisition and use of children and women
other than in their following that path along which we first directed
them. Presumably we attempted in the argument to establish the men
as guardians of a herd."

"Yes."

"So let's follow this up by prescribing the birth and rearing that go   *d*
along with it and consider whether they suit us or not."

"How?" he said.

"Like this. Do we believe the females of the guardian dogs must
guard the things the males guard along with them and hunt with them,
and do the rest in common; or must they stay indoors as though they

451 d   were incapacitated as a result of bearing and rearing the puppies, while
the males work and have all the care of the flock?"

e   "Everything in common," he said, "except that we use the females
as weaker and the males as stronger."

"Is it possible," I said, "to use any animal for the same things if
you don't assign it the same rearing and education?"

"No, it's not possible."

"If, then, we use the women for the same things as the men, they
must also be taught the same things."

452 a   "Yes."

"Now music and gymnastic were given to the men."

"Yes."

"Then these two arts, and what has to do with war, must be
assigned to the women also, and they must be used in the same ways."

"On the basis of what you say," he said, "it's likely."

"Perhaps," I said, "compared to what is habitual, many of the
things now being said would look ridiculous if they were to be done as
is said."

"Indeed they would," he said.

"What's the most ridiculous thing you see among them?" I said.
"Or is it plain that it's the women exercising naked with the men in the
b   palaestras,9 not only the young ones, but even the older ones, too, like
the old men in the gymnasiums who, when they are wrinkled and not
pleasant to the eye, all the same love gymnastic?"

"By Zeus!" he said, "that would look ridiculous in the present
state of things."

"Well," I said, "since we've started to speak, we mustn't be afraid
of all the jokes—of whatever kind—the wits might make if such a
c   change took place in gymnastic, in music and, not the least, in the bearing of arms and the riding of horses."

"What you say is right," he said.

"But since we've begun to speak, we must make our way to the
rough part of the law, begging these men, not to mind their own
business,10 but to be serious; and reminding them that it is not so
long ago that it seemed shameful and ridiculous to the Greeks—as
it does now to the many among the barbarians—to see men naked;
and that when the Cretans originated the gymnasiums, and then the
Lacedaemonians, it was possible for the urbane of the time to make
d   a comedy of all that. Or don't you suppose so?"11

"I do."

"But, I suppose, when it became clear to those who used these
practices that to uncover all such things is better than to hide them,

then what was ridiculous to the eyes disappeared in the light of what's   *452 d*
best as revealed in speeches. And this showed that he is empty who
believes anything is ridiculous other than the bad, and who tries to produce laughter looking to any sight as ridiculous other than the sight of
the foolish and the bad; or, again, he who looks seriously to any stan-   *e*
dard of beauty he sets up other than the good."

"That's entirely certain," he said.

"Mustn't we then first come to an agreement whether these things
are possible or not, and give anyone who wants to dispute—whether
it's a man who likes to play or one who is serious—the opportunity to
dispute whether female human nature can share in common with the   *453 a*
nature of the male class in all deeds or in none at all, or in some things
yes and in others no, particularly with respect to war? Wouldn't one
who thus made the finest beginning also be likely to make the finest
ending?"

"By far," he said.

"Do you want us," I said, "to carry on the dispute and represent
those on the other side ourselves so that the opposing argument won't
be besieged without defense?"

"Nothing stands in the way," he said.   *b*

"Then, on their behalf, let's say: 'Socrates and Glaucon, there's no
need for others to dispute with you. For at the beginning of the settlement of the city you were founding, you yourselves agreed that each
one must mind his own business according to nature.'"

"I suppose we did agree. Of course."

"'Can it be that a woman doesn't differ in her nature very much   *c*
from a man?'"

"But of course she differs."

"'Then isn't it also fitting to prescribe a different work to each according to its nature?'"

"Certainly."

"'How can it be, then, that you aren't making a mistake now and
contradicting yourselves, when you assert that the men and the women
must do the same things, although they have a nature that is most
distinct?' What have you as an apology in the light of this, you surprising
man?"

"On the spur of the moment, it's not very easy," he said. "But I
shall beg you, and do beg you, to interpret the argument on our behalf
too, whatever it may be."

"This, Glaucon, and many other things of the sort," I said,
"foreseeing them long ago, is what I was frightened of, and I shrank   *d*
from touching the law concerning the possession and rearing of the
women and children."

453 d　　　　　"By Zeus," he said, "it doesn't seem an easy thing."

"It isn't," I said. "However, it is a fact that whether one falls into a little swimming pool or into the middle of the biggest sea, one nevertheless swims all the same."

"Most certainly."

"Then we too must swim and try to save ourselves from the argument, hoping that some dolphin might take us on his back or for some other unusual rescue."[12]

e　　　　　"It seems so," he said.

"Come, then," I said, "let's see if we can find the way out. Now we agree that one nature must practice one thing and a different nature must practice a different thing, and that women and men are different. But at present we are asserting that different natures must practice the same things. Is this the accusation against us?"

"Exactly."

454 a　　　　　"Oh, Glaucon," I said, "the power of the contradicting art is grand."

"Why so?"

"Because," I said, "in my opinion, many fall into it even unwillingly and suppose they are not quarreling but discussing, because they are unable to consider what's said by separating it out into its forms.[13] They pursue contradiction in the mere name of what's spoken about, using eristic, not dialectic, with one another."[14]

"This is surely what happens to many," he said. "But this doesn't apply to us too at present, does it?"

b　　　　　"It most certainly does," I said. "At least we run the risk of unwillingly dealing in contradiction."

"How?"

"Following the name alone, we courageously, and eristically, insist that a nature that is not the same must not have the same practices. But we didn't make any sort of consideration of what form of different and same nature, and applying to what, we were distinguishing when we assigned different practices to a different nature and the same ones to the same."

"No," he said, "we didn't consider it."

c　　　　　"Accordingly," I said, "it's permissible, as it seems, for us to ask ourselves whether the nature of the bald and the longhaired is the sǎme or opposite. And, when we agree that it is opposite, if bald men are shoemakers, we won't let the longhaired ones be shoemakers, or if the longhaired ones are, then the others can't be."

"That," he said, "would certainly be ridiculous."

"Is it," I said, "ridiculous for any other reason than that we didn't refer to every sense of same and different nature but were guarding

only that form of otherness and likeness which applies to the pursuits   454 c
themselves? For example, we meant that a man and a woman whose   d
souls are suited for the doctor's art have the same nature. Or don't you
suppose so?"

"I do."

"But a man doctor and a man carpenter have different ones?"

"Of course, entirely different."

"Then," I said, "if either the class of men or that of women shows
its superiority in some art or other practice, then we'll say that that art
must be assigned to it. But if they look as though they differ in this
alone, that the female bears and the male mounts, we'll assert that it   e
has not thereby yet been proved that a woman differs from a man with
respect to what we're talking about; rather, we'll still suppose that our
guardians and their women must practice the same things."

"And rightly," he said.

"After that, won't we bid the man who says the opposite to teach
us this very thing—with respect to what art or what practice connected   455 a
with the organization of a city the nature of a woman and a man is not
the same, but rather different?"

"At least that's just."

"Well, now, perhaps another man would also say just what you
said a little while ago: that it's not easy to answer adequately on the
spur of the moment; but upon consideration, it isn't at all hard."

"Yes, he would say that."

"Do you want us then to beg the man who contradicts in this way
to follow us and see if we can somehow point out to him that there is no   b
practice relevant to the government of a city that is peculiar to
woman?"

"Certainly."

"'Come, now,' we'll say to him, 'answer. Is this what you meant?
Did you distinguish between the man who has a good nature for a thing
and another who has no nature for it on these grounds: the one learns
something connected with that thing easily, the other with difficulty;
the one, starting from slight learning, is able to carry discovery far forward in the field he has learned, while the other, having chanced on a
lot of learning and practice, can't even preserve what he learned; and
the bodily things give adequate service to the thought of the man with
the good nature while they oppose the thought of the other man? Are
there any other things than these by which you distinguished the man   c
who has a good nature for each discipline from the one who hasn't?'"

"No one," he said, "will assert that there are others."

"Do you know of anything that is practiced by human beings in
which the class of men doesn't excel that of women in all these respects? Or

455 c

d

e

456 *a*

b

shall we draw it out at length by speaking of weaving and the care of baked and boiled dishes—just those activities on which the reputation of the female sex is based and where its defeat is most ridiculous of all?"

"As you say," he said, "it's true that the one class is quite dominated in virtually everything, so to speak, by the other. However, many women are better than many men in many things. But, as a whole, it is as you say."

"Therefore, my friend, there is no practice of a city's governors which belongs to woman because she's woman, or to man because he's man; but the natures are scattered alike among both animals; and woman participates according to nature in all practices, and man in all, but in all of them woman is weaker than man."

"Certainly,"

"So, shall we assign all of them to men and none to women?"

"How could we?"

"For I suppose there is, as we shall assert, one woman apt at medicine and another not, one woman apt at music and another unmusical by nature."

"Of course."

"And isn't there then also one apt at gymnastic and at war, and another unwarlike and no lover of gymnastic?"

"I suppose so."

"And what about this? Is there a lover of wisdom and a hater of wisdom? And one who is spirited and another without spirit?"

"Yes, there are these too."

"There is, therefore, one woman fit for guarding and another not. Or wasn't it a nature of this sort we also selected for the men fit for guarding?"

"Certainly, that was it."

"Men and women, therefore, also have the same nature with respect to guarding a city, except insofar as the one is weaker and the other stronger."

"It looks like it."

"Such women, therefore, must also be chosen to live and guard with such men, since they are competent and akin to the men in their nature."

"Certainly."

"And mustn't the same practices be assigned to the same natures?"

"The same."

"Then we have come around full circle to where we were before and agree that it's not against nature to assign music and gymnastic to the women guardians."

"That's entirely certain."

456 b

"Then we weren't giving laws that are impossible or like prayers, since the law we were setting down is according to nature. Rather, the way things are nowadays proves to be, as it seems, against nature."

c

"So it seems."

"Weren't we considering whether what we say is possible and best?"

"Yes, we were."

"And that it is possible, then, is agreed?"

"Yes."

"But next it must be agreed that it is best?"

"Plainly."

"In making a woman fit for guarding, one education won't produce men for us and another women, will it, especially since it is dealing with the same nature?"

d

"No, there will be no other."

"What's your opinion about this?"

"What?"

"Conceiving for yourself that one man is better and another worse? Or do you believe them all to be alike?"

"Not at all."

"In the city we were founding, which do you think will turn out to be better men for us—the guardians who get the education we have described or the shoemakers, educated in shoemaking?"

"What you ask is ridiculous," he said.

"I understand," I said. "And what about this? Aren't they the best among the citizens?"

e

"By far."

"And what about this? Won't these women be the best of the women?"

"That, too, by far," he said.

"Is there anything better for a city than the coming to be in it of the best possible women and men?"

"There is not."

"And music and gymnastic, brought to bear as we have described, will accomplish this?"

457 a

"Of course."

"The law we were setting down is therefore not only possible but also best for a city."

"So it is."

"Then the women guardians must strip, since they'll clothe themselves in virtue instead of robes, and they must take common part in war and the rest of the city's guarding, and must not do other things.

457 a   But lighter parts of these tasks must be given to the women than the
         men because of the weakness of the class. And the man who laughs at

b   naked women practicing gymnastic for the sake of the best, 'plucks
         from his wisdom an unripe fruit for ridicule'[15] and doesn't
         know—as it seems—at what he laughs or what he does. For this is
         surely the fairest thing that is said and will be said—the beneficial is
         fair and the harmful ugly."

         "That's entirely certain."

         "May we then assert that we are escaping one wave,[16] as it
         were, in telling about the woman's law,[17] so that we aren't entirely
         swept away when we lay it down that our guardians, men and women,

c   must share all pursuits in common; rather, in a way the argument is in
         agreement with itself that it says what is both possible and benefi-
         cial?"

         "And indeed," he said, "it's not a little wave you're escaping."

         "You'll say that it's not a big one either," I said, "when you see
         the next one."

         "Tell me, and let me see it," he said.

         "The law that follows this one," I said, "and the others that went
         before is, as I suppose, this."

         "What?"

         "All these women are to belong to all these men in common, and

d   no woman is to live privately with any man. And the children, in their
         turn, will be in common, and neither will a parent know his own off-
         spring, nor a child his parent."

         "This one is far bigger than the other," he said, "so far as con-
         cerns doubt both as to its possibility and its beneficialness."

         "As to whether it is beneficial, at least, I don't suppose it would be
         disputed that the community of women and the community of children
         are, if possible, the greatest good," I said. "But I suppose that there
         would arise a great deal of dispute as to whether they are possible or
         not."

e   "There could," he said, "very well be dispute about both."

         "You mean that there is a conspiracy of arguments against me," I
         said. "I thought I would run away from the other argument, if in your
         opinion it were beneficial; then I would have the one about whether it's
         possible or not left."

         "But you didn't run away unnoticed," he said, "so present an
         argument for both."

         "I must submit to the penalty," I said. "Do me this favor,

458 a   however. Let me take a holiday like the idle men who are accustomed
         to feast their minds for themselves when they walk along. And such
         men, you know, before finding out in what way something they desire

can exist, put that question aside so they won't grow weary deliberating   458 *a*
about what's possible and not. They set down as given the existence of
what they want and at once go on to arrange the rest and enjoy giving a
full account of the sort of things they'll do when it has come into being,
making yet idler a soul that is already idle. I too am by now soft myself,   *b*
and I desire to put off and consider later in what way it is possible; and
now, having set it down as possible, I'll consider, if you permit me,
how the rulers will arrange these things when they come into being and
whether their accomplishment would be most advantageous of all for
both the city and the guardians. I'll attempt to consider this with you
first, and the other later, if you permit."

"I do permit," he said, "so make your consideration."

"Well, then," I said, "I suppose that if the rulers are to be worthy
of the name, and their auxiliaries likewise, the latter will be willing to   *c*
do what they are commanded and the former to command. In some of
their commands the rulers will in their turn be obeying the laws; in
others—all those we leave to their discretion—they will imitate the
laws."

"It's likely," he said.

"Well, then," I said, "you, their lawgiver, just as you selected the
men, will hand over the women to them, having selected them in the
same way too, with natures that are as similar as possible. And all of
them will be together, since they have common houses and mess, with
no one privately possessing anything of the kind. And, mixed together   *d*
in gymnastic exercise and the rest of the training, they'll be led by an
inner natural necessity to sexual mixing with one another, I suppose.
Or am I not, in your opinion, speaking of necessities?"

"Not geometrical but erotic necessities," he said, "which are
likely to be more stinging than the others when it comes to persuading
and attracting the bulk of the people."

"Very much so," I said. "But, next, Glaucon, to have irregular intercourse with one another, or to do anything else of the sort, isn't holy
in a city of happy men nor will the rulers allow it."   *e*

"No," he said, "it's not just."

"Then it's plain that next we'll make marriages sacred in the
highest possible degree. And the most beneficial marriages would be sacred."[18]

"That's entirely certain."

"So then, how will they be most beneficial? Tell me this, Glaucon.   459 *a*
For I see hunting dogs and quite a throng of noble cocks in your house.
Did you, in the name of Zeus, ever notice something about their mar-
riages and procreation?"

"What?" he said.

459 *a*   "First, although they are all noble, aren't there some among them
who are and prove to be best?"

"There are."

"Do you breed from all alike, or are you eager to breed from the
best as much as possible?"

"From the best."

b   "And what about this? From the youngest, or from the oldest, or
as much as possible from those in their prime?"

"From those in their prime."

"And if they weren't so bred, do you believe that the species of
birds and that of dogs would be far worse for you?"

"I do," he said.

"And what do you think about horses and the other animals?" I
said. "Is it in any way different?"

"That would be strange," he said.

"My, my, dear comrade," I said, "how very much we need
eminent rulers after all, if it is also the same with the human species."

c   "Of course it is," he said, "but why does that affect the rulers?"

"Because it will be a necessity for them to use many drugs," I
said. "Presumably we believe that for bodies not needing drugs, but
willing to respond to a prescribed course of life, even a common doctor
will do. But, of course, when there is also a need to use drugs, we know
there is need of the most courageous doctor."

"True, but to what purpose do you say this?"

"To this," I said. "It's likely that our rulers will have to use a
throng of lies and deceptions for the benefit of the ruled. And, of
d   course, we said that everything of this sort is useful as a form of
remedy."

"And we were right," he said.

"Now, it seems it is not the least in marriages and procreations,
that this 'right' comes into being."

"How so?"

"On the basis of what has been agreed," I said, "there is a need
for the best men to have intercourse as often as possible with the best
women, and the reverse for the most ordinary men with the most ordinary women; and the offspring of the former must be reared but not that
e   of the others, if the flock is going to be of the most eminent quality. And
all this must come to pass without being noticed by anyone except the
rulers themselves if the guardians' herd is to be as free as possible from
faction."

"Quite right," he said.

"So then, certain festivals and sacrifices must be established by   459 e
law at which we'll bring the brides and grooms together, and our poets
must make hymns suitable to the marriages that take place. The num-   460 a
ber of the marriages we'll leave to the rulers in order that they may
most nearly preserve the same number of men, taking into consideration wars, diseases, and everything else of the sort; and thus our city
will, within the limits of the possible, become neither big nor little."

"Right," he said.

"I suppose certain subtle lots must be fabricated so that the ordinary man will blame chance rather than the rulers for each union."

"Quite so," he said.

"And, presumably, along with other prizes and rewards, the   b
privilege of more abundant intercourse with the women must be given
to those of the young who are good in war or elsewhere, so that under
this pretext the most children will also be sown by such men."

"Right."

"And as the offspring are born, won't they be taken over by the
officers established for this purpose—men or women, or both, for presumably the offices are common to women and men—and . . ."

"Yes."

"So, I think, they will take the offspring of the good and bring   c
them into the pen[19] to certain nurses who live apart in a certain section of the city. And those of the worse, and any of the others born
deformed, they will hide away in an unspeakable and unseen place, as
is seemly."

"If," he said, "the guardians' species is going to remain pure."

"Won't they also supervise the nursing, leading the mothers to the
pen when they are full with milk, inventing every device so that none   d
will recognize her own, and providing others who do have milk if the
mothers themselves are insufficient? And won't they supervise the
mothers themselves, seeing to it that they suckle only a moderate time
and that the wakeful watching and the rest of the labor are handed over
to wet nurses and governesses?"

"It's an easy-going kind of child-bearing for the women guardians, as you tell it," he said.

"As is fitting," I said. "Let's go through the next point we proposed. We said, of course, that the offspring must be born of those in
their prime."

"True."

"Do you share the opinion that a woman's prime lasts, on the   e
average, twenty years and a man's thirty?"

"Which years?" he said.

460 e   "A woman," I said, "beginning with her twentieth year, bears for the city up to her fortieth; and a man, beginning from the time when he passes his swiftest prime at running, begets for the city up to his fifty-fifth year."

461 a   "Of course," he said, "this is the prime of body and prudence for both."

"Then, if a man who is older than this, or younger, engages in re-production for the commonwealth, we shall say that it's a fault neither holy nor just. For he begets for the city a child that, if it escapes notice, will come into being without being born under the protection of the sacrifices and prayers which priestesses, priests, and the whole city offer at every marriage to the effect that ever better and more beneficial offspring may come from good and beneficial men. This child is born, *b*   rather, under cover of darkness in the company of terrible incontinence."

"Right," he said.

"And the same law applies," I said, "when a man still of the age to beget touches a woman of that age if a ruler has not united them. We'll say he's imposing a bastard, an unauthorized and unconsecrated child, on the city."

"Quite right," he said.

"Now I suppose that when the women and the men are beyond the age of procreation, we will, of course, leave them free to have in-*c*   tercourse with whomsoever they wish, except with a daughter, a mother, the children of their daughters and the ancestors of their mother, and, as for the women, except with a son and a father and the descendants of the one and the ancestors of the other; and all this only after they have been told to be especially careful never to let even a single foetus see the light of day, if one should be conceived, and, if one should force its way, to deal with it on the understanding that there's to be no rearing for such a child."

"That is certainly a sensible statement," he said. "But how will *d*   they distinguish one another's fathers and daughters and the others you just mentioned?"[20]

"Not at all," I said. "But of all the children born in the tenth month, and in the seventh, from the day a man becomes a bridegroom, he will call the males sons and the females daughters; and they will call him father; and in the same way, he will call their offspring grandchildren, and they in their turn will call his group grandfathers and grandmothers; and those who were born at the same time their mothers and fathers were procreating they will call sisters and brothers. Thus, as *e*   we were just saying, they won't touch one another. The law will grant

that brothers and sisters live together if the lot falls out that way and
the Pythia concurs."²¹

"Quite right," he said.

"So, Glaucon, the community of women and children for the
guardians of your city is of this kind. That it is both consistent with the
rest of the regime and by far best, must next be assured by the argument. Or what shall we do?"

"That, by Zeus," he said.

"Isn't the first step toward agreement for us to ask ourselves what we
can say is the greatest good in the organization of a city—that good aiming
at which the legislator must set down the laws—and what the greatest
evil; and then to consider whether what we have just described harmonizes with the track of the good for us and not with that of the
evil?"

"By all means," he said.

"Have we any greater evil for a city than what splits it and makes
it many instead of one? Or a greater good than what binds it together
and makes it one?"

"No, we don't."

"Doesn't the community of pleasure and pain bind it together, when to the greatest extent possible all the citizens alike rejoice
and are pained at the same comings into being and perishings?"

"That's entirely certain," he said.

"But the privacy of such things dissolves it, when some are overwhelmed and others overjoyed by the same things happening to the city
and those within the city?"

"Of course."

"Doesn't that sort of thing happen when they don't utter such
phrases as 'my own' and 'not my own' at the same time in the city, and
similarly with respect to 'somebody else's'?"

"Entirely so."

"Is, then, that city in which most say 'my own' and 'not my own'
about the same thing, and in the same way, the best governed city?"

"By far."

"Then is that city best governed which is most like a single human
being? For example, when one of us wounds a finger, presumably the
entire community—that community tying the body together with the
soul in a single arrangement under the ruler within it—is aware of the
fact, and all of it is in pain as a whole along with the afflicted part; and
it is in this sense we say that this human being has a pain in his finger.
And does the same argument hold for any other part of a human being,
both when it is afflicted by pain and when eased by pleasure?"

462 d

"Yes, it does," he said. "And, as to what you ask, the city with the best regime is most like such a human being."

e

"I suppose, then, that when one of its citizens suffers anything at all, either good or bad, such a city will most of all say that the affected part is its own, and all will share in the joy or the pain."

"Necessarily," he said, "if it has good laws."

"It must be high time for us to go back to our city," I said, "and consider in it the things agreed upon by the argument, and see whether this city possesses them most, or whether some other city does to a greater extent."

"We have to," he said.

463 a

"What about this? There are presumably both rulers and a people in other cities as well as in this one."

"There are."

"Then do all of them call one another citizens?"

"Of course."

"And in addition to citizens, what does the people call the rulers in the other cities?"

"In the many, masters; in those with a democracy, that very name: rulers."22

"And what about the people in our city? What, in addition to citizens, does it say the rulers are?"

b

"Saviors and auxiliaries," he said.

"And what do they call the people?"

"Wage givers and supporters."

"And what do the rulers in the other cities call the people?"

"Slaves," he said.

"And what do the rulers call one another?"

"Fellow rulers," he said.

"And what about ours?"

"Fellow guardians."

"Can you say whether any of the rulers in the other cities is in the habit of addressing one of his fellow rulers as his kin and another as an outsider?"23

"Many do so."

"Doesn't he hold the one who is his kin to be his own, and speak

c

of him as such, while the outsider he does not hold to be his own?"

"That's what he does."

"What about your guardians? Would any one of them be in the habit of holding one of his fellow guardians to be an outsider or address him as such?"

"Not at all," he said. "With everyone he happens to meet, he'll   463 c
hold that he's meeting a brother, or a sister, or a father, or a mother, or
a son, or a daughter or their descendants or ancestors."

"What you say is very fine," I said, "but tell me this too. Is it only
the names of kinship you set down in the laws for them, or also the
doing of all the actions that go with the names—with fathers, all that   d
law prescribes about shame before fathers, and about providing for
parents and having to obey them—under pain of not being in good
stead with gods or human beings, since a man would do what is neither
holy nor just if he did anything other than this? Will these sayings[24]
from the mouths of your citizens ring in the ears of the children in their
earliest age, or will there be others about fathers—whomever one
points out to them as fathers—and the other relatives?"

"No, it will be these sayings," he said. "It would be ridiculous if   e
they only mouthed, without deeds, the names of kinship."

"Therefore in this city more than any other, when someone is
doing well or badly, they will utter in accord the phrase that we used
just now, 'my own' affairs are doing well or badly."

"Very true," he said.

"Weren't we saying that close on the conviction expressed in this   464 a
phrase follows a community of pleasures and pains?"

"And we were right to say so."

"Won't our citizens more than others have the same thing in common, which is that very thing they will name 'my own'? And having
that in common, will they thus more than others have a community of
pain and pleasure?"

"Far more than others."

"Is the cause of this—in addition to the rest of the organization—the community of women and children among the guardians?"

"Certainly, most of all," he said.

"But we further agreed that the community of pain and pleasure is   b
the greatest good for a city, likening the good governing of a city to a
body's relation to the pain and pleasure of one of its parts."

"And what we agreed was right," he said.

"The community of children and women among the auxiliaries
has therefore turned out to be the cause of the greatest good to our
city."

"Quite so," he said.

"And, then, we also agree with what went before. For we were
saying, of course, that there mustn't be private houses for them, nor
land, nor any possession. Instead they must get their livelihood from   c

464 c   the others, as a wage for guarding, and use it up in common all
together, if they are really going to be guardians."

"Right," he said.

"So, as I am saying, doesn't what was said before and what's being
said now form them into true guardians still more and cause them not
to draw the city apart by not all giving the name 'my own' to the same
thing, but different men giving it to different things—one man drag-
ging off to his own house whatever he can get his hands on apart from
d   the others, another being separate in his own house with separate
women and children, introducing private pleasures and griefs of
things that are private? Rather, with one conviction about what's
their own, straining toward the same thing, to the limit of the possible, they are affected alike by pain and pleasure."

"Entirely so," he said.

"And what about this? Won't lawsuits and complaints against one
another virtually vanish from among them thanks to their possessing
nothing private but the body, while the rest is in common? On this
basis they will then be free from faction, to the extent at any rate that
e   human beings divide into factions over the possession of money, children, and relatives?"

"Yes," he said, "it's quite necessary that they be rid of factions."

"And further, there would justly be no suits for assault or insult
among them. For we'll surely say that it is fine and just for men to take
care of their own defense against others of the same age, thus imposing
on them the necessity of taking care of their bodies."

"Right," he said.

465 a   "This law is also right," I said, "in that, if a man's spiritedness is
aroused against someone, he would presumably satisfy it in this way
and be less likely to get into bigger quarrels."

"Most certainly."

"Further, an older man will be charged with ruling and punishing all the younger ones."

"Plainly."

"And, further, unless rulers command it, it's not likely that a
younger man will ever attempt to assault or strike an older one. And he
won't, I suppose, dishonor one in any other way. For there are two
sufficient guardians hindering him, fear and shame: shame preventing
b   him from laying hands as on parents, fear that the others will come to the
aid of the man who suffers it, some as sons, others as brothers, and
others as fathers."

"So it turns out," he said.

"Then will the men, as a result of the laws, live in peace with one
another in all respects?"

"Very much so."   465 b

"Since they are free from faction among themselves, there won't ever be any danger that the rest of the city will split into factions against these guardians or one another."

"Surely not."

"Because of their unseemliness, I hesitate to mention the pettiest of the evils of which they would be rid: poor men flattering rich, all the   c
want and grief they have in rearing children and making money for the necessary support of the household, making debts and repudiating them, doing all sorts of things to provide for the allowances that they turn over to the women and the domestics to manage. What and how they suffer from these things, my friend, is perfectly plain, ignoble, and not worth mentioning."

"Yes, it is plain," he said, "even to a blind man."   d

"So they'll be rid of all this and live a life more blessed than that most blessed one the Olympic victors live."

"In what way?"

"Surely the Olympic victors are considered happy for a small part of what belongs to these men. Their victory is not only fairer but the public support is more complete.[25] The victory they win is the preservation of the whole city, and they are crowned with support and everything else necessary to life—both they themselves and their children as well; and they get prizes from their city while they live and   e
when they die receive a worthy burial."

"That's very fine," he said.

"Do you remember," I said, "that previously an argument—I don't know whose—reproached us with not making the guardians happy; they, for whom it's possible to have what belongs to the citizens,   466 a
have nothing? We said, I believe, that if this should happen to come up at some point, we would consider it later, but that now we were making the guardians guardians and the city as happy as we could, but we were not looking exclusively to one group in it and forming it for happiness."

"I remember," he said.

"Well, then, if the life of our auxiliaries now appears far finer and better than that of the Olympic victors, is there any risk that it will in some way appear comparable to that of the shoemakers or any other   b
craftsmen or to that of the farmers?"

"Not in my opinion," he said.

"Moreover, it is just to say here too, as I said there, that if the guardian attempts to become happy in such a way that he is no longer a guardian, and such a moderate, steady, and (as we assert) best life won't satisfy him; but, if a foolish adolescent opinion about happiness

466 c   gets hold of him, it will drive him to appropriate everything in the city
with his power, and he'll learn that Hesiod was really wise when he said
that somehow 'the half is more than the whole.' "26

"If he follows my advice," he said, "he'll stay in this life."

"Then," I said, "as we've described it, do you accept the community of the women with the men in education, children, and guarding the rest of the citizens; and that both when they are staying in the
d   city and going out to war, they must guard and hunt together like dogs,
and insofar as possible have everything in every way in common; and
that in doing this they'll do what's best and nothing contrary to the
nature of the female in her relationship with the male, nothing contrary
to the natural community of the two with each other?"

"I do accept it," he said.

"Then," I said, "doesn't it remain to determine whether after all it
is possible, as it is among other animals, that this community come into
being among human beings too, and in what way it is possible?"

"You were just ahead of me," he said, "in mentioning what I was
going to take up."

e   "For, as to war," I said, "I suppose it's plain how they'll make war."

"How?" he said.

"That they'll carry out their campaigns in common, and, besides,
they'll lead all the hardy children to the war, so that, like the children
of the other craftsmen, they can see what they'll have to do in their
467 a   craft when they are grown up. Besides seeing, they'll help out and serve
in the whole business of war, and care for their fathers and mothers. Or
haven't you noticed in the other arts that, for example, potters' sons
look on as helpers for a long time before putting their hands to the
wheel?"

"Quite so."

"Must they be more careful than the guardians in educating their
children by experience and observation of their duties?"

"That would be quite ridiculous," he said.

"And further, every animal fights exceptionally hard in the pres-
b   ence of its offspring."

"That's so. But, Socrates, there's no small risk that in defeats,
which are of course likely in war, they will lose the children along with
themselves and make it impossible even for the rest of the city to
recover."

"What you say is true," I said. "But do you believe that one must
first provide for the avoidance of all risks?"

"Not at all."

"And what about this? Since risks must presumably be run,

shouldn't it be those from which they will emerge better men when suc-   467 *b*
cessful?"

"Plainly."

"But do you suppose it makes only a small difference, and one not   *c*
worth a risk, whether children who are to be men skilled in war look on
the business of war or not?"

"No, it does make a difference for what you are talking about."

"Then this must be the beginning, making the children spectators
of war. And, if we further contrive something for their security, everything will be fine. Won't it?"

"Yes."

"In the first place," I said, "won't their fathers, insofar as is human, be not ignorant but knowledgeable about all the campaigns that
are risky and all that are not?"   *d*

"It's likely," he said.

"Then they'll lead them to the ones and beware of the others."

"Right."

"And as rulers," I said, "they'll presumably set over them not the
most ordinary men but those adequate by experience and age to be
leaders and tutors."27

"Yes, that's proper."

"But, we'll say, many things for many men also turn out contrary
to their opinions."

"Indeed."

"Therefore, in view of such things, my friend, they'll have to be
equipped with wings right away as little children, so that, if need be,
they can fly and get away."

"How do you mean?" he said.   *e*

"At the earliest possible age, they must be mounted on horses," I
said, "and when they've been taught how to ride, they must be led to
the spectacle on horses, not spirited and combative ones, but the
swiftest and most easily reined. Thus they will get the fairest look at
their own work and, if need be, will make the surest escape to safety
following older leaders."

"In my opinion," he said, "what you say is right."

"Now what about the business of war?" I said. "How must your   468 *a*
soldiers behave toward one another and the enemies? Is the way it
looks to me right or not?"

"Just tell me," he said, "what that is."

"If one of them," I said, "leaves the ranks or throws away his
arms, or does anything of the sort because of cowardice, mustn't he be
demoted to craftsman or farmer?"

468 a   "Most certainly."
               "And the man who's taken alive by the enemy, won't we give him
        as a gift to those who took him, to use their catch as they wish?"
  b   "Exactly."
               "Is it or isn't it your opinion that the man who has proved best
        and earned a good reputation must first be crowned by each of those
        who made the campaign with him, youths and boys in turn?"
               "It surely is."
               "And what about this? Must his right hand be shaken?"
               "That too."
               "But I suppose," I said, "you wouldn't go so far as to accept this
        further opinion."
               "What?"
               "That he kiss and be kissed by each."
               "Most of all," he said. "And I add to the law that as long as they
  c   are on that campaign no one whom he wants to kiss be permitted to
        refuse, so that if a man happens to love someone, either male or female,
        he would be more eager to win the rewards of valor."
               "Fine," I said. "That marriages will be more readily available for
        a man who's good than for the others, and that he will frequently be
        chosen for that sort of thing in preference to the others, so that the most
        children will be born of such a man, has already been said."
               "Yes," he said, "we did say that."
               "Further, according to Homer too, it's just to honor in such ways
  d   whoever is good among the young. For Homer said that Ajax, when he
        earned a good reputation in the war, 'received as prize the whole back-
        bone,' as though the honor appropriate for a man who is in the bloom of
        youth and courageous is that by which he will at the same time be
        honored and increase his strength."[28]
               "Quite right," he said.
               "Therefore we'll believe Homer in this at least," I said. "And at
        sacrifices and all such occasions we'll honor the good, insofar as they
        have shown themselves to be good, with hymns and the things we were
        mentioning just now and, besides that, with 'seats and meats and full
  e   cups,'[29] so that we'll give the good men and women what is con-
        ducive to their training at the same time as honoring them."
               "What you say," he said, "is quite fine."
               "All right. As for those who die on a campaign, won't we first say
        that the man who died in earning a good reputation is a member of the
        golden class?"[30]
               "Most of all."
               "Won't we believe Hesiod that when any of that class die,

They become holy demons dwelling on earth,   *469*   *a*
Good, warders-off of evil, guardians of humans
      endowed with speech?"³¹

"We certainly will believe him."

"We'll inquire, therefore, of the god how the demonic and divine beings should be buried and with what distinction, and we'll bury them as he indicates."

"Of course we shall."

"And for the rest of time we'll care for their tombs and worship at them as at those of demons. And we'll make the same conventions for   *b* any one of those who have been judged exceptionally good in life when dying of old age or in some other way."

"That is only just," he said.

"And what about this? How will our soldiers deal with enemies?"

"In what respect?"

"First, as to enslavement: which seems just, that Greek cities enslave Greeks; or that they, insofar as possible, not even allow another city to do it but make it a habit to spare the Greek stock, well aware of   *c* the danger of enslavement at the hands of the barbarians?"

"Sparing them," he said, "is wholly and entirely superior."

"And, therefore, that they not themselves possess a Greek as slave, and give the same advice to the other Greeks?"

"Most certainly," he said. "At any rate in that way they would be more inclined to turn to the barbarians and keep off one another."

"What about this?" I said. "When they win, is it a fine practice to strip the dead of anything more than their arms? Or doesn't it provide a pretext for cowards not to attack the man who's still fighting, as though   *d* they were doing something necessary in poking around the dead, while many an army before now has been lost as a consequence of this plundering?"

"Quite so."

"Doesn't it seem illiberal and greedy to plunder a corpse, and the mark of a small, womanish mind to hold the enemy to be the body of the dead enemy who's flown away and left behind that with which he fought? Or do you suppose that the men who do this are any different from the dogs who are harsh with the stones thrown at them but don't   *e* touch the one who is throwing them?"

"Not in the least," he said.

"They must, therefore, leave off stripping corpses and preventing their recovery?"

"Yes indeed," he said, "they must, by Zeus."

"And, further, we surely won't bring the arms to the temples as

469 *e*   votive offerings, especially those of the Greeks, if we care at all about
470 *a*   the good will of the other Greeks. Rather we'll be afraid it would be a
defilement to bring such things from our kin to a temple, unless, of
course, the god should say otherwise."

"Quite right," he said.

"And what about ravaging the Greek countryside and burning
houses? What sort of thing will your soldiers do to the enemies?"

"I would be glad," he said, "to hear you present your opinion."

"Well, in my opinion," I said, "they'll do neither of these things,
b   but they'll take away the year's harvest; and do you want me to tell you
why?"

"Certainly."

"It appears to me that just as two different names are used, war
and faction, so two things also exist and the names apply to differences
in these two. The two things I mean are, on the one hand, what is one's
own and akin, and what is alien, and foreign, on the other. Now the
name faction is applied to the hatred of one's own, war to the hatred of
the alien."

"What you're saying," he said, "is certainly not off the point."

c   "Now see whether what I say next is also to the point. I assert that
the Greek stock is with respect to itself its own and akin, with respect
to the barbaric, foreign and alien."

"Yes," he said, "that is fine."

"Then when Greeks fight with barbarians and barbarians with
Greeks, we'll assert they are at war and are enemies[32] by nature,
and this hatred must be called war; while when Greeks do any such
thing to Greeks, we'll say that they are by nature friends, but in this
case Greece is sick and factious, and this kind of hatred must be called
d   faction."

"I, for one," he said, "agree to consider it in that way."

"Now observe," I said, "in what is nowadays understood to be
faction, that wherever such a thing occurs and a city is split, if each
side wastes the fields and burns the houses of the others, it seems that
the faction is a wicked thing and that the members of neither side are
lovers of their city. For, otherwise, they would never have dared to
ravage their nurse and mother. But it seems to be moderate for the vic-
e   tors to take away the harvest of the vanquished, and to have the frame
of mind of men who will be reconciled and not always be at war."

"This frame of mind," he said, "belongs to far tamer men than the
other."

"Now what about this?" I said. "Won't the city you are founding
be Greek?"

"It must be," he said.   470 e

"Then won't they be good and tame?"

"Very much so."

"And won't they be lovers of the Greeks? Won't they consider Greece their own and hold the common holy places along with the other Greeks?"

"Very much so."

"Won't they consider differences with Greeks—their kin—to be   471 a
faction and not even use the name war?"

"Of course."

"And they will have their differences like men who, after all, will be reconciled."

"Most certainly."

"Then they'll correct³³ their opponents in a kindly way, not punishing them with a view to slavery or destruction, acting as correctors, not enemies."

"That's what they'll do," he said.

"Therefore, as Greeks, they won't ravage Greece or burn houses, nor will they agree that in any city all are their enemies—men, women, and children—but that there are always a few enemies who are to blame for the differences. And, on all these grounds, they won't be   b
willing to ravage lands or tear down houses, since the many are friendly; and they'll keep up the quarrel until those to blame are compelled to pay the penalty by the blameless ones who are suffering."

"I for one," he said, "agree that our citizens must behave this way toward their opponents; and toward the barbarians they must behave as the Greeks do now toward one another."

"So, shall we also give this law to the guardians—neither waste countryside nor burn houses?"   c

"Let it be given," he said. "And this and what went before are fine. But, Socrates, I think that if one were to allow you to speak about this sort of thing, you would never remember what you previously set aside in order to say all this. Is it possible for this regime to come into being, and how is it ever possible? I see that, if it should come into being, everything would be good for the city in which it came into being. And I can tell things that you leave out—namely, that they would be best at fighting their enemies too because they would least   d
desert one another, these men who recognize each other as brothers, fathers, and sons and who call upon each other using these names. And if the females join in the campaign too, either stationed in the line itself, or in the rear, to frighten the enemies and in case there should ever be any need of help—I know that with all this they would be un-

471 d
e

beatable. And I see all the good things that they would have at home and are left out in your account. Take it that I agree that there would be all these things and countless others if this regime should come into being, and don't talk any more about it; rather, let's now only try to persuade ourselves that it is possible and how it is possible, dismissing all the rest."

472 a

"All of a sudden," I said, "you have, as it were, assaulted my argument, and you have no sympathy for me and my loitering.[34] Perhaps you don't know that when I've hardly escaped the two waves, you're now bringing the biggest and most difficult, the third wave.[35] When you see and hear it, you'll be quite sympathetic, recognizing that it was, after all, fitting for me to hesitate and be afraid to speak and undertake to consider so paradoxical an argument."

b

"The more you say such things," he said, "the less we'll let you off from telling how it is possible for this regime to come into being. So speak, and don't waste time."

"Then," I said, "first it should be recalled that we got to this point while seeking what justice and injustice are like."

"Yes, it should," he said. "But what of it?"

"Nothing. But if we find out what justice is like, will we also insist that the just man must not differ at all from justice itself but in every

c

way be such as it is? Or will we be content if he is nearest to it and participates in it more than the others?"

"We'll be content with that," he said.

"It was, therefore, for the sake of a pattern," I said, "that we were seeking both for what justice by itself is like, and for the perfectly just man, if he should come into being, and what he would be like once come into being; and, in their turns, for injustice and the most unjust man. Thus, looking off at what their relationships to happiness and its opposite appear to us to be, we would also be compelled to agree in our

d

own cases that the man who is most like them will have the portion most like theirs. We were not seeking them for the sake of proving that it's possible for these things to come into being."

"What you say is true," he said.

"Do you suppose a painter is any less good who draws a pattern of what the fairest human being would be like and renders everything in the picture adequately, but can't prove that it's also possible that such a man come into being?"

"No, by Zeus, I don't," he said.

"Then, what about this? Weren't we, as we assert, also making a

e

pattern in speech of a good city?"

"Certainly."

"Do you suppose that what we say is any less good on account of our not being able to prove that it is possible to found a city the same as the one in speech?"

"Surely not," he said.

"Well, then, that's the truth of it," I said. "But if then to gratify you I must also strive to prove how and under what condition it would be most possible, grant me the same points again for this proof."

"What points?"

"Can anything be done as it is said? Or is it the nature of acting to attain to less truth than speaking, even if someone doesn't think so? Do you agree that it's so or not?"

"I do agree," he said.

"Then don't compel me necessarily to present it as coming into being in every way in deed as we described it in speech. But if we are able to find that a city could be governed in a way most closely approximating what has been said, say that we've found the possibility of these things coming into being on which you insist. Or won't you be content if it turns out this way? I, for my part, would be content."

"I would, too," he said.

"So, next, as it seems, we must try to seek out and demonstrate what is badly done in cities today, and thereby keeps them from being governed in this way, and with what smallest change—preferably one, if not, two, and, if not, the fewest in number and the smallest in power—a city would come to this manner of regime."

"That's entirely certain," he said.

"Well, then," I said, "with one change—not, however, a small or an easy one, but possible—we can, in my opinion, show that it would be transformed."

"What change?" he said.

"Well here I am," I said, "coming to what we likened to the biggest wave. But it shall be said regardless, even if, exactly like an uproarious wave, it's going to drown me in laughter and ill repute. Consider what I am going to say."

"Speak," he said.

"Unless," I said, "the philosophers rule as kings or those now called kings and chiefs genuinely and adequately philosophize, and political power and philosophy coincide[36] in the same place, while the many natures now making their way to either apart from the other are by necessity excluded, there is no rest from ills for the cities, my dear Glaucon, nor I think for human kind, nor will the regime we have

473 e now described in speech ever come forth from nature, insofar as possible, and see the light of the sun. This is what for so long was causing my hesitation to speak: seeing how very paradoxical it would be to say. For it is hard to see that in no other city would there be private or public happiness."

And he said, "Socrates, what a phrase and argument you have let burst out. Now that it's said, you can believe that very many men, and

474 a not ordinary ones, will on the spot throw off their clothes, and stripped for action, taking hold of whatever weapon falls under the hand of each, run full speed at you to do wonderful deeds. If you don't defend yourself with speech and get away, you'll really pay the penalty in scorn."

"Isn't it you," I said, "that's responsible for this happening to me?"

"And it's a fine thing I'm doing," he said. "But no, I won't betray you, and I'll defend you with what I can. I can provide good will and encouragement; and perhaps I would answer you more suitably than

b another. And so, with the assurance of such support, try to show the disbelievers that it is as *you* say."

"It must be tried," I said, "especially since you offer so great an alliance. It's necessary, in my opinion, if we are somehow going to get away from the men you speak of, to distinguish for them whom we mean when we dare to assert the philosophers must rule. Thus, when they have come plainly to light, one will be able to defend oneself,

c showing that it is by nature fitting for them both to engage in philosophy and to lead a city, and for the rest not to engage in philosophy and to follow the leader."

"It would be high time," he said, "to distinguish them."

"Come, now, follow me here, if we are somehow or other to set it forth adequately."

"Lead," he said.

"Will you need to be reminded," I said, "or do you remember that when we say a man loves something, if it is rightly said of him, he mustn't show a love for one part of it and not for another, but must cherish all of it?"

d "I need reminding, as it seems," he said. "For I scarcely understand."

"It was proper for another, Glaucon, to say what you're saying," I said. "But it's not proper for an erotic man to forget that all boys in the bloom of youth in one way or another put their sting in an erotic lover of boys and arouse him; all seem worthy of attention and delight. Or don't you people behave that way with the fair? You praise the boy

with a snub nose by calling him 'cute'; the hook-nose of another you
say is 'kingly'; and the boy between these two is 'well proportioned';
the dark look 'manly'; and the white are 'children of gods.' And
as for the 'honey-colored,' do you suppose their very name is the
work of anyone other than a lover who renders sallowness endearing
and easily puts up with it if it accompanies the bloom of youth? And, in
a word, you people take advantage of every excuse and employ any
expression so as to reject none of those who glow with the bloom of
youth."

474 d

e

475 a

"If you want to point to me while you speak about what erotic
men do," he said, "I agree for the sake of the argument."

"And what about this?" I said. "Don't you see wine-lovers doing
the same thing? Do they delight in every kind of wine, and on every
pretext?"

"Indeed, they do."

"And further, I suppose you see that lovers of honor, if they can't
become generals, are lieutenants,[37] and if they can't be honored by
greater and more august men, are content to be honored by lesser and
more ordinary men because they are desirers of honor as a whole."

b

"That's certainly the case."

"Then affirm this or deny it: when we say a man is a desirer of
something, will we assert that he desires all of that form, or one part of
it and not another?"

"All," he said.

"Won't we also then assert that the philosopher is a desirer of
wisdom, not of one part and not another, but of all of it?"

"True."

"We'll deny, therefore, that the one who's finicky about his learning, especially when he's young and doesn't yet have an account of
what's useful and not, is a lover of learning or a philosopher, just as we
say that the man who's finicky about his food isn't hungry, doesn't
desire food, and isn't a lover of food but a bad eater."

c

"And we'll be right in denying it."

"But the one who is willing to taste every kind of learning with
gusto, and who approaches learning with delight, and is insatiable, we
shall justly assert to be a philosopher, won't we?"

And Glaucon said, "Then you'll have many strange ones. For all
the lovers of sights are in my opinion what they are because they enjoy
learning; and the lovers of hearing would be some of the strangest to
include among philosophers, those who would never be willing to go
voluntarily to a discussion and such occupations but who—just as
though they had hired out their ears for hearing—run around to every

d

475 d   chorus at the Dionysia, missing none in the cities or the villages.[38]
Will we say that all these men and other learners of such things and the
e   petty arts are philosophers?"

"Not at all," I said, "but they are like philosophers."

"Who do you say are the true ones?" he said.

"The lovers of the sight of the truth," I said.

"And that's right," he said. "But how do you mean it?"

"It wouldn't be at all easy to tell someone else. But you, I suppose, will grant me this."

"What?"

"Since fair is the opposite of ugly, they are two."

476 a   "Of course."

"Since they are two, isn't each also one?"

"That is so as well."

"The same argument also applies then to justice and injustice,
good and bad, and all the forms; each is itself one, but, by showing up
everywhere in a community with actions, bodies, and one another,
each is an apparitional many."

"What you say," he said, "is right."

"Well, now," I said, "this is how I separate them out. On one side
I put those of whom you were just speaking, the lovers of sights, the
lovers of arts, and the practical men; on the other, those whom the argu-
b   ment concerns, whom alone one could rightly call philosophers."

"How do you mean?" he said.

"The lovers of hearing and the lovers of sights, on the one hand,"
I said, "surely delight in fair sounds and colors and shapes and all that
craft makes from such things, but their thought is unable to see and
delight in the nature of the fair itself."

"That," he said, "is certainly so."

"Wouldn't, on the other hand, those who are able to approach the
fair itself and see it by itself be rare?"

c   "Indeed they would."

"Is the man who holds that there are fair things but doesn't hold
that there is beauty itself and who, if someone leads him to the
knowledge of it, isn't able to follow—is he, in your opinion, living in a
dream or is he awake? Consider it. Doesn't dreaming, whether one is
asleep or awake, consist in believing a likeness of something to be not a
likeness, but rather the thing itself to which it is like?"

"I, at least," he said, "would say that a man who does that
dreams."

"And what about the man who, contrary to this, believes that
d   there is something fair itself and is able to catch sight both of it and of
what participates in it, and doesn't believe that what participates is it

itself, nor that it itself is what participates—is he, in your opinion, living in a dream or is he awake?"

"He's quite awake," he said.

"Wouldn't we be right in saying that this man's thought, because he knows, is knowledge, while the other's is opinion because he opines?"

"Most certainly."

"What if the man of whom we say that he opines but doesn't know, gets harsh with us and disputes the truth of what we say? Will we have some way to soothe and gently persuade him, while hiding from him that he's not healthy?"

"We surely have to have a way, at least," he said.

"Come, then, and consider what we'll say to him. Or do you want us to question him in this way—saying that if he does know something, it's not begrudged him, but that we would be delighted to see he knows something—but tell us this: Does the man who knows, know something or nothing? You answer me on his behalf."

"I'll answer," he said, "that he knows something."

"Is it something that *is* or *is not?*"

"That *is*. How could what *is not* be known at all?"

"So, do we have an adequate grasp of the fact—even if we should consider it in many ways—that what *is* entirely, is entirely knowable; and what in no way *is*, is in every way unknowable?"

"Most adequate."

"All right. Now if there were something such as both to be and not to be, wouldn't it lie between what purely and simply *is* and what in no way *is?*"

"Yes, it would be between."

"Since knowledge depended on what *is* and ignorance necessarily on what *is not*, mustn't we also seek something between ignorance and knowledge that depends on that which is in between, if there is in fact any such thing?"

"Most certainly."

"Do we say opinion is something?"

"Of course."

"A power[39] different from knowledge or the same?"

"Different."

"Then opinion is dependent on one thing and knowledge on another, each according to its own power."

"That's so."

"Doesn't knowledge naturally depend on what *is*, to know of what *is* that it is and how it is? However, in my opinion, it's necessary to make this distinction first."

"What distinction?"

477 c   "We will assert that powers are a certain class of beings by means
of which we are capable of what we are capable, and also everything
else is capable of whatever it is capable. For example, I say sight and
hearing are powers, if perchance you understand the form of which I
wish to speak."
               "I do understand," he said.
               "Now listen to how they look to me. In a power I see no color or
shape or anything of the sort such as I see in many other things to
which I look when I distinguish one thing from another for myself.
d   With a power I look only to this—on what it depends and what it accomplishes; and it is on this basis that I come to call each of the powers
a power; and that which depends on the same thing and accomplishes
the same thing, I call the same power, and that which depends on
something else and accomplishes something else, I call a different
power. What about you? What do you do?"
               "The same," he said.
               "Now, you best of men, come back here to knowledge again. Do
you say it's some kind of power, or in what class do you put it?"
               "In this one," he said, "as the most vigorous of all powers."
e   "And what about opinion? Is it among the powers, or shall we
refer it to some other form?"
               "Not at all," he said. "For that by which we are capable of
opining is nothing other than opinion."
               "But just a little while ago you agreed that knowledge and opinion
are not the same."
               "How," he said, "could any intelligent man count that which
doesn't make mistakes the same as that which does?"
478 a   "Fine," I said, "and we plainly agree that opinion is different
from knowledge."
               "Yes, it is different."
               "Since each is capable of something different, are they, therefore,
naturally dependent on different things?"
               "Necessarily."
               "Knowledge is presumably dependent on what *is*, to know of what
is that it is and how it is?"
               "Yes."
               "While opinion, we say, opines."
               "Yes."
               "The same thing that knowledge knows? And will the knowable
and the opinable be the same? Or is that impossible?"
               "On the basis of what's been agreed to, it's impossible," he said.
"If different powers are naturally dependent on different things and

both are powers—opinion and knowledge—and each is, as we say, dif-   *478 b*
ferent, then on this basis it's not admissible that the knowable and the
opinable be the same."

"If what *is*, is knowable, then wouldn't something other than that
which *is* be opinable?"

"Yes, it would be something other."

"Then does it opine what *is not*? Or is it also impossible to opine
what *is not*? Think about it. Doesn't the man who opines refer his opinion to something? Or is it possible to opine, but to opine nothing?"

"No, it's impossible."

"The man who opines, opines some one thing?"

"Yes."

"But further, that which *is not* could not with any correctness be   *c*
addressed as some one thing but rather nothing at all."

"Certainly."

"To that which *is not*, we were compelled to assign ignorance, and
to that which *is*, knowledge."

"Right," he said.

"Opinion, therefore, opines neither that which *is* nor that which *is
not*."

"No, it doesn't."

"Opinion, therefore, would be neither ignorance nor knowledge?"

"It doesn't seem so."

"Is it, then, beyond these, surpassing either knowledge in clarity
or ignorance in obscurity?"

"No, it is neither."

"Does opinion," I said, "look darker than knowledge to you and
brighter than ignorance?"

"Very much so," he said.

"And does it lie within the limits set by these two?"   *d*

"Yes."

"Opinion, therefore, would be between the two."

"That's entirely certain."

"Weren't we saying before that if something should come to light
as what *is* and what *is not* at the same time, it lies between that which
purely and simply *is* and that which in every way *is not*, and that
neither knowledge nor ignorance will depend on it, but that which in its
turn comes to light between ignorance and knowledge?"

"Right."

"And now it is just that which we call opinion that has come to
light between them."

"Yes, that is what has come to light."

478 e   "Hence, as it seems, it would remain for us to find what participates in both—in *to be* and *not to be*—and could not correctly be
addressed as either purely and simply, so that, if it comes to light, we
can justly address it as the opinable, thus assigning the extremes to the
extremes and that which is in between to that which is in between. Isn't
that so?"

"Yes, it is."

"Now, with this taken for granted, let him tell me, I shall say, and
479 a   let him answer—that good man who doesn't believe that there is anything fair in itself and an *idea* of the beautiful itself, which always stays
the same in all respects, but does hold that there are many fair things,
this lover of sights who can in no way endure it if anyone asserts the
fair is one and the just is one and so on with the rest. 'Now, of these
many fair things, you best of men,' we'll say, 'is there any that won't
also look ugly? And of the just, any that won't look unjust? And of the
holy, any that won't look unholy?' "

b   "No," he said, "but it's necessary that they look somehow both
fair and ugly, and so it is with all the others you ask about."

"And what about the many doubles? Do they look any less half
than double?"

"No."

"And, then, the things that we would assert to be big and little,
light and heavy—will they be addressed by these names any more than
by the opposites of these names?"

"No," he said, "each will always have something of both."

"Then is each of the several manys what one asserts it to be any
more than it is not what one asserts it to be?"

"They are like the ambiguous jokes at feasts," he said, "and the
c   children's riddle about the eunuch, about his hitting the bat—with
what and on what he struck it.[40] For the manys are also ambiguous,
and it's not possible to think of them fixedly as either being or not
being, or as both or neither."

"Can you do anything with them?" I said. "Or could you find a
finer place to put them than between being and not to be? For presumably nothing darker than not-being will come to light so that something could *not be* more than it; and nothing brighter than being will
d   come to light so that something could *be* more than it."

"Very true," he said.

"Then we have found, as it seems, that the many beliefs[41] of
the many about what's fair and about the other things roll around[42]
somewhere between not-being and being purely and simply."

"Yes, we have found that."

"And we agreed beforehand that, if any such thing should come to   *479 d*
light, it must be called opinable but not knowable, the wanderer between, seized by the power between."

"Yes, we did agree."

"And, as for those who look at many fair things but don't see the   *e*
fair itself and aren't even able to follow another who leads them to it,
and many just things but not justice itself, and so on with all the rest,
we'll assert that they opine all these things but know nothing of what
they opine."

"Necessarily," he said.

"And what about those who look at each thing itself—at the
things that are always the same in all respects? Won't we say that they
know and don't opine?"

"That too is necessary."

"Won't we assert that these men delight in and love that on which
knowledge depends, and the others that on which opinion depends? Or   *480 a*
don't we remember that we were saying that they love and look at fair
sounds and colors and such things but can't even endure the fact that
the fair itself is something?"

"Yes, we do remember."

"So, will we strike a false note in calling them lovers of opinion
rather than lovers of wisdom? And will they be very angry with us if we
speak this way?"

"No," he said, "that is, if they are persuaded by me. For it's not
lawful to be harsh with what's true."

"Must we, therefore, call philosophers rather than lovers of opinion those who delight in each thing that is itself?"

"That's entirely certain."

BOOK VI

"And so, Glaucon," I said, "through a somewhat lengthy argument, who the philosophers are and who the nonphilosophers has, with considerable effort, somehow been brought to light."

484 a

"Perhaps," he said, "that's because it could not easily have been done through a short one."

"It doesn't look like it," I said. "Still, in my opinion at least, it would have been better done if this were the only question that had to be treated, and there weren't many things left to treat for one who is going to see what the difference is between the just life and the unjust one."

"What's after this for us?" he said.

b

"What else but what's next?" I said. "Since philosophers are those who are able to grasp what is always the same in all respects, while those who are not able to do so but wander among what is many and varies in all ways are not philosophers, which should be the leaders of a city?"

"How should we put it so as to speak sensibly?" he said.

"Those who look as if they're capable of guarding the laws and practices of cities should be established as guardians."

c

"Right," he said.

"But is it plain," I said, "whether it's a blind guardian or a sharp-sighted one who ought to keep watch over anything?"

"Of course it's plain," he said.

484 c   "Well, does there seem to be any difference, then, between blind
men and those men who are really deprived of the knowledge of what
each thing is; those who have no clear pattern in the soul, and are
hence unable—after looking off, as painters do, toward what is truest,
d   and ever referring to it and contemplating it as precisely as
possible—to give laws about what is fine, just, and good, if any need to
be given, and as guardians to preserve those that are already established?"

"No, by Zeus," he said, "there isn't much difference."

"Shall we set these men up as guardians rather than those who not
only know what each thing is but also don't lack experience or fall
short of the others in any other part of virtue?"

"It would be strange to choose others," he said, "if, that is, these
men don't lack the rest. For the very thing in which they would have
the advantage is just about the most important."

485 a   "Then shouldn't we say how the same men will be able to possess
these two distinct sets of qualities?"

"Most certainly."

"Well, then, as we were saying at the beginning of this argument,
first their nature must be thoroughly understood. And, I suppose, if we
should come to an adequate agreement about that, we'll also agree that
the same men will be able to possess both and that there should be no
other leaders of cities than these."

"How shall we do it?"

"About philosophic natures, let's agree that they are always in
b   love with that learning which discloses to them something of the being
that *is* always and does not wander about, driven by generation and decay."

"Yes, let's agree to that."

"And, further," I said, "that just like the lovers of honor and the
erotic men we described before, they love all of it and don't willingly
let any part go, whether smaller or bigger, more honorable or more
contemptible."

"What you say is right," he said.

"Well, next consider whether it is necessary in addition that those
who are going to be such as we were saying have this further charac-
c   teristic in their nature."

"What?"

"No taste for falsehood; that is, they are completely unwilling to
admit what's false but hate it, while cherishing the truth."

"It's likely," he said.

"It's not only likely, my friend, but also entirely necessary that a

man who is by nature erotically disposed toward someone care for   485 c
everything related and akin to his boy."[1]

"Right," he said.

"Now could you find anything more akin to wisdom than truth?"

"Of course not," he said.

"Now is it possible that the same nature be both a lover of wisdom
and a lover of falsehood?"   d

"In no way."

"Therefore the man who is really a lover of learning must from
youth on strive as intensely as possible for every kind of truth."

"Entirely so."

"But, further, we surely know that when someone's desires incline
strongly to some one thing, they are therefore weaker with respect to
the rest, like a stream that has been channeled off in that other direction."

"Of course."

"So, when in someone they have flowed toward learning and all
that's like it, I suppose they would be concerned with the pleasure of
the soul itself with respect to itself and would forsake those pleasures
that come through the body—if he isn't a counterfeit but a true
philosopher."   e

"That is most necessary."

"Such a man is, further, moderate and in no way a lover of money. Money and the great expense that accompanies it are pursued for
the sake of things that any other man rather than this one is likely to
take seriously."

"That's so."

"And you too must of course also consider something else when   486 a
you're going to judge whether a nature is philosophic or not."

"What?"

"You mustn't let its partaking in illiberality get by you unnoticed.
For petty speech is of course most opposite to a soul that is always
going to reach out for the whole and for everything divine and human."

"Very true," he said.

"To an understanding endowed with magnificence[2] and the contemplation of all time and all being, do you think it possible that human life seem anything great?"

"Impossible," he said.

"Won't such a man also believe that death is not something terri-   b
ble?"

"Not in the least."

486 b

"So, a cowardly and illiberal nature would not, as it seems, participate in true philosophy."

"Not in my opinion."

"What then? Is there any way in which the orderly man, who isn't a lover of money, or illiberal, or a boaster, or a coward, could become a hard-bargainer or unjust?"

"There isn't."

"And further, when you are considering whether a soul is philosophic or not, you'll also take into consideration whether, from youth on, it is both just and tame or hard to be a partner with and savage."

"Most certainly."

c

"And you won't leave this out either, I suppose."

"What?"

"Whether he learns well or with difficulty. Or do you ever expect anyone would care sufficiently for a thing that, when he does it, he does painfully, accomplishing little with much effort?"

"That could not be."

"And what if he were able to preserve nothing of what he learns, being full of forgetfulness? Would it be possible he be not empty of knowledge?"

"Of course not."

"So, toiling without profit, don't you suppose he'll finally be compelled to hate both himself and an activity of this sort?"

"Of course."

d

"Let us never, then, admit a forgetful soul into the ranks of those that are adequately philosophic; in our search, let us rather demand a soul with a memory."

"Most certainly."

"Further, we would deny that what has an unmusical and graceless nature is drawn in any direction other than that of want of measure."[3]

"Of course."

"Do you believe that truth is related to want of measure or to measure?"

"To measure."

"Then, besides the other things, let us seek for an understanding endowed by nature with measure and charm, one whose nature grows by itself in such a way as to make it easily led to the *idea* of each thing that is."

"Of course."

e

"What then? Have we, in your opinion, gone through particular qualities that are in any way unnecessary and inconsequent to one

another in a soul that is going to partake adequately and perfectly in   486 e
what *is*?"

"They are," he said, "certainly most necessary."   487 a

"Is there any way, then, in which you could blame a practice like
this that a man could never adequately pursue if he were not by nature
a rememberer, a good learner, magnificent, charming, and a friend and
kinsman of truth, justice, courage, and moderation?"

"Not even Momus,"[4] he said, "could blame a practice like that."

"When such men," I said, "are perfected by education and age,
wouldn't you turn the city over to them alone?"

And Adeimantus said: "Socrates, no one could contradict you in   b
this. But here is how those who hear what you now say are affected on
each occasion. They believe that because of inexperience at questioning and answering, they are at each question misled a little by the argument; and when the littles are collected at the end of the arguments, the
slip turns out to be great and contrary to the first assertions. And just as
those who aren't clever at playing draughts are finally checked by those
who are and don't know where to move, so they too are finally checked
by this other kind of draughts, played not with counters but speeches,
and don't know what to say. However, the truth isn't in any way affected by this. In saying this, I look to the present case. Now someone
might say that in speech he can't contradict you at each particular thing
asked, but in deed he sees that of all those who start out on
philosophy—not those who take it up for the sake of getting educated
when they are young and then drop it, but those who linger in it for a   d
longer time—most become quite queer, not to say completely vicious;
while the ones who seem perfectly decent, do nevertheless suffer at
least one consequence of the practice you are praising—they become
useless to the cities."

And when I heard this, I said: "Do you suppose that the men who
say this are lying?"

"I don't know," he said, "but I should gladly hear your opinion."

"You would hear that it looks to me as if they were speaking the
truth."

"Then, how," he said, "can it be good to say that the cities will   e
have no rest from evils before the philosophers, whom we agree to be
useless to the cities, rule in them?"

"The question you are asking," I said, "needs an answer given
through an image."[5]

"And you, in particular," he said, "I suppose, aren't used to
speaking through images."

"All right," I said. "Are you making fun of me after having involved me in an argument so hard to prove? At all events, listen to the   488 a

[167]

488 a   image so you may see still more how greedy I am for images. So hard is
the condition suffered by the most decent men with respect to the cities
that there is no single other condition like it, but I must make my
image and apology on their behalf by bringing it together from many
sources—as the painters paint goatstags and such things by making
mixtures. Conceive something of this kind happening either on many
ships or one. Though the shipowner surpasses everyone on board in
b   height and strength, he is rather deaf and likewise somewhat
shortsighted, and his knowledge of seamanship is pretty much on the
same level. The sailors are quarreling with one another about the pilot-
ing, each supposing he ought to pilot, although he has never learned the
art and can't produce his teacher or prove there was a time when he
was learning it. Besides this, they claim it isn't even teachable and are
ready to cut to pieces the man who says it is teachable. And they are always crowded around the shipowner himself, begging and doing every-
c   thing so that he'll turn the rudder over to them. And sometimes, if they
fail at persuasion and other men succeed at it, they either kill the others
or throw them out of the ship. Enchaining the noble shipowner with
mandrake, drink, or something else, they rule the ship, using what's in
it; and drinking and feasting, they sail as such men would be thought
likely to sail. Besides this, they praise and call 'skilled sailor,' 'pilot,'
d   and 'knower of the ship's business' the man who is clever at figuring out
how they will get the rule, either by persuading or by forcing the
shipowner, while the man who is not of this sort they blame as useless. They don't know that for the true pilot it is necessary to pay
careful attention to year, seasons, heaven, stars, winds, and everything that's proper to the art, if he is really going to be skilled at rul-
e   ing a ship. And they don't suppose it's possible to acquire the art and
practice of how one can get hold of the helm whether the others
wish it or not, and at the same time to acquire the pilot's skill. So
with such things happening on the ships, don't you believe that the
489 a   true pilot will really be called a stargazer,[6] a prater and useless to
them by those who sail on ships run like this?"

"Indeed, he will," said Adeimantus.

"Now," I said, "I don't suppose you need to scrutinize the image
to see that it resembles the cities in their disposition toward the true
philosophers, but you understand what I mean."

"Indeed, I do," he said.

"First of all, then, teach the image to that man who wonders at the
philosophers' not being honored in the cities, and try to persuade him
b   that it would be far more to be wondered at if they were honored."

"I shall teach him," he said.

"And, further, that you are telling the truth in saying that the most   489 *b*
decent of those in philosophy are useless to the many. However, bid
him blame their uselessness on those who don't use them and not on the
decent men. For it's not natural that a pilot beg sailors to be ruled by
him nor that the wise go to the doors of the rich. The man who invented that subtlety lied.[7] The truth naturally is that it is necessary
for a man who is sick, whether rich or poor, to go to the doors of doctors, and every man who needs to be ruled to the doors of the man who
is able to rule, not for the ruler who is truly of any use to beg the ruled
to be ruled. You'll make no mistake in imagining the statesmen now
ruling to be the sailors we were just now speaking of, and those who are
said by them to be useless and gossipers about what's above to be the
true pilots."

sick go to doctors. Doctors don't go to the sick.

"Quite right," he said.
"Well, then, on this basis and under these conditions, it's not easy
for the best pursuit to enjoy a good reputation with those who practice
the opposite. But by far the greatest and most powerful slander[8] comes   *d*
to philosophy from those who claim to practice such things—those
about whom you say philosophy's accuser asserts that, 'most of those
who go to it are completely vicious and the most decent useless,' and I
admitted that what you say is true. Isn't that so?"
"Yes."
"Haven't we gone through the cause of the uselessness of the decent ones?"
"Yes indeed."
"Do you want us next to go through the necessity of the
viciousness of the many and to try to show, if we are able, that philosophy isn't to blame for that?"   *e*
"Most certainly."
"Then, let us begin our listening and speaking by reminding ourselves of the point at which we started our description of the kind of
nature with which the man who is to be a gentleman is necessarily en-
dowed. First, if it's present to your mind, truth guided him, and he had   490 *a*
to pursue it entirely and in every way or else be a boaster who in no
way partakes of true philosophy."
"Yes, that was said."
"Now isn't this one point quite contrary to the opinions currently
held about him?"
"Very much so," he said.
"So then, won't we make a sensible apology in saying that it is the
nature of the real lover of learning to strive for what *is*; and he does not
tarry by each of the many things opined to *be* but goes forward and   *b*

490 b   does not lose the keenness of his passionate love nor cease from it
before he grasps the nature itself of each thing which *is* with the part of
the soul fit to grasp a thing of that sort; and it is the part akin to it that
is fit. And once near it and coupled with what really is, having begotten
intelligence and truth, he knows and lives truly, is nourished and so
ceases from his labor pains, but not before."[9]

"Nothing," he said, "could be more sensible."

"What then? Will this man have any part in caring for falsehood,
or, all to the contrary, will he hate it?"

c   "He'll hate it," he said.

"If truth led the way, we wouldn't, I suppose, ever assert a
chorus[10] of evils could follow it?"

"Of course not."

"But a healthy and just disposition, which is also accompanied by
moderation."

"Right," he said.

"Why, then, must I also force the rest of the philosophic nature's
chorus into order all over again from the beginning? You surely remember that, appropriate to these, courage, magnificence, facility at
learning, and memory went along with them. And you objected, saying

d   that everyone would be forced to agree to what we are saying, but if
they let the arguments go and looked to the men themselves whom the
argument concerns, they would say they see that some of them are
useless and the many bad, possessing vice entire. In considering the
cause of the slander, we've come now to this point: why are the many
bad? And it's for just this reason that we brought up the nature of the
true philosophers again and defined what it necessarily is."

"That's so," he said.

e   "Then we must," I said, "look at the corruptions of this nature
and see how it is destroyed in many, while a small number escape—just
those whom they call not vicious but useless. And after that, in turn, we

491 a   must look at the natures of the souls that imitate the philosophic nature
and set themselves up in its practice, and see what sort they are who
approach a practice that is of no value for them and beyond them, and
who often strike false notes, thereby attaching to philosophy everywhere and among all men a reputation such as you say."

"What corruptions do you mean?" he said.

"I shall try," I said, "if I am able, to go through them for you.
Now I suppose everybody will agree with us about this. Such a
nature—possessing everything we prescribed just now for the man who
is going to become a perfect philosopher—such natures are few and

b   born only rarely among human beings. Or don't you suppose so?"

Rare to be Perfect Philo.

"Indeed, I do."

"Now consider how many great sources of ruin there are for these few."

"Just what are they?"

"What is most surprising of all to hear is that each one of the elements we praised in that nature has a part in destroying the soul that has them and tearing it away from philosophy. I mean courage, moderation, and everything we went through."

"Yes," he said, "that is strange to hear."

"And what's more," I said, "besides these, all the things said to be goods corrupt it and tear it away—beauty, wealth, strength of body, relatives who are powerful in a city, and everything akin to these. You see the type of thing I mean?"

"I do," he said, "and I would gladly learn more precisely what you mean."

"Well, then," I said, "grasp it correctly as a whole, and it will look perfectly plain to you, and what was said about them before won't seem strange."

"What do you bid me do?" he said.

"Concerning every seed or thing that grows, whether from the earth or animals," I said, "we know that the more vigorous it is, the more it is deficient in its own properties when it doesn't get the food, climate, or place suitable to it. For surely bad is more opposed to good than to not-good."

"Of course."

"So I suppose it is reasonable that the best nature comes off worse than an ordinary one from an inappropriate rearing."

"Yes, it is."

"Won't we say for souls too, Adeimantus," I said, "that, similarly, those with the best natures become exceptionally bad when they get bad instruction? Or do you suppose an ordinary nature is the source of great injustices and unmixed villainy? Don't you suppose, rather, that it's a lusty one corrupted by its rearing, while a weak nature will never be the cause of great things either good or bad?"

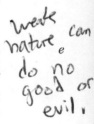

weak nature can do no good or evil.

"Yes," he said, "that's the case."

"Well, then, I suppose that if the nature we set down for the philosopher chances on a suitable course of learning, it will necessarily grow and come to every kind of virtue; but if it isn't sown, planted, and nourished in what's suitable, it will come to all the opposite, unless one of the gods chances to assist it. Or do you too believe, as do the many, that certain young men are corrupted by sophists, and that there are certain sophists who in a private capacity corrupt to an extent worth

492 a
  b

mentioning? Isn't it rather the very men who say this who are the biggest sophists, who educate most perfectly and who turn out young and old, men and women, just the way they want them to be?"

"But when do they do that?" he said.

"When," I said, "many gathered together sit down in assemblies, courts, theaters, army camps, or any other common meeting of a multitude, and, with a great deal of uproar, blame some of the things said or done, and praise others, both in excess, shouting and clapping; and,

  c

besides, the rocks and the very place surrounding them echo and redouble the uproar of blame and praise. Now in such circumstances, as the saying goes, what do you suppose is the state of the young man's heart? Or what kind of private education will hold out for him and not be swept away by such blame and praise and go, borne by the flood, wherever it tends so that he'll say the same things are noble and base as they do, practice what they practice, and be such as they are?"

  d

"The necessity is great, Socrates," he said.

"And yet," I said, "we still haven't mentioned the greatest necessity."

"What?" he said.

"What these educators and sophists inflict in deed when they fail to persuade in speech. Or don't you know that they punish the man who's not persuaded with dishonor, fines, and death?"

"Yes," he said, "they punish very severely."

"So, what other sophist or what sort of private speeches do you suppose will go counter to these and prevail?"

  e

"I don't suppose any will," he said.

"No," I said, "but even the attempt is a great folly. For, a character receiving an education contrary to theirs does not, has not, and will not become differently disposed toward virtue, a human character that is, my comrade; for the divine, according to the proverb, let's make an exception to the argument. You should be well aware that, if anything

493 a

should be saved and become such as it ought to be in regimes in this kind of condition, it won't be bad if you say that a god's dispensation saved it."

"I am of no other opinion," he said.

"Well, then," I said, "besides that one, be of this opinion too."

"What?"

"That each of the private wage earners whom these men call sophists and believe to be their rivals in art, educates in nothing other than these convictions[11] of the many, which they opine when they are gathered together, and he calls this wisdom. It is just like the case of a man who learns by heart the angers and desires of a great, strong

beast he is rearing, how it should be approached and how taken hold   *493 b*
of, when—and as a result of what—it becomes most difficult or most
gentle, and, particularly, under what conditions it is accustomed to utter its several sounds, and, in turn, what sort of sounds uttered by
another make it tame and angry. When he has learned all this from
associating and spending time with the beast, he calls it wisdom and,
organizing it as an art, turns to teaching. Knowing nothing in truth
about which of these convictions and desires is noble, or base, or good,
or evil, or just, or unjust, he applies all these names following the great   *c*
animal's opinions—calling what delights it good and what vexes it bad.
He has no other argument about them but calls the necessary just and
noble, neither having seen nor being able to show someone else how
much the nature of the necessary and the good really differ. Now, in
your opinion, wouldn't such a man, in the name of Zeus, be out of
place as an educator?"

"Yes," he said, "in my opinion, he would indeed."

"So, does this man seem any different from the man who believes
it is wisdom to have figured out the anger and pleasures—whether in   *d*
painting, music, or, particularly, in politics—of the multifarious many
who assemble? However a man associates with them, whether he makes
a display of poetry, or any other product of craft, or any service to the
city—making the many his masters beyond what is necessary—the so-
called necessity of Diomede[12] will compel him to produce the things
these men praise. But that those things are in truth good and
noble—have you up to now ever heard anyone presenting an argument
for this that isn't ridiculous?"

"No," he said, "nor do I suppose I shall hear one."   *e*

"Well, then, keep all this in mind and recall this question: Can a
multitude accept or believe that the fair itself, rather than the many fair
things, or that anything itself, *is*, rather than the many particular   *494 a*
things?"

"Not in the least," he said.

"Then it's impossible," I said, "that a multitude be philosophic."

"Yes, it is impossible."

"And so, those who do philosophize are necessarily blamed by
them."

"Necessarily."

"As well as by all those private men who consort with the mob
and desire to please it."

"Plainly."

"So, on this basis, what salvation do you see for a philosophic
nature so that it will remain in its practice and reach its end? Think it

494 b over on the basis of what went before. We did agree that facility at learning, memory, courage, and magnificence belong to this nature."

"Yes."

"Won't such a one be first among all in everything, straight from the beginning, especially if his body naturally matches his soul?"

"Of course he will," he said.

Family use
Philo to
attain
power

"Then I suppose kinsmen and fellow citizens will surely want to make use of him, when he is older, for their own affairs."

"Of course."

"They will, therefore, lie at his feet begging and honoring him, taking possession of and flattering beforehand the power that is going to be his."

"At least," he said, "that's what usually happens."

"What do you suppose," I said, "such a young man will do in such circumstances, especially if he chances to be from a big city, is rich and noble in it, and is, further, good-looking and tall? Won't he be overflowing with unbounded hope, believing he will be competent to mind the business of both Greeks and barbarians, and won't he, as a result, exalt himself to the heights, mindlessly full of pretension and empty conceit?"[13]

"Indeed he will," he said.

"Now, if someone were gently to approach the young man in this condition and tell him the truth—that he has no intelligence in him although he needs it, and that it's not to be acquired except by slaving for its acquisition—do you think it will be easy for him to hear through a wall of so many evils?"

"Far from it," he said.

"But if," I said, "thanks to his good nature and his kinship to such speeches, one young man were to apprehend something and be turned and drawn toward philosophy, what do we suppose those will do who believe they are losing his use and comradeship? Is there any deed they won't do or any word they won't say, concerning him, so that he won't be persuaded, and concerning the man who's doing the persuading, so that he won't be able to persuade; and won't they organize private plots and public trials?"

495 a "It's very necessary," he said.

"Is it possible that such a man will philosophize?"

"Not at all."

"Do you see," I said, "it wasn't bad when we said that the very elements of the philosophic nature, when they get a bad rearing, are, after all, in a way the cause of its being exiled from the practice, and so are the so-called goods—wealth and all equipment of the sort."

"No, it wasn't," he said. "What was said is right."

[174]

"Then, you surprising man," I said, "such is the extent and
character of this destruction and corruption of the best nature with
respect to the best pursuit. And such a nature is a rare occurrence in any
event, we say. And particularly from these men come those who do the
greatest harm to cities and private men, as well as those who do the
good, if they chance to be drawn in this direction. No little nature ever
does anything great either to private man or city."

"Very true," he said.

"So these men, for whom philosophy is most suitable, go thus into
exile and leave her abandoned and unconsummated. They themselves
live a life that isn't suitable or true; while, after them, other unworthy
men come to her—like an orphan bereft of relatives—and disgrace her.
These are the ones who attach to her reproaches such as even you say
are alleged by the men who reproach her—namely, that of those who
have intercourse with her, some are worthless and the many worthy of
many bad things."

"Yes," he said, "that is what is said."

"And what is said is fitting," I said. "For other manikins see that
this place has become empty although full of fine names and pretensions; and, just like those who run away from prisons to temples, these
men too are overjoyed to leap out of the arts into philosophy, those
who happen to be subtlest in their little art. For, although philosophy is
faring thus, it still retains a more magnificent station in comparison with
the other arts at least. Aiming at this, many men with imperfect
natures—just as their bodies are mutilated by the arts and crafts, so too
their souls are doubled up and spoiled as a result of being in mechanical occupations—or isn't that necessary?"[14]

"Quite so," he said.

"Do you suppose," I said, "that they are any different to see than
a little, bald-headed worker in bronze who has gotten some silver, and,
newly released from bonds, just washed in a bathhouse, wearing a new-
made cloak and got up like a bridegroom, is about to marry his
master's daughter because he's poor and destitute?"[15]

"Hardly at all different," he said.

"What sort of things are such men likely to beget? Aren't they
bastard and ordinary?"

"Quite necessarily."

"And what about this? When men unworthy of education come
near her and keep her company in an unworthy way, what sort of notions and opinions will we say they beget? Won't they be truly fit to be
called sophisms,[16] connected with nothing genuine or worthy of true
prudence?"

"That's entirely certain," he said.

496 a   "Then it's a very small group, Adeimantus," I said, "which re-
  b mains to keep company with philosophy in a way that's worthy;
perhaps either a noble and well-reared disposition, held in check by exile, remains by her side consistent with nature, for want of corruptors;
or when a great soul grows up in a little city, despises the business of
the city and looks out beyond; and, perhaps, a very few men from
another art, who justly despise it because they have good natures, might
come to her. And the bridle of our comrade Theages might be such as
  c to restrain him. For in Theages' case all the other conditions for an exile from philosophy were present, but the sickliness[17] of his body,
shutting him out of politics, restrains him. My case—the demonic[18]
sign—isn't worth mentioning, for it has perhaps occurred in some one
other man, or no other, before. Now the men who have become members of this small band have tasted how sweet and blessed a possession
it is. At the same time, they have seen sufficiently the madness of the
many, and that no one who minds the business of the cities does virtually
anything sound, and that there is no ally with whom one could
go to the aid of justice and be preserved. Rather—just like a human
being who has fallen in with wild beasts and is neither willing to join
them in doing injustice nor sufficient as one man to resist all the
savage animals—one would perish before he has been of any use to city
or friends and be of no profit to himself or others. Taking all this into
the calculation, he keeps quiet and minds his own business—as a man
in a storm, when dust and rain are blown about by the wind, stands
aside under a little wall. Seeing others filled full of lawlessness, he is
content if somehow he himself can live his life here pure of injustice
  e and unholy deeds, and take his leave from it graciously and cheerfully
with fair hope."
497 a   "Well," he said, "he would leave having accomplished not the
least of things."
    "But not the greatest either," I said, "if he didn't chance upon a
suitable regime. For in a suitable one he himself will grow more and
save the common things along with the private.
    "Now the reasons why philosophy is slandered, and that it isn't
just that it be, have in my opinion been sensibly stated, unless you still
have something else to say."
    "I have nothing further to say about this," he said. "But which of
the current regimes do you say is suitable for it?"
  b   "None at all," I said, "but this is the very charge I'm bringing; not
one city today is in a condition worthy of the philosophic nature. And
this is why it is twisted and changed; just as a foreign seed sown in alien
ground is likely to be overcome and fade away into the native stock, so

too this class does not at present maintain its own power but falls away   497 b
into an alien disposition. But if it ever takes hold in the best regime,
just as it is itself best, then it will make plain that it really is divine as   c
we agreed it is and that the rest are human, both in terms of their
natures and their practices. Of course, it's plain that next you'll ask
what this regime is."

"You've not got it," he said. "That's not what I was going to ask,
but whether it is the same one we described in founding the city or
another."

"It is the same in the other respects," I said, "and, in this very one
too, which was stressed in connection with it—that there would always
have to be present in the city something possessing the same understanding of the regime as you, the lawgiver, had when you were set-   d
ting down the laws."

"Yes," he said, "that point was made."

"But it wasn't made sufficiently plain," I said, "from fear of what
you people, with your insistence, have made plain—that its demonstration would be long and hard. And now what's left is by no means the
easiest to go through."

"What is it?"

"How a city can take philosophy in hand without being destroyed.
For surely all great things carry with them the risk of a fall, and, really
as the saying goes, fine things are hard."

"All the same," he said, "let the proof get its completion by clear-   e
ing this up."

"It won't be hindered by a lack of willingness, but, if by anything,
by a lack of capacity," I said. "You'll be on hand to see my eagerness
at least. Consider how eagerly and recklessly I am going to say now that
the way a city takes up this practice should be just the opposite of what
is done nowadays."

"How?"

"Nowadays," I said, "those who take it up at all are lads fresh
from childhood; in the interval before running a household and making   498 a
money, *they approach its hardest part and then leave, those, that is,*
who are fancied to be complete philosophers. I mean by the hardest
part that which has to do with speeches.[19] In later life, if others are
doing this and they are invited, they believe it's a great thing if they are
willing to be listeners, thinking it ought to be done as a hobby. Toward
old age, except of course for a certain few, they are far more extinguished than Heracleitus' sun,[20] inasmuch as they are not rekindled again."
                                                                                 b
"How ought it to be?" he said.

498 b   "Entirely opposite. When they are youths and boys they ought to take up an education and philosophy suitable for youths, and take very good care of their bodies at the time when they are growing and blooming into manhood, thus securing a helper for philosophy. And as they advance in age to the time when the soul begins to reach maturity, it ought to be subjected to a more intense gymnastic. And when strength begins to fail and they are beyond political and military duties, at this

c   time they ought to be let loose to graze and do nothing else, except as a spare-time occupation—those who are going to live happily and, when they die, crown the life they have lived with a suitable lot in that other place."

"In my opinion, you truly are speaking eagerly, Socrates," he said. "However, I suppose that the many among the hearers are even more eager to oppose you and won't be persuaded at all, beginning with Thrasymachus."

"Don't make a quarrel between Thrasymachus and me when

d   we've just become friends, though we weren't even enemies before," I said. "We'll not give up our efforts before we either persuade him and the others, or give them some help in preparation for that other life when, born again, they meet with such arguments."

"That's a short time you are speaking about," he said.

"No time at all," I said, "if you compare it to the whole. However, it's no wonder that the many are not persuaded by these speeches. For they never saw any existing thing that matches the pres-

e   ent speech. Far rather they have seen such phrases purposely 'balanced' with one another, not falling together spontaneously as they are now. But as for a man who to the limit of the possible is perfectly 'likened' to and 'balanced'21 with virtue, in deed and speech, and

499 a   holds power in a city fit for him, they have never seen one or more. Or do you suppose so?"

"No, I don't at all."

"Nor, you blessed man, have they given an adequate hearing to fair and free speeches of the sort that strain with every nerve in quest of the truth for the sake of knowing and that 'nod a distant greeting'22 to the subtleties and contentious quibbles that strain toward nothing but opinion and contention in trials as well as in private groups."

"No, they haven't," he said.

"Well, it was on account of this," I said, "foreseeing it then, that

b   we were frightened; but, all the same, compelled by the truth, we said that neither city nor regime will ever become perfect, nor yet will a man become perfect in the same way either, before some necessity chances to constrain those few philosophers who aren't vicious, those now called useless, to take charge of a city, whether they want to or

not, and the city to obey;[23] or a true erotic passion for true philoso-   499 *b*
phy flows from some divine inspiration into the sons of those who hold   *c*
power[24] or the office of king, or into the fathers themselves. I deny
that there is any reason why either or both of these things is impossible.
If that were the case we would justly be laughed at for uselessly saying
things that are like prayers. Or isn't that so?"

"Yes, it is."

"Therefore, if, in the endless time that has gone by, there has been
some necessity for those who are on the peaks of philosophy to take
charge of a city, or there even now is such a necessity in some barbaric
place somewhere far outside of our range of vision, or will be later, in   *d*
this case we are ready to do battle for the argument that the regime
spoken of has been, is, and will be when this Muse has become master
of a city. For it's not impossible that it come to pass nor are we speaking of impossibilities. That it's hard, we too agree."

"That," he said, "in my opinion, is so."

"Will you," I said, "say that in the opinion of the many it isn't
so?"

"Perhaps," he said.

"You blessed man," I said, "don't make such a severe accusation
against the many. They will no doubt have another sort of opinion, if   *e*
instead of indulging yourself in quarreling with them, you soothe them
and do away with the slander against the love of learning by pointing
out whom you mean by the philosophers, and by distinguishing, as was
just done, their nature and the character of their practice so the many   500 *a*
won't believe you mean those whom they suppose to be philosophers.
And if they see it this way, doubtless you'll say that they will take on
another sort of opinion and answer differently. Or do you suppose
anyone of an ungrudging and gentle character is harsh with the man
who is not harsh or bears grudges against the man who bears none? I
shall anticipate you and say that I believe that so hard a nature is in a
few but not the multitude."

"I, too," he said, "of course, share your supposition."

"Don't you also share my supposition that the blame for the many's   *b*
being harshly disposed toward philosophy is on those men from outside who don't belong and have burst in like drunken revelers, abusing
one another and indulging a taste for quarreling, and who always make
their arguments about persons,[25] doing what is least seemly in
philosophy?"

"Very much so," he said.

"For, presumably, Adeimantus, a man who has his understanding
truly turned toward the things that *are* has no leisure to look down
toward the affairs of human beings and to be filled with envy and ill   *c*

500 c   will as a result of fighting with them. But, rather, because he sees and contemplates things that are set in a regular arrangement and are always in the same condition—things that neither do injustice to one another nor suffer it at one another's hands, but remain all in order according to reason—he imitates them and, as much as possible, makes himself like them. Or do you suppose there is any way of keeping someone from imitating that which he admires and therefore keeps company with?"

"It's not possible," he said.

d   "Then it's the philosopher, keeping company with the divine and the orderly who becomes orderly and divine, to the extent that is possible for a human being. But there is much slander abroad."

"In every way that's most certain."

"If some necessity arises," I said, "for him to practice putting what he sees there into the dispositions of men, both in private and in public, instead of forming only himself, do you suppose he'll prove to be a bad craftsman of moderation, justice, and vulgar[26] virtue as a whole?"

"Least of all," he said.

e   "Now, if the many become aware that what we are saying about this man is true, will they then be harsh with the philosophers and distrust us when we say that a city could never be happy otherwise than by having its outlines drawn by the painters who use the divine pattern?"

"No, they won't be harsh," he said, "provided they do gain this
501 a   awareness. But what kind of drawing do you mean?"

"They would take the city and the dispositions of human beings, as though they were a tablet," I said, "which, in the first place, they would wipe clean. And that's hardly easy. At all events, you know that straight off in this they would differ from the rest—in not being willing to take either private man or city in hand or to draw laws before they receive it clean or themselves make it so."

"And they are right," he said.

"Next, don't you think they would outline the shape of the regime?"

"Of course."

b   "After that, I suppose that in filling out their work they would look away frequently in both directions, toward the just, fair, and moderate by nature and everything of the sort, and, again, toward what is in human beings; and thus, mixing and blending the practices as ingredients, they would produce the image of man,[27] taking hints

from exactly that phenomenon in human beings which Homer too   501 *b*
called god-like and the image of god."

"Right," he said.

"And I suppose they would rub out one thing and draw in another
again, until they made human dispositions as dear to the gods as they   *c*
admit of being."

"The drawing," he said, "would at any rate be fairest that way."

"Are we then somehow persuading those men who you said were
coming at us full speed," I said, "that the man we were then praising to
them is such a painter of regimes? It was on his account that they were
so harsh, because we were handing the cities over to him. Are they any
gentler on hearing it now?"

"Yes, and very much so," he said, "if they are moderate."

"For how will they be able to dispute it? Will they say the   *d*
philosophers aren't lovers of that which *is* and of truth?"

"That would be strange," he said.

"Or that their nature as we described it isn't akin to the best?"

"Not that either."

"Or this—that such a nature, when it chances on suitable
practices, will not be perfectly good and philosophic if any is? Or
are those men whom we excluded by nature more so?"28

"Surely not."   *e*

"Will they still be angry when we say that before the philosophic
class becomes master of a city, there will be no rest from ills either
for city or citizens nor will the regime about which we tell tales in
speech get its completion in deed?"

"Perhaps less," he said.

"If you please," I said, "let's not say that they are less angry but
that they have become in every way gentle and have been persuaded, so   502 *a*
that from shame, if nothing else, they will agree."

"Most certainly," he said.

"Now, let's assume they have been persuaded of this," I said.
"And, as to the next point, will anyone argue that there is no chance
that children of kings, or of men who hold power, could be born
philosophers by their natures?"

"There won't," he said, "even be one who will argue that."

"And if such men came into being, can anyone say that it's quite
necessary that they be corrupted? That it's hard to save them, we too
admit. But that in all of time not one of all of them could ever be saved,   *b*
is there anyone who would argue that?"

"How could he?"

502 b   "But surely," I said, "the birth of one, if he has an obedient city, is sufficient for perfecting everything that is now doubted."

"Yes," he said, "one is sufficient."

"For, of course, when a ruler sets down the laws and practices that we have gone through," I said, "it's surely not impossible that the citizens be willing to carry them out."

"Not at all."

"But, then, is it anything wonderful or impossible if others also have the same opinions as we do?"

c   "I don't suppose so," he said.

"And further, that it is best, granted it's possible, we have, I believe, already gone through sufficiently."

"Yes, it was sufficient."

"Now, then, as it seems, it turns out for us that what we are saying about lawgiving is best if it could come to be, and that it is hard for it to come to be; not, however, impossible."

"Yes," he said, "that's the way it turns out."

"Now that this discussion has after considerable effort reached an end, mustn't we next speak about what remains—in what way and as a

d   result of what studies and practices the saviors will take their place within our regime for us and at what ages each will take up each study?"

"Indeed we must," he said.

"It hasn't," I said, "turned out to have been very wise of me to have left aside previously the unpleasantness about the possession of women, nor to have left aside procreation, as well as the institution of the rulers either. I did so because I knew that the wholly and completely true institution is a thing both likely to arouse resentment and hard to bring into being. But, as it was, the necessity of going through

e   these things nonetheless arose. Well, what particularly concerns women and children has been completed, but what concerns the rulers must be pursued as it were from the beginning. We were saying, if you re-

503 a   member, that they must show themselves to be lovers of the city, tested in pleasures and pains, and that they must show that they don't cast out this conviction in labors or fears or any other reverse. The man who's unable to be so must be rejected, while the one who emerges altogether pure, like gold tested in fire, must be set up as ruler and be given gifts and prizes both when he is alive and after he has died. These were the kinds of things that were being said as the

b   argument, covering its face, sneaked by, for fear of setting in motion what now confronts us."

"What you say is quite true," he said. "I do remember."

"My friend, I shrank from saying what has now been dared

anyhow," I said. "And let's now dare to say this: philosophers must be   *503 b*
established as the most precise[29] guardians."

"Yes, let it be said," he said.

"Then bear in mind that you'll probably have but a few. For the
parts of the nature that we described as a necessary condition for them
are rarely willing to grow together in the same place; rather its many
parts grow forcibly separated from each other."

"How do you mean?" he said.   *c*

"You know that natures that are good at learning, have memories,
are shrewd and quick and everything else that goes along with these
qualities, and are as well full of youthful fire and magnificence—such
natures don't willingly grow together with understandings that choose
orderly lives which are quiet and steady. Rather the men who possess
them are carried away by their quickness wherever chance leads and all
steadiness goes out from them."

"What you say is true," he said.

"And, on the other hand, those steady, not easily changeable
dispositions, which one would be inclined to count on as trustworthy   *d*
and which in war are hard to move in the face of fears, act the same
way in the face of studies. They are hard to move and hard to teach, as
if they had become numb;[30] and they are filled with sleep and yawn-
ing when they must work through anything of the sort."

"That's so," he said.

"But we are saying that this nature must participate in both in
good and fair fashion, or it mustn't be given a share in the most precise
education, in honor, or in rule."

"Right," he said.

"Don't you suppose this will be rare?"

"Of course."

"Then it must be tested in the labors, fears, and pleasures we   *e*
mentioned then; and moreover—what we passed over then but mention now—it must also be given gymnastic in many studies to see
whether it will be able to bear the greatest studies, or whether it will
turn out to be a coward, as some turn out to be cowards in the other   *504 a*
things."

"Well, that's surely the proper way to investigate it," he said.
"But exactly what kinds of studies do you mean by the greatest?"

"You, of course, remember," I said, "that by separating out three
forms in the soul we figured out what justice, moderation, courage, and
wisdom each is."

"If I didn't remember," he said, "it would be just for me not to
hear the rest."

"And also what was said before that?"

504 a   "What was it?"

b   "We were, I believe, saying that in order to get the finest possible look at these things another and longer road around would be required, and to the man who took it they would become evident, but that proofs on a level with what had been said up to then could be tacked on. And you all said that that would suffice. And so, you see, the statements made at that time were, as it looks to me, deficient in precision. If they were satisfactory to you, only you can tell."

      "They were satisfactory to me, within measure," he said. "And it looks as though they were for the others too."

c   "My friend," I said, "a measure in such things, which in any way falls short of that which *is*, is no measure at all. For nothing incomplete is the measure of anything. But certain men are sometimes of the opinion that this question has already been adequately disposed of and that there is no need to seek further."

      "Easygoingness," he said, "causes quite a throng of men to have this experience."

      "Well," I said, "it's an experience a guardian of a city and of laws hardly needs."

      "That's likely," he said.

      "Well then, my comrade," I said, "such a man must go the longer
d   way around and labor no less at study than at gymnastic, or else, as we were just saying, he'll never come to the end of the greatest and most fitting study."

      "So these aren't the greatest," he said, "but there is something yet greater than justice and the other things we went through?"

      "There is both something greater," I said, "and also even for these very virtues it won't do to look at a sketch, as we did a while ago, but their most perfect elaboration must not be stinted. Or isn't it ridiculous
e   to make every effort so that other things of little worth be as precise and pure as can be, while not deeming the greatest things worth the greatest precision?"

      "That's a very worthy thought," he said. "However, as to what you mean by the greatest study and what it concerns, do you think anyone is going to let you go without asking what it is?"

      "Certainly not," I said. "Just ask. At all events, it's not a few times already that you have heard it; but now you are either not think-
505 a   ing or have it in mind to get hold of me again and cause me trouble. I suppose it's rather the latter, since you have many times heard that the *idea* of the good is the greatest study and that it's by availing oneself of it along with just things and the rest that they become useful and beneficial. And now you know pretty certainly that I'm going to say

this and, besides this, that we don't have sufficient knowledge of it.   *505 a*
And, if we don't know it and should have ever so much knowledge
of the rest without this, you know that it's no profit to us, just as there
would be none in possessing something in the absence of the good.
Or do you suppose it's of any advantage to possess everything except   *b*
what's good? Or to be prudent about everything else in the absence of
the good, while being prudent about nothing fine and good?"

"No, by Zeus," he said. "I don't."

"And, further, you also know that in the opinion of the many the
good is pleasure, while in that of the more refined it is prudence."

"Of course."

"And, my friend, that those who believe this can't point out what
kind of prudence it is, but are finally compelled to say 'about the
good.'"

"And it's quite ridiculous of them," he said.

"Of course, it is," I said, "if they reproach us for not knowing the   *c*
good, and then speak as though we did know. For they say it is prudence about the good as though we, in turn, grasped what they mean
when they utter the name of the good."

"Very true," he said.

"And what about those who define pleasure as good? Are they any
less full of confusion than the others? Or aren't they too compelled to
agree that there are bad pleasures?"

"Indeed they are."

"Then I suppose the result is that they agree that the same things
are good and bad, isn't it?"

"Of course."   *d*

"Isn't it clear that there are many great disputes about it?"

"Of course."

"And what about this? Isn't it clear that many men would choose
to do, possess, and enjoy the reputation for things that are opined to be
just and fair, even if they aren't, while, when it comes to good things,
no one is satisfied with what is opined to be so but each seeks the things
that *are*, and from here on out everyone despises the opinion?"

"Quite so," he said.

"Now this is what every soul pursues and for the sake of which it
does everything. The soul divines that it is something but is at a loss   *e*
about it and unable to get a sufficient grasp of just what it is, or to have
a stable trust such as it has about the rest. And because this is so, the
soul loses any profit there might have been in the rest. Will we say that
even those best men in the city, into whose hands we put everything,
must be thus in the dark about a thing of this kind and importance?"   *506 a*

506 a

"Least of all," he said.

"I suppose, at least," I said, "that just and fair things, when it isn't known in what way they are good, won't have gotten themselves a guardian who's worth very much in the man who doesn't know this. I divine that no one will adequately know the just and fair things themselves before this is known."

"That's a fine divination of yours," he said.

"Won't our regime be perfectly ordered if such a guardian, one who knows these things, oversees it?"

b

"Necessarily," he said. "But now, Socrates, do you say that the good is knowledge, or pleasure, or something else beside these?"

what is Good?

"Here's a real man!" I said. "It's been pretty transparent all along that other people's opinions about these things wouldn't be enough for you."

"It doesn't appear just to me, Socrates," he said, "to be ready to tell other people's convictions but not your own when you have spent so

c

much time occupied with these things."

"And what about this?" I said. "Is it your opinion that it's just to speak about what one doesn't know as though one knew?"

"Not at all as though one knew," he said; "however, one ought to be willing to state what one supposes, as one's supposition."

"What?" I said. "Haven't you noticed that all opinions without knowledge are ugly? The best of them are blind. Or do men who opine something true without intelligence seem to you any different from blind men who travel the right road?"

"No," he said.

"Do you want to see ugly things, blind and crooked, when it's

d

possible to hear bright and fair ones from others?"

"No, in the name of Zeus, Socrates," said Glaucon. "You're not going to withdraw when you are, as it were, at the end. It will satisfy us even if you go through the good just as you went through justice, moderation and the rest."

"It will quite satisfy me too, my comrade," I said. "But I fear I'll not be up to it, and in my eagerness I'll cut a graceless figure and have to pay the penalty by suffering ridicule. But, you blessed men, let's

e

leave aside for the time being what the good itself is—for it looks to me as though it's out of the range of our present thrust to attain the opinions I now hold about it. But I'm willing to tell what looks like a child of the good and most similar to it, if you please, or if not, to let it go."

"Do tell," he said. "Another time you'll pay us what's due on the father's narrative."

507 a

"I could wish," I said, "that I were able to pay and you were able

to receive it itself, and not just the interest, as is the case now. Anyhow,   507 *a*
receive this interest and child of the good itself. But be careful that I
don't in some way unwillingly deceive you in rendering the account of
the interest fraudulent."³¹

"We'll be as careful as we possibly can," he said. "Just speak."

"Yes," I said, "as soon as I've come to an agreement and reminded you of the things stated here earlier and already often repeated
on other occasions."

"What are they?" he said.   *b*

"We both assert that there are," I said, "and distinguish in speech,
many fair things, many good things, and so on for each kind of thing."

"Yes, so we do."   .

"And we also assert that there is a fair itself, a good itself, and so
on for all the things that we then set down as many. Now, again, we
refer them to one *idea* of each as though the *idea* were one; and we address it as that which really *is*."

"That's so."

"And, moreover, we say that the former are seen but not intellected, while the *ideas* are intellected but not seen."

"That's entirely certain."

"With what part of ourselves do we see the things seen?"   *c*

"With the sight," he said.

"Isn't it with hearing," I said, "that we hear the things heard, and
with the other senses that we sense all that is sensed?"

"Of course."

"Have you," I said, "reflected on how lavish the craftsman of the
senses was in the fabrication of the power of seeing and being seen?"

"Not very much," he said.

"Well consider it in this way. Is there a need for another class of
thing in addition to hearing and sound in order that the one hear and
the other be heard—a third thing in the absence of which the one won't   *d*
hear and the other won't be heard?"

"No," he said.

"I suppose," I said, "that there are not many other things, not to
say none, that need anything of the kind. Or can you tell of any?"

"Not I," he said.

"Don't you notice that the power of seeing and what's seen do
have such a need?"

"How?"

"Surely, when sight is in the eyes and the man possessing them
tries to make use of it, and color is present in what is to be seen, in the
absence of a third class of thing whose nature is specifically directed to

507 e   this very purpose, you know that the sight will see nothing and the colors will be unseen."

"What class of thing are you speaking of?" he said.

"It's that which you call light," I said.

"What you say is true," he said.

"Then the sense of sight and the power of being seen are yoked together with a yoke that, by the measure of an *idea* by no

508 a   means insignificant, is more honorable than the yokes uniting other teams, if light is not without honor."

"But, of course," he said, "it's far from being without honor."

"Which of the gods in heaven can you point to as the lord responsible for this, whose light makes our sight see in the finest way and the seen things seen?"

"The very one you and the others would also point to," he said. "For it's plain your question refers to the sun."

"Is sight, then, naturally related to this god in the following way?"

"How?"

"Neither sight itself nor that in which it comes to be—what we

b   call the eye—is the sun."

"Surely not."

"But I suppose it is the most sunlike[32] of the organs of the senses."

"Yes, by far."

"Doesn't it get the power it has as a sort of overflow from the sun's treasury?"

"Most certainly."

"And the sun isn't sight either, is it, but as its cause is seen by sight itself?"

"That's so," he said.

"Well, then," I said, "say that the sun is the offspring of the good I mean—an offspring the good begot in a proportion with itself: as the

c   good is in the intelligible region with respect to intelligence and what is intellected, so the sun is in the visible region with respect to sight and what is seen."

"How?" he said. "Explain it to me still further."

"You know," I said, "that eyes, when one no longer turns them to those things over whose colors the light of day extends but to those over which the gleams of night extend, are dimmed and appear nearly blind as though pure sight were not in them."

"Quite so," he said.

d   "But, I suppose, when one turns them on those things illuminated by the sun, they see clearly and sight shows itself to be in these same eyes."

"Surely."   *508 d*

"Well, then, think that the soul is also characterized in this way. When it fixes itself on that which is illumined by truth and that which *is*, it intellects, knows, and appears to possess intelligence. But when it fixes itself on that which is mixed with darkness, on coming into being and passing away, it opines and is dimmed, changing opinions up and down, and seems at such times not to possess intelligence."

"Yes, that's the way it seems."

"Therefore, say that what provides the truth to the things known   *e*
and gives the power to the one who knows, is the *idea* of the good. And, as the cause of the knowledge and truth, you can understand it to be a thing known; but, as fair as these two are—knowledge and truth—if you believe that it is something different from them and still fairer than they, your belief will be right. As for knowledge and t.uth, just as in the other region it is right to hold light and sight sunlike, but   *509 a*
to believe them to be sun is not right; so, too, here, to hold these two to be like the good is right, but to believe that either of them is the good is not right. The condition which characterizes the good must receive still greater honor."

"You speak of an overwhelming beauty," he said, "if it provides knowledge and truth but is itself beyond them in beauty. You surely don't mean it is pleasure."

"Hush,[33] Glaucon," I said. "But consider its image still further in this way."

"How?"   *b*

"I suppose you'll say the sun not only provides what is seen with the power of being seen, but also with generation, growth, and nourishment although it itself isn't generation."

"Of course."

"Therefore, say that not only being known is present in the things known as a consequence of the good, but also existence and being are in them besides as a result of it, although the good isn't being but is still beyond being, exceeding it in dignity[34] and power."

And Glaucon, quite ridiculously, said, "Apollo, what a demonic   *c*
excess."

"You," I said, "are responsible for compelling me to tell my opinions about it."

"And don't under any conditions stop," he said, "at least until you have gone through the likeness with the sun, if you are leaving anything out."

"But, of course," I said, "I am leaving out a throng of things."

"Well," he said, "don't leave even the slightest thing aside."

509 c   "I suppose I will leave out quite a bit," I said. "But all the same, insofar as it's possible at present, I'll not leave anything out willingly."

"Don't," he said.

d   "Well, then," I said, "conceive that, as we say, these two things *are*, and that the one is king of the intelligible class and region, while the other is king of the visible. I don't say 'of the heaven' so as not to seem to you to be playing the sophist with the name.[35] Now, do you have these two forms, visible and intelligible?"

"I do."

"Then, take a line cut in two unequal segments, one for the class that is seen, the other for the class that is intellected—and go on and cut each segment in the same ratio. Now, in terms of relative clarity and obscurity, you'll have one segment in the visible part for

e   images. I mean by images first shadows, then appearances produced in

510 a   water and in all close-grained, smooth, bright things, and everything of the sort, if you understand."

"I do understand."

"Then in the other segment put that of which this first is the likeness—the animals around us, and everything that grows, and the whole class of artifacts."

"I put them there," he said.

"And would you also be willing," I said, "to say that with respect to truth or lack of it, as the opinable is distinguished from the knowable, so the likeness is distinguished from that of which it is the likeness?"

b   "I would indeed," he said.

"Now, in its turn, consider also how the intelligible section should be cut."

"How?"

"Like this: in one part of it a soul, using as images the things that were previously imitated, is compelled to investigate on the basis of hypotheses and makes its way not to a beginning but to an end; while in the other part it makes its way to a beginning[36] that is free from hypotheses;[37] starting out from hypothesis and without the images used in the other part, by means of forms themselves it makes its inquiry through them."

"I don't," he said, "sufficiently understand what you mean here."

c   "Let's try again," I said. "You'll understand more easily after this introduction. I suppose you know that the men who work in geometry, calculation, and the like treat as known the odd and the even, the figures, three forms of angles, and other things akin to these in each kind of inquiry. These things they make hypotheses and don't think it worthwhile to give any further account of them to themselves or others,

as though they were clear to all. Beginning from them, they go ahead   *510 d*
with their exposition of what remains and end consistently at the object
toward which their investigation was directed."

"Most certainly, I know that," he said.

"Don't you also know that they use visible forms besides and
make their arguments about them, not thinking about them but about
those others that they are like? They make the arguments for the sake
of the square itself and the diagonal itself, not for the sake of the
diagonal they draw, and likewise with the rest. These things themselves   *e*
that they mold and draw, of which there are shadows and images in
water, they now use as images, seeking to see those things themselves,
that one can see in no other way than with thought."

"What you say is true," he said.   *511 a*

"Well, then, this is the form I said was intelligible. However, a
soul in investigating it is compelled to use hypotheses, and does not go
to a beginning because it is unable to step out above the hypotheses.
And it uses as images those very things of which images are made by
the things below, and in comparison with which they are opined to be
clear and are given honor."

"I understand," he said, "that you mean what falls under geome-   *b*
try and its kindred arts."

"Well, then, go on to understand that by the other segment of the
intelligible I mean that which argument itself grasps with the power of
dialectic, making the hypotheses not beginnings but really hypotheses—that is, steppingstones and springboards—in order to reach
what is free from hypothesis at the beginning of the whole.[38] When
it has grasped this, argument now depends on that which depends on
this beginning and in such fashion goes back down again to an end;
making no use of anything sensed in any way, but using forms them-   *c*
selves, going through forms to forms, it ends in forms too."

"I understand," he said, "although not adequately—for in my
opinion it's an enormous task you speak of—that you wish to distinguish
that part of what is and is intelligible contemplated by the knowledge of dialectic as being clearer than that part contemplated by what
are called the arts. The beginnings in the arts are hypotheses; and although those who behold their objects are compelled to do so with
the thought and not the senses, these men—because they don't
consider them by going up to a beginning, but rather on the basis of
hypotheses—these men, in my opinion, don't possess intelligence   *d*
with respect to the objects, even though they are, given a beginning, intelligible; and you seem to me to call the habit of geometers
and their likes thought and not intelligence, indicating that thought
is something between opinion and intelligence."

511 d   "You have made a most adequate exposition," I said. "And, along with me, take these four affections arising in the soul in relation to the four segments: intellection in relation to the highest one, and thought in

e   relation to the second; to the third assign trust, and to the last imagination.[39] Arrange them in a proportion, and believe that as the segments to which they correspond participate in truth, so they participate in clarity."

      "I understand," he said. "And I agree and arrange them as you say."

BOOK VII

"Next, then," I said, "make an image of our nature in its education and want of education, likening it to a condition of the following kind. See human beings as though they were in an underground cave-like dwelling with its entrance, a long one, open to the light across the whole width of the cave. They are in it from childhood with their legs and necks in bonds so that they are fixed, seeing only in front of them, unable because of the bond to turn their heads all the way around. Their light is from a fire burning far above and behind them. Between the fire and the prisoners there is a road above, along which see a wall, built like the partitions puppet-handlers set in front of the human beings and over which they show the puppets."

"I see," he said.

"Then also see along this wall human beings carrying all sorts of artifacts, which project above the wall, and statues of men and other animals wrought from stone, wood, and every kind of material; as is to be expected, some of the carriers utter sounds while others are silent."

"It's a strange image," he said, "and strange prisoners you're telling of."

"They're like us," I said. "For in the first place, do you suppose such men would have seen anything of themselves and one another other than the shadows cast by the fire on the side of the cave facing them?"

515 a
   b

"How could they," he said, "if they had been compelled to keep their heads motionless throughout life?"

"And what about the things that are carried by? Isn't it the same with them?"

"Of course."

"If they were able to discuss things with one another, don't you believe they would hold that they are naming these things going by before them that they see?"[1]

"Necessarily."

"And what if the prison also had an echo from the side facing them? Whenever one of the men passing by happens to utter a sound, do you suppose they would believe that anything other than the passing shadow was uttering the sound?"

"No, by Zeus," he said. "I don't."

   c

"Then most certainly," I said, "such men would hold that the truth is nothing other than the shadows of artificial things."

"Most necessarily," he said.

"Now consider," I said, "what their release and healing from bonds and folly would be like if something of this sort were by nature to happen to them. Take a man who is released and suddenly compelled to stand up, to turn his neck around, to walk and look up toward the light; and who, moreover, in doing all this is in pain and, because he is dazzled, is unable to make out those things whose shadows he saw

   d

before. What do you suppose he'd say if someone were to tell him that before he saw silly nothings, while now, because he is somewhat nearer to what *is* and more turned toward beings, he sees more correctly; and, in particular, showing him each of the things that pass by, were to compel the man to answer his questions about what they are? Don't you suppose he'd be at a loss and believe that what was seen before is truer than what is now shown?"

"Yes," he said, "by far."

   e

"And, if he compelled him to look at the light itself, would his eyes hurt and would he flee, turning away to those things that he is able to make out and hold them to be really clearer than what is being shown?"

"So he would," he said.

"And if," I said, "someone dragged him away from there by force along the rough, steep, upward way and didn't let him go before he had dragged him out into the light of the sun, wouldn't he be distressed and

516 a

annoyed at being so dragged? And when he came to the light, wouldn't he have his eyes full of its beam and be unable to see even one of the things now said to be true?"

"No, he wouldn't," he said, "at least not right away."   516 a

"Then I suppose he'd have to get accustomed, if he were going to see what's up above. At first he'd most easily make out the shadows; and after that the phantoms of the human beings and the other things in water; and, later, the things themselves. And from there he could turn to beholding the things in heaven and heaven itself, more easily at night—looking at the light of the stars and the moon—than by   b day—looking at the sun and sunlight."

"Of course."

"Then finally I suppose he would be able to make out the sun—not its appearances in water or some alien place, but the sun itself by itself in its own region—and see what it's like."

"Necessarily," he said.

"And after that he would already be in a position to conclude about it that this is the source of the seasons and the years, and is the steward of all things in the visible place, and is in a certain way the   c cause of all those things he and his companions had been seeing."

"It's plain," he said, "that this would be his next step."

"What then? When he recalled his first home and the wisdom there, and his fellow prisoners in that time, don't you suppose he would consider himself happy for the change and pity the others?"

"Quite so."

"And if in that time there were among them any honors, praises, and prizes for the man who is sharpest at making out the things that go by, and most remembers which of them are accustomed to pass before, which after, and which at the same time as others, and who is   d thereby most able to divine what is going to come, in your opinion would he be desirous of them and envy those who are honored and hold power among these men? Or, rather, would he be affected as Homer says and want very much 'to be on the soil, a serf to another man, to a portionless man,'[2] and to undergo anything whatsoever rather than to opine those things and live that way?"

"Yes," he said, "I suppose he would prefer to undergo everything   e rather than live that way."

"Now reflect on this too," I said. "If such a man were to come down again and sit in the same seat, on coming suddenly from the sun wouldn't his eyes get infected with darkness?"

"Very much so," he said.

"And if he once more had to compete with those perpetual prisoners in forming judgments about those shadows while his vision was still dim, before his eyes had recovered, and if the time   517 a needed for getting accustomed were not at all short, wouldn't he be

517 a

Other prisoners would kill the person who tried to free them

the source of laughter, and wouldn't it be said of him that he went up and came back with his eyes corrupted, and that it's not even worth trying to go up? And if they were somehow able to get their hands on and kill the man who attempts to release and lead up, wouldn't they kill him?"

"No doubt about it," he said.

b

"Well, then, my dear Glaucon," I said, "this image as a whole must be connected with what was said before. Liken the domain revealed through sight to the prison home, and the light of the fire in it to the sun's power; and, in applying the going up and the seeing of what's above to the soul's journey up to the intelligible place, you'll not mistake my expectation, since you desire to hear it. A god doubtless knows if it happens to be true. At all events, this is the way the phenomena look to me: in the knowable the last thing to be seen, and

c

that with considerable effort, is the *idea* of the good; but once seen, it must be concluded that this is in fact the cause of all that is right and fair in everything—in the visible it gave birth to light and its sovereign; in the intelligible, itself sovereign, it provided truth and intelligence —and that the man who is going to act prudently in private or in public must see it."

"I, too, join you in supposing that," he said, "at least in the way I can."

"Come, then," I said, "and join me in supposing this, too, and don't be surprised that the men who get to that point aren't willing to mind the business of human beings, but rather that their souls are al-

d

ways eager to spend their time above. Surely that's likely, if indeed this, too, follows the image of which I told before."

"Of course it's likely," he said.

"And what about this? Do you suppose it is anything surprising," I said, "if a man, come from acts of divine contemplation to the human evils, is graceless and looks quite ridiculous when—with his sight still dim and before he has gotten sufficiently accustomed to the surrounding darkness—he is compelled in courts or elsewhere to contest about the shadows of the just or the representations of which they are the

e

shadows, and to dispute about the way these things are understood by men who have never seen justice itself?"

"It's not at all surprising," he said.

518 a

2 disturbances

"But if a man were intelligent," I said, "he would remember that there are two kinds of disturbances of the eyes, stemming from two sources—when they have been transferred from light to darkness and when they have been transferred from darkness to light. And if he held that these same things happen to a soul too, whenever he saw one that is confused and unable to make anything out, he wouldn't laugh

without reasoning but would go on to consider whether, come from a   518 a
brighter life, it is in darkness for want of being accustomed, or whether,
going from greater lack of learning to greater brightness, it is dazzled
by the greater brilliance. And then he would deem the first soul happy   b
for its condition and its life, while he would pity the second. And, if he
wanted to laugh at the second soul, his laughing in this case would be
less a laugh of scorn than would his laughing at the soul which
has come from above out of the light."

"What you say is quite sensible," he said.

"Then, if this is true," I said, "we must hold the following about
these things: education is not what the professions of certain men assert
it to be. They presumably assert that they put into the soul knowledge
that isn't in it, as though they were putting sight into blind eyes."   c

"Yes," he said, "they do indeed assert that."

"But the present argument, on the other hand," I said, "indicates
that this power is in the soul of each,[3] and that the instrument with
which each learns—just as an eye is not able to turn toward the light
from the dark without the whole body—must be turned around from
that which *is coming into being* together with the whole soul until it is
able to endure looking at that which *is* and the brightest part of that
which *is*. And we affirm that this is the good, don't we?"   d

"Yes."

"There would, therefore," I said, "be an art of this turning
around, concerned with the way in which this power can most easily
and efficiently be turned around, not an art of producing sight in it.
Rather, this art takes as given that sight is there, but not rightly turned
nor looking at what it ought to look at, and accomplishes this object."

"So it seems," he said.

"Therefore, the other virtues of a soul, as they are called, are probably somewhat close to those of the body. For they are really not there
beforehand and are later produced by habits and exercises, while the   e
virtue of exercising prudence is more than anything somehow more divine, it seems; it never loses its power, but according to the way it is
turned, it becomes useful and helpful or, again, useless and harmful. Or
haven't you yet reflected about the men who are said to be vicious but   519 a
wise, how shrewdly their petty soul sees and how sharply it distinguishes those things toward which it is turned, showing that it
doesn't have poor vision although it is compelled to serve vice; so
that the sharper it sees, the more evil it accomplishes?"

"Most certainly," he said.

"However," I said, "if this part of such a nature were trimmed
in earliest childhood and its ties of kinship with becoming were cut
off—like leaden weights, which eating and such pleasures as well as   b

519 b   their refinements naturally attach to the soul and turn its vision downward—if, I say, it were rid of them and turned around toward the true
things, this same part of the same human beings would also see them
most sharply, just as it does those things toward which it now is
turned."

"It's likely," he said.

"And what about this? Isn't it likely," I said, "and necessary, as a
consequence of what was said before, that those who are without
education and experience of truth would never be adequate stewards of

c   a city, nor would those who have been allowed to spend their time in
education continuously to the end—the former because they don't have
any single goal in life at which they must aim in doing everything they
do in private or in public, the latter because they won't be willing to
act, believing they have emigrated to a colony on the Isles of the
Blessed[4] while they are still alive?"

"True," he said.

"Then our job as founders," I said, "is to compel the best natures
to go to the study which we were saying before is the greatest, to see the

d   good and to go up that ascent; and, when they have gone up and seen
sufficiently, not to permit them what is now permitted."

"What's that?"

"To remain there," I said, "and not be willing to go down again
among those prisoners or share their labors and honors, whether they
be slighter or more serious."

"What?" he said. "Are we to do them an injustice, and make them
live a worse life when a better is possible for them?"

e   "My friend, you have again forgotten," I said, "that it's not the
concern of law that any one class in the city fare exceptionally well, but
it contrives to bring this about in the city as a whole, harmonizing the
citizens by persuasion and compulsion, making them share with one

520 a   another the benefit that each is able to bring to the commonwealth. And it produces such men in the city not in order to let them
turn whichever way each wants, but in order that it may use them in
binding the city together."

"That's true," he said. "I did forget."

"Well, then, Glaucon," I said, "consider that we won't be doing
injustice to the philosophers who come to be among us, but rather that
we will say just things to them while compelling them besides to care
for and guard the others. We'll say that when such men come to be

b   in the other cities it is fitting for them not to participate in the labors of
those cities. For they grow up spontaneously against the will of the
regime in each; and a nature that grows by itself and doesn't owe its
rearing to anyone has justice on its side when it is not eager to pay off

the price of rearing to anyone. 'But you we have begotten for your- 520*b*
selves and for the rest of the city like leaders and kings in hives; you
have been better and more perfectly educated and are more able to participate in both lives. So you must go down, each in his turn, into the   *c*
common dwelling of the others and get habituated along with them to
seeing the dark things. And, in getting habituated to it, you will see ten
thousand times better than the men there, and you'll know what each of
the phantoms is, and of what it is a phantom, because you have seen the
truth about fair, just, and good things. And thus, the city will be
governed by us and by you in a state of waking, not in a dream as the
many cities nowadays are governed by men who fight over shadows
with one another and form factions for the sake of ruling, as though it
were some great good. But the truth is surely this: that city in which   *d*
those who are going to rule are least eager to rule is necessarily
governed in the way that is best and freest from faction, while the one
that gets the opposite kind of rulers is governed in the opposite
way.'"

whoever wants to rule less will rule best

"Most certainly," he said.

"Do you suppose our pupils will disobey us when they hear this
and be unwilling to join in the labors of the city, each in his turn, while
living the greater part of the time with one another in the pure region?"

"Impossible," he said. "For surely we shall be laying just injunc-   *e*
tions on just men. However, each of them will certainly approach
ruling as a necessary thing—which is the opposite of what is done by
those who now rule in every city."

"That's the way it is, my comrade," I said. "If you discover a life
better than ruling for those who are going to rule, it is possible that   521 *a*
your well-governed city will come into being. For here alone will the
really rich rule, rich not in gold but in those riches required by the happy man, rich in a good and prudent life. But if beggars, men hungering
for want of private goods, go to public affairs supposing that in them
they must seize the good, it isn't possible. When ruling becomes a thing
fought over, such a war—a domestic war, one within the family—destroys these men themselves and the rest of the city as well."

"That's very true," he said.

"Have you," I said, "any other life that despises political offices   *b*
other than that of true philosophy?"

"No, by Zeus," he said. "I don't."

"But men who aren't lovers of ruling must go[5] to it; otherwise.
rival lovers will fight."

"Of course."

521 b

"Who else will you compel to go to the guarding of the city than the men who are most prudent in those things through which a city is best governed, and who have other honors and a better life than the political life?"

"No one else," he said.

c

"Do you want us now to consider in what way such men will come into being and how one will lead them up to the light, just as some men are said to have gone from Hades up to the gods?"[6]

"How could I not want to?" he said.

"Then, as it seems, this wouldn't be the twirling of a shell[7] but the turning of a soul around from a day that is like night to the true day; it is that ascent to what *is* which we shall truly affirm to be philosophy."

"Most certainly."

d

"Then mustn't we consider what studies have such a power?"

"Of course."

"What then, Glaucon, would be a study to draw the soul from becoming to being? And, as I speak, I think of this. Weren't we saying that it's necessary for these men to be champions in war when they are young?"[8]

"Yes, we were saying that."

"Then the study we are seeking must have this further characteristic in addition to the former one."

"What?"

"It mustn't be useless to warlike men."

"Of course, it mustn't," he said, "if that can be."

"Now previously they were educated by us in gymnastic and music."

e

"That was so," he said.

"And gymnastic, of course, is wholly engaged with coming into being and passing away. For it oversees growth and decay in the body."

"It looked that way."

"So it wouldn't be the study we are seeking."

522 a

"No, it wouldn't."

"And is music, so far as we described it before?"

"But it," he said, "was the antistrophe[9] to gymnastic, if you remember. It educated the guardians through habits, transmitting by harmony a certain harmoniousness, not knowledge, and by rhythm a certain rhythmicalness. And connected with it were certain other habits, akin to these, conveyed by speeches, whether they were tales or speeches of a truer sort. But as for a study directed toward something

b

of the sort you are now seeking, there was nothing of the kind in it."

[200]

"Your reminder to me is quite precise," I said. "For, really, it had   *522 b*
nothing of the sort. But Glaucon, you demonic man, what could
there be that is like this? For all the arts surely seemed to be mechanical."

"Certainly they were. And, yet, what other study is left now separate
from music, gymnastic, and the arts?"

"Come, then," I said, "if we have nothing left to take besides
these, let's take something that applies to them all."

"What kind of thing?"

"For example, this common thing that all kinds of art, thought,   *c*
and knowledge use as a supplement to themselves, a thing that it is
necessary for everyone to learn among his first studies."

"What's that?" he said.

"The lowly business," I said, "of distinguishing the one, the two,
and the three. I mean by this, succinctly, number and calculation. Or
isn't it the case with them that every kind of art and knowledge is compelled to participate in them?"

"Very much so," he said.

"The art of war too?" I said.

"Most necessarily," he said.

"At all events," I said, "in the tragedies Palamedes is constantly   *d*
showing up Agamemnon as a most ridiculous general. Or haven't you
noticed that he says that by discovering number he established the
dispositions for the army at Ilium and counted the ships and everything
else, as though before that they were uncounted and Agememnon
didn't know how many feet he had, if he really didn't know how to
count?[10] And, if this is the case, what kind of general do you suppose
he was?"

"A strange one," he said, "if this was true."

"Shall we not then," I said, "set down as a study necessary for a   *e*
warrior the ability to calculate and to number?"

"Most of all," he said, "if he's going to have any professional knowledge of the order of the army, but I should say rather, if he's going to be a
human being."

"Do you," I said, "notice the same thing I do in this study?"

"What?"

"It probably is one of those things we are seeking that by nature   *523 a*
lead to intellection; but no one uses it rightly, as a thing that in every
way is apt to draw men toward being."

"How do you mean?" he said.

"I shall attempt to make at least my opinion plain. Join me in
looking at the things I distinguish for myself as leading or not leading

523 *a*   to what we are speaking of; and agree or disagree so that we may see
more clearly whether this is as I divine it to be."

"Show," he said.

"Here, I show," I said, "if you can make it out, that some objects

b   of sensation do not summon the intellect to the activity of investigation
because they seem to be adequately judged by sense, while others bid it
in every way to undertake a consideration because sense seems to produce nothing healthy."

"Plainly you mean things that appear from far off," he said, "and
shadow paintings."

"You have hardly got my meaning," I said.

"Then, what do you mean?" he said.

"The ones that don't summon the intellect," I said, "are all those

c   that don't at the same time go over to the opposite sensation. But the
ones that do go over I class among those that summon the intellect,
when the sensation doesn't reveal one thing any more than its opposite,
regardless of whether the object strikes the senses from near or far off.
But you will see my meaning more clearly this way: these, we say,
would be three fingers—the smallest, the second, and the middle."[11]

"Certainly," he said.

"Think of them while I'm speaking as if they were being seen up close.
Now consider this about them for me."

"What?"

"Surely each of them looks equally like a finger, and in this

d   respect it makes no difference whether it's seen in the middle or on the
extremes, whether it's white or black, or whether it's thick or thin, or
anything else of the sort. In all these things the soul of the many is not
compelled to ask the intellect what a finger is. For the sight at no point
indicates to the soul that the finger is at the same time the opposite of a
finger."

"No," he said, "it doesn't."

"Then," I said, "it isn't likely that anything of the sort would be

e   apt to summon or awaken the activity of intellect."

"No, it's not likely."

"Now what about this? Does the sight see their bigness and lit-
tleness adequately, and does it make no difference to it whether a finger
lies in the middle or on the extremes? And similarly with the touch, for
thickness and thinness or softness and hardness? And do the other
senses reveal such things without insufficiency? Or doesn't each of

524 *a*   them do the following: first, the sense set over the hard is also compelled to be set over the soft; and it reports to the soul that the same
thing is sensed by it as both hard and soft?"

"So it does," he said.   524 *a*

"Isn't it necessary," I said, "that in such cases the soul be at a loss as to what this sensation indicates by the hard, if it says that the same thing is also soft, and what the sensation of the light and of the heavy indicates by the light and heavy, if it indicates that the heavy is light and the light heavy?"

"Yes, indeed," he said, "these are strange interpretations received   *b* by the soul and require further consideration."

"Therefore," I said, "it's likely that in such cases a soul, summoning calculation and intellect, first tries to determine whether each of the things reported to it is one or two."

"Of course."

"If it appears to be two, won't each of the two appear to be different and to be one?"

"Yes."

"Then, if each is one and both two, the soul will think the two as separate. For it would not think the inseparable as two but as one."   *c*

"Right."

"But sight, too, saw big and little, we say, not separated, however, but mixed up together. Isn't that so?"

"Yes."

"In order to clear this up the intellect was compelled to see big and little, too, not mixed up together but distinguished, doing the opposite of what the sight did."

"True."

"Isn't it from here that it first occurs to us to ask what the big and the little are?"

"That's entirely certain."

"And so, it was on this ground that we called the one intelligible and the other visible."

"Quite right," he said.   *d*

"Well, then, this was what I was just trying to convey in saying that some things are apt to summon thought, while others are not, defining as apt to summon it those that strike the sense at the same time as their opposites, while all those that do not, are not apt to arouse intellection."

"Well, now I understand," he said, "and in my opinion it is so."

"What then? To which of the two do number and the one seem to belong?"

"I can't conceive," he said.

"Figure it out on the basis of what was said before," I said. "For if the one is adequately seen, itself by itself, or is grasped by

524 e   some other sense, it would not draw men toward being, as we were
saying about the finger. But if some opposition to it is always seen at
the same time, so that nothing looks as though it were one more than
the opposite of one, then there would now be need of something to
judge; and in this case, a soul would be compelled to be at a loss and
to make an investigation, setting in motion the intelligence within it,
and to ask what the one itself is. And thus the study of the one would
525 a   be among those apt to lead and turn around toward the contemplation of what *is*."

"Surely," he said, "the sight, with respect to the one, possesses
this characteristic to a very high degree. For we see the same thing at
the same time as both one and as an unlimited multitude."

"If this is the case with the one," I said, "won't it be the same for
all number?"

"Of course."

"And, further, the arts of calculation and number are both wholly
concerned with number."[12]

"Quite so."

b   "Then it looks as if they lead toward truth."

"Preternaturally so."

"Therefore, as it seems, they would be among the studies we are
seeking. It's necessary for a warrior to learn them for the sake of his
dispositions for the army, and for a philosopher because he must rise
up out of becoming and take hold of being or else never become skilled
at calculating."

"That's so," he said.

"And our guardian is both warrior and philosopher."

"Certainly."

"Then it would be fitting, Glaucon, to set this study down in law
and to persuade those who are going to participate in the greatest
c   things in the city to go to calculation and to take it up, not after the
fashion of private men, but to stay with it until they come to the contemplation of the nature of numbers with intellection itself, not practicing it for the sake of buying and selling like merchants or tradesmen,
but for war and for ease of turning the soul itself around from becoming to truth and being."

"What you say is very fine," he said.

"And further," I said, "now that the study of calculation has been
d   mentioned, I recognize how subtle it is and how in many ways it is
useful to us for what we want, if a man practices it for the sake of coming to know and not for trade."

"In what way?" he said.

"In the very way we were just now saying. It leads the soul power-   *525 d*
fully upward and compels it to discuss numbers themselves. It won't at
all permit anyone to propose for discussion numbers that are attached
to visible or tangible bodies. For surely, you know the way of men who
are clever in these things. If in the argument someone attempts to cut
the one itself, they laugh and won't permit it. If you try to break it up   *e*
into small coin, they multiply, taking good care against the one's ever
looking like it were not one but many pieces."

"What you say is very true," he said.

"What, Glaucon, do you suppose, would happen if someone   *526 a*
were to ask them, 'you surprising men, what sort of numbers are
you discussing, in which the one is as your axiom claims it to be—
each one equal to every other one, without the slightest difference
between them, and containing no parts within itself?' What do you
suppose they would answer?"

"I suppose they would answer that they are talking about those
numbers that admit only of being thought and can be grasped in no
other way."

"Do you see, then, my friend," I said, "that it's likely that this   *b*
study is really compulsory for us, since it evidently compels the soul
to use the intellect itself on the truth itself?"

"It most certainly does do that," he said.

"What about this? Have you already observed that men who
are by nature apt at calculation are naturally quick in virtually all
studies, while those who are slow, if they are educated and given
gymnastic in it, all make progress by becoming quicker than they
were, even if they are benefited in no other way?"

"That's so," he said.

"And, further, I don't suppose you would easily find many studies   *c*
that take greater effort in the learning and in the practice than this."

"Certainly not."

"Then, for all these reasons this study shouldn't be neglected, and
the best natures must be educated in it."

"I join my voice to yours," he said.

"Therefore we have settled on this one," I said. "And let's consider whether the study adjoining this one is in any way suitable."

"What is it?" he said. "Or do you mean geometry?"

"That's exactly it," I said.

"As much of it as applies to the business of war is plainly   *d*
suitable," he said. "In pitching camp, assaulting places, gathering the
army together and drawing it up in line, and in all other maneuvers ar-

526 d   mies make in the battle itself and on marches, it would make quite a
difference to a man whether he were skilled in geometry or not."

"However," I said, "for such things only a small portion of
geometry—as of calculation—would suffice. It must be considered
whether its greater and more advanced part tends to make it easier to
e   make out the *idea* of the good. And we say that this tendency is
possessed by everything that compels the soul to turn around to the
region inhabited by the happiest part of what is, which is what the soul
must by all means see."

"What you say is right," he said.

"Then if geometry compels one to look at being, it is suitable; if at
becoming, it is not suitable."

"That is what we affirm."

527 a   "Well, then," I said, "none of those who have even a little experience with geometry will dispute it with us: this kind of knowledge
is exactly the opposite of what is said about it in the arguments of those
who take it up."

"How?" he said.

"In that they surely speak in a way that is as ridiculous as it is
necessary. They speak as though they were men of action and were making
all the arguments for the sake of action, uttering sounds like 'squaring,'
'applying,' 'adding,' and everything of the sort, whereas the whole study is
b   surely pursued for the sake of knowing."

"That's entirely certain," he said.

"Mustn't we also come to an agreement about the following
point?"

"What?"

"That it is for the sake of knowing what is always, and not at all
for what is at any time coming into being and passing away."

"That may well be agreed," he said. "For geometrical knowing is
of what is always."

"Then, you noble man, it would draw the soul toward truth and be
productive of philosophic understanding in directing upward what we
now improperly direct downward."

"It does so," he said, "to the greatest extent possible."

c   "Then to the greatest extent possible," I said, "the men in your
beautiful city[13] must be enjoined in no way to abstain from geometry. For even its by-products aren't slight."

"What are they?" he said.

"What you said about war, of course," I said, "and, in addition,
with respect to finer reception of all studies, we surely know there is a
general and complete difference between the man who has been
devoted to geometry and the one who has not."

"Yes, by Zeus," he said, "the difference is complete."   527 c

"Then, shall we set this down as the second study for the young?"

"Yes," he said, "we shall set it down."

"And what about this? Shall we set astronomy down as the third?   d
Or doesn't it seem to be the thing?"

"It does, at least to me," he said. "A better awareness of seasons, months and years is suitable not only for farming and navigation, but no less so for generalship."

"You are amusing," I said. "You are like a man who is afraid of the many in your not wanting to seem to command useless studies. It's scarcely an ordinary thing, rather it's hard, to trust that in these studies a certain instrument of everyone's soul—one that is destroyed and   e
blinded by other practices—is purified and rekindled, an instrument more important to save than ten thousand eyes. For with it alone is truth seen. To those who share your opinion about this, what you say will seem indescribably good, while all those who have had no awareness at all of it can be expected to believe you are talking non-sense. They see no other benefit from these studies worth mentioning. Consider right here with which of these two kinds of men you are   528 a
discussing. Or are you making the arguments for neither but chiefly for your own sake, without, however, grudging anyone else who might be able to get some profit from them?"

"I choose the latter," he said, "to speak and ask and answer mostly for my own sake."

"Well, then," I said, "retreat a way.[14] What we took up as following geometry just now wasn't right."

"Where was the mistake?" he said.

"After a plane surface," I said, "we went ahead and took a solid in motion before taking it up by itself. But the right way is to take up   b
the third dimension[15] next in order after the second, and this is surely the dimension of cubes and what participates in depth."

"Yes, it is," he said. "But, Socrates, it doesn't seem to have been discovered yet."[16]

"Of that," I said, "there are two causes. Because no city holds it in honor, it is feebly sought due to its difficulty. And those who seek for it need a supervisor, without whom they would not find it. And, in the first place, he's hard to come by; and then, even when he's there, as things stand he wouldn't be obeyed by those given to seeking it because of their high opinion of themselves. But if a whole city should join in   c
supervising it and take the lead in honoring it, these men would obey; and, with it being continuously and eagerly sought for, its character would come to light; for even now, although it is despised and cut short by the many, and by those who seek it, since they have no account to

528 c   give of the way it is useful, nevertheless in the face of all this it grows
per force, due to its charm. So it wouldn't be at all surprising if it came
to light."

d   "Yes, indeed," he said, "it is exceptionally charming. But tell me
more clearly what you meant just now; you presumably set geometry
down as that which treats of the plane."

"Yes," I said.

"Then," he said, "at first you set down astronomy after geometry,
but later you withdrew."

"My haste to go through everything quickly is the cause of my
being slowed down," I said. "The investigation of the dimension with
depth was next in order, but, due to the ridiculous state of the search
for it, I skipped over it after geometry and said astronomy, which treats
e   the motion of what has depth."

"What you say is right," he said.

"Well, then," I said, "as the fourth study let's set down astronomy, assuming that the study that is now being left aside will be
present if a city pursues it."

"That's likely," he said. "And on the basis of the reproach you
just made me for my vulgar praise of astronomy, Socrates, now I shall
529 a   praise it in the way that you approach it. In my opinion it's plain to
everyone that astronomy compels the soul to see what's above and leads
it there away from the things here."

"Perhaps it's plain to everyone except me," I said. "In my
opinion, that's not the way it is."

"Then how is it?" he said.

"As it is taken up now by those who lead men up to philosophy, it
has quite an effect in causing the soul to look downward."

"How do you mean?" he said.

"In my opinion," I said, "it's no ignoble conception you have for
yourself of what the study of the things above is. Even if a man were to
b   learn something by tilting his head back and looking at decorations on
a ceiling, you would probably believe he contemplates with his intellect
and not his eyes. Perhaps your belief is a fine one and mine innocent. I,
for my part, am unable to hold that any study makes a soul look upward other than the one that concerns what *is* and is invisible. And if a
man, gaping up[17] or squinting down, attempts to learn something of
sensible things, I would deny that he ever learns—for there is no
c   knowledge of such things—or that his soul looks up, rather than down,
even if he learns while floating on his back on land or sea."

"I am paying the just penalty," he said. "You are right in reproaching me. But just what did you mean when you said that

astronomy must be studied in a way contrary to the one in which   529 *c*
they now study it, if it's going to be studied in a way that's helpful
for what we are talking about?"

"As follows," I said. "These decorations in the heaven, since they
are embroidered on a visible ceiling, may be believed to be the fairest
and most precise of such things; but they fall far short of the true ones,   *d*
those movements in which the really fast and the really slow—in true
number and in all the true figures—are moved with respect to one
another and in their turn move what is contained in them. They, of
course, must be grasped by argument and thought, not sight. Or do you
suppose otherwise?"

"Not at all," he said.

"Therefore," I said, "the decoration in the heaven must be used as
patterns for the sake of learning these other things, just as if one were
to come upon diagrams exceptionally carefully drawn and worked out   *e*
by Daedalus or some other craftsman or painter. A man experienced in
geometry would, on seeing such things, presumably believe that they
are fairest in their execution but that it is ridiculous to consider them
seriously as though one were to grasp the truth about equals, doubles,
or any other proportion in them."   530 *a*

"How could it be anything but ridiculous?" he said.

"Then," I said, "don't you suppose that a man who is really an as-
tronomer will have the same persuasion in looking at the movements of
the stars? He will hold that the craftsman[18] of heaven composed it
and what's in it as beautifully as such works can be composed. But as
for the proportion of night to day, of these to a month, of a month to a
year, and of the rest of the stars to these and to one another, don't you
think he will consider strange the man who holds that these are always   *b*
the same and deviate in no way at all? For these things are connected
with body and are visible. Hence won't he consider it strange to seek in
every way to grasp their truth?"

"That is my opinion," he said, "at least now that I am listening to
you."

"Therefore," I said, "by the use of problems, as in geometry, we
shall also pursue astronomy; and we shall let the things in the heaven
go, if by really taking part in astronomy we are going to convert the
prudence by nature in the soul from uselessness to usefulness."   *c*

"The task you prescribe," he said, "is many times greater than
what is now done in astronomy."

"And," I said, "I suppose our prescriptions in the rest will also be
of the same kind, if we are to be of any help as lawgivers. But have you
any suitable study to suggest?"

530 c

"No, I haven't," he said, "at least not right now."

"However," I said, "motion presents itself not in one form but
d   several, as I suppose. Perhaps whoever is wise will be able to tell them
all, but those that are evident even to us are two."

"What are they?"

"In addition to astronomy," I said, "there is its antistrophe."

"What's that?"

"It is probable," I said, "that as the eyes are fixed on astronomy,
so the ears are fixed on harmonic movement, and these two kinds of
knowledge are in a way akin, as the Pythagoreans say and we, Glaucon,
agree. Or what shall we do?"

"That," he said.

e   "Then," I said, "since it's a big job, we'll inquire of the
Pythagoreans what they mean about them and if there is anything else
besides them. But throughout all of this we shall keep a guard over our
interest."

"What's that?"

"That those whom we shall be rearing should never attempt to
learn anything imperfect, anything that doesn't always come out at the
point where everything ought to arrive, as we were just saying about as-
531 a   tronomy. Or don't you know that they do something similar with harmony too? For, measuring the heard accords and sounds against one
another, they labor without profit, like the astronomers."[19]

"Yes, by the gods," he said, "and how ridiculous they are. They
name certain notes 'dense'[20] and set their ears alongside, as though
they were hunting a voice from the neighbors' house. Some say they
distinctly hear still another note in between and that this is the smallest
interval by which the rest must be measured, while others insist that it
b   is like those already sounded. Both put ears before the intelligence."

"You mean," I said, "those good men who harass the strings and
put them to the torture, racking them on the pegs. I won't prolong the
image with the blows struck by the plectrum, and the accusation
against the strings, and their denial and imposture.[21] I will put an
end to the image by saying that it isn't these men I mean but those
whom we just now said we are going to question about harmony. They
c   do the same thing the astronomers do. They seek the numbers in these
heard accords and don't rise to problems, to the consideration of which
numbers are concordant and which not, and why in each case."

"The thing you are speaking of," he said, "is demonic."

"Useful, rather, for the quest after the fair and the good," I said,
"but pursued in any other way it is useless."

"That's likely," he said.

"And I suppose," I said, "that if the inquiry into all the things we   *531 c*
have gone through arrives at their community and relationship with   *d*
one another, and draws conclusions as to how they are akin to one
another, then the concern with them contributes something to what we
want, and is not a labor without profit, but otherwise it is."

"I, too, divine that this is the case," he said. "But it's a very big
job you speak of, Socrates."

"Do you mean the prelude or what?" I said. "Or don't we know
that all of this is a prelude to the song²² itself which must be
learned? For surely it's not your opinion that the men who are clever at
these things are dialecticians."   *e*

"No, by Zeus," he said, "with the exception of a very few whom I
have encountered."

"But," I said, "was it ever your opinion that men who are unable
to give an account and receive one will ever know anything of what we
say they must know?"

"To this question too," he said, "the answer is no."

"Glaucon," I said, "isn't this at last the song itself that dialectic   *532 a*
performs? It is in the realm of the intelligible, but it is imitated by the
power of sight. We said that sight at last tries to look at the animals
themselves and at stars themselves and then finally at the sun itself. So,
also, when a man tries by discussion—by means of argument without
the use of any of the senses—to attain to each thing itself that *is* and
doesn't give up before he grasps by intellection itself that which is good   *b*
itself, he comes to the very end of the intelligible realm just as that
other man was then at the end of the visible."

"That's entirely certain," he said.

"What then? Don't you call this journey dialectic?"

"Of course."

"Then," I said, "the release from the bonds and the turning
around from the shadows to the phantoms and the light, the way up
from the cave to the sun; and, once there, the persisting inability to
look at the animals and the plants and the sun's light, and looking instead at the divine appearances in water and at shadows of the things   *c*
that *are*, rather than as before at shadows of phantoms cast by a light
that, when judged in comparison with the sun, also has the quality of
a shadow of a phantom—all this activity of the arts, which we
went through, has the power to release and leads what is best in the
soul up to the contemplation of what is best in the things that *are*,
just as previously what is clearest in the body was led to the contemplation of what is brightest in the region of the bodily and the
visible."   *d*

532 d   "I accept this as so," he said. "It seems to me extremely hard to
accept, however, but in another way hard not to accept. All the
same—since it's not only now that these things must be heard, but they
must all be returned to many times in the future—taking for granted
that this is as has now been said, let's proceed to the song itself and go
through it just as we went through the prelude. So tell what the character of the power of dialectic is, and, then, into exactly what forms it is
e   divided; and finally what are its ways. For these, as it seems, would lead
at last toward that place which is for the one who reaches it a haven
from the road, as it were, and an end of his journey."

533 a   "You will no longer be able to follow, my dear Glaucon," I said,
"although there wouldn't be any lack of eagerness on my part. But you
would no longer be seeing an image of what we are saying, but rather
the truth itself, at least as it looks to me. Whether it is really so or not
can no longer be properly insisted on. But that there is some such thing
to see must be insisted on. Isn't it so?"

          "Of course."

          "And, also, that the power of dialectic alone could reveal it to a
man experienced in the things we just went through, while it is in no
other way possible?"

          "Yes," he said, "it's proper to insist on that too."

b   "At least," I said, "no one will dispute us when we say that some
other inquiry methodically[23] attempts with respect to everything to
grasp—about each several thing itself—what each *is*. For all the other
arts are directed to human opinions and desires, or to generation and
composition, or to the care of what is grown or put together. And as for
the rest, those that we said do lay hold of something of what
is—geometry and the arts following on it—we observe that they do
dream about what *is*; but they haven't the capacity to see it in full
c   awakeness so long as they use hypotheses and, leaving them untouched,
are unable to give an account of them. When the beginning is what one
doesn't know, and the end and what comes in between are woven out of
what isn't known, what contrivance is there for ever turning such an
agreement into knowledge?"

          "None," he said.

          "Then," I said, "only the dialectical way of inquiry proceeds in
this direction, destroying the hypotheses, to the beginning itself in order to make it secure; and when the eye of the soul is really buried in a
d   barbaric bog,[24] dialectic gently draws it forth and leads it up above,
using the arts we described as assistants and helpers in the turning
around. Out of habit we called them kinds of knowledge several times,
but they require another name, one that is brighter than opinion but

dimmer than knowledge. Thought was, I believe, the word by which we   533 d
previously distinguished it. But, in my opinion, there is no place for
dispute about a name when a consideration is about things so great as   e
those lying before us."

"No, there isn't," he said.25

"Then it will be acceptable," I said, "just as before, to call the first
part knowledge, the second thought, the third trust, and the fourth
imagination; and the latter two taken together, opinion, and the former   534 a
two, intellection. And opinion has to do with coming into being and intellection with being; and as being is to coming into being, so is intellection to opinion; and as intellection is to opinion, so is knowledge
to trust and thought to imagination. But as for the proportion between
the things over which these are set and the division into two parts of
each—the opinable and the intelligible—let's let that go, Glaucon, so
as not to run afoul of arguments many times longer than those that have
been gone through."

"Well," he said, "about the rest, insofar as I am able to follow, I   b
share your opinion."

"And do you also call that man dialectical who grasps the reason
for the being of each thing? And, as for the man who isn't able to do so,
to the extent he's not able to give an account of a thing to himself and
another, won't you deny that he has intelligence with respect to it?"

"How could I affirm that he does?" he said.

"Isn't it also the same with the good? Unless a man is able to
separate out the *idea* of the good from all other things and distinguish it   c
in the argument, and, going through every test, as it were in battle—eager to meet the test of being rather than that of opinion—he
comes through all this with the argument still on its feet; you will deny
that such a man knows the good itself, or any other good? And if he
somehow lays hold of some phantom of it, you will say that he does so
by opinion and not knowledge, and that, taken in by dreams and slum-
bering out his present life, before waking up here he goes to Hades and
falls finally asleep there?"   d

"Yes, by Zeus," he said. "I shall certainly say all that."

"Then, as for those children of yours whom you are rearing and
educating in speech, if you should ever rear them in deed, I don't suppose that while they are as irrational as lines26 you would let them
rule in the city and be the sovereigns of the greatest things."

"No, I wouldn't," he said.

"Then will you set it down as a law to them that they pay special
attention to the education on the basis of which they will be able to
question and answer most knowledgeably?"

534 e   "I shall join with you," he said, "in setting down this law."

"Is it your opinion," I said, "that we have placed dialectic at the top of the studies like a coping stone, and that no other study could rightly be set higher than this one, but that the treatment of the studies
535 a   has already reached its end?"

"Yes, it is my opinion," he said.

"Well, then," I said, "the distribution is still ahead of you. To whom shall we give these studies and how shall we do it?"

"That's plainly the next question," he said.

"Do you remember, in the former selection of the rulers, what sort of men we selected?"

"How could I not remember?" he said.

"Well, then, so far as most of the requirements go, suppose that those are the natures that must be chosen," I said. "The steadiest and most courageous must be preferred and, insofar as possible, the best
b   looking. But besides this, one must seek for men who are not only by disposition noble and tough, but who also possess those qualities in their nature that are conducive to this education."

"What do you determine them to be?"

"Keenness at studies, you blessed man," I said, "is a prerequisite for them, and learning without difficulty. For souls, you know, are far more likely to be cowardly in severe studies than in gymnastic. The labor is closer to home in that it is the soul's privately and not shared in common with the body."

"True," he said.

c   "And, of course, a man with a memory and who is firm and wholly a lover of labor must be sought. Or in what way do you suppose anyone will be willing both to perform the labors of the body and to complete so much study and practice?"

"No one would," he said, "unless he has an entirely good nature."

"At any rate," I said, "the current mistake in philosophy—as a result of which, as we also said before, dishonor has befallen philosophy—is that men who aren't worthy take it up. Not bastards, but the genuine should have taken it up."

"What do you mean?" he said.

d   "In the first place," I said, "the man who is to take it up must not be lame in his love of labor, loving half the labor while having no taste for the other half. This is the case when a man is a lover of gymnastic and the hunt and loves all the labor done by the body, while he isn't a lover of learning or of listening and isn't an inquirer, but hates the labor involved in all that. Lame as well is the man whose love of labor is directed exclusively to the other extreme."

"What you say is very true," he said.   535 *d*

"And likewise with respect to truth," I said, "won't we class as
maimed a soul that hates the willing lie, both finding it hard to endure   *e*
in itself and becoming incensed when others lie, but is content to
receive the unwilling lie and, when it is caught somewhere being
ignorant, isn't vexed but easily accommodates itself, like a swinish beast, to
wallowing in lack of learning?"

"That's entirely certain," he said.   536 *a*

"And with respect to moderation," I said, "and courage and
magnificence and all the parts of virtue, a special guard must be kept for
the man who is bastard and the one who is genuine. When a private
man and a city don't know how to make a complete consideration of
such things, for whatever services they happen to need they unawares
employ lame men and bastards as friends or rulers."

"That's just the way it is," he said.

"So," I said, "we must take good care of all such things since, if
we bring men straight of limb and understanding to so important a   *b*
study and so important a training and educate them, Justice herself will
not blame us, and we shall save the city and the regime; while, in
bringing men of another sort to it, we shall do exactly the opposite
and also pour even more ridicule over philosophy."

"That," he said, "would indeed be shameful."

"Most certainly," I said. "But I seem to have been somewhat
ridiculously affected just now."

"How's that?" he said.

"I forgot," I said, "that we were playing and spoke rather in-   *c*
tensely. For, as I was talking I looked at Philosophy and, seeing her
underservingly spattered with mud, I seem to have been vexed and said
what I had to say too seriously as though my spiritedness were aroused
against those who are responsible."

"No, by Zeus," he said, "that's not the way you seemed to me, the
listener."

"But to me, the speaker," I said. "And let's not forget that in our
former selection we were picking old men, but in this one that isn't admissible. For we mustn't trust Solon when he says that in growing old a man   *d*
is able to learn much; he's less able to do that than to run, and all the
great and numerous labors belong to the young."

"Necessarily," he said.

"Well then, the study of calculation and geometry and all the preparatory education required for dialectic must be put before them as
children, and the instruction must not be given the aspect of a compulsion to learn."

536 d

e

537 a

b

c

d

"Why not?"

"Because," I said, "the free man ought not to learn any study slavishly. Forced labors performed by the body don't make the body any worse, but no forced study abides in a soul."

"True," he said.

"Therefore, you best of men," I said, "don't use force in training the children in the studies, but rather play. In that way you can also better discern what each is naturally directed toward."

"What you say makes sense." he said.

"Don't you remember," I said, "that we also said that the children must be led to war on horseback as spectators; and, if it's safe anywhere, they must be led up near and taste blood, like the puppies?"

"I do remember," he said.

"Then in all these labors, studies, and fears," I said, "the boy who shows himself always readiest must be chosen to join a select number."

"At what age?" he said.

"After they are released from compulsory gymnastic." I said. "For this is a time, whether it is two or three years, during which it is impossible to do anything else. Weariness and sleep are enemies of studies. And, at the same time, one of their tests, and that not the least, is what each will show himself to be in gymnastic."

"Of course," he said.

"Then, after this time," I said, "those among the twenty-year-olds who are given preference will receive greater honors than the others. And the various studies acquired without any particular order by the children in their education must be integrated into an overview[27] which reveals the kinship of these studies with one another and with the nature of that which *is*."

"At least, only such study," he said, "remains fast in those who receive it."

"And it is the greatest test," I said, "of the nature that is dialectical and the one that is not. For the man who is capable of an overview is dialectical while the one who isn't, is not."

"I share your belief," he said.

"Well, then," I said, "in terms of these tests, you will have to consider who among them most meets them and is steadfast in studies and steadfast in war and the rest of the duties established by law.[28] And to these men, in turn, when they are over thirty, you will give preference among the preferred and assign greater honors; and you must

consider, testing them with the power of dialectic, who is able to   537 *d*
release himself from the eyes and the rest of sense and go to that which
is in itself and accompanies truth. And here, my comrade, you have a
job requiring a great deal of guarding."

"Of what in particular?" he said.

"Don't you notice," I said, "how great is the harm coming from   *e*
the practice of dialectic these days?"

"What's that?" he said.

"Surely its students," I said, "are filled full with lawlessness."

"Very much so," he said.

"Do you suppose it's any wonder," I said, "that they are so affected, and don't you sympathize?"

"Why exactly should I?" he said.

"It is like the case of changeling child," I said, "reared in much
wealth, in a numerous and great family amidst many flatterers, who on   538 *a*
reaching manhood becomes aware that he does not belong to these pre-
tended parents and isn't able to find those who really gave him birth.
Can you divine how he would be disposed toward the flatterers and
toward those who made the change, in the time when he didn't know
about the change, and then again when he did know it? Or do you want
to listen while I do the divining?"

"That's what I want," he said.

"Well, then," I said, "I divine that in the time when he doesn't
know the truth he would be more likely to honor his father and his   *b*
mother and the others who seem to be his kin than those who flatter
him. And he would be less likely to overlook any of their needs, less
likely to do or say anything unlawful to them, and less likely to disobey
them in the important things than the flatterers."

"That's to be expected," he said.

"And, when he has become aware of that which *is*, I divine that
now he would relax his honor and zeal for these people and intensify
them for the flatterers, be persuaded by them a great deal more than
before, and begin to live according to their ways, and have unconcealed   *c*
relations with them. For that father and the rest of the adoptive kin,
unless he is by nature particularly decent, he wouldn't care."

"Everything you say," he said, "is just the sort of thing that would
happen. But how does this image apply to those who take up arguments?"

"Like this. Surely we have from childhood convictions about
what's just and fair by which we are brought up as by parents, obeying
them as rulers and honoring them."

538 c

d

"Yes, we do."

"And then there are other practices opposed to these, possessing pleasures that flatter our soul and draw it to them. They do not persuade men who are at all sensible;[29] these men rather honor the ancestral things and obey them as rulers."

"That's so."

"Then what?" I said. "When a question is posed and comes to the man who is so disposed, 'What is the fair?'—and after answering what he heard from the lawgiver, the argument refutes him, and refuting him many times and in many ways, reduces him to the opinion that what the law says is no more fair than ugly, and similarly about the just and good and the things he held most in honor—after that, what do you suppose he'll do about honoring and obeying as rulers the things he heard from the lawgiver?"

e

"Necessarily," he said, "he'll neither honor nor obey them any longer in the same way."

"Then," I said, "when he doesn't believe, as he did before, that these things are honorable or akin to him, and doesn't find the true ones, is it to be expected that he will go to any other sort of life than the one that flatters him?"[30]

539 a

"No, it isn't," he said.

"Then, I suppose, he will seem to have become an outlaw from having been a law-abiding man."

"Necessarily."

"Isn't it to be expected," I said, "that this is what will happen to those who take up the study of arguments in this way; and as I was just saying, don't they deserve much sympathy?"

"And pity, too," he said.

"Lest your thirty-year-olds be recipients of this pity, mustn't you take every kind of precaution when they turn to arguments?"

"Quite so," he said.

b

"Isn't it one great precaution not to let them taste of arguments while they are young? I suppose you aren't unaware that when lads get their first taste of them, they misuse them as though it were play, always using them to contradict; and imitating those men by whom they are refuted, they themselves refute others, like puppies enjoying pulling and tearing with argument at those who happen to be near."

"They certainly have," he said, "a preternatural tendency in that direction."

c

"Then when they themselves refute many men and are refuted by many, they fall quickly into a profound disbelief of what they formerly

believed. And as a result of this, you see, they themselves and the   *539 c*
whole activity of philosophy become the objects of slander among the
rest of men."

"Very true," he said.

"An older man, however," I said, "wouldn't be willing to participate in such madness. He will imitate the man who's willing to
discuss and consider the truth rather than the one who plays and contradicts for the sake of the game. And he himself will be more sensible
and will make the practice of discussion more honorable instead of   *d*
more dishonorable."

"That's right," he said.

"And wasn't everything that was said before this also directed to
precaution—that those with whom one shares arguments are to have
orderly and stable natures, not as is done nowadays in sharing them
with whoever chances by and comes to it without being suited for
it."

"Most certainly," he said.

"If a man is to devote himself exclusively to steady and strenuous
participation in arguments—exercising himself in a gymnastic that is
the antistrophe of the bodily gymnastic—will double the number of
years devoted to gymnastic suffice?"

"Do you mean six years," he said, "or four?"   *e*

"Don't worry about that," I said. "Set it down at five. Now, after
this, they'll have to go down into that cave again for you, and they must
be compelled to rule in the affairs of war and all the offices suitable for
young men, so that they won't be behind the others in experience. And
here, too, they must still be tested whether they will stand firm or give   *540 a*
way when pulled in all directions."

"How much time do you assign to this?" he said.

"Fifteen years," I said. "And when they are fifty years old, those
who have been preserved throughout and are in every way best at
everything, both in deed and in knowledge, must at last be led to the
end. And, lifting up the brilliant beams of their souls, they must be
compelled to look toward that which provides light for everything.
Once they see the good itself, they must be compelled, each in his turn,
to use it as a pattern for ordering city, private men, and themselves for   *b*
the rest of their lives. For the most part, each one spends his time in
philosophy, but when his turn comes, he drudges in politics and rules
for the city's sake, not as though he were doing a thing that is fine, but
one that is necessary. And thus always educating other like men and
leaving them behind in their place as guardians of the city, they go off

540 b   to the Isles of the Blessed and dwell. The city makes public memorials
         and sacrifices to them as to demons, if the Pythia is in accord; if not, as
c   to happy[31] and divine men."

         "Just like a sculptor, Socrates," he said, "you have produced
         ruling men who are wholly fair."

         "And ruling women, too, Glaucon," I said. "Don't suppose that
         what I have said applies any more to men than to women, all those who
         are born among them with adequate natures."

         "That's right," he said, "if they are to share everything in com-
         mon equally with the men, as we described it."

d   "What then?" I said. "Do you agree that the things we have said
         about the city and the regime are not in every way prayers; that they
         are hard but in a way possible; and that it is possible in no other way
         than the one stated: when the true philosophers, either one or more,
         come to power in a city, they will despise the current honors and
         believe them to be illiberal and worth nothing. Putting what is right
e   and the honors coming from it above all, while taking what is just as
         the greatest and the most necessary, and serving and fostering it, they
         will provide for their own city."

         "How?" he said.

         "All those in the city who happen to be older than ten they will
541 a   send out to the country; and taking over their children, they will rear
         them—far away from those dispositions they now have from their
         parents—in their own manners and laws that are such as we described
         before. And, with the city and the regime of which we were speaking
         thus established most quickly and easily, it will itself be happy and
         most profit the nation in which it comes to be."

         "That is by far the quickest and easiest way," he said. "And how
         it would come into being, if it ever were to come into being, you have,
b   in my opinion, Socrates, stated well."

         "Isn't that enough already," I said, "for our arguments about this
         city and the man like it? For surely it's plain what sort of man we'll say
         he has to be."

         "It is plain," he said. "And as for what you ask, in my opinion
         this argument has reached its end."

BOOK VIII

"All right. This much has been agreed, Glaucon: for a city that is going to be governed on a high level, women must be in common, children and their entire education must be in common, and similarly the practices in war and peace must be in common, and their kings must be those among them who have proved best in philosophy and with respect to war."

"Yes," he said, "it has been agreed."

"Furthermore, we also accepted that when the rulers are once established, they must take the lead and settle the soldiers in houses—such as we spoke of before—that have nothing private for anyone but are common for all. And, in addition to such houses, as to possessions, if you remember, we presumably came to an agreement about what sort they are to have."

"Yes, I do remember," he said, "that we supposed that no one must possess any of the things the others nowadays have; but that like champions of war and guardians, they will receive a wage annually from the others consisting of the bare subsistence required for their guarding, and for this wage they must take care of themselves and the rest of the city."

"What you say is right," I said. "But come, since we have completed this, let's recall where we took the detour that brought us here so that we can go back to the same way."

543 a

b

c

543 c

d

544 *a*

b

c

d

e

"That's not hard," he said. "You were presenting your arguments pretty much as you are doing now, as though you had completed your description of what concerns the city, saying that you would class a city such as you then described, and the man like it, as good. And you did this, as it seems, in spite of the fact that you had a still finer city and man to tell of. Anyhow, you were saying that the other cities are mistaken if this one is right. Concerning the remaining regimes, as I remember, you asserted that there are four forms it is worthwhile to have an account of, and whose mistakes are worth seeing; and similarly with the men who are like these regimes; so that, when we have seen them all and agreed which man is best and which worst, we could consider whether the best man is happiest and the worst most wretched, or whether it is otherwise. And just as I was asking which four regimes you meant, Polemarchus and Adeimantus interrupted. That's how you picked up the argument and got here."

"What you remember," I said, "is quite correct."

"Well, then, like a wrestler, give me the same hold again; and when I put the same question, try to tell what you were going to say then."

"If I am able," I said.

"And, in fact," he said, "I myself really desire to hear what four regimes you meant."

"It won't be hard for you to hear them," I said. "For those I mean are also the ones having names; the one that is praised by the many, that Cretan and Laconian regime; and second in place and second in praise, the one called oligarchy, a regime filled with throngs of evils; and this regime's adversary, arising next in order, democracy; and then the noble tyranny at last, excelling all of these, the fourth and extreme illness of a city. Or have you some other *idea* of a regime that fits into some distinct form? For dynasties and purchased kingships and certain regimes of the sort are somewhere between these, and one would find them no less among the barbarians than the Greeks."[1]

"At any rate," he said, "many strange ones are talked about."

"Do you know," I said, "that it is necessary that there also be as many forms of human characters as there are forms of regimes? Or do you suppose that the regimes arise 'from an oak or rocks'[2] and not from the dispositions of the men in the cities, which, tipping the scale as it were, draw the rest along with them?"

"No," he said. "I don't at all think they arise from anything other than this."

"Therefore if there are five arrangements of cities, there would also be five for the soul of private men."

"Surely."

"Well, we have already described the man who is like the   *544 e*
aristocracy, a man of whom we rightly assert that he is both good and
just."

"Yes, we have described him."   *545 a*

"Must we next go through the worse men—the man who loves
victory and honor, fixed in relation to the Laconian regime; and then,
in turn, an oligarchic and a democratic man, and the tyrannic man, so
that seeing the most unjust man, we can set him in opposition to the
most just man? If so, we can have a complete consideration of how
pure justice is related to pure injustice with respect to the happiness
and wretchedness of the men possessing them. In this way we may be
persuaded either by Thrasymachus and pursue injustice, or by the
argument that is now coming to light and pursue justice."   *b*

"That," he said, "is most certainly what must be done."

"Then, just as we began by considering the various dispositions in
the regimes before considering them in the private men, supposing that
to be the more luminous way; so must we now consider first the regime
that loves honor—I can give no other name that is used for it in common parlance; it should be called either timocracy or timarchy.³ And,
in relation to this regime, we shall consider the like man, and after that
oligarchy and an oligarchic man. Later, after having looked at   *c*
democracy, we'll view a democratic man; and fourth, having gone to
the city that is under a tyranny and seen it, then looking into a tyrannic soul, we shall try to become adequate judges of the subject we proposed for ourselves."

"It would, in any case," he said, "be a reasonable way for the observation and judgment to take place."

"Well, come, then," I said, "let's try to tell the way in which a
timocracy would arise from an aristocracy. Or is it simply the case that
change in every regime comes from that part of it which holds the   *d*
ruling offices—when faction arises in it—while when it is of one mind,
it cannot be moved, be it composed of ever so few?"

"Yes, that's so."

"Then, Glaucon," I said, "how will our city be moved and in what
way will the auxiliaries and the rulers divide into factions against each
other and among themselves? Or do you want us, as does Homer, to
pray to the Muses to tell us how 'faction first attacked,'⁴ and shall we   *e*
say that they speak to us with high tragic talk, as though they were
speaking seriously, playing and jesting with us like children?"

"How?"

"Something like this. A city so composed is hard to be moved.   *546 a*
But, since for everything that has come into being there is decay, not
even a composition such as this will remain for all time; it will be

546 a   dissolved. And this will be its dissolution: bearing and barrenness of soul and bodies come not only to plants in the earth but to animals on the earth when revolutions complete for each the bearing round of circles; for ones with short lives, the journey is short; for those whose lives are the opposite, the journey is the opposite. Although they are

b   wise, the men you educated as leaders of the city will nonetheless fail to hit on the prosperous birth and barrenness of your kind with calculation aided by sensation, but it will pass them by, and they will at some time beget children when they should not. For a divine birth there is a period comprehended by a perfect number; for a human birth, by the first number in which root and square increases, comprising three distances and four limits, of elements that make like and unlike, and that wax and wane, render everything conversable and rational. Of

c   these elements, the root four-three mated with the five, thrice increased, produces two harmonies. One of them is equal an equal number of times, taken one hundred times over. The other is of equal length in one way but is an oblong; on one side, of one hundred rational diameters of the five, lacking one for each; or, if of irrational diameters, lacking two for each; on the other side, of one hundred cubes of the three. This whole geometrical number is sovereign of better and worse

d   begettings.[5] And when your guardians from ignorance of them cause grooms to live with brides out of season, the children will have neither good natures nor good luck. Their predecessors will choose the best of these children; but, nevertheless, since they are unworthy, when they, in turn, come to the powers of their fathers, they will as guardians first begin to neglect us by having less consideration than is required, first, for music, and, second, for gymnastic; and from there your young will become more unmusical. And rulers chosen from them won't be guar-

e   dians very apt at testing Hesiod's races[6] and yours—gold and silver

547 a   and bronze and iron. And the chaotic mixing of iron with silver and of bronze with gold engenders unlikeness and inharmonious irregularity, which, once they arise, always breed war and hatred in the place where they happen to arise. Faction must always be said to be 'of this ancestry'[7] wherever it happens to rise."

      "And we'll say," he said, "that what the Muses answer is right."

      "Necessarily," I said. "For they are Muses."

b   "What," he said, "do the Muses say next?"

      "Once faction had arisen," I said, "each of these two races, the iron and bronze, pulled the regime toward money-making and the possession of land, houses, gold, and silver; while the other two, the gold and the silver—not being poor but rich by nature—led the souls toward virtue and the ancient establishment. Struggling and straining against one another, they came to an agreement on a middle way: they

[224]

Distribute land
enslave free friends

distributed land and houses to be held privately, while those who pre-   547 c
viously were guarded by them as free friends and supporters they then
enslaved and held as serfs and domestics; and they occupied themselves
with war and with guarding against these men."

"In my opinion," he said, "this is the source of this transformation."

"Wouldn't this regime," I said, "be a certain middle between
aristocracy and oligarchy?"

"Most certainly."

"This will be the way of the transformation. But once transformed,
how will it be governed? Or is it evident that in some things it will imitate   d
the preceding regime; in others oligarchy, because it is a middle; and
that it will also have something peculiar to itself?"

"That's the way it is," he said.

"In honoring the rulers, and in the abstention of its war-making
part from farming and the manual arts and the rest of money-making;
in its provision for common meals and caring for gymnastic and the exercise of war—in all such ways won't it imitate the preceding regime?"

"Yes."

"But in being afraid to bring the wise to the ruling offices—be-   e
cause the men of that kind it possesses are no longer simple and
earnest, but mixed—and in leaning toward spirited and simpler men,
men naturally more directed to war than to peace; in holding the wiles
and stratagems of war in honor; and in spending all its time making   548 a
war; won't most such aspects be peculiar to this regime?"

"Yes."

"And such men," I said, "will desire money just as those in oligarchies do, and under cover of darkness pay fierce honor to gold and silver, because they possess storehouses and domestic treasuries where
they can deposit and hide them; and they will have walls around their
houses, exactly like private nests, where they can make lavish expenditures on women and whomever else they might wish."

Men will desire $. Material things

b

"Very true," he said.

"Then they will also be stingy with money because they honor it
and don't acquire it openly; but, pushed on by desire, they will love to
spend other people's money; and they will harvest pleasures stealthily,
running away from the law like boys from a father. This is because they
weren't educated by persuasion but by force—the result of neglect of
the true Muse accompanied by arguments and philosophy while giving
more distinguished honor to gymnastic than music."   c

"You certainly speak of a reigme," he said, "which is a mixture of
bad and good."

"Yes, it is mixed," I said, "but due to the dominance of

Mixed regime
∴ Good and Bad.

548 c   spiritedness one thing alone is most distinctive in it: love of victories and of honors."

"Very much so," he said.

"Then," I said, "this is the way this regime would come into being and what it would be like—given the fact that we are only outlining a

d   regime's figure in speech and not working out its details precisely, since even the outline is sufficient for seeing the justest man and the unjustest one, and it is an impractically long job to go through all regimes and all dispositions and leave nothing out."

"Right," he said.

"Who, then, is the man corresponding to this regime? How did he come into being and what sort of man is he?"

"I suppose," said Adeimantus, "that as far as love of victory goes, he'd be somewhere near to Glaucon here."

e   "Perhaps in that," I said, "but in these other respects his nature does not, in my opinion, correspond to Glaucon's."

"Which respects?"

"He must be more stubborn," I said, "and somewhat less apt at music although he loves it, and must be a lover of hearing although he's

549 a   by no means skilled in rhetoric. With slaves such a man would be brutal, not merely despising slaves as the adequately educated man does. But with freemen he would be tame and to rulers most obedient. He is a lover of ruling and of honor, not basing his claim to rule on speaking or anything of the sort, but on warlike deeds and everything connected with war; he is a lover of gymnastic and the hunt."

"Yes," he said, "that is the disposition belonging to this regime."

"Wouldn't such a man," I said, "when he is young also despise

b   money, but as he grows older take ever more delight in participating in the money-lover's nature and not be pure in his attachment to virtue, having been abandoned by the best guardian?"

"What's that?" Adeimantus said.

"Argument mixed with music," I said. "It alone, when it is present, dwells within the one possessing it as a savior of virtue throughout life."

"What you say is fine," he said.

"Such, then," I said, "is the timocratic youth, like the timocratic city."

c   "Most certainly."

"And this is how he comes into being," I said. "Sometimes he is the young son of a good father who lives in a city that is not under a good regime, a father who flees the honors, the ruling offices, the law-

Mother of father
father
son

suits, and everything of the sort that's to the busybody's taste, and who   549 *c*
is willing to be gotten the better of so as not to be bothered."

"In what way, then, does he come into being?" he said.

"When," I said, "in the first place, he listens to his mother com-
plaining. Her husband is not one of the rulers and as a result she is at a
disadvantage among the other women. Moreover, she sees that he isn't   *d*
very serious about money and doesn't fight and insult people for its
sake in private actions in courts and in public but takes everything of
the sort in an easygoing way; and she becomes aware that he always
turns his mind to himself and neither honors nor dishonors her very
much. She complains about all this and says that his father is lacking in
courage and too slack, and, of course, chants all the other refrains such   *e*
as women are likely to do in cases of this sort."

"Yes, indeed," said Adeimantus, "it's just like them to have many
complaints."

"And you know," I said, "that the domestics of such men—those
domestics who seem well-disposed—sometimes also secretly say
similar things to the sons, and if they see someone who owes him
money or does some other injustice and whom the father doesn't
prosecute, they urge the son to punish all such men when he becomes a
man, and thus to be more of a man than his father. And when the son   550 *a*
goes out, he hears and sees other similar things—those in the city who
mind their own business called simpletons and held in small account,
and those who don't, honored and praised. Now when the young man
hears and sees all this, and, on the other hand, hears his father's arguments and sees his practices at close hand contrasted with those of the
others, he is drawn by both of these influences. His father waters the
calculating part of his soul, and causes it to grow; the others, the desiring and spirited parts. Because he doesn't have a bad man's nature, but   *b*
has kept bad company with others, drawn by both of these influences,   *Young man will be in the middle*
he came to the middle, and turned over the rule in himself to the mid-
dle part, the part that loves victory and is spirited; he became a
haughty-minded man who loves honor."

"In my opinion," he said, "you have given a complete description
of this man's genesis."

"Therefore," I said, "we have the second regime and the second   *c*
man."

"We have," he said.

"Then, next, shall we, with Aeschylus, tell of 'another man set
against another city,'[8] or rather, shall we follow our plan and tell first
of the city?"

[227]

550 c

Oligarchy

"Most certainly," he said.

"And, I suppose, oligarchy would come after such a regime."

"What kind of arrangement do you mean by oligarchy?" he said.

d

Rule by Rich

"The regime founded on a property assessment,"[9] I said, "in which the rich rule and the poor man[10] has no part in ruling office."

"I understand," he said.

"Mustn't it first be told how the transformation from timarchy to oligarchy takes place?"

"Yes."

"And really," I said, "the way it is transformed is plain even to a blind man."

Transformation

"How?"

Spend & pervert laws

"The treasure house full of gold," I said, "which each man has, destroys that regime. First they seek out expenditures for themselves and pervert the laws in that direction; they themselves and their wives disobey them."

Enter into rivalry w/other men

"That's likely," he said.

e

"Next, I suppose, one man sees the other and enters into a rivalry with him, and thus they made the multitude like themselves."

"That's likely."

↑ Money making
↓ Virtue

"Well, then," I said, "from there they progress in money-making, and the more honorable they consider it, the less honorable they consider virtue. Or isn't virtue in tension with wealth, as though each were lying in the scale of a balance, always inclining in opposite directions?"

"Quite so," he said.

551 a

"Surely, when wealth and the wealthy are honored in a city, virtue and the good men are less honorable."

"Plainly."

"Surely, what happens to be honored is practiced, and what is without honor is neglected."

"That's so."

"Instead of men who love victory and honor, they finally become lovers of money-making and money; and they praise and admire the wealthy man and bring him to the ruling offices, while they dishonor the poor man."

"Certainly."

b

"Therefore, don't they then set down a law defining an oligarchic regime by fixing an assessment of a sum of money—where it's more of an oligarchy, the sum is greater, where less of an oligarchy, less? Prescribing that the man whose substance is not up to the level of the fixed assessment shall not participate in the ruling offices, don't

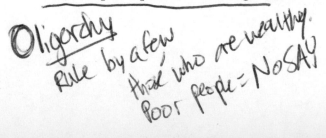

Oligarchy
Rule by a few
those who are wealthy.
Poor people = No SAY

they either put this into effect by force of arms or, before it comes to   551 b
that, they arouse fear and so establish this regime? Or isn't it that
way?"

"It certainly is."

"This is, then, speaking generally, its establishment."

"Yes," he said. "But what is the character of the regime? And
what are the mistakes which we were saying it contains?"

"First," I said, "the very thing that defines the regime is one.   c
Reflect: if a man were to choose pilots of ships in that way—on the basis of
property assessments—and wouldn't entrust one to a poor man, even if he
were a more skilled pilot—"

"They would make a poor sailing," he said.

"Isn't this also so for any other kind of rule watsoever?"

"So I suppose, at least."

"Except for a city?" I said. "Or does it also apply to a city?"

"Certainly," he said, "most of all, insofar as it is the hardest and
greatest kind of rule."

"Then oligarchy would contain this one mistake that is of such   d
proportions."

"It looks like it."

"And what about this? Is this a lesser mistake than the former
one?"

"What?"

"Such a city's not being one but of necessity two, the city of the
poor and the city of the rich, dwelling together in the same place, ever
plotting against each other."

"No, by Zeus," he said, "that's no less of a mistake."

"And further, this isn't a fine thing: their being perhaps unable to
fight any war, first, on account of being compelled either to use the
multitude armed and be more afraid of it than the enemy, or not to use
it and thus show up as true oligarchs[11] on the field of battle; and,   e
besides, on account of their not being willing to contribute money because they love it."

"No, it's not a fine thing."

"And what about this? That tendency to be busybodies we were
condemning long ago—the same men in such a regime engaged in
farming, money-making and war-making at the same time—does that   552 a
seem right?"

"In no way whatsoever."

"Now see whether this regime is the first to admit the greatest of
all these evils."

552 a   "What?"

"Allowing one man to sell everything that belongs to him and another to get hold of it; and when he has sold it, allowing him to live in the city while belonging to none of its parts, called neither a money-maker, nor a craftsman, nor a knight, nor a hoplite, but a poor man without means."

b   "Yes," he said, "it is the first."

"Then this sort of thing is at least not prevented in oligarchies. Otherwise some wouldn't be super rich while others are out-and-out poor."

"Right."

"Reflect on this. When such a man was wealthy and was spending, was he then of any more profit to the city with respect to the functions we were mentioning just now? Or did he seem to belong to the rulers, while in truth he was neither a ruler nor a servant of the city but a spender of his means?"

c   "That's the way it was," he said, "he seemed, but was nothing other than a spender."

"Do you wish us," I said, "to say of him that, as a drone growing up in a cell is a disease of a hive, such a man growing up in a house is a drone and a disease of a city?"

"Most certainly, Socrates," he said.

"Hasn't the god made all drones with wings stingless, Adeimantus, but only some drones with feet stingless while others have terrible stings? From the stingless ones come those who end up as beggars in
d   old age, while from those who have stings come all who are called wrongdoers."

"Very true," he said.

"It's plain, therefore," I said, "that in a city where you see beggars, somewhere in the neighborhood thieves, cutpurses, temple robbers, and craftsmen of all such evils are hidden."

"It is plain," he said.

"What then? In cities under oligarchies don't you see beggars present?"

"Just about everyone except the rulers," he said.

e   "Aren't we to suppose," I said, "that there are also many wrongdoers with stings among them, whom the ruling offices diligently hold down by force?"

"We must certainly suppose so," he said.

"Shall we assert that such men arise there as a result of want of education, bad rearing, and a bad arrangement of the regime?"

"We shall assert it."   552 *e*

"Well, anyhow, such would be the city under an oligarchy and it would contain all these evils, and perhaps even more."

"That's pretty nearly it," he said.

"Then let's take it," I said, "that we have developed the regime   553 *a* called oligarchy, one that gets its rulers on the basis of a property assessment, and next let's consider how the man similar to it comes into being and what he's like once he has come into being."

"Most certainly," he said.

"Is this the principal way in which the transformation from that timocratic man to an oligarchic one takes place?"

"How?"

"When his son is born and at first emulates his father and follows in his footsteps, and then sees him blunder against the city as against a   *b* reef and waste his property as well as himself. He had either been a general or had held some other great ruling office, and then got entangled with the court—suffering at the hands of sycophants—and underwent death, exile, or dishonor[12] and lost his whole substance."

"That's likely," he said.

"And the son, my friend, seeing and suffering this and having lost his substance, is frightened, I suppose, and thrusts love of honor and spiritedness headlong out of the throne of his soul; and, humbled by   *c* poverty, he turns greedily to money-making; and bit by bit saving and working, he collects money. Don't you suppose that such a man now puts the desiring and money-loving part on the throne, and makes it the great king within himself, girding it with tiaras, collars, and Persian swords?"[13]

"I do," he said.

"And, I suppose, he makes the calculating and spirited parts sit by   *d* it on the ground on either side and be slaves, letting the one neither calculate about nor consider anything but where more money will come from less; and letting the other admire and honor nothing but wealth and the wealthy, while loving the enjoyment of no other honor than that resulting from the possession of money and anything that happens to contribute to getting it."

"There is," he said, "no other transformation so quick and so sure from a young man who loves honor to one who loves money."

"Is this, then," I said, "the oligarchic man?"   *e*

"At least he is transformed out of a man who was like the regime out of which oligarchy came."

"Then, let's consider if he would be like."

554 a   "Yes, let's consider that."

"In the first place, wouldn't he be similar in giving the highest place to money?"

"Of course."

"And, further, in being stingy and a toiler, satisfying only his necessary desires and not providing for other expenditures, but enslaving the other desires as vanities."

"Most certainly."

"A sort of squalid man," I said, "getting a profit out of everything, filling up his storeroom—exactly the kind of men the multitude

b   praises—isn't this the one who is like such a regime?"

"In my opinion, at least," he said. "Money, in any event, is held in honor above all by the city and by the man like it."

"For I don't suppose," I said, "such a man has devoted himself to education."

"Not in my opinion," he said. "Otherwise he wouldn't have set a blind leader[14] over the chorus and honored it above all."

"Good," I said. "But consider this. Won't we say that due to lack of education dronelike desires come to be in him—some of the beggar

c   variety, others of the wrongdoing variety—held down forcibly by his general diligence."

"Surely," he said.

"Do you know," I said, "to what you must look if you want to see the wrongdoings of these men?"

"To what?" he said.

"To their guardianship of orphans and any occasion of the kind that comes their way and gives them a considerable license to do injustice."

"True."

"Isn't it plain from this that when such a man has a good reputation in other contractual relations—because he seems to be just—he is

d   forcibly holding down bad desires, which are there, with some decent part of himself. He holds them down not by persuading them that they 'had better not' nor by taming them with argument, but by necessity and fear, doing so because he trembles for his whole substance."

"Very much so," he said.

"And, by Zeus, my friend," I said, "you'll find the desires that are akin to the drone present in most of them when they have to spend what belongs to others."

"Indeed you most certainly will," he said.

"Such a man, therefore, wouldn't be free from faction within himself; nor would he be simply one, but rather in some sense twofold, al-

though for the most part his better desires would master his worse   554 e
desires."

"That's so."

"Then on this account, I suppose such a man would be more
graceful than many, but the true virtue of the single-minded and harmonized soul would escape far from him."

"That's my opinion."

"Furthermore, the stingy man is a poor contestant when with his
private means he competes for some victory or any other noble object   555 a
of ambition in a city; he's not willing to spend money for the sake of
good reputation or any such contests. Afraid to awaken the spendthrift
desires and to summon them to an alliance and a love of victory, he
makes war like an oligarch, with a few of his troops, is defeated most of
the time, and stays rich."

"Quite so," he said.

"Do we then still doubt," I said, "that the stingy, money-making
man, in virtue of his likeness, corresponds to the oligarchic city?"

"Not at all," he said.   b

"Then, democracy, must, as it seems, be considered next—in
what way it comes into being and, once come into being, what it is
like—so that when we know the character of such a man in his turn, we
can bring him forward for judgment."

"In that," he said, "we would at least be proceeding just as we
were."

"Doesn't," I said, "the transformation from an oligarchy to a
democracy take place in something like the following way, as a result
of the insatiable character of the good that oligarchy proposes for itself—the necessity of becoming as rich as possible?"

"How?" he said.

"I suppose that because the rulers rule in it thanks to possessing   c
much, they are unwilling to control those among the youth who become
licentious by a law forbidding them to spend and waste what belongs
to them—in order that by buying and making loans on the property
of such men they can become richer and more honored."

"That they do above all."

"Isn't it by now plain that it's not possible to honor wealth in a
city and at the same time adequately to maintain moderation among
the citizens, but one or the other is necessarily neglected?"   d

"That's fairly plain," he said.

"Then, by their neglect and encouragement of licentiousness in
oligarchies, they have sometimes compelled human beings who are not
ignoble to become poor."

555 d

Poor
made at
Rich who
have wronged
them

"Quite so."

"Then I suppose these men sit idly in the city, fitted out with stings and fully armed, some owing debts, some dishonored, and some both, hating and plotting against those who acquired what belongs to them and all the rest too, gripped by a love of change."

"That's so."

"And these money-makers, with heads bent down, not seeming to see these men, wound with injections of silver any man among the remainder who yields; and carrying off from the father a multiple off-

556 a

spring in interest,[15] they make the drone and the beggar great in the city."

"Very great indeed," he said.

"And, at all events," I said, "they aren't willing to quench this kind of evil—as it is bursting into flame—either by preventing a man from doing what he wants with his property, or, alternatively, by instituting another law that resolves such cases."

"What law?"

"The one that takes second place to the former law and which compels the citizens to care for virtue. For if someone were to

b

prescribe that most voluntary contracts are to be made at the contractor's own risk, the citizens would make money less shamelessly in the city and fewer evils of the kind we were just describing would grow in it."

"Far fewer," he said.

"But, as it is," I said, "for all these reasons, the rulers in the city treat the ruled in this way. And as for themselves and their own, aren't their young luxurious and without taste for work of body or of soul, too

c

soft to resist pleasures and pains, and too idle?"

"What else could they be?"

"And haven't they themselves neglected everything except money-making and paid no more attention to virtue than the poor?"

"Yes, they have."

"When the rulers and the ruled, each prepared in this fashion, come alongside of each other—either wayfaring or in some other community, on trips to religious festivals or in campaigns, becoming ship-

d

mates or fellow soldiers, or even observing one another in dangers themselves—the poor are now in no wise despised by the rich. Rather it is often the case that a lean, tanned poor man is ranged in battle next to a rich man, reared in the shade, surrounded by a great deal of alien flesh, and sees him panting and full of perplexity. Don't you suppose he believes that it is due to the vice of the poor that such men are rich, and when the poor meet in private, one passes the word to the other: 'Those men are ours. For they are nothing'?"

"I certainly know very well," he said, "that this is what they do."   556 e

"Just as a sickly body needs only a slight push from outside to become ill, and sometimes even without any external influence becomes divided by factions within itself, so too doesn't a city that is in the same kind of condition as that body, on a small pretext—men brought in as allies from outside, from a city under an oligarchy, by the members of one party, from a city under a democracy by the members of the other—fall sick and do battle with itself, and sometimes even without any external influence become divided by faction?"

"That is very much the case."   557 a

"Then democracy, I suppose, comes into being when the poor win, killing some of the others and casting out some, and share the regime and the ruling offices with those who are left on an equal basis; and, for the most part, the offices in it are given by lot."

Democracy occurs when poor win!

"Yes," he said, "this is the establishment of democracy, whether it comes into being by arms or by the others' withdrawing due to fear."

"In what way do these men live?" I said. "And what is the character of such a regime? For it's plain that the man who is like it will turn out to be democratic."   b

"Yes, it is plain," he said.

"In the first place, then, aren't they free? And isn't the city full of freedom and free speech? And isn't there license in it to do whatever one wants?"

"That is what is said, certainly," he said.

"And where there's license, it's plain that each man would organize his life in it privately just as it pleases him."

"Yes, it is plain."

"Then I suppose that in this regime especially, all sorts of human beings come to be."   c

"How could they fail to?"

"It is probably the fairest of the regimes," I said. "Just like a many-colored cloak decorated in all hues, this regime, decorated with all dispositions, would also look fairest, and many perhaps," I said, "like boys and women looking at many-colored things, would judge this to be the fairest regime."

"Quite so," he said.

"And, what's more, you blessed man," I said, "it's a convenient place to look for a regime."   d

"Why is that?"

"Because, thanks to its license, it contains all species of regimes, and it is probably necessary for the man who wishes to organize a city, as we were just doing, to go to a city under a democracy. He would choose the sort that pleases him, like a man going into a general store

557 d of regimes, and, once having chosen, he would thus establish his regime."

e "Perhaps," he said, "he wouldn't be at a loss for patterns at least."

"And the absence of any compulsion to rule in this city," I said, "even if you are competent to rule, or again to be ruled if you don't want to be, or to make war when the others are making war, or to keep peace when the others are keeping it, if you don't desire peace; and, if some law prevents you from ruling or being a judge, the absence of any

558 a compulsion keeping you from ruling and being a judge anyhow, if you long to do so—isn't such a way of passing the time divinely sweet for the moment?"

"Perhaps," he said, "for the moment."

"And what about this? Isn't the gentleness toward[16] some of the condemned exquisite? Or in such a regime haven't you yet seen men who have been sentenced to death or exile, nonetheless staying and carrying on right in the middle of things; and, as though no one cared or saw, stalking the land like a hero?"[17]

"Yes, many," he said.

b "And this regime's sympathy and total lack of pettiness in despising what we were saying so solemnly when we were founding the city—that unless a man has a transcendent nature he would never become good if from earliest childhood his play isn't noble and all his practices aren't such—how magnificently it tramples all this underfoot and doesn't care at all from what kinds of practices a man goes to

c political action, but honors him if only he says he's well disposed toward the multitude?"

"It's a very noble regime," he said.

"Then, democracy," I said, "would have all this and other things akin to it and would be, as it seems, a sweet regime, without rulers and many-colored, dispensing a certain equality to equals and unequals alike."

"What you say," he said, "is quite well known."

"Reflect, then," I said, "who is the private man like this? Or, just as we did in the case of the regime, must we first consider how he comes to be?"

"Yes," he said.

d "Isn't it this way? I suppose a son would be born to that stingy, oligarchic man, a son reared by his father in his dispositions."

"Of course."

"Now, this son too, forcibly ruling all the pleasures in himself that are spendthrifty and do not conduce to money-making, those ones that are called unnecessary—"

"Plainly," he said.

[236]

"So that we don't discuss in the dark," I said, "do you want us to   *558 d*
define the necessary and the unnecessary desires?"

"Yes," he said, "that's what I want."

"Wouldn't those we aren't able to turn aside justly be called
necessary, as well as all those whose satisfaction benefits us? We are by
nature compelled to long for both of these, aren't we?"

"Quite so."

"Then we shall justly apply the term necessary to them."   *559 a*

"That is just."

"And what about this? If we were to affirm that all those are unnecessary of which a man could rid himself if he were to practice from
youth on and whose presence, moreover, does no good—and sometimes
even does the opposite of good—would what we say be fine?"

"Fine it would be."

"Then shall we choose an example of what each of them is so that
we can grasp their general types?"

"Yes, we must."

"Wouldn't the desire of eating—as long as it is for health and
good condition, the desire of mere bread and relish—be necessary?"

"I suppose so."

"The desire for bread, at least, is presumably necessary on both
counts, in that it is beneficial and in that it is capable of putting an end
to life."

"Yes."

"And so is the desire for relish, if in any way it is beneficial to
good condition."

"Most certainly."

"But what about the desire that goes beyond toward sorts of food
other than this, of which the many can be rid if it is checked in
youth and educated, and is harmful to the body and to the soul with
respect to prudence and moderation? Wouldn't it rightly be called un-   *c*
necessary?"

"Most rightly indeed."

"Then wouldn't we also assert that the latter desires are
spendthrifty, while the former are money-making because they are
useful[18] for our works?"

"Surely."

"Then won't we also assert the same about sex and the other
desires?"

"Yes, we'll assert the same."

"And weren't we also saying that the man we just named a drone
is full of such pleasures and desires and is ruled by the unnecessary
ones, while the stingy oligarchic man is ruled by the necessary ones?"   *d*

559 d

"Of course we were."

"Well, then, going back again," I said, "let's say how the democratic man comes out of the oligarchic one. And it looks to me as though it happens in most cases like this."

"How?"

"When a young man, reared as we were just saying without education and stingily, tastes the drones' honey, and has intercourse with fiery, clever beasts who are able to purvey manifold and subtle pleasures with every sort of variety, you presumably suppose that at

e
this point he begins his change from an oligarchic regime within himself to a democratic one."

"Most necessarily," he said.

"Then, just as the city was transformed when an alliance from outside brought aid to one party, like to like, is the young man also transformed in the same way when desires of a kindred and like form from without bring aid to one party of desires within him?"

"That's entirely certain."

"And, I suppose, if a counteralliance comes to the aid of the oligarchic party in him, either from the advice and scolding of his father

560 a
or from other relatives, then faction and counterfaction arise in him and he does battle with himself."

"Surely."

"And I suppose that at times the democratic party gives way to the oligarchic; and, with some of the desires destroyed and others exiled, a certain shame arose in the young man's soul, and order was reestablished."

"Sometimes that does happen," he said.

"But I suppose that once again other desires, akin to the exiled

b
ones, reared in secret due to the father's lack of knowledge about rearing, came to be, many and strong."

"At least," he said, "that's what usually happens."

"Then, drawn to the same associations, their secret intercourse bred a multitude."

"Of course."

"And, finally, I suppose they took the acropolis of the young man's soul, perceiving that it was empty of fair studies and practices and true speeches, and it's these that are the best watchmen and guardians in the thought of men whom the gods love."

c
"They are by far the best," he said.

"Then, in their absence, false and boasting speeches and opinions ran up and seized that place in such a young man."

"Indeed they did," he said.

[238]

"Doesn't he go back again to those Lotus-eaters and openly settle   *560 c*
among them? And if some help should come to the stingy element in
his soul from relatives, those boasting speeches close the gates of the
kingly wall within him; they neither admit the auxiliary force itself nor
do they receive an embassy of speeches of older[19] private men, but   *d*
doing battle they hold sway themselves; and naming shame simplicity,
they push it out with dishonor, a fugitive; calling moderation
cowardliness and spattering it with mud, they banish it;[20] persuading
that measure and orderly expenditure are rustic and illiberal, they join
with many useless desires in driving them over the frontier."

"Indeed they do."

"Now, once they have emptied and purged these from the soul of
the man whom they are seizing and initiating in great rites, they pro-   *e*
ceed to return insolence, anarchy, wastefulness, and shamelessness
from exile, in a blaze of light, crowned and accompanied by a
numerous chorus, extolling and flattering them by calling insolence
good education;[21] anarchy, freedom; wastefulness, magnificence;
and shamelessness, courage. Isn't it in some such way," I said, "that a   *561 a*
man, when he is young, changes from his rearing in necessary desires to
the liberation and unleashing of unnecessary and useless pleasures?"

"Yes," he said, "it's quite manifestly that way."

"Then, I suppose that afterward such a man lives spending no
more money, effort, and time on the necessary than on the unnecessary
pleasures. However, if he has good luck and his frenzy does not go
beyond bounds—and if, also, as a result of getting somewhat older and
the great disturbances having passed by, he readmits a part of the exiles   *b*
and doesn't give himself wholly over to the invaders—then he lives his
life in accord with a certain equality of pleasures he has established. To
whichever one happens along, as though it were chosen by the lot, he
hands over the rule within himself until it is satisfied; and then again to
another, dishonoring none but fostering them all on the basis of
equality."

"Most certainly."

"And," I said, "he doesn't admit true speech or let it pass into the
guardhouse, if someone says that there are some pleasures belonging to
fine and good desires and some belonging to bad desires, and that the   *c*
ones must be practiced and honored and the others checked and
enslaved. Rather, he shakes his head at all this and says that all are
alike and must be honored on an equal basis."

"That's exactly," he said, "what a man in this condition does."

"Then," I said, "he also lives along day by day, gratifying the
desire that occurs to him, at one time drinking and listening to the

561 c

d

Very Fickle

No Order

e

flute, at another downing water and reducing; now practicing gymnastic, and again idling and neglecting everything; and sometimes spending his time as though he were occupied with philosophy. Often he engages in politics and, jumping up, says and does whatever chances to come to him; and if he ever admires any soldiers, he turns in that direction; and if it's money-makers, in that one. And there is neither order nor necessity in his life, but calling this life sweet, free, and blessed he follows it throughout."²²

"You have," he said, "described exactly the life of a man attached to the law of equality."

"Well," I said, "I suppose that this man is all-various and full of the greatest number of dispositions, the fair and many-colored man, like the city. Many men and women would admire his life because it contains the most patterns of regimes and characters."

"Yes, that is he," he said.

562 a

Democracy

↓

b

tyranny

Greediness for what democracy defines as good destroys it.

c

"What then? Shall we set the man of this sort over against democracy as the one who would rightly be called democratic?"

"Let's do so," he said.

"Then," I said, "the fairest regime and the fairest man would be left for us to go through, tyranny and the tyrant."

"Certainly," he said.

"Come, now, my dear comrade, what is the manner of tyranny's coming into being? For it is pretty plain that it is transformed out of democracy."

"Yes, it is plain."

"Does tyranny come from democracy in about the same manner as democracy from oligarchy?"

"How?"

"The good that they proposed for themselves," I said, "and for the sake of which oligarchy was established, was wealth, wasn't it?"

"Yes."

"And then the greediness for wealth and the neglect of the rest for the sake of money-making destroyed it."

"True," he said.

"And does the greediness for what democracy defines as good also dissolve it?"

"What do you say it defines that good to be?"

"Freedom," I said. "For surely in a city under a democracy you would hear that this is the finest thing it has, and that for this reason it is the only regime worth living in for anyone who is by nature free."

"Yes indeed," he said, "that's an often repeated phrase."

[240]

Democracy defines [Freedom] as the good.

"Then," I said, "as I was going to say just now, does the insatiable   562 *c*
desire of this and the neglect of the rest change this regime and prepare
a need for tyranny?"

"How?" he said.

"I suppose that when a democratic city, once it's thirsted for freedom, gets bad winebearers as its leaders and gets more drunk than it   *d*
should on this unmixed draught, then, unless the rulers are very gentle
and provide a great deal of freedom, it punishes them, charging them
with being polluted and oligarchs."

"Yes," he said, "that's what they do."

"And it spatters with mud those who are obedient, alleging that
they are willing slaves of the rulers and nothings," I said, "while it
praises and honors—both in private and in public—the rulers who are
like the ruled and the ruled who are like the rulers. Isn't it necessary in
such a city that freedom spread to everything?"   *e*

"How could it be otherwise?"

"And, my friend," I said, "for it to filter down to the private
houses and end up by anarchy's being planted in the very beasts?"

"How do we mean that?" he said.

"That a father," I said, "habituates himself to be like his child and
fear his sons, and a son habituates himself to be like his father and to
have no shame before or fear of his parents—that's so he may be free;
and metic is on an equal level with townsman and townsman with
metic, and similarly with the foreigner."[23]   563 *a*

"Yes," he said, "that's what happens."

"These and other small things of the following kind come to
pass," I said. "As the teacher in such a situation is frightened of the
pupils and fawns on them, so the students make light of their teachers,
as well as of their attendants. And, generally, the young copy their el-
ders and compete with them in speeches and deeds while the old come
down to the level of the young; imitating the young, they are overflowing with facility and charm, and that's so that they won't seem to be   *b*
unpleasant or despotic."

"Most certainly," he said.

"And the ultimate in the freedom of the multitude, my friend," I
said, "occurs in such a city when the purchased slaves, male and
female, are no less free than those who have bought them. And we almost forgot to mention the extent of the law of equality and of freedom
in the relations of women with men and men with women."

"Won't we," he said, "with Aeschylus, 'say whatever just came to   *c*
our lips'?"[24]

"Certainly," I said, "I shall do just that. A man who didn't have

563 c   the experience couldn't be persuaded of the extent to which beasts subject to human beings are freer here than in another city. The bitches follow the proverb exactly and become like their mistresses;[25] and, of course, there come to be horses and asses who have gotten the habit of making their way quite freely and solemnly, bumping into whomever they happen to meet on the roads, if he doesn't stand aside, and all else

d   is similarly full of freedom."

    "You're telling me my own dream," he said. "I, myself, repeatedly suffer that very thing when journeying to the country."

    "Then, summing up all of these things together," I said, "do you notice how tender they make the citizens' soul, so that if someone proposes anything that smacks in any way of slavery, they are irritated and can't stand it? And they end up, as you well know, by paying no attention to the laws, written or unwritten, in order that they may avoid hav-

e   ing any master at all."

    "Of course, I know it," he said.

    "Well, then, my friend," I said, "this is the beginning, so fair and heady, from which tyranny in my opinion naturally grows."

    "It surely is a heady beginning," he said, "but what's next?"

    "The same disease," I said, "as that which arose in the oligarchy and destroyed it, arises also in this regime—but bigger and stronger as a result of the license—and enslaves democracy. And, really, anything that is done to excess is likely to provoke a correspondingly great change in the opposite direction—in seasons, in plants, in bodies, and,

564 a   in particular, not least in regimes."

    "That's probable," he said.

    "Too much freedom seems to change into nothing but too much slavery, both for private man and city."

    "Yes, that's probable."

    "Well, then," I said, "tyranny is probably established out of no other regime than democracy, I suppose—the greatest and most savage slavery out of the extreme of freedom."

    "Yes," he said, "that's reasonable."

    "But I suppose you weren't asking that," I said, "but rather what

b   disease, growing naturally in oligarchy and democracy alike, enslaves the latter."

    "What you say is true," he said.

    "Well, then," I said, "I meant that class of idle, extravagant men. The most courageous part of them leads, the less courageous part follows. It's just these whom we liken to drones, some equipped with stings, others without stings."

    "That's right," he said.

"Well, then," I said, "when these two come into being in any   564 *b*
regime, they cause trouble, like phlegm and bile in a body. And it's
against them that the good doctor and lawgiver of a city, no less than a   *c*
wise beekeeper, must take long-range precautions, preferably that they
not come into being, but if they do come into being, that they be cut out
as quickly as possible, cells and all."

"Yes, by Zeus," he said, "completely."

"Well, then," I said, "let's take it like this so that we may more
distinctly see what we want."

"How?"

"In the argument let's divide the city under a democracy into three
parts, which is the way it actually is divided. One class is surely that which,
thanks to the license, grows naturally in it no less than in the oligarchic city."

"That's so."

"But it's far fiercer here than in the other."

"How's that?"

"There, due to its not being held in honor but being driven from
the ruling offices, it is without exercise and isn't vigorous. But in a
democracy, presumably, this class, with few exceptions, leads, and its
fiercest part does the speaking and the acting, while the rest alight near
the platform and buzz and don't endure the man who says anything
else; the result is that everything, apart from a certain few exceptions,   *e*
is governed by this class in such a regime."

"Quite so," he said.

"Well, there is also another class that always distinguishes itself
from the multitude."

"What class?"

"Presumably when all are engaged in money-making, the men
most orderly by nature become, for the most part, richest."

"Likely."

"Then I suppose that it is there that the most honey, and that
easiest to get to, can be squeezed out by the drones."

"How," he said, "could one squeeze it out of those who have little?"

"Then I suppose such rich men are called the drones' pasture."

"Just about," he said.

"And the people would be the third class, all those who do their   565 *a*
own work, don't meddle in affairs, and don't possess very much.
Whenever they assemble, they constitute the most numerous and most
sovereign class in a democracy."

"Yes, they do," he said. "But they aren't willing to assemble very
frequently unless they get some share of the honey."

[handwritten margin note: Democracy is divided into 3 parts]   *d*

[243]

565 a

"Therefore, they always get a share," I said, "to the extent that the leaders, in taking away the substance of those who have it and distributing it among the people, are able to keep the greatest part for themselves."

"Yes," he said, "they do get a share in that way."

"Then I suppose that those men whose property is taken away are compelled to defend themselves by speaking before the people and by doing whatever they can."

"Of course."

"For this they are charged by the others, even if they don't desire to make innovations, with plotting against the people and being oligarchs."

"Of course."

"And, therefore, when they see that the people are trying to do them an injustice, not willingly but out of ignorance and because they are deceived by the slanderers, they at last end up, whether they want to or not, by becoming truly oligarchs; they do not do so willingly, but the drone who stings them engenders this evil too."

"That's entirely certain."

"And then come impeachments, judgments, and contests against one another."

"Quite so."

"Aren't the people always accustomed to set up some one man as their special leader and to foster him and make him grow great?"

"Yes, they are accustomed to do that."

"It's plain, therefore," I said, "that when a tyrant grows naturally, he sprouts from a root of leadership and from nowhere else."

"That is quite plain."

"What is the beginning of the transformation from leader to tyrant? Or is it plainly when the leader begins to act out the tale that is told in connection with the temple of Lycaean Zeus in Arcadia?"[26]

"What's that?"

"That the man who tastes of the single morsel of human inwards cut up with those of other sacrificial victims must necessarily become a wolf. Or haven't you heard that speech?"

"I have."

"Isn't it also the same for the leader of a people who, taking over a particularly obedient mob, does not hold back from shedding the blood of his tribe but unjustly brings charges against a man—which is exactly what they usually do—and, bringing him before the court, murders him, and, doing away with a man's life, tastes of kindred blood

with unholy tongue and mouth, and banishes, and kills, and hints at   *565 e*
cancellations of debts and redistributions of land; isn't it also   *566 a*
necessarily fated, I say, that after this such a man either be slain by his
enemies or be tyrant and turn from a human being into a wolf?"

"Quite necessarily," he said.

"Then this," I said, "is the man who incites faction against those
who have wealth."

"This is he."

"If he's exiled and comes back in spite of his enemies, does he
come back a complete tyrant?"

"Plainly."

"But if they are unable to exile him or to kill him by slandering
him to the city, they plot to do away with him stealthily by a violent
death."

"At least," he said, "that's what usually happens."

"All those, then, whose careers have progressed to this stage now
hit upon the notorious tyrannical request—to ask the people for some
bodyguards to save the people's defender for them."

"Quite so," he said.

"Then I suppose the people grant the request, frightened for him
and sure of themselves."

"Quite so."

"Consequently when a man sees this, one who possesses money
and is charged not only with having money but also with hating the
people, he, my comrade, then follows the oracle that was given to
Croesus and

> Flees along many-pebbled Hermus;
> He doesn't stay nor is he ashamed to be a coward."[27]

"For he couldn't be ashamed a second time," he said.

"And I suppose," I said, "that if he's caught, he's given death."

"Necessarily."

"And surely it's plain that this leader himself doesn't lie 'great in
his greatness' on the ground, but, having cast down many others, stands   *d*
in the chariot of the city, now a perfected tyrant instead of a
leader."[28]

"Of course," he said.

"Then let us," I said, "go through the happiness of the man and
the city in which such a mortal comes to be."

"Most certainly," he said, "let's go through it."

"In the first days of his time in office," I said, "doesn't he smile at
and greet whomever he meets, and not only deny he's a tyrant but prom-

566 e

ise much in private and public, and grant freedom from debts and distribute land to the people and those around himself, and pretend to be gracious and gentle to all?"

"Necessarily," he said.

"But I suppose that when he is reconciled with some of his enemies outside and has destroyed the others, and there is rest from concern with them, as his first step he is always setting some war in motion, so that the people will be in need of a leader."

"That's likely."

567 a

"And, also, so that, becoming poor from contributing money, they will be compelled to stick to their daily business and be less inclined to plot against him?"

"Plainly."

"Then, too, I suppose—if he suspects certain men of having free thoughts and not putting up with his ruling—so that he can have a pretext for destroying them by giving them to the enemy? For all these reasons isn't it necessary for a tyrant always to be stirring up war?"

"It is necessary."

b

"And is, consequently, all this activity a preparation for being more hateful to the citizens?"

"Of course."

"Also, don't some of those who helped in setting him up and are in power—the manliest among them—speak frankly to him and to one another, criticizing what is happening?"

"That's likely."

"Then the tyrant must gradually do away with all of them, if he's going to rule, until he has left neither friend nor enemy of any worth whatsoever."

"Plainly."

c

"He must, therefore, look sharply to see who is courageous, who is great-minded, who is prudent, who is rich. And so happy is he that there is a necessity for him, whether he wants to or not, to be an enemy of all of them and plot against them until he purges the city."

"A fine purgation," he said.

"Yes," I said, "the opposite of the one the doctors give to bodies. For they take off the worst and leave the best, while he does the opposite."

"For it seems," he said, "to be a necessity for him, if he is to rule."

d

"Therefore," I said, "he is bound by a blessed necessity that prescribes that he either dwell with the ordinary many, even though hated by them, or cease to live."

"That is precisely his situation," he said.

[246]

"To the extent that he is more hateful to the citizens for doing   *567 d*
these things, won't he have more need of more—and more trustworthy
—armed guards?"

"Of course."

"Who are these trustworthy men? And where will he send for
them?"

"On their own, many will come flying," he said, "if he gives the
wages."

"These are drones, by the dog," I said, "of whom you are, in my
opinion, again speaking, foreign ones of all sorts."   *e*

"Your opinion is true," he said.

"And who are the trustworthy ones on the spot? Wouldn't he be
willing—"

"What?"

"—to take away the slaves from the citizens, free them and
include them among the armed guards surrounding himself?"

"Oh, he would be very willing," he said, "since these are,
doubtless, the men most trustworthy for him."

"The tyrant of whom you speak," I said, "is a blessed thing, if he
uses such men as friends and trustworthy helpers after he has destroyed   *568 a*
his former ones."

"But he certainly does use such men," he said.

"And these companions admire him," I said, "and the new
citizens have intercourse with him, while the decent men hate him and
flee from him."

"What else would they do?"

"It's not for nothing," I said, "that tragedy in general has the
reputation of being wise and, within it, Euripides of being particularly
so."

"Why is that?"

"Because, among other things, he uttered this phrase, the product
of shrewd thought, 'tyrants are wise from intercourse with the   *b*
wise.'29 And he plainly meant that these men we just spoke of are the
wise with whom a tyrant has intercourse."

"And he and the other poets," he said, "extol tyranny as a condition 'equal to that of a god'30 and add much else, too."

"Therefore," I said, "because the tragic poets are wise, they pardon us, and all those who have regimes resembling ours, for not admit-
ing them into the regime on the ground that they make hymns to
tyranny."

"I suppose," he said, "they pardon us, at least all the subtle ones
among them."   *c*

"And I suppose that, going around to the other cities, gathering

568 c crowds, and hiring fine, big and persuasive voices, they draw the regimes toward tyrannies and democracies."

"Quite so."

"And, besides this, they get wages and are honored too, most of all by tyrants, as is to be expected, and, in the second place, by democracy. But the higher they go on the slope of the regimes, the

d more their honor fails, as though it were unable to proceed for want of breath."

"Most certainly."

"But here we've digressed," I said. "Let's return to the tyrant's camp, that fair, numerous, many-colored thing that is never the same, and tell from where its support will come."

Lavish Life

"It's plain," he said, "that if there is sacred money in the city, he'll spend it as long as it lasts, along with the property of the men he has destroyed,[31] so that people won't be compelled to bring in such large contributions."

e "And what happens when that source gives out?"

"It's plain," he said, "that he and his drinking fellows and comrades, male and female, will get their support from his father's property."

"I understand," I said. "The people that begot the tyrant will support him and his comrades."

"A great necessity will compel it," he said.

"But what do you have to say to this?" I said. "What if the people are discontented and say that it is not just for a son in his prime to be supported by his father, but the reverse, the father should be supported

569 a by the son; and that they didn't beget and set him up so that when he had grown great they should be slaves to their own slaves and support him and the slaves along with other flotsam, but so that with him as leader they would be freed from the rich and those who are said to be gentlemen in the city; and they now bid him and his comrades to go away from the city—like a father driving a son along with his troublesome drinking fellows out of the house?"

"By Zeus, how this kind of a people will then know," he said, "the kind

b of a beast they have begotten, welcomed, and made great, and that they are the weaker driving out the stronger!"

"What are you saying?" I said. "Will the tyrant dare to use force on his father, and if he doesn't obey, strike him?"

"Yes," he said, "once he's taken away his father's arms."

"You speak of the tyrant as a parricide and a harsh nurse of old age,"[32] I said, "and, as it seems, this would at last be self-admitted tyranny and, as the saying goes, the people in fleeing the smoke of

enslavement to free men would have fallen into the fire of being under   *569 c*
the mastery of slaves; in the place of that great and unseasonable freedom they have put on the dress of the harshest and bitterest enslavement to slaves."

"That's exactly what happens," he said.

"Well then," I said, "wouldn't we be speaking appropriately if we
asserted that we have given an adequate presentation of how a tyranny
is transformed out of a democracy, and what it is like when it has come
into being?"

"Most certainly," he said, "it was adequate."

BOOK IX

"Well," I said, "the tyrannic man himself remains to be considered—how he is transformed out of the democratic man, and, once come into being, what sort of man he is and how he lives, wretchedly or blessedly."

"Yes," he said, "he is the one who still remains."

"Do you know," I said, "what I still miss?"

"What?"

"In my opinion we haven't adequately distinguished the kinds and number of the desires. And with this lacking, the investigation we are making will be less clear."

"Isn't it," he said, "still a fine time to do so?"

"Most certainly. And just consider that aspect of them I wish to observe. It's this. Of the unnecessary pleasures and desires, there are, in my opinion, some that are hostile to law and that probably come to be in everyone; but, when checked by the laws and the better desires, with the help of argument, in some human beings they are entirely gotten rid of or only a few weak ones are left, while in others stronger and more numerous ones remain."

"Which ones do you mean?" he said.

"Those," I said, "that wake up in sleep when the rest of the soul—all that belongs to the calculating, tame, and ruling part of it—slumbers, while the beastly and wild part, gorged with food or

571 *a*

b

c

[251]

571 c   drink, is skittish and, pushing sleep away, seeks to go and satisfy its dispositions. You know that in such a state it dares to do everything as though it were released from, and rid of, all shame and prudence. And it doesn't shrink from attempting intercourse, as it supposes, with a
d   mother or with anyone else at all—human beings, gods, and beasts; or attempting any foul murder at all, and there is no food from which it abstains. And, in a word, it omits no act of folly or shamelessness."

"What you say," he said, "is very true."

"But, on the other hand, I can suppose a man who has a healthy and moderate relationship to himself and who goes to sleep only after he does the following: first, he awakens his calculating part and feasts it on fair arguments and considerations, coming to an understanding with
e   himself; second, he feeds the desiring part in such a way that it is neither in want nor surfeited—in order that it will rest and not disturb
572 a   the best part by its joy or its pain, but rather leave that best part alone pure and by itself, to consider and to long for the perception of something that it doesn't know, either something that has been, or is, or is going to be; and, third, he soothes the spirited part in the same way and does not fall asleep with his spirit aroused because there are some he got angry at. When a man has silenced these two latter forms and set the third—the one in which prudent thinking comes to be—in motion, and only then takes his rest, you know that in such a state he most lays hold of the truth and at this time the sights that are hostile to
b   law show up least in his dreams."

"I suppose," he said, "it's exactly that way."

"Well now, we have been led out of the way and said too much about this. What we wish to recognize is the following: surely some terrible, savage, and lawless form of desires is in every man, even in some of us who seem to be ever so measured. And surely this becomes plain in dreams. Now reflect whether I seem to be saying something and whether you agree with me."

"I do agree."

"Well then, recall the character we attributed to the man of the
c   people. He was presumably produced by being reared from youth by a stingy father who honored only the money-making desires while despising the ones that aren't necessary but exist for the sake of play and showing off. Isn't that so?"

"Yes."

"And once having had intercourse with subtler men who are full of those desires we just went through, he began by plunging himself into every insolence and assuming the form of these men, out of hatred of his father's stinginess. But, because he has a nature better than that of

his corrupters, he was drawn in both directions, and settled down ex-   *572 c*
actly in the middle between the two ways; and enjoying each in   *d*
measure, as he supposed, he lives a life that is neither illiberal nor
hostile to law, a man of the people come from an oligarchic man."

"That was and is," he said, "the opinion about this kind of man."

"Well, then," I said, "assume again that such a man, now grown
older, has a young son reared, in turn, in his father's dispositions."

"I shall assume that."

"Well, assume further that those same things happen to the son
that also happened to his father and he is drawn to complete hostility to
law, though it is named complete freedom by those who are introducing   *e*
him to it, and that his father and his other relatives bring aid to those
middle desires while these dread enchanters and tyrant-makers give aid
to the other side. And when they have no hope of getting hold of the
young man in any other way, they contrive to implant some love in
him—a great winged drone—to be the leader of the idle desires that insist on all available resources being distributed to them. Or do you sup- *573 a*
pose that love in such men is anything other than a winged drone?"

"I suppose," he said, "that it is nothing but this."

"Then, when the other desires—overflowing with incense, myrrh,
crowns, wines and all the pleasures with which such societies are
rife—buzz around the drone, making it grow great and fostering it,
they plant the sting of longing in it. Now this leader of the soul takes
madness for its armed guard and is stung to frenzy. And if it finds in   *b*
the man any opinions or desires accounted good and still admitting of
shame, it slays them and pushes them out of him until it purges him of
moderation and fills him with madness brought in from abroad."

"Your account," he said, "of a tyrannic man's genesis is quite
perfect."

"Is it for this reason, too," I said, "that love has from old been
called a tyrant?"

"That's likely," he said.

"And, my friend," I said, "doesn't a drunken man also have something of a tyrannic turn of mind?"   *c*

"Yes, he does."

"And, further, the man who is mad and deranged undertakes and
expects to be able to rule not only over human beings but gods, too."

"Quite so," he said.

"And, you demonic man," I said, "a man becomes tyrannic in
the precise sense when, either by nature or by his practices or both, he
has become drunken, erotic, and melancholic."[1]

"That's perfectly certain."

573 c   "This, as it seems, is also the way such a man comes into being. Now how does he live?"

d   "As those who play say," he said, "you'll tell me this too."[2]

"I shall," I said. "I suppose that next there are among them feasts, revels, parties, courtesans, and everything else of the sort that belongs to those in whom the tryant love dwells and pilots all the elements of the soul."

"Necessarily," he said.

"Don't many terrible and very needy desires sprout up beside it every day and night?"

"They are indeed many."

"So that whatever revenues there may be are quickly used up."

"Of course."

e   "And next surely come borrowing and the stripping away of his estate."

"What else?"

"Then when all this gives out, won't the crowd of intense desires hatched in the nest necessarily cry out; and won't these men, driven as it were by the stings of the other desires but especially by love itself, which guides all the others as though they were its armed guards, rage and consider who has anything they can take away by deceit or

574 a   force?"

"Very much so," he said.

"Then it is necessary to get contributions from every source or be caught in the grip of great travail and anguish."

"Yes, it is necessary."

"Then, just as the pleasures that came to be in him later got the better of the old ones and took away what belonged to them, so won't he, a younger man, claim he deserves to get the better of his father and mother and, if he has spent his own part, take away and distribute the paternal property?"

"Of course," he said.

b   "And then if they won't turn it over to him, wouldn't he first attempt to steal from his parents and deceive them?"

"Exactly."

"And where he's not able to, won't he next seize it and use force?"

"I suppose so," he said.

"And then, you surprising man, if the old man and the old woman hold their ground and fight, would he watch out and be reluctant to do any tyrannic deeds?"

"I'm not," he said, "very hopeful for such a man's parents."

"But, in the name of Zeus, Adeimantus, is it your opinion that for   *574 b*
the sake of a newly-found lady friend and unnecessary concubine such   *c*
a man will strike his old friend and necessary mother, or that for the
sake of a newly-found and unnecessary boy friend, in the bloom of
youth, he will strike his elderly and necessary father who is no longer in
the bloom of youth and is the oldest of friends, and that he will enslave
his parents to them if he should bring them into the same house?"

"Yes, by Zeus," he said, "it is."

"How very blessed it seems to be," I said, "to bear a tyrannic
son."

"Oh, quite," he said.

"What then? When what belongs to his father and mother gives   *d*
out on such a man and there's already quite a swarm of pleasures densely
gathered in him, won't he begin by taking hold of the wall³ of
someone's house or the cloak of someone who goes late at night,
and next, sweep out some temple? And throughout all this, those
opinions he held long ago in childhood about fine and base things, the
opinions accounted just,⁴ are mastered by the opinions newly released from slavery, now acting as love's bodyguard and conquering
along with it. These are the opinions that were formerly released as
dreams in sleep when, still under laws and a father, there was a dem-   *e*
ocratic regime in him. But once a tyranny was established by love,
what he had rarely been in dreams, he became continuously while
awake. He will stick at no terrible murder, or food, or deed. Rather,
love lives like a tyrant within him in all anarchy and lawlessness; and,   *575 a*
being a monarch, will lead the man whom it controls, as though he
were a city, to every kind of daring that will produce wherewithal for it
and the noisy crowd around it—one part of which bad company
caused to come in from outside; the other part was from within and
was set loose and freed by his own bad character. Or isn't this the life
of such a man?"

"It certainly is," he said.

"And if," I said, "there are few such men in a city and the rest of
the multitude is behaving moderately, they emigrate and serve as   *b*
bodyguards to some other tyrant or as auxiliaries for wages, if there is
war somewhere. And if they come to be in a period of peace and quiet,
then they remain there in the city and do many small evil deeds."

"What kind of deeds do you mean?"

"Oh, they steal, break into houses, cut purses, go off with people's
clothes, rob temples, and lead men into slavery; at times they are sycophants, if they are able to speak, and they bear false witness and take
bribes."

575 c

"These are small evils you speak of," he said, "if such men are few."

"That's because small things," I said, "are small compared to big ones; and for the badness and wretchedness of a city all of these things together surely don't, as the saying goes, come within striking distance of a tyrant. But when such men and the others who follow them become many in a city, and they become aware of their own multitude, it is then that they, together with the folly of the people, generate the tyrant, that one among them who in particular has the biggest and most

d

extreme tyrant within his own soul."

"Fitting," he said. "For he would be the most tyrannic."

"That's if they submit willingly. But if the city doesn't offer itself, just as he then punished his mother and father, so now he will, if he can, punish the fatherland, bringing in new comrades; and his way of keeping and cherishing his dear old motherland—as the Cretans say—and fatherland will be to enslave them to these men. And this must surely be the end toward which such a man's desire is directed."

e

"That's exactly it," he said.

"When these men are in private life, before they rule, aren't they like this: in the first place, as to their company, either they have intercourse with their flatterers, who are ready to serve them in everything, or, if they have need of anything from anyone, they themselves cringe and dare to assume any posture, acting as though they belonged

576 a

to him, but when they have succeeded they become quite alien."

"Very much so," he said.

"Therefore, they live their whole life without ever being friends of anyone, always one man's master or another's slave. The tyrannic nature never has a taste of freedom or true friendship."

"Most certainly."

"Wouldn't we be right in calling such men faithless?"

"Of course."

"And, further, could we call them as unjust as they can be, if our

b

previous agreement about what justice is was right?"

"But surely it was right," he said.

"Well, then," I said, "let's sum up the worst man. He is awake, presumably, what we described a dreaming man to be."

"Most certainly."

"And he comes from a man who is by nature most tyrannic and gets a monarchy; and the longer he lives in tyranny, the more he becomes like that."

"Necessarily," Glaucon said, as he took over the argument.

"The man who turns out to be worst," I said, "will he also turn

out to be most wretched? And he who is for the longest time the most a   *576 c*
tyrant, will he also have been most wretched for the longest time—in
the light of the truth? However, the many have many opinions."

"But, regardless," he said, "this is necessarily so."

"With respect to likeness," I said, "does the tyrannic man correspond to anything other than the city under a tyranny, and the man of
the people to anything other than the city under a democracy, and similarly with the other men?"

"Of course not."   *d*

"And as city is to city with respect to virtue and happiness so is man to
man?"

"Of course."

"With respect to virtue, what is the relation between a city under
a tyranny and the one under a kingship such as we first described?"

"Everything is the opposite," he said. "The one was the best, the
other the worst."

"I won't ask you which you mean," I said. "It's plain. But as to
their happiness and wretchedness, do you judge similarly or differently? And let's not be overwhelmed at the sight of the tyrant—one
man—or a certain few around him; but, as one must, let's go in and
view the city as a whole, and, creeping down into every corner and   *e*
looking, only then declare our opinion."

"What you suggest is right," he said. "And it's plain to everyone
that there is no city more wretched than one under a tyranny and none
happier than one under a kingship."

"And about these same things, as they exist in the men," I said,
"would I also be right in suggesting that that man should be deemed fit   *577 a*
to judge them who is able with his thought to creep into a man's disposition and see through it—a man who is not like a child looking from outside and overwhelmed by the tyrannic pomp set up as a facade for those
outside, but who rather sees through it adequately? And what if I were
to suppose that all of us must hear that man who is both able to judge
and has lived together with the tyrant in the same place and was
witness to his actions at home and saw how he is with each of his own,
among whom he could most be seen stripped of the tragic gear; and, again, *b*
has seen him in public dangers; and, since he has seen all that,
we were to bid him to report how the tyrant stands in relation to the
others in happiness and wretchedness?"

"You would," he said, "be quite right in suggesting these things
too."

"Do you want us," I said, "to pretend that we are among those
who would be able to judge and have already met up with such men, so
that we'll have someone to answer what we ask?"

577 b   "Certainly."

c   "Come, then," I said, "and consider it in this way for me.
Recalling for yourself the likeness of the city and the man, and reflecting on each in turn, tell of the states of both."

               "Which ones?" he said.

               "In the first place," I said, "speaking of a city, will you say that
one under a tyranny is free or slave?"

               "Slave," he said, "in the highest possible degree."

               "However, you do see masters and free men in it too."

               "I do," he said, "see a small part of the kind, but virtually the
whole of it and the most decent part is slave, without honor, and wretched."

d   "If, then," I said, "a man is like his city, isn't it also necessary that
the same arrangement be in him and that his soul be filled with much
slavery and illiberality, and that, further, those parts of it that are most
decent be slaves while a small part, the most depraved and maddest, be
master?"

               "That is necessary," he said.

               "What, then? Will you assert that such a soul is slave or free?"

               "Slave, of course."

               "And, further, doesn't the city that is slave and under a tyranny
least do what it wants?"

               "By far."

e   "And therefore, the soul that is under a tyranny will least do what
it wants—speaking of the soul as a whole. Always forcibly drawn by a
gadfly, it will be full of confusion and regret."

               "Of course."

               "And is the city under a tyranny necessarily rich or poor?"

               "Poor."

578 a   "And, therefore, the tyrannic soul is necessarily always poverty-
ridden and insatiable."

               "That's so," he said.

               "And what about this? Isn't such a city necessarily as full of fear as such a man?"

               "Quite necessarily."

               "Do you suppose you'll find more complaining, sighing, lamenting
or suffering in any other city?"

               "Not at all."

               "But, in a man, do you believe there is more of this sort of thing
in anyone other than this tyrannic man maddened by desires and
loves?"

               "How could I?" he said.

b   "I suppose, then, that you looked to all these things and others like them and judged this city to be the most wretched of cities."   578 *b*

"Wasn't I right in doing so?" he said.

"Quite right," I said. "But, now, what do you say about the tyrannic man in looking at these same things?"

"That he is by far," he said, "the most wretched of all men."

"In saying that," I said, "you are no longer right."

"How's that?" he said.

"This man," I said, "is not yet, I suppose, the most wretched."

"Then who is?"

"Perhaps this man will, in your opinion, be even more wretched than the other."

"What man?"

"The man," I said, "who is tyrannic and doesn't live out a   *c*
private life but has bad luck and by some misfortune is given the occasion to become a tyrant."

"I conjecture," he said, "on the basis of what was said before, that what you say is true."

"Yes," I said. "But in an argument such as this, one must not just suppose such things but must consider them quite well. For, you know, the consideration is about the greatest thing, a good life and a bad one."

"Quite right," he said.

"Well, then, consider whether, after all, I am saying anything. In   *d*
my opinion we must reflect on it from this point of view."

"Which one?"

"The point of view of the individual private men who are rich in cities and possess many bondsmen. For they are similar to the tyrant in ruling many, although the multitude of the tyrant is greater."

"Yes, it is greater."

"You know that they are confident, and not frightened, of the domestics?"

"What would they be frightened of?"

"Nothing," I said. "But do you recognize the cause?"

"Yes, that the city as a whole defends the individual private man."

"What you say is fine," I said. "But what if some one of the gods   *e*
were to lift one man who has fifty or more bondsmen out of the city—him, his wife, and his children—and set them along with the rest of his property and the domestics in a desert place where none of the free men is going to be able to help him? What do you suppose will be the character and extent of his fear that he, his children, and his wife will be destroyed by the domestics?"

"I think it will be extreme," he said.

579 a
"Wouldn't he now be compelled to fawn on some of his own slaves and promise them much and free them although there is no obligation for him to do so? And wouldn't he himself turn out to be the flatterer of servants?"

"He's certainly compelled to," he said, "or else be destroyed."

"And," I said, "what if the god settled many other neighbors all around him who won't stand for any man's claiming to be another's master, and if they ever can get their hands on such a one, they subject him to extreme punishments."

b
"He would," he said, "I suppose, be in an even greater extreme of evil, watched on all sides by nothing but enemies."

"Isn't the tyrant bound in such a prison, he who has a nature such as we described, full of many fears and loves of all kinds? And he, whose soul is so gourmand, alone of the men in the city can't go anywhere abroad or see all the things the other free men desire to see; but, stuck in his house for the most part, he lives like a woman, envying any of the

c
other citizens who travel abroad and see anything good."

"That's entirely certain," he said.

"Therefore, it is a harvest greater by such ills that is reaped by a man who has a bad regime in himself—the one you just now judged most wretched, the tyrannic man—and who doesn't live out his life as a private man but is compelled by some chance to be a tyrant, and while not having control of himself attempts to rule others, just as if a man with a body that is sick and without control of itself were com-

d
pelled to spend his life not in a private station but contesting and fighting with other bodies."

"The case is in every way most similar," he said, "and what you say, Socrates, is most true."

"My dear Glaucon," I said, "isn't this a perfectly wretched condition, and doesn't the man who is a tyrant have a still harder life than the man judged by you to have the hardest life?"

"That's entirely so," he said.

"Therefore, the real tyrant is, even if he doesn't seem so to someone, in truth a real slave to the greatest fawning and slavery,

e
and a flatterer of the most worthless men; and with his desires getting no kind of satisfaction, he shows that he is most in need of the most things and poor in truth, if one knows how to look at a soul as a whole. Throughout his entire life his is full of fear, overflowing with convulsions and pains, if indeed he resembles the disposition of the city he rules. And he does resemble it, doesn't he?"

"Quite so," he said.

580 a
"And, besides, shouldn't we attribute to the man too the

things we spoke of before? Isn't it necessary that he be—and due   580 *a*
to ruling become still more than before—envious, faithless, unjust,
friendless, impious, and a host and nurse for all vice; and, thanks
to all this, unlucky in the extreme; and then, that he make those close
to him so?"

"No one with any sense," he said, "will contradict you."

"Come, then," I said, "just as the man who has the final decision
in the whole contest[5] declares his choice, you, too, choose now for me   *b*
who in your opinion is first in happiness, and who second, and the others
in order, five in all—kingly, timocratic, oligarchic, democratic, tyrannic."

"The choice is easy," he said. "For, with respect to virtue and
vice, and happiness and its opposite, I choose them, like choruses, in
the very order in which they came on stage."

"Shall we hire a herald then," I said, "or shall I myself announce
that Ariston's son has decided that the best[6] and most just man is
happiest, and he is that man who is kingliest and is king of himself;   *c*
while the worst and most unjust man is most wretched and he, in his
turn, happens to be the one who, being most tyrannic, is most tyrant of
himself and of the city?"

"Let it have been announced by you," he said.

"And shall I," I said, "add this to the proclamation: whether or
not in being such they escape the notice of all human beings and
gods?"

"Do add that to the proclamation," he said.

"All right, then," I said. "That would be one proof for us. Look at
this second one and see if there seems to be anything to it."   *d*

"What is it?"

"Since," I said, "just as a city is divided into three forms, so the
soul of every single man also is divided in three, the thesis will admit
yet of another proof, in my opinion."

"What is it?"

"This. It looks to me as though there were also a threefold division of pleasures corresponding to these three, a single pleasure
peculiar to each one; and similarly a threefold division of desires and
kinds of rule."

"How do you mean?" he said.

"One part, we say, was that with which a human being learns, and
another that with which he becomes spirited; as for the third, because
of its many forms, we had no peculiar name to call it by, but we named   *e*
it by what was biggest and strongest in it. For we called it the desiring
part on account of the intensity of the desires concerned with eating,
drinking, sex, and all their followers; and so, we also called it the

581 *a*   money-loving part, because such desires are most fulfilled by means of money."

"That was right," he said.

"Then if we were to say that its pleasure and love is of gain, would we most satisfactorily fix it in one general form for the argument, so that when we speak of this part of the soul we will plainly indicate something to ourselves; and would we be right in calling it money-loving and gain-loving?"

"In my opinion, at least," he said.

"And what about this? Don't we, of course, say that the spirited part is always wholly set on mastery, victory and good reputation?"

b   "Quite so."

"If we were to designate it victory-loving, and honor-loving, would that strike the right note?"

"Very much the right note."

"And, moreover, it's plain to everyone that the part with which we learn is always entirely directed toward knowing the truth as it is; and of the parts, it cares least for money and opinion."

"By far."

"Then would it be appropriate for us to call it learning-loving and wisdom-loving?"

"Of course."

"And," I said, "doesn't this part rule in the souls of some men, while in that of others another of these parts rules, whichever it hap-

c   pens to be?"

"That's so," he said.

"Then that's why we assert that the three primary classes of human beings are also three: wisdom-loving, victory-loving, gain-loving."

"Entirely so."

"Then, also of pleasures, are there three forms, one underlying each of these?"

"Certainly."

"Do you know," I said, "that if you were willing to ask three such men, each in turn, what is the sweetest of these lives, each would most

d   laud his own? The money-maker will assert that, compared to gaining, the pleasure in being honored or in learning is worth nothing, unless he makes some money from them."

"True," he said.

"And what about the lover of honor?" I said. "Doesn't he believe the pleasure from money to be a vulgar thing and, on the other hand, the pleasure from learning—whatever learning doesn't bring honor—to be smoke and nonsense?"

"That's so," he said.

"As for the lover of wisdom," I said, "what do we suppose he will
hold about the other pleasures as compared with that of knowing the
truth as it is and always being in some such state of pleasure while
learning? Won't he hold them to be far behind in pleasure? And won't
he call them really necessary since he doesn't need all the others if
necessity did not accompany them?"

"That we must know well," he said.

"Since, then," I said, "the pleasures of each form, and the life itself, dispute with one another, not about living more nobly or
shamefully or worse or better but about living more pleasantly and
painlessly, how would we know which of them speaks most truly?"

"I certainly can't say," he said.

"Consider it in this way. By what must things that are going to be
finely judged be judged? Isn't it by experience, prudence, and argument? Or could anyone have better criteria than these?"

"How could he?" he said.

"Now, consider. Of the three men, which is most experienced in all
the pleasures of which we were speaking? Does the lover of gain, because he learns the truth itself as it is, seem to you to be more experienced in the pleasure that comes from knowing than the lover of
wisdom is in the pleasure that comes from gaining?"

"There's a great difference," he said. "It's necessary for the
latter to taste of the other pleasures starting in childhood. But for
the lover of gain it's not necessary to taste, or to have experience of,
how sweet is the pleasure of learning the natural characteristics of
the things which *are*; rather even if he were eager to, it wouldn't be
easy."

"There's a great difference, then," I said, "between the lover of
wisdom and the lover of gain in their experience of both the pleasures."

"Great indeed."

"And what about the lover of wisdom's relation to the lover of
honor? Is he less experienced in the pleasure that comes from being
honored than the lover of honor is in the pleasure that comes from
thinking?"

"No," he said. "Honor accompanies them all, if each achieves its
aim. For the wealthy man is honored by many; and so are the
courageous man and the wise one. Therefore, all have experience of the
kind of pleasure that comes from being honored. But the kind of
pleasure connected with the vision of what *is* cannot be tasted by
anyone except the lover of wisdom."

582 d   "Therefore," I said, "as for experience, he is the finest judge among the three men."

"By far."

"And, moreover, only he will have gained his experience in the company of prudence."

"Of course."

"Furthermore, as to the instrument by means of which judgment must be made, it is not the instrument of the lover of gain or the lover of honor but that of the lover of wisdom."

"What's that?"

"We surely said that it is by means of arguments that judgment must be made, didn't we?"

"Yes."

"And arguments are especially the instrument of the philosopher."

"Of course."

"Now, if what is being judged were best judged by wealth and
e   gain, what the lover of gain praised and blamed would necessarily be most true."

"Very much so."

"And if by honor, victory, and courage, wouldn't it be what the lover of honor and victory praised and blamed?"

"Plainly."

"But since it's by experience, prudence, and argument—"

"What the lover of wisdom and the lover of argument praise would necessarily be most true," he said.

583 a   "Therefore, of the three pleasures, the most pleasant would belong to that part of the soul with which we learn; and the man among us in whom this part rules has the most pleasant life."

"Of course he has," he said. "At least it is as a sovereign praiser that the prudent man praises his own life."

"What life," I said, "does the judge say is in second place and what pleasure is in second place?"

"Plainly that of the warlike man and lover of honor. For it is nearer to him than that of the money-maker."

"Then the pleasure of the lover of gain is in last place, as it seems."

"Of course," he said.

b   "Well then, that makes two in a row, and twice the just man has been victorious over the unjust one. Now the third, in Olympic fashion, to the savior and the Olympian Zeus.[7] Observe that the other men's pleasure, except for that of the prudent man, is neither entirely true nor pure but is a sort of shadow painting, as I seem to have heard from

some one of the wise. And yet this would be the greatest and most   583 *b*
sovereign of the falls."

"By far. But what do you mean?"

"With you answering and me seeking," I said, "I'll find out."   *c*

"Ask," he said.

"Tell me," I said, "don't we say pain is the opposite of pleasure?"

"Quite so."

"Don't we also say that being affected by neither joy nor pain is
something?"

"We do indeed say that it is."

"Is it in the middle between these two, a certain repose of the soul
with respect to them? Or don't you say it's that way?"

"Just so," he said.

"Don't you remember," I said, "the words of sick men, spoken
when they are sick?"

"What words?"

"That after all nothing is more pleasant than being healthy, but
before they were sick it had escaped them that it is most pleasant."   *d*

"I do remember," he said.

"And don't you also hear those who are undergoing some intense
suffering saying that nothing is more pleasant than the cessation of suffering?"

"I do hear them."

"And I suppose you are aware of many other similar circumstances in which human beings, while they are in pain, extol as
most pleasant not enjoyment but rather the absence of pain and repose
from it."

"For," he said, "at that time repose perhaps becomes pleasant and
enough to content them."

"And when a man's enjoyment ceases," I said, "then the repose   *e*
from pleasure will be painful."

"Perhaps," he said.

"Therefore, what we were just saying is between the two—repose
—will at times be both, pain and pleasure."

"So it seems."

"And is it possible that what is neither can become both?"

"Not in my opinion."

"And, moreover, the pleasant and the painful, when they arise in
the soul, are both a sort of motion, aren't they?"

"Yes."

"And didn't what is neither painful nor pleasant, however, just   584 *a*
come to light as repose and *in the middle* between these two?"

"Yes, that's the way it came to light."

584 a   "Then how can it be right to believe that the absence of suffering is pleasant or that the absence of enjoyment is grievous?"

"In no way."

"Therefore it is not so," I said, "but when it is next to the painful, repose looks pleasant and next to the pleasant, painful; and in these appearances there is nothing sound, so far as truth of pleasure goes, only a certain wizardry."

"So the argument indicates, at least," he said.

b   "Well, then," I said, "look at pleasures that don't come out of pains, so that you won't perhaps suppose in the present instance that it is naturally the case that pleasure is rest from pain and pain rest from pleasure."

"Where shall I look," he said, "and what pleasures do you mean?"

"There are many others, too," I said, "but, if you are willing to reflect on them, the pleasures of smells in particular. For these, without previous pain, suddenly become extraordinarily great and, once having ceased, leave no pain behind."

"Very true," he said.

c   "Then, let's not be persuaded that relief from pain is pure pleasure or that relief from pleasure is pure pain."

"No, let's not," he said.

"However," I said, "of the so-called pleasures stretched through the body to the soul, just about most, and the greatest ones, belong to this form; they are kinds of relief from pains."

"Yes, they are."

"Isn't this also the case with the anticipatory pleasures and pains arising from expectation of pleasures and pains that are going to be?"

"Yes, it is."

d   "Do you," I said, "know what sort of things they are and what they are most like?"

"What?" he said.

"Do you," I said, "hold that up, down, and middle are something in nature?"

"I do."

"Do you suppose that a man brought from the downward region to the middle would suppose anything else than that he was being brought up? And standing in the middle and looking away to the place from which he was brought, would he believe he was elsewhere than in the upper region since he hasn't seen the true up?"

"No, by Zeus," he said. "I don't suppose such a man would suppose otherwise."

"And if he were brought back," I said, "would he suppose he was   *584 e*
being brought down and suppose truly?"

"Of course."

"And wouldn't he undergo all this due to being inexperienced in
what is truly above, in the middle, and below?"

"Plainly."

"Then would you be surprised if those who are inexperienced in
truth, as they have unhealthy opinions about many other things, so too they
are disposed toward pleasure and pain and what's between them in such
a way that, when they are brought to the painful, they suppose truly and   *585 a*
are really in pain, but, when brought from the painful to the in-
between, they seriously suppose they are nearing fulfillment and
pleasure; and, as though out of lack of experience of white they looked
from gray to black, out of lack of experience of pleasure they look from
pain to the painless and are deceived?"

"No, by Zeus," he said, "I wouldn't be surprised; I'd be far more
so if this weren't the case."

"Reflect on it this way," I said. "Aren't hunger, thirst, and such
things kinds of emptiness of the body's condition?"   *b*

"Of course."

"Aren't ignorance and imprudence in their turn emptiness of the
soul's condition?"

"Quite so."

"And wouldn't the man who partakes of nourishment and the one
who gets intelligence become full?"

"Surely."

"As to fullness, is the truer fullness that of a thing which *is* less or of one
which *is* more."

"Plainly that of one which *is* more."

"Which of the classes do you believe participates more in pure
being: the class of food, drink, seasoning, and nourishment in general,
or the form of true opinion, knowledge, intelligence and, in sum, of all   *c*
virtue? Judge it in this way: In your opinion which thing *is* more: one
that is connected with something always the same, immortal and true,
and is such itself and comes to be in such a thing; or one that is connected with something never the same and mortal, and is such itself and
comes to be in such a thing?"

"That," he said, "which is connected with what is always the same
far exceeds."

"And the being of that which is always the same, does it participate in being any more than in knowledge?"[8]

"Not at all."

585 c   "Any more than in truth?"

"No, not that either."

"And if less in truth, less in being also?"

"Necessarily."

d   "Generally, isn't it the case that the classes that have to do with the care of the body participate less in truth and being than those having to do with the care of the soul?"

"Far less."

"Don't you suppose the same is the case with body itself as compared to soul?"

"I do."

"Isn't what is full of things that *are* more, and itself *is* more, really fuller than what is full of things that *are* less and itself *is* less?"

"Of course."

"Therefore, if it is pleasant to become full of what is by nature suitable, that which is more really full of things that *are* more would

e   cause one to enjoy true pleasure more really and truly, while what partakes in things that *are* less would be less truly and surely full and would partake in a pleasure less trustworthy and less true."

"Most necessarily," he said.

586 a   "Therefore, those who have no experience of prudence and virtue but are always living with feasts and the like are, it seems, brought down and then back again to the middle and throughout life wander in this way; but, since they don't go beyond this, they don't look upward toward what is truly above, nor are they ever brought to it; and they aren't filled with what really *is*, nor do they taste of a pleasure that is sure and pure; rather, after the fashion of cattle, always looking down and with their heads bent to earth and table, they feed, fattening them-

b   selves, and copulating; and, for the sake of getting more of these things, they kick and butt with horns and hoofs of iron, killing each other because they are insatiable; for they are not filling the part of themselves that *is*, or can contain anything, with things that *are*."

"That, Socrates," said Glaucon, "is exactly the life of the many presented in the form of an oracle."

"Then isn't it also necessary that the pleasures they live with be mixed with pains—mere phantoms and shadow paintings of true

c   pleasure? Each takes its color by contrast with the others, so that they look vivid and give birth to frenzied loves of themselves in the foolish and are fought over, like the phantom of Helen that Stesichorus says the men at Troy fought over out of ignorance of the truth."[9]

"It's most necessary," he said, "that it be something like that."

"And what about this? In what concerns the spirited part, won't other like things necessarily come to pass for the man who brings this

part to its fulfillment—either by envy due to love of honor, or by   586 *c*
violence due to love of victory, or by anger due to ill-temper—pursuing
satisfaction of honor, victory, and anger without calculation and in-   *d*
telligence?"

"Concerning this part, too," he said, "such things are necessary."

"What then?" I said. "Shall we be bold and say this: Of the
desires concerned with the love of gain and the love of victory,
some—followers of knowledge and argument—pursue in company
with them the pleasures to which the prudential part leads and take
only these; such desires will take the truest pleasures, so far as they can
take true ones—because they follow truth—and those that are most
their own—if indeed what is best for each thing is also most properly   *e*
its own?"

"But, of course," he said, "that is what is most its own."

"Therefore, when all the soul follows the philosophic and is not
factious, the result is that each part may, so far as other things are concerned, mind its own business and be just and, in particular, enjoy its
own pleasures, the best pleasures, and, to the greatest possible extent,
the truest pleasures."   587 *a*

"That's entirely certain."

"And, therefore, when one of the other parts gets control, the
result is that it can't discover its own pleasure and compels the others
to pursue an alien and untrue pleasure."

"That's so," he said.

"Doesn't what is most distant from philosophy and argument produce such results?"

"By far."

"And is what is most distant from law and order most distant
from argument?"

"Plainly."

"And didn't the erotic and tyrannic desires come to light as most
distant?"   *b*

"By far."

"And the kingly and orderly ones least distant?"

"Yes."

"Then I suppose the tyrant will be most distant from a pleasure
that is true and is properly his own, while the king is least distant."

"Necessarily."

"And therefore," I said, "the tyrant will live most unpleasantly
and the king most pleasantly."

"Quite necessarily."

"Do you know," I said, "how much more unpleasant the tyrant's
life is than the king's?"

587 b   "I will, if you tell me," he said.

             "There are, as it seems, three pleasures—one genuine, and two
  c   bastard. The tyrant, going out beyond the bastard ones, once he has
       fled law and argument, dwells with a bodyguard of certain slave
       pleasures; and the extent of his inferiority isn't at all easy to tell, except
       perhaps as follows."

             "How?" he said.

             "The tyrant, of course, stood third from the oligarchic man; the
       man of the people was between them."

             "Yes."

             "Then wouldn't he dwell with a phantom of pleasure that with
       respect to truth is third from that other, if what went before is true?"

             "That's so."

             "And the oligarchic man is in his turn third from the kingly man,
  d   if we count the aristocratic and the kingly man as the same."

             "Yes, he is third."

             "Therefore," I said, "a tyrant is removed from true pleasure by a
       number that is three times three."

             "It looks like it."

             "Therefore," I said, "the phantom of tyrannic pleasure would,
       on the basis of the number of its length, be a plane?"[10]

             "Entirely so."

             "But then it becomes clear how great the distance of separation is
       on the basis of the square and the cube."

             "It's clear," he said, "to the man skilled in calculation."

             "Then if one turns it around and says how far the king is removed
  e   from the tyrant in truth of pleasure, he will find at the end of the mul-
       tiplication that he lives 729 times more pleasantly, while the tyrant
       lives more disagreeably by the same distance."

             "You've poured forth," he said, "a prodigious calculation of the
588 a   difference between the two men—the just and the unjust—in pleasure
       and pain."

             "And yet the number is true," I said, "and appropriate to lives
       too, if days and nights and months and years are appropriate to
       them."[11]

             "But, of course, they are appropriate," he said.

             "Then if the good and just man's victory in pleasure over the bad
       and unjust man is so great, won't his victory in grace, beauty, and vir-
       tue of life be greater to a prodigious degree?"

             "To a prodigious degree, indeed, by Zeus," he said.

  b   "All right, then," I said. "Since we are at this point in the argu-
       ment, let's take up again the first things said, those thanks to which we
       have come here. It was, I believe, said that doing injustice is profitable

for the man who is perfectly unjust but has the reputation of being just. *588 b*
Or isn't that the way it was said?"

"Yes, it was."

"Now then," I said, "let's discuss with him, since we have agreed
about the respective powers of doing injustice and doing just things."

"How?" he said.

"By molding an image of the soul in speech so that the man who
says these things will see just what he has been saying."

"What sort of image?" he said.   *c*

"One of those natures such as the tales say used to come into being in olden times—the Chimæra, Scylla, Cerberus, and certain others, a
throng of them, which are said to have been many *ideas* grown
naturally together in one."[12]

"Yes," he said, "they do tell of such things."

"Well then, mold a single *idea* for a many-colored, many-headed
beast that has a ring of heads of tame and savage beasts and can
change them and make all of them grow from itself."

"That's a job for a clever molder," he said. "But, nevertheless,   *d*
since speech is more easily molded than wax and the like, consider it as
molded."

"Now, then, mold another single *idea* for a lion, and a single one
for a human being. Let the first be by far the greatest, and the second,
second in size."

"That's easier," he said, "and the molding is done."

"Well, then, join them—they are three—in one, so that in some
way they grow naturally together with each other."

"They are joined," he said.

"Then mold about them on the outside an image of one—that of
the human being—so that to the man who's not able to see what's inside, but sees only the outer shell, it looks like one animal, a human   *e*
being."

"The outer mold is in place," he said.

"Then let's say to the one who says that it's profitable for this human being to do injustice, and that it's not advantageous for him to do
just things, that he's affirming nothing other than that it is profitable for
him to feast and make strong the manifold beast and the lion and
what's connected with the lion, while starving the human being and
making him weak so that he can be drawn wherever either of the others *589 a*
leads and doesn't habituate them to one another or make them friends
but lets them bite and fight and devour each other."

"That," he said, "is exactly what would be meant by the man who
praises doing injustice."

"On the other hand, wouldn't the one who says the just things

589 a   are profitable affirm that it is necessary to do and say those things
from which the human being within will most be in control of the hu-

b   man being and take charge of the many-headed beast—like a farmer, nourishing and cultivating the tame heads, while hindering the
growth of the savage ones—making the lion's nature an ally and,
caring for all in common, making them friends with each other and
himself, and so rear them?"

"That is exactly what in turn is meant by the man who praises the
just."

"In every respect, surely, the man who lauds the just things would

c   speak the truth and the man who lauds the unjust ones would lie. For,
considering pleasure, good reputation, and benefit, the praiser of the
just tells the truth, while the blamer says nothing healthy and blames
without knowing what he blames."

"In my opinion," he said, "he doesn't know it at all."

"Well, then, let's persuade him gently—for he isn't willingly
mistaken—by questioning him: 'You blessed man, wouldn't we affirm
that lawful noble and base things have come into being on
such grounds as these; the noble things cause the bestial part of our

d   nature to be subjected to the human being—or, perhaps, rather to the divine part—while the base things enslave the tame to the savage?' Will
he agree or not?"

"He will, if he's persuaded by me," he said.

"Is it possible," I said, "on the basis of this argument, that it be
profitable for anyone to take gold unjustly if something like this happens: he takes the gold and at the same time enslaves the best part of

e   himself to the most depraved? Or, if he took gold for enslaving his son
or daughter, and to savage and bad men, it wouldn't have profited him
no matter how much he took for it; now if he enslaves the most divine
part of himself to the most godless and polluted part and has no pity,
won't he then be wretched and accept golden gifts for a destruction

590 a   more terrible by far than Eriphyle's accepting the necklace for her husband's soul?"[13]

"Far more terrible indeed," said Glaucon. "I'll answer you on his
behalf."

"Don't you suppose that being licentious has also long been
blamed for reasons of this kind, since by that sort of thing that terrible,
great, and many-formed beast is given freer rein than it ought to
have?"

"Plainly," he said.

"And aren't stubbornness and bad temper blamed when they inharmoniously strengthen and strain the lion-like and snake-like part?"   590 *b*

"Most certainly."

"And aren't luxury and softness blamed for slackening and relaxing this same part when they introduce cowardice in it?"

"Of course."

"And aren't flattery and illiberality blamed when a man subjects this same part, the spirited, to the mob-like beast; and, letting it be insulted for the sake of money and the beast's insatiability, habituates it from youth on to be an ape instead of a lion?"

"Quite so," he said.   *c*

"And why do you suppose mechanical and manual art bring reproach? Or shall we say that this is because of anything else than when the form of the best is by nature so weak in a man that he isn't capable of ruling the beasts in himself, but only of serving them, and is capable of learning only the things that flatter them?"

"So it seems," he said.

"In order that such a man also be ruled by something similar to what rules the best man, don't we say that he must be the slave of that best man who has the divine rule in himself? It's not that we suppose   *d* the slave must be ruled to his own detriment, as Thrasymachus supposed about the ruled; but that it's better for all to be ruled by what is divine and prudent, especially when one has it as his own within himself; but, if not, set over one from outside, so that insofar as possible all will be alike and friends, piloted by the same thing."

"Yes," he said, "that's right."

"And the law," I said, "as an ally of all in the city, also makes it   *e* plain that it wants something of the kind; and so does the rule over the children, their not being set free until we establish a regime in them as in a city, and until—having cared for the best part in them with the like   591 *a* in ourselves—we establish a similar guardian and ruler in them to take our place; only then, do we set them free."

"Yes," he said, "they do make that plain."

"Then in what way, Glaucon, and on the basis of what argument, will we affirm that it is profitable to do injustice, or be licentious, or do anything base, when as a result of these things one will be worse, even though one acquires more money or more of some other power?"

"In no way," he said.

"And in what way is it profitable to get away with doing injustice and not pay the penalty? Or doesn't the man who gets away with it be-   *b* come still worse; while, as for the man who doesn't get away with it and is punished, isn't the bestial part of him put to sleep and tamed, and the

591 b   tame part freed, and doesn't his whole soul—brought to its best nature, acquiring moderation and justice accompanied by prudence—gain a habit more worthy of honor than the one a body gains with strength and beauty accompanied by health, in proportion as soul is more honorable than body?"

"That's entirely certain," he said.

c   "Then won't the man who has intelligence strain all of his powers to that end as long as he lives; in the first place, honoring the studies that will make his soul such, while despising the rest?"

"Plainly," he said.

"Next," I said, "not only won't he turn the habit and nourishment of the body over to the bestial and irrational pleasure and live turned in that direction, but he'll not even look to health, nor give precedence to being

d   strong, healthy, or fair unless he's also going to become moderate as a result of them; rather he will always be seen adjusting the body's harmony for the sake of the accord in the soul."

"That's entirely certain," he said, "if he's going to be truly musical."

"And won't he also maintain order and concord in the acquisition of money?" I said. "And, since he's not impressed with what the many deem to be blessedness, will he give boundless increase to the bulk of his property and thus possess boundless evils?"

"I don't suppose he will," he said.

"Rather, he looks fixedly at the regime within him," I said, "and

e   guards against upsetting anything in it by the possession of too much or too little substance. In this way, insofar as possible, he governs his additions to, and expenditure of, his substance."

"That's quite certain," he said.

592 a   "And, further, with honors too, he looks to the same thing; he will willingly partake of and taste those that he believes will make him better, while those that would overturn his established habit he will flee, in private and in public."

"Then," he said, "if it's that he cares about, he won't be willing to mind the political things."

"Yes, by the dog," I said, "he will in his own city, very much so. However, perhaps he won't in his fatherland unless some divine chance coincidentally comes to pass."

"I understand," he said. "You mean he will in the city whose foundation we have now gone through, the one that has its place in

b   speeches, since I don't suppose it exists anywhere on earth."

"But in heaven," I said, "perhaps, a pattern is laid up for the man   592 *b*
who wants to see and found a city within himself on the basis of what
he sees. It doesn't make any difference whether it is or will be
somewhere. For he would mind the things of this city alone, and of no
other."

"That's likely," he said.

BOOK X

"And, indeed," I said, "I also recognize in many other aspects of this city that we were entirely right in the way we founded it, but I say this particularly when reflecting on poetry."

"What about it?" he said.

"In not admitting at all any part of it that is imitative. For that the imitative, more than anything, must not be admitted looks, in my opinion, even more manifest now that the soul's forms have each been separated out."

"How do you mean?"

"Between us—and you all won't denounce me to the tragic poets and all the other imitators—all such things seem to maim the thought of those who hear them and do not as a remedy have the knowledge of how they really are."

"What are you thinking about in saying that?" he said.

"It must be told," I said. "And yet, a certain friendship for Homer, and shame before him, which has possessed me since childhood, prevents me from speaking. For he seems to have been the first teacher and leader of all these fine tragic things. Still and all, a man must not be honored before the truth, but, as I say, it must be told."

"Most certainly," he said.

"Then listen, or rather, answer."

"Ask."

595 a

b

c

595 c   "Could you tell me what imitation in general is? For I myself scarcely comprehend what it wants to be."

"Then it follows," he said, "that I, of course, will comprehend it."

"That wouldn't be anything strange," I said, "since men with
596 a   duller vision have often, you know, seen things before those who see more sharply."

"That's so," he said. "But with you present I couldn't be very eager to say whatever might occur to me, so look yourself."

"Do you want us to make our consideration according to our customary procedure, beginning from the following point? For we are, presumably, accustomed to set down some one particular form for each of the particular 'manys' to which we apply the same name. Or don't you understand?"

"I do."

"Then let's now set down any one of the 'manys' you please; for
b   example, if you wish, there are surely many couches and tables."

"Of course."

"But as for *ideas* for these furnishings, there are presumably two, one of couch, one of table."

"Yes."

"Aren't we also accustomed to say that it is in looking to the *idea* of each implement that one craftsman makes the couches and another the chairs we use, and similarly for other things? For presumably none of the craftsmen fabricates the idea itself. How could he?"

"In no way."

"Well, now, see what you call this craftsman here."
c   "Which one?"

"He who makes everything that each one of the manual artisans makes separately."

"That's a clever and wonderful man you speak of."

"Not yet. In an instant you'll say that even more. For this same manual artisan is not only able to make all implements but also makes everything that grows naturally from the earth, and he produces all animals—the others and himself too—and, in addition to that, produces earth and heaven and gods and everything in heaven and everything in Hades under the earth."
d   "That's quite a wonderful sophist you speak of," he said.

"Are you distrustful?" I said. "And tell me, in your opinion could there be altogether no such craftsman; or in a certain way, could a maker of all these things come into being and in a certain way not? Or aren't you aware that you yourself could in a certain way make all these things?"

"And what," he said, "is that way?"   596 *d*

"It's not hard," I said. "You could fabricate them quickly in many ways and most quickly, of course, if you are willing to take a mirror and carry it around everywhere; quickly you will make the sun and the   *e* things in the heaven; quickly, the earth; and quickly, yourself and the other animals and implements and plants and everything else that was just now mentioned."

"Yes," he said, "so that they look like they *are;* however, they surely *are* not in truth."

"Fine," I said, "and you attack the argument at just the right place. For I suppose the painter is also one of these craftsmen, isn't he?"

"Of course he is."

"But I suppose you'll say that he doesn't truly make what he makes. And yet in a certain way the painter too does make a couch, doesn't he?"

"Yes," he said, "he too makes what looks like a couch."

"And what about the couchmaker? Weren't you just saying that   597 *a* he doesn't make the form, which is what we, of course, say is just a couch, but a certain couch?"

"Yes," he said, "I was saying that."

"Then, if he doesn't make what *is*, he wouldn't make the being but something that is like the being, but is not being. And if someone were to assert that the work of the producer of couches or of any other manual artisan is completely being, he would run the risk of saying what's not true."

"Yes," he said, "at least that would be the opinion of those who spend their time in arguments of this kind."

"Therefore, let's not be surprised if this too turns out to be a dim thing compared to the truth."

"No, let's not."   *b*

"Do you," I said, "want us on the basis of these very things to investigate who this imitator is?"

"If you want to," he said.

"There turn out, then, to be these three kinds of couches: one that *is* in nature, which we would say, I suppose, a god produced. Or who else?"

"No one else, I suppose."

"And then one that the carpenter produced."

"Yes," he said.

"And one that the painter produced, isn't that so?"

"Let it be so."

597 b   "Then painter, couchmaker, god—these three preside over three forms of couches."

"Yes, three."

c   "Now, the god, whether he didn't want to or whether some necessity was laid upon him not to produce more than one couch in nature, made only one, that very one which is a couch. And two or more such weren't naturally engendered by the god nor will they be begotten."

"How's that?" he said.

"Because," I said, "if he should make only two, again one would come to light the form of which they in turn would both possess, and that, and not the two, would be the couch that *is*."

"Right," he said.

d   "Then, I suppose, the god, knowing this and wanting to be a real maker of a couch that really *is* and not a certain couchmaker of a certain couch, begot it as one by nature."

"So it seems."

"Do you want us to address him as its nature-begetter or something of the kind?"

"That's just at any rate," he said, "since by nature he has made both this and everything else."

"And what about the carpenter? Isn't he a craftsman of a couch?"

"Yes."

"And is the painter also a craftsman and maker of such a thing?"

"Not at all."

"But what of a couch will you say he is?"

e   "In my opinion," he said, "he would most sensibly be addressed as an imitator of that of which these others are craftsmen."

"All right," I said, "do you, then, call the man at the third generation from nature an imitator?"

"Most certainly," he said.

"Therefore this will also apply to the maker of tragedy, if he is an imitator; he is naturally third from a king and the truth, as are all the other imitators."

"Probably."

"Then we have agreed about the imitator. Now tell me this

598 a about the painter. In your opinion, does he in each case attempt to imitate the thing itself in nature, or the works of the craftsmen?"

"The works of the craftsmen," he said.

"Such as they are or such as they look? For you still have to make this further distinction."

"How do you mean?" he said.

"Like this. Does a couch, if you observe it from the side, or   598 a
from the front, or from anywhere else, differ at all from itself? Or
does it not differ at all but only look different, and similarly with the
rest?"

"The latter is so," he said. "It looks different, but isn't."

"Now consider this very point. Toward which is painting directed   b
in each case—toward imitation of the being as it is or toward its looking
as it looks? Is it imitation of looks or of truth?"

"Of looks," he said.

"Therefore, imitation is surely far from the truth; and, as it
seems, it is due to this that it produces everything—because it lays
hold of a certain small part of each thing, and that part is itself only a
phantom. For example, the painter, we say, will paint for us a shoemaker, a carpenter, and the other craftsmen, although he doesn't
understand the arts of any one of them. But, nevertheless, if he is a   c
good painter, by painting a carpenter and displaying him from far
off, he would deceive children and foolish human beings into thinking that it is truly a carpenter."

"Of course."

"But, in any event, I suppose, my friend, that this is what
must be understood about all such things: when anyone reports to
us about someone, saying that he has encountered a human being
who knows all the crafts and everything else that single men severally know, and there is nothing that he does not know more precisely
than anyone else, it would have to be replied to such a one that he   d
is an innocent human being and that, as it seems, he has encountered
some wizard and imitator and been deceived. Because he himself is
unable to put knowledge and lack of knowledge and imitation to the
test, that man seemed all-wise to him."

"Very true," he said.

"Then, next," I said, "tragedy and its leader, Homer, must be
considered, since we hear from some that these men know all arts   e
and all things human that have to do with virtue and vice, and the
divine things too. For it is necessary that the good poet, if he is going to make fair poems about the things his poetry concerns, be in
possession of knowledge when he makes his poems or not be able
to make them. Hence, we must consider whether those who tell us
this have encountered these imitators and been deceived; and
whether, therefore, seeing their works, they do not recognize that
these works are third from what *is* and are easy to make for the man   599 a
who doesn't know the truth—for such a man makes what look like
beings but are not. Or, again, is there also something to what they

599 a   say, and do the good poets really know about the things that, in the
opinion of the many, they say well?"

"Most certainly," he said, "that must be tested."

"Do you suppose that if a man were able to make both, the thing
to be imitated and the phantom, he would permit himself to be serious
about the crafting of the phantoms and set this at the head of his own
b   life as the best thing he has?"

"No, I don't."

"But, I suppose, if he were in truth a knower of these things that
he also imitates, he would be far more serious about the deeds than the
imitations and would try to leave many fair deeds behind as memorials
of himself and would be more eager to be the one who is lauded rather
than the one who lauds."

"I suppose so," he said. "For the honor and the benefit coming
from the two are hardly equal."

"Well, then, about the other things, let's not demand an account
c   from Homer or any other of the poets by asking, if any one of them was
a doctor and not only an imitator of medical speeches, who are the men
whom any poet, old or new, is said to have made healthy, as Asclepius
did; or what students of medicine he left behind as Asclepius did his
offspring.[1] Nor, again, will we ask them about the other arts, but
we'll let that go. But about the greatest and fairest things of which
Homer attempts to speak—about wars and commands of armies and
d   governances of cities, and about the education of a human being—it
is surely just to ask him and inquire, 'Dear Homer, if you are not
third from the truth about virtue, a craftsman of a phantom, just the
one we defined as an imitator, but are also second and able to recognize what sorts of practices make human beings better or worse in
private and in public, tell us which of the cities was better governed
thanks to you, as Lacedaemon was thanks to Lycurgus, and many
e   others, both great and small, were thanks to many others? What
city gives you credit for having proved a good lawgiver and benefited them? Italy and Sicily do so for Charondas, and we for Solon;[2] now who does it for you?' Will he have any to mention?"

"I don't suppose so," said Glaucon. "At least, the Homeridae
themselves do not tell of any."

"Well, is any war in Homer's time remembered that was well
600 a   fought with his ruling or advice?"

"None."

"Well, then, as is appropriate to the deeds of a wise man, do they
tell of many ingenious devices for the arts or any other activities,
just as for Thales the Milesian or Anacharsis the Scythian?"[3]

"Not at all; there's nothing of the sort."

"Well, then, if there is nothing in public, is it told that Homer,   *600 a*
while he was himself alive, was in private a leader in education for
certain men who cherished him for his intercourse and handed down
a certain Homeric way of life to those who came after, just as Py-   *b*
thagoras himself was particularly cherished for this reason, and his
successors even now still give Pythagoras' name to a way of life that
makes them seem somehow outstanding among men."

"Again," he said, "nothing of the sort is said. For Creophylos,
Homer's comrade, would, Socrates, perhaps turn out to be even
more ridiculous in his education than in his name,⁴ if the things
said about Homer are true. For it is told that Homer suffered considerable neglect in his own day, when he was alive."   *c*

"Yes, that is told," I said. "But, Glaucon, if Homer were really
able to educate human beings and make them better because he is in
these things capable not of imitating but of knowing, do you suppose
that he wouldn't have made many comrades and been honored and
cherished by them? But Protagoras, the Abderite, after all, and Prodicus, the Cean,⁵ and very many others are able, by private intercourse, to impress upon the men of their time the assurance that they
will be able to govern neither home nor city unless they themselves   *d*
supervise their education, and they are so intensely loved for this
wisdom that their comrades do everything but carry them about on
their heads. Then do you suppose that if he were able to help human
beings toward virtue, the men in Homer's time would have let him or
Hesiod go around being rhapsodes and wouldn't have clung to them
rather than to their gold? And wouldn't they have compelled these
teachers to stay with them at home; or, if they weren't persuaded,   *e*
wouldn't they themselves have attended⁶ them wherever they went,
until they had gained an adequate education?"

"In my opinion, Socrates," he said, "what you say is entirely
true."

"Shouldn't we set down all those skilled in making, beginning
with Homer, as imitators of phantoms of virtue and of the other subjects of their making? They don't lay hold of the truth; rather, as we
were just now saying, the painter will make what seems to be a
shoemaker to those who understand as little about shoemaking as he   *601 a*
understands, but who observe only colors and shapes."

"Most certainly."

"Then, in this way, I suppose we'll claim the poetic man also
uses names and phrases to color each of the arts. He himself doesn't
understand; but he imitates in such a way as to seem, to men whose
condition is like his own and who observe only speeches, to speak
very well. He seems to do so when he speaks using meter, rhythm,

601 a
b

and harmony, no matter whether the subject is shoemaking, general-ship, or anything else. So great is the charm that these things by na-ture possess. For when the things of the poets are stripped of the colors of the music and are said alone, by themselves, I suppose you know how they look. For you, surely, have seen."

"I have indeed," he said.

"Don't they," I said, "resemble the faces of the boys who are youthful but not fair in what happens to their looks when the bloom has forsaken them?"

"Exactly," he said.

"Come now, reflect on this. The maker of the phantom, the imitator, we say, understands nothing of what *is* but rather of what

c

looks like it *is*. Isn't that so?"

"Yes."

"Well, then, let's not leave it half-said, but let's see it adequately."

"Speak," he said.

"A painter, we say, will paint reins and a bit."

"Yes."

"But a shoemaker and a smith will make them."

"Certainly."

"Then does the painter understand how the reins and the bit must be? Or does even the maker not understand—the smith and the leather-cutter—but only he who knows how to use them, the horseman?"

"Very true."

"And won't we say that it is so for everything?"

"How?"

d

"For each thing there are these three arts—one that will use, one that will make, one that will imitate."

"Yes."

"Aren't the virtue, beauty, and rightness of each implement, animal, and action related to nothing but the use for which each was made, or grew naturally?"

"That's so."

"It's quite necessary, then, that the man who uses each thing be most experienced and that he report to the maker what are the good or bad points, in actual use, of the instrument he uses. For example, about flutes, a flute player surely reports to the flute-maker which ones would

e

serve him in playing, and he will prescribe how they must be made, and the other will serve him."

"Of course."

"Doesn't the man who knows report about good and bad flutes, and won't the other, trusting him, make them?"

"Yes."

"Therefore the maker of the same implement will have right trust   *601 e*
concerning its beauty and its badness from being with the man who
knows and from being compelled to listen to the man who knows, while
the user will have knowledge."   *602 a*

"Certainly."

"And will the imitator from using the things that he paints have
knowledge of whether they are fair and right or not, or right opinion
due to the necessity of being with the man who knows and receiving
prescriptions of how he must paint?"

"Neither."

"Therefore, with respect to beauty and badness, the imitator will
neither know nor opine rightly about what he imitates."

"It doesn't seem so."

"The imitator, in his making, would be a charming chap, so far as
wisdom about what he makes goes."

"Hardly."

"But all the same, he will imitate, although he doesn't know in   *b*
what way each thing is bad or good. But as it seems, whatever looks to
be fair to the many who don't know anything—that he will imitate."

"Of course he will."

"Then it looks like we are pretty well agreed on these things: the
imitator knows nothing worth mentioning about what he imitates;
imitation is a kind of play and not serious; and those who take up tragic
poetry in iambics and in epics are all imitators in the highest possible
degree."

"Most certainly."

"In the name of Zeus," I said, "then, isn't this imitating con-   *c*
cerned with something that is third from the truth? Isn't that so?"

"Yes."

"Now, then, on which one of the parts of the human being does it
have the power it has?"

"What sort of part do you mean?"

"This sort. The same magnitude surely doesn't look equal to our
sight from near and from far."

"No, it doesn't."

"And the same things look bent and straight when seen in water
and out of it, and also both concave and convex, due to the sight's
being misled by the colors, and every sort of confusion of this kind is
plainly in our soul. And, then, it is because they take advantage of this   *d*
affection in our nature that shadow painting, and puppeteering, and
many other tricks of the kind fall nothing short of wizardry."

"True."

"And haven't measuring, counting, and weighing come to light as

602 d   most charming helpers in these cases? As a result of them, we are not
ruled by a thing's looking bigger or smaller or more or heavier; rather
we are ruled by that which has calculated, measured, or, if you please,
weighed."

"Undeniably."

e   "But this surely must be the work of the calculating part in a
soul."

"Yes, it is the work of that part."

"And to it, when it has measured and indicates that some things
are bigger or smaller than others, or equal, often contrary appearances
are presented at the same time about the same things."

"Yes."

"Didn't we say that it is impossible for the same thing to opine
contraries at the same time about the same things?"

"And what we said is right."

603 a   "Therefore, the part of the soul opining contrary to the measures
would not be the same as the part that does so in accordance with the
measures."

"No, it wouldn't."

"And, further, the part which trusts measure and calculation
would be the best part of the soul."

"Of course."

"Therefore, the part opposed to it would be one of the ordinary
things in us."

"Necessarily."

"Well, then, it was this I wanted agreed to when I said that painting and imitation as a whole are far from the truth when they produce
their work; and that, moreover, imitation keeps company with the part
b   in us that is far from prudence, and is not comrade and friend for any
healthy or true purpose."

"Exactly," he said.

"Therefore, imitation, an ordinary thing having intercourse with
what is ordinary, produces ordinary offspring."

"It seems so."

"Does this," I said, "apply only to the imitation connected with
the sight or also to that connected with the hearing, which we name
poetry?"

"It is likely," he said, "that it applies also to this."

"Well, then," I said, "let's not just trust the likelihood based on
painting; but let's now go directly to the very part of thought with
c   which poetry's imitation keeps company and see whether it is ordinary
or serious."

"We must."

"Let's present it in this way. Imitation, we say, imitates human beings performing forced or voluntary actions, and, as a result of the action, supposing themselves to have done well or badly, and in all of this experiencing pain or enjoyment. Was there anything else beyond this?"

"Nothing."

"Then, in all this, is a human being of one mind? Or, just as with respect to the sight there was faction and he had contrary opinions in himself at the same time about the same things, is there also faction in him when it comes to deeds and does he do battle with himself? But I am reminded that there's no need for us to come to an agreement about this now. For in the previous arguments we came to sufficient agreement about all this, asserting that our soul teems with ten thousand such oppositions arising at the same time."   *d*

"Rightly," he said.

"Yes, it was right," I said. "But what we then left out, it is now necessary to go through, in my opinion."   *e*

"What was that?" he said.

"A decent man," I said, "who gets as his share some such chance as losing a son or something else for which he cares particularly, as we were surely also saying then, will bear it more easily than other men."

"Certainly."

"Now let's consider whether he won't be grieved at all, or whether this is impossible, but that he will somehow be sensible in the face of pain."

"The latter," he said, "is closer to the truth."

"Now tell me this about him. Do you suppose he'll fight the pain   604 *a* and hold out against it more when he is seen by his peers, or when he is alone by himself in a deserted place?"

"Surely," he said, "he will fight it far more when seen."

"But when left alone, I suppose, he'll dare to utter many things of which he would be ashamed if someone were to hear, and will do many things he would not choose to have anyone see him do."

"That's so," he said.

"Isn't it argument and law that tell him to hold out, while the suffering itself is what draws him to the pain?"   *b*

"True."

"When a contradictory tendency arises in a human being about the same thing at the same time, we say that there are necessarily two things in him."

"Undeniably."

604 b   "Isn't the one ready to be persuaded in whatever direction the law leads?"

"How so?"

"The law presumably says that it is finest to keep as quiet as possible in misfortunes and not be irritated, since the good and bad in such things aren't plain, nor does taking it hard get one anywhere, nor are

c   any of the human things worthy of great seriousness; and being in pain is an impediment to the coming of that thing the support of which we need as quickly as possible in these cases."

"What do you mean?" he said.

"Deliberation," I said, "about what has happened. One must accept the fall of the dice and settle one's affairs accordingly—in whatever way argument declares would be best. One must not behave like children who have stumbled and who hold on to the hurt place and spend their time in crying out; rather one must always habituate the

d   soul to turn as quickly as possible to curing and setting aright what has fallen and is sick, doing away with lament by medicine."

"That," he said, "at all events, would be the most correct way for a man to face what chance brings."

"And, we say, the best part is willing to follow this calculation—"

"Plainly."

"—whereas the part that leads to reminiscences of the suffering and to complaints and can't get enough of them, won't we say that it is irrational, idle, and a friend of cowardice?"

"Certainly we'll say that."

e   "Now then, the irritable disposition affords much and varied imitation, while the prudent and quiet character, which is always nearly equal to itself, is neither easily imitated nor, when imitated, easily understood, especially by a festive assembly where all sorts of human beings are gathered in a theater. For the imitation is of a condition that is surely alien to them."

605 a   "That's entirely certain."

"Then plainly the imitative poet isn't naturally directed toward any such part of the soul, and his wisdom isn't framed for satisfying it—if he's going to get a good reputation among the many—but rather toward the irritable and various disposition, because it is easily imitated."

"Plainly."

"Therefore it would at last be just for us to seize him and set him beside the painter as his antistrophe. For he is like the painter in making things that are ordinary by the standard of truth; and he is also

b   similar in keeping company with a part of the soul that is on the same

level and not with the best part. And thus we should at last be justified   *605 b*
in not admitting him into a city that is going to be under good laws, because he awakens this part of the soul and nourishes it, and, by making
it strong, destroys the calculating part, just as in a city when someone,
by making wicked men mighty, turns the city over to them and corrupts the superior ones. Similarly, we shall say the imitative poet produces a bad regime in the soul of each private man by making phan-   *c*
toms that are very far removed from the truth and by gratifying the
soul's foolish part, which doesn't distinguish big from little, but
believes the same things are at one time big and at another little."

"Most certainly."

"However, we haven't yet made the greatest accusation against
imitation. For the fact that it succeeds in maiming even the decent
men, except for a certain rare few, is surely quite terrible."

"Certainly, if it does indeed do that."

"Listen and consider. When even the best of us hear Homer or
any other of the tragic poets imitating one of the heroes in mourning
and making quite an extended speech with lamentation, or, if you like,   *d*
singing and beating his breast, you know that we enjoy it and that we
give ourselves over to following the imitation; suffering along with the
hero in all seriousness, we praise as a good poet the man who most puts
us in this state."

"I know it, of course."

"But when personal sorrow comes to one of us, you are aware
that, on the contrary, we pride ourselves if we are able to keep quiet
and bear up, taking this to be the part of a man and what we then   *e*
praised to be that of a woman."

"I do recognize it," he said.

"Is that a fine way to praise?" I said. "We see a man whom we
would not condescend, but would rather blush, to resemble, and,
instead of being disgusted, we enjoy it and praise it?"

"No, by Zeus," he said, "that doesn't seem reasonable."

"Yes, it is," I said, "if you consider it in this way."   *606 a*

"In what way?"

"If you are aware that what is then held down by force in our own
misfortunes and has hungered for tears and sufficient lament and
satisfaction, since it is by nature such as to desire these things, is that
which now gets satisfaction and enjoyment from the poets. What is by
nature best in us, because it hasn't been adequately educated by argument or habit, relaxes its guard over this mournful part because it sees
another's sufferings, and it isn't shameful for it, if some other man who   *b*
claims to be good laments out of season, to praise and pity him; rather

606 b   it believes that it gains the pleasure and wouldn't permit itself to be deprived of it by despising the whole poem. I suppose that only a certain few men are capable of calculating that the enjoyment of other people's sufferings has a necessary effect on one's own. For the pitying part, fed strong on these examples, is not easily held down in one's own sufferings."

c   "Very true," he said.

"Doesn't the same argument also apply to the laughing part? If there are any jokes that you would be ashamed to make yourself, but that you enjoy very much hearing in comic imitation or in private, and you don't hate them as bad, you do the same as with things that evoke pity. For that in you which, wanting to make jokes, you then held down by argument, afraid of the reputation of buffoonery, you now release, and, having made it lusty there, have unawares been carried away in your own things so that you become a comic poet."

d   "Quite so," he said.

"And as for sex, and spiritedness, too, and for all the desires, pains, and pleasures in the soul that we say follow all our action, poetic imitation produces similar results in us. For it fosters and waters them when they ought to be dried up, and sets them up as rulers in us when they ought to be ruled so that we may become better and happier instead of worse and more wretched."

"I can't say otherwise," he said.

e   "Then, Glaucon," I said, "when you meet praisers of Homer who say that this poet educated Greece, and that in the management and education of human affairs it is worthwhile to take him up for study and for living, by arranging one's whole life according to this poet, you

607 a   must love and embrace them as being men who are the best they can be, and agree that Homer is the most poetic and first of the tragic poets; but you must know that only so much of poetry as is hymns to gods or celebration of good men should be admitted into a city. And if you admit the sweetened muse in lyrics or epics, pleasure and pain will jointly be kings in your city instead of law and that argument which in each instance is best in the opinion of the community."

"Very true," he said.

b   "Well," I said, "since we brought up the subject of poetry again, let it be our apology that it was then fitting for us to send it away from the city on account of its character. The argument determined us. Let us further say to it, lest it convict us for a certain harshness and rusticity, that there is an old quarrel between philosophy and poetry. For that 'yelping bitch shrieking at her master,' and 'great in the empty eloquence of fools,' 'the mob of overwise men holding sway,' and 'the

c   refined thinkers who are really poor'[7] and countless others are signs of

this old opposition. All the same, let it be said that, if poetry directed   607 c
to pleasure and imitation have any argument to give showing that they
should be in a city with good laws, we should be delighted to receive
them back from exile, since we are aware that we ourselves are
charmed by them. But it isn't holy to betray what seems to be the truth.
Aren't you, too, my friend, charmed by it, especially when you contemplate it through the medium of Homer?"   d

"Very much so."

"Isn't it just for it to come back in this way—when it has made an
apology in lyrics or some other meter?"

"Most certainly."

"And surely we would also give its protectors, those who aren't
poets but lovers of poetry, occasion to speak an argument without
meter on its behalf, showing that it's not only pleasant but also beneficial to regimes and human life. And we shall listen benevolently. For
surely we shall gain if it should turn out to be not only pleasant but also   e
beneficial."

"We would," he said, "undeniably gain."

"But if not, my dear comrade, just like the men who have once
fallen in love with someone, and don't believe the love is beneficial,
keep away from it even if they have to do violence to themselves; so we
too—due to the inborn love of such poetry we owe to our rearing in
these fine regimes—we'll be glad if it turns out that it is best and truest.   608 a
But as long as it's not able to make its apology, when we listen to it,
we'll chant this argument we are making to ourselves as a coun-
tercharm, taking care against falling back again into this love, which is
childish and belongs to the many. We are, at all events, aware that such
poetry mustn't be taken seriously as a serious thing laying hold of truth,
but that the man who hears it must be careful, fearing for the regime in   b
himself, and must hold what we have said about poetry."

"Entirely," he said. "I join you in saying that."

"For the contest is great, my dear Glaucon," I said, "greater than
it seems—this contest that concerns becoming good or bad—so we
mustn't be tempted by honor or money or any ruling office or, for that
matter, poetry, into thinking that it's worthwhile to neglect justice and
the rest of virtue."

"I join you in saying that," he said, "on the basis of what we have
gone through. And I suppose anyone else would too."

"And, yet," I said, "we haven't gone through the greatest rewards   c
and prizes proposed for virtue."

"You are speaking of an inconceivable greatness," he said, "if
there are others greater than those mentioned."

"What that is great could come to pass in a short time?" I said.

608 c   "For surely, the whole of the time from childhood to old age would be short when compared with all time."

"Rather, it's nothing at all," he said.

"What then? Do you suppose that an immortal thing ought to be

d   serious about so short a time and not about all time?"

"I do suppose so," he said. "But what do you mean by this?"

"Haven't you perceived," I said, "that our soul is immortal and is never destroyed?"

And he looked me in the face with wonder and said, "No, by Zeus, I haven't. Can you say that?"

"If I am not to do an injustice," I said. "And I suppose you can, too, for it's nothing hard."

"It is for me," he said. "But I would gladly hear from you this thing that isn't hard."

"You must hear it," I said.

"Just speak," he said.

"Do you," I said, "call something good and something bad?"

"I do."

e   "Then do you have the same understanding of them as I do?"

"What's that?"

"What destroys and corrupts everything is the bad, and what saves and benefits is the good."

"I do," he said.

"And what about this? Do you say there is something bad and something good for each thing—for example, ophthalmia for the eyes,

609 a   and sickness for the entire body, blight for grain, rot for wood, rust for iron and bronze, and, as I say, for nearly all things is there an evil and illness naturally connected with each?"

"I do," he said.

"When one of these attaches itself to something, doesn't it make the thing to which it attaches itself bad and, in the end, wholly dissolve and destroy it?"

"Undeniably."

"Therefore the evil naturally connected with each thing and its particular badness destroys it, or if this doesn't destroy it, surely there

b   is nothing else that could still corrupt it. For surely the good would never destroy anything, nor, again, would what is neither bad nor good."

"How could they?" he said.

"Therefore, if we find any existing thing that has an evil that makes it bad but is, however, not able to dissolve and destroy it, then won't we know that for a thing that is naturally so there is no destruction?"

[292]

"That's likely," he said.   *609 b*

"What then?" I said. "Doesn't the soul have something that makes it bad?"

"Very much so," he said, "all the things we were just going through—injustice, licentiousness, cowardice, and lack of learning."   *c*

"Does any one of them dissolve and destroy it? And reflect, so that we won't be deceived into supposing that the unjust and foolish human being, when he is caught doing injustice, is then destroyed due to the injustice, which is a badness of soul. But do it this way: just as the badness of body, which is disease, melts and destroys a body and brings it to the point where it is not even a body, similarly all the things of which we were just speaking are corrupted by their own specific vice, which attaches itself to them and is present in them, and they   *d* finally come to the point where they *are* not. Isn't that so?"

"Yes."

"Come, then, and consider soul in the same way. Do injustice and the rest of vice, when they are present in it, by being present and attaching themselves, corrupt and wither it until, brought to the point of death, they separate it from the body?"

"That's not at all the way it is," he said.

"But it is, on the contrary, unreasonable," I said, "that a thing be destroyed by a badness that is alien and not by one that is its own."

"It is unreasonable."

"Reflect, Glaucon," I said, "that we don't suppose a body should   *e* be destroyed by the badness of foods, whatever it may be—whether it is their oldness, rottenness, or anything else. But if the badness of the foods themselves introduces the badness of body into the body, we shall say that due to them it was destroyed by its own vice, which is disease. But we shall never admit that the body, which is one thing, is corrupted   *610 a* by the badness of food, which is another thing, if the alien evil does not introduce the evil that is naturally connected with the body."

"What you say," he said, "is quite right."

"Well, then," I said, "according to the same argument, if badness of body doesn't introduce badness of soul into a soul, we would never admit that a soul is destroyed by an alien evil that does not bring with it the specific badness of a soul—that is, we would not admit that one thing is destroyed by the evil of another."

"That's reasonable," he said.

"Well then, either let's refute what we are saying and show that it's not fine, or, as long as it's unrefuted, let's never assert that by fever,   *b* or by another illness, or, again, by slaughter—even if someone cuts the whole body up into the smallest pieces—a soul is ever closer to being destroyed as a result of these things, before someone proves that due to

610 b   these sufferings of the body the soul itself becomes unjuster and unholier. But when an alien vice comes to be in something else and its

c   own peculiar vice does not come to be in it, let's not permit anyone to assert that a soul or anything else is destroyed."

"On the contrary," he said, "no one will ever show that when men are dying their souls become unjust due to death."

"And," I said, "if someone dares to come to close quarters with the argument and say that the dying man becomes worse and unjuster, just so as not to be compelled to agree that souls are immortal, we shall surely insist that, if the man who says this says the truth, injustice is

d   fatal to him who has it, even as disease is, and that, since by its nature it kills, those who get it die from it—those who get most, more quickly, those who get less, in more leisurely fashion. They would be unlike the unjust men who, as things now stand, do indeed die from injustice, but at the hands of other men who administer the penalty."

"By Zeus," he said, "then injustice won't look like such a very terrible thing if it will be fatal to the one who gets it. For it would be a relief from evils. But I suppose rather that it will look, all to the con-

e   trary, like it kills other men, if it can, but makes its possessor very much alive and, in addition to alive, sleepless. So far surely, as it seems, does its camp lie from fatality."

"What you say is fine," I said. "For surely, whenever its own badness and its own evil are not sufficient to kill and destroy a soul, an evil assigned to the destruction of something else will hardly destroy a soul, or anything else except that to which it is assigned."

"Yes, hardly," he said, "at least as is likely."

"Therefore, since it's not destroyed by a single evil—either its

611 a   own or an alien—it's plainly necessary that it be always and, if it is always, that it be immortal."

"That is necessary," he said.

"Well, then," I said, "let this be so. And if it is, you recognize that there would always be the same souls. For surely they could not become fewer if none is destroyed, nor again more numerous. For if any of the immortal things should become more numerous, you know that they would come from the mortal, and everything would end up by being immortal."

"What you say is true."

"But," I said, "let's not suppose this—for the argument won't per-

b   mit it—nor that soul by its truest nature is such that it is full of much variety, dissimilarity, and quarrel with itself."

"How do you mean?" he said.

"It's not easy," I said, "for a thing to be eternal that is both com-

posed out of many things and whose composition is not of the finest, as   *611 b*
the soul now looked to us."

"No; at least it's not likely."

"Well then, that soul is immortal both the recent argument and
the others would compel us to accept. But it must be seen such as it is
in truth, not maimed by community with body and other evils, as we   *c*
now see it. But what it is like when it has become pure must be examined sufficiently by calculation. And one will find it far fairer and
discern justice and injustice[8] and everything we have now gone
through more distinctly. Now we were telling the truth about it as it
looks at present. However that is based only on the condition in which
we saw it. Just as those who catch sight of the sea Glaucus[9] would no   *d*
longer easily see his original nature because some of the old parts of his
body have been broken off and the others have been ground down and
thoroughly maimed by the waves at the same time as other things have
grown on him—shells, seaweed, and rocks—so that he resembles any
beast rather than what he was by nature, so, too, we see the soul in such
a condition because of countless evils. But, Glaucon, one must look
elsewhere."

"Where?" he said.

"To its love of wisdom, and recognize what it lays hold of and   *e*
with what sort of things it longs to keep company on the grounds that it
is akin to the divine and immortal and what *is* always, and what it
would become like if it were to give itself entirely to this longing and
were brought by this impulse out of the deep ocean in which it now is,
and the rocks and shells were hammered off—those which, because it
feasts on earth, have grown around it in a wild, earthy, and rocky profu-   *612 a*
sion as a result of those feasts that are called happy. And then one
would see its true nature—whether it is many-formed or single-formed,
or in what way it is and how. But now, as I suppose, we have fairly
gone through its affections and forms in its human life."

"That's entirely certain," he said.

"In the argument," I said, "haven't we both cleared away the
other parts of the criticism and also not brought in the wages and   *b*
reputations connected with justice as you said Hesiod and Homer do?
But we found that justice by itself is best for soul itself, and that the
soul must do the just things, whether it has Gyges' ring or not, and, in
addition to such a ring, Hades' cap."[10]

"What you say is very true," he said.

"Then, Glaucon," I said, "isn't it now, at last, unobjectionable, in
addition, also to give back to justice and the rest of virtue the
wages—in their quantity and in their quality—that they procure for   *c*

612 c   the soul from human beings and gods, both while the human being is
still alive and when he is dead?"

"That's entirely certain," he said.

"Then, will you give back to me what you borrowed in the argument?"

"What in particular?"

"I gave you the just man's seeming to be unjust and the unjust
man just. You both asked for it; even if it weren't possible for this to
escape gods and human beings, all the same, it had to be granted for the
argument's sake so that justice itself could be judged as compared with
d   injustice itself. Or don't you remember?"

"If I didn't," he said, "I should indeed be doing an injustice."

"Well, then," I said, "since they have been judged, on justice's
behalf I ask back again the reputation it in fact has among gods and
among human beings; and I ask us to agree that it does enjoy such a
reputation, so that justice may also carry off the prizes that it gains
from *seeming* and bestows on its possessors, since it has made clear that
it bestows the good things that come from *being* and does not deceive
those who really take possession of it."

e   "What you ask," he said, "is only just."

"Then," I said, "won't you first give this back: that it doesn't
escape the notice of gods, at least, what each of the two men is?"

"Yes," he said, "we shall give that back."

"And if they don't escape notice, the one would be dear to the
gods and the other hateful, as we also agreed at the beginning?"

"That's so."

"And won't we agree that everything that comes to the man dear
613 a   to the gods—insofar as it comes from gods—is the best possible, except
for any necessary evil that was due to him for former mistakes?"

"Most certainly."

"Thus, it must be assumed in the case of the just man that, if he
falls into poverty, diseases, or any other of the things that seem bad, for
him it will end in some good, either in life or even in death. For, surely,
gods at least will never neglect the man who is eagerly willing to become just and, practicing virtue, likens himself, so far as is possible for
b   a human being, to a god."

"It's quite likely," he said, "that such a man isn't neglected by his
like."

"And, in the case of the unjust man, mustn't we think the opposite
of these things?"

"Very much so."

"Then such would be some of the prizes from gods to the just
man."

"In my opinion, at least," he said.   *613 b*

"And what does he get from human beings?" I said. "Or, if that which *is* must be asserted, isn't it this way? Don't the clever unjust men do exactly as do all those in a race who run well from the lower end of the course but not from the upper?[11] At the start they leap sharply away but end up by becoming ridiculous and, with their ears on their shoulders,[12] run off uncrowned? But those who are truly runners come to the end, take the prizes, and are crowned. Doesn't it also for the most part turn out that way with the just? Toward the end of every action, association, and life they get a good reputation and bear off the prizes from human beings."   *c*

"Quite so."

"Will you, then, stand for my saying about them what you yourself said about the unjust? For I shall say that it's precisely the just, when they get older, who rule in their city if they wish ruling offices, and marry wherever they wish and give in marriage to whomever they want. And everything you said about the unjust, I now say about these men. And, again, about the unjust, I shall say that most of them, even if they get away unnoticed when they are young, are caught at the end of the race and ridiculed; and when they get old, they are insulted in their wretchedness by foreigners and townsmen. As for being whipped and the things that you, speaking truly, said are rustic—that they will be racked and burned—suppose that you have also heard from me that they suffer all these things. But, as I say, see if you'll stand for it."   *d*

                                    e

"Very much so," he said. "For what you say is just."

"Well, then," I said, "such would be the prizes, wages, and gifts coming to the just man while alive from gods and human beings, in addition to those good things that justice itself procured."   *614 a*

"And they are," he said, "quite fair and sure ones."

"Well," I said, "they are nothing in multitude or magnitude compared to those that await each when dead. And these things should be heard so that in hearing them each of these men will have gotten back the full measure of what the argument owed him."

"Do tell," he said, "since there aren't many other things that would be more pleasant to hear."   *b*

"I will not, however, tell you a story of Alcinous," I said, "but rather of a strong man, Er, son of Armenius, by race a Pamphylian.[13] Once upon a time he died in war; and on the tenth day, when the corpses, already decayed, were picked up, he was picked up in a good state of preservation. Having been brought home, he was about to be buried on the twelfth day; as he was lying on the pyre, he came back to life, and, come back to life, he told what he saw in the other world. He said that when his soul departed, it made a journey in

614 c   the company of many, and they came to a certain demonic place, where there were two openings in the earth next to one another, and, again, two in the heaven, above and opposite the others. Between them sat judges who, when they had passed judgment, told the just to continue their journey to the right and upward, through the heaven; and they attached signs of the judgments in front of them. The unjust they told to continue their journey to the left and down, and they had behind them

d   signs of everything they had done. And when he himself came forward, they said that he had to become a messenger to human beings of the things there, and they told him to listen and to look at everything in the place. He saw there, at one of the openings of both heaven and earth, the souls going away when judgment had been passed on them. As to the other two openings, souls out of the earth, full of dirt and dust, came up from one of them; and down from the other came other souls, pure from heaven. And the souls that were ever arriving looked as

e   though they had come from a long journey: and they went away with delight to the meadow, as to a public festival, and set up camp there. All those who were acquaintances greeted one another; and the souls that came out of the earth inquired of the others about the things in the other place, and those from heaven about the things that had happened to those from the earth. And they told their stories to one another, the

615 a   ones lamenting and crying, remembering how much and what sort of things they had suffered and seen in the journey under the earth—the journey lasts a thousand years—and those from heaven, in their turn, told of the inconceivable beauty of the experiences and the sights there. Now to go through the many things would take a long time, Glaucon. But the sum, he said, was this. For all the unjust deeds they had done anyone and all the men to whom they had done injustice, they had paid the penalty for every one in turn, ten times over for each. That is, they were punished for each injustice once every hundred years; taking this

b   as the length of human life, in this way they could pay off the penalty for the injustice ten times over. Thus, for example, if some men were causes of the death of many, either by betraying cities or armies and had reduced men to slavery, or were involved in any other wrongdoing, they received for each of these things tenfold sufferings; and again, if they had done good deeds and had proved just and holy, in the same

c   measure did they receive reward. And about those who were only just born and lived a short time, he said other things not worth mentioning. And he told of still greater wages for impiety and piety toward gods and parents and for murder. For he said he was there when one man was asked by another, 'Where is Ardiaeus the Great?' This Ardiaeus

had been tyrant in a certain city of Pamphylia just a thousand years   615 c
before that time; he had, as was said, killed his old father and elder
brother and done many other unholy deeds.[14] Now Er said that the   d
man asked responded, 'He hasn't come. Nor will he come here,' he
asserted. 'For this too, of course, was one of the terrible sights we saw.
When we were near the mouth about to go up and had suffered everything else, we suddenly saw him and others. Just about all of them were
tyrants, but there were also some private men, of those who had committed great faults. They supposed they were ready to go up, but the   e
mouth did not admit them; it roared when one of those whose badness
is incurable or who had not paid a sufficient penalty attempted to go
up. There were men at that place,' he said, 'fierce men, looking fiery
through and through, standing by and observing the sound, who took
hold of some and led them away, but who bound Ardiaeus and others
hands, feet, and head, threw them down and stripped off their skin.   616 a
They dragged them along the wayside, carding them like wool on
thorns; and they indicated to those who came by for what reason this
was done and that these men would be led away and thrown into Tar-
tarus.' They had experienced many fears of all kinds, he said, but more
extreme than any was the fear that each man experienced lest the sound
come as he went up; and when it was silent, each went up with the
greatest delight. Such then were the penalties and punishments; and, on
the other hand, the bounties were the antistrophes of these.

"When each group had spent seven days in the plain, on the   b
eighth they were made to depart from there and continue their journey.
In four days they arrived at a place from which they could see a
straight light, like a column, stretched from above through all of heaven
and earth, most of all resembling the rainbow but brighter and purer.
They came to it after having moved forward a day's journey. And
there, at the middle of the light, they saw the extremities of its bonds   c
stretched from heaven; for this light is that which binds heaven, like the
undergirders of triremes, thus holding the entire revolution together.
From the extremities stretched the spindle of Necessity, by which all
the revolutions are turned. Its stem and hook are of adamant, and its
whorl is a mixture of this and other kinds. The nature of the whorl is
like this: its shape is like those we have here; but, from what he said, it d
must be conceived as if in one great hollow whorl, completely scooped
out, lay another like it, but smaller, fitting into each other as bowls fit
into each other; and there is a third one like these and a fourth, and
four others. For there are eight whorls in all, lying in one another with
their rims showing as circles from above, while from the back they   e

616 e   form one continuous whorl around the stem, which is driven right
through the middle of the eighth.[15] Now the circle formed by the lip
of the first and outermost whorl is the broadest; that of the sixth, second; that of the fourth, third; that of the eighth, fourth; that of the seventh, fifth; that of the fifth, sixth; that of the.third, seventh; and that of
the second, eighth. And the lip of the largest whorl is multicolored; that

617 a   of the seventh, brightest; that of the eighth gets its color from the seventh's shining on it; that of the second and the fifth are like each
other, yellower than these others; the third has the whitest color; the
fourth is reddish; and the sixth is second in whiteness. The whole
spindle is turned in a circle with the same motion, but within the
revolving whole the seven inner circles revolve gently in the opposite
direction from the whole; of them, the eighth goes most quickly, second

b   and together with one another are the seventh, sixth and fifth. Third in
swiftness, as it looked to them, the fourth circled about; fourth, the
third; and fifth, the second. And the spindle turned in the lap of
Necessity. Above, on each of its circles, is perched a Siren, accompanying its revolution, uttering a single sound, one note; from all eight is
produced the accord of a single harmony. Three others are seated

c   round about at equal distances, each on a throne. Daughters of
Necessity, Fates—Lachesis, Clotho, and Atropos[16]—clad in white
with wreaths on their heads, they sing to the Sirens' harmony, Lachesis
of what has been, Clotho of what is, and Atropos of what is going to be.
And Clotho puts her right hand to the outer revolution of the spindle
and joins in turning it, ceasing from time to time; and Atropos with her
left hand does the same to the inner ones; but Lachesis puts one hand
to one and the other hand to the other, each in turn.

d   "Now, when they arrived, they had to go straight to Lachesis. A
certain spokesman first marshaled them at regular distances from each
other; then, he took lots and patterns of lives from Lachesis' lap, and
went up to a high platform and said, 'This is the speech of Necessity's
maiden daughter, Lachesis. Souls that live a day, this is the beginning
of another death bringing cycle for the mortal race. A demon will not

e   select you, but you will choose a demon. Let him who gets the first lot
make the first choice of a life to which he will be bound by necessity.
Virtue is without a master; as he honors or dishonors her, each will have
more or less of her. The blame belongs to him who chooses; god is
blameless.'

"When he had said this, he cast the lots among them all, and each
picked up the one that fell next to him—except for Er who wasn't permitted to do so. To the man who picked it up it was plain what number
he had drawn. After this, in turn, he set the patterns of the lives on the

ground before them; there were far more than there were souls present.
There were all sorts; lives of all animals, and, in particular, all the
varieties of human lives. There were tyrannies among them, some lasting to the end, others ruined midway, ending both in poverty and exile
and in beggary. And there were lives of men of repute—some for their
forms and beauty and for strength in general as well as capacity in
contests; others for their birth and the virtues of their ancestors—and   *b*
there were some for men without repute in these things; and the same
was the case for women, too. An ordering of the soul was not in them,
due to the necessity that a soul become different according to the life it
chooses. But all other things were, mixed with each other and with
wealth and poverty and with sickness and health, and also with the
states intermediate to these.

"Now here, my dear Glaucon, is the whole risk for a human
being, as it seems. And on this account each of us must, to the neglect
of other studies, above all see to it that he is a seeker and student of   *c*
that study by which he might be able to learn and find out who will give
him the capacity and the knowledge to distinguish the good and the bad
life, and so everywhere and always to choose the better from among
those that are possible. He will take into account all the things we have
just mentioned and how in combination and separately they affect the
virtue of a life. Thus he may know the effects, bad and good, of beauty
mixed with poverty or wealth and accompanied by this or that habit of   *d*
soul; and the effects of any particular mixture with one another of good
and bad birth, private station and ruling office, strength and weakness,
facility and difficulty in learning, and all such things that are connected
with a soul by nature or are acquired. From all this he will be able to
draw a conclusion and choose—in looking off toward the nature of the
soul—between the worse and the better life, calling worse the one that   *e*
leads it toward becoming more unjust, and better the one that leads it
to becoming juster. He will let everything else go. For we have seen
that this is the most important choice for him in life and death. He
must go to Hades adamantly holding to this opinion so that he won't be
daunted by wealth and such evils there, and rush into tyrannies and
other such deeds by which he would work many irreparable evils, and
himself undergo still greater suffering; but rather he will know how always to choose the life between such extremes and flee the excesses in
either direction in this life, so far as is possible, and in all of the next
life. For in this way a human being becomes happiest.   *b*

"And the messenger from that place then also reported that the
spokesman said the following: 'Even for the man who comes forward
last, if he chooses intelligently and lives earnestly, a life to content him

619 b   is laid up, not a bad one. Let the one who begins not be careless about his choice. Let not the one who is last be disheartened.'

     "He said that when the spokesman had said this the man who had drawn the first lot came forward and immediately chose the greatest tyranny, and, due to folly and gluttony, chose without having con-

c   sidered everything adequately; and it escaped his notice that eating his own children and other evils were fated to be a part of that life. When he considered it at his leisure, he beat his breast and lamented the choice, not abiding by the spokesman's forewarning. For he didn't blame himself for the evils but chance, demons, and anything rather than himself. He was one of those who had come from heaven, having lived in an orderly regime in his former life, participating in virtue by

d   habit, without philosophy. And, it may be said, not the least number of those who were caught in such circumstances came from heaven, because they were unpracticed in labors. But most of those who came from the earth, because they themselves had labored and had seen the labors of others, weren't in a rush to make their choices. On just this account, and due to the chance of the lot, there was an exchange of evils and goods for most of the souls. However, if a man, when he comes to the life here, always philosophizes in a healthy way and the

e   lot for his choice does not fall out among the last, it's likely, on the basis of what is reported from there, that he will not only be happy here but also that he will journey from this world to the other and back again not by the underground, rough road but by the smooth one, through the heavens.

     "He said that this was a sight surely worth seeing: how each of the

620 a   several souls chose a life. For it was pitiable, laughable, and wonderful to see. For the most part the choice was made according to the habituation of their former life. He said he saw a soul that once belonged to Orpheus choosing a life of a swan, out of hatred for womankind; due to his death at their hands, he wasn't willing to be born, generated in a woman. He saw Thamyras' soul choosing the life of a nightingale. And he also saw a swan changing to the choice of a human life; other musical animals did the same thing. The soul that got the twentieth lot

b   chose the life of a lion; it was the soul of Ajax, son of Telamon, who shunned becoming a human being, remembering the judgment of the arms. And after him was the soul of Agamemnon; it too hated humankind as a result of its sufferings and therefore changed to the life of an eagle. Atalanta's soul had drawn one of the middle lots; she saw the great honors of an athletic man and couldn't pass them by but took

c   them. After this soul he saw that of Epeius, son of Panopeus, going into the nature of an artisan woman. And far out among the last he saw the

soul of the buffoon Thersites, clothing itself as an ape.[17] And by   *620 c*
chance Odysseus' soul had drawn the last lot of all and went to choose;
from memory of its former labors it had recovered from love of honor;
it went around for a long time looking for the life of a private man who
minds his own business; and with effort it found one lying somewhere,
neglected by the others. It said when it saw this life that it would have   *d*
done the same even if it had drawn the first lot, and was delighted to
choose it. And from the other beasts, similarly some went into human
lives and into one another—the unjust changing into savage ones, the
just into tame ones, and there were all kinds of mixtures.

"When all the souls had chosen lives, in the same order as the lots
they had drawn, they went forward to Lachesis. And she sent with each
the demon he had chosen as a guardian of the life and a fulfiller of what   *e*
was chosen. The demon first led the soul to Clotho—under her hand as
it turned the whirling spindle—thus ratifying the fate it had drawn and
chosen. After touching her, he next led it to the spinning of Atropos,
thus making the threads irreversible.[18] And from there, without
turning around, they went under Necessity's throne. And, having come   *621 a*
out through it, when the others had also come through, all made their
way through terrible stifling heat to the plain of Lethe.[19] For it was
barren of trees and all that naturally grows on earth. Then they made
their camp, for evening was coming on, by the river of Carelessness
whose water no vessel can contain. Now it was a necessity for all to
drink a certain measure of the water, but those who were not saved by
prudence drank more than the measure. As he drank, each forgot
everything. And when they had gone to sleep and it was midnight,   *b*
there came thunder and an earthquake; and they were suddenly carried
from there, each in a different way, up to their birth, shooting like
stars.[20] But he himself was prevented from drinking the water.
However, in what way and how he came into his body, he did not
know; but, all of a sudden, he recovered his sight and saw that it was
morning and he was lying on the pyre.

"And thus, Glaucon, a tale was saved and not lost;[21] and it
could save us, if we were persuaded by it, and we shall make a good   *c*
crossing of the river of Lethe and not defile our soul. But if we are persuaded by me, holding that soul is immortal and capable of bearing all
evils and all goods, we shall always keep to the upper road and practice
justice with prudence in every way so that we shall be friends to ourselves and the gods, both while we remain here and when we reap the
rewards for it like the victors who go about gathering in the prizes. And   *d*
so here and in the thousand year journey that we have described we
shall fare well."[22]

INTERPRETIVE ESSAY

INTERPRETIVE ESSAY

The *Republic* is the true *Apology* of Socrates, for only in the *Republic* does he give an adequate treatment of the theme which was forced on him by Athens' accusation against him. That theme is the relationship of the philosopher to the political community.

Socrates was accused of doing unjust things—of not believing in the gods which the city believed in and of corrupting the youth. These charges do not relate simply to the man Socrates who happens to be a philosopher but are meant to be a condemnation of the philosophic activity itself—and not on behalf simply of the city of Athens, but on behalf of the political community as such. From the city's point of view, there seems to be something about the thought and way of life of the philosopher which calls into question the city's gods, who are the protectors of its laws, and which hence makes him a bad citizen, or rather no citizen at all. Such a man's presence in the city and his association with the most promising young men make him a subversive. Socrates is unjust not only because he breaks Athens' laws but also because he apparently does not accept those fundamental beliefs which make civil society possible.

Philosophy required a defense if it was to be admitted into civil society. At the time of Socrates' trial, philosophy was new to the cities, and it could easily have been crushed. The philosopher had to defend himself before the city, or the city would have been legitimated in discouraging philosophy's entrance into it as vigorously as possible. Socrates' trial was the crisis of philosophy, and its life was at stake. And, contrary to what modern men might be inclined to believe, it is not simply clear that philosophy is salutary, or even harmless, for the city. Socrates indicates this by the fact that he is at pains in the *Apology* to distinguish himself from other philosophers. He seems to agree that it is somewhat questionable whether a city which wants its sons to care for it should permit them to consort with philosophers.

The city sees only the apparent atheism of the philosopher and his effect on the young; the poet Aristophanes, who ridiculed Socrates in the *Clouds* and paved the way for his later official accusation, shows why the philosopher is subversive. He depicts Socrates as a man "who has investigated all the things in the air and under the earth and who makes the weaker argument stronger." The meaning of this charge is that the philosopher studies nature, particularly the heavens, and there he finds a true account of the celestial phenomena differing widely from that given in the religious myths; for example, he learns of a purely mechanical explanation of Zeus' thunderbolt. The philosopher's contemplation of the heavens dissolves the perspective of the city, the laws of which now seem to be mere conventions with no natural status. His way of life turns him from the duties of citizenship, and what he learns teaches him to despise the human, political things. What is more, the philosopher's understanding of the causes of all things makes it impossible for him to grasp man on his own level; man is reduced to non-man, the political to the subpolitical. The philosophers are alienated from the human things, which only poetry can adequately reproduce. The poet, in a more profound way, joins the city in its condemnation of philosophy as an enemy of political man.

Socrates must show, then, that the philosopher is just and that it is he, not the poet, who is the one able to treat of political things responsibly. This is not easy to do since it would appear that the philosopher calls into question the natural character of justice as a virtue and that his science of being has no special place for man in it. The *Apology* does not adequately accomplish this task, since it is a description of Socrates' life directed to a large, hostile audience composed of generally ignorant jurors sworn to uphold the defective laws of Athens. The *Republic*, on the other hand, is a leisurely discussion among cultivated, friendly men. The *Apology*, in which Socrates defends himself against the charge of injustice, makes no attempt to define justice: his accusers mean by an unjust man one who breaks the laws; and Socrates' justice is surely not that of a law-abiding man. Only the *Republic* makes the attempt to define justice and elaborate the science which can give ground to such a definition. In it, Socrates—who had argued in the

Apology that his only knowledge was ignorance and who had thus apparently admitted his incompetence in political things—presents a teaching about the nature of things political.

That teaching culminates in the famous declaration that "unless philosophers rule as kings, or those now called kings and chiefs genuinely and adequately philosophize . . . there is no rest from ills for the cities . . . nor, I think, for human kind. . . ." This means that there is a perfect harmony between philosophy and the city, science and society. Socrates has reformed philosophy so that it is now the one thing most needful for the city; and the philosopher is its greatest benefactor. We are, however, likely to be misled by this apparent Socratic optimism concerning the best case—the regime where philosophers rule. Careful reading will reveal that this alleged harmony is more of a paradox than a solution, that it covers a host of tensions which come to light in the less than perfect cases. Socrates may well have reformed philosophy so that it was no longer indifferent to politics, but it was certainly no less subversive of all existing regimes than was the older philosophy. If philosophers are the natural rulers, they are the rivals of all the actual rulers; philosophy, rather than being simply useless, seems to be conspiratorial. Philosophy may very well be harmful to real regimes, and it is very unlikely that the regime at which it aims can come into being. In fact, the *Republic* tacitly admits the truth of the charges made against Socrates: he is not orthodox in his beliefs about the gods and sets up new beings, the *ideas*, which are superior to the gods; the philosophers he trains will be men who both know the nature of things in the air and below the earth and are able to speak with consummate skill; and he teaches young men to despise Athens because he teaches them to love a regime in which philosophers are kings. Socrates denies that he is unjust because of this, but there must be a revolution in men's understanding of justice for just deeds to be recognized as such. In all imperfect regimes, his presence is problematic, and he must behave prudently: he undermines the attachment to the regime and laws of the city, but he is the salvation of all those in it who wish to live the good life.

The *Republic* shows us why Socrates was accused and why there was good reason to accuse him. Not only does he tell us about the good regime, but we see his effect on the young men he was said to have corrupted. Socrates, in leading them to a justice which is not Athenian, or even Greek, but is rather human, precisely because it is rational, shows the way to the truth about political things and develops the extremely complex relationship of that truth to civil society. These questions are most relevant to modern man, although they are perhaps harder for him to understand than for men of any previous generation. They are relevant to him because he admits his need for "values" and because the progress of publicly useful science now threatens him with destruction; they are harder for him to understand because he has been taught that "values" cannot be established by reason and that science is simply salutary for society.

For these reasons it behooves us to study the *Republic*. For it is the first book which brings philosophy "down into the cities"; and we watch in it the foundation of political science, the only discipline which can bring the blessings of reason to the city. We will learn that the establishment of political science cannot be carried out without sacrifice of the dearest convictions and interests of most men; these sacrifices are so great that to many they do not seem worthwhile: one of the most civilized cities which has ever existed thought it better to sacrifice philosophy in the person of Socrates rather than face the alternative he presented. This is why philosophy needs an *apology*; it is a dangerous and essentially questionable activity. Socrates knew that his interests were not, and could not be, the interests of most men and their cities. We frequently do not see this and assume that his execution was a result of the blind prejudices of the past. Therefore we do not see the true radicalness of the philosophic life. The *Republic* is the best antidote to our prejudice. The proper starting point for the study of Socratic philosophy is the nonphilosophic orientation of the city within which philosophy must take its place. Hostility to philosophy is the natural condition of man and the city. Socrates, in admitting his guilt, will show what higher concerns pardon him for it.

(*327a–328b*) As in the *Apology* the city compels Socrates to speak and defend himself, so in the *Republic* a group of men compels Socrates to remain with them and finally to give an account of himself. Apparently he does not wish to do so; other activities might be more to his taste, and he would like to hurry to them. But these men who accost him have power, and Socrates must adjust to them. If he cannot carry on his preferred activities unimpeded by the need for a compromise with his fellows, he must earn their good will and teach them to respect his tastes. Otherwise he would have to give up his way of life. He will only give as much of himself as is required to regain his freedom. This situation is a paradigm of the relation of the philosopher to the city. The difference between the *Republic* and the *Apology* is that the threat of compulsion used in the *Republic* is only playful while that of the Athenian law court in the *Apology* is in deadly earnest. In the *Apology* Socrates is condemned to death because a compromise acceptable to the people would have meant his spiritual death; in the *Republic*, dealing with a different audience, he emerges as the ruler of a tamed city which may not understand him but which is at least willing to permit him the unbridled pursuit of philosophy and access to the noble youth.

Socrates had accompanied Glaucon to the Piraeus both to pray and to see; he was motivated by piety and by theory—in the primitive and most revealing sense of that term, idle curiosity. The Athenians were introducing a new goddess into their cult. Socrates hints that it is the Athenians who bring in new divinities; if he, too, does so, he only imitates the democracy, with which he has more kinship than appears on the surface. (Adeimantus finally persuades Socrates to stay in the Piraeus by the promise of another innovation: a torch race on horseback. The conversation, also an innovation and itself innovating, takes the place of that torch race and is parallel to it. Socrates has a taste for newness which is antithetical to the best political orders and which he shares with the democracy. The difference between Athenian and Socratic tastes, however, can be measured by the difference between a torch race in honor of the goddess and a friendly discussion about justice.) Socrates' piety brings him down to the Piraeus with Glaucon and puts him into the situation where he must discuss the city, and that piety disposes him to care for the city. But his piety is somewhat lax; it is open to change and mixed with curiosity. He does not tell us the result of his prayers, but his observations led him to the recognition that the Athenian procession was no better than that of the Thracians. Socrates' theory stands above the enthusiasm of national pride and is somehow beyond mere citizenship. His piety belongs to the city; his thought does not.

Polemarchus sees him hurrying off and orders a slave to order him to stay. This little scene prefigures the three-class structure of the good regime developed in the *Republic* and outlines the whole political problem. Power is in the hands of the gentlemen, who are not philosophers. They can command the services of the many, and their strength is such that they always hold the philosophers in their grasp. Therefore it is part of the philosophers' self-interest to come to terms with them. The question becomes: to what extent can the philosophers influence the gentlemen? It is this crucial middle class which is the primary object of the *Republic* and the education prescribed in it. In this episode, the first fact is brute force, leading to the recognition that no matter how reasonable one may be, everything depends upon the people's willingness to listen. There is a confrontation here between wisdom, as represented by Socrates, and power, as represented by Polemarchus and his friends. At first the opposition of the two principles is complete, but Adeimantus and Polemarchus try to make Socrates choose to remain by offering him pleasant occupations if he does so. Glaucon accepts on behalf of his friend, and Socrates grudgingly gives in to the *fait accompli*. Hence wisdom and power reach a compromise, and a miniature community is formed. This accomplished, they take a vote and ratify their decision, and a new principle of rule emerges: consent. It is a mixture of powerless wisdom and unwise power. All political life will be founded on such compromises, more or less satisfactory, until the means can be discovered to permit the absolute rule of wisdom. Since he is forced to become a member of this community, Socrates soon establishes himself as its ruler by overcoming the other aspirants to the office, and then he proceeds to found a political regime in which philosophers will rule.

(328b–331d) Having made their social contract, the members of the group go to Polemarchus' house where they find his father, Cephalus, who dominates the scene, and who does so precisely because he is the father. Age is his title to rule, as it is in almost all regimes governed by ancestral custom. Age is a practical substitute for wisdom because, unlike wisdom, it is politically recognizable and easily defined. It is more feasible to teach force to respect age than to teach it to respect wisdom. The reverence for age, and hence antiquity, is one of the strongest ties which can bind a civil society together. But in order to carry on a frank discussion about justice, this reverence must be overcome, and the philosopher must take the place of the father at the center of the circle. Socrates must induce Cephalus to leave the scene, because Cephalus is beyond reason, and it would be impious to dispute him.

Once authority has been banished, Socrates and his companions can begin a critical examination of the ancestral code, of the conventional view of justice. This is the burden of the rest of Book I. All traditional opinions are discredited; and unaided reason, free of limiting prejudices, can begin the search for an understanding of justice which is not merely opinion. This criticism is a destructive activity in the name of liberation. It is a perilous undertaking for men who must remain members of civil society and could not properly take place under the eyes of Cephalus. He stands for those restraints on body and soul which are essential to the preservation of the city. There are certain uncomfortable issues, the raising of which usually indicates an inclination to vice on the part of those who do so. The practice of posing the extreme questions is a bad one, for one of its necessary consequences is corruption of the habits of the virtues. The only justification for questioning the old way would be that as a result a new, superior, way which Cephalus does not know of might emerge. The ancestral is by its nature silent about its own foundations; it is an imposing presence that awes those who might be tempted to look too closely.

Cephalus typifies the ancestral which cannot, but must, be questioned. Although his appearance is brief, by means of a few circumspect inquiries Socrates manages to reveal his character and his principles and, hence, those of the tradition he represents. Then the old man is delicately set aside. He is a father in the fullest sense—he was once very erotic and he possesses a considerable store of money. He presents himself as a lover of speeches, and thereby a friend of Socrates. But he loves speeches only in his old age, and it is doubtful whether he considers that his prime. The passions of youth led him to bodily pleasures, and it is only with the body's decline that he turns to the things of the soul. For Cephalus, speeches are a way of spending his old age, for Socrates they constitute the highest human activity. Cephalus' youthful passions, however appealing, seem to have led him into activities that are contrary to justice, and his old age is spent worrying about them and atoning for them. Thus, from the point of view of justice, *eros* is a terrible thing, a savage beast. For a man like Cephalus, life is always split between sinning and repenting. Only by the death of *eros* and its charms can such a gentleman become fully reliable, for his *eros* leads neither to justice nor philosophy but to intense, private bodily satisfaction.

Cephalus says that it is character, an attribute of the soul, which enables him to be contented in old age. Socrates poses a rather crude question: doesn't money help? Aren't the things with which Cephalus is concerned really tied to money? Isn't the insistence on character merely a way of hiding the fact of dependence on money and of attributing one's happiness to oneself rather than to the true material source of one's well being? Must not the overriding concern of private men, families and cities be the acquisition of wherewithal? The answer is yes and no. Cephalus would be very different and much less happy without money; he is not like Socrates who is poor and needs nothing more. But Cephalus is not a simple money-maker. Money is necessary, but it frees him for the fulfillment of certain family and religious duties which sublimate his life. He inherits the money and whatever improprieties were committed in the first making of it are lost in the mists of time. It would be unseemly, and lead to an undue concentration on money if one were to insist too much on its importance. Characteristic of Cephalus and men like him is a salutary forgetting of the preconditions of their kind of life.

The greatest good Cephalus has enjoyed from money is the avoidance of injustice and impiety. Here for the first time we touch on the subject which is to become the theme of the *Republic*. The question of money seems to lead him to the question of justice. The old man is afraid of punishment after death, so he does not want to depart owing debts to men or sacrifices to gods, or having cheated or deceived anyone. With his money he can pay his debts and offer his sacrifices, and because he possesses money he is not so dependent on others that he need deceive in order to stay alive. The tales told by the poets about punishments in another world for injustices committed in this one concerned Cephalus little when he was younger. He was inclined to laugh them off; accordingly, he worried little about injustices he might be committing. Only as death and death's perspective approaches does fear cause him to become concerned about his duties to men and gods. He is not sure that there are such punishments or even that he had really done unjust deeds, but prudence counsels a punctilious attention to his accounts with men and gods. Justice is a matter of self-interest: one should care about others if there are gods who defend justice.

In response to Cephalus' moving account of how he wishes to use his money in such a way as to live out his life in justice and piety, Socrates becomes argumentative. Instead of encouraging the old man in his laudable intentions, Socrates as much as tells him that he does not know what justice is and thereby undermines his life. This is one of the most decisive moments of the dialogue, for, with his question, Socrates takes command of the little community, forces Cephalus to leave, and makes the nature of justice the problem of the discussion. Socrates acts as though Cephalus had tried to define justice and objects to the definition he himself constructs out of Cephalus' statement. Justice, according to Socrates' rendition of Cephalus' view, is telling the truth and paying one's debts. Socrates' procedure is quite strange. In the first place he says nothing about half of what interests Cephalus: he does not mention piety, whether this is because he thinks Cephalus' understanding of piety is adequate or because he is not interested in piety. Second, in his discussion of paying one's debts, Socrates is silent about the gods and the sacrifices owed to them. In a word, Socrates forgets the divine, which is Cephalus' prime preoccupation, and makes the discussion one concerning human justice alone. This, along with his unwillingness to face the fact that he might be ignorant of the very obligations he is trying so hard to meet, is what causes Cephalus to leave. While the discussion is going on, he is elsewhere performing sacrifices to the gods, concerned with what is forgotten in that discussion.

Socrates' objection is very simple. Everyone knows that it is just to pay one's debts, but everyone is also aware that there are occasions when one need not and should not do so. Thus, it is impossible, without contradicting oneself, to say that justice is paying one's debts. One must seek a noncontradictory definition of justice. Cephalus, too, is aware that one must sometimes deviate from the principles of justice in the name of justice, but he has never considered what the consequences of that fact are. He must adhere to the laws, human and divine, or he would have to spend his time in finding out what justice is rather than in doing it. If everyone had to decide whether the laws properly apply in each case that arises, the political result would be anarchy; and, individually, a task beyond the capacities and energies of most men would be imposed on them. For Cephalus the just is identical to the law of the city, and the law is protected by the gods. The problem of justice is simply expressed in his view: if there are no gods, there is no reason to be just or to worry; if there are, we must simply obey their laws, for that is what they wish. But common sense tells us that laws are not always conducive to the good of those they are intended to benefit. Cephalus, however, is content to forget this fact in his sacrifices, even though his actions may be harming others. His lighthearted piety can seem extreme selfishness. He leaves to his son the consideration of what is truly good for other men, for it would force him to make a distinction between the just and the legal. And he leaves to all thoughtful selfish men the consideration of what the profitable life would be if there are no punishments after death. The unity of things expressed in the identification of the just and the legal under the protection of the gods has been rent asunder by Socrates' simple objection to Cephalus' assertion that a man should pay his debts. Now the members of this group must try to find out what justice is and whether justice is good for the man who practices it.

Although the definitions of justice proposed by Cephalus, Polemarchus, and Thrasymachus are all found wanting and must be abandoned, the discussions concerning them are not simply critical nor is their result only negative. From each something is learned which is of the essence of political life and which is reflected in the final definition and the regime that embodies it.

From Cephalus we learn that for most men justice can mean only law-abidingness, and that rewards and punishments in this life and the next are necessary to insure obedience which does not seem to them desirable in itself. Cephalus' definition fails because it cannot account for those instances in which one is admittedly exempted from obeying the law. He has no grasp of the intention or principle of law. He believes in the sanctity of private property: injustice is taking what belongs to others; justice, respecting what belongs to them. Belonging is defined by the law. But insanity and the intention to injure are sufficient grounds for taking away from a man what is thought to belong to him. Rationality and good will, or to put it otherwise, capacity to use a thing well and attachment to the community and its laws, are apparently conditions of the respect of a man's right to ownership. The simple example of the insane man who demands the return of his weapon, if generalized, leads far from the letter of the law, which men like Cephalus must respect. It becomes Polemarchus' responsibility to explain what standard should be looked to when one deviates from the letter of the law—which is equivalent to stating the purpose for which laws are instituted.

(331d–336a) Polemarchus inherits his father's duty of defending the law and hence of defending that property which he is going to inherit. He fails in his attempt to define justice in a way which is consistent with the maintenance of private property, and the *Republic* culminates in the elaboration·of a regime in which the only title to property is virtue and which is hence communistic. Polemarchus' original intention when he interrupted was merely to support his father's contention that one should pay what is owed. He does so by citing the authority of a poet. In his case, however (as opposed to that of Cephalus), poetic authority apparently does not refer to the even greater authority of the gods; he expresses his own view. Socrates can, with greater propriety, call into question the opinions of the young Polemarchus based on the authority of Simonides than the dogmas of the pious old Cephalus based on the authority of the traditions about the gods. But even here Socrates does not criticize the authority; he merely asks Polemarchus to interpret. Socrates makes the ironic assumption that Simonides must be right and that, since he is right, his views must accord with the results of rational argument. Polemarchus is compelled to learn how to argue; this is the first step on the road from unconditional acceptance of the ancestral order to the new regime based on reason in which the authority of the father's opinions and the power of his property play no role. By the end of his discussion with Socrates, Polemarchus is aware that he cannot get help from Simonides and that he must himself find reasons if he is to be satisfied with his beliefs about justice. Finally he and Socrates join in agreeing that Simonides could not have said what Polemarchus asserted he said, for it is unreasonable and base. Simonides remains respectable, but only because it is assumed that he accepts the authority of Polemarchus and Socrates who are now free of him. Polemarchus is the last participant in the discussion who attempts to use an authority as a sufficient cause for belief. Immediately after him comes Thrasymachus with his own definition of justice.

Polemarchus insists that justice is paying what one owes, but Socrates again poses the same objection that silenced his father. In order to save his definition Polemarchus must alter the sense of owing. Now justice is not giving back to any man what he has deposited but giving good things to friends. In general this would mean following Cephalus' rule, but it accounts for the exceptions: one need not aid a man who intends to do one damage—he must be a friend; and one must look to the good of the other party, as Cephalus did not do. Two great themes emerge: friendship, or community, and the good—infinite themes which it now becomes necessary to understand if one wishes to understand justice. Polemarchus, of course, does not recognize what has happened, for he does not see any problem in knowing what is good for a friend.

Socrates explains Polemarchus' definition of justice—doing good, and no harm, to friends—in terms of the example he used to embarrass Cephalus. A thing is not owed if it works harm to render it. But Socrates changes the thing deposited in this case: it is money, not a weapon. This small change is most revealing, for it broadens the scope of the exceptions and changes their sense. Cephalus would not return the weapon because its owner might hurt him with it; his justification is the selfish one of his own defense; justice must be practiced until it is manifestly harmful to oneself. Money in the hands of a madman is not so manifestly dangerous to another man as is a weapon. If one withholds his money, the justification for so doing is not likely to be that he will harm others but rather that he will harm himself. Now the focus of attention is on what it does to the one who receives rather than to the one who gives, a question to which Cephalus was profoundly indifferent. Cephalus was interested in what justice would profit himself, Polemarchus is interested in its advantage for others. He is really much more of a gentleman than his father. He presents the other side of the problem of justice—the good it does the community, as opposed to the individual. The relation between justice conceived as one's own good and justice conceived as the common good is the abiding concern of the *Republic*; Cephalus and Polemarchus represent the two poles. Also at this point, with the recognition that a man's property in money only extends so far as he can use that money well—only so far as is good for him—private property becomes radically questionable.

After more prodding by Socrates, Polemarchus is led to complete his definition by asserting that enemies are owed harm. Justice is benefiting friends and harming enemies. This is Polemarchus' and the gentleman's view of justice. As Lessing approvingly put it, "for the ancient Greeks moral greatness consisted in a love of friends that is as constant as the hatred of one's enemies is unchanging." Although Socrates finds this understanding of justice ultimately inadequate, he clearly agrees with Lessing that it is the formula for gentlemanly and heroic nobility and higher than most alternatives. It sounds harsh to our ears, for it is far from the morality of universal love to which we are accustomed, and we must make great efforts if we are to understand its dignity. That dignity consists in unswerving loyalty, loyalty to the first, most obvious attachments a man forms—loyalty to his family and his city. Our admiration for this character is manifest in our horror at the man who is willing to betray family or friends for gain, out of fear, or even in the pursuit of an ideal. Such loyalty seems natural, for it springs up in us with our first appetites and tastes; it is identical with love of our own. It does not have the abstract aspect of the love of a humanity which a man cannot know in its entirety, a love which does not make distinctions among men. It is more powerful because of its exclusiveness; it stays within the limits of possible human concern.

But, although many might be willing to admit that one's duties toward one's own take precedence over those toward mankind at large, it might well be asked why it is necessary to harm enemies, or why there need be enemies at all. The answer is twofold. There are unjust men who would destroy the good things and the good life of one's own family or nation if one did not render them impotent. And, even though there were not men who are natively unjust, there is a scarcity of good things in the world. The good life of one group of men leaves other groups outside who would like, and may even be compelled, to take away the good things of the first group. To have a family or a city that is one's own implies the distinction between insiders and outsiders; and the outsiders are potential enemies. Justice as helping friends and harming enemies is peculiarly a political definition of justice, and its dignity stands or falls with the dignity of political life. Every nation has wars and must defend itself; it can only do so if it has citizens who care for it and are willing to kill the citizens of other nations. If the distinction between friends and enemies, and the inclination to help the former and harm the latter, were obliterated from the heart and mind of man, political life would be impossible. This is the necessary political definition of justice, and it produces its specific kind of human nobility expressed in the virtue of the citizen. Socrates does not simply reject it as he appears to do. The warriors in his best regime, whom he compares to noble dogs, share in the most salient characteristic of noble dogs: gentleness toward acquaintances and harshness toward strangers. This is the key to the strengths and weaknesses of the political man.

Socrates' analysis of the definition is divided into three parts: (1) a discussion of how one can do good to friends (332c–334b); (2) an attempt to define a friend (334c–335b); and (3) a critique of the notion that a just man can do harm (335b–336a).

Socrates begins by asserting that Simonides meant that the owed is the fitting. The deposit is no longer important. Whether a man has deposited something or not is irrelevant; the only consideration is what is fitting for him. Justice might mean depriving him of what he thinks belongs to him or giving him something to which he appears to have no claim. In this reformulation, doing good to friends and harm to enemies is equivalent to giving to each what is fitting. Polemarchus meant that one gives to friends the things they want and denies to enemies the things they want. Socrates changes Polemarchus' meaning by concentrating not on the wants of men but on what is objectively proper for them. A sick friend is justly treated when given medicine whether he likes it or not. This shift in emphasis implies that the primary concern of the just man must be something Polemarchus has never considered: what counts is not so much the disposition to give the good things to friends, but knowing what those good things are. Justice must be some kind of knowledge.

Therefore Socrates turns to the most evident, perhaps the only sure, models of knowledge of what is fitting—the arts. A doctor wishes to give what is fitting to bodies and knows what is fitting and how to give it. The just man, if he is to succeed in his intention, must also possess an art. Now the problem becomes to identify the art of justice which, to put it mildly, common sense does not apprehend so quickly as it does the other arts. Formally, it must be the art which gives good to friends and harm to enemies, just as cookery gives seasoning to foods.

However, it immediately comes to light that justice is not the only art capable of benefiting friends and harming enemies. Medicine and navigation are of even greater use than justice to men who are sick or sailing. As a matter of fact, each of the arts aims at some good, and hence each is capable of working the benefactions or injuries called for by the definition of justice. The question is to find what justice does that no other art does, and this is obviously a difficult, or, rather, an impossible, task. Polemarchus suggests that justice is most useful and indispensable in the affairs of war, and, in peacetime, in keeping money deposits. This response is more helpful for learning about Polemarchus' view of justice than for solving the problem of justice's subject matter. The connection of war and money is obvious; and the kind of good things Polemarchus means and the sense in which the just citizen is a warrior emerge more clearly. But, as he does in the other cases, Socrates could easily show that a skilled soldier is a better partner in war than a just man, and a trained banker a better partner in peacetime than a just man. Socrates has indicated by the examples he uses that, for Polemarchus at least, justice is concerned with the acquisition and distribution of good things in communities of men while keeping off the outsiders (332c–d, 333a, 333b). The extraordinary result of this conversation is that justice is useless in the enterprise of doing good to friends and harm to enemies. What has happened is that Socrates and Polemarchus discover that the world is divided up among the arts and there is nothing left for an art of justice. A doctor may do good to his friends and hence be just, but justice is nothing beyond the exercise of his art, which is something other than justice. Arts are the means of doing good and harm; arts have subject matters but justice does not; hence justice is not an art and cannot do good. Justice has disappeared.

Moreover, Socrates insists on pointing out that the arts are neutral, that they can effect opposite results with equal ease. This fact is particularly shocking to Polemarchus, for its consequence is that the practitioner of the art of justice would be as adept at stealing as at guarding a thing and would lie as well as he tells the truth. Nothing in the art would guide a man as to which he should do; he would merely be technically proficient. Instead of being the model of reliability, the just man becomes the archetype of untrustworthiness, the possessor of power without guiding principle. He is a thief and a liar, the contrary of the debt-paying, truth-telling just man defined by Polemarchus' father —a definition which Polemarchus has inherited and the substance of which he is trying to defend.

Of course, it has been admitted that the just man sometimes would not pay his debts and would lie even to his friends, so the result of this argument should not be surprising. But Polemarchus is unwilling to accept it. He is a gentleman, and there are certain things— dishonorable things—a gentleman is never supposed to do. He may admit that they must be done, and even do them, but he refuses to recognize the consequences of what he does. If he did so, it would seem to end in the loss of all standards. Life is ordered according to fixed rules, and the exceptions are hidden in silence. Polemarchus could be accused of hypocrisy, and the limitations of his kind of moralism are exposed here. Socrates hints that the good things which Polemarchus defends might well have been acquired in less than decent ways, the memory of which is lost in the mists of time. But, even worse, his character is such that he would probably rather work harm than use ungentlemanly means to a good end. Socrates, as the *Republic* reveals, is not averse to lies and is certainly no respecter of private property.

However that may be, the assumption that justice is an art does lead to serious difficulties, expressed ironically in the notion that the just man is both useless and a thief. It would seem that arts require particular subject matters and that they are morally neutral. We are forced to abandon the assumption, and one might very well ask why it was made in the first place. We all sense that justice is a disposition, as Cephalus originally suggested, one which every man must possess in addition to his skill. A doctor must be disposed to heal his patients as well as be able to do so; otherwise he might just as well kill them for profit as cure them. Just why did Socrates turn the conversation in this direction?

In the first place, it must be remembered that, with the banishment of Cephalus, ancestral authority was replaced by what men can know for themselves, by the evidence of reasoned experience. The arts are the most obvious sources of knowledge available to all men as men without the need of any act of faith or the instruction of a particular tradition. The desire to know what one owes other men would most immediately lead in the direction of trying to discern an art which can guide us just as medicine guides us in matters of health. Moreover, however much habit may play a role in the character we call just, it is also clear that it is simply insufficient for a man to follow rules without any knowledge of the reasons behind them. Cephalus is proof enough of that. Our doctors are supposed to obey the Hippocratic oath, and that obedience would, in a sense, make them reliable. But, ultimately, the most important thing is the knowledge of the goodness of that oath, of the reasons why following it is salutary. The worthwhileness of a doctor's activity depends on this; and, no matter how technically proficient he may be, his talents are useless or dangerous if there is no knowledge about this first question. Justice necessarily and primarily demands a knowledge of what is good for man and the community; otherwise the knowledge and skills of the arts are in the service of authoritative myths.

Now, this discussion with Polemarchus outlines in a negative way what the character of the requisite knowledge must be. It cannot be like any of those arts which are always present in every community—shoemaking, weaving, carpentry, etc. This is what Socrates meant in the *Apology* when he told of his quest for wise men. Poets and statesmen, he found, knew literally nothing, whereas artisans did indeed know something. Unfortunately their knowledge was limited and partial, and Socrates said that he would prefer to be ignorant as he was than knowledgeable as they were. For they were content with their competence and closed to the larger questions. To be ignorant in Socrates' way is to be open to the whole. The artisans are models of knowledge, but their kind of knowledge is not applicable to the domain of poets and statesmen. The problem is to combine the concerns of poets and statesmen with knowledge as artisans possess it. Such knowledge is what Socrates is seeking.

The discussion with Polemarchus leads to the same result as the questioning of the artisans described in the *Apology*. The artisans are found insufficient, and the insufficiency of the arguments here shows why. These arguments are based on the premise that the arts like medicine are self-sufficient; but this is not so. The doctor can produce health, but that health is good he does not learn from medicine, and similarly with all of the arts. They deal with partial goods which presuppose a knowledge of the whole good to which they minister. The error of the discussion was to look for a specific subject matter for justice, to make it one among many arts, to act as though only the doctor had anything to say about medicine. To help a sick friend one needs not only a doctor but someone who knows to whom health is fitting and how many other goods should be sacrificed to it, and who can direct the doctor to do what will most help the patient. There are master arts which rule whole groups of ministerial arts and are necessary to them. These are what Aristotle calls architectonic arts. The carpenter, the mason, the roofer, etc.—all are in need of an architect if a house is to be produced. He is more important than they are, he guides them, and he does not need to be a carpenter, a mason, or a roofer himself. Without the architect, all the other arts connected with building lack an end and are useless or worse. Similarly, justice must be a master art, ruling the arts which produce partial goods so as to serve the whole good. In other words, justice must be knowledge of that good which none of the other arts knows but which each presupposes. Lawgivers actually organize all the arts and tell their practitioners what they can and cannot do. What Socrates proposes is a legislative or political science. If each of the artisans obeys the law established by a legislator who is wise in this science, he would be just, and justice would take care of itself in law-abiding practice of the arts. In this way the arts would provide what is fitting to each man.

The very inadequacy of this argument, which divides the world among the arts without reflecting on that world which is divided, points to an art which does so; that art must be justice. Hence Socrates teaches that in order to be just in the full sense one must be a philosopher, and that philosophy is necessary to justice. Philosophy does have a subject matter which helps in doing good to friends and harm to enemies, for it alone knows what is good or fitting. And it alone is not neutral, for, by its very definition, it seeks the whole good. Justice in this way would be knowledge, would be useful, and would not be able indifferently to produce opposite results. This is the solution which the argument compels us to seek. And a community of artisans ruled by philosophers would be one in which good would be done to friends. This solution, however, must wait until later, for Polemarchus really has no notion of what philosophy is, and its discovery is impossible on this level of thought. The poets and the laws tell Polemarchus the proper place of each thing, and this is why he sees no difficulty in doing good to friends. His is a prephilosophic world, and its authorities must be completely discredited before philosophy can even be sought.

After thoroughly confusing Polemarchus about the way to do good to friends and harm to enemies, Socrates turns to the question of what a friend is. He and Polemarchus agree that men consider as friends those they believe to be good. The problem is whether they must really be good men or only seem to be so in order to be friends. Polemarchus answers sensibly that the reality is not so important but rather what is thought about it. Almost all men have friends, and many are not able to judge the true character of those they call friends. Friendship would be very rare if both parties had to be good men and know it. But from this simple admission follows a consequence which is intolerable to Polemarchus: to the extent that the just man erred about the goodness of men, he would benefit bad men and harm good ones and hence be unjust. A simple reformulation solves the problem: friends are properly those who appear to be good and are.

But this little change, if it were taken seriously, would have the profoundest of effects on Polemarchus' life. His first admission that his friends were those who seemed to him good reflected the way he really thinks. It is an easygoing outlook, typical of most men. He knows who friends are. Our friends are those around us, and the insistence that they must be good is a secondary consideration, one that has an abstract ring to it. This condition is admitted in speech but has little effect in deed. And this means that men who loyally serve their friends are constantly and thoughtlessly doing injustice. This consequence cannot be avoided simply by making more effort, for Polemarchus' view is not merely a result of his laziness but a product of his attachment to family and city. He makes the primitive identification of the good with his own. He is like his father who wanted Socrates as a friend and invited him to become a member of the family. Men who are outsiders can become friends only by becoming "naturalized" members of the family; blood ties are what count. Even the loyalty to the city is understood as an extension of the family. This tendency to see the good in one's own and to devote oneself to it is one of the most powerful urges of human nature and the source of great devotion and energy. Once the distinction between what is good and one's own is made, the principle of loyalty to family and city is undermined. In order to be just, one must seek good men wherever they may be, even in nations fighting one's own nation. If the good must be pursued, then caring for one's own must be extinguished, or it will make one unjust and impede the quest for the good. This undermines family and city; and they must attempt to prevent the distinction from even coming to light. Certainly, Polemarchus would regard the abandonment of his primary loyalties as the destruction of the purpose and dignity of his life. If, however, he is to be consistent with the argument, he must make this sacrifice. A man who wishes to be just must be cosmopolitan.

Thus far, Socrates has led us to the observation that in order to do good to friends and harm to enemies one need only be a philosopher and give up one's attachments to those whom most men call friends. Now he attacks the entire view implied by the definition. He asserts that no just man would harm anyone, thereby opposing his own understanding of justice to that of the gentleman. His is an utterly unpolitical view, one that seems to deny the distinction between friend and enemy. It takes no account of the desire to avenge insults and appears to be predicated on the notion that life is not essentially competitive. Socrates does not suggest that the just man would want to benefit all men, only that he would want to benefit his friends and remain indifferent to the others. Polemarchus believes that it is impossible to benefit friends without harming enemies, for every city is in competition with other cities for the possession of scarce things. There cannot be cities without enemies, and a man cannot be a good citizen without wishing ill to his city's enemies. One can be indifferent to enemies if one divorces oneself from the city's perspective *and* if the things one considers good are not threatened or scarce. Only the things of the mind are such as to belong to all men without necessary exclusion of some men and the war consequent on that exclusion. Nobody need take a man's knowledge from him in order to enjoy it as one would have to do in order to make use of his money. Socrates' view is that of philosophy, in which knowledge is the highest good; Polemarchus' view is that of the city, in which property is the highest, at least the most needful, good.

In the concluding portion of their discussion, Socrates and Polemarchus actually have entirely different understandings of what it means to harm someone. Socrates says that to harm is to make a person or thing worse, with respect to his or its specific virtue. Justice, he asserts without proof, is human virtue, so to harm someone would be to make him more unjust. Correcting his earlier statement that the arts are simply neutral, Socrates further asserts that the practitioners of arts are dedicated to goals which they cannot, to the extent they are true to their arts, ignore. Therefore the just man cannot by justice make another man more unjust, and thus cannot harm him. Now Polemarchus had no such notion in mind when he spoke of harming enemies. What he meant was taking the enemy's property or life, for those are the good things. Socrates' view is perfectly consistent with stealing from or killing an enemy just so long as he is not made more unjust. Socrates and Polemarchus differ about what is truly good. With all of Polemarchus' admiration for justice, it is not the highest thing, not sought for as such. Justice is more of a means to the end of preserving life and property than itself the end of a good life.

Polemarchus' definition of justice might be regarded as the rule requisite to the satisfaction of collective selfishness: be loyal to the members of your own group so that you can best take advantage of the outsiders. And, in principle, there is no reason why this selfishness should not be extended to the individual if justice is not good in itself. This is why Socrates is able to claim that this definition, which seems so gentlemanly, is the product of a rich tyrant: if wealth is the goal, then the best way to attain it is by breaking all faith and seizing power in one's city and conquering as many nations as one can. Only if justice is an end, not a means, is it reasonable to be unremittingly just.

There is a tension in Polemarchus—of which he is unaware—between his love of property and his love of justice. This is what Socrates exposes and what Thrasymachus is about to exploit. Justice, Thrasymachus says, is the morality of a band of robbers who are face to face with their victims, and only a simpleton would be duped into making something more of it. Polemarchus is in an untenable position somewhere between utter selfishness and total dedication to the common good. Gentlemanly morality is self-contradictory, and the goods desired by the gentlemen would, if he were clear-sighted, lead in the direction of tyranny. Thrasymachus continues on the road to it, a road to which Socrates' questions have directed him.

(336b–354b) Thrasymachus bursts violently into the discussion. He is angry because Socrates and Polemarchus had been engaged in a dialogue. He sees this as a form of weakness. The participants in a dialogue obey certain rules which, like laws, govern their association; they seek a common agreement instead of trying to win a victory. The very art of dialectic seems to impose a kind of justice on those who practice it, whereas rhetoric, the art of making long speeches without being questioned—Thrasymachus' art—is adapted to self-aggrandizement. Thrasymachus sees dialectic as an opponent of rhetoric and wishes to show his audience the superiority of rhetoric. Moreover, Thrasymachus objects to the substance as well as the form of what he has just heard. Justice as doing good to others fits in well with the self-abnegation of dialectic and is just as unsound. It is foolishness, the direct opposite of prudence, which causes a man to hold the position that justice is doing good to others while also supposing that it is good for the doer. Thrasymachus adopts the accents of moral indignation in the cause of immorality. He charges Socrates with wrongdoing, with deceiving other men; since Socrates' method is irony, he is a dissembler or a hypocrite. He imposes a higher good, in which he himself does not believe, and would cause men and cities to neglect their needs and interests.

Thrasymachus wishes to punish Socrates, and, in a book teeming with allusions to Socrates' accusation and trial, Thrasymachus makes the most explicit condemnation of Socrates; his insistence that Socrates, if bested by Thrasymachus, propose an appropriate punishment for himself prefigures that fateful day when the condemned Socrates is forced by the Athenian law to propose his own penalty. To Thrasymachus, as he will to the Athenian jurors, Socrates claims that he has no money; and now, as they will then, his friends offer to provide him with the necessary funds. Thrasymachus and the city are both angry at Socrates for not accepting their point of view, which appears to be as clear as day. The terms of the two accusations seem to be different, but it soon becomes evident that Thrasymachus' definition of justice is really the same as the city's and that he acts as its representative. For, as soon as he asserts that the just is the advantage of the stronger, he explains that by the "stronger" he means those who hold power in a city and constitute its sovereign, whether that sovereign consists of the people, the rich, the well-born, or a single man. The just is whatever the sovereign in its laws says is just. This is precisely what the city says, and Socrates is disloyal to both city and Thrasymachus in suggesting that justice goes beyond the law—that law may not even be necessary if wise men rule. This is a notion that is not only antilegal, but is, in particular, antidemocratic, because it looks to the few wise rather than the many free. Thrasymachus insists that the decree of the sovereign is ultimate, and that there is no recourse beyond it, while Socrates insists that laws are just only to the extent they conform to a standard of justice superior to the laws and independent of the wishes of the sovereign.

Thrasymachus' identification with the city's view of justice helps to explain his previously mentioned moral indignation in the cause of immorality, which also has its counterpart in the actions of the city. The city insists that its laws are just and punishes those who break them. Anger seems a proper reaction to lawbreakers who are thought to harm others for their selfish ends. But Thrasymachus has stripped away the veils that covered the selfishness of the rulers and their laws. Those laws themselves serve the private interest of a part of the city and do harm to the rest of it. Laws are not directed to the common good. And yet the city will continue to put lawbreakers to death as unjust men and enemies of the common good. The anger awakened in men by the sight of indifference or hostility to law is a powerful force in protecting the law and hence the city, but it can also be the enemy of justice and is certainly the greatest enemy of philosophy. Thrasymachus, whose art gives speech to the passions of the city, is its agent in condemning Socrates, and his action in the service of this passion imitates the city's action.

The immediate cause of Thrasymachus' ire is the end of Socrates' argument with Polemarchus. Based on the tacit premise that justice is good, the argument led to the conclusion that justice is an art that does good to those to whom it ministers. The just man profits both others and himself. This means that there is a common good; the community is bound together by justice, and no one sacrifices his own personal advantage to it. On the contrary, if—to use Socrates' hyperbolic expression—justice is human virtue, each gains his fulfillment in the prosperity of the whole. A just man never harms anyone. Thrasymachus, referring to his knowledge of the world and the actual practice of the cities, treats this view as the result of a culpable innocence, an innocence destructive to the happiness of those who are taken in by it. Practically speaking, as Cephalus' example shows, justice is law-abidingness. That is certainly what the city says it is; and, even if there is a natural justice, it must be embodied in a code of political law in order to have a real effect. The city always presents its laws as a constitutive part of itself, like the territory and the populace. But, in fact, those laws can vary as the territory and the populace cannot; they are a function of the regime, of the kind of men who govern the city. When the poor, or the rich, or the old families, or a tyrant take over the rule in a city, its laws change correspondingly. The sovereign makes the laws, and those laws always happen to reflect its interests. Oligarchies make laws which favor and protect oligarchy; democracy makes laws which favor and protect democracy, etc. The regime is the absolute beginning point; there is nothing beyond it. To understand the kind of justice practiced in any city one must look to the regime. The laws have their source in the human, all too human. He who obeys them, in reverence or in fear, is simply serving the advantage of the stronger, whether the stronger is a single man, or the great majority of the people, or any other politically relevant group within the city. If this be the case, however, prudence and self-interest would seem to dictate to the individual that either he should try to evade the law or else become the lawmaker himself. Thrasymachus' thesis is simply that the regime makes the laws and that the members of the regime look to their own good and not the common good. The city is not a unity but a composite of opposed parties, and the party which wins out over the others is the source of the law. There is no fundamental difference between tyranny and other regimes because they all have the same selfish end. Justice, therefore, is not a fundamental phenomenon; the lawgiver cannot base himself upon it, for justice is a result of law.

Socrates does not deny that it is the stronger who rule and establish the law. He silently accepts the view that all existing regimes are as Thrasymachus says they are. The two men thus agree that the character of the ruling group is the core of politics, that the rulers are the stronger, and that justice is a political phenomenon and must be embodied in the laws of a city. The issue between them is whether all rulers, all lawgivers, must be selfish in the way Thrasymachus insists they are. From this point on the question is the regime—who rules; and Socrates tries to find a kind of man, a political class, which is both strong and public-spirited.

Socrates turns, then, to the criticism of Thrasymachus' view of the rulers. He quickly succeeds in embarrassing him by the reflection that sometimes rulers make mistakes; hence obedience to the law may be as much to their disadvantage as their advantage. Justice is not the advantage of the stronger unless the stronger (the rulers) know what their own advantage is. The emphasis now shifts from strength to knowledge. Socrates' question appears to refer to rulers' mistakes about the means to their ends, but could apply to mistakes about the proper ends of action. Socrates, then, is also asking whether the rulers really know what is advantageous and leads Thrasymachus into a region of profound problems on which he has hardly reflected. Like Polemarchus, he takes it for granted that the most common objects of desire—particularly whatever has to do wealth—are advantageous and that knowledge of them is a given. Thrasymachus is the more thoughtful voice of the most thoughtless opinions and desires. He teaches an art by means of which men can get those good things, and a mistaken ruler for him would be one who did not know the appropriate means to the given ends. He wishes to educate a clever, selfish man who knows how to get what he wants. But, as Socrates will show, this artisan of selfish satisfaction is really not in harmony with the vulgar tastes Thrasymachus is also committed to supporting. It is by developing this contradiction that Socrates will be able to tame the wild beast.

Thrasymachus could easily have circumvented the difficulty which Socrates presents. The crude Clitophon, who enters to defend Thrasymachus, shows Polemarchus (who is now Socrates' ally and defender) how obvious this route is. Thrasymachus had only to say, as Clitophon insists he meant, that justice is what *appears* to be the advantage of the stronger. This position is close to that of legal positivism: the just is what the city says is just and nothing more. Clitophon asserts the laws established by the rulers are based on their *apparent* advantage. This position may not be true but it does not defy common sense, and it seems based on the actual practice of cities. The thesis merely asserts that the only source and sanction of law is the sovereign and that it is hence benighted to look for higher justification. There is no need to define rulers by any criterion other than their having the power to make laws in the city, and the question of what is truly advantageous is set aside. Clitophon's solution to Socrates' difficulty does not contain those internal contradictions which bring about Thrasymachus' downfall.

Thrasymachus, however, chooses to respond to Socrates' objection by arguing that the ruler is always right and knows his own advantage. The ruler who makes mistakes is not a ruler; that is, almost all rulers are not really rulers. It is not that rulers *do* behave with scientific selfishness but that they *should*. Thrasymachus, as it were, anticipates Socrates' best regime by developing an alternative opposed to it. As in Socrates' good city, where rulers will be trained who are perfectly public-spirited, so in Thrasymachus' there will be rulers who are perfectly selfish; the rulers in both regimes do have in common, however, the fact that they are knowers. Thrasymachus' regime is as improbable and opposed to experience as is Socrates'. Rather than defend the plausible observation that rulers of selfish intention are the source of law, Thrasymachus encumbers himself with the responsibility for what amounts to a moral imperative, requiring rulers to be selfish with perfect knowledge.

Why does Thrasymachus do so? In the first place, he has simply thought through the consequences of his position, unlike the advocates of a crude positivism. If law has no deeper authority than human convention, any man who reflects at all on what kind of life he should live realizes he cannot rely on the law for guidance. Every man reasonably pursues his own good, and, if there is no common good, he will properly use the law for his own private satisfaction. This is the lesson which the individual can well draw from the teaching that law is nothing more than the sovereign's will; and the intelligent tyrant seems to be the one who has best learned the lesson. The ruler is hence a man who seeks his own advantage; to do so is almost the only alternative, since other goals are illusory. If he fails to attain it, he is a failure as a ruler and a man. Thrasymachus looks at politics from the point of view of the man who wants to live well and has understood the nature of justice; it is this perspective which causes him to go beyond Clitophon's formulation.

Further, to the extent that in this drama Thrasymachus plays the role of the city, he echoes the city's insistence that it knows the truth. For the city could hardly admit that its laws are essentially fallible. Its pronouncements must be authoritative, and all knowledge, divine or human, must be ratified and codified by the sovereign. It has a monopoly of wisdom. Otherwise every individual would have an appeal from it.

And, finally, Thrasymachus as the practitioner and teacher of an art, one which he believes to be the most important art for men who want to live a good life, must make a claim himself to possess knowledge and to be able to convey that knowledge to others. As Socrates suggests, he is in Athens looking for students, whose money he needs in order to live. He directs his appeal to noble, political youths of high ambition. They wish to be rulers. But if there is no art the possession of which makes a man a ruler and enables him to attain the good sought for in the activity of ruling, what would Thrasymachus have to teach them? Clitophon's argument implies that the ruler is defined only by holding office, not by any particular skill which gives him the capacity to attain his end. This would be disastrous for Thrasymachus' profession. He therefore claims he teaches a skill which can make men rulers, in the sense that they will be able to fulfill their wishes. The ordinary ruler is potentially the completely successful selfish ruler. He cannot be understood without reference to this end any more than the doctor can be understood without reference to the end of curing sick men. A ruler who errs about his advantage is not as such a ruler any more than a mathematician who errs in calculation is as such a mathematician. Thrasymachus promises political success to his students. His definition of the rulers "in the precise sense" is part of his professional propaganda.

In the discussion of this definition of the ruler who is a perfect knower of an art, we see that Thrasymachus is not merely a lover of gain. He is also, in his way, a lover of knowledge. He is a model of that not uncommon phenomenon, "the intellectual." His passions are in the service of things other than knowledge although he devotes himself to a life of knowledge. Knowledge is not pursued for the sake of knowledge, but he recognizes a certain superiority in the life devoted to knowing for its own sake. It is this contradiction that defeats him, for taking knowledge seriously leads beyond preoccupation with one's private advantage toward a disinterested life devoted to universal concern. Thrasymachus' respect for art and reason enables Socrates to tame him, both because Thrasymachus is compelled by the argument as a less rational man would not be when an argument goes counter to his passions, and because he is intrigued by Socrates' art and skill. Even though his arguments are not always simply good, Socrates manages to get the advantage over the great rhetorician. This is an impressive feat. The city, when confronted with Socrates, itself destroys him; Thrasymachus, charmed by his arguments, finally becomes his friend. The intellectual voice of the city can become tractable as the city never will. The *Republic*, a book about a perfect city, is characterized by having perfect interlocutors, that is, men without whom a city could not be founded and who are, at the same time, persuadable, whom argument can convince to adapt to a new kind of world which is contrary to their apparent advantage. Just as one must have almost unbelievable conditions to found the best city in deed, so one must have exceptional interlocutors to found it in speech.

After Thrasymachus posits the precise definition of the ruler, a definition which assumes that ruling is an art and that art is a great good, it is a simple matter for Socrates to refute—or rather to silence —him. This argument is of particular interest because it poses the problem of justice in a most radical form. Socrates proceeds to show that all arts are directed to subject matters and that they are concerned with those subject matters and not with themselves; all arts rule something, and they are interested in the good of the thing ruled. The practitioner of an art, at least in the precise sense, does not serve himself; on the contrary, he forgets himself completely. Thrasymachus' definition leads to the furthest extreme from his intention. If one wanted to have a city of men who cared only for the public rather than the private, one would only have to find a way of constituting one peopled by artisans in the precise sense—which is just the solution of the *Republic*. To the extent to which a man is devoted to his calling, he forgets his own advantage.

Thrasymachus rebels at the conclusion to which the argument compels him; in attempting to refute it, he cites the way of the world. Shepherds care for their sheep in order that they may be eaten, not in order to have happy sheep. Rulers look on the people as shepherds do sheep: as objects of exploitation. A shepherd who looked to the good of the sheep would not help them but would only serve the appetites of his master. Similarly, the man who cares for the people and devotes himself to the common good only makes the people fatter for the exploitation of the city's masters. It is much more reasonable for the shepherd to deceive his masters and eat the sheep himself or to make himself the master. Now Thrasymachus makes it explicit that justice is bad for a man and that the best way of life is the most unjust one—the tyrant's life. His indignation at Socrates' argument is understandable, since one must wonder who or what takes care of the artisan-ruler who is also a human being and has needs and wishes of his own. Why would he be willing to be a ruler? Thrasymachus is unable to find an answer to this question because his own assertions have bound him.

It is Socrates himself who provides an answer, although it is an enigmatic and ironic one. Reiterating this principle that a shepherd—or a ruler—by definition cares for nothing but his flock, Socrates adds that, since the artisan gets nothing for himself from his art, he must be paid a wage. A man who earns a wage is, according to Socrates, a practitioner of the wage-earner's art; in point of fact, every artisan practices two arts—the one from which he gets his title and the wage-earner's art. With the latter art he cares for himself; with the former, for others. Wage earning, then, is the rubric that covers the side of a man's life concerned with his personal advantage; he must provide himself with the necessities, and he pursues his own good as well as that of others; he is not a selfless servant.

Thus a new art, and a new kind of art, comes to light. This art, however, contradicts the definition of the arts which has been the basis of the discussion. The wage-earner's art is not concerned with the good of the art's object, but rather with the good of the practitioner. After all, the wage earner does not care for the well-being of money, he cares for his own well-being. Moreover, there being no pre-established harmony between the two arts practiced by a man, there is every probability of there being conflicts between their demands. For example, what is the doctor to do who is offered a bribe for harming his patient? His two arts each make rigorous and contradictory claims upon him, and there is no evident principle for choosing which should be preferred. Socrates makes this explicit when he tells Glaucon that wages must always be paid to political men, and that there is a perpetual conflict between their interests as wage earners and their interests as good rulers. The tension between the public good and private good of the individual which Socrates had explicitly denied is admitted with this introduction of the wage-earner's art. Thrasymachus, however, is not quick enough to notice this and take advantage of it.

This wage-earner's art is ubiquitous. It accompanies all of the arts and directs their action. It is thus an architectonic art. Contrary to Socrates' argument that each art is complete and perfect in itself, needing nothing beyond itself, a super art is necessary to supplement all the arts. For they must be related to each other and to the whole of which their subject matters are a part. The carpenter's, bricklayer's, and plasterer's arts are not sufficient unto themselves; they must be guided by the architect's art. Money, or what we would call the economic system, is a sort of architectonic principle; for in ordinary cities the amount of money paid for the products of the arts determines what arts are practiced, how they are practiced, and what kind of men practice them. Money is the common denominator running through all the arts; it seems to establish their value and provides the motivation for practicing them. Thrasymachus, who is seeking students in Athens, is surely a part of this system. His rhetoric is of use to him only if people desire it and are willing to pay for learning it.

Socrates, by means of this fabrication of an art of wage earning, points, as he did in the discussion with Polemarchus, to the need for a master art to supplement the other arts. Money is manifestly an inadequate architectonic or regal principle, and its inadequacies serve to indicate what a true architectonic art would have to be and accomplish. Money cannot discern the nature of each of the arts nor evaluate the contribution their products make to happiness; the price paid for the services of the arts is merely the reflection of the untutored tastes of the many or the rich. Money constitutes an artificial system which subordinates the higher to the lower. And the man who serves for money becomes the slave of the most authoritative voices of his own time and place, while renouncing the attempt to know, and live according to, the natural hierarchy of value. He is always torn between the demands of his art and the needs of the marketplace.

The wage-earner's art is a kind of political substitute for philosophy. The intention of philosophy is to understand the nature of the arts and order them toward the production of human happiness, and to educate men to desire those things which most conduce to happiness. It can claim to rule all the arts for it alone tries to know the whole, the true whole, as opposed to the view of the whole of this time or place, and it restores the unity to a man's life. It demands total dedication to its objects, as was required of the arts, while giving ample reward to its practitioner in that it is the perfection of his nature and his greatest satisfaction. Only in philosophy is there an identity of the concern for the proper practice of the art and that for one's own advantage. Socrates embodies a solution to the conflicting demands which render Thrasymachus' life meaningless: Socrates combines in a single way of life the satisfactions of the lover of knowledge and the lover of gain. All other lives are essentially self-contradictory. In the philosopher we can find both the public-spirited ruler and the satisfied man.

Thus Socrates, whose explicit intention was to show that the practitioners of arts—and hence Thrasymachus' rulers—cannot be concerned with their own advantage, has, by the introduction of the wage-earner's art, tacitly admitted the necessity and legitimacy of that concern. He has only shown that men cannot consistently at the same time be both rulers in the precise sense defined by Thrasymachus and seekers of their own advantage, while hinting that philosophy is the only resolution of the conflict between art or science and self-interest. As it appears to Thrasymachus, Socrates is madly insisting that a man spend his life in total dedication to others without any reason for so doing and in blind indifference to the facts of life. Thrasymachus cannot defend his position because of his earlier assertions, and he is prevented by them from making his powerful appeal to men's lust and their respect for knowledge. His definition of justice as the advantage of the stronger fails, but only because his definition of the ruler is indefensible. He sees this as a result of having become entangled in Socrates' dishonest arguments. And no reader can be satisfied that Thrasymachus' definition has been refuted or that this discussion has proved that there is sufficient reason to devote oneself to the common good. The discussion has only served to heighten the sense of the disproportion between the private and the public good, to make justice more problematic than ever.

Instead of abandoning or attempting to improve Thrasymachus' definition of justice, the conversation curiously changes its theme. Without having established what justice is, Socrates turns to the question of whether it is good or not. It is most unusual to attempt to determine the desirability of a thing whose character one does not know. Socrates' reason for this procedure is that this is what interests the other men present whose attention he is trying to attract and who believe they have a fair sense of what justice is. They are not particularly interested in a philosophic investigation of the nature of justice, but in how they will live profitably or well. Thrasymachus has told them that they will do so by becoming tyrants, by disregarding the laws. Socrates appears to disagree. They want to know whether Thrasymachus' ruler lives a good life. Thrasymachus has stated that it is bad to be just, in the sense of caring for others, or obeying the law, or being dedicated to the common good. Socrates until now, along with Cephalus and Polemarchus, has seemed to believe that one must be just, that the only problem is to define more precisely what justice is. Now, following Thrasymachus, he makes the whole discussion much more radical in permitting the goodness of justice and the just life to become doubtful. Although justice has not been defined, an example of it has been present in the discussion and the members of the group look to that. That example is the deposit. Cephalus says that, though it may be a desirable object, one must return it for fear of divine punishment for not doing so. Polemarchus says that one must not, in deciding whether to return it, consider whether it is desirable for oneself or not, in the case of a friend, but only whether it will do the friend good. Thrasymachus says, that since the gods do not punish and there is no common good, one should keep deposits and try to get as much more as possible, the only consideration being one's own advantage. Glaucon and Adeimantus who are about to enter the discussion understand quite well what Thrasymachus is telling them; and Socrates *seems* to be saying that it is bad to keep deposits and break faith. This is what draws their attention, and Socrates makes them anxious to know why he thinks it is bad to become a tyrant. The question of the goodness of justice, the nature of which they think they know, will be the spur to their quest for the discovery of its true nature.

To refute Thrasymachus' contention that it is disadvantageous to be just, Socrates makes three arguments.

First, he establishes that Thrasymachus holds the unconventional position that injustice is a virtue, meaning by injustice getting the better of, or more than, others. Life, in his view, is a competition, and he who is most talented at the struggle possesses the greatest virtue. At the end of a complicated, specious, and amusing chain of reasoning, Socrates makes injustice appear to be a vice because it is contrary to wisdom, which is a virtue. The wise man, understood again by Socrates as the possessor of an art, does not seek to win out over other possessors of the same art. As a matter of fact they are, as such, in fundamental harmony, accepting the same general rules, at one, the same as each other. Mathematicians are all seeking the same result to the same problem, and, as mathematicians, there is no competition among them. The just man is more like the wise man in this than is the unjust man. Hence justice is virtue and injustice vice.

Now this would only be convincing if justice were wisdom and if, therefore, the objects of human action could be gained without taking them away from others. This is by no means evident. The result of the argument serves to point toward a realm of noble human activity which is not essentially competitive, and to show that the desire to have more for oneself is a goal which contradicts the character of art or science which, like law, deals not with the individual, but rather with the universal. But this argument does not suffice to convince anyone that it is possible to live well without being a sturdy competitor and re-enforces the doubt about the desirability of being devoted to art or wisdom.

Socrates only succeeded in this discussion because of Thrasyma-chus' incapacity to make the proper distinctions and to see the problem in the analogy to the arts. Surely, it is impossible to hold that life is simply getting more; but in the character of civil society and the pre-cariousness of human life and property there is a substantial basis for Thrasymachus' observations which he has been unable to defend. Soc-rates, rather than refuting him, humiliates and punishes him. At the end of this argument he is shown to be unjust but unwise, discredited before an audience in his claim to wisdom, and, worst of all, shown to be an inferior rhetorician. The apparently shameless Thrasymachus, willing to say anything, is revealed in all his vanity, for he blushes. He has no true freedom of mind, because he is attached to prestige, to the applause of the multitude and hence their thought. He gives voice merely to common opinions which are usually kept quiet and therefore appears wiser than most men. But he is really conventional and petty, a lover of applause more than of truth.

The next argument advanced by Socrates in favor of justice is that it is necessary. It begins from a more conventional understanding of justice: obedience to common rules which enable a group to act in com-mon. Socrates proves that the acquisition of any of the goals previously praised by Thrasymachus requires at least some justice. This is un-deniably true, but it does not prove that those goals are unattractive; it only shows that justice may be an unpleasant necessity in gaining them—a repulsive means to a desirable end. In this sense, the justice of a city would be no different from that of a band of robbers. Each is forced to make some sacrifices of immediate individual advantage for the sake of long-range self-interest. There is nothing intrinsically more noble about the city. At this point it would almost seem as though Soc-rates were accusing Thrasymachus of being too "idealistic." The latter thinks the strong man can simply ignore justice, while Socrates teaches that justice must be a matter of concern to him who wants to get more than others; it is an unfortunate fact of life.

The third argument is to the effect that justice is to be desired be-cause it is the health and perfection of the soul. In the course of the first argument, Thrasymachus had somehow agreed with Socrates that justice is virtue. But what is virtue, if not that which allows a thing to perform its work well? Nobody would want to have a sick body or a horse that could not pull its load. It therefore follows that justice, as the virtue of the soul, is desirable in itself. In addition to its other weaknesses, this argument is purely formal and empty. Everyone wishes to have a healthy soul. But what it consists in is the question. Above all, it is not clear that the justice spoken of in this third argument is identical with that spoken of in the second one. Is the man who obeys the laws of the community for the sake of ultimate gain precisely the same man as the one who is perfecting his soul? Are there not two definitions of justice implied here that have no necessary connection, so that the man who fulfills the commands of the one is not necessarily fulfilling the commands of the other and may even be contradicting them?

Thus ends the inconclusive argument with Thrasymachus, and he is shunted aside. But two important objects have been accomplished by the confrontation. The traditional definitions of justice have been reduced to a shambles, revealing the need for a fresh start. Furthermore, although, as Socrates disarmingly admits, they have not defined justice but have wandered, their wandering has not been purposeless—they have not defined justice, but they have succeeded in defining the problem of justice. Justice is either what makes a city prosper or it is a virtue of the soul and hence necessary to the happiness of the individual. *The* question is whether the two possibilities are identical, whether devotion to the common good leads to the health of the soul or whether the man with a healthy soul is devoted to the common good. It is left to Glaucon and Adeimantus to pose this question which is the distillation of the arguments of Book I.

(*357a–367e*) With Glaucon and Adeimantus, Socrates becomes a teacher. We watch him educating those Athenian youths he was accused of corrupting. The action of the *Republic* now becomes a formal response to the charge made in Aristophanes' *Clouds* which showed Socrates leaving the scene and permitting the unjust speech to overcome the just one. Here he becomes the defender of justice; indeed the whole *Republic* represents the triumph of the just speech. The two youths, brothers of Plato, introduce a new element into the dialogue. (For another account of Socrates' relationship to Glaucon, cf. Xenophon, *Memorabilia*, III, vi.) They are potential Athenian statesmen, men whose goals transcend the horizon of sensuality and money which limited the interlocutors of the first book. They are lovers of honor, which lends nobility to their souls, frees them from the goals which rendered Thrasymachus' notion of advantage so crude and narrow, and gives them the spiritual substance required for the sublimating experience of Socratic education.

They have often heard the arguments of rhetoricians and sophists, all of which, according to Glaucon, propound the thesis of Thrasymachus. This teaching is the application to politics of what has come to be known as pre-Socratic philosophy. The results of the study of nature led the earlier philosophers to believe that there is no cosmic support for justice, that the gods, if they exist at all, have no care for men. Justice is, then, merely human convention and hence a matter of indifference to those who wish to live according to nature. This does not necessarily lead to the consequence that one must desire to become a tyrant, for it is possible to care for things which cannot be procured by political life, for example, philosophy. But, in general, most men do care for the political life or things which can best be procured by it. Sophists and rhetoricians extract the political significance from the philosophers' knowledge of nature. They teach that the proper study of politics is not the laws or justice, for they are phantasms, but rhetoric, the means of getting one's way. At best, then, the study of nature apparently leads to indifference to the city and its laws; at worst it leads to tyranny. This was the suspicion of the Athenian *demos*, and it may very well be the case. Devotion to justice or the opposite is not simply a question of decency or corruption but one of the truth of things. And if what Thrasymachus teaches is the truth, the city in self-defense must suppress that truth.

It may be recalled that Socrates was accused of being a proponent of this pre-Socratic philosophy so inimical to the city's interest and a teacher of rhetoric. The *Republic* defends Socrates against this accusation: here he is shown to be the protector of justice against a rhetorician. Of course, he does not simply defend the justice of the ancestral laws of the city; his is a philosophic response to a philosophic challenge, and therefore it, too, is subversive of the ancestral. This response cannot merely be an exhortation to the practice of justice; it must also attempt to find a natural support for justice. The study of justice therefore leads to the study of nature; the character of justice depends on the character of nature as a whole. Hence the *Republic*, beginning with justice, must be a comprehensive book. In being forced to defend justice, Socrates is forced to enter forbidden realms and to expound novel conceits. Innocence once lost cannot be regained; the substitute is philosophizing in the fullest sense.

Although Socrates is not depicted as a practitioner of rhetoric, his appeal to Glaucon and Adeimantus stems from a kind of rhetoric which succeeded in silencing the master rhetorician Thrasymachus without truly refuting him. Socrates controlled the discussion from the outset in such a way as to involve them while, and in, posing the problem of justice in its most radical form. The confrontation with Thrasymachus was in a sense carried on for Glaucon's benefit. Socrates' success at perplexing and attracting Glaucon was seen when Glaucon could not restrain himself from interrupting to express his wonder at Socrates' assertion that punishment is a form of wage for rulers. Both Socrates and Thrasymachus, for their various reasons, are interested in these two men—young, teachable, and ambitious. Among the best of the youth, Glaucon and Adeimantus are powerfully drawn to excel in the most honored pursuits, those in which they can most benefit both others and themselves. That is to say they are drawn to politics. And Thrasymachus offers them the means of success, both by the tools of persuasion he can provide and by the liberating insight into the nature of political life on which his teaching is based. In effect, Thrasymachus tells them that in their pursuit of glory they need not be hampered by considerations of justice. This is an attractive teaching, for it simplifies things and gives them a reasoned ground for giving way to those temptations which political life always presents, temptations which are usually resisted at the command of law and shame. They are ready to become Thrasymachus' students since reason and passion combine to support him. But Socrates proves to be the superior speaker. Somehow what he represents is stronger; he arouses their curiosity by showing that his rhetoric is more powerful and by appealing to their nobility and love of justice. Socrates' paradoxical argument touches something in them. This is the beginning of an education that will lead them very far from anything they have ever known, but the end of which follows inevitably from the concerns with which they began. Before they can turn to Thrasymachus, they will have to overcome Socrates.

The daring and manly Glaucon has seen that Socrates has at best shown only the necessity of justice and not its desirability. More urbane than Thrasymachus, he recognizes the power of the reputation of justice. Therefore he does not himself praise injustice but puts the argument on its behalf in the mouth of others. He presents his motivation as a desire to see justice vindicated. Of course, he does not have to sell a teaching about justice as did Thrasymachus. The contradiction between the public teaching of injustice and the public necessity for the profession of justice was inherent in Thrasymachus' situation, and Glaucon's situation does not involve him in it. He profits from the lesson of Thra-symachus' discomfiture; hiding his personal doubts, he is able never-theless to satisfy his curiosity about the goodness of justice. His very mode of presenting his discourse is a model of the hypocritical use of public professions of justice.

Glaucon asks whether justice is good by nature or only by law or convention, and is thus the first participant in the dialogue who turns to nature as his standard. He is a daring man whose desire not to be hood-winked by common opinions about the good gives him a certain in-tellectual force lacked by Thrasymachus. The latter is perhaps too con-cerned with, and dependent on, what men usually hold to be good to look for a standard independent of civil society which might divorce him from it. And he also is so convinced of the power of art, and of his art in particular, to accomplish whatever one wants that he does not feel compelled to look for the permanent limits and ends which cannot be altered by art. At all events, it is Glaucon who goes to the roots by elaborating—though in the name of others—a teaching about nature which denies that man's nature is essentially political. Bound by its ancestral laws and myths, the city, like Thrasymachus, does not raise the question of nature; in fact it hinders the question from arising. It wishes to give the accidents of this time and place the same status as the unchanging principles of all things. It presents a certain combina-tion of nature and convention as the horizon within which its citizens must live and act. The cosmic phenomena are interpreted by the city as expressions of the same divine will which supports its laws; the ways of the heavens and those of city are in its view the same. The first effort of philosophy or science was to sort out the various elements in our ex-perience, to discover the true cause of lightning, eclipses, etc., by means of investigation unhampered by authority. It had to liberate it-self from the weight of respectable opinion and to become aware of the existence of rationally comprehensible principles of the phenomena seen in the heavens; in other words, nature had to be discovered against the will of the city. The consequence of this investigation was to deny the naturalness of the city, to deny that the lightning which strikes the man has any relation to justice, to deny that eclipses are signs from the gods. In this perspective, justice is merely human and is only punished if seen by human beings. Glaucon, who assumes this philosophic background in·his speech, draws the conclusion that if a man could be invisible to human beings, there would be no reason for him to be just in his pursuit of the good. Recalling to our minds Thrasymachus' shepherd, he tells the story of Gyges, the shepherd, who, with his ring that made him invisible, deposed his master and exploited his master's flocks, animal and human. And, by means of Thrasymachus' rhetoric, men can make their acts change appearance, which is tantamount to making them invisible. One should be indifferent to the city or use it for one's own purposes, but one need never take it seriously for itself. Glaucon challenges Socrates with the problem at its most extreme. He honestly wishes to be convinced that justice is best, but he does not want to be duped. He must know; for above all he seeks what is good for himself and does not care to be taken in by edifying preaching which will cause him to miss the enjoyment of the objects of his desires. Glaucon presents the political supplement to pre-Socratic natural philosophy: the city limits men in the pursuit of the good things, but its only justification for doing so is the need to preserve itself.

According to Glaucon, the character of justice can be discovered in its origin; the nature of a thing, in his view, is to be understood by that from which it comes, by its beginning and not its end. Nature dictates the pursuit of one's own good, but because of the scarcity of good things, this pursuit must be carried on at the expense of others. It is good to take from others what belongs to them, and it is bad to have things taken which belong to oneself; but the badness of the latter exceeds the goodness of the former. For those who cannot succeed at taking without also being taken from, it is better to compromise, giving up the one and gaining immunity from the other. Such a compromise, however, constitutes no more than a human construction, a contract. It does not overcome nature, which still impels a man to get what he wants without considering the contract; it is simply a recognition of the imprudence of doing so. Since the city's justice does not make men good or happy, able men who have the arts of force and deception can, and in all reason should, continue to follow the dictates of nature. In other words, superior men are not bound by the contract for they do not receive any advantage from it. In this perspective, justice is the simple, unadorned will, following the contract, to avoid injuring other men, whether this means obeying the laws set down to this end or equitably correcting the law so as to fulfill its intention. There is, then, no particular knowledge or ability implied in being just; it is merely the performance of a difficult task that goes against the grain of one's desires. Thrasymachus had said that the laws were made for the advantage of the stronger, meaning by "the stronger" whatever party happens to hold power. Glaucon implicitly accuses him of holding a conventional view of the stronger. There is a naturally strong man, and for him to obey the laws would serve the advantage of the conventionally, or politically, stronger but of the naturally weaker. But, from either standpoint, the law-abiding man is an innocent, and Glaucon adopts

Thrasymachus' notion of the just man as the simple, honest server of other men's interest. And it is this understanding of justice that Glaucon asks Socrates to defend. Socrates must show that the man who is whipped, racked, chained, and has his eyes burned out because men believe him to be unjust will be blessedly happy if only he possesses justice; while the prudent, courageous, skilled server of his own interest is miserable because he lacks justice. Socrates is commanded to prove that selfless dedication is rewarded by nature, that justice is the one thing most needful.

After Glaucon completes his exposition of the nature of justice and makes his demands for its defense, his brother enters the scene to state his problem. Although the two speeches seem supplementary, they are really quite different and set conflicting tasks for Socrates. As Glaucon was daring, Adeimantus is moderate; as Glaucon turned to nature, Adeimantus turns to opinion; as Glaucon paid attention to what he saw, Adeimantus pays attention to what he hears. He is particularly addicted to poetry. He does not make an argument for the superiority of injustice, but is perplexed by what he hears about justice. Although justice is praised, it is not praised for itself but for its rewards, and those rewards consist in certain pleasures which can be enjoyed by men who are unjust. It is not justice but the reputation for justice which gets these rewards. The accounts of gods and men contained in the classic poems support this conclusion. According to these poems, some just men are unhappy, and unjust men can win the favor of the gods. Everything that is known about men's duties comes from the poetic tradition, the laws, and parental training; and all in effect agree that justice itself does not produce happiness, that there are substitutes for justice, that just acts are not pleasant or good. It may be improper to question the tradition; but, once questioned, its internal contradictions lead to the same conclusion as that of both Thrasymachus and Glaucon. Either the tales are true, and one should *seem* rather than *be* just; or they are not true, in which case nature, the only substitute for them, teaches the same thing. We live within a horizon constructed by the poets, a horizon bounded by the presence of the gods. Cephalus, who spends his old age using his money to placate the gods' possible wrath at his earlier unjust deeds, is most representative of this human condition. There is no other available account of the sanctions of justice, and this one is not adequate to make it choiceworthy.

Thus Adeimantus, too, wishes to hear a new and adequate praise of justice, but what he asks for is different from what his brother asked for. Just as the latter desired an argument for pure and earnest dedication, so Adeimantus now reveals his deepest wishes by insisting that justice be easy and pleasant. It should in itself incorporate the advantages conventionally said to result from its practice. The poets promise just men great honors and sensual pleasures in this life and the next. Without making it quite explicit, Adeimantus longs for justice itself to be like or to be an adequate substitute for these honors and pleasures. Justice is always said to be hard, and there are ways to get around its necessity. If it is so unpleasant, why be just? As he says, in these conditions only a man whose divine nature renders injustice distasteful to him, *or* one who has knowledge, would resist the opportunity to do injustice. In order to be convincing to both Glaucon and Adeimantus, Socrates must show that justice satisfies even the man who loses everything for it, and that his happiness is akin to the sensations of the man immersed in the pleasures of the senses.

At the conclusion of the unjust arguments of Glaucon and Adeimantus, Socrates professes his incapacity to succeed at a task of the magnitude of the one imposed on him. But he recognizes that piety forbids him to abandon justice under attack. Under pressure from the entire group he agrees to defend justice. However, he does not respond directly to the questions of his young companions. Rather than criticize their arguments or present a counter argument of his own, he invites them to share an adventure with him. They are to join together in the greatest and most revealing of political acts, the founding of a city. Socrates thus engages their desire for glory; although they are not indifferent to the desires which moved the other speakers, they, and particularly Glaucon, are animated by a different passion: it is not money that they love so much, but honor. Thrasymachus had offered them tyranny, the highest position in the city. Socrates inflames their imagination with even grander dreams. The founders of a city are more powerful and more revered than are its tyrants. All succeeding generations honor them; they have none of the obloquy attached to the tyrant. Socrates outdoes Thrasymachus and offers more attractive food for reflection. Thrasymachus, with his training in rhetoric, also offers the means of attaining the object he proposes, and Socrates has no substitute for that. But the very attractiveness of the goal proposed causes them to neglect its impracticality. Socrates succeeds with them because he begins by giving them at least part of what they want. Socrates takes Glaucon and Adeimantus to the limits of politics, and it is at the limits that one can see both the nature and the problems of politics. We have learned that justice is a political question: can there be a regime whose laws are such as to serve the common good while allowing each of its members to reach his natural perfection? If not, life will be eternally torn between duty to the city and duty to oneself. In pretending that they are founders, Glaucon and Adeimantus at once discover that they must care for justice. In this case at least, the satisfaction of their desires is identical with the concern for justice.

Socrates, momentarily at least, accepts Glaucon's view that things can be understood by their origins. They are about to watch justice coming into being in order to see if Glaucon's account was correct. The decision to look for justice in a city first, and the consequent distinction between justice in a city and justice in an individual man, keep constantly before us the question whether the justice which makes a city healthy is the same as that which makes a man healthy. On the answer to this question depends the answer to the question whether it is advantageous for a man to devote himself to the city. We must first discover what a healthy city is and what a healthy soul is. The very coming to awareness of such a city and soul transforms and educates these young men.

(369b–372e) The first city is constructed by Socrates and Adeimantus, without the help of Glaucon. Thus it reflects the tastes of Adeimantus. It is an easy place: there is no scarcity, and justice takes care of itself. Men join together because they are incomplete, because they cannot provide for their needs themselves. Their intention is not to have more than others but to have enough for themselves. As long as there is no scarcity they will be peaceful, and the arts, with the cooperation of nature, produce enough to content them. Each man chooses an art according to his natural capacities so that nothing in life goes against the grain of the inhabitants' desires or talents. Each contributes according to his ability and receives according to his needs. In such a city, there is an immediate identity between selfish interest and the common good. Hence there is no need for men to be governed. The city is really the perfect community of artisans envisaged in the discussion with Thrasymachus, for each man devotes himself exclusively to his own art, his own good resulting from that dedication. The invention of money makes this possible. In this city it is not of value in itself and is not pursued as an end in itself. That development would be the result of inflamed desires. Here money simply facilitates exchange so that every artisan, as a result of practicing his own art, will have access to the products of the other arts. There is no separate wage-earner's art, for each art by itself produces the equivalent of money; and there is no need of an organizing principle other than that provided by money, which represents the needs of the body. It sets the various arts and artisans in motion in the service of satisfying those needs. This is a city which takes the bodily needs as the only real ones; and whatever efforts of the soul and intelligence it calls into play are entirely directed to the preservation and comfort of the body.

By means of the example of this city, Socrates, in opposition to Glaucon, suggests that the bodily desires are very simple and easy to satisfy. In this he is not unlike Rousseau in his opposition to Hobbes. The more complicated desires, the ones that cause the injustice of which Glaucon has spoken, are the result of a mixture of the desires of the body with the desires of the soul. Although the entrance of these desires connected with the soul serves to corrupt this first city, Socrates looks on them with more favor than does Rousseau, for they are the first manifestations of a longing for a natural perfection higher than that of the body; he admits Glaucon's dissatisfaction as a legitimate objection to this city. Glaucon is a man of intense desires, and his daring is in the service of those desires. He is, to use Socratic language, an erotic man, one who lusts to have as his own all things which appear beautiful and good. His desires are inchoate expressions of his inclination to a fulfillment of which he is as yet unaware. His view of nature is actually a conventional one, ignorant of the distinction between the body and the soul and of the distinct and divergent demands of the two. A natural man, for him, pursues the same goals as do men in conventional societies but without the restraints those societies always impose on their members. He takes ruling to be merely a means to the acquisition of certain things which most men believe to be good and which all serve the body's desires. Actually his desire to rule is the expression of an independently noble impulse which, if fully developed, would find its satisfaction only in contemplation and would wish to overcome the body's desires in order to enjoy its own peculiar pleasure undisturbed. His passionate nature has been tutored by the common opinions about what is good and by the materialist philosophy of which he has heard. Glaucon is thus a dangerous man but also an eminently interesting and educable one. His desires lead him to despise law and convention; as long as his limitless desires have as their objects the things he lists as desirable in his speech, he will long for tyranny. But it is precisely this freedom from law and convention combined with his passion that may enable him to climb to the human peaks. As is the case with all the young men most attractive to Socrates, Glaucon has a potential for good or evil. The conduct of his companions Critias and Alcibiades, both subverters of the Athenian democratic regime, caused Socrates to be suspected as a corrupter of the youth. Critias and Alcibiades were liberated but not educated. With Glaucon, we have the opportunity of seeing how Socrates educates and his effect on the young. He undertakes a perilous activity but one full of promise.

Adeimantus is much more moderate than Glaucon, and he is made a part of his brother's education. What he represents is also necessary to the founding of the just city as well as to the philosophic life, both of which are judicious blendings of moderation and courage or manliness. A city, if it is to be well governed, requires citizens whose desires are not too great and are well controlled; and it must possess some men who are willing to risk their lives in its defense. A philosopher's bodily needs must be minimal and his soul must be daring. These are the simplest senses of moderation and courage and the role they play in a city and a philosopher. Glaucon, with his manly intransigence, makes the most important contribution of the two interlocutors; he gives the conversation its power and its height. Glaucon cannot endure his brother's satisfaction with what he calls a city of sows and causes a new and luxurious city to be founded. But Adeimantus purges that luxurious city and makes it possible for its better potential to be realized.

This first city is obviously impossible. It depends on an unfounded belief in nature's providential generosity, in a "hidden hand" which harmonizes private and public interest, a belief to which Adeimantus would like to subscribe. This city is also undesirable, as will soon become clear. The fact that Socrates says that it is the true city does not mean that he thinks it could come into being or that he would wish it to do so. Rather, by this assertion, he implies that the city really exists to serve the body and that this city, devoted to the satisfaction of the simplest desires, serves the body best. The emergence of other forms of desire complicates the city and brings misery to it. But that corruption is the condition of the growth of more perfect human beings. Perhaps Socrates' assertion that it is the true city is not in contradiction, but in agreement, with Glaucon's characterization of it as a city of sows.

Glaucon rejects the first city because it does not appeal to his taste: he does not like the food. His manliness always leads him to make a direct assault on the good as he sees it. He has been promised a dinner which seems to have been postponed indefinitely. At the first mention of eating, he looks on the bill of fare with the eye of a hungry man who has a delicate palate and imagines how he would like to satisfy his hunger. He finds the simple city does not meet his gastronomic standards; in it food is only nourishment, only for keeping men alive and healthy. Merely to live and be healthy is the way of sows. Human beings require more than life; they demand unnecessary refinements and pleasures. Desire causes him to sharpen his demands on the city. He may think his is only bodily hunger, but it is a spiritual hunger which will cause him to transcend this city and lead him toward another kind of fulfillment. He is getting an unwilling lesson in austerity, which will aid him in sublimating his hunger. His wishes are always contradictory, for he always mistakes all of his great longings for bodily desires but cannot find satisfaction for them thus understood. His first long speech is another example of this tendency: while asserting the naturalness of perfect self-indulgence, he was at the same time insisting on a notion of justice which is the direct opposite of self-indulgence. He is an "idealist," in whatever direction he turns. He admires both the man who is perfectly self-indulgent and the one who is perfectly abstinent; in order to satisfy himself he would have to discover a way of life which combined both great eroticism and great moderation. This is an apparent impossibility, but he has before his eyes a man who has actually succeeded in making such a combination of opposites, and Glaucon need only recognize him for what he is to solve his dilemma concerning the best way of life. Socrates, according to his own account, is an erotic man, but his *eros* does not lead him, as it did Cephalus, to injure others or take what belongs to them. In order to satisfy his *eros*, he need not compete with other men to their detriment. He has no wealth and no honor; in fact he is despised and believed to be unjust. Yet he is happy. Finally he is executed for his very justice, but this will not cause him to regret his choice of way of life. He fulfills the harsh conditions Glaucon set for the just man, but also lives in great pleasure. He does not live without the ordinary pleasures because he is an ascetic, but because the intensity of his joy in philosophy makes him indifferent to them. Once Glaucon can see the possibility of such a way of life he will be cured of his desire for tyranny; already he has somehow divined the presence of such a way of life in Socrates. To be sure, he is not yet conscious of the nature of his own desires, or of desire in general, but in the revolt against the simple city he and Socrates are really allies. Glaucon finds no satisfaction in it; and there could be no Socrates living there, both because it is not advanced enough to give him the basis for a philosophic understanding and because such an idle, unproductive man would starve to death. Perhaps the objections of the two men are ultimately the same: the solution to the political problem embodied in this city is not a human one. A human solution requires the emancipation of desire, for only then can virtue arise. Humanity requires a self-overcoming; not because life is essentially struggle, but because man's dual nature is such that the goods of the soul cannot be brought to light without the body's being tempted and, therefore, without a tyranny of soul over body.

(372e–376c) Socrates agrees to join Glaucon in observing a feverish city, as opposed to the healthy one they had just been observing. One would think that they would do this only as a study in pathology, keeping the healthy model constantly before their eyes. Actually, the healthy city is forgotten and the good city is constituted by a reform of the feverish city rather than by a return to the healthy one. No serious attempt is even made to look for justice in the healthy city. The new city founded by Glaucon's desire begins with an act of injustice. Since luxury creates scarcity, land must be taken from others. Not everyone can have a city which is sufficient to support a life of satisfaction. Hence, the city proper is formed, that is, the band of brothers who have enemies, who must make war and be warriors. It would appear from this presentation that war is requisite to the emergence of humanity; as the city of sows was gentle and reflected a fundamental harmony among men, so the city of warriors is harsh and reflects a fundamental conflict among men. Paradoxically this is the first human city. It cannot claim that it does not harm other men; its justification can only be in the quality of life it provides for its citizens.

Here there emerges a new class of men devoted to the art of war, and in their souls emerges a new principle, spiritedness. The warriors must be men who like to fight, who are capable of anger, who rush to the defense of their city and of justice. Spiritedness is a difficult motive to understand, and its character can only be seen by contrasting it with desire. Desires are directed to the satisfaction of a need: they express an incompleteness and yearn for completeness. Hunger, thirst, sexual desire, etc., are all immediately related to a goal and their meaning is simple. The goal of spiritedness is much harder to discern. Its simplest manifestation is anger, and it is not immediately manifest what needs are fulfilled by anger. Spiritedness seems characterized more by the fact that it overcomes desire than by any positive goal of its own. Moreover, the desires related to the body—which are the only ones that have appeared thus far—all have a self-preservative function, whereas spiritedness, on the contrary, is characterized by an indifference to life. It may indeed aid in the preservation of life, but it can just as well place honor above life. The city may exist for the sake of life, but it needs men who are willing to die for it.

At first sight, the warriors look like the practitioners of just another art, to be set alongside the arts of shoemaking and farming, but they are really the first ruling class and introduce the first principle of hierarchy into the city. Similarly, spiritedness at first sight seems to be just another quality of soul, like the qualities which made a man a farmer or a blacksmith, but it really represents a new part of the soul, one which will rule the desires and establish a principle of hierarchy in the soul. The various arts present in the first city, however diverse in skill or product, all serve bodily satisfaction and are practiced for money. Ultimately they are the same; their practitioners are all included together in what will be called the wage-earning class; although there are many differences among its members in activity and intelligence, from the decisive point of view they are the same—mere life is their goal. They do not represent any fundamental diversity of principle. The warriors' art, however, is really different, and its services cannot be measured by money, for money is a standard for evaluating the contributions made toward the satisfaction of desire or the preservation of life. Spiritedness is beyond the economic system. The founders of modern economic science, who wanted it to be a universal political science, could do so only by denying the existence of spiritedness or understanding it as merely a means to self-preservation. Only men who pursue self-preservation and the gratification of bodily desire can be counted on to act according to the principles of economic "rationality."

Now there are two classes in the city, and the distinction between them is a purely natural one: one class is motivated by bodily desire, the other by spiritedness. The former can be counted on to pursue what we would call the economic goals. The latter has liberated itself from the single-minded concern for mere life. But the purposes of this class are not as yet clear. It seems that it is in the nature of spiritedness to be in the service of something, just as it is in the nature of soldiers to be in the service of something. Neither spiritedness nor the class which embodies it can be ends in themselves; their purposes come from outside of themselves. This class could be understood as a servant of the wage-earning class, but this would mean that the superior exists for the sake of the inferior. To understand the dignity of this element in the soul and in the city requires the discovery of a third and highest class which spiritedness serves and the end of which is as clear as that of the wage-earning class. This necessity for a third class is implied in the description of the warriors as noble dogs who guard a flock. Sheep dogs require shepherds. The warrior class would then be the link between the highest and lowest class, gaining its meaning from its service to the higher. The parallel of city and soul would apply in this case too. However that may be, the city needs defenders, and it also now needs rulers, for its feverish desires make living together impossible without control.

It is inevitable that the spirited warriors will rule in this city, for they are strong. In every civil society, there is one group that has the greatest strength, and it can and always does set down the laws in the terms suitable to it. Whatever the character of this class, the city's way of life will be determined by it. This is what Thrasymachus meant when he said that justice is the advantage of the stronger. The members of this class do not necessarily possess wisdom or any other element of virtue. If Socrates and his companions wish to establish a good regime without having to compromise with mere power, it is this crucial class they must control and train. They need not preoccupy themselves with the wage-earning class, for it will be unable to resist the commands of the warriors. The instrument for controlling the warriors is education and, therefore, from this point forward education is the central theme of the *Republic*. The city's way of life depends on the character and hence the education of the rulers.

Socrates and Glaucon have established this class of spirited warriors to protect the city from its enemies, but they quickly become aware of its problematic character. What is to prevent these men who are so savage to foreigners from being savage with their fellow citizens? Although they are supposed to guard the flock, they are likely to exploit it. What in their nature will permit them to be gentle to their charges? Gentleness and harshness seem very like contrary characteristics, and good guardians thus appear to be impossible. But Socrates, on second thought, recognizes that the animals to whom they compared the guardians do combine gentleness and harshness: dogs are gentle to those they know and harsh to those they do not know. Socrates most surprisingly draws the conclusion that the good guardian is possible if, in addition to being spirited, his nature is philosophic. Judging friends and enemies by the criterion of knowledge and ignorance is, he says, the way of philosophy, and thus philosophy is the principle of gentleness. In a book famous for the proposal that philosophers be kings, this is the first mention of philosophy or philosophers. Philosophy is invoked in the city only for the purpose of solving a political problem.

This identification of dog-like affection for acquaintances with philosophy is, of course, not serious. It only serves to prepare the way for the true emergence of philosophy in Book V and to heighten the difference between philosopher and warrior. The philosophers are gentle men because they pursue knowledge and not gain; their object does not entail exploitation of others. The love of knowledge is a motive necessary to the rulers of this city in order to temper their love of victory and wealth. But the philosophers are the opposites of the dogs inasmuch as they are always questing to know that of which they are ignorant, whereas the dogs must cut themselves off from the unknown and are hostile to foreign charms. They love their own and not the good. And this must be so, for otherwise they would not make the necessary distinction between their flock and those who are likely to attack it. The warrior principle is doing good to friends and harm to enemies. It is true that their love of the known extends their affections beyond themselves to the city; it partakes of the universalizing or cosmopolitan effect of philosophy. But that love ends at the frontier of the city. They remain the irrational beasts who love those who mistreat them as well as those who are kind to them. No mention is made of the fact that dogs do not characteristically love the flocks but the masters to whom the flock belongs and who teach them and command them to care for the flock. These dogs as yet have no masters and are therefore incomplete. The masters whom they will know and hence love are philosophers and knowers. The dogs' nature opens them to the command of philosophy but does not make them philosophers.

(376c–383c) After Socrates and Glaucon have established the necessity of a nature combining spiritedness and gentleness for the warriors, Adeimantus takes his brother's place in the discussion, and he and Socrates begin the education of that nature. On the basis of the description of the warriors' function, one would have expected that their education would be in the art of bearing arms—but this is not even mentioned. The entire discussion concerns the character of their souls and largely deals with the effects of music—the lovely domain of the Muses in which men charm their passions when at peace. Socrates focuses on the contents of poems, thereby implying that the other elements of poetry are only accessories used for the purpose of better conveying a theme or a teaching. The poets are taken most seriously as the makers of the horizon which constitutes the limit of men's desire and aspiration; they form the various kinds of men, who make nations various. Men's views about the highest beings and their choice of heroes are decisive for the tone of their lives. He who believes in the Olympian gods is a very different man from the one who believes in the Biblical God, just as the man who admires Achilles is different from the one who admires Moses or Jesus. The different men see very different things in the world and, although they may partake of a common human nature, they develop very different aspects of that nature; they hardly seem to be of the same species, so little do they agree about what is important in life. Everything in the city stems from the beliefs of those who hold power and are respected in it. If poetry is so powerful, its character must be a primary concern of the legislator.

The reform of poetry is most immediately directed to Adeimantus and the teaching he drew from poetry in his speech in favor of injustice. On the basis of the "reformed" poetry, Adeimantus could not have come to his conclusions. The gods do not give evil lots to good men, or good ones to bad men, nor can they be moved by prayer. Just men and just deeds are the only ones celebrated. There is nothing in the poetic universe which would make men think that injustice profits men or gods.

The critique of poetry is divided according to the most important effects its representations have on men's beliefs, in particular, their beliefs about the gods, courage, and moderation. Justice cannot be treated here, Socrates says, because they have not yet decided whether justice is good or not, and that would be essential to such a discussion. The beliefs about the gods and the poetic depiction of them are the first topic Socrates and Adeimantus undertake. Courage, moderation, and justice—three of the four cardinal virtues defined in the *Republic*—are each mentioned in the context of the critique of poetry, but the fourth, wisdom, is not. It would seem necessary to infer that the warriors are not to be wise and that the beliefs about the gods are their substitute for wisdom. Those beliefs about the gods are a nonphilosophic equivalent of knowledge of the whole. The first segment of the study of poetry constitutes, therefore, a theology, a theology not true but salutary. Its doctrines are simple: the gods are good; they are the cause of the good; and they do not deceive. Nothing is said about the nature of the gods' relations with men or whether they care for men at all. Similarly, there is no assurance that these are the Olympian gods or that they have anything in common with what Adeimantus understands a god to be. Certainly Cephalus' piety, based on appeals to the gods for leniency, becomes, in this light, highly questionable. It is not even clear that it is sensible to pray to such gods.

A closer look at Socrates' prescriptions for the representations of the gods shows that they are not, in his view, all powerful and that they are subordinated to rational principle. They must be good and can only cause good; the deeper teaching implied here is that the good is the highest and most powerful principle of the *cosmos*. As opposed to the earlier views of the first things which the poets express, chaos is not the origin of all things; and the universe is fundamentally a *cosmos*, not a battlefield of contrary and discordant elements, as the poets represent it to be in their terrible tales of the family lives and wars of the gods. Those earlier views are not proved false here, but it is manifest that in such a world nobility and justice have no cosmic support; low can win over high, and the noble things can be in conflict with the necessary ones and with each other. In the new theology the higher is not derived from the lower, and the good is first. Similarly, the gods themselves are not representatives of becoming as opposed to being; of all things, they are the most unchanging; they are not moved by the desires of the body which are the sign of weakness and change and dependence. Primacy is given to rest and eternity over motion and time. The gods are a prefiguration of the *ideas* which are known to the philosophers. The man who believes in these gods, while loving the city and justice, will not hate and consider impious the philosopher who teaches the *ideas*.

A further important consequence of the discussion about the gods follows from the fact that the gods do not lie. In the discussion with Cephalus it was indicated that just as human justice sometimes requires not repaying debts, so it sometimes requires not telling the truth. That gods never lie would seem to imply that they have nothing to do with men and are not their friends. The world in which men live contains evil as well as good, and, although the dominance of the good in the *cosmos* at large is reassuring for the human estate, it does not perfect it. Men cannot live like the gods. Later we are told that rulers must lie; hence the gods are not rulers, and rulers cannot imitate the virtues of gods. Statesmen require a human prudence in which the gods can give them no guidance. This reform of the poetic account of the gods leads to the consequence that in the future the poetic depictions of the gods cannot serve as models for human conduct.

(*386a–392c*) These beliefs about the gods, Socrates says, will make the warriors men who honor the gods and ancestors and who are serious about their friendship with one another. This means that the proper opinions about the gods will cause the warriors to be both pious and just in the common meanings of these terms. Next comes courage, the virtue governing and perfecting spiritedness. It does not depend so much on beliefs about the gods, whose place is usually held to be in the heavens, but on beliefs about Hades, the home of the dead, which is generally thought to be beneath the earth. Homer's description of Hades is repulsive and frightening, and Socrates asserts that men who believe it cannot be courageous. Here Socrates' critique is completely negative; he simply says such things must not be said. He does not, as he did with the gods, tell what must be said. He does not even say that Hades exists or that there is any life after death. The existence of some kind of gods seems less questionable than the existence of an afterlife. Strangely, Socrates insists only that death should not be frightening, without paying any attention to the salutary effect such fear might have. Apparently, it is not only the warriors who are liberated from their terrors about a life to come, but also men like Cephalus. This terror caused Cephalus to try to live justly in his old age. But it also made him unable to participate in this discussion. Socrates is looking for another way to make men love justice, one which does not force them to turn away from this life and to be hostile to reason.

Socrates wishes ɔ expunge all of these disagreeable stories about Hades from the literature. But in so doing he seems to destroy the virtue of courage. If there is nothing terrible in death, then the sacrifice of life is not particularly praiseworthy. It would not require the overcoming of fear. Socrates' intention is not, however, to turn the warriors into dependable automatons. His true intention comes to light in the seven quotations from Homer, concerning Hades, he cites at the beginning of this part of the discussion. All but the central one have to do more or less directly with Achilles; so indeed do most of the Homeric passages cited in what remains of the discussion of poetry. Socrates brings Achilles to the foreground in order to analyze his character and ultimately to do away with him as *the* model for the young. The figure of Achilles, more than any teaching or law, compels the souls of Greeks and all men who pursue glory. He is the hero of heroes, admired and imitated by all. And this is what Socrates wishes to combat; he teaches that if Achilles is the model, men will not pursue philosophy, that what he stands for is inimical to the founding of the best city and the practice of the best way of life. Socrates is engaging in a contest with Homer for the title of teacher of the Greeks—or of mankind. One of his principal goals is to put himself in the place of Achilles as the authentic representation of the best human type. One need only look at their physical descriptions to recognize that they are polar opposites. Socrates is attempting to work a fantastic transformation of men's tastes in making the ugly old man more attractive than the fair youth.

Now, it is perfectly obvious that Achilles, although he believed that Hades was a dreadful place, was still able to be courageous. Socrates cannot seriously mean that the view of Hades presented by Homer necessarily makes a man a coward. In the *Apology*, where he most forcefully states his superiority to the fear of death, Socrates identifies himself with Achilles. It is not for a failure of courage that Socrates is reproaching the heroes. What he objects to is the price such men, given their understanding of death, must pay in order to face it. With his analysis of Achilles, Socrates is actually beginning a critique of the courage based on spiritedness which is thus also a critique of the warrior class of his city. The surface presentation of spiritedness and spirited men in the *Republic* is that they are easily educable and can become the foundation of the good city. This is a necessary presupposition of the good city. But beneath that surface runs a current which shows that spiritedness is a most problematic element of the soul and the city, and that the good city is hence most improbable.

Spiritedness first appeared in the city as the means to protect its stolen acquisitions. And this is a key to the nature of spiritedness: it is very much connected with the defense of one's own. This is particularly true in the case of Achilles whose anger is aroused by Agamemnon's taking away his prize of war, the maid Briseis, and whose rage is the result of the loss of his friend, Patroclus. If we take Achilles as the model of the spirited man, we see that anger is particularly directed toward punishment of those who take away one's own. Although anger causes men to be willing to sacrifice life, it is somehow connected with preserving those things which make life possible. Now, it is in the nature of human anger to seek for justification. It is difficult for a man to be angry when he is convinced that what is taken from him does not belong to him or that his losses or sufferings are his own fault. Anger requires something or someone to blame; it attributes responsibility to what injures, and it is closely allied with the sense of justice and injustice. Unfortunately, it is unreasoning and can easily mistake its sense of injustice for the fact of injustice. It can support reason in legitimate defense and punishment, but it may also oppose reason, for it is unwilling to admit anything that calls into question the rightness of its cause. Anger may be educated to become a very generous passion, arousing itself at the sight of whatever appears to be injustice; but no matter what the substance of the charges of injustice it makes, no matter how selfish the interest it is really protecting, it is always accompanied by the conviction that it is just. Anger is always self-righteous; it is at the root of moral indignation, but moral indignation is a dangerous and, although necessary, often unreasonable and even immoral passion. The tendency of anger is to give the color of reason and morality to selfishness. This has been revealed by the only character in the dialogue who has expressed anger; Thrasymachus' anger defends the city's own against philosophy when philosophy threatens the city's injustice. Spiritedness is the only element in the city or man which by its very nature is hostile to philosophy.

In order to overcome fear of death, spiritedness requires an almost fanatic fury; for, although the hero loves honor, he admits that it is better to be a slave on earth than a king in Hades. For him to be heroic is literally unreasonable; he must overcome his reason in order to be a hero. He is an enemy of reason. The alternatives as he sees them are either a reasonable but ignoble attachment to life or a noble but unreasonable willingness to die. Anger permits him to conquer the fear of terrible things; but in so doing it exacts a high price, for it forces the man, whose existence is threatened and whose prospects are so bleak, to attach too high a value and cosmic significance to the sacrifice of that existence. It cannot face the senselessness or accidental quality of a particular death and violently resists anything which would rob it of its meaning. In other words, anger provides unreasonable reasons for heroic action. It sees acts of injustice and duties of punishment everywhere. That is why Achilles treats lifeless bodies as though they were men and scourges them; that is why rivers that resist him become gods who defy him. This does have the effect of elevating his heroism to fantastic heights and of making him capable of the most extraordinary deeds, but only at the cost of investing the world with absurd meaning, only by believing in, and perhaps fabricating, demonic beings who minister to and justify his anger. By changing this view of death, Socrates hopes to curb the extremes of the warriors' spiritedness without giving up the advantages it brings.

The discussion of courage, which can be viewed as an analysis of the character of Achilles, is followed by a discussion of moderation; and once again Achilles assumes a central role. In the curious account given by Socrates, moderation is not, as would be expected, primarily control of the bodily desires but obedience to rulers. Though Socrates does not say so explicitly, it is clear that anger is the main cause of disobedience to rulers, and that Achilles is the very model of the disobedient subject. His anger, closely allied with his self-respect, makes him an unreliable subject of rulers. Socrates charges Achilles with love of money, of being mercenary. Superficially this is unfair. He is not avaricious; it is Phoenix who suggests that he accept gifts, and not because of their value but because they would be evidence of Agamemnon's humiliation. Achilles does not follow the advice. But in a deeper sense, it *is* just to accuse Achilles of attaching undue significance to property, for he does destroy his friends and countrymen because his possessions have been taken from him by the ruler. Such a man would make a poor citizen of the good regime which is being founded. In it there is no private property and the rulers decide what belongs to a man. Achilles would resist them, as he did Agamemnon, claiming that it is just that he keep what belongs to him. His resistance to Agamemnon appears to stem from noble pride, but that pride has its roots in excessive love of one's own. Spiritedness is the cause of phenomena as diverse as kicking the chair over which one has stumbled, disobedience to rulers, punishment of philosophers, and insolence to gods; and the true character of these phenomena can only be seen in their common source. The real problem treated in these passages is, therefore, not that of making the guardians courageous but of converting that primitive courage they possess by nature into civil courage. And that is the work of a poetry which leads to moderation.

The pure form of spiritedness—that exhibited by Achilles —implies a certain "tragic view of life and the world," according to which justice receives no reward in eternity, and noble things are no more supported by nature than base ones. The only cure for this illness is that philosophy which consists of "learning how to die," the philosophy of which Socrates was the master. Philosophy leads to lack of concern with one's own; it is concerned with things that are not threatened, that exist always. The activity of philosophy—the soul's contemplation of the principles of all things—brings with it a pleasure of a purity and intensity that causes all other pleasures to pale. For the philosopher, living as most men do is equivalent to living in Hades as conceived by most men. He need not live according to myths which assure the permanence and significance of things which are not permanent or significant. Death is overcome by a lack of concern with one's individual fate, by forgetting it, in the contemplation of eternity. This is a life both noble and reasonable. The central quote among the seven at the beginning of Book III refers to Teiresias, a man who was wise on earth and who alone among the shades in Hades still possesses prudence or wisdom. Perhaps even Homer suggests that wisdom can exempt a man from the miseries of Hades. But the warriors are not wise and cannot enjoy the consolation of philosophy; therefore they need consoling myths which make death less frightening, which lessen the need for that furious spiritedness that consumes the element of gentleness in its flames.

Socrates' intention in these passages of the *Republic* is made clearer by his behavior in the *Apology*. When he identifies himself with Achilles there, he is trying to impress his audience with his dedication to philosophy; and nothing impresses the vulgar so much as a man who is willing to die for a cause. Therefore Socrates assimilates himself to the most popular example of such a man. He indicates that the members of the jury are men who fear death and that he himself does not. The jurors are like Achilles inasmuch as they hold that property, family, friends, and city are the good things. The only way they could overcome their fear of death, their fear of the loss of these perishable things, is as Achilles did—in defense of those things, in defense of their own. But this spirited defense of one's own is precisely what Socrates is suffering from; he is being condemned because he threatens Athens. Socrates' own fearlessness stems from other sources. After his condemnation he divides his jurors into two groups, those who had voted for condemnation and those who had voted for acquittal. To the former he speaks directly and in their own terms. They assume that death is the worst thing, and so he threatens them; they will suffer for what they have done, and suffer what they most fear. Their anger will not protect them; Socrates' death will precipitate the worst rather than fend it off. To those who voted for acquittal he tells consoling myths to the effect that death is not to be feared. They are gentle men. Although they did not understand him, they were favorably disposed to him. He strengthens that gentleness within them by weakening the fears which would cause them to hate the cosmopolitanism of the accused man. Thus, imitating the function of tragedy, Socrates attempts to purge them of the pity and fear which can lead to fanaticism and enables them to share something of his own calm without knowing its source. The myths he tells the jurors who believed him to be innocent are akin to those he wants the poets to tell the warriors, who are potential jurors. Achilles and Socrates are both superior to the many, in particular in their mastery over death. But the difference between the mad Achilles and the Socrates whose death is depicted in the *Phaedo* is the measure of the difference between the two sources of that mastery. Socrates' death and the mysterious power it reveals are the new model of the heroic and must replace the Achillean one.

To understand the meaning and uses of music, as Socrates taught them, it is most helpful to turn to Shakespeare who reflected that teaching in Lorenzo's great speech to Jessica in *The Merchant of Venice*, Act V. This scene takes place at the end of a dark, unhappy play the theme of which was the struggle between Shylock and Antonio, each defending his own to the detriment of the other. Only here, in Belmont, is there harmony and beauty. In this utopia, love reigns. The discussion of music explains the possibility of that love and beauty. There is a cosmic harmony, music and love in the universe. Earthly music is the audible imitation of the inaudible music of the spheres. These heard harmonies have a mathematical structure which is akin to the mathematical principles at the base of the whole. Of all the arts, music is the one which most directly represents to the senses the intelligible order of things. We forget that cosmic music because we are "grossly closed in by a muddy vesture of decay." Our mortality leads us to be full of rage; earthly music ministers to that rage, calms us and makes us gentle. It reminds us, in all our separateness and opposition, of the dominance of harmony in our universe. Socrates' musical education of the warriors gives their passions that music without which a man, according to Lorenzo, cannot be trusted.

(*392c–403c*) If poetry is to be salutary for the warriors, it is not, according to Socrates, sufficient to change its content, but its form must also be changed. He forces the poetically inclined Adeimantus to give up the greatest charm of poetry—imitation. These are his reasons: the poet can make men believe that they see and hear his characters. This constitutes his real power—he enchants men so that they live the experiences he wishes to present. The poet hides himself behind his work, and the audience forgets, for the moment, that the world into which they enter is not the real one. The spectators have the sense of the reality of men and events which are more interesting and more beautiful than any they know in their own lives. This is what makes poetry so peculiarly attractive. The poet's hold on men is such that he can conceive a very high opinion of himself and a great sense of superiority over those whom he moves. But he is much less powerful than he thinks he is. Precisely because he must make his audience join in the world he wishes to present to them, he must appeal to its dominant passions. He cannot force the spectators to listen to him or like and enter into the lives of men who are repulsive to them. He must appeal to and flatter the dominant passions of the spectators. Those passions are fear, pity, and contempt. The spectators want to cry or to laugh. If the poet is to please, he must satisfy that demand. He is capable of making men cry or laugh; he can refine the expressions of the passions connected with tears and laughter; he can even, within limits, change the objects which move those passions; but he cannot alter the fact that he thrives on the existence and intensification of those passions. But it is precisely those passions which Socrates says the warriors must try to overcome. In the beautiful and exalted figure of Achilles who revolts against Agamemnon and grieves over the loss of his friends, they could find justification for their own temptations and fears. Men believe that in Achilles they see the reality of human perfection whereas he is only a distillation of themselves.

Moreover, poetry seems to require diversity of character and action and the intensity of passion; unhappy, suffering men or ludicrous ones are its favorite subjects. Virtuous men tend to be alike and are less likely to give way to the actions which poetry best imitates; and certainly moderation is not a virtue favored by poets. There is a certain tendency in poetry to make vice and even crime interesting because of the attractiveness of the men drawn to them. In other words, virtue is not necessarily the best choice of subject for a man who wants to write a beautiful epic or drama; the poet must subordinate his love of virtue to the requirements of his art.

Finally, and most important, the poet is unable to imitate the best kind of man, the philosopher. The philosopher would ruin a tragedy; and, although he might appear in a comedy, only certain effects of his activity, and not that activity itself, could be shown. A ruler can be shown ruling on the stage; and most other human types can also be shown as they are. But it is impossible to show a philosopher philosophizing. The Socratic critique of poetry is not only that the epic, tragic, and comic poets have not chosen as heroes the most admirable human types, but that their forms make it impossible for them to do so. What is needed is a form of poetry which is not compelled to make what is not truly highest appear to be highest. Ultimately the Platonic dialogue with its hero, Socrates, is that form. At this level of the discussion, however, Socrates leaves it at banishing most poets and insisting on a simple poetry which uses little imitation and, when it does use imitation, imitates only good men in their good moments. He does so because he wishes to protect the warriors' hard-won moderation. He also does so because he does not want them to believe that the heroes of poetry are the best men, for they are to be ruled by men very different from those heroes and must respect them.

Just as Socrates deprived Adeimantus of the greater part of the charm derived from imitation, so he deprives Glaucon of much of the charm of the powerful accompaniments of poetry, harmony and rhythm, to which he is particularly inclined and at the mention of which he rejoins the dialogue. Harmony and rhythm move the passions in the most primitive way, speechlessly appealing to irrational fears and pleasures—which are themselves speechless. They possess a man and give him a deep sense of the significance of his sentiments. Socrates ruthlessly subjects harmony and rhythm to the tales he wants told. Only those rhythms and harmonies which evoke the feelings appropriate to the new heroes are acceptable. Instead of letting words follow music, a temptation apparently involved in the nature of music's appeal, speech, *logos*, guides the music completely. Thus Socrates has made himself the master of poetry; he controls what it represents, how it represents, and the accompaniments which intensify its appeal. This mastery has been gained, though, only at the cost of what lovers of poetry find attractive in it.

However, with Glaucon, as opposed to his brother, it is not only sacrifice that is demanded. Adeimantus' disposition is such as to accept severe austerity when he sees its necessity for the preservation of the city he is in the process of founding or the furtherance of that comfortable justice he asked for in his speech and was contented with in the city of sows. But Glaucon, on the other hand, insists on what is good for himself, and the community is only of secondary interest insofar as it serves that goal. He, therefore, must have sufficient reasons for his sacrifices; and to him Socrates reveals the positive purpose of the warriors' education. The warriors are to be lovers of the beautiful, particularly of beautiful souls. The products of the fine arts are to be used to surround them with imitations of the beautiful things; those imitations will give the warriors the habit of seeing beauty in the deeds, characters, and speeches of virtuous men and hence teach them to love the virtue whose various aspects they see represented. Imitation must not flatter the passions, but transform and sublimate them. The severe moderation of the bodily desires which Socrates has imposed is the condition of the liberation of the love of the fair and the virtuous. The needs of the body, if dominant, lead to ugliness, no matter how it is adorned; for their satisfaction requires discord and vice. The warriors, prepared by restraint of their desires and habituated to the vision of noble men, will shun Thrasymachus' thieves and tyrants, not as a result of moral principle but as a matter of taste. The warriors will be more politically reliable because the *eros* of the beautiful, a grace and delicacy of sentiment and action, will temper their pursuit of their self-interest. Glaucon now sees that *eros*, properly educated, has a place in the new order and thus accepts the efforts requisite to that new order. In attempting to grasp what Socrates is trying to achieve here, it is again most helpful to turn to Shakespeare's poetry. The wise Prospero, who must rule unwise men in his little island city of the *Tempest*, uses three kinds of motivations to insure their political good conduct. The slavish Caliban can be motivated only by pinches and blows. The covetous Alfonso and his cohorts are, like Cephalus, restrained by the equivalents of conscience and the fear of divine punishment. But Prospero's favorites, to whom he intends to hand over his rule, are lovers of the beautiful who need no harsher constraints. Ferdinand and Miranda are each struck with wonder at the aspect of the other's beauty. Each longs to be worthy of the other and is eager to perform the deeds which will win approval. This is a gentler, surer, and more human path to virtue.

(*403c–412b*) After music, which would seem to be the training of the warriors' souls, Socrates turns to gymnastic which would seem to be the training of the warriors' bodies. One might have expected that this would be the most important part of the education since these men are being trained for combat; they are artisans of victory in battle and they must learn their art at least as well as any of the other artisans. However, Socrates treats the subject as though the men did not have bodies and as though the use of arms was not the cause of victory. He asserts that the possession of virtue assures victory; technical skill and chance play no role. This is an unwarranted assertion, as any experience of life will show. But it is not entirely implausible within the context of this city. It will soon become evident that these warriors will do little if any fighting outside the city, that the city will have little foreign policy, and that their function is much more to control the vices of the desiring or wage-earning class. Therefore the control of the warriors' predatary inclinations and the encouragement of their dedication to the common good is more important than their fighting skill. But, still, Socrates' whole treatment of the good city seems to neglect the problems involved in getting and keeping the things which make the good city possible. This neglect, however, is deliberate, and recognizing it makes one aware of the problem of the good city and the good life—that is, that there is a tension between the activities necessary to preserve life and those necessary to live it well. The satisfaction of the body's demands, which is the pre-condition of living any kind of good life at all, can easily become an end in itself. Socrates directs his attention exclusively to the perfection of the soul, as though its demands were in perfect harmony with those of the body, for the difficulty posed by the body is made clear and precise only by acting as though it did not exist, or at least as though its demands never contradict those of a good city or philosophy.

The discussion of gymnastic is in keeping with the neglect of the body which characterizes the entire *Republic*. But in this case the body is peculiarly difficult to neglect, and it would seem that here Socrates would have to admit that man is a dual being and discuss the relation of body and soul. However he continues to insist that his warriors are simple, as opposed to complex, beings. The cause of a healthy body is a healthy soul; and if a body does become diseased, nature must be allowed to take its course. In other words, we are asked to believe that the soul controls the body perfectly, that good souls cannot be joined to bad bodies and, at the same time, are told to forget the evidence to the contrary provided by sick men and the existence of an art of medicine which ministers to men's bodies and not their souls.

Inevitably, then, since gymnastic has little to do in keeping men's bodies healthy, the discussion turns from a description of gymnastic into an attack on medicine which looks to the care of diseased bodies without regard to the health of the soul. Doctors, according to Socrates, are required in cities for the same reason as judges—because there is a failure of moderation. When men desire too much, they take from others and must appear before a judge; the same inflamed desire also disrupts the body's harmony, and the men thus diseased must submit themselves to a doctor. Immoderation is the cause of all ills of body and city. Both judges and doctors should be kept out of the city as much as possible. The particular object of Socrates' apparent scorn is Herodicus, the founder of advanced and complex medicine, who was a sickly man and invented an art which kept his ruined body alive. The valetudinarian is ridiculous and dangerous because he subordinates everything to keeping himself alive and has nothing to live for but that life; if his kind of caring for life were to become general in a city, the city's virtue would be undermined, everything in it would be harnessed to that purpose—the soul would exist for the body rather than the body for the soul.

Socrates opposes complex medicine with a simple, good medicine which was founded by the divine Asclepius and is described by Homer. Asclepius used ready methods which did not require the quest for rare medicines or any change in the patient's way of life. If these methods did not suffice, the patient was allowed to die. This may seem like a crude art of medicine, but Asclepius did not adopt it out of ignorance but because he was political or statesmanlike, meaning he adapted the art of medicine to the common good. This kind of medicine does not threaten the practice of the virtues and the simple devotion to them; it does not emancipate the body and permit it to have a life of its own. Thus Socrates finds in Homer a twin to the simple poetry he has just elaborated in opposition to Homer. Complex poetry causes men to attach too much significance to what is perishable, to what is their own; complex medicine causes men to attach too much significance to their bodies. Perhaps the two errors are really the same. As the new poetry is intended to make men strong in the loss of their lives, their properties, and their loved ones, the old medicine was intended to make them strong in the disease of their bodies.

Although Socrates' concern with the citizens' performing their duties makes his banishment of Herodicus' medicine comprehensible and even justifiable, it does not do away with the fact that Herodicus knew much more about the body than did Asclepius; nor does it do away with the fact that his art reveals the untruth of the myth concerning the simplicity or unity of man. To understand man one must understand his complexity, and to do that one must study his illness as well as his health, his vices as well as his virtues. Such a study is impossible in this city because it is too simple. Glaucon recognizes this when he warns Socrates that it will be difficult to have good judges in their city because the men in it will not have sufficient experience with the diversity of souls to be able to diagnose and treat them properly. Socrates chooses to ignore the question, but it is clear that he has more to learn from the experience of Herodicus and Homer—from complex medicine and complex poetry which know not only the good but also the bad—than he is here willing to admit. It seems that the arts—and hence intellectual perfection—flourish in an atmosphere which is inimical to the citizen virtue of the warriors. A soldier or an artisan who forgets his body and concentrates on his work is surely better at his trade, but the body cannot be forgotten by the man who wishes to have knowledge of the body and its relation to the soul. The demands of citizen virtue and intellectual virtue are different. What appears to be a concentration on the warriors' souls is actually a concern for the power of their bodies. If the warriors were to see the truth about bodies, they could not be trusted to control them. Their education is incomplete and so are they.

Socrates' denigration of the body goes so far that he ends by denying that gymnastic has anything to do with the body at all. Its real purpose is to train the soul. Just as the spirited part of the soul needed softening, so the gentle or philosophic part needs hardening. Reason tends to be weak in that it puts itself into the service of the passions or gives way to the rage of spiritedness. It must be strengthened so that it can resist particular desires and angers in its quest for the universal truth. Gymnastic serves that function. In the preparation of the warriors' souls for good citizenship, Socrates also looks to their openness to philosophy and the salvation of any potential philosophers among them. Spiritedness and gentleness are the warp and woof of the soul, each necessary to its healthy functioning but in a delicate balance with one another. To alter the metaphor, the soul must be tuned like an instrument, by relaxing and tightening the strings; this is what education in music and gymnastic does. The proper tuning of the instrument is the precondition of citizenship and of philosophy.

At the end of the warriors' education—an education intended to make them good guardians of a peaceful people—it becomes evident that *the* virtue which has been encouraged is moderation. This education is now complete and the warriors are about to assume their functions, but there has been no training in justice. It seems possible to have good guardians who are not just. This can be explained only if moderation is an equivalent of justice. And moderation is, at least from the city's standpoint, such an equivalent. The main source of civic strife is competition for scarce good things, and those who can control their desires for these things are least likely to find it to their advantage to be seditious and break the laws. In the city of sows, the harmony of public and private interest was insured by the simplicity of desire, natural plenty, and the skill of the arts. Once desire has been emancipated, the virtue of moderation—understood as the control of spiritedness as well as desire—is used to re-establish that harmony.

(*412b–416d*) The next step in the establishment of the regime is the selection of rulers. These must be the older warriors who also possess prudence and military capacity and who care for the city. Although the other qualifications seem equally important, the only one discussed is that of caring for the city. The severe education of the warriors has not rendered them free of the temptations which might ultimately make them wolves instead of watchdogs. They still think of the good things as those which are scarce and which men wish to keep privately for themselves. Nothing in their education has as yet attached them to this city and its well-being. If they are to care for the city they must love it, and if they are to love it they must connect it with their own self-love: they will love the city most if they are of the opinion that the city's advantage is their own advantage. Apparently, this opinion is constantly threatened, either because it is not simply evident to natural reason or because reason can so easily be mastered by sophistic arguments or by passions. Thus the most important criterion in the selection of the rulers is that they hold this opinion most solidly. The most elaborate techniques are used to test them. And even this does not suffice to guarantee that they will love the city. They must be showered with honors and rewards which will give them even more palpable proof of how advantageous the city is for them. But all the education, testing, and honors are not enough to re-establish the harmony between private and public interest which disappeared with the city of sows. The only remedy that Socrates can find is a great lie—the noble lie.

This famous lie consists of two very diverse parts. According to the first part, all the members of the city, and particularly the warriors, were born from the earth and educated and equipped prior to emerging from it. If the citizens believe the tale, they will have a blood tie to the country; their relationship to it will have the same immediacy as does their relationship to the family. Loyalty to a particular city always seems somehow questionable: why affection for these men rather than any or all others? The tale makes them brothers and relates them to this particular patch of land. It identifies city and regime with country, which is the object of the most primitive political loyalty; it gives the motherland life and the principles of the city body. Short of a universal state, nothing but such a tale can make a natural connection of the individual to one of the many existing cities. Moreover, in this way, the regime itself is lent the color of naturalness. The fact that regimes require human institution, as other natural things do not, calls their naturalness into question. But here the very functions which the regime has educated the citizens to fulfill are attributed to nature; the citizens grow into their political roles as acorns grow into oaks. Each might have wondered why he should be devoted to his particular specialty to the exclusion of all others; but now they see that the equipment of their arts belongs to them in the same way their bodies do. This regime is also vulnerable because it conquered or stole the land in which it is established; this imperfect beginning gives ground for later men to argue the right of the stronger in their own interest. This tale provides for that eventuality by concealing the unjust origin of this regime (which we have seen) by a just account of its origin. On the basis of the lie, the citizens can in all good faith and conscience take pride in the justice of their regime, and malcontents have no justification for rebellion. Such are the advantages of autochthony.

The second part of the lie gives divine sanction to the natural hierarchy of human talents and virtues while enabling the regime to combine the political advantages of this hierarchy with those of mobility. In the Socratic view, political justice requires that unequal men receive unequal honors and unequal shares in ruling. This is both advantageous and fitting. In order to be effective and be preserved, the inequality of right and duty must receive institutional expression. But, in practice, if inequality is an accepted principle it finds its expression in a fixed class to which one belongs as a result of birth and/or wealth, rather than virtue. Where there is no such class, equality is the principle that dominates; and, if in an egalitarian society there are hierarchies, they are based on standards like wealth or technical skill. The problem is to establish a regime in which the hierarchy established by law reflects the natural one, or in which virtue is the only title to membership in the ruling class. All unjust conventional inequalities must be overcome without abandoning the respect for the inequality constituted by differences in virtue. The difficulty, of course, stems from private interest and property. The more powerful always want to have more, and the weaker are willing to settle for equality. In order to demote the ruler, his special privileges and property must be taken from him; such changes meet the strongest resistance. Fathers are not inclined to see their sons deprived of their birthright. And it is not easy to make men without virtues see and accept their inferiority and give up hopes of rising. Reason and sentiment demand a solution by means of which men get what they deserve. But in all actual regimes there are one of two practical solutions: there is a hierarchy, but one that mixes nature with convention by making ruling depend on some more easily recognized and accepted title than virtue; or there is no standard or hierarchy at all. Each solution reflects a part of the truth, but each is incomplete. The lie provides a basis for a satisfactory solution, giving the hierarchy solidity while at the same time presenting men with a rationale designed to overcome their primitive inclination to value themselves at least as highly as their neighbors. The lie accomplishes this by introducing a god who fashions the citizens, and who at their birth mixes various metals into them to indicate their various values—gold for rulers, silver for warriors, and bronze and iron for artisans. If the citizens believe this, and if the citizens also accept the notion that there are means of seeing the various metals, they will have at least some counterpoise to their self-love. The lie implies that the city must have some wise ruler who can distinguish the qualities of souls, but here that is not underlined, and the emphasis is on preparing the citizens to accept both a stability and a movement which go against their grain. The first part of the lie differs from the second in that the former attempts to make the conventional attachment to the city and its regime seem natural, while the latter must provide a conventional support for natural differences which men have reason to want to forget. This is why, in the second part of the lie, a god must be invoked.

The lie, because it is a lie, points up the problems it is designed to solve. Perhaps no rational investigation of them could yield a basis for political legitimacy. In any event, the character of men's desires would make it impossible for a rational teaching to be the public teaching. Today it is generally admitted that every society is based on myths, myths which render acceptable the particular form of justice incorporated in the system. Socrates speaks more directly: the myths are lies. As such, they are unacceptable to a rational man. But he does not hold that because all civil societies need myths about justice, there is no rational basis to be found for justice. His teaching cannot serve as an excuse for accepting whatever a society asserts is justice. The noble lie is precisely an attempt to rationalize the justice of civil society; it is an essential part of an attempt to elaborate a regime which most embodies the principles of natural justice and hence transcends the false justice of other regimes. The thoughtful observer will find that the noble lie is a political expression of truths which it itself leads him to consider. In other words, there are good reasons for every part of this lie, and that is why a rational man would be willing to tell it.

The Socratic teaching that a good society requires a fundamental falsehood is the direct opposite of that of the Enlightenment which argued that civil society could dispense with lies and count on selfish calculation to make men loyal to it. The difference between the two views can be reduced to a difference concerning the importance of moderation, both for the preservation of civil society and for the full development of individual men's natures. The noble lie is designed to give men grounds for resisting, in the name of the common good, their powerful desires. The great thinkers of the Enlightenment did not deny that such lies are necessary to induce men to sacrifice their desires and to care for the common good. They were no more hopeful than Socrates concerning most men's natural capacity to overcome their inclinations and devote themselves to the public welfare. What they insisted was that it was possible to build a civil society in which men did not have to care for the common good, in which desire would be channeled rather than controlled. A civil society which provided security and some prospect of each man's acquiring those possessions he most wishes would be both a more simple and more sure solution than any utopian attempt to make men abandon their selfish wishes. Such a civil society could count on men's rational adhesion, for it would be an instrument in procuring their own good as they see it. Therefore moderation of the appetites would be not only unnecessary but undesirable, for it would render a man more independent of the regime whose purpose it is to satisfy the appetites.

The Socratic response to this argument would be twofold. First, he would simply deny the possibility of a regime which would never be compelled to call for real sacrifices from its citizens. This is particularly true in time of war. A man cannot reasonably calculate that dying in battle will serve the long-range satisfaction of his desires. Therefore every civil society will require myths which can make citizens of private men. But in the case of such a selfish society it will be both very difficult to provide such myths, and they will be a distasteful parody of the reason on which the society prides itself; what pretends to be philosophy will have to be propaganda.

Second, such a civil society can be founded only by changing the meaning of rationality. For this society, rationality consists in the discovery of the best means of satisfying desires. The irrationality of those desires must be neglected; in particular, men must neglect the irrationality of their unwillingness to face the fact that they must die, of their constant search for the means of self-preservation as if they could live forever. Socrates teaches that only a man who masters the desires of the body can see the true human situation and come to terms with it. Such mastery is the precondition of living a rational and satisfying life, but it is very difficult to attain, and men need all the help they can get if they are to succeed in attaining it. The civil society proposed by the men of the Enlightenment, far from encouraging such moderation, positively discourages it. It also ridicules those sometimes simple beliefs which would help to support a man's self-restraint and remind him of his mortality. Such a society would produce a race of self-forgetting, philistine men who would demand as their rulers men like themselves. According to Socrates, a noble lie is the only way to insure that men who love the truth will exist and rule in a society. The noble lie was intended to make both warriors and artisans love the city, to assure that the ruled would be obedient to the rulers, and, particularly, to prevent the rulers from abusing their charge. Apparently, though, it is not completely successful in overcoming the warriors' temptations. Socrates goes yet further: they are deprived of all private property, of everything which they might call their own to which they might become privately attached, particularly money, which admits of infinite increase and extends the possibility of private desire. And they are also deprived of privacy; they have no place where they might store illegally acquired things or enjoy forbidden pleasures. They are always seen by men, if not by gods, so that the secrecy needed for successful lawbreaking and the gaining of an unfounded good reputation are lacking. Injustice cannot be profitable for them. They are now completely political, the realization of Socrates' perfect artisan who cares only for what he rules and not at all for himself. They can have no concern other than the common good.

(419c–427c) It is not surprising that Adeimantus rebels at this point. He has accepted much that is distasteful to him and given up many of the charms of life for the sake of the founding on which he has embarked. He wants good guardians for his city. But the comparison of the life of the guardians with what he himself would desire is too much for Adeimantus. His original demands showed him to be a friend of justice and the political community, but he wanted an easy-going sort of life which the city would defend. He was content with the city of sows; nothing that has come afterward in the construction of the good city has given him back the personal satisfaction he experienced there. He has the capacity for self-restraint, a certain austerity not shared by Glaucon. But this is in the name of that comfortable existence which too much desire would destroy. Now, in making the life of the guardians so hard, Socrates has taken away Adeimantus' motive for having allowed them to be trained so severely. Adeimantus, following the procedure he and Glaucon adopted in their attacks on justice, puts his objection in the mouth of another. The anonymous accuser asserts that Socrates is not making the guardians happy, and Adeimantus asks Socrates to make an *apology* to the charge. He joins Thrasymachus in bring-

ing Socrates to trial. Thrasymachus charged Socrates with undermining the city, with teaching a doctrine which would lead to dis-
respect for the law. Adeimantus' charge is not entirely dissimilar. As a
founder, Socrates is taking away from the citizens that for which they
founded the civil order, their property, their privacy—their own. Socrates subordinates happiness to something else, or he robs men of their
happiness. His teaching is a threat to that end for which everything is
done. Here, as in the earlier accusation, the accuser's selfishness
motivates his charge that Socrates is unjust. But there is also no doubt
that Socrates is guilty as charged.

Socrates' defense is not, as might be expected, that these guardians are happy. One could have responded that they get a specific
pleasure from doing their duty, that devotion to the city is naturally
good for them. Evidently Socrates does not believe that this is the case.
Men who engage in politics for the sake of private gain have a sufficient motivation for their conduct; but total devotion to the common
good does not yet have a sufficient justification in the *Republic*, and the
guardians are asked to serve without adequate compensation. Socrates'
response is that he is talking about a happy city and not a happy group
within it. Looking at it from the city's point of view, one can see the
advantage of its possessing such a group of totally dedicated public servants. But this only postpones discussing the problem of the individual's relation to the city, which has already been postponed by the
decision to see justice in a city first, and renders it more acute. Socrates
treats the city as though it were an organism, as though there could be a
happy city without happy men.

With this response, Socrates has not met Adeimantus' objection.
It is a powerful objection, one that can be made by wiser men than the
youthful, unphilosophic Adeimantus. Aristotle himself agrees that the
guardians are not happy and that this speaks against the desirability of
the regime. Even Aristotle, whom no one could accuse of encouraging a
lax morality, compromises with men's wish to have something of their
own, and the rulers in his best regime are property owners. Why then
does Socrates insist on making such high demands on his rulers?
Perhaps it is because he is more interested in revealing a problem than
in making a practical suggestion. By pushing the demand for dedication to the extreme, he brings to light precisely what it is in man that
makes such dedication impossible and thereby indicates to practical
men what compromises have to be made. Any deviation from this standard of dedication is indeed a compromise; for example, the devotion
of Aristotle's rulers to the city is not quite pure, and the regime has to
accept the injustice of making wealth one of the titles to rule. Virtue

without wealth has no place in Aristotle's best regime; convention must be mixed with nature. Socrates is attempting to satisfy Glaucon's request; he is trying to show that political justice is good in itself, not because it can be a source of other advantages. Perhaps that request cannot be satisfied, at least on the level of Glaucon's original intention.

However, strictly political considerations are not sufficient to account for Socrates' procedure; it can be explained ultimately only in the light of the trans-political considerations which emerge later. On political grounds it would be wise to make the compromises necessary to make the guardians happy. But the concentration on the public and the common, the forgetfulness of the demands of the body, prepares the way for the introduction of philosophy which is the most universal concern. It is the concern with the private or particular as such that must be overcome if individuals are to philosophize and cities are to be ruled by philosophy. The guardian who is totally devoted to the common good is the prototype of the philosopher who is devoted to knowing *the* good.

Adeimantus is a secret lover of wealth, as is revealed by his rebellion at the abolition of private property. Therefore Socrates immediately turns to an attack on the effects of wealth on the city. This provokes Adeimantus into making a last stand in its favor. He objects that the city will not be rich enough to defend itself. Wars require money, and so some amount of acquisitiveness must be permitted. Perhaps sound domestic policy would discourage the acquisition of wealth, but priority must be given to foreign policy since the city's very existence depends on it. Adeimantus' objection, then, is the same as Machiavelli's: the best regime is a mere dream, for a good city cannot avoid ruin if it does not do the things which will enable it to survive among vicious cities. It is foreign policy which makes the devotion to the good life within a city impossible. One must be at least as powerful as one's neighbors and must adopt a way of life such as to make this possible. Poverty, smallness, and unchangingness cannot compete with wealth, greatness, and innovation. The true policy is outward-looking, and cities and men are radically dependent on others for what they must be. Without a response to this objection—which Machiavelli thought to be decisive for the rejection of classical political thought—the very attempt to elaborate a utopia is folly.

In his attempt to meet the objection, Socrates formulates a Machiavellian foreign policy in order to preserve the anti-Machiavellian domestic policy of his city. The city will be too poor to be very attractive as an object of conquest; its tough fighters will make it a dangerous enemy and it will join its potential attacker in attacking soft, rich cities. Furthermore, in order to prevent the allied city from becoming all-powerful, it will foment civil discord within it, siding with the poor, although the guardians' city does not believe the poor have justice on their side. In this way the city can live as though it had no neighbors and devote itself to whatever way of life it deems best. In relation to its neighbors, the city is not motivated by considerations of justice but by those of preservation. Justice has to do with the domestic life of the city and cannot be extended beyond its borders. This is a point to be considered when examining the analogy between city and man: justice is supposed to be the same in both, so one would expect that a man should behave toward other men as does a city toward other cities.

Socrates' argument persuades at least Adeimantus, and therewith his last reserves about the regime have been overcome. He becomes Socrates' whole-hearted ally. He now uses his moralizing severity against all enemies of the regime, particularly against poets and ordinary statesmen. Anything that might weaken his newly founded city is his enemy, and he is angry with those whom he regards as vicious. His conduct can be explained by reference to an observation he himself made in his long speech on justice. There he asserted that a man who truly knows that justice is better than injustice is not angry with those who do injustice; rather, he sympathizes with their ignorance, knowing that they are not responsible. The implication is that those who are angry at injustice do not know its inferiority, that their anger is a way of suppressing their own temptations, that they blame others for giving way to temptations that beset themselves. After the curious fashion of moral indignation, they attribute responsibility where there is none. For those who want to be just but hold the objects of injustice to be good, self-restraint is necessary; anger and blame are the means of that restraint. In these passages the contrast between Socrates' gentleness and Adeimantus' indignation is striking, suggesting that they represent the alternatives of knowledge and ignorance of the superiority of justice. It almost seems as though Socrates is incapable of the anger so necessary to political justice, and, therefore, can use Adeimantus to advantage here and elsewhere. Adeimantus' particular form of spiritedness, when tamed, is a scourge of injustice, a source of primitive justice.

(427c–445e) With the establishment of rules concerning the worship of the gods, the city is asserted to be complete and perfect. Its perfection must consist in its being the only city in which the rulers rule for the advantage of the ruled and hence of the weaker—the exact opposite of Thrasymachus' description of rulers, but in accord with Socrates' and Thrasymachus' joint understanding of the artisan in the precise sense.

At last Socrates and his companions are ready to begin the investigation for which all their previous efforts were only the preparation. They must now look for justice and injustice in the city founded in their discourse. Socrates, at the urging of Glaucon, who here takes over from Adeimantus, suggests the following procedure for locating it: since the city is perfectly good, it must be wise, moderate, courageous, and just; therefore, they need only recognize in it the virtues they do know in order to identify what remains as justice. This procedure, however, is open to several obvious objections. Nothing has been done to establish that these four—and only these four—virtues are what makes a city good. Nor is there any indication that the interlocutors know what wisdom, moderation, and courage are, any more than they know what justice is. These virtues have not been thematically discussed here, but we know from other Socratic dialogues that they are as problematic as justice. But, most important of all, Socrates, without stating any grounds for so doing, assumes what he and his companions had set out to prove—that justice is good. Originally the question was: What is justice, and is it good? Now it has become: What good thing is justice? One is compelled to wonder why Glaucon accepts so great a change without comment. It may be because Glaucon is so eager to hear what justice is, because he is of the opinion that he and the others are finally at the borders of the promised land, that he does not, as it were, read the fine print. Moreover, this is his city, and for that reason alone it is good. Common sense dictates the notion that justice is something that has to do with a city and that a good city must possess justice. Glaucon has accepted this city and justice along with it. He could hardly announce that a city he has founded is not just.

However, Glaucon's original question has not been answered. In opposition to Thrasymachus, he had suggested that justice means that the strong man serves the weak to the neglect of his own advantage. The life of the rulers in this regime seems to support that suggestion. For the ruled to obey the rulers is strictly to their own advantage since the rulers are dedicated to them. But the doubt remains as to whether it is to the rulers' advantage to care for the ruled. A founder, for his own selfish reasons, may want the rulers to be just, but he does not thereby prove that it is good for them to be just. The assumption that justice is good and must be in the city is perfectly legitimate from the point of view of founders or men who are discussing a city. But the real question is postponed until the discussion of the individual: Is justice in the individual man the same as that in the city *and* does justice in the individual lead to good citizenship? First we look at the perfected city, and then at the perfected man. The issue is in their relation: Can a perfect man become and remain perfect in a perfect city? Is justice good for him? This is identical with the question: Is the city natural? For man, and hence the good man, is surely natural.

Socrates and his companions experience greater difficulty in discerning justice than in discerning the other virtues. Justice, rather than far away in the heavens, is in a dark place at their feet. Even a cursory examination of what they find there reveals that justice is not necessary in this city. This is not too surprising, for the city came into being without justice being included in the specific way that courage, moderation, and wisdom were included. Indeed, when defined as each man doing his job or minding his own business, justice adds nothing to the city that is not accomplished by the other three virtues. The city needs wise men to command; it needs courageous men to overcome resistance to the wise commands; and it needs moderation to bind the city together into a whole and maintain the proper hierarchy of its parts. But where does that leave justice? Justice disappears here, even as it did when Polemarchus asserted that justice consists of doing good to friends, only to discover that it is the various arts that do good to men. This seemed unsatisfactory because of the fact that the arts can do harm as well as good—a doctor can kill as well as cure—so that something more than the arts is required. But now it appears that it is not justice which is necessary to supplement the arts; they need only belong to the proper order or whole. If the rulers are interested in the good of the whole city and its individuals, and if they command the artisans as to how they are to use their arts, nothing further is needed. Moderation, not justice, causes the artisans to obey the rulers. There is no temper or disposition of justice demanded of the citizens. Justice, in the city at least, means only the presence of the three other virtues.

Nevertheless, minding one's own business is not an unilluminating formula for expressing what is ordinarily meant by justice. Justice seems to involve doing good to others, but the busybody or meddler is somehow an imperfect type. In this city, if each does what properly is his to do, he also does good to others. Each keeps and does his own while benefiting others. Moreover, the simplest sense of justice, that expressed by Cephalus, is also satisfied here: obedience to the law is vindicated for the laws are good. Hence this city, in which justice is not a concern, meets the demands of justice defined by Cephalus and Polemarchus who are its advocates. And in this city Thrasymachus will no longer be able to allege the same reasons for despising justice. He will soon join Socrates' group of friends.

Socrates now turns to the investigation of the justice of the individual man, which is so crucial for Glaucon. This investigation quickly moves to a discussion of the soul; by treating the soul as the whole man, Socrates tacitly assumes the irrelevance of the body to the question of what justice in a man is. He and Glaucon attempt to determine whether the soul has three parts, as does the city; if it does, the analogy would incline them to believe that they are of the same character and order as are the parts of a city and that a soul's virtues are the same as those of a city. They easily distinguish desire and reason as separate parts of the soul. Then, as might be expected, the crucial part and the one most difficult to determine is spiritedness. Is it separate or does it belong to one of the two other classes? Glaucon gives an obvious answer and one that accords with his own experience: it belongs to the desiring part. He is probably most angry when he does not get what he wants; surely his specific form of spiritedness leads him off to war in pursuit of satisfaction of desire for pleasure and victory. Socrates responds with an example in which spiritedness purportedly overcomes desire. Spiritedness is ambiguous: it may support or oppose bodily desire, or it may even itself be a kind of desire. But Socrates goes much further. He tries to make spiritedness look like a loyal ally of reason, as it were, reason's army, which forces the desires along the path of reason's commands. Socrates acts as though it were only in the cases of the most perverse kind of man that spiritedness opposes reason. Hence the soul is a unity in diversity and is strictly parallel to the city. The analogy to the auxiliary class in the city makes it plausible to assert that spiritedness is reason's companion and of a distinctly higher order than the desires.

But this is a most "optimistic" account of spiritedness, one that accords with that hopefulness about its control which is *the* condition of the founding of the city and that depreciation of the desires that is necessary to the city. Socrates, in order to prove the point that spiritedness is different from desire and serves to control it, tells the story of a certain Leontius who, on his way up to Athens from the Piraeus, observed that there were corpses on the public executioner's ground and desired to look at them. Something within him resisted the desire, but after a struggle, he gave way and looked. He then cursed his eyes and bid them take their fill of "the fair [or noble] spectacle." Careful reflection on this example reveals that it does not so simply support Socrates' thesis that spiritedness is essentially an ally of reason. One must ask why spiritedness opposes the desire to look at corpses and becomes angry with the eyes? Either it must be because the sight of death is repulsive to it and thus it cooperates with the desire for life, or because the contemplation of the corpses of criminals is ignoble and goes counter to the sense of shame induced by spiritedness. Whatever the explanation, its resistance to Leontius does not seem rational. As a matter of fact, spiritedness is fighting curiosity, a close kin of the desire to know, either because that desire is opposed by other powerful desires, or because it seeks to know the forbidden. Spiritedness appears to be capable both of allying itself with desire and of opposing the quest for knowledge. In the city the spirited class, although its education presented some difficulties, was largely salutary; but in the soul it is more problematic. Socrates, because he is trying to persuade Glaucon to be a good citizen of the good city, gives him an inadequate account of spiritedness in the soul—one which gives spiritedness the same role in the soul as it performed in the city, while forgetting the differences between a soul and a city.

Primarily, what Socrates chooses to forget in his incomplete picture of spiritedness as merely reason's trusty tool is the fact that in some sense reason in the soul is a desire, and that spiritedness, to the extent that it opposes desire, opposes reason also. He was enabled to do this by asserting that reason in the soul is merely calculation, as it is in the city. A dry, calculating reason, concerned with directing the desires to a fulfillment consonant with the common good, is distinct from desire and need not conflict with spiritedness; but a reason erotically striving to know the first causes of all things, with a life of its own, indifferent to the needs of the here and now, is one of the most powerful desires and far removed from the city's primary concerns. Spiritedness will oppose it as surely as it does any of the other forms of *eros*. Reason exists in cities but only in the form of political prudence. Timocracy, the regime founded on spiritedness, is the regime most openly hostile to philosophy (547e). A city, like a man, desires wealth, needs food, and deliberates. But a city cannot reproduce or philosophize; all forms of *eros* are cut off from it. In this sense a city cannot be properly compared to a man. It can use the offspring of *eros*, whether children or thoughts, but it must merely make use of, or conventionalize, the activities which produce them. In order to make a man thoroughly political, one must suppress or distort all expressions of his eroticism.

In order to see what Socrates leaves out here, it is helpful to look again at the warrior class which is supposed to perform the same function in the city as does spiritedness in the soul. The warriors can, in the service of desires, take from foreigners as conquerors, or they can, in the service of the city as a whole and the rulers, defend against invaders. Within the city, they can side with the people, and hence the desires, against the rulers and reason, or they can side with the rulers, not against the people, but for the purpose of controlling and guiding them. The warriors are guided by general opinions, or rules, whose grounds they do not know and exceptions to which they cannot recognize. For example, they must detest men who do not appear to care for the city, who love foreign things, who call the law into question. Most such men would indeed be vicious, but Socrates would also be among them. They would instinctively hate him and want to punish him as an enemy, for, in their lack of reason and identification of all good with the city's good, they would be unable to distinguish him from the others. The rulers might be able to make the necessary distinctions, and the warriors would most likely obey them; but one could foresee a situation in which the warriors rebelled against the rulers because the rulers broke the rules of morality they had inculcated in the warriors. But, at all events, from the point of view of the healthy city, perhaps men like Socrates should be repressed. In practice, spiritedness frequently rules over wisdom in cities, leading to crimes committed in the name of justice. Moral indignation led to the execution of the generals who were in command at the great Athenian victory of Arginusae, but who, because of a storm, were unable to satisfy the pious duty of recovering the corpses of their dead from the sea; this execution was carried out over the strenuous objections of the wise Socrates. Moreover, Socrates' own execution was a result of the same moral indignation. In both cases the general principle of the people was a valid one; but in both they failed to see the mitigating circumstances, not to say the moral superiority of the lawbreakers.

Within the individual soul, spiritedness expresses itself in similar ways. It can lead to the voracious conqueror or the proud protector of his own. It can also produce the angry, petulant man who flies into a fury at what opposes his desires. And, most interesting of all, it can result in the morally indignant man who punishes his own desires as well as those of others. But in the case of the soul this punishment of offending desires is more harmful than in the city. The soul in which reason is most developed will—like Leontius' eyes—desire to see all kinds of things which the citizen is forbidden to see; it will abound with thoughts usually connected with selfishness, lust, and vice. Such a soul will be like that banished poetry which contained images of vice as well as of virtue. Spiritedness, in the form of anger and shame, will oppose reason's desiring. This is why the austere, moral Adeimantus is much more opposed to philosophy than is the victory-loving, erotic Glaucon. Thus, spiritedness, which protected the city's health, stands in the way of the development of the soul's theoretical capacities and hence its health. Socrates in this passage abstracts from all other aspects of spiritedness and focuses solely on one of its functions—the control of desire. In so doing he makes explicit its political advantages and hints at the threat it poses to philosophy. The harmony of the parts of the soul is most questionable.

Socrates concludes that the soul has the same parts as the city and will be perfected by the same virtues. Thus the discussion of justice should be at an end; and Socrates does indeed try to turn to the discussion of injustice, which must be discerned if it is to be compared to justice. But, he will not be permitted to continue in that direction, for his interlocutors are not yet persuaded that it is desirable to be a member of this city, and want to know more about it. The identification of the good of the soul with that of the city has not been convincing to them. This is understandable, since it is purely formal to assert that a just soul is one in which each of its parts does its own work when one does not know the nature of those parts or precisely what their work is. It cannot be assumed merely that they exactly parallel the parts of the city and their work.

Nothing as yet has indicated that the man who has a healthy soul will be identical with the citizen of the regime which has been established. Is the wise man, who makes full use of the powers of his reason, the same as the prudent statesman, who issues commands to the warriors and the artisans? Is his courage that of the warrior who holds the belief that what is good for the city is good for him, and is thus willing to die on the battlefield? Is his moderation that of an obedient subject, or that of a ruler who cares for the citizens and wishes to rule them for their good? And does his justice consist in doing some work which the city prescribes to him and is useful to it? Affirmative answers to all or any of these questions seem highly improbable. Glaucon's real question, however, was whether his happiness depended on being a good citizen, a law-abiding man. Socrates tries to give the impression that there is a harmony between the justice of the city and that of man by never suggesting that there might not be.

But it is a glaring problem, and Socrates' mode of presentation has rendered it even more obtrusive. As we have already observed, if the parallel of city and man is to hold true, then a man, like the city, should be interested only in himself and merely use others for his own advantage, as the city does. And in the present discussion Socrates has made it appear that the soul's health can be attained in isolation; as the good city's neighbors were only a hindrance in its quest for the good life, a man's neighbors might also be understood to be hindrances. In that case, he would want to strive for the greatest self-sufficiency. This impression is intensified by the fact that the body, whose needs tie a man to his fellows, has been treated here as though it did not exist. The parallel of city and man presented would tend to support the view that the just man—in the sense of the man with a healthy soul—would not want to be a good citizen in the good city. It would also seem that he would not want to be a tyrant, for his perfection seems to be independent of the city. When Socrates points out that a man with a healthy soul would not be likely to steal deposits, break oaths, commit adultery, etc., he does not prove that the just individual abstains from such deeds because he respects the laws or even cares for other men. The fact that the just man does not try to take advantage of other men could be as easily explained by a lack of desire for the objects involved as by attachment to the common good. In describing the conduct of such a man in relation to others, Socrates only tells of things he does not do, but never mentions any positive deeds of citizen virtue which he does do. It would seem possible to be a just man without being a just citizen, which goes further than anything Glaucon had suggested.

The apparent answer to the question of justice has only heightened the difficulty of that question, for we now have the just city and the just soul, and their relations are as mysterious as are the relations of body and soul. As a result of the spurious identification of city and soul, the nature of the soul has emerged as the decisive consideration in the understanding of justice. Given the magnitude of this consideration, it is no wonder that Socrates is eager, as he was in the beginning of the dialogue, to hurry away. It is also no wonder that his companions once again join together to stop him, for he owes them much more.

(449a–473c) In a scene that recapitulates the beginning of the dialogue, Polemarchus again joins with Adeimantus to "arrest" Socrates. They are more formidable this time, for they have now added Glaucon and Thrasymachus to their ranks. The dialogue begins anew. Socrates' companions have recognized, if only in a peripheral way, the incompleteness of the discussion of the soul, which they take to be an incompleteness of the discussion of the city. They want to know more about his statement that friends in the city have all things in common—including women and children—for this total lack of privacy means that a man cannot have a life of his own. Therefore a man's soul must be satisfied by the community or not be satisfied at all. They accuse Socrates of a crime, of doing injustice by robbing them of a part of the discussion. And they are right. Socrates wanted to do his duty to men and the city without devoting himself to them completely; he was keeping his way of life private. All the others could find their satisfaction and dignity in the city that has been established. But can Socrates? He is compelled to appear before the bar of that city; here he cannot

give a mythical account of his life (as he did in the *Apology*) but must explain himself as he really is. This city claims to be the greatest good for men, to call for the highest loyalty, to satisfy the human potential. Now it must be expanded to see if it can include Socrates. This is the crucial test, for, if the highest activity of the city is identical to the highest activity of man, there is no justification for going beyond the city, for rebellion in heart or deed. The status of the city depends on this attempt.

Now Socrates proceeds to try to make public or common everything that remains private. Full communism, from Socrates' point of view the only form of just regime, requires not only the abolition of private property but also the sharing of women and children and the rule of philosophers. Women, family, and philosophy are all of the domain of the erotic, which seems to be what is most intransigently private. Up to now what Socrates has suggested has been severe, but not outlandish. The city is merely an improved Sparta, correcting its worst vices, while preserving its virtues. He has adopted the opinions of his well-born Laconophile interlocutors; Adeimantus is attached to Sparta because it is austere, secure, and aristocratic; Glaucon because it is warlike. Socrates has improved on the Spartan regime by stopping the ruling class from persecuting the poor, by suppressing the secret lust for wealth, and by moderating the exclusive orientation to war. At the same time, he has softened the warlike temper of the men and given them the possibility of a certain openness. Now he must take advantage of that possibility and attempt to infuse the Athenian element into the Spartan regime. In order to complete his work, he will have to face three fantastic waves which threaten to engulf him. The first two waves—the same way of life for women as men and the community of wives and children—have never existed in reality or in the thoughts of serious men; they are the absurd conceits of a comic poet who only suggested them in order to ridicule them. And the last wave, the rule of philosophers, is a total innovation, beyond the wildest thoughts of that same comic poet who had also ridiculed philosophy.

Book V is preposterous, and Socrates expects it to be ridiculed. It provokes both laughter and rage in its contempt for convention and nature, in its wounding of all the dearest sensibilities of masculine pride and shame, the family, and statesmanship and the city. As such it can only be understood as Socrates' response to his most dangerous accuser, Aristophanes, and his contest with him. In the *Ecclesiazusae* Aristophanes had attacked the public in the name of the private, and in the *Clouds* he had attacked philosophy in the name of poetry. Here Socrates suggests that, if philosophy rules, the political can triumph over the private life. If he is right, he can show that Aristophanes did not understand the city because he did not understand philosophy, and he did not understand philosophy because he did not understand that philosophy could grasp the human things and particularly the city. The *Republic* is the first book of political philosophy, and attempts to show that philosophy can shed light on human things as no other discipline can. Socrates is the founder of the city in speech and, hence, of political philosophy. In Book V he tries to show the superiority of the philosopher to the comic poet in deed; he does so by producing a comedy which is more fantastic, more innovative, more comic, and more profound than any work of Aristophanes. Socrates with an air of utmost seriousness undertakes absurd considerations; in this he is already comic. If what he appears to teach seriously is impossible, as will prove to be the case, Socrates' comedy will be akin to the *Ecclesiazusae*. In that play the women of Athens try to institute what is just but politically impossible, and thereby they create ridiculous situations; Socrates surpasses them by radicalizing their proposals. If the perfection of the city cannot comprehend the perfection of the soul, the city will look ugly in comparison to the soul's beauty and be a proper subject of comedy; its pretensions will be ludicrous. Such a comedy will be a divine comedy, one calling for a more divine laughter. Only philosophy could produce it, for, as Socrates will explain, only philosophy has the true standard of beauty. In appearing to disagree with Aristophanes about the city, Socrates shows that only he knows the true grounds of its inadequacy. Plato believes that his Socrates can argue better about man than Aristophanes, and that his arguments can culminate in better comedies. If this proves to be true, the total superiority of Socrates and his way of life will be manifest.

Socrates proposes that women should have the same education and way of life as the men; there should be a full equality of the sexes, and they must, as it were, share the same locker room. Socrates is aware that poets will laugh at this proposal and that it will be a subject of ridicule for men like Aristophanes. But Socrates asserts that the comic poets are in this merely serving Greek convention, either because they cannot themselves transcend convention, or because they are dependent on an audience of Greek men to whom they must appeal. Once Greeks, like the barbarians, were ashamed to see each other naked, but they were able to overcome that shame. A naked man would look ridiculous in a crowd of clothed men, to be sure, but why should men be clothed? In the gymnasium, public nakedness is no longer laughable. The Greeks showed that civilized men can be both moderate and unclad. Now they must go even further and make greater demands on their moderation. But does it make sense to say that it is only convention which prohibits the public association of naked men and women? Nakedness is forbidden because it encourages licentiousness, because civilized men need some mastery over their sexual appetites. Public nakedness is permissible where sexual desire is not likely to be aroused by it. Men can be naked together because it is relatively easy to desexualize their relations with one another; but the preservation of the city requires the mutual attraction of men and women. The city can forbid homosexual relations, and shame and habit can make the very notion inconceivable to them. But it cannot forbid heterosexual relations, and men and women could hardly be expected to be above attraction to one another at any particular moment. Hence the purpose of the gymnasia would be subverted. Law would at the same time encourage and forbid the mutual attraction of the sexes. The comic poets are not without justification; the sexual is necessary and must remain private. This is part of Socrates' attempt to politicize the erotic, to act as though it made no demands that cannot conform to the public life of the city. Once more, Socrates "forgets" the body, and this forgetting is the precondition of the equality of women. As a political proposal, the public nakedness of men and women is nonsense. Shame is an essential component of the erotic relations between men and women. The need for overcoming shame becomes clear in relation to what Socrates considers to be another form of eros—intellectual or philosophic eros. Souls, in order to know, must strip away the conventions which cover their nature. Shame prevents them from doing this just as it prevents them from stripping their bodies. The comic poets, because of this shame, are able to ridicule what is natural and thus to discourage it. The comic poet is too much motivated by shame, for he is unaware of the kind of eros which justifies shamelessness. In other words, the comic poet will ridicule philosophy just as he will ridicule lasciviousness and do so because both conflict with conventional demands which are enforced by shame. This point is also made by Homer. When the angry Haephaestus binds his unfaithful wife Aphrodite together with her lover Ares and exposes them naked to the other gods, all but one are convulsed with laughter at the sight. But Hermes says that he would be willing to undergo such humiliation if he could lie with Aphrodite. Shame cannot induce his eros to forsake the pursuit of the beautiful and the good, even if all the goddesses were to join the gods in observing and laughing at him. Ultimately, from the Socratic point of view, Hermes is right.

According to Socrates, the institution of the same practices for women as men is possible because it is natural; and it is proved to be natural by arguing that the difference between men and women is no more important than the difference between bald men and men with hair. However, Socrates also admits that the best women are always inferior in capacity to the best men; it is then highly improbable that any women would even be considered for membership in the higher classes. Thus the whole consideration of their education as guardians is unnecessary. If the fact that women bear children is to be ignored and does not play a role in their selection as guardians, if ability is the only criterion, there will not be a sufficient number of women in the guardian class to reproduce it. It is evident that the women are placed among the guardians not because they possess the same capacities as the men, but precisely because they are different, because they can bear children and the men cannot. To treat dissimilar persons similarly is unjust and unnatural. Maybe the souls are the same, but the influence of the body is powerful; the necessity of the body makes justice to souls difficult. In order to legitimate treating the women in the same way as the men, Socrates must fabricate a convention about the nature of women.

Why then does Socrates insist on the same training for men and women? Women had hardly been mentioned in the first four books. Why not let the men run the city and leave the women at home? Two reasons may be suggested, one political, the other trans-political. In the first place, neglect of the virtue of women may be said to be another Spartan error. Men need women and can easily be controlled by them. The character of the women in a society has a great deal to do with the character of the men; for when the men are young, the women have a great deal to do with their rearing, and when they are older, they must please the women. In particular, women have a more powerful attachment to the home and the children than do men. They are involved with the private things which are likely to oppose the city. They characteristically do not like to send their sons off to war. Further, women have much to do with men's desire to possess money. Women's favor can be won by gifts, and they have a taste for adornment and public display. Women play a great role in the corruption of regimes, as will be shown in Books VIII and IX. If half the city is not educated to the city's virtues, the city will not subsist. This is a city without homes, and the women have more to overcome if they are to accept it, for their natures lead them to love the private things most and draw the men to a similar love. They must share the men's tastes, or they will resist the changes in the family Socrates is about to propose.

In the second place, the exclusive maleness, so much connected with battle, is not the whole of human nature, although it may appear so to the men. The female represents gentleness, and the complete soul must embrace both principles. Pheidippides, in the *Clouds*, and Callicles, in the *Gorgias*, think of Socrates as unmanly, a pale-faced individual who sits around and gossips rather than engaging in the activities of real men. In the *Theaetetus* Socrates compares himself to a kind of woman, a midwife; and in the *Symposium* he recounts that he learned the secrets of his erotic science from a woman. Just as a city needs the female, so does the soul, but perhaps in a more fundamental way. Full humanity is a discrete mixture of masculinity and femininity. When talking about warrior-guardians the feminine could be forgotten; but this latest discussion is a harbinger of the philosopher-guardians.

Having successfully met the first wave—the same education and way of life for women as for men, Socrates and Glaucon prepare to face the second—the community of women and children. In the discussion of this proposal there is less emphasis on the comic element; the problems touched on here have been themes of tragedy—*Antigone* and *Oedipus* come most immediately to mind—as well as comedy. Socrates and Glaucon agree to postpone the question of the possibility of this institution—that is, according to the procedure they have adopted, the question of whether it is natural—in favor of first describing it and its advantages.

The sexual relations of the guardian and auxiliary classes are treated as though they exist only for the production of children for the city. An attempt is made to rationalize sexual desire in making it responsive to the command of the law. Attraction and love in themselves know no limits of propriety, exigency, law or country. They are most dangerous to a city because their power is such as to drown all other sentiments in their intensity, and they indicate an element of man which is by nature unpolitical. The sexual passion can be trained and repressed, but it is not usually thought possible to make it respond only to those objects chosen by the city, in a way and at a time deemed fitting by the city. But here Socrates acts as though it were feasible, if not easy, to channel *eros* for the benefit of the city; otherwise it would have to be left private, repressed and exhorted, but always a somewhat hostile beast, even when asleep. Now the rulers must tell many lies. And these lies must be bigger ones than the noble lie. The noble lie is more easily believable than these lies will be, inasmuch as the former concerns the origins and, after a period of time, there will be no witnesses of those origins left to gainsay it; inclination will be a constant witness against the lies of the rulers in sexual matters. So Socrates invokes the gods. Marriages, he says, are sacred. But in this arrangement of things, marriage means nothing more than a temporary sexual relationship, for there are no private homes, no private children, and the citizens may be expected to have many such marriages. Socrates explains that the sacred is what is beneficial to the city. Appetizing and frequent sexual relations are to be the reward for excellence in public service; this will motivate the citizens to perform their responsibilities well and will insure that those who are of the greatest virtue will produce the most children. In order to make this system work, the rulers will have many concerns not shared by rulers in less perfect cities; these concerns could well be the subject of comedy in these other cities.

Just as erotic activity becomes a part of a man's public duty, so the offspring of the unions must become part of public property. The family is abolished, unless one considers the city as one family. The problem of Antigone cannot arise, for there can be no conflict between the family and the city. The intention of the noble lie is furthered: men are finally deprived of everything which they might love more than the city; all men are brothers. But the effect of this is to remove whatever is natural in the family and replace it with an entirely conventional base. A father, if he is anything, is the one who engenders the child. A father who did not do so would be a completely artificial entity, at best a substitute for the natural father. Law or convention must take the place of nature in order to insure the possibility of this city. Children are to transfer to the city what they would give to their parents. This, too, is completely unnatural. It is, however, not entirely without foundation in our understanding of human nature. If the family, which is surely somehow natural, remains the only object of loyalty, the clan or tribe can never be surpassed. To become either a member of a city—or a philosopher—one must break with one's primary loyalty. The bodily or blood ties are not the only thing that is natural to man; nor are they the most important thing. Men do not only love members of their family, but also those whom they believe to be good. Nevertheless, a man who loved the better children of others more than his own inferior children would be considered monstrous. The blood ties bind and have a morality of their own which keeps the mind from wandering freely over the world; they stand in the way of natural fulfillment. Men are usually torn between duty to their own and duty to the good. The communism of women and children, by suppressing family ties, serves to emancipate men's love of the good.

If the family is to become the city, and the city is to be self-sufficient, the most sacred and awesome of prohibitions must be defied. There must be incest in this city. By law all members of the city are the closest of relatives, and they will not know their natural relatives. To most men nothing could seem more terrible than incest; so powerful is the prohibition against incest that it even removes desire where objects of satisfaction are closest at hand; it is accepted without question and hardly needs to be taught. The crime of Oedipus and his tragedy, the archetype of tragedy, concerns this prohibition. When asked about the problem, Socrates treats it as though he were speaking of regulations no more controversial than those concerning rivers and harbors. He thus justifies the accusation of Aristophanes: he is the enemy of the family and its fundamental principle. The particular crime of Oedipus is indeed prohibited here, but only because he and Jocasta would not be of the proper age for breeding. When Socrates says that in special instances, and if the Delphic oracle permits, brothers and sisters can wed, he understates the case. As Glaucon sees (463c), Socrates' prescriptions about the family actually mean that everybody in the city is closely related; there are no cousins; everyone is at least the brother or sister of everyone else. Examination of the marriage regulations would suggest that it is unlikely that even more serious breaches of the incest prohibition can be avoided in this city. The relationships in the entire city will be as tangled as those in the family of Oedipus. And Socrates asks for divine sanction for such incestuous loves. Given that there will be many erotic improprieties in this city—as Aristotle makes clear (*Politics* II, iv)—it seems that Socrates' approach to the matter is quite light-hearted.

What, then, is this radical policy meant to achieve? Socrates argues that the city will be one, and the demon of private, selfish interest will be exorcised. He compares the city to a body all parts of which share the same pleasures and pains. This city does not attain to that degree of unity, however, for one thing cannot be made public: the body. Everyone's body is his own. The minds could conceivably be made to think similar thoughts (a possibility not so obnoxious as it sounds; for minds contemplating the same truths are, for that moment and in that way, the same). But if a man stubs his toe, no other man can share his pain. Thus the unity of the city depends on that same forgetting of the body which has been a golden thread running through the whole discourse. The body is what stands in the way of devotion to the common good; it is the source of the desire and the need for privacy. The problem is that the body's demands lead to the establishment of an entire way of life and a set of beliefs contrary to those which would be most conducive to the perfection of a man's soul or the pursuit of truth. The way of life based on the body is directed to acquisition of the means of preserving and gratifying the body. The set of beliefs which protects that way of life concerns private property, the family, the civil order, and even the gods. Although these beliefs only serve the selfish interests related to the body and do not express the truth about nature, they are enormously respectable. Men hold strongly to them, and it seems very important that they be maintained. These beliefs fetter men's minds; they are the conventions which veil nature.

Socrates is here trying to construct a political regime which is not dominated by such conventions, one in which philosophy does not have to be a private, hidden activity because it contradicts the authoritative prejudices. Aristophanes can help us to understand the character of these prejudices. In the *Clouds*, Strepsiades burns Socrates' dwelling when he discovers that Socrates had taught his son things which threaten the sanctity of the family. Only a man who did not care too much about the family would be prepared to tolerate Socrates' teaching. Socrates has elaborated a regime in which no citizen has a family and thus no one can be unreasonable in the name of the family. Socrates' demand that the city be unified is identical to the demand that the body and its extensions—property and the family—be perfectly mastered. If that mastery is impossible, so is the city. We would learn from this fact that philosophy is essentially a private activity and that the city must always be ruled by prejudices. Moreover, from the example of the city in speech, a man would learn what he must overcome in himself in order to become a philosopher. Socrates forgets the body in order to make clear its importance.

To put the matter more simply: only in a city such as Socrates and his companions have constructed will no obloquy be attached to Socrates' deplorable neglect of his family and his indifference to the labor necessary to making a comfortable living. This city, which is constructed in response to Aristophanes' charge that Socrates had to break the law in order to feed and clothe himself and in order to replenish his society of male companions, will take care of him, and his children will be talented youths of the kind he sought out in Athens. In all other cities Socrates must be morally suspect as a poor husband and father. Socrates has the strength to endure this opprobrium; if he were seriously concerned about it, he would fetter his mind in trying to avoid it. In the passage under consideration, then, we see the conditions of philosophy and what must be sacrificed to it. As yet the citizens of this city have no sufficient reason to make these sacrifices. But if philosophy is desirable, so are these efforts to conquer everything that attaches one to particularity. Socrates can contemplate going naked where others go clothed; he is not afraid of ridicule. He can also contemplate sexual intercourse where others are stricken with terror; he is not afraid of moral indignation. In other words, he treats the comic seriously and the tragic lightly. He can smile where others cry and remain earnest where others laugh. In the *Symposium* he says that the true poet must be both tragedian and comedian, implying that the true poet is the philosopher. Here he shows that the man who has both gifts must use them to oppose the ways the vulgar tragic and comic poets use them; he must treat the tragic lightly and the comic seriously, hence reversing their usual roles. The man who is able to do this is already a philosopher. In both cases, it is shame which must be opposed; for shame is the wall built by convention which stands between the mind and the light. The ordinary poetry appeals to that shame, accepting its edicts as law, while philosophic poetry overcomes it. Shame, in both the case of nakedness and that of incest, is spiritedness' means of controlling *eros* for the sake of preservation and the city. The effect of that shame is pervasive and subtle, making the thinkable appear unthinkable. The mind requires heroic efforts in order to become aware of the distortions of its vision caused by shame and to overcome them.

Having discussed the community of women and children and its advantages, Socrates and Glaucon turn to the question of the possibility of this regime. But Socrates, who seems anxious to avoid this question, turns the discussion to the foreign relations of their completed city, particularly to the way in which it will fight wars. The changes within the city bring about changes in the character of inter-city relations. In this discussion, although Socrates provides some satisfactions to be derived from war for Glaucon's erotic and warlike temper, the general intention is to temper and humanize war. To this end, Socrates proposes a pan-Hellenic policy of hostility toward the barbarians. As the relations among the members of the city are to be like the relations among the members of a family, so the relations among the Greek cities are to become like the relations which prevail among the parties in a city and the relations between Greeks and non-Greeks are to become like the relations of Greek cities. Thus there is a general reduction of hostility along the line (without expectation that it can be done away with altogether), and even the barbarians profit from the change. In this way, all men are brought closer to one another by extending the sentiments connected with love of one's own to all of humanity: fellow citizens are to be brothers, Greeks are to be fellow citizens, and barbarians are to be Greeks. At this point Socrates accepts the Greek, or conventional, distinction between Greek and barbarian. One should not, however, assume that he is limited by this horizon; he is speaking to Glaucon who is subject to such limitations. Later, when Glaucon has learned more, Socrates asserts that this good city can be either Greek or barbarian. This discussion of the relation among cities mixes convention with nature in the intention of bringing men closer together and removing the obstacles which prevent the recognition of a common humanity, without at the same time undermining the principles which make political life possible.

The eager Glaucon finally insists that Socrates must stop trying to avoid *the* question. Socrates must tell whether the regime is possible. Glaucon, however, no longer means by possible what had earlier been meant. He wants to know how the regime will come into being; he is interested only in its actualization. He thus abandons the standard which he set in his first speech about justice, that is, nature. What he wanted then was a proof that justice is good according to nature and not merely according to convention or human agreement; justice was to be shown to conduce to human happiness in the same way health does. This standard was maintained in the discussion of the desirability of assigning the same way of life to women as to men. By showing that women's natures are the same as men's and supporting this proof with examples of natural animal behavior, Glaucon and Socrates were satisfied that the proposal was possible and good. Now Glaucon, only wants to know whether the city can exist without determining whether it is natural and hence good. At the end, he seems willing to accept the city and its justice without having found out that thing which he himself had insisted was decisive for accepting or rejecting the city. And it is clear that the community of women and children, if it were to exist, would not be a product of nature but of art; it would be a triumph of art over nature. Glaucon's desire to see his city come into being has caused him to forget to ask whether it is good for man or not. The lesson of this change in the meaning of possibility would seem to be that, though man exists by nature, the city does not and is hence of a lower status than man.

Socrates, in a preamble to his discussion of the possibility of the regime, contributes to the depreciation of the city which was just begun by abandoning the question of its naturalness. He makes it clear that this regime which is to be brought into being will not be simply just. Justice itself exists more in speech than deed. After all of this effort, the product is admitted to be imperfect and not lovable for itself but because it is an imitation of justice. At the peak of the insistence that everything be given to the city, it becomes manifest that no city deserves such attention and that one must look beyond the city for the reality. This is a great disappointment and prepares the way for a transcendence of the city.

(473c–487a) At last, however, Socrates allows the final wave—the philosopher-kings—to roll in on them, and he introduces his own way of life into the city. It is no wonder that he hesitated to speak, for he asserts:

> Unless the philosophers rule as kings or those now called kings and
> chiefs genuinely and adequately philosophize, and political power
> and philosophy coincide in the same place, while the many natures
> now making their way to either apart from the other are by neces-
> sity excluded, there is no rest from ills for the cities, my dear
> Glaucon, nor I think for human kind, nor will the regime we have
> now described in speech ever come forth from nature, insofar as
> possible, and see the light of the sun.

Socrates expects to be drowned in tides of ridicule for this paradoxical
assertion. Glaucon wholeheartedly agrees that this will be the case, and
anticipates that the scorn will be mixed with anger. The laughter and
indignation, which played so important a role in the discussion of the
first two waves, reappear together here in a more intense form.

It is, however, hard for modern men to be particularly shocked by
Socrates' pronouncement; it seems much less comic or reprehensible to
us than the other waves. It is not that we would take the notion very
seriously, but we are in some sense the heirs and beneficiaries of Socrates' work, even as we are the children of the Enlightenment which
radicalized that work. Partly because Socrates and Plato were so effective in arguing the usefulness of philosophy to civil society, and
partly because the meaning of philosophy has changed, we no longer
believe that there is a tension between philosophy and civil society. Although we might doubt whether philosophers have the gift of ruling, we
do not consider the activity of philosophy to be pernicious to political
concerns. Hence the notion of philosopher-kings is not in itself
paradoxical for us. But, precisely because we take it for granted that
the hatred of philosophy was merely prejudice, and that history has
helped us to overcome that prejudice, we are in danger of missing the
point which Socrates makes here. In order to understand this passage,
we must see philosophy against the nonphilosophic and hostile
background from which it emerged. It is not merely historical curiosity
which should lead us to make this effort. We must rediscover the
forgotten reasons for Socrates' difficulties in order to evaluate the role
of philosophy and science within our world, for their role may be more
problematic than we are wont to believe. Philosophy is a rare plant,
one which has flourished only in the West; it is perhaps the essence of
that West. Its place is not simply assured everywhere and always as is
the city's. The writings of Plato and a few others made it respectable.
The *Republic* thus represents one of the most decisive moments of our
history. In this work Socrates presents the grounds of his being brought
to trial and shows why philosophy is always in danger and always in
need of a defense.

The best way to see the fantastic character of Socrates' proposal for the rule of philosopher-kings is to look at Aristophanes' *Clouds,* which shows how the philosopher appears to the city. Socrates stays in his think-tank discussing the nature of the heavens with unhealthy men. He is graceless and unprepossessing, a ridiculous personage in the eyes of any man of the world. His experiments in natural philosophy allow him to be besmirched by lizards, and he spends his time looking at gnats, a thing no gentleman would do; these insects even infest his clothes. He does not believe in the gods of Athens and has other extraordinary divinities of his own; he draws promising young men away from the political life into his unusual researches. He is a marginal figure who seems both odd and corrupt, utterly without common sense. With this picture of himself in mind, Socrates seems to say here, "All right, this is the man who should rule." He is ridiculous in his pretensions and subversive in his intentions, thus provoking reactions of laughter and anger.

At this point in the discussion, Socrates argues that philosophy is needed in this city; he does not argue that philosophy is the best human activity. Philosophy is not the theme of the discussion, but justice, and particularly a just city. Nevertheless, the most comprehensive discussion of the city leads—against the will of Socrates, as it were—to a discussion of philosophy. Beginning from the common sense of political men and maintaining their perspective throughout, Socrates demonstrates that they must tolerate and encourage philosophy. This constitutes a defense of philosophy from the political point of view. Philosophy is necessary to this regime, to the best regime, because without philosophy the regime cannot find impartial rulers who have considered the proper distribution of the good things. In other words, the philosopher is the only kind of knower whose attention is devoted to the whole. Statesmen are always preoccupied with the here-and-now, but the interpretation of the here-and-now depends on some knowledge of the whole. If justice means giving each man what is fitting for him, a statesman must know what man is and his relation to the other beings.

In asserting that philosophers should rule, Socrates formulates a view of the relation between wisdom and power opposed to that of the Enlightenment. Beginning from the common assumption that knowledge of the ends of man and civil society is necessary to civil society, or that wisdom should rule, the two teachings differ as to whether the rule of wisdom requires that the wise rule. The thinkers of the Enlightenment teach that wisdom can rule without philosophers having to take political power; that is, they teach that the dissemination of knowledge will inevitably lead to the establishment of good regimes.

Socrates teaches that wisdom and political power are distinct. Their coming together can only be due to the coincidence that a man who is wise happens also to be a ruler, thus uniting the two things; nothing in their two natures leads the one to the other. Political power serves the passions or desires of the members of a city, and a multitude cannot philosophize. It may use the results of science or philosophy, but it will use them to its own ends and will thereby distort them. Moreover, the wise man by himself is more of a threat to a regime than a helper. Intellectual progress is not the same as political progress, and, because there is not a simple harmony between the works of the mind and the works of the city, the philosopher without power must remain in an uneasy relationship with the city and its beliefs. Enlightenment endangers philosophy because it tempts philosophers to sacrifice their quest for the truth in favor of attempting to edify the public; in an "enlightened" world, philosophy risks being made a tool of unwise and even tyrannical regimes, thus giving those regimes the color of reason and losing its function as the standard for criticism of them. Enlightenment also endangers the city by publicly calling into question its untrue but essential beliefs. If philosophers cannot rule, philosophy must be disproportionate to the city. This means that its truths must remain fundamentally private, and that the philosopher, for his own good and that of the city, must hide himself. He must adapt his public teachings to his particular situation while keeping his thought free of its influence. The philosopher's public speech must be guided by prudence rather than love of the truth; his philosophic activity seems essentially private. Philosopher-kings are, therefore, truly a paradox. The formulation points up the salutary effect of philosophy in a city and the necessity of the city for philosophy, hence justifying each to the other; but the high degree of improbability of actualization of the *coincidence* of philosophers and kings also points up the enduring tension between philosophy and the city. The city cannot do without philosophy, but it also cannot quite tolerate philosophy.

Socrates expects a spirited attack on his position by his opponents, so he must prepare his defenses. He begins by distinguishing the philosophers from the nonphilosophers. This distinction is made by referring to two salient aspects of the philosopher. In the first place, he has a voracious appetite for all learning. His curiosity is not like that of a craftsman who learns only what is useful in the narrow sense and whose interest is limited by his craft. The philosopher learns as other men love—simply because it seems good and an end in itself; as a matter of fact, learning is an erotic activity for him. Love of learning is another expression of man's *eros*, of his longing for completeness. Such a man wants to know everything, aware that no part can be understood without being considered in relation to the whole. Socrates simply describes that rare but revealing phenomenon, the theoretical man, he who proves the possibility of disinterested knowledge. He is the man who can preserve his disinterestedness even in the difficult human questions which concern him most immediately, because he is more attracted by clarity than life, satisfaction of desire, or honor. The philosopher introduces to the city a dimension of reason that had not been discerned in the earlier discussion of it.

Glaucon objects that on the basis of this description of the philosopher, all the lovers of sights and hearing—particularly the lovers of the festivals where the poets display their dramas—would have to be considered philosophers. In response to this objection, Socrates defines the second salient characteristic of the philosopher: he is a lover of the one *idea* of each thing and not the many things which participate in the *ideas*, of being and not becoming, of knowledge and not opinion. Thus Socrates introduces the teaching for which he is most renowned and which constitutes the most difficult ·part of his thought—the *ideas*. Here this teaching is presented to a young man who is not a philosopher in a context where it is not the primary concern. Hence the treatment of it is most inadequate, and the existence of the *ideas* is assumed rather than proved. Socrates only tries to satisfy Glaucon that the philosopher has concern for a reality other than that of most men. In so doing, Socrates appeals particularly to Glaucon's own experience with the beautiful things he loves so much. That experience shows Glaucon that all the beautiful things he knows are also in some ways ugly, and that what was once beautiful becomes ugly. These beautiful things seem to be understood to be beautiful in relation to some standard which is entirely beautiful, the approach to which makes them beautiful. That standard *is* beautiful, while the things which imitate it *are* and *are not* beautiful at the same time. Things which come into being and pass away *are* only to the extent that they partake of what does not come into being or pass away. The *ideas* are the permanent *ones* behind the changing *manys* to which we apply the same name. Thus they are the causes of the things seen and heard— causes not in the sense that they explain the coming-into-being of a particular thing but in the sense that they explain its character. The *idea* of man is the cause of a particular man's being a man rather than a collection of the elements to which he can be reduced. The *ideas*, then, are the justification of the philosophic life. If there are no permanent entities, if everything is in flux, there can be no knowledge. Knowledge, or science, requires universals of which the particulars are imperfect examples; as knowing beings we care only for the universals. The *ideas* give reality to the universals and hence make it possible to explain the fact that man possesses knowledge. The *ideas* are the being of things. They constitute an account of the first causes of things which also does justice to the observed heterogeneity of the visible universe, unlike earlier, pre-Socratic accounts of being which required the reduction of all things to a single kind of being—like the atoms—thus making the specific characters of those things unintelligible. This teaching provides those intelligible, diverse, permanent, universal beings which the mind seems to seek when it attempts to define or to explain. In undertaking to look for justice, Socrates and his companions were looking for something real, which has a higher dignity than, and can act as a standard for, the imperfect justice which they found in men and cities. If there is not something like an *idea* of justice, their quest is futile.

And it is in this quest for the universal principles that the theoretical man first meets the opposition of the unphilosophic men who make up a city. They are loyal not to cities in general but to their own city; they love not men in general, but this particular man or woman; they are not interested in the nature of the species, but their own fates. However, all the things to which citizens are most passionately attached have a lessened reality in the eyes of the theoretical man; what is peculiar to these things, what constitutes their charm for the practical man, must be overcome in order to understand them. For the practical man the particular things to which he is attached are the real things, and he will resist any attempt to go beyond them to "the more general case," which would destroy their character and his capacity to possess them as his very own. The city in speech of the philosopher comes into being only by depreciating Athens, and any other city in which men can live. To the philosopher the city in speech is more lovable and more real than any of the particular cities which are to him poor imitations of the city in speech. In order to love what *is*, he must be a man who does not have the same needs as other men; he must have overcome, at least in thought, his own becoming. For the theoretical man, particular things are real only insofar as they "participate" in the *ideas*. They *are* not but are like what *is*. Hence the practical men who love particular things make the mistake of taking a thing to *be* that which it is like. They thus dream their lives away, never laying hold of a reality. But they cannot be told this. They must be soothed and deceived, and it is questionable how far they can afford to be tolerant of the philosopher whose interests are so different and conflicting.

Here, again, poetry seems to be in the service of the characteristic weakness of the many. Thus, in mentioning the unphilosophic men who are like the philosophers, Glaucon chooses the example of those who love theatrical spectacles. Poetry itself deals in images of particular things; and it uses its images to give added significance to one's particular attachments, beautifying one's country, one's loves, one's aspirations. In the beginning of the discussion Thrasymachus, the rhetorician, was refuted because he made the error of saying that a thing is that which it is like. And the discussion of imitation in Book III addressed this same question. It is a theme which runs throughout the *Republic*. Poetry, in its most common usage, adorns the particular and renders it more attractive, hence making it more difficult to transcend. It does so because it must appeal to audiences of men who cannot and do not wish to make that transcendence. It is thus an opponent of philosophy.

Glaucon agrees that philosophers, since they are awake while others are dreaming and are like painters who can use the truth as their model, would be the best rulers *if* they possessed the other virtues. Socrates responds to the doubt implied in Glaucon's condition by attempting to show that all the virtues are involved in the philosophers' very vocation and that thus they are good citizens. As a result of their love of wisdom, all the lovers of wisdom possess all the virtues, and more reliably than anyone else because they have a sufficient reason for being virtuous. They do not have to make an effort to become virtuous or concentrate on the virtues; the virtues follow of themselves from the greatest love and pleasure of the philosophers. In the case of other men, as Adeimantus has made clear, everything they love has to be sacrificed on the altar of virtue. By way of contrast, without sacrifice the philosopher, in addition to possessing the intellectual virtues, will be moderate, courageous, and just. At last there appears to be a resolution of the disharmony between happiness and devotion to the city that arose after the destruction of the city of sows. For the philosophers constitute a class of men who can safely be made rulers and whose happiness is identical with their virtuous activity.

However, this solution may be more apparent than real, for it is questionable whether the virtues of the philosopher are quite the same as those of the citizen. One has only to consider the case of the philosopher's love of truth, which Socrates assimilates to the warriors' truthfulness. It is obvious that a man can love the truth without telling it and can also regularly tell what he understands to be the truth without any love for or questing after the real truth. Similarly, the philosopher's courage and moderation are not the same as those of the simple citizen. The philosopher is courageous because his constant preoccupation with the eternal makes him somewhat oblivious to life, and not because he is obedient to the city's rules about what is fearful and what not. And he is moderate because he has an immoderate love of the truth, not because he restrains his desires. Most important of all, Socrates indicates that the philosopher is just only by showing that there are certain kinds of things he is likely to abstain from. This is the same procedure Socrates adopted in Book IV when he tried to prove that a man with a healthy soul will be just, and he admitted there that this is only a crude test. Thus the philosopher is likely to be indifferent to money because it plays only a small role in helping him acquire what he cares for, but there is nothing here that indicates he has a disposition to render unto others what is due to them. Moreover, there is also nothing in his nature which would attach him to the city. Socrates hints at this by repeating a catalogue of the philosopher's virtues several times; the virtues listed change slightly in the course of these repetitions. The most significant change is that justice is finally omitted (cf. 487a and 494b). The silent lesson would seem to be that it is indeed possible to possess intellectual virtue without what later came to be called moral virtue.

The problem appears to be something like the following. As presented in the *Republic*, the virtues can be derived from two possible sources: the necessities of the city and the necessities of philosophy. The virtues stemming from these two sources have much in common, but they are far from identical. Nonetheless, Socrates' procedure is to identify the two and thus to assert that the philosopher is identical with the virtuous man in the civic sense. In the very act of making this questionable identification, however, he helps us to see the distinction between the two. It is a new way of stating the already familiar tension between the needs of the body and those of the soul. The virtues connected with the city help to preserve the city and thereby its inhabitants; preservation, or mere life, is the goal. The virtues connected with philosophy aid in the quest for the comprehensive truth; the good life is the goal. Both goals make their demands, and those demands conflict. There are, then, two kinds of virtue: philosophic virtue and demotic, or vulgar, virtue.

Moreover, in both instances, virtue is loved not for virtue's sake but for some other good beyond it; or, to use Kantian language, the system of the virtues presented by Socrates is heteronomous. What Glaucon had asked for is a proof that justice is good in itself. The implicit Socratic teaching is that no such proof is possible, that nature does not give a ground for a virtue not connected with some other end. He differs from the utilitarians only in that the needs of the body do not constitute the only end. In Socratic thought, the demands of philosophy, or of the soul, provide a second polar star for the guidance of human conduct. This tempers the unmitigated pursuit of the goods connected with the body and the city which characterizes the tradition begun by Machiavelli and Hobbes; and it adds a sublimity to the account of the virtues which is also lacking in the later thought. Still, this leaves the virtues of the warrior class in a kind of limbo. They are asked to live and die for the city. They are asked to have more virtues than their self-preservation would demand, yet they are not philosophers. What, then, is the status of their virtues? Socrates seems to deny the existence of the independent moral virtues. These are the virtues presented by Aristotle as ends in themselves, pursued only because they are noble. Socrates presents instead two kinds of virtues, one low and one high, but both mercenary in the sense that they are pursued for the sake of some reward. The warrior's virtue is somewhere between them. Virtue, if pursued for other reasons, is no longer what we mean by true virtue; the great tradition stretching from Aristotle to Kant is evidence for that. But virtue pursued for its own sake is without ground and has a tincture of folly. This is the Socratic teaching. Moral virtue is a halfway house, partaking of the *grandeur et misère* of its two sources.

(*487b–503b*) Adeimantus, sensing the inadequacy of this proof of the philosopher's public virtue and comparing it with the experience of the cities, for the fourth and last time stops Socrates in the name of the city. Once more, his interruption takes the form of an accusation, but an accusation no longer directed against certain political proposals but rather against the philosophers themselves, against the true source of the difficulties. According to Adeimantus, philosophers mislead men by their superior power of speech, making the weaker argument appear the stronger; at best they are useless to the city, at worst, and most usually, they are completely vicious. Of all men, their dedication to the city appears to be most questionable. Philosophy always has a bad reputation, and it becomes Socrates' duty to show that its ill-repute is the fault of those who hate it rather than of its practitioners. In the performance of that duty, he will also prove to Glaucon that philosophy is one thing that a man would want to pursue even if it brings him a bad reputation or the reputation for injustice. If philosophy is the health of the soul, and hence justice in the highest sense, justice is desirable in itself, regardless of reputation. This is the praise of justice Glaucon asked for in the beginning.

The explanation of philosophy's plight is divided into three parts: the true philosophers are misunderstood and neglected, the potential philosophers are corrupted, and impostors have taken on the guise of philosophers. Philosophy is exculpated and is useful to the city if properly used. The appeal is directed to the people as a whole, whom Adeimantus seems to represent. The people's hostility is explained as a result of misunderstanding and the deceptions of vicious men. The people are represented as persuadable because they are decent, and there are no real conflicts of interest. This gentleness of the people is a necessary condition of the actualization of the good city and is therefore somewhat overstated in an account which tries to show that a city will accept philosophers as kings.

Socrates begins his *apology* with an image, the first of several that are to come. These images constitute a kind of Socratic poetry and serve to counterbalance the powerful attack Socrates has made on poetry. Just as we learned that the poets know the human passions, here we learn that they are in possession of one of the most powerful tools for leading men to the truth. The intellect does not perceive the *ideas* directly; it knows of their existence only through particulars. Man must reason about the things he perceives in order to know their causes. Without a full and profound experience of the phenomena, the intellect is a void. Images are the food of the mind; and poetry can make the most fruitful images. In poetry one can find representations of man which are richer and more typical than any experiences of men that one is likely to have. The poetic images should be used as geometers use representations of circles—to understand something of which the particular circle is only an imperfect image. Poetry characteristically causes men to forget that its images are only images, that is, like the circle drawn in the sand which is not *the* circle; but it need not always be abused in this way. The image Socrates presents to Adeimantus has a double function: it tells him a lovely tale which charms him into a more favorable disposition toward philosophy; and it causes him to think about the meaning of the image. Adeimantus must see how the image applies to philosophy as he knows it, and in what respects the image differs from the reality it indicates. Thus he is beginning to think about philosophy, and in a way he is philosophizing.

In Socrates' image, the city is compared to a ship which belongs to the people, who are compared to a big and strong shipowner who is also somewhat deaf, short of vision, and ignorant of navigation. Incapable of running the ship himself, the owner turns it over to sailors who are more preoccupied with securing the positions of power than they are with the art of sailing. They should be subordinate to a pilot, but the mechanics of the struggle for power become an art that is treated as an end in itself. The true pilot is not interested in fighting for his proper position and is excluded. In this image, the sailors are akin to the warrior class without rulers; the chiefs of that class remain preoccupied with the human world, unaware that a good sailing requires knowledge of mathematics and astronomy, that is, of the *cosmos* as a whole. This knowledge appears irrelevant to their concerns, and the true pilot is ridiculed. The philosopher, who, contrary to the indications of the *Apology*, must know nature, and particularly the nature of the heavens, is as necessary to the city as a pilot is to a ship. He is merely misunderstood, and the people are misled. His knowledge is not described here as something desirable in itself for him, but it is acquired for the sake of the city; it is like the pilot's or the doctor's art. He is ready and fit to serve if only the ship's owner can perceive how necessary he is. The philosopher's situation might well be compared to that of Gulliver in Lilliput. He is too big and too different to be trusted, too much beyond the temptations of the small ambitious men to be their tool; but if the Lilliputians could have maintained their faith in him, they would have both profited and become more just. This explanation of the philosopher's lack of reputation also serves as a defense against the accusation that he pries into the secrets of the heavens and Hades, not by denying that he does but by insisting on the value to the city of his doing so.

After having by means of the image disposed of the objection that the philosopher is useless to the city, Socrates turns to the explanation of why gifted young men turn away from philosophy. According to Socrates, their talents make them able to succeed at anything; healthy young people usually try to excel at what is most respectable within their community. The honors given by the city attract the potential philosophers to political life. Because these young men seem to have great political futures, corrupt and ambitious statesmen hope to make use of them, promising them all sorts of advantages if they are willing to adopt the current practices of the city. It is not, as is often said, the sophists who corrupt the young. The sophists, Socrates says, are harmless men who are only servants of the city's passions. The true sophist, the true educator, is the public assembly—the sovereign body of the people; it forms the tastes of the young by its thunderous expressions of approval and disapproval. It is almost impossible for a noble youth to resist the city's praise and blame and the prospects it offers him. The man who undertakes to teach the truth to such a youth faces many difficulties. The youth himself is disinclined to renounce the charms which draw him. And, if the teacher succeeds in influencing him, the unruly sailors will persecute the teacher who is robbing them of a great prop of their power. First the teacher will be intimidated by threats;

finally he will be brought to trial and condemned to death as a corruptor of the youth. All he was trying to do was teach the true politics which would enable the young man to do good for the city while punishing its deceivers. Such a teacher, to be sure, takes his pupil away from the immediate and most visible concerns of the people, but his intention is to provide the people with the kind of men they would pray to have as rulers. Socrates claims that men such as himself do not corrupt the youth but try to save them from corruption.

By thus showing that those who could be genuine philosophers abandon the practice of philosophy, Socrates tries to explain away the fact that some philosophers seem vicious by claiming that they are impostors. Incomplete, little men move into the positions left free by the corruption of those who might truly have filled them. Such impostors are motivated by vanity, and they are less interested in being wise than in being reputed wise and in winning arguments. Willing to make the worse argument appear the stronger, they are the source of the accusation that the philosophers are teachers of rhetoric. In this terrible situation, the true philosophers are isolated, defenseless, and unable to help the city. For their own preservation they therefore reluctantly withdraw into private life, though their real vocation is ruling.

These arguments in defense of philosophy are directed to soothing the people's anger and apprehension. They show how Socrates believes the people must be talked to. They must, above all, be shown that he is a good citizen, even though he may appear useless or even vicious. Thus he insists that these appearances are the result of a fatal misunderstanding. He is truly the people's friend; he appeals to them over the heads of their rulers. He responds to the great accusations against him—that he is a meddler in things in the heavens and below the earth, a corruptor of the youth, and a deceiver. However, he is silent about the charge of atheism.

Having argued that the charges against philosophy are unjust, Socrates now proceeds to suggest that the people could accept the rule of philosophers. It is altogether a difficult business to bring city and philosopher together, but in these passages the problem appears principally to be to persuade the people to overcome their anger. And Socrates' defense seems to persuade at least one man who is vitally connected with the people—Thrasymachus. In any event Socrates now announces that Thrasymachus has just become his friend. Perhaps this is because Thrasymachus now believes that Socrates is no longer a threat to the city; perhaps it is because he now sees that his rhetoric has a place in Socrates' enterprise for which philosophy alone does not suffice. Socrates has tamed the lion and can now use him in the taming of the people. And Socrates, with Thrasymachus' help, will succeed in doing in the dream of the *Republic* what he could not do in the real situation of the *Apology*. If he cannot persuade the people directly, perhaps his philosophic rhetoric, which we see in the course of this dialogue, can persuade the political rhetorician who will in turn persuade the people. The problem is to overcome the people's moral indignation at what appears to be a threat to their own. Socrates insists that the people will ultimately be gentle; but in doing so, he mentions so many obstacles which stand in the way of that gentleness that he undermines his case. He argues that there is a possibility that the people will not be angered by an attempt to transform their lives and put them under the absolute rule of philosophers who will take their property away. His arguments only serve to underline the great improbability, not to say impossibility, of the consummation of the project.

(503b–540c) Socrates, however, takes it as proven that the city, which cannot philosophize, will accept philosophy, and he now turns to the problem of training the philosophers. But this means that he must treat of philosophy itself and no longer of philosophy as it affects the city. As a result, a whole new world of incredible beauty emerges; Glaucon and Adeimantus are shown an unexpected realm, from the standpoint of which everything looks different. If the *Republic* can be understood as a gradual ascent, we have reached the peak. Now everything must be accomplished by means of images, for Socrates' students have no personal experience of philosophy, but they must respect it in order to have the proper perspective on the whole political question. Socrates introduces the new theme when he tells Adeimantus that the study of justice, far from being the most important subject, is worthless unless it is completed by another. The true science, to which the others are only ministerial, is the study of the good. This comes as a surprise to Adeimantus, who is totally devoted to the city. It is a step beyond the earlier recognition that the *idea* of justice transcends any possible city. In turn, the *idea* of justice is only one of many *ideas*, which are treated in the comprehensive study of the good.

Glaucon insists that Socrates tell more of the *idea* of the good, and again takes his brother's place in the discussion. He was the first to ask for an account of justice in terms of the good, and his eroticism impels him to possess the good things. Socrates formulates his account of the good in such a way as to appeal to Glaucon's interest and passion. Glaucon is informed of a good which makes questionable all the good things of which he spoke in his original attack on justice, and the attainment of which requires a way of life very different from the tyrant's way of life. Socrates leads Glaucon toward the apprehension of the good by means of the things which Glaucon knows and of which he has already spoken. He agrees that all action is directed toward the attainment of some good and that none of the things he desires is unambiguously good. There are many good things, but none of them are *the* good. The discussion at the end of Book V concluded that where there is a *many* to which we give a name, there must also be a *one* which is the cause of the particulars that constitute that many, which *is* the thing in itself without qualification. Hence there must be a good in itself, an *idea* of the good in which the good things participate. A man does not desire those things, but desires the good, which is somehow in them but *is* not them. The good, however, must also be a super *idea*, an *idea* of *ideas*, for the other *ideas*, for example, justice, man, beauty, are also good. Therefore these other ideas, the many *ideas*, are participations in the one *idea* of the good. Since the *ideas are*, the good, then, is the source of being, but beyond being, in the sense that it exists in a way different from the other beings. The good is the transcendent principle of the whole, the cause of the being of things and of the apprehension of being, uniting knower and known, the lover of the good and the good things. As experienced by man, the good is an overpowering combination of pleasure and knowledge.

Socrates tells Glaucon that an account of the good cannot be given to him, because he, Socrates, is incapable of giving it and Glaucon is incapable of understanding it. But he agrees to give him an account of the offspring of the good, the sun. The sun is the cause both of things being seeable and their being seen, and is also the cause of the existence of living things. What the sun is in the visible world, the good is in the intelligible world. On the basis of what we know of the visible world with its sun, we can conjecture about the intelligible world with its *idea* of the good. This Socrates does by drawing the divided line which describes the being of things and the faculties which apprehend them. It shows that reality extends far beyond anything the practical man ever dreams and that to know it one must use faculties never recognized by the practical man. The divided line is a sketch of a *cosmos* which can give ground to the aspirations of the philosophic soul. The splendor of this vision is meant to dazzle the mind's eye as the sun dazzles the body's eye. The erotic Glaucon is told that *eros* is the soul's longing for completeness, to be full of being, to know everything which *is*. Philosophy, which was introduced as a means to actualize the city's good and is being used as a means to discover *the* good, turns out to be the end, the human good.

After initiating Glaucon into the mysteries of this divine beauty, Socrates turns to an elaboration of the relationship of the philosophic soul to the city. The divided line described the soul's progress from its lowest level of cognition, imagination, to trust, thought, and finally intellection, its highest level. But now Socrates makes clear that this is not a simple movement depending only on talent and effort. There are powerful forces that stand in the way of the philosophic quest. The discovery of that quest has the character of a liberation from bondage. In the most moving of all his many images, Socrates compares our situation to that of prisoners in a cave. We are surrounded by darkness, our only access to ourselves and the world coming from the observation of shadows on the wall. But, although there is darkness, there is also a light in the cave; the pale shadows we possess are made possible by that light. Moreover, a few human beings can emerge from the cave. Our lives are a combination of ugliness and sublime possibility. The Enlightenment, taken literally, believed that the light could be brought into the cave and the shadows dispelled; men, in that view, could live in perfect light. This Socrates denies; the philosopher does not bring light to the cave, he escapes into the light and can lead a few to it; he is a guide, not a torchbearer. The attempt to illuminate the cave is self-defeating: a part of man craves the shadows. The light would be dimmed and distorted; it would not provide real clarity within the cave. And, at the same time, those who have the urge to ascend to the light would be discouraged from the endeavor by the myth, apparently based on reason, that there is no other light to which they can ascend. Thus the only source of liberation and inspiration would disappear from the cave. The Enlightenment teaches that the cave can be transformed; Socrates teaches that it must be transcended and that this transcendence can be accomplished only by a few.

Only by constant reference back to the divided line can one understand the cave. In what sense does the cave represent the human situation with respect to education? The prisoners are said to be in bonds and forced to look at images of images—shadows on the wall of the cave. The lowest level of the line belongs to shadows and reflections, and the faculty which apprehends them is called imagination. This is the level of distorted and unclear images, and the faculty related to them is completely unreliable. To judge of images one must compare them to the things of which they are images. These latter are the things of which we have a natural consciousness—plants, animals, artifacts, etc.—the various *manys* of which we become aware through the senses. The faculty which apprehends them may be called trust, and it is the beginning point of knowledge We do not have sufficient knowledge of these things, nor can we explain how we know of them or how we are sure of their existence, but they are our entry into reality, the hints which lead us toward the causes or the *ideas*; the higher levels of the line are devoted to the explanation of these phenomena. Our awareness of them is not perfectly sure, but a universal doubt of them would lead us into a void; it would leave us with nothing. It is called trust precisely because it resists doubt of the existence of what it apprehends. Knowledge or philosophy is the clarification and articulation of this natural consciousness. Imagination is no beginning point for knowledge because it cannot distinguish between what is merely a shadow, a distortion caused by the idiosyncrasies of our mental vision or those of the reflecting medium, and what is an accurate reflection of the objects. Only the awareness that an image is an image makes it possible to judge its true character, and in order to have that awareness imagination must be aided by the faculty of trust.

But who regularly believes that images are real things; who mistakes reflections for what is reflected? Why does Socrates insist that our situation is that of men who mistake images for realities? It would seem more sensible to say that we take objects too seriously, that we do not recognize the importance and superior reality of the causes or first principles. How can it be said that we are bound to the lowest level of the line? The answer seems to be that the cave is the city and that our attachment to the city binds us to certain authoritative opinions about things. We do not see men as they are but as they are represented to us by legislators and poets. A Greek sees things differently from the way a Persian sees them. One need only think of the question of nakedness as discussed in Book V, or the significance of cows to Hindus as opposed to other men, to realize how powerful are the various horizons constituted by law or convention. Legislators and poets are the makers of these horizons; or, to use the symbols of the cave image, they are the men who carry the statues and the other things the reflections of which the prisoners see. These objects are not natural; they are themselves images of natural objects produced with cunning art so as to look like their originals, but are adapted to serve the special interests of the artists. In other words, we do not see things directly, but through the opinions we are taught about them. Those opinions are not accurate reflections of nature but are adapted to serve the needs of the city. They are designed to make a man love his city, and therefore they have to invest the city with all sorts of special significance and have no basis in nature. The theoretical man would not believe such opinions and would, as theoretical man, have no particular concern for them or, therefore, for the city they defend. But the citizens' world is always a mixture of nature and convention, and that is the world of all of us. The first and most difficult of tasks is the separation of what exists by nature from what is merely made by man. The pictures on the wall of our cave look very real, and the two sources of the representations are artfully intertwined. We are attached to the illusion because it constitutes our own world and gives meaning to our particular existence.

Philosophy or science is concerned only with man or the city, not with this particular man or this particular city. Few men—and no cities—can live with this perspective. Socrates illustrates this in the account of his beliefs and practices given by Xenophon (*Memorabilia,* I, i). He was in the habit of telling his friends that art or science could teach a man how to sow a field well or how to build a house well, but it cannot tell him whether he will reap what he has sown or live in what he has built. Science is indifferent to the fate of individuals. Those for whom this is intolerable need a supplement to reason; they must turn to the Delphic oracle, to the divine, in order to satisfy themselves. Thus our love of our own ties us to the cave, and that powerful passion must be overcome in order to move upward on the line of knowledge. And he who does must leave his kin, be regarded as a traitor by them, forego the rewards offered to the man who joins in their self-deception, and run the risks of punishment prescribed by their laws. These are the bonds which tie us to the cave and its images. To break them requires rare passion and courage, for the lion in our souls, spiritedness, guards the gates of the dungeon.

The divided line and the cave teach that there are two fatal temptations of the mind. The first is that of the men who insist on the significance of the images in the cave and constitute themselves as their defenders and hence the accusers of the philosophers. They are often men of very high intelligence who are forced to hate reason by their unwillingness to renounce the charm and significance of their particular experiences and those of their people. They are enemies of whatever leads in the direction of universality, of anything that would tend to break down the heterogeneity, the particularity and distinctiveness, of the ways to which they are attached. Their dominant trait is piety, which frequently turns into fanaticism. These men are among the leaders of peoples and are protectors of the people's beliefs. This account of their nature acts as a corrective of the view that the people can easily be persuaded to accept philosophers as kings.

The other great temptation is that of those who are too easily liberated and do not learn in the cave what must be learned about man and the soul. These men dwell on the third level of the line and are best represented by the mathematicians. They escape to a world of universality and are charmed by the competence of their reason to order and explain that world. The homogeneity of numbers which can apply to all things permits them to reduce all the particularities in the world to unities. They tend to forget the questionableness of their own beginnings or principles and the natural heterogeneity of the different kinds of things; they are forgetful of qualitative differences and, hence, of the *ideas*. As the pious men were hostile to the *ideas* because the *ideas* threatened the heterogeneity of their world, these competent men are hostile to the *ideas* because they threaten the homogeneity of their world. Such were the early philosophers who while watching the sky fell into holes, the men ridiculed by Aristophanes because their science could not understand man, the only being who understands. These two temptations are aided by two of man's most noble arts: poetry and mathematics. Both of these arts are necessary and useful, but both tend to emancipate themselves from philosophy and re-enforce the hostility to it. In order to resist these temptations, a man's reason must be both daring and moderate. Socrates, in his reform of philosophy, showed the way in which these virtues must be combined. A man must be daring in his quest for the first causes of all things and in his refusal to accept the sacred opinions of the cave. But he must be moderate and not look directly at the sun for fear of being blinded and losing the distinctions among the various kinds of things. He must look at the reflection of the sun and the things it illuminates; that is, he must not try to apprehend being directly but must try to discern it in the opinions about the various kinds of beings. Dialectic, the art of friendly conversation, as practiced by Socrates, is this combination of daring and moderation.

In the account of the cave given here, a man is liberated from his bonds not by his own efforts but by a teacher who compels him to turn to the light. The actual mode of this turning is represented in the action of the *Republic*. Old Cephalus has opinions about justice; in the investigation of justice, one does not begin by trying to look at justice, or by constructing definitions, but by examining these opinions about it. Cephalus holds two contradictory opinions about justice, but both seem necessary for his understanding of justice. One is thus forced to seek for another and more adequate opinion which can comprehend the phenomena covered by the contradictory opinions. The thoughtful observer recognizes that the opinions of the men in the cave are self-contradictory and thus meaningless as they stand. But their very contradiction points beyond them to more intelligible opinions and to objects which do not admit of such ambiguity. The many contradictory opinions are solicited by the one, comprehensive, opinion. Dialectic, beginning from the commonly held opinions, will lead to an ultimate agreement. It is this activity which can guide us to the discovery of the natural objects, and it implies that we begin from the phenomena as we see them, taking them seriously in an effort to clarify them. It is only by way of our imprisonment that a liberation can be effected; and our speech about things, if properly examined, is the reflection of the light in the cave.

The liberation, once effected, results in great happiness; the soul carries on its proper activity with its proper objects. And, as a result, the freed man has a great contempt for the cave, its shadows and its inhabitants. He wants always to live out in the light; the others do not know they are slaves, so they are content; but he knows it and cannot bear to live among them. Nothing in the city contributes to his specific pleasures, and he wants nothing from it; he is not, as are all others, a potential exploiter of the city. At last the problem of finding disinterested rulers is solved. But it also becomes clear that the philosophers do not want to be rulers and that they must be compelled. Compulsion is necessary since rhetoric could not deceive philosophers. Now the tables are turned. Previously it appeared that the philosophers are anxious to rule and must persuade a recalcitrant populace. In the investigation of the philosophic nature it has by accident, as it were, emerged that philosophers want nothing from the city and that their contemplative activity is perfectly engrossing, leaving neither time nor interest for ruling. So, if philosophers are to rule, it must be the city that forces them to do so; and it is in the philosophers' interest to keep the knowledge of their kingly skills from the people. It is a perfect circle. The people must be persuaded to accept the philosophers; but the philosophers must be compelled to persuade the people to compel them to rule. And who would do that? This is not an accidental difficulty of communication between the two sides; it is grounded on real conflicts of interest.

Glaucon objects to the injustice of forcing the philosophers to return to the cave. This is injustice in the fullest sense of the word: it would be contrary to their good to return. Or to put it into the formula for justice: the city would force one man to do two jobs, to be both philosopher and king. It has become perfectly manifest that the life of reason, contrary to the political view stated in Book IV, has a character of its own far different from the calculation of the practical man. The activity of a king is not the same as that of a philosopher. It is at this point in the elaboration of the good city that we see that it cannot fulfill its intention and is hence a failure. The attempt was to found a city in which every member's duty was identical to his self-interest, in which total dedication was possible, in which the universal demands of justice did not undermine the laws of the city, and in which there was no claim that went beyond the city limits. This was to be a city without limits. But now it is evident that in the decisive respect the city is not natural: it cannot comprehend the highest activity of man. We modern men are accustomed to insist that almost every claim against civil society is valid, but Socrates denies this. There is only one claim the dignity of which is greater than that of the city; only at this point do the limits of the city become clear.

In the light of the splendor of the soul's yearning after the whole, the city looks very ugly. This is the true comedy—taking the city with infinite seriousness, beautifying it with every artifice, making it a veritable Callipolis, and then finding that compared to the soul which was supposed to be like it, it is a thing to be despised. This fair city, the goal of so many aspirations, now looks like a cave, and its happy citizens like prisoners; it is comparable to the Hades of which Achilles complained, and the attachment to it is a species of folly. From the point of view of the city, the philosopher looks ridiculous; but from the point of view of the whole, the citizen looks ridiculous. Socrates asks which of the two contexts is the more authoritative. Aristophanes' comedy is the human comedy, Socrates' the divine.

Only the philosophers can provide the city with an end that can direct its actions. The ordinary statesmen serve the city and seek to provide for its preservation, which is only a condition of action, not an end. Only knowledge seems to have the character of an end in itself. But the philosopher has nothing to do with the city. The practical virtues can only be justified if they are understood to be the means to the theoretical virtues. But the city cannot consider itself a means to philosophy. This union of philosophy and the city is a shotgun wedding. The citizens would not be slaves to the philosophers' well-being, considering themselves means to an end in which they do not partake; and the philosopher, although he too needs preservation, can arrange that in less burdensome fashion than ruling.

This disproportion between city and philosophy becomes ever more evident during the presentation of the philosophic education. Glaucon and Socrates agree that the studies must serve war and thought because these are two essential activities of kings who are philosophers. But in the course of the discussion the politically relevant content of the studies progressively decreases, and finally they are forced to abandon the notion that philosophic studies have anything to do with action in the city. Socrates even reproaches Glaucon with hindering and distorting the philosophic education by his practical concern, on which he himself had previously insisted. Now the only justification of the higher learning is philosophy.

Socrates has proved in the course of the dialogue that all cities need the rule of wisdom and that wisdom means knowledge of the true whole or the first causes. He has shown that only the philosopher is concerned with such knowledge and hence is potentially the only true ruler. But he has not shown that such knowledge is possible, that any man can actually convert himself from a lover of wisdom into a wise man by knowing everything there is to know. This is also a condition of the city's possibility. Just as Socrates has overstated the case for the possibility of the city's accepting wisdom, he overstates the case for the possibility of a man's becoming wise. He seems to say that the philosophers will complete their labors and come to know the *idea* of the good. But it is doubtful whether the mind's eye can look directly at the good without being dazzled any more than the body's eye can look directly at the sun without being dazzled. Philosophy, as Socrates usually teaches, has the character of an unfinished and unfinishable quest. If this is true, it means that the philosopher cannot rule because he does not know what he would need to know in order to rule. He is the good citizen because he is seeking to acquire what the city most needs, but he has not yet succeeded in acquiring it, so that both he and the city are incomplete. Further, the philosopher has less time to rule than would a wise man, because his urgent business is unfinished. Both the philosopher's ignorance and his lack of available free time caused by that ignorance militate against his being able to rule.

The final condition for the actualization of the best regime is that those who have compelled the philosophers to become kings must abandon their city, lands, and children, leaving no one over ten years of age in the city, so that an entirely new formation of the soul can be given to the children. Socrates blandly announces this condition as though the renunciation of all they live for by the whole citizen body were easy to accomplish. And it would have to be a voluntary renunciation because the philosophers have not yet educated a defense force with which to compel the people. The perfect city is revealed to be a perfect impossibility.

What then was the use of spending so much time and effort on a city that is impossible? Precisely to show its impossibility. This was not just any city, but one constructed to meet all the demands of justice. Its impossibility demonstrates the impossibility of the actualization of a just regime and hence moderates the moral indignation a man might experience at the sight of less-than-perfect regimes. The extreme spirit of reform or revolution loses its ground if its end is questionable. If the infinite longing for justice on earth is merely a dream or a prayer, the shedding of blood in its name turns from idealism into criminality. The revolutions of Communism or Fascism are made in the name of perfect regimes which are to be their consequence. What matter if a few million die now, if one is sure that countless generations of mankind will enjoy the fruits of justice? Socrates thinks about the end which is ultimately aimed at by all reformers or revolutionaries but to which they do not pay sufficient attention. He shows what a regime would have to be in order to be just and why such a regime is impossible. Regimes can be improved but not perfected; injustice will always remain. The proper spirit of reform, then, is moderation. Socrates constructs his utopia to point up the dangers of what we would call utopianism; as such it is the greatest critique of political idealism ever written. The *Republic* serves to moderate the extreme passion for political justice by showing the limits of what can be demanded and expected of the city; and, at the same time, it shows the direction in which the immoderate desires can be meaningfully channeled. At the beginning of the dialogue, Glaucon and Adeimantus set the severest standards for political justice. In order to try to meet those standards, they would have to establish a terrible tyranny and would fail nevertheless. Socrates leads them first to the fulfillment of their wishes, and then beyond, to a fullfillment which does not depend on the transformation of human nature. The striving for the perfectly just city puts unreasonable and despotic demands on ordinary men, and it abuses and misuses the best men. There is gentleness in Socrates' treatment of men, and his vision is never clouded by the blackness of moral indignation, for he knows what to expect of men. Political idealism is the most destructive of human passions.

All of Western man's aspirations to justice and the good life are given expression and fulfillment in Socrates' proposals for a city. This is a regime where men's faculties are not denied their exercise by poverty, birth, or sex, where the accidental attachments of family and city do not limit a man's understanding and pursuit of the good; it is a regime, finally, where wise, public-spirited men rule for the common good. But this regime can only be achieved at the sacrifice of other treasured things to which we are less reasonably, but perhaps more powerfully, inclined. These are property, family, and the city of one's birth—all the things a man can love as his own; they exist everywhere and existed long before the emergence of philosophy. Not only do these things constitute the charm of life for most men, they also provide the occasion for the acquisition and the exercise of most of the virtues which can give ordinary men dignity. If reason requires Socrates' city, love of family and friends, patriotism, and even heroism demand the older kind of city. Man's dual nature makes it impossible to solve the problem posed by the two kinds of goods. Every decent regime is some kind of uneasy compromise between them. Socrates' scheme, in a spirit of comedy, proposes the triumph of the side which represents the soul, the side to which the best kind of man can be almost totally devoted, the only rational side. The non-barbaric society is defined by openness to this part of man's longing; this openness to philosophy is the very definition of civilization and carries with it a tendency to wish for the actualization of the regime of the philosopher-kings. It is the light in the cave which Socrates and those near him fought to preserve when its infancy was so severely threatened. But to forget the other side of man—to neglect the irony of Socrates' proposals—is also a fatal error. The cosmopolitan communistic society of egalitarian man is a distortion of man and the city which is more terrible than barbarism. In acting as though the eternal tension between body and soul has been overcome by history, a society is constituted which satisfies neither body nor soul. Such a society creates one universal cave illuminated by an artificial light, for men have not made the sacrifices necessary to the attainment of true cosmopolitanism but have been robbed of those attachments which can give them depth. The thinkers of the Enlightenment, culminating in Marx, preserved Socrates' ultimate goals but forgot his insistence that nature made them impossible for men at large. Only by distorting or narrowing man's horizon can the permanent duality in his nature be overcome.

The *Republic* finally teaches that justice as total dedication to the city cannot be simply good for the philosopher, and that hence it is somewhat questionable for other men as well. For the philosopher to dedicate himself to the city would not result either in the salvation of mankind or the promotion of his own wisdom. He has to live in a city, however, and must count on other men to preserve him; therefore he must care for at least a modicum of justice in the city. But this care is only necessary, not desirable in itself. The answer to Glaucon's question—Is justice good in itself or only instrumentally?—is that justice conceived as dedication to the city is only instrumentally good. But there is one kind of doing good to one's friends which is also beneficial to the philosopher. There are some young men in whom his soul delights, for they have souls akin to his own and are potential philosophers; these are men who may even aid him in his uncompleted quest for wisdom. Glaucon himself may well be one of them. In the case of most citizens, the philosopher's concern is only that he do them no harm, and his justice thus has the character of a burdensome duty. In the case of the promising young, he is concerned with doing them a positive good, and his justice has the character of love. He must always carry on a contest with the city for the affections of its sons. Although he has a duty to the city, he is always at war with it.

(543a–569c) The elaboration of the best regime and the way of life corresponding to it is not a sufficient response to Glaucon's original demand, which was to compare the life of the just man and that of the unjust man with respect to their happiness. In his speech in favor of injustice Glaucon described the advantages of the unjust man's life; those alleged advantages must be looked at again in the light of what Glaucon has learned in the course of the dialogue. If Glaucon is to be converted, he must compare what previously attracted him with what he has come to admire. This calls for a presentation of the bad regimes of city and soul as well as the good.

Following the hypothesis of the dialogue, according to which the city is the soul writ large, Socrates turns first to the discussion of the inferior cities. The parallelism of the city and the soul is maintained here (as it was in Book IV) in spite of the fact that it has become most questionable. This procedure has the rhetorical advantage of making justice, which is admittedly desirable in a city, appear equally desirable in the soul. When Glaucon sees and is forced to admit that the city ruled by a tyrant is a terrible place, he is more easily induced to view the tyrant as a terrible man.

In preparing the direct confrontation of philosopher and tyrant for Glaucon's benefit, Socrates makes use of Adeimantus and his particular qualities. Throughout, Glaucon and Adeimantus have balanced each other, and they are perfectly matched as interlocutors. Without their specific characters and Socrates' judicious blending of them, the founding of the city in speech would have been impossible. Glaucon is the daring, manly lover of victory whose *eros* leads him directly to the conquest of the good things as he sees them, and whose spiritedness aids him in his endeavor. He is responsible for the progress of the dialogue: it is Glaucon who wanted to go to the Piraeus to see the festival, and who decided for both Socrates and himself that they would heed Polemarchus and Adeimantus and stay. It is Glaucon who was perplexed and interested by Socrates' discussion of payments for ruling; it is he who insisted on continuing the argument about justice and most convincingly portrayed the advantages of injustice. Moreover, it is Glaucon whose appetites forced the abandonment of the city of sows, who compelled Socrates to tell of all the virtues, to introduce the philosopher-kings, and to discuss the good. Glaucon's feverish intensity is the impulse that carries the discussion forward to the greatest innovations and the most extreme satisfaction.

Adeimantus, by contrast, is a moderate man and a lover of tragic poetry. His spiritedness is directed inward and it makes him austere. He is thus a more reliable citizen than Glaucon with his many and powerful desires. He is a moralist and a defender of civil life. He was the one who, by the promise of interesting sights, persuaded Glaucon and Socrates to join the little community of men in the Piraeus. It is Adeimantus who helped Socrates to build the healthy city, and he was contented with it. He is the agent of the purification of the feverish city. And, above all, he is the accuser of Socrates, the one who forces him to stop and justify himself to the city. Adeimantus speaks in the name of the political men who are offended and threatened by both Glaucon's and Socrates' unconventional notions. He accuses Socrates of not making the warriors happy, of robbing his friends of an adequate discussion of communism, and of imposing useless or vicious philosophers on the city as rulers. He is necessary to the building of a city; and he is necessary to that punishment of the bodily passions which is the condition of Glaucon's reformation. Just as Glaucon is dangerous because he is a potential subverter of the laws, Adeimantus is dangerous because he is a potential accuser of philosophy. Just as Glaucon can be useful because he tends toward philosophy, so Adeimantus can be useful because he tends toward public spiritedness.

In Books VIII and IX Adeimantus finally ceases being Socrates' opponent and becomes his wholehearted ally. For at this point a city has been founded in speech of which Socrates is a member; thus, in defending this city, Adeimantus is also defending Socrates. His moralism and moral indignation are now in the service of a city devoted to philosophy, and he is its protector against what threatens it. Adeimantus was previously an admirer of Sparta and used it as a standard to criticize men and cities; Socrates induces him to abandon that standard in favor of the city of the *Republic,* by showing him that the new city has all the virtues of Sparta and is a great improvement on it. The Spartan standard caused Adeimantus to condemn behavior which did not conform to it, which means that he condemned philosophy along with many vices. Now, with his new standard, he will still condemn those vices, but he will see in the philosopher a blessed remnant of the best regime rather than a sign of the corruption of the times. In order to reenforce Adeimantus' belief in the reality of this regime and hence in the correctness of using it as a standard, Socrates constructs a myth which assures him that the good city did indeed exist a long time ago. This regime is not only possible, but it (not Sparta or any old regime of Athens) is the truly ancestral regime, and therefore deserves the respect of men like Adeimantus who have the tendency to regard the ancestral as the good. Moreover, Socrates tells the tale in such a way that Adeimantus will not commit any follies in attempting to reinstitute the ancestral regime. It is irrevocably in the past, and any changes in the present regime can only lead to a worse regime. Thus Socrates turns Adeimantus into a conservative and neutralizes his potentially dangerous idealism. Adeimantus will not love the democracy under which he lives, but he will also not want to see it overturned; he will support what is best in that regime and respect the philosopher who lives in the city governed by it. With this altered perspective, Adeimantus joins Socrates in judging the various imperfect regimes and men, and thereby they set the stage for Glaucon's judgment of the tyrannic life.

In Books VIII and IX Socrates sketches the outlines of a political science. This presentation schematizes five fundamental kinds of regimes and five ways of life or types of men who are related to those regimes. Thus a basis is provided for categorizing political phenomena and understanding their causes; such knowledge, in turn, provides guidance in political deliberation and choice. The regime is treated as the most important political fact and the cause of all the other facts. The regime is identical with the class, or kind, of men who hold the ruling offices. As this class varies, so does the way of life of the city. The regime determines the character of law, education, property, marriage, and the family. Therefore, the regime is what must be studied by anyone who is interested in the effect of politics on his life or his pursuit of the good life. This is the most important question, and a relevant political science is designed to answer it. The different kinds of regime are distinguished by their explicit goals, which derive from the ways of life men can choose. Truly different regimes, and men, stem from significant and irreducible differences of principle. Socrates suggests that wisdom, honor, money, freedom, and love are the ends which men pursue and for which they can use the political order; the dominance of one principle or another brings forth very different dimensions in the lives of men. The healthy soul is the standard for the judgment of regimes and the key to understanding them; the healthy regime is the one that allows for the development of healthy souls. Such a political science is more akin to medicine than to mathematics. Political science must be evaluative; just as a doctor must know what a healthy body is, a political scientist must know what a healthy regime is. Such a political science provides a much richer and more comprehensive framework than that provided by our contemporary political science with its oversimplified dichotomies, democratic versus totalitarian or developed versus underdeveloped. These represent a pale reminiscence of the Socratic approach, impoverished both because we rely too much on the narrow experience of our own time and because of our attempts to erect a value-free science on the foundation of that narrow experience.

Socrates' political science as presented here is not quite serious because it is absurdly severe, using as its standard a regime which can never exist. Socrates still insists that the regime of philosopher-kings can exist and that all other regimes are corruptions of it. His procedure is justified by his desire to include all the highest capacities in the city, to make the complete man a part of the complete city. But the inclusion of the philosopher stretches the limits of the city beyond the realm of the possible. Aristotle elaborated Socrates' sketch and turned it into a true political science by adjusting his standard to the possibilities of political life. Aristotle treats the gentlemen as though their virtue were complete and self-sufficient, thus making it possible to base decent regimes on the gentlemen. In his view, any regime in which the rulers care for the common good is legitimate, and there are a variety of such regimes. Socrates, on the other hand, subjects the nonphilosophic virtues to a harsher scrutiny which reveals that they are seriously flawed. There is hence only one good regime; this is ruled by philosophers, who are the only men with no temptation to get the better of others and exploit the city. Thus, on the basis of a regime which can never be, he is able to cast doubt on the legitimacy of all possible regimes.

Socrates presents political life in this way with the intention of benefiting Glaucon and Adeimantus. He is in the process of leading them back to the level of ordinary political life after their brief ascent toward the sun. They must live in the city, as must most men. But he wishes them to see the city in the light of what they have learned in their ascent; their vision of their world must be transformed. Adeimantus must no longer see philosophy as an enemy of the city, and Glaucon must no longer be tempted by tyranny. Socrates accomplishes this by taking the highest kind of individual and constructing a regime around him. He thus appeals to Adeimantus, by giving political status to that human type, and to Glaucon, by showing him a ruler for whom the practice of justice appears to be an unqualified good. The young man who wishes to live well will pray for that city and its way of life. But this ultimately means that he will, in the absence of that regime, desire to live a private life, for that good life is shown to be possible without the regime; it does not depend, as do the other ways of life, on ruling in the city. It is self-sufficient and always available to him who chooses it. Socrates' political science, paradoxically, is meant to show the superiority of the private life. The most important point made in this section is that while the best city exists only in myth, the best man exists actually.

Socrates' account of the regimes diverges from common sense in that he insists that the best regime came first and that after it there is a necessary downward movement of decay to timocracy, oligarchy, democracy, and finally, tyranny. This is supported neither by argument nor by history. Aristotle in his discussion of the various regimes does not argue that one regime must necessarily emerge from another; worse regimes can certainly precede better ones. The argument of the *Republic* itself has indicated that the regime of the philosophers, or aristocracy, is not first but necessarily last in time. It is furthest away from innocence; it requires experience; it is the result of a great and recent progress in understanding, the discovery of philosophy. As has been suggested, Socrates, contrary to fact, places the best regime first in order that the quest for wisdom not appear to be in conflict with the political prejudice in favor of the ancestral. Aristophanes, in the *Clouds*, accused Socrates of teaching wise sons to beat unwise fathers. If Socrates describes the decay of regimes correctly, there would never be a legitimate ground for beating one's father; in each successive downward step the son is inferior to the father. The quest for self-improvement would be identical to respect for one's forebears. Moreover, the belief in perfect beginnings here expressed is the response to Glaucon's suggestion that civil society is a mere compact between men who prefer to do, rather than suffer, injustice, and who joined together only because of the suffering involved in their original estate. In the account given by Socrates, the foundings or origins of civil society are not in injustice and the blood of the innocent, and the past does not provide a model for tyrannic methods of rule. The harsh facts of the foundings of cities are covered over because of the temptations engendered by their example. Glaucon, in his first speech on justice, asserted that a thing could be understood by its origin, or that its origin is its nature. Socrates taught, in the discussion of the *ideas*, that the end, not the origin, of a thing is its nature. Here he appeals to Glaucon's faulty philosophic understanding by putting what is really the end at the origin. Finally, it must be stressed again that there is a downward movement of the regimes, that there is no indication that this trend can be reversed, and that the final tyranny does not lead back again toward one of the superior regimes. It is the fault of man, not of gods or nature, that decay occurs, but once having occurred, the original state of innocence cannot be recovered. At best men can struggle against further decay, but they cannot hope to establish the best regime by their own effort. By this mode of presentation Socrates teach- es Glaucon and Adeimantus that the ancestral is truly respectable because it was wise and just, and that it cannot be improved upon. Thus he makes them moderate without being closed to reason, as respect for what is truly ancestral would make them.

Socrates and Adeimantus discuss each of the regimes before they discuss the man corresponding to it. Therefore, they have the tendency (as was the case in Book IV) to see in the man what they saw in the city. This predetermines the somewhat questionable result that men have the same rank order of goodness which was found in regimes. For example, there is some doubt whether a man who pursues money alone is simply preferable to one who devotes himself to spending it in a variety of pleasures. But the anti-democratic Adeimantus readily agrees that oligarchy is superior to democracy; thus it appears, from his connection with the oligarchic regime, that the oligarchic man is the superior human type. This is obviously not an exhaustive account of the men under consideration, but it serves Socrates' intention, which is to condemn the tyrannic man. To do this, the desires must be condemned, particularly the erotic desires. This condemnation of the desires is the key to the rank order of the men—the more desire is dominant in them, the lower they are on the scale. However, this principle of order is not manifest to desiring men such as Glaucon. It is given plausibility by the fact that in the cities selfish desire is what most leads to injustice. From a strictly political standpoint, the denigration of desire is necessitated; from the standpoint of an individual who wants to be happy, it is not so easily accepted or seen to be necessary. This hidden tension between the two standpoints is most revealing and must be watched in the description which explicitly argues for their sameness. The similarity of the life of the city to that of the man actually diminishes in the downward progress from timocracy to tyranny. The timocratic man is largely devoted to the same goals as the timocratic city and his description is like that of the city, but the democratic man seems to be able to lead a private life and his description is quite different from that of the city. And, although all would agree that a tyrannically ruled city is the unhappiest of cities, it is hardly clear that the tyrant is the unhappiest of men. In a timocracy, as the city fares, so fares the man. This is not so evidently the case in democracies and tyrannies.

The order of the cities in dignity and goodness—timocracy, oligarchy, democracy, and tyranny—accords with Adeimantus' tastes and common sense, although it is not in any way demonstrated. Following the principles tacitly established in the *Republic*, a city must provide for the sustenance of the body, be able to defend itself, and have as rulers men who care for the common good. The cities' ranks seem to correspond to their capacity to meet these conditions. Only aristocracy meets them fully, but timocracy comes closest to so doing. Sparta, the model of the timocratic regime, is a republic with a long history of stability and is able to defend its liberty courageously and skillfully. Although the rulers secretly lust for money, their love of honor protects their devotion to the public, and they are too ashamed to sacrifice their duty to acquisition. Moreover, if their courage is not that of the educated auxiliaries who are convinced that death is nothing terrible, and if they are somewhat too savage, it is undeniable that they can fight very well.

Next in order comes the oligarchic regime, which has neither the perfect rulers of the aristocratic regime nor the love of honor, and hence the courage, of the timocratic regime. The oligarchs turn all of the city's resources to their private gain and are both unwilling and unable to fight. But their continence and sobriety in acquiring and keeping property lend to the regime a certain stability. Because it lacks even the stability of oligarchy, democracy comes fourth. The democrats are incapable of ruling themselves, so they must choose leaders. These demogogues despoil the rich for their own profit while trying to satisfy the demands of the poor. Finally, the city's property is wasted. Democracy is essentially a transitional regime because its principle, freedom, does not encourage the respect for law requisite to the maintenance of a regime. It prepares the way for tyranny, admitted by all to be the worst of regimes, the regime in which the ruler exploits the city simply for his personal benefit.

In his treatment of the destruction of these regimes, Socrates sets down the rule that a regime can be destroyed only by the vice intrinsic to its principle. Oligarchy, for example, because of its attachment to money, necessarily impoverishes vulnerable members of its own class and thus swells the ranks of the poor with able, disaffected men. This regime has to encourage prodigality and hence saps public spiritedness. Oligarchy, in this view, can never be overthrown by an unprovoked, surprise attack by a more powerful neighbor. Its downfall must be a result of its own faults. This assertion of Socrates is akin to his insistence in Book III that the soul is the cause of the body's illness. The regime is the soul of the city, and it causes everything that happens in it; thus domestic policy is all that counts. Socrates abstracts here from accident and particularly from foreign policy. This serves to focus attention on what is most essential in the city, its virtues; these depend entirely on the regime, and its good character is the chief responsibility of the statesmen.

This treatment of the regimes contrasts strongly with the way Socrates treats the men who are supposed to be like them. The man in each case seems to be a member, not of the city he resembles, but of a democratic city and does not share the character of the city in which he lives. (Even the democratic man is not the poor, lean citizen described by Socrates when he spoke of the democratic city.) The various kinds of soul can apparently reach their fulfillment on their own in a democratic city; they are not encouraged by it, nor are they hindered by it. Socrates describes democracy as a general store stocked with all kinds of regimes; he follows his own suggestion and goes to that store when he wants to select the various kinds of men. Athens is where one has to live in order to know the range of human possibilities. The only type he cannot find there is the tyrant actualizing his potential, but there is a young man present in the discussion who might well like to be one. The change from one kind of man to the next and lower kind is understood by Socrates as a failure of education within the family. It is in each case a superior father who is unable to make his son like himself. And here, as opposed to the discussion of the regimes, the changes in the crucial instances are in part caused by what might be called problems of foreign policy. The cities were isolated, and their difficulties arose out of the relations of the parts within them. But the aristocratic and timocratic men have difficulties in their relations with the city, and because of the unsatisfactory character of those relations, the sons reject the fathers' ways of life in favor of ways which are more suited to success in the city. Thus they become inferior men. Socrates appears to be teaching that the fatal error consists in taking the city too seriously and adapting to its demands, thus that men need not be like the regimes, that the regimes need not be the primary fact of their lives, particularly if they live in a democracy.

The good city's corruption was mysterious and shrouded in myth; the very existence of that city was questionable. The only nonmythical account one can give of it is that drawn from a comparison with the causes of the corruption of the inferior regimes: the preoccupation with the acquisition of property and the difficulties involved in its distribution make it impossible for the city to devote itself to the good use of that property or, simply, to the good life. The body cannot be forgotten, and thus it is impossible to renounce everything connected with private property and concentrate only on the soul. The possession of private property is the crucial change from the best regime to the second best, and all the ills which beset the various regimes follow from that change. The city's primary business becomes the management of property and is, hence, the dedication to mere life. It is no accident that in the list of regimes the central one is oligarchy, for in its pursuit of money, it incarnates the concern of the real city. The private desires which money represents and can fulfill and which are at a tension with public spirit become more and more dominant as one goes down the slope of the regimes. Socrates indicates that because a city is a composite of many kinds of men, of whom very few are capable of love of knowledge, no city can avoid the fundamental compromise with private property.

The corruption of the aristocrat's son, on the other hand, can be seen by all. Unlike the aristocratic city, the aristocratic man really exists; he is a philosopher. Moreover, he is exactly like Socrates. He devotes himself to learning; he is totally indifferent to his body and other men's opinions of him; he is utterly dedicated and single-minded. But his wife, like Xanthippe, cannot endure the fact that her husband, and thereby she herself, is unhonored and despised. She, along with other like-minded people, convinces his son that this is no way to live. She echoes Callicles, who in the *Gorgias* accused the philosopher of being unmanly, of being incapable of honorably avenging insults. Man's fall from the state of innocence is a result of a woman's temptings. The son's spiritedness is awakened, and he lives the life of a proud man, performing those deeds which will make him respected by others. Such a life entails the abandonment of philosophy, both because he no longer has time for it and because the questions raised by it are not appropriate to a gentleman. He now lives for the opinions of other men and no longer for himself. His father was not truly a citizen—he was in the city but not of it; but that father's son becomes a part of the city by adapting himself to it.

The timocrat's son, in turn, is corrupted when he sees his father mistreated by the people. He was too proud to court the people and lost everything. Fear becomes the son's motivation; he abandons pride, for it is dangerous. His father was spiritually dependent on the people; his condemnation ruins his life. The son recognizes that the father's apparent independence was groundless. Now life, bodily life, becomes dominant. The only source of security is in money which can guarantee the means of life. The father had money and did not pay sufficient attention to the need he had for it. Spiritedness cannot maintain itself against this awareness. The son is completely dependent on things outside himself, and desire has become the principle of his life. The example of Socrates teaches that a man should live in the city like a sovereign nation unto himself, with only such relations to other citizens as are dictated by a defensive prudence.

In order to show how this oligarchic man's son becomes a democratic man, Socrates makes a distinction between the necessary and unnecessary desires, which explains the difference between the oligarch and the democrat. The necessary desires are those which contribute to the maintenance of life; the unnecessary ones are those that we could do without. Socrates appears to include even sex in this latter category. Presumably because of his father's success at providing money, the democratic son has devoted himself to many desires and not limited himself to the necessary ones as did his austere father. On the basis of Socrates' description, it is not at all clear why the democratic son should be considered inferior to his oligarchic father who has spent his life pursuing money, despoiling others. The young democrat seems to be a rather charming, if aimless, fellow. It is easy to see why a democratic regime might well be considered inferior to an oligarchic one, but this would only serve to show the difference between the solid life of the city and the agreeable life of man. Neither the oligarchic nor democratic regime or man is devoted to any virtue, but at least the democratic man's principle does not preclude the practice of virtue. As has been observed, this judgment against the democratic man is part of a general condemnation of desire leading to the condemnation of the tyrant, who is taken to be *the* man of desire. The desires are interpreted as the bodily desires which, when emancipated, are infinite and make man's needs infinite. Their moderation is necessary both for political stability and for the possibility of philosophizing. For the many, the praise of desire is the praise of bodily desire, and this must be controlled for the sake of both philosophy and politics.

But this is only a partial account, for among the objects that the disorganized democrat pursues, on the same level as flute-playing and dieting, is philosophy. To him it is not a serious occupation, but democracy is nevertheless the only one of the practicable regimes in which philosophy makes an appearance. Democracy is merely indifferent to philosophy, while the other regimes are positively hostile to it. The moral or fiscal austerity of timocracy and oligarchy preclude the leisure necessary to philosophy and condemn the thought produced by it; at the same time, life in these regimes is too organized for philosophy to be able to escape unnoticed for long. And the tyrant is frightened by the wise and free-minded. Philosophy is among the unnecessary desires and hence finds its home in democracy. Timocracy, the best practicable regime, is the regime furthest removed from philosophy; paradoxically, Socrates the citizen praises timocracy, while Socrates the philosopher desires democracy. He is actually engaged in a defense of democracy against its enemies, the potential tyrants and the lovers of Sparta, not because he can be dedicated to democracy but precisely because it does not demand dedication. After showing the impossibility, and perhaps the undesirability, of a regime to which he could be dedicated, he progressively abandons it in favor of the regime which leaves him free, the only real regime in which he can prosper.

Socrates' harsh and apparently insensitive criticism of tragedy as a servant of democracy, and particularly of tyranny, is part of the same condemnation of desire which leads him in this context to prefer the oligarch to the democrat. Tragedy is indeed the taste of democracies and tyrannies, as opposed to timocracies and oligarchies. The other cities are too busy to develop such tastes and consider them a danger to moral virtue or to sound economics. Tragedy requires the emancipation of, and the appeal to, desires which are denied or suppressed in the other regimes. Tragedy, therefore, encourages those desires and must be condemned insofar as those regimes are inferior. But if democracy and tyranny contain elements of humanity lacking in other regimes, tragedy's alliance with them may be partially justified. Specifically, the very desires which existed but were denied to exist in other regimes are the themes of tragedy. Thus, tragedy can both learn and teach about man in the inferior regimes where these desires are permitted. In one sense, it is a mistake to give way to these desires, but to turn one's back on them is to misunderstand man. And the suppression of these desires is allied with the suppression of philosophy. Just as philosophy is unnecessary, so is poetry. The real quarrel with tragedy does not concern its implicit rejection of the self-control requisite to timocracy and oligarchy, but rather the absence in it of any knowledge of the true aristocracy and, because it lacks that counterpoise, the consequent inclination to take the desires and passions too seriously. This criticism of poetry in Book VIII prepares the way for the re-examination of philosophy's powerful opponent in Book X.

(571a–592b) At last Socrates comes to his description of the tyrant. He is the public fulfillment of the private desires which first quietly entered the city hidden in the soul of the timocratic man. Once the pleasure of philosophy has disappeared, man is split between duty and desire with no adequate motive for the choice of duty over desire. Socrates indicates that the tyrant's life would be the appropriate choice of a way of life if philosophy did not exist, if the bodily pleasures were the only pleasures and the mind had no pleasures of its own. The self-control demanded by morality has no cosmic support if it is not in the service of a higher pleasure. The timocratic man's devotion to duty is groundless, and the oligarchic and democratic men represent unsteady compromises between duty and desire. Socrates can only prove the inferiority of the tyrannic life to Glaucon by way of the superiority of the philosophic life, of which Glaucon has only a glimmering. To be sure, he has been prepared for the choice by the beautiful images of the philosophic life in Book VII and by the moral indignation evoked by the decay of political life depicted in Book VIII. But, although all men readily admit that to live under a tyranny is the worst of political fates, they are not so ready to admit that the tyrant is the unhappiest of men, precisely because he has succeeded in winning the struggle for those scarce goods which reputedly make a man happy. It is to this problem that Socrates addresses himself in Book IX.

Socrates characterizes the tyrant as the erotic man; and *eros,* as Cephalus said in the very beginning of the dialogue, is a mad master. Socrates now makes a further distinction among the unnecessary desires; some of them are law-abiding, and others are law-breaking. The erotic desires lead to breaking of the law, to daring everything, to that omnivorous taste for all good things which makes a man the enemy of law and other men. The democratic man was unerotic, and this gave him an easygoing, harmless quality and rendered him innocuous. His lack of erotic passion prevented him from taking anything very seriously. This is not the case with a man whose sexual passion is very intense. Glaucon is such a man, and it is the wish to satisfy this part of his nature that attracts him to tyranny; for tyranny is the only regime in which no satisfaction can be denied him—it provides the freedom, power, and money a lover needs. *Eros* is the most dangerous and powerful of the desires, an infinite longing which consumes all other attachments in its heat. It, too, however, is ambiguous. Up to this point the *Republic* has continuously attacked *eros* when it has not overlooked it. It is hard to imagine that its author is also the author of the *Symposium* and the *Phaedrus.* But it must be observed that the *eros* attacked is the lust for other bodies, and that this is done in the name of both politics and philosophy. Politics seems to be hostile to any form of extreme eroticism, but what about philosophy? It is clear in Books VI and VII that love of wisdom is a form of *eros,* and that the hostility to *eros* is limited to the kind which precludes the development of philosophic *eros.* The political and philosophic critiques of *eros* are therefore not in total harmony. If the radically incomplete discussion of the soul in the *Republic* were to be made comprehensive, it would have to be enlarged to provide an adequate account of *eros.* (For example, in Book IX it becomes clear that the spirited and rational parts of the soul have their specific desires; desire is not limited to the lowest part which has been called the desiring part.) The present interpretation of *eros* does serve the purpose of moderating Glaucon's passion, which is both anti-political and anti-philosophic. But the obvious incompleteness of this understanding of *eros* leads to an awareness of a hidden kinship between the tyrant and the philosopher. There are certain kinds of things (for example, incest) which a gentleman is not even willing to think about, let alone do. Sometimes against his will such things find expression in his dreams. The tyrant is willing both to think about them and to do them when wide awake. The philosopher, as we have seen in the *Republic,* is at least willing to think about them, and they hold none of the peculiar horror for him that they do for the gentleman. This is because both tyrant and philosopher depreciate law or convention *(nomos)* in their quest for nature *(physis)*. *Eros* is nature's demonic voice. The tyrant and the philosopher are united in their sense of their radical incompleteness and their longing for wholeness, in their passion and in their singlemindedness. They are the truly dedicated men.

The potential tyrant, if saved from corruption, may also very well be the potential philosopher. The young man drawn to tyranny, like the philosopher, is allowed to flourish only in the democracy. Socrates, by curing Glaucon of his lust for tyrannic pleasures, can indulge his own lust for beautiful souls while at the same time acting the part of the good citizen who defends his city's regime. The democracy satisfies everything: it lets Socrates be a philosopher, at least until he is seventy; it provides him with students by allowing the emergence of unnecessary and unlawful desires; and by permitting him to convert those possessed by these desires to philosophy, it gives him the opportunity to show that he loves his country.

Socrates attempts to prove to Glaucon that the tyrant is the unhappiest of men. His argument consists of two parts. In the first place, the tyrant cannot fulfill his desires; he must always continue his longing, become hated, and do every terrible deed. In sum, he is the least self-sufficient of men, utterly dependent on external things and thus full of anxiety. Second, the tyrannic life is not the pleasantest life. The latter argument is again divided into two parts. According to the first, each of the three parts of the soul has its own specific pleasure. The man who knows all three pleasures would be the best judge of which is the greatest pleasure. Only the philosopher knows all three, however, and he chooses the pleasure of philosophy. According to the second part of the argument, the tyrant's pleasures are all mixed and allied to pain, while the philosophic pleasures are pure. The tyrant's pleasures are unreal because they are linked to becoming which is itself somehow unreal; the philosopher is attached to being, and hence his pleasures are real. It will be noted that Socrates makes the choice between tyranny and philosophy depend on pleasure.

This aspect of the teaching of the *Republic* is powerfully presented by Aristotle in *Politics* (II, vii). In criticizing an economic solution of the political problem advanced by Phaleas of Chalcedon, Aristotle asserts that there are three causes of men's doing injustice: want of the necessities, desire for more than what is necessary, and desire to enjoy independent pleasures which are pure and unmixed with pain. In Socrates' presentation the oligarch is preoccupied with the necessary, the democrat with the unnecessary, and the tyrant with the unlawful pleasures. Aristotle explicitly identifies the man who wishes the pleasures which have no admixture of pain with the one who commits the greatest crimes and longs for tyranny. He also indicates that this is the most interesting kind of man. He suggests three cures for the three causes of injustice: a small amount of property and work, moderation, and philosophy. The quest for pure pleasures is the motivation of the higher kind of free man who no longer has to worry about the necessary. But this quest can only be fulfilled through philosophy because "the other [pleasures] require human beings." Only philosophy is pure pleasure and is self-sufficient, not entailing the use of other men. Most radically posed, the moral problem consists in a simple alternative: either philosophy or tyranny is the best way of life. Other solutions are only halfway measures. If philosophy did not exist, tyranny would be the desideratum which only a lack of vigor would cause one to reject.

This choice between the philosophic and tyrannic lives explains the plot of the *Republic*. Socrates takes a young man tempted by the tyrannic life and attempts to give him at least that modicum of awareness of philosophy which will cure him of the lust for tyranny. Any other exhortation would amount to empty moralism. The young man drawn to tyranny is the illustration of Aristotle's maxims that man is both the best and the worst of animals, and that the man living outside the city (in the sense of not participating in its law) must be either a god or a beast. In the *Republic* Socrates has included both god and beast in the city, and this accounts for the difference between his political science and Aristotle's. Socrates, unlike Aristotle, makes *eros* a political principle. Although tyranny and the tyrannic man are in one way the furthest from philosophy, they are in another the nearest to it. This is why Socrates is attracted to those dangerous young men, the potential tyrants, who are products of the democracy. With some of these young men (for example, Critias and Alcibiades) his training failed, and as a result he was condemned. But with others (for example, Xenophon and Plato) he succeeded, and they have exculpated him.

Since the time when Glaucon first asked for a comparison of the lives of the just and unjust men, the action of the *Republic* has steadily moved toward it. The question has changed en route, for the comparison is now between the philosopher and the tyrant; this would not have satisfied Glaucon at the beginning, nor does it prove the superiority of justice over injustice, unless justice is philosophy and injustice tyranny. But such a comparison does cast light on the original problem; although the just man on the rack is not proved to be happy, it is clear that happiness does not depend on anything tyranny can acquire. Glaucon's notion of the good things has been altered by the marvelous things he has experienced in this conversation. Previously he thought that both just and unjust man desired the same things; now he sees the possibility of a life—the life of Socrates—which is self-sufficient and happy. The needfulness of tyranny has become questionable, and Glaucon will never again be able to pose the problem as he once did. Happiness is not connected with the exploitation of other human beings. Socrates makes an image of the soul for Glaucon's benefit; the desiring part is compared to a many-headed beast, the spirited part to a lion, and the rational part to a man. Socrates thus explains that the laws which impose moderation are not made in the interest of an exploiter but in the interest of the soul as opposed to the body, of reason as opposed to desire. This would, of course, hold true only in the best regime, but Glaucon himself is now able to say that that makes no difference. Previously it had appeared that one must found a city and live within it to be a complete man, but now it appears that a man can be happy on his own. The good city exists only in speech and is a pattern in the sky for those who want to live well; justice is obedience to the laws of that regime. At last man can break from the earthly city, and Glaucon has gained an inner freedom from its claims and its charms.

(595a–608b) With the confrontation of the philosopher and the tyrant, the discussion appears to have reached its end, but Socrates once more raises the subject of poetry. This is surprising, and it is difficult to see why we should return to this topic after the lengthy discussion of it in Book III. That treatment, however, dealt only with the uses and disadvantages of poetry in the education of the warriors, men who needed courage and the salutary tales which would encourage it. Homer is the teacher of the Greeks, and his title to that role must be examined. In the earlier discussion, Homer's hero, Achilles, was the theme; in this discussion, Homer himself is the theme. The light tone adopted by Socrates here, the ease with which he apparently dismisses poetry, must not cause one to forget that he is taking it very seriously indeed. Poetry is *the* opponent, and there is an ancient quarrel between it and philosophy. Homer is read or listened to by all the Greeks; he speaks of all things in their interrelations, and he tells of the gods. Homer and the other great poets constitute the respectable tribunal before which philosophy is tried. Socrates is afraid of being denounced to them, as though they were the law; and in a sense they do reflect that law and determine the opinions that make it. However, Book X attempts to reverse this situation. Socrates begins by making an *apology* to the poets and ends by opening the way for them to make an *apology* to him. Socrates does not wish to destroy poetry; he only wishes to judge it, rather than be judged by it.

The other themes of Book X help to clarify the grounds for this final consideration of poetry. The immortality of the soul and the rewards of justice are also discussed, particularly the rewards after death. Moreover, Book X culminates in a poetic myth; after appearing to reject poetry, Socrates uses it to describe the *cosmos* and the fate of man, the broadest possible objects of human discourse. Poetry is necessary to Socrates' project of reforming Glaucon, but it must be a new kind of poetry, one which can sustain Glaucon in a life of moral virtue and respect for philosophy. It is not, then, that poetry must be entirely banished but that it must be reformed. Book X begins with a criticism of Homeric poetry and ends with an example of Socratic poetry. Separating the two is a discussion of the immortality of the soul. The difference between the old poetry and the new lies in their understanding of the soul; the old poetry seems to lead necessarily to a view of the soul which is inimical to philosophy. The *cosmos* or *chaos* of pre-Socratic poetry contained no support for either the moral or theoretical life. The River Ocean which surrounds Homer's world is a thing of constant, meaningless change. Poetry, taken on its own ground, portraying those subjects on which it can best reveal its powers, culminates in the hero Achilles. And it is Achilles who bemoans his fate and asserts his preference for serfdom on earth to the kingdom over the dead. Life, mere life, is all that counts, for what is beyond it is a void, justifying neither a life of nobility nor one of learning.

The text for *Republic*, Book X, is *Odyssey*, Book XI, the account of Odysseus' visit to the dead. The difference between Odysseus' experiences among the dead and those of Er is an indication of what Socrates is trying to teach. Er found rewards and punishments for just and unjust souls; but, more important, he also found an order of the universe which makes this world intelligible and provides a ground for the contemplative life. At the source of all things, Er saw that soul is the first principle of the cosmic order; hence the proper study of the universe is the study of the soul. What is best in man is not in conflict but in harmony with the nature of things. The myth of Er is only a tale, just as is Odysseus' descent to Hades; there is small likelihood that Socrates believed in the survival of the individual soul. But this tale is a poetic reflection of the view which makes philosophy possible just as it is indicated that Homer's tale reflects the view connected with an autonomous poetry. Men need poetry, but the kind of poetry which nourishes their souls makes all the difference in their understanding of their nonpoetic lives. Socrates outlines a new kind of poetry which leads beyond itself, which does not present man's only alternatives as tragic or comic, which supports the philosophic life. He gives the principle which Aristotle developed in the *Poetics,* and which is embodied in the works of men such as Dante and Shakespeare. It is still poetry, but poetry which points beyond itself.

Socrates begins his quarrel with Homer by asking Glaucon what he would think of a craftsman who "is not only able to make all implements but also makes everything that grows naturally from the earth, and produces all animals—the others and himself too—and, in addition, produces earth and heaven and gods and everything in heaven and everything in Hades under the earth." Glaucon responds that such a man must be a most amazing sophist, but Socrates hastens to assure him that this maker's power is nothing surprising and is within everyone's reach. Socrates tells Glaucon, ". . . if you are willing to take a mirror and carry it around everywhere, quickly you will make the sun and the things in the heaven; quickly, the earth; and quickly, yourself and the other implements and plants and everything else that was just now mentioned" (596c–e). This seems an almost unbelievably crude and insensitive way to depreciate the value of poetry's representations. Socrates accuses the poet of being a charlatan who deceives men and who has no claim to wisdom whatsoever. However, a closer examination of the passages cited will show that Socrates' point here is subtler than immediately appears. The man who carries the mirror around will not catch the reflections of some of the things which appeared in the sophist's mirror: no ordinary mirror can reflect the gods and the things in Hades; the sun would have to take their place. Only the poets and the painters can reproduce the gods and the life after death, and they have no models for their imitation of them in the works of other craftsmen or in the visible universe. The poets are the authentic, the only, teachers about the gods.* The great mystery is how they find out about them, how they are able to present them to men. Socratic poetry

*The difference between the mirror held to nature and the product of the imitative sophist is parallel to the difference between the lowest level of the divided line—where things are seen reflected in water or on smooth surfaces—and the wall of the cave—where the prisoners see the reflections of artifacts, only some of which have natural models. The prisoners' problem is ascending toward truth. The cause of their errors is connected with this mixture of natural and man-made things. In this discussion of poetry Socrates elaborates that problem and reveals the essential character of the cave.

also must tell about the gods and the afterlife. This does not constitute the difference between the old poetry and the new; the gods are the center, not to say the essence, of both. The real quarrel between Socrates and Homer concerns the way in which one finds out about the gods, or the view of the whole which causes a poet to present the gods in one way rather than another. Socrates' criticism of Homeric poetry is really a study of the principles of his theogony or theology, a study of the nature of the Homeric gods.

Socrates' first step in his analysis of Homeric wisdom is to attempt to establish the nature of a poem. A poem, he asserts, like a painting, is a particular being which has a curious sort of existence. It represents other particular beings which are beings because they, in turn, partake of a single, self-subsistent being. Poetry is dependent on the world around us; it does not make its objects, and its strength comes from the depth of its grasp of those objects. Socrates makes the point that Homer's book presupposes knowledge of the book of the world, which Homer does not make; he is not creative and must be judged by that external standard. Poetry is imitation. Now Socrates takes the strange step of testing the poet's knowledge by comparing it to the knowledge of the artisan who makes the thing imitated. This procedure has a kind of surface plausibility, in that the poem does indeed imitate the objects of the various arts, and that the knowledge of the latter belongs to the practitioners of those arts. In this way the poet comes off very badly indeed because he is surely not a knower of all the diverse arts; his representation is only a shadow of the competent opinions of the artisans. But all of this is somehow very wrong. In the first place, not everything represented in poetry is an artifact; indeed, its most interesting objects are not products of art. Second, poetry presents its objects in their interrelations, as no particular art can do. The specialist in health does not as such know the proper uses of a healthy body. Poetry is essentially comprehensive or synoptic, and this distinguishes it from the special arts. The poem is a collection of imitations, but it is informed by the vision of the poet, a vision that transcends the level of the special arts.

The further development of the argument gradually reveals the reasons for this unusual presentation. Since it has been determined that the artisans are the standard of knowledge, it follows that if Homer is to be authoritative, he must have exercised all of the arts or at least the most important ones. Homer, if he was so skilled and is an appropriate teacher of the Greeks, should be famous for his deeds as well as his speeches. His favorite themes are human virtues and vices, so it is proper to see what he did as a legislator, general, educator, etc. It is evident that he had a reputation in none of these fields, and it is even said that he was neglected and abandoned in his own lifetime. It therefore follows that Homer is not a reliable teacher of the most important human things. The tacit assumption of the argument is that it is better to be a doer than a knower, or that knowledge is only tested in action—in benefits to other men.

But a moment's reflection makes one aware that these charges against Homer apply at least as well to Socrates. He was not a lawgiver, a leader in war, an inventor, or a professor in the manner of Protagoras; there was also no way of life named after Socrates as there was a Pythagorean way of life. He was worse than neglected by his contemporaries. Yet he, too, understood himself to be wise in human things. The authority to talk about human things does not come from the study of any of the arts, and Homer and Socrates are one in their neglect of the arts and their divorce from the practical life. What Socrates shows in this presentation is that the ordinary standards for judgment of the worth of an activity or depth of wisdom are not applicable to Homer or himself. Wisdom has another source than art, and there is another kind of relation to the *ideas* than that of the artisan. A wise man is judged, not by any deed that he performs, but by the quality of his knowledge. And that knowledge is not like that of the artisan who produces something which can be used and who deals with a special subject matter. Wisdom is sought for its own sake, and it is comprehensive, interrelating the various arts and their products. Both Homer and Socrates in some way possess this kind of knowledge; they both have a view of the whole. Homer produces a product as the artisans do, but that product is distinguished from the artisans' products in that it reflects a view of the whole, and its maker is by his very nature a man who must reflect on the whole.

What Socrates implicitly criticizes Homer for is that he cannot explain the grounds for that view of the whole or for the way of life devoted to knowing it. Homer appears as a celebrator of heroes, of men of action, and hence as their inferior. Speech seems to be subordinate to deed. Nothing in the Homeric poems indicates the dignity of the poet; there are no heroes who give an account of the poet's own doings, nor is there a picture of a universe which makes it possible to comprehend the possibility of wisdom. Socrates accuses Homer of not reflecting on himself, and hence making a world in which there is no place for himself. His poem is not a compendium of imitations of the various arts because it is animated by a view of the whole. But because he does not provide a basis for that view, because the truth of that view is not the center of the poet's concern, Socrates is legitimated in treating him as though he were merely a universal imitator of the arts to be judged by every artisan, or an incompetent statesman. This line of reasoning serves to point up the way in which Homer differs from the artisans and the men of action and is like Socrates. They are both devoted to the most comprehensive understanding of things. The real question, then, is what is the source and status of the view of the whole which informs Homer's works?

In the next part of the discussion Socrates explores this question. He had earlier asserted that the painter, or, implicitly, the poet, is one of three craftsmen who in a way make the same product and that he stands farthest of the three from what *is*. A divine craftsman makes the idea, for example, of a bed. (The *ideas* were in this context understood not as eternal but as the product of art, thus constituting a world in which artisans or makers, rather than knowers, are the highest human beings.) A human craftsman looks to the *idea* of a bed and makes a bed. And the painter or poet looks to the bed made by the human craftsman and makes an image of a bed. He is thus an imitator of an imitator and his products have very little reality. Now, however, Socrates abandons the reference to the *ideas* and their maker, and no longer asserts that the craftsman look to *ideas* in their making. He substitutes a common-sense notion for all of this. The craftsman is indeed dependent, however, not on an *idea* but on the command of the man who uses his products. The poet is still at the bottom, but now there is a human being at the top who practices what Socrates calls the user's art. The horseman, who knows the equipment necessary to using a horse well, can tell the artisans what he needs and give them their impulse without knowing their arts; he is more important than they are, and the end of their activity is his activity. The user's art comes closer to poetry and philosophy in that it, too, deals with the relations of things and is not restricted to any single art. The broadest such art would be the one that treats of happiness—the legislator's art. The legislator organizes the whole city with a view to the good life—the end of all action—and the various arts ultimately are guided by the role their products play in that life. The horseman who told the saddlemaker and the blacksmith what he needed, is, in turn, told by the general what is needed from the cavalry; and the general, finally, is told by the statesmen or the legislator what the army must do. Only the legislator oversees the whole; and by looking to the legislator, the artisans know what the purpose or end of their products is. There is no *idea* which the legislator can look to and imitate mechanically; his art comprises wisdom entire. *The* user's art is political science, of which Socrates is the founder. To follow out the image of the *Republic*, the sheep are guarded by dogs who are obedient to shepherds who are in the service of owners: the people are guarded by warriors who are obedient to guardians who are ultimately obedient to philosophers or who are philosophers themselves. In the best case the legislators are philosophers, but in any case the legislator is the master of the city.

In this perspective it becomes clear what Socrates means when he says that the poet is an imitator of an imitator. The poet imitates the legislator. He must appeal to an audience; and in that sense he imitates the tastes and passions of that audience. But the tastes and passions of the audience have been formed by the legislator, who is understood to be the craftsman who builds the city according to the pattern provided by his view of nature. Thus the poet, who looks to the audience which looks to the legislator, is at the third remove from nature. The poet's function leads him to be a servant of convention; his works give the illusion of nature, but are fundamentally affected by convention, and thus they deceive man in his quest for nature. To put the same thing in a different way, the poet must imitate heroes in his poems. But those heroes are the heroes of his nation who are also children of the legislator or the founder of the Greek way of life. Because the poet looks to what is around him or is conveyed by the tradition, and because he must appeal to an audience, he is peculiarly prone to become involved in the popular prejudices. Rousseau, in his *Letter to d'Alembert*, has accurately reproduced this aspect of Socrates' critique of poetry and given it a modern force. What Socrates stresses is that there is nothing in the poet's art which impels him to the discovery of what is truly natural and much that inclines him to serve convention. If a poet shares the perspective of the philosophic legislator, if he is capable of the moral and intellectual virtue required for such a liberation, and if that perspective can inform his poetry, Socrates has no quarrel with him.

From this viewpoint, one can also understand what Socrates meant by treating the poet as an imitator of artifacts. In one sense man is a natural being, but in another he is a product of *nomos*, convention. Men and men's ways differ from place to place as trees and their ways do not. The law transforms men to such an extent that many can doubt whether there is such a thing as human nature at all. Even if there is a natural man, or, more classically expressed, a man who lives according to nature, civil society and its laws must aid in his coming to be. Civil men, the dwellers in the cave, are in the decisive sense the artifacts of the legislator: their opinions are made by him. Human making has a great deal to do with our perception of even the things which seem most unambiguously natural. Men see the beautiful sunset, the noble river, the terrifying storm or the sacred cow. To know these things we must separate what belongs to them naturally from what opinion adds to them. Poetry tends to blend the natural and conventional elements in things; and it charms men in such a way that they no longer see the seams of the union of these two elements.

It is not sufficient, however, to say that the poet is an imitator of an imitator, for Socrates knows that the poet is not simply slavishly subservient to the law and the legislator. The tragic poet depicts men's misfortunes and their lamentations. In Book III it was stated that good men do not suffer at the loss of those dear to them, and the poets had been commanded to so depict them. Now Socrates admits that they do indeed lament, but they do so in private. The poet's fault lies in publicizing what is properly private. His crime consists of breaking the legislator's command that moral virtue must always be represented as leading to happiness. In other words, the poet tells the truth about the passions, a truth suppressed by the law. Men are attached to their own things, and much of the significance of life comes from those things, which are not necessarily acquired or kept by the exercise of the moral virtues. The legislator taught that nobility and happiness are one; the poets separate the two and reveal the truth. As a matter of fact, the legislator, as we saw in Book III, turns to the poet when he wishes to learn the nature of the human passions. In order to know what in man has to be overcome in order to establish a good regime, Socrates studies Homer.

Homer, then, is not Socrates' opponent because he knows nothing of nature. It is rather because he knows only that part of nature which causes men to laugh or cry, the part that makes human life appear either ridiculous or miserable. The poets deal with the failures of acting men and show what the *Republic* has also shown—that the practical or moral life is essentially self-contradictory and is hence either comic or tragic. But the poets do not show, and perhaps do not believe in, the possibility of a noncontradictory life lived by a man who is neither comic nor tragic. They water man's laughter and his pity without giving him a counterpoise; hence they justify laughter and pity as ultimate responses to the human situation. Pity, in particular, is a passion connected with one's own possible sufferings; it sees the losses suffered by even the noblest of men and recognizes how threatened are the things for which a man lives. Pity, grown great, ends in terror caused by the misery of man's existence. The man overwhelmed by pity and fear is the man least of all able to forget himself and his own, and hence the things that will protect him and give his life meaning. Most of all, he looks to the laws and the gods, and his pity can well make him a fanatic. The natural passions of men which Homer knows and appeals to are those that most attach a man to convention and hence to bondage in the cave. And the Homeric gods are such as to encourage and satisfy the pitying part of man's soul.

Socrates admits the overwhelming charm of poetry, a charm composed of elements drawn on the one hand, from the attachment to one's particular existence and what is connected with it, and, on the other hand, from the pleasure which accompanies the contemplation of the truth. But the truth which poetry reveals is only a partial truth, and, in liberating from the conventions or laws of a city, it can contribute to an enslavement to the source of convention, the love of one's own. Reason is the only instrument with which to fight laughter and pity. But poetry belongs essentially to the faculty of imagination, a faculty necessary to reasoning, one, however, which can also be at war with it. The overcoming of the attachment to one's own is a monstrous endeavor, and the passions served by poetry rebel against it; but that endeavor is necessary to philosophy.

This, then, is the essence of the quarrel between philosophy and poetry. Socrates banishes poetry once more, but this time offers it a return if it can learn to argue, to justify itself before the bar of philosophy. He points the way to Aristotle's understanding of tragedy as a purgation of the passions of pity and fear rather than their satisfaction. Such tragedy would prepare a man to be reasonable and moderate after having purged those terrible passions; it would pay due attention to man's necessary love of his own, but would temper it in such a way as to allow him some freedom from it. Thus tragedy would neither give way to these passions nor deny their existence. It would then be an important part of the education of decent, unfanatic men. Poetry will return, but only after having learned to subordinate itself, to mitigate its unguided tendencies toward indulgence and fanaticism. When the poets depict the gods they must no longer look to laughter and pity but to the *ideas*.

(*608c–621d*) The discussion of poetry is a preparation for a discussion of the rewards and punishments of justice and injustice. Poetry will tell, as it always has, the tales of the wages of virtue in this life and the next. The theme appears to be more appropriate to poetic than philosophic treatment, both in terms of the things discussed and the audience to which it is relevant. Socrates, in undertaking this discussion, disobeys Glaucon's explicit command, for the latter had insisted that a true praise of justice in itself would have to abstract from any rewards extrinsic to justice which might accrue to it. Socrates thus returns to the conventional way of praising justice which Adeimantus has criticized. Glaucon and Adeimantus permit Socrates to do so because they are now more favorably disposed to justice; Socrates must do so because the dialogue has not sufficiently demonstrated that citizen virtue is choiceworthy for itself, and Glaucon and Adeimantus are not capable of philosophic virtue.

The first step of the praise is to extend the range of consideration beyond this life to eternity because eternity is the proper study of man, and because the promiscuity of fortune in this life would tend to make men believe that justice goes unrewarded and injustice unpunished. So Socrates undertakes to convince Glaucon that the soul is immortal. This discussion can hardly rank as a proof, and there is no attempt at all to show that the *individual* soul is immortal, which is the only thing a man anxious about his fate after life would care about. Moreover, Socrates admits that we know nothing about the soul, which denies the value of the argument, calling into question the teaching of the whole dialogue which was based on an understanding of the soul. This discussion then serves two purposes: to cause the unphilosophic man to be concerned about justice for fear of what will happen to him in another world, and to turn philosophic men to the study of the soul. The soul is *the* philosophic question, and it is his concern for this question that distinguishes Socrates from his predecessors; the most characteristic part of his teaching is that soul is irreducible and that it is somehow the principle of the *cosmos*. The shade of Achilles in Hades is offensive not only to good morals but to the possibility of philosophy, for Achilles seems to show that the human soul has no support in the *cosmos*. Socratic thought combines the apparently contradictory concerns of earlier poetry and earlier philosophy; he can understand man and understand nature, for the two are informed by the same principle, soul. The *Republic*, which seems to give a completed teaching about politics and the soul, ends with a return to philosophic doubt, to the conviction that one's opinions are open to unanswered, if not unanswerable, questions. In one sense one can even say that the book has taught us nothing other than the necessity of philosophy and its priority and superiority to the political life.

The myth of Er merely reiterates this message. According to this myth there is a rational cosmic order to which each individual's fate is attached. In the afterlife happiness and misery are distributed according to virtues and vices practiced during life. This encourages decent men to persist in their efforts to be virtuous; for if they succeed, a wonderful thousand-year voyage through the heavens awaits them. But the myth also makes clear that the civic virtues do not suffice for a man's salvation for all eternity, and that, unless he has philosophized on earth, this voyage will profit him nothing. For each man must choose a new life, and that new life will determine whether he will fare well or ill in his next thousand-year sojourn among the dead; the correct choice of a life depends on knowledge of the soul, not on the practice of moral virtue. Those who have been rewarded for moral virtue in the afterlife are less well prepared than are those who have been punished to make the proper choice of life. We see a decent man, one like Cephalus, who has just come from his rewards, choose a tyrant's life; for only law and convention had kept him in bounds in his earlier life, and his real view of happiness led him to envy tyrants. He has learned nothing in the afterlife; there is apparently no philosophy in the afterlife for those who did not practice it on earth; the soul is not perfected by the separation from the body. For all men other than the philosopher, there is a constant change of fortune from happiness to misery and back. The myth attributes full responsibility to men for what happens to them and thus teaches that there is no sin but ignorance.

The key to Er's account of his visit to the other world is the absence of Achilles. He says that Ajax was the twentieth soul he saw. Ajax was the twentieth shade seen by Odysseus on his voyage to Hades; one of the shades which accompanied Ajax and the one with which Odysseus spoke just prior to speaking with Ajax was that of Achilles, who at that point made his complaint about Hades quoted at the beginning of Book III. Er makes no mention of whom he saw with Ajax. Achilles no longer exists, alive or dead, in the new poetry or the new Socratic world. Correspondingly, the wise voyager Odysseus gains higher status. All he needed was to be cured of love of honor (a form of spiritedness), and he could live the obscure but happy life of Socrates. In this Socrates also gets his inspiration from Homer, and thus he lets us know that there may be another side to Homer's poetry than that which the tradition had popularized. At all events, the teaching of the myth is a strictly human one—man in this life, without being other worldly—can attain self-sufficient happiness in the exercise of his natural powers and only in this way will he partake of eternity to the extent a human being can do so. Otherwise stated, only the philosopher has no need of the myth.

On this note the discussion ends, Glaucon having learned his lesson in moderation, and Socrates thereby having made his *apology*—the *apology* of a man who benefits others because he first of all knows how to benefit himself.

NOTES

NOTES

Book I

1. "Republic" is the English equivalent of Cicero's Latin translation of the Greek title *Politeia*. The word does not convey precisely the correct connotation to us, although the great weight of the tradition hinders us from changing the English rendition of the title itself. The word *politeia* is ultimately derived from *polis* (by way of *politēs*, citizen), as are many of the important political terms in Plato's vocabulary.

The *polis* is the city, the community of men sharing a way of life and governing themselves, waging war and preserving the peace. The *polis* is the natural social group, containing all that is necessary for the development and exercise of the human powers. Today *polis* is usually translated as "city-state"; this is done because it is recognized that a polis is not a state in the modern sense (for example, state as distinguished from society), and that the character of ancient political life was radically different from our own. However, to translate *polis* as "city-state" implies that our notion of state is somehow contained in that of the *polis*, although only half-consciously. Hence the ancient understanding of political things is taken as an imperfect prefiguration of the modern one rather than as an alternative to it—an alternative alien and not adequately known to us. In this edition it will always be rendered "city," on the assumption that the phenomena the *polis* comprises can be comprehended by comparing the various uses of the word. Moreover, it should be borne in mind that words like "statesman" and "citizen" are based on the root *polis*. The citizen (*politēs*) is literally "one who belongs to the city," and the statesman (*politikos*) is "one who knows the things of the city." Politics (*politika*) is merely "what has to do with the city." Thus, there is a unity of terminology which reflects the unity of life in the city.

Now the *polis* is given its character and its peculiar way of life is established by the organization of the city's diverse elements. The central political concern is the proper organization of a city, and the *politeia* is that organization. The *politeia* can largely be identified with the class of citizens who rule, for they impress their way on the city and are the source of the laws. The *politeia* is, as it were, the soul of the city; the *politeia* is related to the individuals who compose the city as form is to matter. The best English term for translating it is "regime," as in "the old regime." The book which describes the best political life is appropriately entitled "the regime," the only true or the best regime, just as the book of all books is entitled simply the *Bible*, the book. Such an approach to the political problem is characteristically Platonic, and an attempt to recover the Greek understanding of human things requires a consideration of the sense in which the *politeia* is the single most important political fact and the cause of men's characters and ways of life. The use of this word should, therefore, be followed attentively throughout this book. [Cf. Leo Strauss, *Natural Right and History* (Chicago: University of Chicago Press, 1953), pp. 135–139; and Harry V. Jaffa, "Aristotle," in Strauss and Cropsey, eds., *History of Political Philosophy*, (Chicago: Rand McNally, 1963), pp. 65–68.]

2. *On the Just* is a subtitle which may have been added by later editors. It is not mentioned by Aristotle in his account of the *Republic* in the *Politics* (126la ff.).

3. The Piraeus is the port of Athens, situated some six miles from the city. As the center of Athenian commerce, it was the place to find all the diversity and disorder that come from foreign lands. It was, therefore, the appropriate place in which to consider outlandish ways of life. Furthermore, it was a center of the democratic party. Sometime after the supposed date of the action of this dialogue (probably around 411 B.C.), in 404 B.C., the Piraeus was the stronghold of the resistance against the despotic group of men, known as the "Thirty Tyrants," who ruled Athens after its defeat by Sparta in the Peloponnesian War. In that resistance, the family of Cephalus, especially Lysias (cf. 328b and note 7), played a leading role. Polemarchus was executed by the tyrants. Socrates was suspected of sympathy with and influence over the leaders of the tyranny because several had been among his companions. In the *Apology* (32c–d) he makes a point of showing his disagreement with this oligarchy, and the grounds of that disagreement. But his position in relation to the democracy remains ambiguous. The conversation in the *Republic* takes place in the shadow of the "Thirty." They had much to do with the execution, not only of Polemarchus, but also, indirectly, of Socrates; and the dialogue treats, at least in part, of the tyrannical ambitions of Socrates' companions. The men who gather here in happy days for a theoretical conversation are soon to fall on evil ones in the practice of politics. The problems of that practice, which are later to be revealed in deed, are here discussed. This is the drama of the *Republic*, without which its teaching cannot be understood. This

friendly association of ten men with whom Socrates talks in the Piraeus will be replaced by a committee of ten men who brutally rule there in the name of the "Thirty" and put the host of this meeting to death. The participants discuss the best regime but are to experience the worst.

4. Ariston was Plato's father, and Glaucon and Adeimantus were his brothers (cf. 368a).

5. Apparently the festival of Bendis (cf. 354a). Bendis was a foreign goddess; she was related to the moon by the Thracians who worshiped her. The Piraeus seems to have been a center for innovations in everything, including religion.

6. At the end of this scene, which is a dramatic prefiguration of the whole political problem, Socrates uses this word as it was used in the political assembly to announce that the sovereign authority had passed a law or decree. It is the expression with which the laws begin, "It is resolved by [literally, 'it seems to'] the Athenian people. . . ."

7. One of the classic Attic orators. He played an important role in the overthrow of the "Thirty" and the restoration of the democracy.

8. A man who taught rhetoric, the art of political and legal persuasion, and who earned his living from his teaching.

9. Paeania was a *deme* or township. These were the ancient divisions of Athens which had later been politically submerged in the Cleisthenic division of the city into tribes. They still retained their identity, and Plato frequently uses the name of the *deme* as a substitute for the patronymic in the identification of individuals.

10. There is a short dialogue that bears his name. It is the natural introduction to the *Republic* in that it discusses Socrates' way of teaching virtue, particularly justice, and compares it with that of Thrasymachus. Lysias plays an important role in the dialogue.

11. Cephalus was not an Athenian citizen but a metic, that is, an alien who is allowed to settle in Athens and who pays taxes but enjoys no civil rights. He was originally from Syracuse.

12. The expression means that the man is about to pass into the other world; he is at that stage of old age when he can be said to stand on the threshold of Hades (cf. *Iliad*, XXII, 60, XXIV, 487; *Odyssey*, XV, 246). In the *Iliad*, it occurs both times in the mouth of the wretched Priam.

13. "Like to like" (cf. *Phaedrus*, 240c).

14. The Greek word is *anthrōpos*, the generic word for a member of the human species. The word for a male human being is *anēr*. This is an important distinction in Greek and allows for considerable subtlety in the use of the terms. On the first level, *anthrōpos* is clearly the lower term; it signifies the mere participation in the minimal qualities of the species, whereas an *anēr* is distinctly a real man, one who has developed his male humanity and can participate in the highest functions of a man, politics, and war. But, on a second level, the full or final end of humanity may transcend mere maleness and include activities different from, and contrary to, those of the real man [cf. Callicles' attack on the philosophers from the point of view of manliness

(*Gorgias*, 484c ff.)]. In this sense, *anthrōpos* would be the deeper and more meaningful term. In Book V Socrates suggests that the best regime, and implicitly the best human being, is a combination of male and female. Unfortunately no term in English adequately translates *anēr*; and the word "man" cannot be reserved for it since "man" must often be added where it does not exist in Greek (for example, "the good man" is in Greek merely "the good"). *Anthrōpos* will regularly be translated as "human being."

15. This is Aristophanes' description of Sophocles in *Frogs*, 82.

16. "The many" is a translation of *hoi polloi* and implies all that the latter term means to us. It is frequently translated by "the mass," "the mob," and other such terms which are appropriate in the extent to which they indicate the class to which Plato refers. For Plato, however, the fact of number—the simple fact that this class contains the majority of men—is of decisive importance. The great number of men share common traits, and, when they dominate, they necessarily lend a certain character to the regime. Politically the expression is used in contrast to the one and the few. Ultimately it reflects the theoretical problem of "the one and the many." Every time it is used, it is meant to call up a cluster of meanings.

Here the temptation to translate it by "most people" must be resisted, for such a translation would obscure the fact that Socrates is referring to a class of men, a politically relevant class. This passage presents one element in the definition of that class which is so important for political life. It is dominated by opinions which give too much weight to money. The many have a distorted sense of the importance of the equipment necessary for a good life; they identify the condition of happiness with happiness itself. Socrates finally calls the lowest class, as well as the desiring part of the soul, the money-making part (441a). This is one of the most massive political facts, and, in Plato's way of teaching, it becomes clear only through fidelity to his clear language.

17. The Greek word is *mythos;* first meaning no more than "a speech" (as in Homer), it comes to mean "a story," very often one connected with religious traditions. The poets are the makers of the *mythoi;* the meaning and reliability of *mythoi* is an important question in Plato. The term will always be translated thus.

18. This is the first time one of the words in the family of *dikaiosynē*, "justice," is used in the dialogue. It arises, as it were, accidentally during a discussion of other questions. Justice gradually becomes *the* problem of the dialogue, to the exclusion of other questions; hence the traditional subtitle of the book, *On the Just. Dikaiosynē* is justice, the virtue; *dikaion* is what is just or right, the thing or act to which the virtue is related.

19. In conversation, where we would say "good," or "right," or "true," the Greeks said "you speak well," etc. This has been rendered as "what you say is good," etc. Characteristically there are four possible alternatives used in this formula, meaning true, correct, good, and fine, fair, or noble (*kalon*). The only ones that present a problem are the last two. They have in the past been translated and understood as though they were equivalent, but there is a

nuance of difference which should be preserved. Something that has been said can be good without being fine or noble, just as fine or noble speech is not necessarily good or true. Our idiom does not reveal this difference, but it does not follow therefore that the distinction is not relevant to Socratic thought. The *kalon* is a crucial and ambiguous term in classical moral thought altogether, and we have no precise equivalent for it. It means, in the first place, fair or beautiful, and expresses nobility when qualifying speech or deed. It is always rendered as fine, fair or beautiful; in the formula under discussion, it is almost always rendered as fine. This may often sound strange to our ears, but it is well to maintain the distinction in the hope of becoming aware of a subtlety in Socrates' style, a subtlety based on a forgotten moral viewpoint. The passage to which this note refers is a case in point. For a precise discussion of the difference in the Platonic usages of these terms, cf. Seth Benardete, "The Right, the True, and the Beautiful" [*Glotta*, XLI (1963), pp. 54–62].

20. Another reading, much less well supported by the manuscripts, would give the following translation: " 'Isn't Polemarchus the heir of all that belongs to you?' I said."

21. The word for "sacrifices" is identical with the generic term for the "sacred." This is the very last word concerning Cephalus. He is introduced to, and removed from, the dialogue in the atmosphere of ancestral piety which he represents and by which his situation in this life and the next is protected.

22. The Greek word is *technē*, from which the English words "technical" and "technique" are derived. It does not mean art in the present-day sense, but rather in the older sense implied, for example, by the word artisan. It means a discipline operating on the basis of principles that can be taught. It is, hence, not opposed to science but allied with it, and in Plato the terms "art" and "science" are often indistinguishable; an art is always a model of what is rational and intelligible.

23. The term is derived from the word *koinon*, which means "common" or "public." All the words for partner or partnership used by Socrates in this context are drawn from this root; the last, a few lines farther on, is *koinōnia* which is a classic term for a political community. "Contracts," used by Polemarchus, implies relations having primarily to do with money. Socrates, in introducing the broader term, indicates that the proper context for the solution of the problem of justice is the political community.

24. Apparently this was a game similar to checkers. In Plato, it is often employed as a symbol of dialectic, just as housebuilding or architecture (the next example) frequently stands for lawgiving. In dialectic, premises—like pieces—are set down and are changed in relation to the moves of one's partners. The game can be played over, and one's moves can be improved on the basis of experience with the opponent's moves. It is a friendly combat and an amusement for its own sake (cf. 487b–c).

25. The Greek word is *logos* which most simply means "speech" and is derived from the verb "to speak." It can also mean story, discourse, argument,

and reason; it is speech and what speech implies—human reason as expressed in speech. At this stage in the discussion begins the first reflection on that activity of discussion in which the interlocutors find themselves engaged. In this edition the word will always be translated as "speech" or "argument," except in a few instances where it must be rendered as "reason."

26. *Odyssey*, XIX, 395–396. The other grandfather, previously mentioned (330b), should not be forgotten in this context.

27. This is a translation of the word *aretē*; it is the translation used by Cicero and all other thinkers in the tradition of moral and political thought. It means, broadly stated, "the specific excellence of a thing." "What is virtue?" is the typical Socratic question, and no answer can be given to it in the Platonic context unless all the subtle and various uses of the word itself be followed throughout the work. Contemporary usage has narrowed the sense of the word, but we still can grasp its broader meaning. If we fail to recognize that our understanding of virtue is different from the classical view, we cannot become aware of the very great change in moral understanding that has occurred. The moral sense of virtue can only be developed in relation to its larger sense, and, thus, it is no accident that Socrates' first use of the word is in relation to horses. *Aretē* will always be rendered as "virtue" throughout this translation. Any other procedure would simply render the problem posed by the word invisible.

28. Bias and Pittacus were among the semilegendary "Seven Wise Men." Many wise sayings are attributed to them. Simonides, the source of Polemarchus' definition of justice, was a poet, aptly described by Lessing as "the Greek Voltaire."

29. Periander was a sixth-century tyrant of Corinth [usually counted among the "Seven Wise Men," but not by Socrates (*Protagoras*, 343a)]. Perdiccas II was king of Macedonia, father of Archelaus (*Gorgias*, 471b). Xerxes was the Persian king who led the great expedition against Greece. Ismenias the Theban is not well known, but he is mentioned at *Meno*, 90a, and it is probably the same Ismenias to whom Xenophon refers (*Hellenica*, III, 5, 1–2). He is the only one of these four who was not a monarch. He seems to have been excessively fond of money and to have sold his services to the Persians at a date later than the supposed date (411 B.C.) of the action of the *Republic*].

30. There was a popular belief in antiquity that if a wolf sees a man first, the man is struck speechless.

31. Cf. *Apology*, 38b. This whole scene is a parody of judicial procedure, in which the defendant proposes his own punishment in opposition to the accuser. The rhetorician plays the accuser, and thereby shows how his skills can be of use (cf. Aristophanes, *Clouds*). Plato, contrary to the impression Aristophanes wishes to give, presents Socrates as innocent of judicial rhetoric; rather it is his opponent who knows that powerful and dangerous art.

32. This is a translation of the word *kreitton*, which means "stronger"; however, its use was also expanded to cover all sorts of superiority, and it finally could mean even goodness or excellence. Here the sense is clear, but Plato also plays on a certain popular confusion as to what really constitutes ex-

cellence. The first use of the word occurred at 327c and prefigured Thrasymachus' argument that the stronger should rule and are the standards for justice.

33. *Pancration* was a combination of wrestling and boxing.

34. In modern times the word *sycophant* has come to mean only a "flatterer," especially of the sort who surround kings and tyrants. This meaning is not entirely alien to the Greek sense, but it is at a certain remove from the primary meaning. The sycophants were men who made accusations against Athenian citizens, acting, as it were, as public prosecutors. They were blackmailers; any charge they might make could cause difficulty and, at the least, would be expensive. They distorted the meaning of men's acts and statements, and Socrates, accused of making the worse argument appear the better, could be compared to them. He was trying to cause trouble and make his interlocutors look bad before the public. The sycophants were flatterers of the tyrant public opinion, since their charges usually had to do with alleged crimes against civil society, and since the juries were chosen by lot from the citizen body at large.

35. This is another legal term in a scene that is a sort of mock accusation of Socrates. The word implies any crime of malicious damage or fraud.

36. The term used is *poneros*, one which has strong moral overtones, implying something worthless or vicious. The exact translation would be "villainous," and the word has precisely the same history as the English word villain—originally it refers to someone who works. The use of the term in this context prepares for a technical or scientific treatment of virtue and vice. Just as the body's vice is corrected by the art of medicine, the soul's vice is corrected by the art of politics. The word was translated as "bad" in the discussion at 334c–e.

37. The Greek word is *pleonexia*, which means "greed," "grasping," or "overreaching," but is derived from the words meaning "to have more" or "to get more." This sense is played upon in what follows, and it should be remembered that "to get the better" is an idiomatic English rendering, and that the Greek is "more" rather than "better" (cf. 349e).

38. "Kidnappers" here means those who capture men and sell them into slavery. "Housebreakers" are those who break through the mud or plaster walls of the Athenian homes in order to enter.

39. An attendant in the public bathhouses who brought water and soap and performed some of the offices of a barber. These were proverbially vulgar men and great talkers.

40. This expression refers to the way a nurse feeds a balky child by putting food into its mouth. Thrasymachus becomes the nurse Socrates needs (cf. 343a).

41. The Greek word is *idion* which in its simplest sense means "private" as opposed to public or common (cf. 333a, note 23). It can also mean the individual, as opposed to the general, or the peculiar character of a thing. The opposition between private and public is an important theme in the *Republic* and, in some respects, it is the core of the problem of justice. The private is usually of distinctly lower status than the public; but there are occasions when

the private, as opposed to the political, is treated as superior or more important, for example, when the city is not the best possible and certain individuals can be more fully human in opposition to it. It is most important to note this word in a context in which the arts are compared to a community of men. In almost all cases *idion* will be translated as "private."

42. Cf. 338c, note 32.

43. The word used—*dikastai*—is the one used for members of the Athenian juries. This is another reference to the mock trial of Socrates. Here Socrates suggests another form of rhetoric that would assure his triumph over his accuser and do away with his dependence on popular judgment.

44. The Greek word for innocence, *euētheia,* is composed from words meaning "good habits"; the word for corruption, *kakoētheia,* is composed from words meaning "bad habits." Hence Socrates' transition here is very direct, if not entirely obvious.

45. Cf. 327a and note 5.

Book II

1. This is the first occurrence in the *Republic* of the famed Platonic word *eidos*; it gives its name to what is known as the "theory of ideas or forms," Plato's teaching about the first or most fundamental beings. The meaning of this teaching has always been a subject of controversy. This is another case where an attempt to follow Plato's use of the word from its casual common-sense meaning to its highest theoretical meaning is a precondition of learning, because that highest sense is only a distillation of what is implied in the casual use of the word.

Etymologically, *eidos* is derived from the verb "to see" and means, in the first instance, "the appearance of a thing"—how it looks, the visible characteristics that distinguish it from everything else. In the present passage, it means "a sort of thing," a "class"; the connection of this sense with the former one is obvious. The word *form* will be reserved for *eidos* throughout this translation.

2. The Greek word is *doxa* derived from the word meaning "to seem." This is the classic word for "opinion," as opposed to "knowledge." Its sense is sometimes extended to mean "reputation"; for *doxa* means what is popularly held and is based upon the appearance or seeming of things, as opposed to their reality. Hence, although "opinion" and "reputation" are not pejorative terms in themselves, their relation to mere seeming calls them into question; Plato constantly plays upon this ambiguity. In this context Glaucon and Adeimantus insist on the distinction between opinion or seeming and being, and between the few who are capable of freeing themselves from opinion and the many who are not.

3. The Greek word for "law" is *nomos*. It can also be translated as "convention." (A law is not necessarily what is passed by an assembly; it can be an ancestral practice which governs a group of men. In this sense *nomos* can be understood as the opposite of *physis*, "nature.")

4. Glaucon's account of this story should be compared with Herodotus' (*History*, I, 8–13).

5. Paraphrased from *Seven Against Thebes* (592). The man it describes wishes to be "best."

6. *Seven Against Thebes*, 593–594.

7. Literally: "Let a brother stand by a man."

8. *Works and Days*, 232–234.

9. *Odyssey*, XIX, 109–113. After the second line Adeimantus drops the following line: "Lording over many strong men." Line 114 reads: "All as a result of his good leadership; and the people prosper (live in virtue) under him."

10. Musaeus is a semimythical singer and seer from the heroic times. His poetry is said to have dealt with cosmological themes. He is sometimes alleged to have been the son of Orpheus. By his son, Adeimantus may mean Eumolpus, who, among other things, was reputed to have instituted the Eleusinian Mysteries, one of the central Athenian religious observances. His descendants were the Eleusinian priests. If it is indeed Eumolpus who is meant, Adeimantus is implicitly criticizing the official Athenian understanding of the future life.

A *symposium* is literally a "drinking party," and a Platonic presentation of such a gathering is to be found in the *Symposium*.

11. The expression for prose is composed from words meaning "to speak privately" and could also mean what one says in private. Almost all public speech was written in verse, and Herodotus (443 B.C.) is the first prose writer any of whose works we possess in their entirety. The fact that poetry by nature is addressed to men in large groups is an essential element in Plato's analysis of it. Prose has a naturalness and frankness connected with its private character, and this should provide a basis for reflection on Plato's choice of prose for the presentation of his own thought.

12. Hesiod, *Works and Days*, 287–289. Adeimantus seems to have substituted the word *smooth* for *short* (cf. 328b–d). In Hesiod's text "gods" is qualified by "deathless."

13. Homer, *Iliad*, IX, 497–501. Adeimantus substitutes "can be moved by prayer" for "can be turned," and he leaves out the line following the first in the original: "And they are surely greater in virtue, honor, and strength."

14. The Greek for initiation, *teletē*, means a "making perfect" and is very close to the word Adeimantus has just used for death, *teleutē*.

15. The quote is attributed to Simonides.

16. A shadow painting is a rough sketch designed to produce an effect at a distance. Perhaps Adeimantus means perspective drawing which gives an impression of depth on a two-dimensional surface. (Cf. 523b; 602d.)

17. Archilochus lived at the end of the eighth and beginning of the seventh centuries B.C. He was a lyric poet, famed for his bitter lampoons. Of his works only fragments remain. Apparently the fox epitomized cunning and subtle deception in his works.

18. Most manuscripts read *logoi*, "speeches," rather than *nomoi*, "laws," but the manuscript reading "laws" is regarded as an excellent one; I

follow Burnet in choosing "laws" on the grounds of its intrinsic plausibility. At 366b Adeimantus recapitulates this argument and asserts that it is the cities (instead of the laws) and the poets who tell us of the deliverances from the wrath of the gods. If cities tell anything, it is by their laws. "Laws" in this passage is just a substitute for "cities." Adeimantus undoubtedly refers to parts of the Athenian religious observance. *Nomoi*, in an alternate meaning, are "religious songs."

19. Heroes were the great warrior chieftains of the first ages. They were regarded as divine because they were directly descended from the gods and because they performed superhuman deeds. Some of them were held to be the founders or the ancestors of the founders of the great cities. The citizens were thus descendants of the heroes who provided the link between the cities and the gods.

20. Cf. 338c, note 32.

21. This curious expression occurs only once elsewhere in Plato (at *Philebus*, 36d). It can mean "that well-known man"; or it could imply that Socrates jokingly calls Glaucon and Adeimantus the sons of Thrasymachus, as Adam suggests.

22. Ariston was Plato's father; the name means "best."

23. This could also mean "more important."

24. "Idea" is merely a transliteration of the Greek; it is of the same family as *eidos* (cf. 357c, note 1) and frequently seems to be identical in meaning in Plato's usage. There is, however, a nuance of difference. Primarily, "idea" is closer to the root verb and accentuates the notion of a thing's being seen or its looks.

25. Cf. 328b, note 6.

26. The superlative of the word for necessity here can be construed to mean: (1) this city is composed of the fewest elements possible; (2) this city is most oppressed by necessity, or is most necessitous; or (3) this city is the proper one, the one most needed.

27. The word is *himation* and means a specific sort of loose-fitting outer robe usually worn over undergarments. It was an oblong piece of cloth thrown over the left shoulder and fastened over or under the right. It is familiarly seen on Greek statues.

28. The word for "market" is *agora*. The agora was the central meeting place in the city and the haunt of Socrates, according to his own account.

29. The word for "currency" is *nomisma*. It means something conventional and is derived from the word *nomos*. A strictly literal translation would be "a conventional [or legal] sign of exchange." It is to be noted that the first mention of convention, as opposed to nature, within the city has to do with commerce.

30. The Greek meal was eaten in a reclining posture; usually the individuals would support themselves on one elbow. For this purpose the well-to-do Athenian had special low couches with cushions.

31. Or "truthful."

32. The *hoplite*, or "heavy-armed soldier," who carried a large shield (*hoplon*) and a pike was the most admired and most useful of soldiers. He

fought the great land battles in close combat. He is contrasted with light-armed and mounted soldiers who were used to annoy the enemy on the flanks. The capacity to provide oneself with and use such arms was a test for citizenship in limited democratic regimes, like that of 411 B.C. in Athens. From the point of view of wealth and military skill, this distinguished a man from the majority, who were either light-armed soldiers or sailors. Heavy-armed combat was understood to be the most important kind, from the point of view of strategy and as an occasion for the expression of virtue. The *Iliad* is a hymn to this kind of soldier; in Socrates' time the Spartan was the model of the hoplite.

33. The word here is *thymos*, and it expresses one of the most important notions in the book. *Thymos* is the principle or seat of anger or rage. It might well be translated by that pregnant word "heart," which mirrors the complexity of the Greek. It will always be translated as "spirit" or "spiritedness." Its use should be carefully watched.

34. The word *philosopher* means "lover of wisdom" and is parallel to *philomathēs*, "lover of learning." These first uses of the term and their context are the first steps toward a definition of that difficult notion. Sometimes it will be translated as "philosopher," at other times as "lover of wisdom"; it is always the same Greek word.

35. This expression is composed of the words *kalos* and *agathos*, the former meaning "fair," "fine," or "noble," and the latter "good." It is the formula for what we would call "the gentleman." Whenever feasible, *kaloskagathos* will be translated as "gentleman."

36. "Gymnastic" means the exercise of the unadorned body. "Music" means originally "any activity performed under the guidance of the Muses." This meant especially lyric poetry sung to music, which is not far from our sense. Socrates broadens the sense somewhat and concentrates upon subordinating the rhythmic and melodic elements to the verbal and rational content. This was a change from the traditional emphasis, and the surprise we experience at the way in which he interprets the word is not entirely alien to what the Greek reader was probably supposed to experience at this radical treatment of the subject. To change the word would be to presuppose the effect of Socrates' thought prior to the fact. We have no adequate equivalent for either of the terms, and it is better to let each individual make his own interpretation on the basis of their use. (The larger sense of "music" is expressed at 617b–c, and in Lorenzo's speech at the beginning of Act V of *The Merchant of Venice*.)

37. The word is *poiein* from which the word "poet" is drawn. It means "to make" and is the characteristic expression for the activity of the poet. Poetry is just one form of making, but it is the most revealing kind of making, and the poet becomes *the* maker. In English usage it is impossible to translate it consistently as "making," and so "writing" and "composing" have also been used when necessary. It should be remembered that the word is always *poiein*; for the notion that a thing has been made, and made by the poet, is often part of Plato's meaning. The ancient interpretation of the poet as a maker contrasts with the modern view that the poet is a creator.

38. Hesiod, *Theogony*, 154–210.

39. *Ibid.*, 453–506.

40. The Greek word *aischron* is the opposite of *kalon*, which is always rendered as "fine," "fair," or "noble." It means "base," "ugly," or "shameful."

41. Probably referring to the *peplos* of Athena, the robe embroidered for the goddess by Athenian girls and carried up to the Acropolis during the Panathenaea (cf. *Euthyphro*, 6b). The presentation of the robe is represented on the frieze of the Parthenon.

42. Hephaestus gave his mother a throne containing hidden chains as a means of avenging himself for being rejected by her. There was a play by Epicharmus on this theme.

43. *Iliad*, I, 586–594.

44. *Iliad*, XX, 1–74; XXI, 385–513.

45. The word is *theologia*.

46. *Iliad*, XXIV, 527–532. This is a literal translation of the passage as it stands in Homer:

> Two jars stand on Zeus' threshold of gifts Zeus gives, one of bad ones, the other of good. To whom Zeus, who delights in thunder, gives a mixture, at one time he happens on evil, at another good. But to whom he gives the harmful, he is spitefully treated and evil misery drives him over the divine earth.

Socrates makes several small changes which are untranslatable, but he maintains the meter in his speech. The Homeric Greek would also admit of the following translation of the first two lines: "Two jars of evil gifts stand on Zeus' threshold and another of good ones. . . ."

47. This line is not found in Homer but resembles *Iliad*, IV, 84, in which Zeus is called the dispenser of *war*.

48. *Iliad*, IV, 70 ff.

49. *Iliad*, XX, 1–74.

50. Aeschylus' *Niobe* is not extant.

51. Another formula of the political assembly (cf. 328b, note 6).

52. *Odyssey*, XVII, 485. This citation occurs in a passage in which this characteristic of the gods is invoked to protect Odysseus. And the line that follows is:

> Spying out the insolence and lawfulness of human beings.

53. For Proteus, cf. *Odyssey*, IV, 456–458. For Thetis, cf. Sophocles' *Troilus*, fragment 548; and Pindar, *Nemean*, IV, 60.

54. A line from *The Xantriai*, a lost play by Aeschylus.

55. Demons are gods of lower rank, as it were, links between gods and men. Often the men of the golden age prior to the Trojan War were treated as such deities. They can become identified with personal geniuses. They are one step above heroes. Socrates' voice or *daimonion* is "a kind of demonic thing" (cf. 496c, and *Apology*, 31d, 27d–e).

56. *Iliad*, II, 1–34.

57. The choruses for the tragedies and comedies were part of the public charge and, at Athens, were usually paid for and trained by rich citizens, who did so as part of their civic responsibility and as a mode of display.

Book III

1. *Odyssey*, XI, 489–491. Achilles speaks.
2. *Iliad*, XX, 64–65.
3. *Iliad*, XXIII, 103–104.
4. *Odyssey*, X, 495 (said of Teiresias).
5. *Iliad*, XVI, 856–857.
6. *Iliad*, XXIII, 100–101.
7. *Odyssey*, XXIV, 6–10.
8. The words "as is thought" are generally thought to be corrupt and to have been inserted in the text by a Christian scribe at some late date.
9. The word is *epieikēs*, meaning "fair" or "decent man," the one who does what's fit. *Epieikeia* became the term used for equity in law. It is practically a synonym for the quality of gentlemanliness.
10. *Iliad*, XXIV, 10–12. I have translated Homer's text. Plato substitutes "sailing" or "navigating" for "roaming," "on" for "along," and adds "unharvested." This apparently is a parody, but the text may be corrupt.
11. *Iliad*, XVIII, 23–24.
12. *Iliad*, XXII, 414–415.
13. *Iliad*, XVIII, 54.
14. *Iliad*, XXII, 168–169. Socrates replaces "wall" by "town."
15. *Iliad*, XVI, 433–434.
16. *Iliad*, I, 599–600.
17. 346a, note 41. Here the ruler, *the* public man, is compared to a doctor. Art, or knowledge, gives the title to rule; the private man, in principle, is the man who does not know.
18. This formula brings to mind Swift's Houyhnhnms, who do not say the thing which is not.
19. Here Socrates abruptly introduces a single ruler who guards against lying.
20. *Odyssey*, XVII, 383–384. The next line is:

> Or divine singer whose singing delights.

21. The word is *sōphrosyne*, and its primary sense means what we mean by "temperance"—the control over the bodily pleasures. But it gains a broader sense and gradually, in this work, comes to apply to a control of certain pleasures of the soul that we would hardly designate as temperance. The word "moderation" covers both senses, although not so decisively as "temperance" in the first instance. In order to maintain the unity of the two notions as Socrates develops them, moderation will be used throughout. *Sōphrosynē*

is one of the four cardinal virtues—the others are wisdom, courage, and justice.

22. *Iliad*, IV, 412.

23. The first line is *Iliad*, III, 8, with the words "in silence" dropped; the second is IV, 431.

24. *Iliad*, I, 225.

25. *Odyssey*, IX, 8–10. Odysseus, at the court of the Phæacians, says in this passage that among the "finest of all things" is a whole people in harmony listening to a singer.

26. *Odyssey*, XII, 342. This is not, as might appear, Odysseus speaking, but Eurylochus, urging the companions of Odysseus to eat the Sun's cattle. Punishment is instant, and all die.

27. Zeus' wakefulness and plans are in *Iliad*, II, 1–4. His forgetfulness is in XIV, 294–351. The last words are a quote, not from Zeus, but from Homer speaking of Zeus (XIV, 296).

28. *Odyssey*, VIII, 266 ff.

29. *Odyssey*, XX, 17–18.

30. The source of this passage is unknown. Cf. Euripides, *Medea*, 964, "Gifts and speech persuade gods."

31. The word is *metrion*, derived from the word meaning "measure." The term is frequently equivalent to *sōphrosynē*, but for the sake of making the reader able to follow the latter word, "sensible" will be used for *metrion* where "measure" cannot be properly used in English.

32. *Iliad*, IX, 515 ff.; XIX, 185–281; XXIV, 594.

33. *Iliad*, XXII, 15 and 20.

34. The Scamander, *Iliad*, XXI, 130–132, 212–226, 233 ff.

35. *Iliad*, XXIII, 140–151.

36. From the lost *Niobe* of Aeschylus.

37. The word for "prose writer" here is *logopoios*—literally, a "maker of speeches." It is usually applied to chroniclers and historians, or at Athens to those who write speeches for the use of others in court.

38. The word is *lexis*, which can also mean simply "a speech" but frequently means "manner or style of speech" or "diction in poetry." The word is related to *logos*.

39. Socrates does not mention the very first things in the *Iliad* (I, 1–11), the invocation to the goddess and Homer's claim that she tells the story. Socrates treats the poem as a fabrication of Homer, as not having a divine origin. He is thus able to blame Homer without impiety. Homer becomes an innovator instead of a spokesman of the gods. Socrates' intention is akin to that of certain schools of Biblical criticism.

40. *Iliad*, I, 15–16.

41. *Eponyms*, those names given to gods or heroes from places, deeds, or characteristics.

42. 376c, note 35.

43. The word is *erōs*, which is "sexual passion" or "love." It can some-

times be used synonymously with "desire" in general, as the most characteristic of desires or as representative of the character of desire. It is the second great element of the soul along with *thymos,* and its training is equally one of the primary objectives of the education. In the *Republic* its status is quite low, while that of *thymos* is correspondingly high. From its first manifestation at 329c, through the present passage, to Book IX, where the tyrant is presented as the erotic man par excellence; it is that which must be overcome. For a somewhat different evaluation of *erōs,* the *Symposium* and the *Phaedrus* should be consulted.

44. The word, translated here as "harmonic mode," and in what succeeds as simply "mode," is *harmonia.* "Rhythm" and *harmonia* are defined as follows in *Laws,* 664e: ". . . rhythm is the name given to the order of the motion, while, as for sound, the mixture of high and low would receive the name *harmonia.*" A *harmonia* is simply a scale, and the various scales constitute the different modes Socrates speaks of. Its simplest sense is that implied in the present context—the use of variations of pitch in speaking. Rhythm applies both to music and words and is equivalent to the meter and the accentuation of music following upon it.

45. The word is *themis,* which is "law" or "right," but it has a certain divine connotation lacking in the word *nomos.*

46. Cf. 363c, note 10.

47. There are several myths about the satyr Marsyas and the flute. The story apparently referred to here is the one concerning the contest between Apollo and Marsyas, the former playing the cither and the latter the flute. The Muses judged Apollo the winner. He then proceeded to skin Marsyas alive.

48. The various meters are compounded of feet based on the three basic proportions: the 2/2 or equal, as in the dactyl⁻˘˘ , spondee – –, and anapest˘˘⁻; the 3/2, as in the cretic⁻˘⁻; and the 2/1, as in the iamb˘⁻ and trochee⁻˘. The four forms of sound are apparently the notes of the tetrachord, but the exact sense is unsure, as is the case with all the technical details in this passage and the one that succeeds it. Socrates assumes these details to be a part of the common knowledge of anyone liberally educated in music. This is shown by the way in which he addresses himself to Glaucon, who knows it all but for whom the technical knowledge has no visible relation to any human or political experience.

49. Damon is Socrates' musical authority. Cf. *Laches,* 200b; *Alcibiades* I, 118c; also, Isocrates, *Antidosis,* 251.

50. The Greek is *diairesis.* This is the word used for the activity of discerning the *forms* or classes to which things belong. It is the fundamental task of dialectic to define things according to the natural divisions existing in the world; diairesis is the way of discovering such definitions. Cf. *Sophist,* 267d.

51. In this passage Socrates speaks in the terms of common sense, eschewing the language of the specialists. He translates, as it were, the terminology into everyday speech, but his usage is apparently quite precise.

The *enoplion* (armored or fit for war) foot was apparently a cretic ⁻ ˘ ⁻).

The heroic is apparently a foot that could be composed of either a dactyl (⁻˘ ˘) or a spondee (⁻ ⁻) because they both have the same value and the second member of the foot could be made of either two shorts or one long. "Up and down" refers to arsis and thesis.

"The tempo of the foot" refers to the time. The speed with which the verse is read or sung causes it to produce different effects.

52. The words are *euschēmosynē* and *aschēmosynē*. *Schēmē* means "outward appearance," "posture," "attitude," or "bearing." All the terms in the following enumeration of qualities pertaining to music begin with the prefix *eu*, meaning "good," or *a*, meaning "lack of," which provides them with a unity not visible in English.

53. The same word is used by Thrasymachus (348c) to describe the just man. There it was rendered as "innocence." Here Socrates uses it in its literal and etymologically precise sense. The word suffered the same alterations in sense in Greek as did the word "innocent" in English.

54. Sons of Asclepius. Originally the term meant the family of Asclepius (the founder of medicine), for whom medicine was a family trade. It gradually began to be used for the priests of his cult, and generally all healers, who were his sons by adoption, as it were.

55. *Iliad*, XI, 624–641. It is not Eurypylus who is wounded and receives these attentions, but Machaon, a son of Asclepius and a doctor (cf. *Ion*, 538b where the passage is quoted and Machaon properly referred to). Patroclus is not even present at this scene. Machaon's wound is apparently not serious, and this draught is prepared for him and Nestor as refreshment. Eurypylus, wounded in the same engagement, asks for an entirely different treatment from Patroclus (XI, 828–836). (Cf. 408a, below, and note 59.)

56. The word for "prize" is practically the same as that for "old age" (*geras* and *gēras*).

57. The Phocylides passage is only available in fragmentary form, but its sense may very well have been of this sort: "make a living first, then worry about virtue." Socrates makes this into an exhortation to virtue.

58. *Politikon,* a man who knows the business of the city.

59. *Iliad*, IV, 218–219. In this case it is Machaon alone who treats Menelaus. In the last half of the line Socrates drops a word found in Homer. Homer's text reads: "*In his knowledge* he sprinkled gentle salves on the wound." The half-line as Socrates renders it is to be found in the mouth of Eurypylus as he tells of the treatment he wants (XI, 830); this is the same Eurypylus whom Socrates substitutes for Machaon at 405e (cf. note 55). In these two citations, Socrates deliberately changes Homer's emphasis so as to minimize the attention necessary to the bodies of even heroes, as well as the amount of knowledge required for a true art of medicine. Abstraction from the needs of the body is the condition of the actualization of this best regime. Another such condition is a simplicity and isolation that make the development of the arts highly unlikely. Glaucon raises this question in the immediate sequel.

60. Aeschylus, *Agamemnon*, 1022 ff.; Euripides, *Alcestis*, 3–4; Pindar, *Pythians*, iii, 53.

61. Cf. 400d, note 53.

62. *Iliad*, XVII, 588.

63. A hater of speech or reason. Cf. *Laches*, 188c, and *Phaedo*, 89d ff.

64. The word is *dogma* drawn from the word *dokein*, "to seem," hence meaning "an opinion" but usually an authoritative opinion, a decree of the assembly, the opinion or consensus of the rulers of the people. The word here has both senses; it means "an opinion" and "a public agreement or law."

65. The word is *gennaion* which is, primarily, "noble" in the sense of "nobly born" or "well bred" (cf. 375a and 409c).

66. Probably referring to the Phoenician hero, Cadmus; he founded Thebes with giants who sprang from the earth after the teeth of a slain dragon were sown by him (cf. *Laws*, 663e). It may also refer to the tale telling of Odysseus among the Phæacians.

67. The word is *phēmē*. In its first sense it is an oracle or any saying from a mysterious and obscure source. It gradually becomes what men say about such a thing; it is a "report" or a "rumor," and finally a "tradition."

68. The *syssitia* was a Cretan and Spartan institution. The men always had all meals together.

Book IV

1. This is the Greek word which means "a speech in defense in a trial." This is a trial; Socrates is accused. The facts that Socrates was a man who finally really was accused, who presented an *apology* in a court, and who was put to death play an important role in this drama. All uses of the word *apology* in the *Republic* refer to this event and cast light on it. Socrates' outlandish way of life and the consequences of his thought somehow injure the men and the regimes in existing cities; and from the various instances in which he is forced to make an *apology*, one can piece together the true reasons for Socrates', and hence the philosopher's, conflict with the city. This is a valuable supplement to the dialogue, *Apology*; and every use of the word casts an ominous shadow. For this reason the word is merely transliterated in this edition.

2. Greek statues were painted.

3. At a banquet or symposium the guests reclined, and the wine was passed from left to right. Usually they drank in competition, challenging one another. In the *Symposium*, a competition of speaking is substituted for one of drinking, and the order of speeches is from left to right.

4. Cf. 376a ff.

5. This apparently refers to a form of game of draughts (cf. 333a, note 24). Either the individual sections of the board, or the two halves of the board, were called *cities*. There is also here a play on the similar sound of the words for "many" and "city."

6. *Odyssey*, I, 351–352. Socrates changes two words which alter the

emphasis of the phrase somewhat. The word translated as "esteem," a word whose emphasis is on thought or prudence, replaces a word meaning "to praise or extol." In our text of Homer the second line reads:

which floats newest around those who *hear*.

7. The word is *tropos*. It originally means a "turning," a "direction," or a "way," and from there a moral sense evolves; it is the word for "character"— "the way of a man." It has a technical sense in music, referring to various kinds of songs. They are called *tropoi* because they evoke certain dispositions of the soul.

8. The word is *paranomia*; lawlessness in music is a paradoxical notion, but it is made to sound more plausible by using a word that reminds of the musical *nomos* as well as the political (cf. 365e, note 18).

9. Cf. 348c, note 44.

10. *Eidos*.

11. The shrine at Delphi belonged to Apollo; Socrates leaves the practices of piety to the oldest of the traditional sources; this is the only thing the philosopher-founder does not institute. In the temple, where the oracles were given, there was a golden globe, which was supposed to be the center or the navel of the earth.

12. Wisdom is here identified with the capacity of the political counselor. The word *euboulos* reflects the deliberation in public council (cf. 348d). It was an epithet of several gods.

13. The word for knowledge (*epistēmē*) is said by Socrates (*Cratylus*, 435a) to have the same root (*histēmi*) as that for "supervising," used here (*proistēmi*) and in 443e (*ephistamai*). The supervisors supervise by virtue of knowledge; the teaching that knowledge is the title to rule is thus implied in the very words.

14. Chalestra was a town on the Thermaic gulf in Macedonia. In a nearby lake there was carbonate of soda used in washing.

15. Lawful in the sense of "conforming to or based on law." There is some authority for reading "lasting" (*monimon*) instead of "lawful" (*nomimon*).

16. That is, the courage of a citizen, the courage necessary to a city. Socrates leaves open the possibility that there is a higher form of courage which is radically different from that expressed in the willingness to die at the law's command. Courage, simply, without the qualification political, cannot be based on this form of opinion. It consists precisely in the willingness to question opinions, even the most authoritative ones.

17. The analogy is to the hunt, a frequent analogon of philosophy in Socratic discourse.

18. The Greek sentence has a double sense: (*a*) stretching through every member of the whole city; (*b*) stretching through every note in the scale.

19. The Greek is an exclamation, *iou, iou*, which is usually a shout of grief but can also express joy. It is characteristic of the drama.

20. Cf. 479d.

21. *Eidos*.

22. The Greek word is *methodos,* which means the way one takes, a pursuit, a search, and the manner of that search. "Method" has taken on too rigid a sense in modern science to be used as an accurate translation.

23. Literally, "cause," or "a basis for an imputation."

24. The different stocks of men and the particular political talents connected with them, as formed by the climates of the north, the center, and the south, are constant themes of political thought, beginning with Herodotus Plato, and Aristotle, and continuing through Montesquieu.

25. This is the earliest-known explicit statement of the principle of contradiction—the premise of philosophy and the foundation of rational discourse.

26. *Eidos.*

27. *Logismos,* a derivative of *logos,* is used primarily to denote the computation of numbers, but it can mean the power to reason, particularly deductively. The translation "calculation" indicates both senses and underlines the rather practical or common-sense way in which reason makes its appearance in the *Republic.*

28. *Alogiston,* the part without *logos.*

29. Athens was connected to the Piraeus by two walls, and there was a third which ran to Phalerum. This made a system of enclosed fortified spaces. The two walls leading to the Piraeus were called the North Wall and the Middle Wall.

30. The word for executioner is one that means literally "he who belongs to the people." It is curious to note that the man who kills for the people is the one awarded the generic name.

31. It is not clear whether the passage refers to spirit or the man with spirit. If the latter is the case, "he" should be substituted for "it" throughout the speech.

32. Cf. 390d.

33. Cf. *Odyssey,* XIX, 547.

34. Cf. 428e, note 13.

35. The last words of this sentence, beginning with "to that which. . . ," are based on the reading of inferior manuscripts. The reading of all the best manuscripts yields no tolerable sense, and the passage may be corrupt.

Book V

1. The following scene recapitulates the beginning of the dialogue where Polemarchus is also the agent of Socrates' arrest. There, too, a cloak is held. This signifies a new beginning of the book.

2. *Eidos.*

3. 423e.

4. This is again the language of the democratic political assembly, compelling Socrates' service (cf. 327c–328b, note 6).

5. Literally, "to smelt ore in order to get gold." It is proverbial for some-

one who goes off on a wild goose chase, forgetting the business at hand, in the hope of making a great profit.

6. Another name for Nemesis who punishes the immoderate and arrogant. This name for Nemesis probably stems from Adrastus, ancient king of Argos, who established an altar to her. Aeschylus is the first author in the extant Greek literature to mention Adrasteia ("The wise prostrate themselves before Adrasteia," *Prometheus*, 36). The name of the goddess, the poet brought to mind here, and this context (which is an implicit attack on all existing cities and their most sacred laws) call to mind Adrastus, who led the attack of the *Seven Against Thebes*. All were killed save Adrastus, who made his escape on a winged black horse.

7. This is again legal terminology, referring to the treatment of men who commit accidental homicide. The killer was believed hateful to the gods and polluted by his act. The punishment under the Athenian Draconian law was exile, but the killer could be absolved and purified by a member of the victim's family, or by the victim himself before he died. (Cf. *Laws*, 865 ff., and 869e.)

8. A probable allusion to Aristophanes' *Ecclesiazusae*, which also proposed the emancipation of women and communism.

9. Wrestling schools for the young prior to the age when they could frequent the gymnasium (cf. 452d and note 11). These schools were among Socrates' haunts (cf. *Charmides*, 153a).

10. The formula for justice (cf. 433a ff). If he is referring to comic poets, they could not mind their own business while being serious.

11. A gymnasium is literally a place where one goes naked or strips; "gymnastic" is "the exercise of the naked body," and is specifically Greek. [A gymnasium can also mean a "school," a place where the soul is trained (*Gorgias*, 493d). The stripping of souls is also a Platonic metaphor (*ibid.*, 523e). The significance of this passage can be grasped better with an awareness of these facts.] The difference between Greek and barbarian is epitomized by the capacity to bare the body, the overcoming of shame without becoming shameless (cf. Herodotus, I, 10 and Thucydides, I, 6). Seeing a naked woman was the source of a regicide and a tyranny among the barbarians, according to Herodotus' account of the Gyges story (I, 8). Virtue and clothing seem to go together in demotic morality (457a), and the radical change that culminates in the rule of philosophic frankness is foreshadowed here.

12. Herodotus, I, 23–24.

13. Cf. 400c, note 50.

14. "Eristic" means "contentiousness," argument carried on for the sake of winning; formally it looks like "dialectic," which is friendly conversation; but eristic is not carried on for the sake of truth. This is the first use of the word "dialectic" in the *Republic* and provides a first common-sense view of its meaning.

In *Letter* VII (342a ff.) Plato describes the requisites for the attainment of knowledge of a thing. There are three; name (for example, circle); definition (for example, "that in a plane which is everywhere equidistant from the extremities to the center"); representation or image (for example, the circle drawn by the geometer, which is only an imperfect example and an aid to learning, not the real circle). The eristic disputant misleads his interlocutors by looking only to the names *man* and *woman*, not to their definitions.

15. This is a play on a line from a poem of Pindar of which we possess only a fragment [Bowra, *Pindari Carmina*, fr. 194 (Oxford: 1951)]. The line is simply: "he plucks an unripe fruit of wisdom." Pindar was apparently ridiculing philosophers and the study of nature. This is part of "the old quarrel between philosophy and poetry" (607b). Socrates is turning Pindar's ridicule, not only on comedy, but on Pindar himself and poetry as a whole, to the extent that poetry is hostile to philosophy. Even the tragedian would have to regard Socrates as a comic figure—someone not to be taken seriously, if tragedy is to be taken seriously. (In this sense, Aristophanes' *Clouds* is a play in the service of all poetry—tragedy as well as comedy.) The nakedness of women follows from philosophic investigation; and this shamelessness is a crucial step in the preparation of the rule of philosophers and philosophy (a rule over poetry in particular). Socrates takes a line from the poetic attack on philosophy and uses it as part of the philosophic attack on poetry. He says poetry grounds its appeal on the prejudices of conventional morality.

Socrates uses the emphatically masculine *anēr* (cf. 329c, note 14) at the beginning of the sentence. It is the male who laughs at womanliness; Socrates defends the human being. Poetry is tacitly identified with manliness and hence with the city and the political. The limitations of manliness begin to emerge in this passage. The male, the warrior who defends the city, is not open to philosophy and is only incompletely human.

16. The word translated as "wave" also means "foetus." [Cf. *Theaetetus*, 149 ff. and 210b, where words related to this one (in the latter sense) abound. Socrates claims (at 210b) that he is only an intellectual midwife and not himself capable of a pregnancy. That statement may not be wholly adequate, for here we are to see three of his own brain-children.]

17. This could also be translated "the female song," as in the "female drama" at 451a. (Cf. also 365e, note 18.)

18. The marriage of Zeus and Hera was known as the "Sacred Marriage," and it was celebrated in many Greek cities including Athens. They were, of course, brother and sister.

19. A place where lambs, kids, and calves were raised. This whole passage compares the mating and procreation of men to those of animals. The sacred marriages apparently take their standard, not from the gods, but from the beasts.

20. Aristophanes, *Ecclesiazusae*, 634–638.

21. An examination of this prescription will reveal that the prohibitions against incest are relaxed even more than this generous dispensation would seem to indicate (cf. 463c).

22. The Greek word for "ruler" is *archōn*. In Athens the holders of the chief offices were called "archons."

23. The Greek word translated as "outsider" is *allotrion*, meaning "belonging to another," "alien"; it is the opposite of *oikeion*, "what is one's

own," "what belongs to one's own household." It is the same word used by Thrasymachus in describing justice as "someone else's good" (343c), and this passage refers to that one. In the good city everything is one's own, part of one's household, so there can be no interest for one group to oppress another any more than a normal father is interested in oppressing his children. This tacitly admits that Thrasymachus' characterization of justice applies to existing cities.

24. Cf. 415d, note 67.

25. Cf. *Apology*, 36d.

26. Hesiod, *Works and Days*, 40.

27. *Pedagogue*—a man who took children back and forth from school, a sort of supervisor. Among the Athenians he was usually a slave.

28. *Iliad*, VII, 321. (Cf. Aristophanes, *Ecclesiazusae*, 677–679.)

29. *Iliad*, VIII, 162.

30. Those who live in the golden age celebrated by Hesiod (*Works and Days*, 109–120).

31. Socrates alters Hesiod's text: he uses "they become" instead of "they are called," and "endowed with speech" instead of "mortal." This passage is correctly cited in *Cratylus*, 397e.

32. The Greek words for "being at war" and "enemy" are *polemein* and *polemios*.

33. The word used here, which means to punish or chasten, is *sōphronizein*. Literally, this is "to make moderate"; punishment in this way would be a form of education.

34. The majority of manuscripts have a reading that would mean "my (military) campaign."

35. The third wave in a series coming in to shore was traditionally supposed to be the big one.

36. The meeting of philosophy and political power is precisely coincidental or accidental; there is nothing in the nature of either that leads to the union; they may just happen to "fall together." There is no necessary connection between a man's being born a ruler and his having philosophic talent or passion; nor is there any connection between a man's having philosophic talent and his being born in a city that would ask him to rule (the philosopher has neither the desire to be a ruler nor would he do what is necessary to impose his rule on unwilling people). This statement is indicative of the most fundamental difference between Plato's political teaching and that of the Enlightenment. For the moderns, knowledge necessarily leads to political power. Stated otherwise, the dissemination of knowledge gradually transforms civil society and insures the realization of decent regimes. Plato denies this contention; knowledge as knowledge does not effect desirable political change, and knowledge disseminated is no longer knowledge. The philosopher must also be king. These are two separate functions, and this is the core of the political problem. Knowledge cannot be transformed into wise power except in the person of the wise man, although unwise power can be made more powerful by the use of knowledge gained from the wise. It is

natural for some men to be philosophers and for some men to be kings; but it is not natural for kings to become philosophers or philosophers kings. This is why Plato cannot be characterized as an "optimist."

37. A *stratēgos*, or "general" was, in the Athenian system, the commander of an army. Under him were the ten *taxiarchs*, one for each of the Athenian tribes; under them were the *trittyarchs*, of which there were three in each tribe, one for each *trittys*. *Trittyarch* is here translated as "lieutenant."

38. The greater Dionysia, the festival in honor of the god Dionysus, was held in the spring for six days, three days of which were devoted to the presentation of comedies and tragedies. There were celebrations in the outlying villages around Attica as well as in the city of Athens itself.

39. *Dynamis*—"power," "capacity," "faculty." Power does not have precisely the same meaning in modern usage as it did for the ancient thinkers. They taught that every power must be understood in relation to its end; a power only exists in relation to its end—it is never itself an end. Hence the word might best be rendered "potentiality."

40. The riddle apparently ran as follows:

There is a story that a man and not a man
Saw and did not see a bird and not a bird
Perched on a branch and not a branch
And hit him and did not hit him with a rock and not a rock.

The solution is: a eunuch who did not see well saw a bat perched on a reed and threw a pumice stone at him which missed. (The Greek word *bolē* can mean either throwing, or hitting the mark.)

41. The word *nomima*, which usually means "the customary or lawful," is a derivative of *nomos*. Here popular, unsure opinion is identified with the opinion supported by civil society.

42. Cf. 432d.

Book VI

1. Socrates, in discussion with the erotic Glaucon, uses an ambiguous sentence. It could also be translated: ". . . a man who is by nature in love with *something* cares for everything related to *the object of his love*." Socrates wishes Glaucon to take it as it appears in the text, or, at least, he wishes the overtones of that sense to affect Glaucon's response. Socrates himself means the question in the second sense. However, the relation between the sexual love directed toward human beings and the love of wisdom is not to be forgotten. Socrates constantly uses words with a sexual or military connotation in speaking to Glaucon, thus predisposing him to certain answers by appealing to his particular passions.

2. The Greek word is *megaloprepeia* and means literally "that which is fitting or seemly for a great man."

3. Cf. 390e, note 31.

4. The god of ridicule or fault-finding, a being who is all blame, akin to such gods as Nikē and Erōs.

5. *Eikōn*, from which our word "icon" is drawn. It is a painting, an image, a reflection in a mirror—any likeness (cf. 509e ff.). Socrates gives a demonstration of the proper use of the faculty of imagination here.

6. The charge of studying the heavens was a serious one; astronomers tended to be atheists and were accused of so being. They gave mechanical accounts of the movements of the heavens, denied that the Sun and the Moon are gods, etc. They sought out what should be left inviolate. In the accusation of Socrates heavy weight was given to the allegation that he studied the heavens; it is not casual that this speech is presented as an *apology*.

7. According to Aristotle (*Rhetoric*, II, 16), Simonides was asked by the tyrant Hiero's wife whether he would prefer to be wise or rich. "Rich," he answered, "for I see that the wise spend their time at the doors of the rich." The Scholiast says that Socrates himself made the statement and explained that this is because wise men know their own needs.

8. The Greek word means "false accusation" or "gossip." What is implied is the kind of malicious talk that goes around in the city about someone with a bad reputation.

9. The terminology is that of love, procreation, and childbirth.

10. The reference is to the chorus employed in tragedy and comedy. Socrates treats the characteristics of the soul as though they were the actors in the dramatic poems produced by the city for the public festivals, and acts as though he were their trainer or director.

11. Cf. 412e, note 64.

12. The precise meaning of this expression is not certainly known, but there are two stories that might explain it.

(*a*) After Odysseus and Diomede stole the Palladium from Troy one night, Odysseus, in order to have the glory of the achievement for himself, attempted to kill Diomede. Diomede saw the shadow of Odysseus' sword in the light of the moon and turned on him. He bound Odysseus' hands and drove him to the Greek camp ahead of him, covering his back with blows from the flat of his sword.

(*b*) There was a Thracian named Diomede whose daughters were prostitutes. He forced the strangers who came to him to have intercourse with them, and then killed the strangers (cf. Aristophanes, *Ecclesiazusae*, 1029). The Aristophanes passage indicates that the latter story is the one referred to here.

13. There is a series of puns here on the genitive of the Greek word *nous*, "mind" or "intelligence" (cf. 614b and note 13). Seth Benardete suggests that this clause be translated: ". . . with pretentions and conceits of naughts fraught with thoughtlessness."

14. The sentence is incomplete; Socrates, about to introduce the image, stops to develop the comparison and then asks for his interlocutor's agreement before continuing the original thought.

15. Socrates plays on the words for a worker in bronze, or a blacksmith, and money (*argurion*, which is silver) and calls to mind the metals of the two lower classes in the city (415b–c). The words "released" (*lelymenou*) and

"bathed" (*lelumenou*) are practically the same, and the phrase forms a little jingle.

16. A *sophism* is a clever trick or captious argument; it is the product of a "wise guy." The maker of a sophism would be a sophist.

17. The accent in this word is on the care of ills, perhaps on the over-attentiveness to them (cf. 407b).

18. *Daimonion*—"of or belonging to a demon" (cf. 382e, note 55). For Socrates' *daimonion* see *Apology*, 31d; *Theaetetus*, 151a; *Theages*, 128e; Xenophon, *Memorabilia*, i, 4.

19. *Logoi* (cf. 334a, note 25).

20. Heracleitus, according to Aristotle, said: ". . . every day the sun is new" (Aristotle, *Meteorologica*, ii, 2.9).

21. These are terms used in the art of rhetoric; in the sentence which begins, "For they never saw. . . ," there is a parody of these forms in a little jingle that cannot be rendered in English.

22. Euripides, *Hippolytus*, 102. "I nod her a distant greeting because I am pure."

23. The word for "obey" means "to listen to"; here the Scholiast remarks that now the city will "listen instead of being listened to." This constitutes an additional condition to the possibility of the good city that had not previously been mentioned; for this reason some scholars have been led to alter the passage, but it points to an important difficulty (cf. 473c–d).

24. The word is *dynasteia*, derived from the word meaning "power." It is used here in contrast to kingship, which implies a legitimate exercise of political rule. *Dynasteia* is a chiefdom, free from any of the limitations or advantages of legitimacy. It is classed by Aristotle with tyranny or unlimited democracy, regimes without laws in which the sovereign can do as it wishes (*Politics*, 1242b). In 473d the word translated by *chief* was *dynastēs*. (Cf. *Laws*, 680a–b, where the regime of the Cyclopes is called a *dynasteia*.)

25. Or, "their arguments are always *ad hominem*." Literally, "about human beings."

26. *Demotike*, belonging to the *dēmos*, the people at large, the citizen body in a democracy.

27. The word *andreikelon* also means "a flesh-colored pigment."

28. Another possible reading would be translated as follows: "Or will someone assert that those men whom we excluded are more so?"

29. Cf. 341b.

30. Our word "narcotic" comes from the root of the Greek word (cf. *Meno*, 80b).

31. In the preceding passage the word for "interest," *tokos*, also means "offspring." Hence there is an urbane play on money and reproduction, natural and conventional. Aristotle explains the double sense of *tokos* as follows:

> Usury is hated with good reason because of its being acquisition from currency itself and not from that for which currency is provided. For currency came into being for the sake of exchange. The *tokos* makes it more. And it is from that that it got its name. For as

the offspring are like the parents, so *tokos* breeds currency from currency. And in this way it is of the kinds of moneymaking the most contrary to nature. (*Politics*, 1258b.)

32. Literally, "the most sun-*formed*."

33. The Greek means, literally, "to say something good" or "to use words of good omen." It is primarily a word appropriate to religious observance; its opposite is, literally, "blasphemy," and that is what is to be avoided. It is better to say nothing, rather than to use unpropitious expressions.

34. The Greek word means "age," and it gets the sense "dignity" because of the honor or right belonging to age.

35. The genitive form of the word for visible, *horatou*, is, in the Greek orthography, very close to that for heaven, *ouranou*. The last syllable of *ouranou* is identical with the genitive of the word for intelligence (*nous*), which is the root of the word for intelligible (*noēton*). (Cf. 494d and note 13; 614b and note 13). There is, hence, a play on the words for heaven and visible; and, in addition, the question is raised, on the basis of the words, as to the relation of the heavens to the intelligible world (cf. 528e ff.). According to *Cratylus* (396c), the astronomers say that *ouranos* received its name from intelligence, and rightly so.

36. The word translated as "beginning" can also be rendered as "starting-point," "principle" or "cause"; similarly, "end" can be "conclusion" or "result."

37. An hypothesis is, literally, "a placing under," and should perhaps be rendered as "supposition" (cf. *Meno*, 86 ff., and *Phaedo*, 99d ff.).

38. Or, another possible rendering: ". . . the beginning which is the whole."

39. The word is *eikasia*, derived from the verb meaning "to make an image." "Imagination" was chosen in order to preserve its relation to "image" (*eikōn*), which plays such an important role in the *Republic* and on all levels of the divided line. The importance of this faculty would be obscured if this connection were not obvious. For the best discussion of *eikasia*, and of the divided line as a whole, cf. Jacob Klein, *A Commentary on Plato's Meno* (University of North Carolina Press, 1965), pp. 115 ff.

The divided line looks something like this:

	Forms (*eidē*)	Intellection (*noēsis*)
The mathematical objects (*ta mathēmatica*)		Thought (*dianoia*)
	Things	Trust (*pistis*)
	Images (*eikones*)	Imagination (*eikasia*)

The intelligible (*to noēton*) — top two rows; The visible (*to horaton*) — bottom two rows.

The second and third sections are equal (Klein, p. 119, note 27). The way it is stated, it is impossible to know whether the highest or lowest is larger.

Book VII

1. It is not certain whether the Greek was "these things going by . . ." or "these things present. . . ." An alternative manuscript reading would make the sentence: ". . . they would hold that these things that they see are the beings."

2. Cf. 386c, note 1.

3. J. H. Kells ("Assimilation of Predicate Material to the Object," *Philologus*, Band 108, Heft 1½, 1964) makes a persuasive argument that this clause should be translated: ". . . that this power is the power which already exists in each man's soul . . . ." My interpretation of the sentence as a whole follows his.

4. A happy place where good men live forever. In some accounts they went there before dying, in others afterward.

5. "To go to" can have the sense of "to woo," which is obviously also intended in this context.

6. The reference is not clear. There are several tales of men who died and later became gods; notable among them were Heracles, Pollux, and Asclepius.

7. This refers to a game, in the playing of which a group is divided into two parts—one which runs away and the another which gives chase. Who does what is determined by twirling a shell, one side of which is black and the other white. Twirling the shell is equivalent to tossing a coin (cf. *Phaedrus*, 241b).

8. 403a, 416d. A "champion" is an athlete, generally a runner, who wins the prize. The Greek is *athlētēs*, the root of which is the word for "prize."

9. This is a term that refers to drama, in particular, to the chorus. It is either a movement of the dancers from left to right, corresponding to a previous movement from right to left (the *strophē*), or the song they sing while performing their movement.

10. Palamedes was a hero of the Trojan War and was supposed to have invented the alphabet, numbers, lighthouses, and many other useful things. He does not appear in Homer, but Aeschylus, Sophocles, and Euripides each wrote tragedies about him, none of which are extant.

11. The little finger, the index, and the middle.

12. In Greek mathematics the study of numbers and their attributes (*arithmētikē*) is distinguished from that of calculation (*logistikē*), which involves operations with numbers (addition, subtraction, etc.).

13. Socrates gives a name to the city: the Greek is *Callipolis*. There were towns of that name (cf. Herodotus, VII, 154).

14. This is a military term, as are so many in the conversation with Glaucon.

15. Literally, "increase." The plane was understood to be the *increase* from a point, and the solid the *increase* from a plane.

16. "Discovered" in this context probably means that the problems had not been adequately formulated and that decisive ones had not yet been solved. Socrates indicates that in his time solid geometry was in a state similar to that of plane geometry prior to Pythagoras.

17. Cf. Aristophanes, *Clouds,* 170–173, where the same term is used.

18. The word is *demiurge,* meaning "a man who practices an art for the public." In the exalted sense of this passage, he becomes the craftsman of the *cosmos* of the *Timaeus* and the later tradition. Its original humble sense is not to be forgotten.

19. Ancient musicians measured the concordant intervals (for example, fourth, fifth, and octave) and gave them mathematical proportions on the basis of the length of the strings required to produce them.

20. A technical term in music, here probably meaning notes the intervals of which are so small as to be almost inaudible; condensed or combined notes. The word in its original sense refers to cloth which has tightly woven threads.

21. The comparison is to the judicial torture of slaves on the rack.

22. *Nomos* (cf. 365e, note 18).

23. The Greek (*hodos*) means "a way" or "a path" (cf. 532e). None of the arts has a way of treating being as such, but each sees it in a particular perspective; their particular ways are appropriate only to their particular subject matters. Hence some other discipline is needed, the sole business of which is the study of being.

24. The Greek is *borborōi barbarikōi.*

25. In all but one of the manuscripts there follows a sentence of which there are several versions, none wholly intelligible. Hence I have left it out of the translation. Its point is apparently that if the clarity of the name mirrors the clarity of the soul in the particular faculty, Glaucon will be content.

26. Without trying to interpret the deeper meaning of this expression, it can be stated that it probably refers to the mathematical problem addressed in the *Meno*. It is a great shock to discover that the diagonal of a square is not commensurable with its sides; only an irrational number can express the relationship. This raises far-reaching questions about the relation of physical and geometrical reality to mathematical rationality. Such lines are irrational, not able to give an account of themselves in the terms of whole numbers. This is the discovery of the Pythagorean theorem.

27. The word is *synopsis,* "a seeing together."

28. There is a pun on "steadfast" (*monimos*) and "established by law" (*nomimos*). The phrase is an alliterative jingle.

29. Cf. 390a, note 31.

30. Flattery probably means an appeal to the pleasant as opposed to the good (cf. *Gorgias,* 463b).

31. The word for "demon" is *daimōn* and that for "happy" is *eudaimōn,* "possessing a good demon."

Book VIII

1. For "dynasty," cf. 499c, note 24. It is not certain what is meant by "purchased kingships," but cf. Aristotle, *Politics*, 1273a.

2. *Odyssey*, XIX, 163; *Iliad*, XXII, 126; Hesiod, *Theogony*, 35; *Apology*, 34d.

3. The word *time* means "honor."

4. This is an adaptation of *Iliad*, XVI, 112.

5. The nuptial number is one of the darkest passages in Plato's works. It presents difficulties both because we do not know Greek mathematics sufficiently well and because of the "high tragic" manner of its presentation. Its interpretation has been a subject of dispute since antiquity. For a list of some of the commentaries on it cf. Plato's *Republic*, James Adam, ed. (Cambridge, 1963), Vol. I, pp. xlviii–l.

The number clearly has much to do with the Pythagorean triangle whose sides were 3, 4, 5, and which reflects one of the greatest discoveries and problems of ancient science (cf. Aristotle, *Politics*, 1316a; and 534d, note 26). The surface reason for the number's appearance here is to relate the cosmic principles of science to this perfect regime, to establish a harmony between the knowledge of nature and of politics. In this way the highest human things would not be merely the playthings of chance, and there could be perfect technical control over the conditions of decent political life. The riddlesome character of the number's presentation may well reflect on the reality of that harmony and hence on the naturalness and possibility of this regime, which is supposed to be both possible and according to nature.

This regime was predicated on the emergence of rulers who are knowers or artisans in the precise sense first insisted on by Thrasymachus and later adopted by Socrates. Their highest function was to insure the reproduction of the species, the replenishment of their own numbers. If human reproduction cannot be controlled, if there is no science of eugenics combined with the power to use it well, chance rules human affairs, and regimes must lower their standards and rely on more ordinary rulers. The best regime is the regime of artisans who are able to live according to nature because they have mastery over chance. To this end communism was instituted, women were treated like men, and the family was abolished. The guardians were turned into a herd like a herd of cattle which can be used by a breeder, and all the ordinarily cherished human ways of loving and reproducing were suppressed by the rulers' marriage regulations and manipulations. The perfect artisans rule animals in order to reduce the disproportion that is always present in human herds, as opposed to brutish ones, between nature and convention, between the good and one's own. The nuptial number represents this science of eugenics, and the failure of the regime indicates the failure of its project. This conclusion is supported by the corruption of the son of the aristocratic father (549c ff.) which is meant to be the parallel to the corruption of the aristocratic city. The son falls from his father's way of life because of a disharmony between the mother and the father.

To see this in another light one might well look to Aristophanes' characterization of the problems which beset Socrates. The philosopher believes himself to be independent of convention and devotes himself, along with a society of companions, to study of the highest things for its own sake. But, insists Aristophanes, the philosopher has not reflected sufficiently on the preconditions of such a way of life and is actually dependent on the city and its conventions. He does nothing useful and produces none of the vital necessities, but he needs food and clothing. So he must steal to keep alive. And he needs philosophic companions; but his is an all-male society which cannot reproduce itself; therefore he must, as it were, steal the city's sons away from its concerns in order to recruit them for his society. Aristophanes shows that the city will not tolerate such a lawbreaker in its midst. Socrates responds in the *Republic* by asserting that if the philosopher adopts Aristophanes' two proposals in the *Ecclesiazusae*—the equality of women and total communism—he can construct a regime in which his philosophic life will not be in contradiction with his political life. This city will feed and clothe him. And in it women will give birth to children who are to be philosophers and not members of a family or citizens in the usual sense of the word; natural animal reproduction will replenish the philosophers' society which represents the natural human way of life, thus producing a harmony between the two senses of nature and showing that the tension between city and philosophers is neither natural nor necessary. Socrates with a science of eugenics could, by means of bodily procreation, have children who were potential philosophers and would no longer be forced to abandon his own in quest of good men; body and soul, city and philosopher, would work together. The failure to achieve control over births signals an even more comic failure of Socrates than that ridiculed in the *Clouds*. It is in this way that he proved his superiority to Aristophanes.

6. Hesiod, *Works and Days*, 106–201, should be consulted in reference to the entire discussion of the transformation of regimes.

7. *Iliad*, VI, 211. The context of the quote should be read.

8. Cf. *Seven Against Thebes*, 451, 570.

9. The Greek is *timēma*, allied to the word for honor (cf. 545b, note 3). The connection between the two notions is valuing. This term makes the transition from timocracy to oligarchy more pointed.

10. *Penēs*, a poor man in the sense that he must work for his living.

11. This is a play on the etymological sense of the word, composed of elements meaning "few" and "rulers."

12. This expression can have the technical sense of "loss of civic rights."

13. The great king was the ruler of the Persian empire, and these were luxurious signs of his office.

14. Probably a reference to the god Plutus, who is represented as blind. His name means simply "wealth." (Cf. Aristophanes, *Plutus*, 90.)

15. *Tokos* (cf. 507a, note 31).

16. The sentence is ambiguous; "of" could be substituted for "toward" here.

17. The heroes, divine beings, were present but not seen.

18. The word for "money-making," *chrēmatistikē*, is close to the word for "useful," *chrēsimos*. This is a play on that similarity.

19. The words for "embassy" and "older man" have a common root (cf. 509b, note 34).

20. Cf. Thucydides, III, lxxxii, 4.

21. The passage alludes to the Eleusinian Mysteries, the sacred and secret initiations that took place in Attica. The language here has a religous solemnity. The first days of this festival were devoted to purifications, and then there was a spectacular torchlight procession leading the god Iacchus (Dionysus) from Athens back to Eleusis where the initiations took place. This calls to mind the all-but-forgotten torch race promised at 328a.

22. This description should be compared with Pericles' funeral oration (Thucydides, II, xxvii–xli).

23. Cf. Xenophon, *The Athenian Republic*, I, 8–12.

24. We do not possess the play from which this quote comes, nor do we know anything of its context. It is possible that the phrase was not in a play but was said by Aeschylus in his defense when accused of revealing the secrets of the Mysteries. This would be an appropriate context for Socrates to use an utterance with such overtones (cf. Aristotle, *Ethics*, 1111a, 9 ff.).

25. The proverb was "like mistress, like dog," with the ambiguity that dog was taken in the sense of servant. Socrates takes it literally.

26. Lycaon, an ancient hero, founded a sanctuary on the Lycaean mountains in Arcadia. Among the offerings he sacrificed there was a child. As punishment he was turned into a wolf (Greek, *lykos*). In historical times, the priest who performed the sacrifice every ninth year was forced to flee and wander about until the next sacrifice. According to popular legend, he was a wolf during this period.

27. Herodotus, I, 55.

28. *Iliad*, XVI, 776, XVIII, 26; *Odyssey*, XXIV, 40. (Cf. Herodotus, I, 59–60.)

29. The line is variously attributed to Euripides or Sophocles.

30. Euripides, *The Trojan Women*, 1169.

31. On the basis of an alternative reading, the sentence could be rendered as follows: ". . . if there are sacred riches in the city, he'll spend them wherever the income from putting them up for sale suffices, so that . . ."

32. Cf. 331a.

Book IX

1. This means to possess black bile. The physiological characteristic leads to a bilious or unstable character. However, melancholy, although dangerous, is apparently an attribute of most exceptional men. Cf. Aristotle (*Problems*, XXX, i), who says that all men remarkable in philosophy, politics, poetry, or the arts are melancholic.

2. A mild jest in response to someone who asks a question to which he knows the answer. "You'll give the answer as well as pose the question."

3. Cf. 344b, note 38.

4. According to another reading, with better manuscript support, this

clause would read: ". . . the opinions that act as judges . . ." or ". . . the opinions that pronounce sentences. . . ."

5. This is apparently a reference to the mode of awarding the prizes in the tragic and comic competitions.

6. This is a pun on the name Ariston and the word "best" (*ariston*).

7. In wrestling contests there were apparently three throws. There is here a reference to the competitions at the Olympic games. And the dedication calls to mind the libations at banquets, of which there were three: (1) to Olympian Zeus and the Olympian gods; (2) to the heroes; (3) to Zeus Savior [Zeus was worshipped, as were the other gods, under various aspects; he was thus given special names (*Eponyms*) drawn from places or attributes (cf. 394a and note 4)]. Cf. *Philebus*, 66d; *Charmides*, 167a; *Laws*, 692a; *Letter*, VII, 340a.

8. Adam argues that this sentence is corrupt and suggests a possible emendation that would change the sense here and in the next sentences as follows:

"Does the being of what is never the same participate in being at all more than the being of knowledge does?"
"Not at all."
"Or does the being of what is never the same participate more in truth than knowledge does?"

9. Cf. *Phaedrus*, 243a–b.

10. Socrates is turning the difference between the tyrant's pleasure and the king's into a solid figure so that it can be perceived (cf. *Laws*, 894a). The first step is the "line," derived from the distance between the two pleasures. The line is paradoxically called a "plane" because its length is a number (9) formed of two elements (3 x 3), which could represent length and width. Square numbers were technically called "plane numbers." Then the "plane line" is squared and cubed and results in a solid, the number of which is 729. Why Socrates chooses the values he does, or why he uses multiplication rather than addition, or why a solid must be produced are all unclear, unless he wishes to make the result as large as possible in this prototypical attempt to mathematize human things.

11. Philolaus, the pre-Socratic philosopher of the Pythagorean school, calculated that there were 364½ days in the year. If there are a similar number of nights, the number would be 729. He also held that there is a great year of 729 months. It is probably this to which Socrates refers. In what way the number 729 would express years is unknown.

12. The Chimæra was a lion in front, a dragon behind, and a she-goat in the middle. Scylla had a woman's face and breasts, six dogs' heads, a dragon's tail, and snakes for hair. Plato elsewhere (*Phaedrus*, 229d) mentions Pegasus and Gorgons as members of this class of beings.

13. *Odyssey* XI, 326–327. She accepted a necklace from Polynices to prevail upon her husband, Amphiaraus, to partake in the expedition of the Seven against Thebes (cf. Pindar, *Nemean*, IX, 37 ff.). She was killed by her son in revenge.

Book X

1. Cf. 405d, note 54.

2. Cf. Aristotle, *Politics*, 1273b ff.

3. Thales and Anacharsis were among the classic Seven Wise Men (cf. 335e–336d, and notes 28 and 29). Anacharsis was said to have invented the anchor and the potter's wheel. Thales' knowledge of mathematics made him able to calculate eclipses and discover the solstices, among other things. For the point of this passage, cf. Aristotle *Politics*, 1259a, and *Theaetetus*, 174a ff.

4. The name means "of the meat tribe."

5. They were sophists, contemporaries of Socrates, who are frequently mentioned in the Platonic dialogues. These were men who supported themselves by their teachings. Both appear prominently in the *Protagoras*. For further information on Prodicus, cf. *Meno*, 96d; *Theaetetus*, 151b; and *Apology*, 19e.

6. Cf. 467d, note 27.

7. These are all presumably quotes from poets attacking philosophy and philosophers, but we do not know their sources.

8. The words "justice" and "injustice" are plural in the Greek text, implying that there are a plurality of forms.

9. He was once a fisherman who, for one of a number of alleged reasons, threw himself into the sea where he remained and was made a god. In painting and sculpture, he was represented as a combination of all sorts of elements drawn from the sea which were grafted onto his human form.

10. It, like Gyges' ring, made one invisible. Athena used it to hide from Ares (*Iliad*, V, 844). (Cf. Aristophanes, *Acharnians*, 390.)

11. This apparently refers to a race where the runners ran to one end of a straight racecourse, turned, and came back. They start fast but tire in the stretch.

12. This proverbial expression gets its image from those animals that let their ears droop when tired or dispirited.

13. There is a complicated series of allusions in this sentence:
(a) the word for "story" is *apologon* which is very close to *apology*. The four books of the *Odyssey* (IX–XII) in which Odysseus tells Alcinous, King of the Phaeacians, of his adventures were traditionally known as *The Story of Alcinous*. In this part of the *Odyssey* the descent to Hades is recounted. Moreover, "A story of Alcinous" became a proverbial expression for a long-winded tale. (b) The word for "strong" is *alkimou*, differing only by the measure of an *m* instead of an *n* from the genitive form of the king's name used here, *Alkinou*. In itself this is a play on sounds; but, further, if one were to translate the root words of the name, the sentence would read: ". . . a story of a man not strong of mind, but strong. . . ." (Cf. 494 and note 13; 509d and note 35.)

14. Ardiaeus is apparently of Socrates' invention.

15. Er has reached the extremes of the *cosmos*, and he sees there the structure of the heavens. The whorls represent the spheres of the fixed stars, the planets, the sun, and the moon. The motions of these whorls account for

the visible movements of those bodies; their color, brightness, and distance from each other are accounted for by the description of the lips of the whorls. Hence the whole is organized rationally and is knowable; and in this way the particular fates of individuals gain significance by their connection with the cosmic necessities.

16. They are the Fates (*Moirai*): Lachesis (dispenser of lots) holds sway over the past; Clotho (spinner), the present; and Atropos (inevitable or unturnable), the future.

17. Orpheus and Thamyras were both singers who ended badly. Orpheus, after losing Eurydice, was torn apart by Thracian women; Thamyras was deprived of his sight and his power of song by the Muses whom he rivalled. The unhappy fates of Ajax and Agamemnon are recounted by Sophocles and Aeschylus. [Plutarch remarks, (*Quaestiones conviviales*, IX, 5.3, 1740e–f) that Ajax is the twentieth here because he was the twentieth soul encountered by Odysseus in Hades (*Odyssey*, XI, 543).] Atalanta's story has several versions, some with happy endings, others with unhappy endings. At all events, she was an Artemis-like woman, a hunter and runner, beautiful and chaste, although she finally married. Epeius was the builder of the Trojan Horse. For Thersites, cf. *Iliad*, II, 212 ff.

18. The Greek words for "threads" and "irreversible" call to mind the etymological senses of Clotho and Atropos, respectively (cf. 617c, note 16)

19. *Lēthē* means "forgetfulness." Etymologically the word for "truth" (*alētheia*) can be understood to be its negation. In the *Phaedrus* there is a plain of Alētheia (248b).

20. The last words (from "to . . .") form a line of iambic verse.

21. "Saved" in this context has a double sense. Superficially it means that Er came back, so the tale was preserved. But it also means that it has been given meaning, that it has been supported in a deeper sense that gives the surface plausibility. It is in this way that Aristotle speaks of "saving the phenomena" (cf. *Laws*, 645b; and *Philebus*, 14a).

22. This means both "to have success in action" and "to do what is good." It is Plato's favored salutation. (Cf. *Letters*, III, 315a–b.)

INDEX

INDEX

This index has been constructed in accordance with the purposes of the translation. No modern categories alien to Plato's thought have been introduced, and wherever possible categories have been keyed to specific Greek words.

Only the text of the *Republic* has been indexed. The references are to the standard Platonic pagination—that of the first printed edition of Plato's works published by Stephanus in the sixteenth century—which appears at the side of the printed text. This enables the reader to find passages cited in secondary works with ease.

The index is divided into four parts: (1) an index of names, (2) an index of subjects, (3) an index cataloguing the appearances of all the personages in the dialogue, except for Socrates who is ubiquitous, and (4) an index cataloguing the formulae of familiar address, for those who are interested in following their usage. The index of names and the catalogues of the dramatis personae and formulae of familiar address attempt to be complete, as do all those entries in the subject index marked with asterisks.

A dash between two page citations (for example, 331a–333d) indicates either a high frequency in the occurence of a term or a thematic treatment of a given topic in that passage.

It should be noted that it is impossible to make the lines of this translation accord perfectly with those of the Stephanus edition. Therefore, occasionally there may be a slight imprecision in the index's references to the translation. In such a case, the reader may find, for example, that the word the index tells him is at 439d is actually in the last line of 439c.

No attempt has been made to index the terms having to do with "being," related to the word *einai*, "to be," for they occur too frequently. The thematic discussions of being occur at 475d–479d and 506d–518d. The terms which occur most frequently and their usual translations are: *to on*, "that which is"; *ta onta*, "the things which are"; *to einai*, "being"; *ousia*, "substance" or "being."

INDEX OF NAMES

Zeus (oaths) (*cont'd*)
  400a, 400c, 403b, 407b, 423b, 426b,
  440b, 441b, 443b, 444a, 445b, 452b,
  453d, 459a, 462a, 469e, 472e, 484d,

493c, 505b, 506d, 515b, 521b, 527c,
531e, 534d, 536c, 551d, 554d, 564c,
569a, 574b, 574c, 584d, 585a, 588a,
602c, 605e, 608d, 610d

INDEX OF SUBJECTS

Ignorance (*cont'd*)
598d; *agnoia*, 376b, 382b, 477b, 478c–478d, 585b; *agnōsia*, 477a
°Image, *eikōn* (cf. Imitation, Phantom), 375d, 401b, 402b–402c, 487e–488a, 489a, 509a, 509e, 510b, 510e–511a, 514a, 515a, 517a, 517d, 531b, 533a, 538c, 563a, 588b–588d; imagination, *eikasia*, 511e, 534a
°Imitation, *mimēsis* (cf. Image, Phantom), 373b, 382b, 388c, 392d, 393c–398b, 399a–399c, 399d, 400a, 401a, 458c, 491a, 500c, 510b, 532a, 539b–539c, 547d, 563a, 595a–607c
Immortality, *see* Death
°Insolence, *hybris*, 400b, 403a, 560e, 572c
Intellect, *see* Intelligence
Intelligence, intellect or mind, *nous*; the highest rational faculty (cf. Thought), 431c, 490b, 494d, 506c, 508c–508d, 511d, 517c, 531b, 534b, 549d, 585b, 586d, 591c, 619b
°Irony, 337a

°Judge, *dikastēs*, 348b, 397e, 405a–405c, 408d–410a, 425d, 433e, 557e, 614c–614d; courts and trials, 365d, 405a, 425d, 433e, 464d–464e, 492b, 517d, 549c, 549d, 553b, 565e
°Justice, *dikaiosynē*, 330d–354c, 357b–369a, 371e, 372e, 376d, 380b, 391a, 392b–392c, 405b–405c, 409a–409c, 420b, 427d–427e, 430c–430e, 432b, 433a–435b, 440c, 441d–441e, 442d–445b, 451a, 455a, 458e, 461a, 463d, 464e, 466b, 468e, 469b, 472b–472c, 476a, 478e, 479a, 479e, 484b, 484d, 486b, 487a, 490c, 491e, 493c, 496b, 496d, 497a, 499c, 500c, 500d, 501b, 504a, 504d, 505a, 505d, 506a–506d, 517d–517e, 519d, 520a–520c, 520e, 536b, 538c, 538e, 540e, 544e–545b, 548d, 549e, 554c, 558d, 559a, 565c, 565e, 568e, 574d, 576a–576b, 580a–580c, 583b, 586e, 588a–588b, 588e–589d, 591a–591b, 597d, 599d, 605a–605b, 607d, 608b, 608d, 609c–609d, 610b–610e, 611c, 612b–614a, 614c, 615a–615b, 618e, 620d, 621c

Killing, 360b–360c, 451a–451b, 488c, 517a, 557a, 565e–566b, 567a–567c, 571d, 573b, 574e, 586b, 610b–610e, 615c
°King, *basileus*, 445d, 473c–473d, 474d, 499c, 502a, 509d, 520b, 543a, 544d,

553c, 560c, 576d–576e, 580b–580c, 587b–587e, 597e, 607a
Knowledge, *epistēmē*, 340e, 350a, 366c, 409c–409d, 428b–429a, 438c–438e, 442c, 443e, 477b, 477d–478b, 478d, 505a–511c, 518c, 522a, 522c, 529c, 533c–534d, 540a, 585b–585c, 598c–598d, 602a, 618c; *gnōmē*, 476d; *gnōsis*, 476c, 477a, 478c, 480a, 484c, 527b; *gnōston*, 479d; *synesis*, 376b

Lamentation, wailing, 387d–388d, 395e, 398d–398e, 411a, 578a, 604a–606b
Laughter, *gelōs*, 330e, 331d, 337a, 366c, 382d, 388d–389a, 392d, 398c, 432d, 445a–445b, 451a–457b, 473c, 493d, 499c, 505b, 506d, 509c, 517a–518b, 522d, 525e, 527a–531a, 536b, 600b, 606c, 613c–613d, 620a, 620c
Law, *nomos*, 338e–339c, 359a–359c, 364a, 365e, 380c, 383c, 421a, 424c–427b, 429c–430a, 451a–451b, 456b–458c, 461b–465b, 484b–484d, 497d, 501a, 502b–502c, 519e, 534d–534e, 537d–539a, 548b, 551a, 555c, 556a, 563d, 571b–572a, 587a–587c, 589c, 590e, 604a–604b, 607a; lawgiver, *nomothetēs*, 427a, 429c, 458c, 462a, 497d, 502c, 530c, 538d, 564a, 599e
°Lawful, *themis*, 398a, 417a, 422d, 480a
Learning, lack of, *amathia* (cf. Ignorance), 350b–351a, 382b, 409d, 444a, 444b, 535e
°Learning, love of, *philomathia*, 376b–376c, 411d, 435e, 475c, 485d, 490a, 499e
Leisure, *scholē*, 370b–370c, 374e, 376d, 406b–406d, 500c, 610d, 619c
Lie, falsehood, *pseudos*, 331b–331c, 338b, 366c, 367b, 376e–377a, 377d–377e, 381e–383b, 389b–389d, 391d, 413a, 414b–414c, 414e, 444a, 459c, 485c, 485d, 487d, 489b, 490b, 535e, 560c, 575b, 589c
°Love, *erōs*, as distinguished from friendship (*philia*), 368a, 395e, 396d, 402d–403c, 439d, 458d, 468c, 474d–475a, 485b–485c, 490b, 499c, 501d, 521b, 555e, 572e–573e, 574d–575a, 578a, 579b, 586c, 587b, 607e–608a
°Lyric, 379a

°Madness, *mania*, 329d, 331c, 341c, 359b, 382c, 382e, 396a–396b, 400b, 403a,

INDEX OF PERSONAGES

INDEX OF FAMILIAR ADDRESS

19
7
8   35
7
7
16   42
53
20   00

72